T0202935

Lecture Notes in Computer Science   14370

Founding Editors

Gerhard Goos
Juris Hartmanis

The series Lecture Notes in Computer Science (LNCS), including its subseries Lecture Notes in Artificial Intelligence (LNAI) and Lecture Notes in Bioinformatics (LNBI), has established itself as a medium for the publication of new developments in computer science and information technology research, teaching, and education.

LNCS enjoys close cooperation with the computer science R & D community, the series counts many renowned academics among its volume editors and paper authors, and collaborates with prestigious societies. Its mission is to serve this international community by providing an invaluable service, mainly focused on the publication of conference and workshop proceedings and postproceedings. LNCS commenced publication in 1973.

Guy Rothblum · Hoeteck Wee
Editors

Theory
of Cryptography

21st International Conference, TCC 2023
Taipei, Taiwan, November 29 – December 2, 2023
Proceedings, Part II

 Springer

Editors
Guy Rothblum (iD)
Apple
Cupertino, CA, USA

Hoeteck Wee
NTT Research
Sunnyvale, CA, USA

ISSN 0302-9743 ISSN 1611-3349 (electronic)
Lecture Notes in Computer Science
ISBN 978-3-031-48617-3 ISBN 978-3-031-48618-0 (eBook)
https://doi.org/10.1007/978-3-031-48618-0

This Springer imprint is published by the registered company Springer Nature Switzerland AG
The registered company address is: Gewerbestrasse 11, 6330 Cham, Switzerland

Paper in this product is recyclable.

Preface

The 21st Theory of Cryptography Conference (TCC 2023) was held during November 29 – December 2, 2023, at Academia Sinica in Taipei, Taiwan. It was sponsored by the International Association for Cryptologic Research (IACR). The general chairs of the conference were Kai-Min Chung and Bo-Yin Yang.

The conference received 168 submissions, of which the Program Committee (PC) selected 68 for presentation giving an acceptance rate of 40%. Each submission was reviewed by at least three PC members in a single-blind process. The 39 PC members (including PC chairs), all top researchers in our field, were helped by 195 external reviewers, who were consulted when appropriate. These proceedings consist of the revised versions of the 68 accepted papers. The revisions were not reviewed, and the authors bear full responsibility for the content of their papers.

We are extremely grateful to Kevin McCurley for providing fast and reliable technical support for the HotCRP review software. We also thank Kay McKelly for her help with the conference website.

This was the ninth year that TCC presented the Test of Time Award to an outstanding paper that was published at TCC at least eight years ago, making a significant contribution to the theory of cryptography, preferably with influence also in other areas of cryptography, theory, and beyond. This year, the Test of Time Award Committee selected the following paper, published at TCC 2007: "Multi-authority Attribute Based Encryption" by Melissa Chase. The award committee recognized this paper for "the first attribute-based encryption scheme in which no small subset of authorities can compromise user privacy, inspiring further work in decentralized functional encryption." The author was invited to deliver a talk at TCC 2023.

This year, TCC awarded a Best Young Researcher Award for the best paper authored solely by young researchers. The award was given to the paper "Memory Checking for Parallel RAMs" by Surya Mathialagan.

We are greatly indebted to the many people who were involved in making TCC 2023 a success. First of all, a big thanks to the most important contributors: all the authors who submitted fantastic papers to the conference. Next, we would like to thank the PC members for their hard work, dedication, and diligence in reviewing and selecting the papers. We are also thankful to the external reviewers for their volunteered hard work and investment in reviewing papers and answering questions. For running the conference itself, we are very grateful to the general chairs, Kai-Min Chung and Bo-Yin Yang, as well as the staff at Academia Sinica (Institute of Information Science and Research Center of Information Technology Innovation). For help with these proceedings, we thank the team at Springer. We appreciate the sponsorship from IACR, Hackers in Taiwan, Quantum Safe Migration Center (QSMC), NTT Research and BTQ. Finally, we are thankful to

vi   Preface

Tal Malkin and the TCC Steering Committee as well as the entire thriving and vibrant TCC community.

October 2023   Guy Rothblum
                                                         Hoeteck Wee

Organization

General Chairs

Kai-Min Chung   Academia Sinica, Taiwan
Bo-Yin Yang   Academia Sinica, Taiwan

Program Committee Chairs

Guy N. Rothblum   Apple, USA and Weizmann Institute, Israel
Hoeteck Wee   NTT Research, USA and ENS, France

Steering Committee

Jesper Buus Nielsen   Aarhus University, Denmark
Krzysztof Pietrzak   Institute of Science and Technology, Austria
Huijia (Rachel) Lin   University of Washington, USA
Yuval Ishai   Technion, Israel
Tal Malkin   Columbia University, USA
Manoj M. Prabhakaran   IIT Bombay, India
Salil Vadhan   Harvard University, USA

Program Committee

Prabhanjan Ananth   UCSB, USA
Christian Badertscher   Input Output, Switzerland
Chris Brzuska   Aalto University, Finland
Ran Canetti   Boston University, USA
Nico Döttling   CISPA, Germany
Rosario Gennaro   CUNY and Protocol Labs, USA
Aarushi Goel   NTT Research, USA
Siyao Guo   NYU Shanghai, China
Shai Halevi   AWS, USA
Pavel Hubáček   Czech Academy of Sciences and Charles
                                University, Czech Republic
Yuval Ishai   Technion, Israel

Aayush Jain	CMU, USA
Zhengzhong Jin	MIT, USA
Yael Kalai	Microsoft Research and MIT, USA
Chethan Kamath	Tel Aviv University, Israel
Bhavana Kanukurthi	IISc, India
Jiahui Liu	MIT, USA
Mohammad Mahmoody	University of Virginia, USA
Giulio Malavolta	Bocconi University, Italy and Max Planck Institute for Security and Privacy, Germany
Peihan Miao	Brown University, USA
Eran Omri	Ariel University, Israel
Claudio Orlandi	Aarhus, Denmark
João Ribeiro	NOVA LINCS and NOVA University Lisbon, Portugal
Doreen Riepel	UC San Diego, USA
Carla Ràfols	Universitat Pompeu Fabra, Spain
Luisa Siniscalchi	Technical University of Denmark, Denmark
Naomi Sirkin	Drexel University, USA
Nicholas Spooner	University of Warwick, USA
Akshayaram Srinivasan	University of Toronto, Canada
Stefano Tessaro	University of Washington, USA
Eliad Tsfadia	Georgetown University, USA
Mingyuan Wang	UC Berkeley, USA
Shota Yamada	AIST, Japan
Takashi Yamakawa	NTT Social Informatics Laboratories, Japan
Kevin Yeo	Google and Columbia University, USA
Eylon Yogev	Bar-Ilan University, Israel
Mark Zhandry	NTT Research, USA

Additional Reviewers

Damiano Abram	Benedikt Auerbach
Hamza Abusalah	Renas Bacho
Abtin Afshar	Saikrishna Badrinarayanan
Siddharth Agarwal	Chen Bai
Divesh Aggarwal	Laasya Bangalore
Shweta Agrawal	Khashayar Barooti
Martin Albrecht	James Bartusek
Nicolas Alhaddad	Balthazar Bauer
Bar Alon	Shany Ben-David
Benny Applebaum	Fabrice Benhamouda
Gal Arnon	Jean-François Biasse

Alexander Bienstock
Olivier Blazy
Jeremiah Blocki
Andrej Bogdanov
Madalina Bolboceanu
Jonathan Bootle
Pedro Branco
Jesper Buus Nielsen
Alper Çakan
Matteo Campanelli
Shujiao Cao
Jeffrey Champion
Megan Chen
Arka Rai Choudhuri
Valerio Cini
Henry Corrigan-Gibbs
Geoffroy Couteau
Elizabeth Crites
Hongrui Cui
Marcel Dall'Agnol
Quang Dao
Pratish Datta
Koen de Boer
Leo Decastro
Giovanni Deligios
Lalita Devadas
Jack Doerner
Jelle Don
Leo Ducas
Jesko Dujmovic
Julien Duman
Antonio Faonio
Oriol Farràs
Danilo Francati
Cody Freitag
Phillip Gajland
Chaya Ganesh
Rachit Garg
Gayathri Garimella
Romain Gay
Peter Gaži
Ashrujit Ghoshal
Emanuele Giunta
Rishab Goyal
Yanqi Gu

Ziyi Guan
Jiaxin Guan
Aditya Gulati
Iftach Haitner
Mohammad Hajiabadi
Mathias Hall-Andersen
Shuai Han
Dominik Hartmann
Aditya Hegde
Alexandra Henzinger
Shuichi Hirahara
Taiga Hiroka
Charlotte Hoffmann
Alex Hoover
Yao-Ching Hsieh
Zihan Hu
James Hulett
Joseph Jaeger
Fatih Kaleoglu
Ari Karchmer
Shuichi Katsumata
Jonathan Katz
Fuyuki Kitagawa
Ohad Klein
Karen Klein
Michael Klooß
Dimitris Kolonelos
Ilan Komargodski
Yashvanth Kondi
Venkata Koppula
Alexis Korb
Sabrina Kunzweiler
Thijs Laarhoven
Jonas Lehmann
Baiyu Li
Xiao Liang
Yao-Ting Lin
Wei-Kai Lin
Yanyi Liu
Qipeng Liu
Tianren Liu
Zeyu Liu
Chen-Da Liu Zhang
Julian Loss
Paul Lou

Steve Lu
Ji Luo
Fermi Ma
Nir Magrafta
Monosij Maitra
Christian Majenz
Alexander May
Noam Mazor
Bart Mennink
Hart Montgomery
Tamer Mour
Alice Murphy
Anne Müller
Mikito Nanashima
Varun Narayanan
Hai Nguyen
Olga Nissenbaum
Sai Lakshmi Bhavana Obbattu
Maciej Obremski
Kazuma Ohara
Aurel Page
Mahak Pancholi
Guillermo Pascual Perez
Anat Paskin-Cherniavsky
Shravani Patil
Sikhar Patranabis
Chris Peikert
Zach Pepin
Krzysztof Pietrzak
Guru Vamsi Policharla
Alexander Poremba
Alex Poremba
Ludo Pulles
Wei Qi
Luowen Qian
Willy Quach
Divya Ravi
Nicolas Resch
Leah Namisa Rosenbloom
Lior Rotem
Ron Rothblum
Lance Roy

Yusuke Sakai
Pratik Sarkar
Sruthi Sekar
Joon Young Seo
Akash Shah
Devika Sharma
Laura Shea
Sina Shiehian
Kazumasa Shinagawa
Omri Shmueli
Jad Silbak
Pratik Soni
Sriram Sridhar
Akira Takahashi
Ben Terner
Junichi Tomida
Max Tromanhauser
Rotem Tsabary
Yiannis Tselekounis
Nikhil Vanjani
Prashant Vasudevan
Marloes Venema
Muthuramakrishnan Venkitasubramaniam
Hendrik Waldner
Michael Walter
Zhedong Wang
Gaven Watson
Weiqiang Wen
Daniel Wichs
David Wu
Ke Wu
Zhiye Xie
Tiancheng Xie
Anshu Yadav
Michelle Yeo
Runzhi Zeng
Jiaheng Zhang
Rachel Zhang
Cong Zhang
Chenzhi Zhu
Jincheng Zhuang
Vassilis Zikas

Contents – Part II

Secret Sharing, PIR and Memory Checking

Multi-party Computation II

Broadcast-Optimal Four-Round MPC in the Plain Model

Michele Ciampi[3] , Ivan Damgård[1] , Divya Ravi[1] , Luisa Siniscalchi[2] , Yu Xia[3(✉)] , and Sophia Yakoubov[1]

[1] Aarhus University, Aarhus, Denmark
{ivan,divya,sophia.yakoubov}@cs.au.dk
[2] Technical University of Denmark, Kongens Lyngby, Denmark
luisi@dtu.dk
[3] The University of Edinburgh, Edinburgh, UK
{michele.ciampi,yu.xia}@ed.ac.uk

Abstract. The prior works of Cohen, Garay and Zikas (Eurocrypt 2020), Damgård, Magri, Ravi, Siniscalchi and Yakoubov (Crypto 2021) and Damgård, Ravi, Siniscalchi and Yakoubov (Eurocrypt 2023) study 2-round Multi-Party Computation (where some form of set-up is required). Motivated by the fact that broadcast is an expensive resource, they focus on so-called broadcast optimal MPC, i.e., they give tight characterizations of which security guarantees are achievable, if broadcast is available in the first round, the second round, both rounds, or not at all.

This work considers the natural question of characterizing broadcast optimal MPC in the plain model where no set-up is assumed. We focus on 4-round protocols, since 4 is known to be the minimal number of rounds required to securely realize any functionality with black-box simulation. We give a complete characterization of which security guarantees, (namely selective abort, selective identifiable abort, unanimous abort and identifiable abort) are feasible or not, depending on the exact selection of rounds in which broadcast is available.

1 Introduction

Secure Multi-party Computation (MPC) [7,22,28] allows a set of mutually distrusting parties to compute a joint function on their private inputs, with the guarantee that no adversary corrupting a subset of parties can learn more information than the output of the joint computation. The study of round complexity of MPC protocols in various settings constitutes a phenomenal body of work in the MPC literature [1,3,5,9,19,24,26,27]. However, most of the known round-optimal protocols crucially rely on the availability of a *broadcast channel*. Informally, a broadcast channel guarantees that when a message is sent, this reaches all the parties, without ambiguity.

M. Ciampi—Supported by the Sunday Group.

I. Damgård—Supported by the Villum foundation.

D. Ravi—Funded by the European Research Council (ERC) under the European Unions's Horizon 2020 research and innovation programme under grant agreement No 803096 (SPEC).

G. Rothblum and H. Wee (Eds.): TCC 2023, LNCS 14370, pp. 3–32, 2023.
https://doi.org/10.1007/978-3-031-48618-0_1

In practice, a broadcast channel can be realized using $t+1$ rounds of point-to-point communication, where t denotes the corruption threshold (maximal number of parties the adversary can corrupt). In fact, $t+1$ rounds are necessary for any deterministic protocol that realizes broadcast [16,17]. An alternate way of realizing broadcast would be by means of a physical or external infrastructure, e.g. a public ledger such as blockchain. Both these approaches to realize broadcast are quite demanding and expensive; therefore it is important to minimize its use.

Driven by this motivation, a very recent line of work [13–15] studies if it is plausible to minimize the use of broadcast while maintaining an *optimal* round complexity, at the cost of possibly settling for a weaker security guarantee. More specifically, these works investigate the best achievable guarantees when some or all of the broadcast rounds are replaced with rounds that use only point-to-point communication. All the above works focused on two-round MPC protocols where some form of setup assumption (such as a common reference string (CRS) or public-key infrastructure (PKI)) is required.

We make a study analogous to these works but in the *plain model*, where no prior setup is assumed[1]. Further, we focus on the *dishonest majority* setting where the adversary can corrupt all but one party. In this setting, *four rounds* of communication is known to be necessary [18] and sufficient [2,3,6,9–11,24] for secure computation with black-box security[2]. Notably, all the round-optimal (four-round) protocols in this setting use *broadcast* in every round. This leads us to the following natural question:

What is the trade-off between security and the use of broadcast for 4-round MPC protocols in the plain model in the dishonest majority setting?

As a first step, let us recall what kinds of security guarantees are achievable in the dishonest majority setting. The classic impossibility result of [12] showed that it is in general impossible to achieve the notions of fairness (where either all or none of the parties receive the output) and guaranteed output delivery (where all the parties receive the output of the computation no matter what). In light of this, the protocols in the dishonest majority setting allow the adversary to abort prematurely and still, receive the output (while the honest parties do not). Below are the various relevant flavors of *abort security* studied in the MPC literature.

Selective Abort (SA): A secure computation protocol achieves *selective abort* if every honest party either obtains the correct output or aborts.
Selective Identifiable Abort (SIA): a secure computation protocol achieves *selective identifiable abort* if every honest party either obtains the correct output or aborts, identifying one corrupt party (where the corrupt party identified by different honest parties may potentially be different).

---

[1] The only assumption is that communication channels are available between the parties; it is still required that parties have access to authenticated channels.
[2] By black-box security we mean that the simulator has only black-box access to the adversary. As in prior works, all our results are concerning black-box security.

Unanimous Abort (UA): A secure computation protocol achieves *unanimous abort* if either *all* honest parties obtain the correct output, or they all (unanimously) abort.

Identifiable Abort (IA): A secure computation protocol achieves *identifiable abort* if either all honest parties obtain the correct output, or they all (unanimously) abort, *identifying one corrupt party.*

Of these notions, SA is the weakest, IA the strongest, while SIA (recently introduced in [15]) and UA are "in between", and incomparable.

1.1   Our Contributions

We settle the above question by giving a complete characterization of which of the above four security guarantees is feasible or not w.r.t. all the possible broadcast communication patterns that one can have in 4-rounds, namely, if no broadcast is available, if broadcast is available in just one (two or three) rounds, and in which one(s).

We give a concise overview of our results below, which are described in more detail in Sect. 1.2. We recall that our impossibility results hold w.r.t. black-box simulation, which is also the case for [18].

No Broadcast: We show that if broadcast is not used in any of the four rounds, then *selective abort* is the best notion that can be achieved.

Broadcast in One Round: We show that if broadcast is used in exactly one round, then *unanimous abort* can be achieved if it is used in the *last* round; otherwise *selective abort* continues to remain the best achievable guarantee.

Broadcast in Two Rounds: We show that if broadcast is used in exactly two rounds, the feasibility landscape remains the same as the above.

Broadcast in Three Rounds: We show that if broadcast is used in exactly three rounds, then *selective identifiable abort* can be achieved if it is used in the first three rounds; otherwise it continues to remain impossible. The feasibility of other notions does not change in this setting.

Broadcast in Four Rounds: If broadcast is used in all four rounds, the strongest notion of *identifiable abort* becomes possible [11].

In Table 1 we summarize our findings.

1.2   Technical Overview

We start by presenting the technical overview of our positive results, and in the next section, we will provide a high-level idea about how our impossibility proof works.

Table 1. Complete characterization of feasibility and impossibility for 4-round dishonest majority MPC with different communication patterns in the plain model. We denote the acronym $P2P$ (resp. BC) to indicate the peer-to-peer (resp. broadcast) channel. We use the notation $P2P^x$ (resp. BC^x) to indicate x consecutive rounds of peer-to-peer (resp. broadcast) communications.

Broadcast Pattern	Possible?	Theorem reference
Selective Abort (SA)		
$P2P^4$	✓	Theorem 1
Identifiable Abort (IA)		
BC^4	✓	[11]
BC^3-$P2P$	✗	Theorem 4
Any other 4-round pattern	✗	Follows from the set on impossibilities for SIA, see Table 2 for the corresponding theorems.

Broadcast Pattern	Possible?	Theorem reference
Unanimous Abort (UA)		
BC^3-$P2P$	✗	Theorem 4
$P2P^3$-BC	✓	Theorem 2
Selective Identifiable Abort (SIA)		
BC^3-$P2P$	✓	Theorem 3
Any other 4-round pattern	✗	See Table 2 for the corresponding theorems.

Table 2. Impossibility results for 4-round MPC with SIA security against dishonest majority in the plain model. The third column "Implied Patterns" means that the patterns in this column are implied by the pattern in the first column "Broadcast Patterns". An impossibility in a stronger broadcast pattern setting implies the impossibility in a weaker broadcast pattern setting, where a broadcast pattern BP1 is weaker than a pattern BP2 if BP1 replaces at least one of the broadcast rounds in BP2 with a $P2P$ round (without introducing any additional BC rounds over BP2).

Broadcast Pattern	Implied Patterns
BC^2-$P2P$-BC ✗(Theorem 6)	BC-$P2P^2$-BC, BC-$P2P^3$, $P2P$-BC-$P2P$-BC, $P2P$-BC-$P2P^2$
BC^2-$P2P^2$ ✗(Theorem 5)	
BC-$P2P$-BC^2 ✗(Theorem 8)	BC-$P2P$-BC-$P2P$
$P2P$-BC^3 ✗(Theorem 7)	$P2P^2$-BC^2, $P2P^2$-BC-$P2P$, $P2P$-BC^2-$P2P$, $P2P^3$-BC, $P2P^4$

$P2P^4$ SA Protocol. In our first upper bound, we show that security with selective abort can be achieved when all the rounds are over $P2P$ channels. In particular, we show how to turn any protocol that is proven secure assuming that all the messages are sent over a broadcast channel, into a protocol that is secure even if all the broadcast rounds are replaced with $P2P$ rounds. As a starting point, note that if a round where a secure protocol uses broadcast (say round r) is simply replaced with peer-to-peer channels, the main problem is that the adversary can send different messages (over peer-to-peer channels) to a pair of honest parties in round r and obtain the honest parties' responses in round $(r + 1)$, computed with respect to different round r messages. This potentially violates security as such a scenario would never happen in the original protocol with broadcast in round r (as the honest parties would have a consistent view of the messages sent in round r) (Table 2).

To ensure that honest parties' responses are obtained only if they have a consistent view of the corrupt parties' messages, the two-round construction of Cohen *et al.* [13] adopts the following trick: In addition to sending the round r message[3] over a peer-to-peer channel (as described above), the parties send a garbled circuit which computes their next-round message (by taking as input round r messages, and using the hard-coded values of input and randomness of this party) and additively share labels of this garbled circuit. In the subsequent round, parties send the relevant shares based on the round r messages they received. The main idea is that the labels corresponding to honest parties' garbled circuits can be reconstructed to obtain their round $(r+1)$ messages *only if* the adversary sends the same round r message to every honest party.

While [13] use the above idea to transform a BC-BC protocol into a $P2P$-$P2P$ protocol, we extend it to transform a BC^4 protocol to $P2P^4$ protocol. Applying the above trick of sending the next-message garbled circuits and additive shares in Round 1 and 3 will ensure that if honest parties manage to evaluate the garbled circuits in Round 2 and 4 respectively, it must be the case that the honest parties have a consistent view of the Round 1 and Round 3 messages of corrupt parties. However, there is a slight caveat: The corrupt party could still send different garbled circuits to different honest parties, say in Round 1. This will make the view of honest parties inconsistent with respect to Round 2 of the corrupt party. Note that this was not a concern in [13] as Round 2 corresponds to the last round of the protocol, unlike our case[4].

To address this, we use 'broadcast with abort' [23] to realize a 'weak' broadcast of garbled circuits over two peer-to-peer rounds – In the first round, as before, each party sends its garbled circuit to others. In the second round, parties additionally echo the garbled circuits they received in Round 1. A party 'accepts' a garbled circuit only if it has been echoed by all other parties, or else she aborts. This ensures that if a pair of honest parties does not abort, they must have received the same garbled circuit and therefore would have a consistent view of Round 2 of corrupt parties as well. This approach has still one issue, as it allows the adversary to send different fourth-round messages to different honest parties. We can argue that this is not a problem if the input protocol of our compiler admits a simulator that can extract the inputs of the corrupted parties in the first three rounds. This helps because if the inputs of the corrupted parties are fixed in the third round, so is the output. Intuitively, this means that no matter what fourth round the adversary sends, an honest party receiving this fourth round will either abort or compute the correct output (and all the parties will get an output generated accordingly to the same corrupted and honest parties' inputs). Finally, we note that the protocols proposed in [3,9,24] all satisfy this property, hence, they can be used as input of our compiler.

---

[3] The round r corresponds to the first round in the construction of [13].

[4] The consistency of views with respect to the last round follows from input-independence property of the underlying protocol (elaborated in the relevant technical section).

P2P³-BC *UA Protocol.* This upper bound is based on the observation that when the broadcast channel is available in the last round, it is possible to upgrade the security of the above SA protocol (the one enhanced with the garbled circuit that we have described in the previous paragraph) to UA with the following simple modification: If an honest party is unable to continue computation during Rounds 1–3, she simply broadcasts the signal 'abort' in the last round, which would lead to all honest parties aborting unanimously. (Note that a corrupt party can also choose to broadcast 'abort', this does not violate unanimity as all honest parties would abort in such a case.). This takes care of any inconsistency prior to Round 4. Lastly, an adversary cannot cause inconsistency during Round 4, as we make the parties send all their messages via broadcast in Round 4.

BC³-P2P *SIA Protocol.* To prove this upper bound, we show that a big class of protocols (i.e., those that admit a simulator that can extract the inputs of the corrupted parties in the first three rounds) that are secure with identifiable aborts (which use broadcast in all rounds) can be proven to be secure with selective identifiable abort even if the last round is replaced by peer-to-peer channels. Intuitively, if this is not the case, it means that the adversary can make honest parties obtain inconsistent outputs by sending different versions of the last round message. However, this cannot occur since the output of the protocol must have been fixed before the last round (due to our assumption that the simulator extracts the input in the first three rounds), and since that, if there exists a fourth round that forces honest parties to compute the wrong output, this message could be used and sent in the last broadcast round of the original protocol to force honest parties to output an incorrect value. Finally, we note that the protocol proposed in [11] admits this special simulator. This observation yields a protocol that realizes any function with selective identifiable abort when the communication resources are BC^3-$P2P$.

Impossibility Results. We propose two main categories of impossibility results. In the first category, we show that UA security is impossible to achieve when the communication in the last round is performed over $P2P$. This shows the tightness of our $P2P^3$-BC UA upper bound, completing the picture for UA security. The second category comprises a set of four impossibility results that show that any broadcast pattern that does not use a broadcast channel in each of the first three rounds cannot achieve SIA. This result implies that any SIA secure protocol must rely on the pattern BC^3-$P2P$, hence our protocol is tight. This completes the picture for SIA security. Since IA is stronger than both UA and SIA, both the categories of impossibilities are applicable to IA as well. In particular, by putting everything together we prove that the pattern BC^4 is indeed minimal for realizing security with IA.

BC³-P2P *UA Security.* The main idea of this impossibility is to show that any protocol that enjoys security with UA in this setting in the plain model can be turned into a 3-round oblivious transfer (OT) protocol in the plain model. Since the latter is known to be impossible [25], such a BC^3-$P2P$ UA protocol cannot exist. The transformation occurs in two-steps: First, we show that the

BC^3-$P2P$ UA protocol must be such that it is possible for a set of $n/2$ among the n parties to obtain the output by combining their views at the end of Round 3. Intuitively, this is because it may happen that the only communication an honest party, say P, receives in the last round may be from other honest parties. She may still have to compute the output to maintain unanimity – This is because the last round is over peer-to-peer channels and the adversary may have behaved honestly throughout all the rounds towards her fellow-honest party P' (while behaving honestly only in the first three rounds to P). P' will compute the output due to correctness (from the perspective of P', this was an execution where everyone behaved honestly). This lets us infer that the set of honest parties *together* had enough information about the output at the end of Round 3 itself, as this information sufficed to let P get the output at the end of Round 4. Assuming that there are $n/2$ honest parties, this completes the first step. Next, we show that one can construct a three-round OT protocol, where the receiver P_R emulates the role of the above set of $n/2$ parties and the sender P_S emulates the role of the remaining set of $n/2$ parties. For this, we define the function computed by the n-party BC^3-$P2P$ UA protocol accordingly; and invoke the above claim (of the first step) and security of this n-party protocol to argue correctness and security of the OT protocol respectively.

SIA Security. Here, we give a high-level overview of how we prove that SIA is impossible to achieve when the communication pattern is of the form BC-BC-$P2P$-$P2P$. The impossibility of the other communication patterns follows by similar arguments. Assume by contradiction that there exists a three-party protocol Π that can securely compute any efficiently computable function f with SIA security when the broadcast channel is available only in the first two rounds. We denote the parties running this protocol with P_1, P_2, and P_{out}, and assume that f provides the output only to the party P_{out}. We consider now the following two scenarios.

Scenario 1. $P_1^\star$ is corrupted (we denote the i-th corrupted party with $P_i^\star$), and the other parties are honest. $P_1^\star$ behaves like P_1 would, with the difference that it does not send any message to P_2 in the third and the fourth round. Further, $P_1^\star$ pretends that it did not receive the third and the fourth round (over the point-to-point channel) messages from P_2.

Scenario 2. This time $P_2^\star$ is corrupted, and the other parties are honest. $P_2^\star$ behaves exactly like P_2, but it does not send any message to P_1 in the third and the fourth round. Further, $P_2^\star$ pretends that it did not receive the third and the fourth round (over the point-to-point channel) messages from P_1.

We note that the two scenarios look identical in the eyes of P_{out}. This is because P_{out} cannot access the $P2P$ channel connecting P_1 and P_2, hence, he cannot detect which of the two parties did not send a message. In particular, P_{out} will not be able to detect who is the corrupted party. By the definition of SIA, if P_{out} cannot identify the corrupted party, then it must be able to output the evaluation of the function f. Equipped with this observation, our proof proceeds in two steps.

1. First, we construct a new three-party protocol Π'. We denote the parties running this protocol with P_1', P_2', and P_{out}'. The party P_1' behaves exactly like $P_1^\star$ described in Scenario 1, and similarly P_2' and P_{out}' behave respectively like P_2' and P_{out}' in Scenario 1. We argue that Π' is secure with SA security. In fact, it suffices for our argument to show that Π' is secure for the following two corruption patterns: (a) when P_1' and P_{out}' are corrupt and when (b) P_2' and P_{out}' are corrupt. We refer to the simulators proving security in these cases as $\mathcal{S}_{1,out}^{SIA}$ and $\mathcal{S}_{2,out}^{SIA}$ respectively.

2. Next, we show an attack that allows an adversary $\mathcal{A}^{SA}$ corrupting $P_2^{\star\prime}$ and $P_{out}^{\star\prime}$ in Π' to learn the input of honest P_1'. This step would complete the proof as it contradicts the security of Π' for this corruption setting (which was argued to be secure in the first step). Broadly speaking, we show that this adversary $\mathcal{A}^{SA}$ is able to get access to all the information that the simulator $\mathcal{S}_{1,out}^{SIA}$ has (which must exist, as argued in the first step). Intuitively, since the information that $\mathcal{S}_{1,out}^{SIA}$ has must suffice to 'extract' the input of corrupt P_1' (in order for the simulation to be successful[5]), this allows us to argue that $\mathcal{A}^{SA}$ can use this information to learn the input of honest P_1'.

Before elaborating on each of the above steps, we make the following useful observation: since P_{out}' is the only party getting the output and the security goal of Π' is SA security, we can assume without loss of generality that in Π' **(a)** P_{out}' does not send any message to the other parties in the last round and **(b)** there is no communication between P_1' and P_2' in the last round.

SA Security of $\mathbf{\Pi'}$. In the first step, one can easily observe that the correctness of Π' holds as an honest execution of Π' would result in P_{out}' having a view that is identically distributed to the view of P_{out} at the end of Scenario 1 (which sufficed to compute the correct output). Intuitively, privacy holds as there is less room for attack in Π' as compared to Π, as it involves fewer messages. To formally argue SA security of Π' for the case when $P_2^{\star\prime}$ and $P_{out}^{\star\prime}$ are corrupt, we construct a simulator $\mathcal{S}_{2,out}^{SA}$ for Π'. In particular, we need to argue that the messages of P_1' can still be simulated, despite the fact that it does not send messages to $P_2^{\star\prime}$ in the third and the fourth round. Our simulation strategy works as follows. The simulator $\mathcal{S}_{2,out}^{SA}$ for Π' internally runs the SIA simulator $\mathcal{S}_{2,out}^{SIA}$ of Π for the case where P_1 is honest (recall that this exists by definition). $\mathcal{S}_{2,out}^{SA}$ acts as a proxy between $\mathcal{S}_{2,out}^{SIA}$ and the corrupted parties for the first and the second round, but upon receiving the third round from $\mathcal{S}_{2,out}^{SIA}$ directed to $P_2^\star$, $\mathcal{S}_{2,out}^{SA}$ blocks this message. At this point, a corrupted $P_2^{\star\prime}$ may or may not send a reply, but what is important to observe is that whatever behavior $P_2^{\star\prime}$ has, $P_2^\star$ could have had the same behavior while running Π. Intuitively, $P_2^{\star\prime}$ is always weaker than $P_2^\star$. Hence, the security of Π can be used to argue that the input of P_1' remains protected.

---

[5] Note that $\mathcal{S}_{1,out}^{SIA}$ works against an adversary corrupting P_1' and P_{out}', and must therefore be able to extract the input of P_1'.

We deal with the case where P_2' and P_{out}' are corrupted in Π' in a similar way. We refer to the technical part of the paper for a more detailed discussion.

Attack by $\mathcal{A}^{\text{SA}}$. In the second step, our goal is to show an adversary $\mathcal{A}^{\text{SA}}$ that corrupts $P_2^{\star\prime}$ and $P_{\text{out}}^{\star\prime}$ and runs the simulator $\mathcal{S}_{1,\text{out}}^{\text{SA}}$ to extract the input of the honest P_1'[6] (proofs with a similar spirit have been considered in [21,26]). To make the proof go through, we need to argue that an adversary that runs $\mathcal{S}_{1,\text{out}}^{\text{SA}}$ is a *legit adversary*. In particular, this adversary must not rewind the honest P_1'. Note that in the plain model and dishonest majority setting, the only additional power the black-box simulator has compared to an adversary is to perform rewinds. We show that no matter what rewinds $\mathcal{S}_{1,\text{out}}^{\text{SA}}$ performs, these rewinds do not affect the honest party P_1'. At a very high level, $\mathcal{A}^{\text{SA}}$ is able to obtain the same information as $\mathcal{S}_{1,\text{out}}^{\text{SA}}$ would collect over the rewinds because (a) the rewinds that allow $\mathcal{S}_{1,\text{out}}^{\text{SA}}$ to obtain new messages from $P_{\text{out}}^{\star\prime}$ can be locally computed by $\mathcal{A}^{\text{SA}}$ (as $\mathcal{A}^{\text{SA}}$ also controls $P_{\text{out}}^{\star\prime}$) (b) essentially, no rewinds help to obtain new messages from $P_1^{\star\prime}$ because $P_1^{\star\prime}$ does not send any messages to P_2' (on whose behalf $\mathcal{S}_{1,\text{out}}^{\text{SA}}$ acts) in the last two rounds. In more detail,

Rewinding the Second Round: $\mathbf{P_2'} \to \mathbf{P_1'}$. Changing the second message may influence the third round that will be computed by P_1'. However, note that P_1' does not send any message in the third round to P_2'. Hence, we just need to forward to P_1' only one of the potential multiple second-round messages the simulator generates. The messages we choose to forward need to be picked with some care. We refer the reader to the technical section for more detail.

Rewinding the Second Round: $\mathbf{P_2'} \to \mathbf{P_{\text{out}}^{\star\prime}}$. Changing the second round messages may affect the third round that goes from $P_{\text{out}}^{\star\prime}$ to $P_1^{\star\prime}$, and as such, it may affect the fourth round that goes back from P_1' to $P_{\text{out}}^{\star\prime}$. However, the simulator $\mathcal{S}_{1,\text{out}}^{\text{SA}}$ acting on behalf of P_2' will not see the effect of this rewind, given that in Π', P_2' does not receive any message in the fourth round. We also note that this rewind would additionally allow $\mathcal{S}_{1,\text{out}}^{\text{SA}}$ to obtain new third round messages from $P_{\text{out}}^{\star\prime}$ based on different second round messages of P_2'. However, this can be locally computed by $\mathcal{A}^{\text{SA}}$ in its head, as it controls both $P_{\text{out}}^{\star\prime}$ and $P_2^{\star\prime}$.

The above arguments can be easily extended to infer that any rewind performed in the third round does not affect P_1'. There is one pattern left, which is the one where the simulator rewinds the first round.

Rewinding the First Round: $\mathbf{P_2'} \to \mathbf{P_1'}$. The high-level intuition to argue that the simulator has no advantage in using these rewinds is that $\mathcal{S}_{1,\text{out}}^{\text{SA}}$ must be

---

[6] There are functionalities for which the simulator may not need to extract any input from the adversary. In our impossibility, we will consider a three-party oblivious transfer functionality (where one party does not have the input), where the simulator must be able to extract the input of the corrupted parties.

able to work even against the following adversary. Consider a corrupted $P_1^{\star\prime}$ who is rushing in the first round and computes fresh input (and randomness) by evaluating a pseudo-random function (PRF) on the incoming first-round message from P_2'. Subsequently, the corrupted $P_1^{\star\prime}$ uses this input honestly throughout the protocol. It is clear that against such an adversary, a simulator that rewinds the first round has no advantage. This is because changing the first round would change the input the adversary uses on behalf of $P_1^{\star\prime}$. Therefore, the information collected across the rewinding sessions cannot help to extract the input used by the adversary in the simulated thread (which refers to the transcript that is included in the adversary's view output by the simulator).

Formalizing the above intuition requires some care, and here we provide a slightly more detailed overview of how we do that. Our adversary $\mathcal{A}^{\mathsf{SA}}$ will receive messages of P_1'. $\mathcal{S}_{1,\mathrm{out}}^{\mathsf{SA}}$ (which we recall is run internally by $\mathcal{A}^{\mathsf{SA}}$) may rewind the first round multiple times, and each time $\mathcal{A}^{\mathsf{SA}}$ must reply with a valid first and second round of P_1'. We could simply reply to $\mathcal{S}_{1,\mathrm{out}}^{\mathsf{SA}}$ every time using the first round message we received from the honest P_1'. We then forward the first round received from P_{out}' and P_2' to P_1'. P_1' now will send the second round, which we can forward to $\mathcal{S}_{1,\mathrm{out}}^{\mathsf{SA}}$. Now, $\mathcal{S}_{1,\mathrm{out}}^{\mathsf{SA}}$ may decide to rewind P_1', by sending a new first round. At this point, we would need to forward this message to P_1', as this is the only way to compute a valid second round of P_1'. Clearly, P_1' is not supposed to reply to such queries, and as such, our adversary $\mathcal{A}^{\mathsf{SA}}$ is stuck. To avoid this problem, we adopt the following strategy. Let us assume that we know in advance that the simulator $\mathcal{S}_{1,\mathrm{out}}^{\mathsf{SA}}$ runs for at most κ steps[7]. This means that the simulator can open a new session (i.e., rewind the first round) up to κ times. Our adversary samples a random value $i \in [\kappa]$, and for all the sessions $j \neq i$, the adversary will compute the messages on behalf of P_1' using input and randomness computed by evaluating the PRF on input the messages received from P_2'. Only for the i-th session, the adversary will act as a proxy between the messages of P_1' and the simulator $\mathcal{S}_{1,\mathrm{out}}^{\mathsf{SA}}$. If the $\mathcal{S}_{1,\mathrm{out}}^{\mathsf{SA}}$ returns a simulated transcript consistent with the i-th session, then we also know that the simulator must have queried the ideal functionality with a value that corresponds to the input of P_1'. Given that we can guess the index i with some non-negligible probability, and given that the simulator will succeed with non-negligible probability as well, our attack would be successful. There is still subtlety though. In the session with indices $j \neq i$, $\mathcal{A}^{\mathsf{SA}}$ internally runs the algorithm of P_1' using an input x_1 that is computed by evaluating a PRF on input the messages generated from P_2'. The input used by the honest P_1' may have a different distribution, and as such, the simulator may decide to never complete the simulation of the i-th session. We first note that, formally, the goal of our adversary $\mathcal{A}^{\mathsf{SA}}$ is not really to extract the input of the honest P_1'. But it is about distinguishing whether the messages that it will receive on behalf of P_1' are generated using the honest procedure of P_1', or using the simulated procedure. Note that in such an MPC security game, the

---

[7] If the simulator has expected polynomial time κ, for some polynomial κ, then our adversary will run the simulator up to κ steps. This will guarantee that the simulator will terminate successfully with some non-negligible probability.

adversary knows, and can actually decide[8] what are the inputs of the honest parties (i.e., what inputs the challenger of the security game will use to compute the messages of P_1'). $\mathcal{A}^{\mathsf{SA}}$ then can internally run $\mathcal{S}_{1,\mathsf{out}}^{\mathsf{SA}}$, and when the i-th session comes generate an input x_1 by evaluating the PRF on the messages received on the behalf of P_2'. Now that the input of the honest P_1' is defined, we start the indistinguishability game with a challenger that takes as input x_1 (and some default input for the corrupted parties). In this way, we have the guarantee that when the challenger is not generating simulated messages, all the sessions look identical in the eyes of the simulator $\mathcal{S}_{1,\mathsf{out}}^{\mathsf{SA}}$. Hence, we can correctly state that with some non-negligible probability, it will return a simulated transcript for the i-th session. Note that $\mathcal{S}_{1,\mathsf{out}}^{\mathsf{SA}}$ will return $\tilde{x}_1$ when querying the ideal functionality in the i-th session, and we will have that $\tilde{x}_1 = x_1$ iff the challenger is computing the messages using the honest procedure of P_1'. If instead, the challenger was generating simulated messages on behalf of P_1', then the probability that $\tilde{x}_1 = x_1$ is small[9]. Hence, this will give a non-negligible advantage to $\mathcal{A}^{\mathsf{SA}}$ in distinguishing what the MPC challenger is doing. We refer to the technical sections of the paper for a more formal treatment of this proof.

Rewinding the First Round: $\mathbf{P_2'} \rightarrow \mathbf{P_{\mathsf{out}}^{*'}}$. To argue this case, we note that if $\mathcal{S}_{1,\mathsf{out}}^{\mathsf{SA}}$ acts against the rushing adversary defined in the above case (where $P_1^{*'}$ changes its input based on the output of PRF applied on the first round message from P_2'), then the first and second round messages of $P_1^{*'}$ obtained during the rewinds can be locally emulated by $\mathcal{A}^{\mathsf{SA}}$ (as he controls both $P_2^{*'}$ and $P_{\mathsf{out}}^{*'}$).

In summary, we have argued that $\mathcal{A}^{\mathsf{SA}}$ can internally run the simulator $\mathcal{S}_{1,\mathsf{out}}^{\mathsf{SA}}$ which enables the adversary to be able to extract the input of P_1'.[10] We refer to the technical section of the paper for a much more formal proof, and for the proof of impossibility results related to the other communication patterns.

1.3   Related Work

The work of [13] initiated the study of broadcast-optimal MPC. They investigated the question of the best security guarantees that can be achieved by all possible broadcast patterns in two-round secure computation protocols, namely no broadcast, broadcast (only) in the first round, broadcast (only) in the second round, and broadcast in both rounds. Their results focused on the dishonest majority setting and assumed a setup (such as PKI or CRS)[11]. The works of [14,15] investigate the same question for two-round MPC with setup (such as PKI or CRS), but in the honest-majority setting. We refer the reader to [13–15] for a detailed overview of the state of the art on 2-round MPC and their use of

---

[8] The security of MPC states that security holds for any honest parties' inputs (decided before the experiment starts), and these inputs may be known to the adversary.

[9] This will depend on the domain size of P_1' input and on the type of function we are computing.

[10] The simulator may be expected polynomial time, hence we need to cut the running time of the simulator to make sure that $\mathcal{A}^{\mathsf{SA}}$ remains PPT.

[11] It is necessary to assume setup for two-round protocols in dishonest majority setting.

broadcast. The work of [20] studies the best achievable security for two-round MPC in the plain model for different communication models such as only broadcast channels, only peer-to-peer channels, or both. Unlike the previously mentioned line of work, this work does not consider communication patterns where broadcast is limited to one of the two rounds. Going beyond two rounds, the work of [4] studies broadcast-optimal three-round MPC with guaranteed output delivery given an honest majority and CRS, and shows that the use of broadcast in the first two rounds is necessary. None of the above works consider the dishonest majority setting without setup (i.e. the plain model). In this setting, there are several existing round-optimal (four round) constructions, namely protocols with unanimous abort in [2,3,6,9,24] and with identifiable abort in [11]. However, these works do not restrict the use of broadcast in any round. To the best of our knowledge, we are the first to investigate the question of optimizing broadcast for round optimal (four-round) protocols in the dishonest majority setting without setup (i.e. in the plain model).

2   Preliminaries and Notations

Due to lack of space, we assume familiarity with the standard definition of secure Multi-party Computation (MPC), the garbling schemes, additive secret sharing, and also the notion of pseudo-random functions. We refer to the full version for the formal definitions.

In this paper, we mainly focus on four-round secure computation protocols. Rather than viewing a protocol Π as an n-tuple of interactive Turing machines, it is convenient to view each Turing machine as a sequence of multiple algorithms: $\mathtt{frst\text{-}msg}_i$, to compute P_i's first messages to its peers; $\mathtt{nxt\text{-}msg}_i^k$, to compute P_i's $(k+1)$-th round messages for $(1 \leq k \leq 3)$; and $\mathtt{output}_i$, to compute P_i's output. Thus, a protocol Π can be defined as $\{(\mathtt{frst\text{-}msg}_i, \mathtt{nxt\text{-}msg}_i^k, \mathtt{output}_i)\}_{i\in[n], k\in\{1,2,3\}}$.

The syntax of the algorithms is as follows:

- $\mathtt{frst\text{-}msg}_i(x_i; r_i) \to (\mathsf{msg}_{i\to 1}^1, \ldots, \mathsf{msg}_{i\to n}^1)$ produces the first-round messages of party P_i to all parties. Note that a party's message to itself can be considered to be its state.
- $\mathtt{nxt\text{-}msg}_i^k(x_i, \{\mathsf{msg}_{j\to i}^l\}_{j\in[n], l\in\{1,2,\ldots,k\}}; r_i) \to (\mathsf{msg}_{i\to 1}^{k+1}, \ldots, \mathsf{msg}_{i\to n}^{k+1})$ produces the $(k+1)$-th round messages of party P_i to all parties.
- $\mathtt{output}_i(x_i, \mathsf{msg}_{1\to i}^1, \ldots, \mathsf{msg}_{n\to i}^1, \ldots, \mathsf{msg}_{1\to i}^j, \ldots, \mathsf{msg}_{n\to i}^j; r_i) \to y_i$ produces the output returned to party P_i.

When the first round is over broadcast channels, we consider $\mathtt{frst\text{-}msg}_i$ to return only one message—msg_i^1. Similarly, when the $(k+1)$-th round is over broadcast channels, we consider $\mathtt{nxt\text{-}msg}_i^k$ to return only msg_i^{k+1}. We also note that, unless needed, to not overburden the notation, we do not pass the random coin r as an explicit input of the cryptographic algorithms. We denote "$\leftarrow$" as the assigning operator (e.g. to assign to a the value of b we write $a \leftarrow b$). We denote the acronym BC to indicate a round where broadcast is available and the acronym $P2P$ to indicate a round where only peer-to-peer channels are available. We use the notation $P2P^x$ (BC^x) to indicate x rounds of peer-to-peer (broadcast) communications. To strengthen our results, our lower bounds assume that the BC rounds allow peer-to-peer communication as well; our upper bounds assume that the BC rounds involve only broadcast messages (and no peer-to-peer messages).

3 Positive Results

$P2P^4$, SA, Plain Model, $n > t$. In this section, we want to demonstrate that it is feasible to construct a 4-round protocol with SA security, in order to do so we show a compiler that on input a 4-round protocol Π_{bc} with unanimous abort which makes use of the broadcast channel in the dishonest majority setting gives us a 4-round protocol $\Pi_{\text{p2p}^4}^{\text{SA}}$ with the same threshold corruption for selective abort, but relying only on $P2P$ communication. Further, we assume that the exists a simulator for Π_{bc} which extracts the inputs of the adversary from the first three rounds. For instance, one can instantiate Π_{bc} using the protocol of [9][12].

At a very high level, our compiler follows the approach of Cohen et al. [13]. The approach of Cohen et al. focuses on the 2-round setting (using some form of setup) and compiles a 2-round protocol Π_{bc} which uses broadcast in both rounds into one that works over peer-to-peer channels. This core idea of the compiler is to guarantee that honest parties have the same view of the first-round message when they need to compute their second-round message. To achieve this goal the parties, in the first round, generate a garbled circuit which computes their second-round message of Π_{bc} and they secret share their labels using additive secret sharing. The parties send the first-round message of Π_{bc}. In the second round, each party sends her garbled circuit and for each received first-round message of Π_{bc} she sends her appropriate share corresponding to the label in everyone else's garbled circuit. The important observation is that the labels are reconstructed only when parties send the same first-round message to *every* other party. In this work, we extend the following approach for four rounds executing the above idea for Rounds 1–2 and subsequently for Rounds 3–4. If at any round a-party detects any inconsistency (e.g., the garbled circuit outputs $\perp$, or she did not receive a message from another party) she simply aborts. Moreover, the protocol requires some changes w.r.t. the original approach since a corrupted party can send (in the second round) different garbled circuits to the honest party obtaining different 2nd rounds of Π_{bc}. We need to ensure that honest parties abort if the adversary does so, to guarantee that the adversary does not obtain honest parties' responses computed with respect to different versions, in

---

[12] To the best of our knowledge, simulators of all existing 4-round construction in the plain model (e.g., [3,9,24]) have this property of input extraction before the last round. In particular, see page 42 of [8] for details regarding input extraction by the simulator of the UA protocol in [9].

the subsequent rounds. Therefore, the garbled circuits are sent in the round that they are generated in and echoed in the next round.

In more detail, the security follows from the security of Π_{bc} because of the following: the only advantage the adversary has in comparison to Π_{bc} is that she can send inconsistent first (resp., third-round messages) over $P2P$ channels. However, additive sharing of the labels of the honest party's garbled circuit ensures that the adversary can obtain second round (resp., fourth-round) of an honest party only if she sent identical first-round (resp., third-round) to *all* honest parties. Therefore, if the honest parties do not abort, it must be the case that they have a consistent view with respect to the first and third-round messages of the adversary. Further, since the honest parties also echo the garbled circuits sent by the adversary (computing the corrupt parties' second-round messages), if they proceed to evaluate those, it would mean that the honest parties are agreeing with respect to the second-round messages of the adversary. Note that this does not constitute an issue in the 4th round. If the adversary manages to send garbled circuits resulting in honest parties obtaining different valid fourth rounds of Π_{bc} that result in different outputs, this would violate the security of Π_{bc}. This follows from our assumption that the simulator of Π_{bc} extracts the input of the adversary in the first three rounds, which guarantees that the adversarial inputs of Π_{bc} are fixed before the last round. Intuitively, in the last round of Π_{bc}, the adversary can only decide if the honest parties obtain the output or not. Finally, it is important to observe that the compiler avoids using zero-knowledge proofs (as any misbehavior that the adversary does such as garbling an incorrect function can be translated to the adversary broadcasting the corresponding second and fourth-round message in the underlying protocol Π_{bc}) and uses only tools that can be instantiated from one-way functions. In Fig. 3.1 we formally describe our protocol $\Pi_{p2p^4}^{SA}$ and refer the reader to the full version for the formal proof.

Figure 3.1: $\Pi_{p2p^4}^{SA}$

Primitives: A four-broadcast-round protocol Π_{bc} that securely computes f with unanimous abort security against $t < n$ corruptions, and a garbling scheme (garble, eval, simGC). For simplicity assume that each round message has the same length and it is ℓ bits long, so each circuit has $L = n \cdot \ell$ input bits.

Notation: Let $C_{i,x}^j(\text{msg}_1^j, \ldots, \text{msg}_n^j)$ denote the boolean circuit with hard-wired values x that takes as input the j-th round messages $\text{msg}_1^j, \ldots, \text{msg}_n^j$ and computes nxt-msg_i^j. We assume that when a party aborts she also signals the abort to all other parties.

Private input: Every party P_i has a private input $x_i \in \{0,1\}^*$.

First round $(P2P)$: Every party P_i does the following:

1. Let $\text{msg}_i^1 \leftarrow \text{frst-msg}_i(x_i)$ be P_i's first round message in Π_{bc}.

2. Compute $(\mathsf{GC}_i, \mathbf{K}_i) \leftarrow \mathsf{garble}(1^\lambda, \mathsf{C}^1_{i,x_i})$, where $\mathbf{K}_i = \{\mathbf{K}^b_{i,\alpha}\}_{\alpha \in [\mathsf{L}], b \in \{0,1\}}$.

3. For every $\alpha \in [\mathsf{L}]$ and $b \in \{0,1\}$, sample n uniform random strings $\{\mathbf{K}^b_{i \to k,\alpha}\}_{k \in [n]}$, such that $\mathbf{K}^b_{i,\alpha} = \bigoplus_{k \in [n]} \mathbf{K}^b_{i \to k,\alpha}$.

4. Send to every party P_j the message $(\mathsf{msg}^1_i, \mathsf{GC}_i, \{\mathbf{K}^b_{i \to j,\alpha}\}_{\alpha \in [\mathsf{L}], b \in \{0,1\}})$

Second round $(P2P)$: Every party P_i does the following:

1. If P_i does not receive a message from some other party (or an abort message), she aborts;

2. Otherwise, let $(\mathsf{msg}^1_{j \to i}, \mathsf{GC}_i, \{\mathbf{K}^b_{j \to i,\alpha}\}_{\alpha \in [\mathsf{L}], b \in \{0,1\}})$ be the first round message received from P_j.

3. Concatenate all received messages $\{\mathsf{msg}^1_{j \to i}\}_{j \in [n]}$ as $(\mu^1_{i,1}, \ldots, \mu^1_{i,\mathsf{L}}) \leftarrow (\mathsf{msg}^1_{1 \to i}, \ldots, \mathsf{msg}^1_{n \to i}) \in \{0,1\}^{\mathsf{L}}$.

4. Let $\overline{\mathsf{GC}}_i$ be the set of garbled circuits received from the other parties in the first round.

5. Send to all parties the message $(\overline{\mathsf{GC}}_i, \{\mathbf{K}^{\mu^1_{i,\alpha}}_{j \to i,\alpha}\}_{j \in [n], \alpha \in [\mathsf{L}]})$.

Third round $(P2P)$: Every party P_i does the following:

1. If P_i does not receive a message from some other party (or receives an abort message), she aborts; Otherwise, let $(\{\overline{\mathsf{GC}}_l\}_{l \in [n]}, \{\mathbf{K}_{1 \to j,\alpha}\}_{\alpha \in [\mathsf{L}]}, \ldots, \{\mathbf{K}_{n \to j,\alpha}\}_{\alpha \in [\mathsf{L}]})$ be the second round message received from party P_j, and let GC_j be the garbled circuit received from P_j in the first round.

2. Check if the set of garbled circuits $\{\overline{\mathsf{GC}}_l\}_{l \in [n]}$ echoed in Round 2 are consistent with the garbled circuits received in Round 1. If this is not the case, abort.

3. For every $j \in [n]$ and $\alpha \in [\mathsf{L}]$, reconstruct each garbled label by computing $\mathbf{K}_{j,\alpha} \leftarrow \bigoplus_{k \in [n]} \mathbf{K}_{j \to k,\alpha}$.

4. For every $j \in [n]$, evaluate the garble circuit as $\mathsf{msg}^2_j \leftarrow \mathsf{eval}(\mathsf{GC}_j, \{\mathbf{K}_{j,\alpha}\}_{\alpha \in [\mathsf{L}]})$. If any evaluation fails, aborts. Let $\mathsf{msg}^3_i \leftarrow \mathsf{nxt\text{-}msg}^2(x_i, \{\mathsf{msg}^1_{j \to i}\}_{j \in [n]}, \{\mathsf{msg}^2_j\}_{j \in [n]})$ be the P_i's third round message in Π_{bc}.

5. Compute $(\widetilde{\mathsf{GC}}_i, \widetilde{\mathbf{K}}_i) \leftarrow \mathsf{garble}(1^\lambda, \mathsf{C}^3_{i,x_i})$, where $\widetilde{\mathbf{K}}_i = \{\widetilde{\mathbf{K}}^b_{i,\alpha}\}_{\alpha \in [\mathsf{L}], b \in \{0,1\}}$.

6. For every $\alpha \in [\mathsf{L}]$ and $b \in \{0,1\}$, sample n uniform random strings $\{\widetilde{\mathbf{K}}^b_{i \to j,\alpha}\}_{j \in [n]}$, such that $\widetilde{\mathbf{K}}^b_{i,\alpha} = \bigoplus_{k \in [n]} \widetilde{\mathbf{K}}^b_{i \to k,\alpha}$.

7. Send to every party P_j the message $(\mathsf{msg}^3_i, \{\widetilde{\mathbf{K}}^b_{i \to j,\alpha}\}_{\alpha \in [\mathsf{L}], b \in \{0,1\}})$

Fourth round $(P2P)$: Every party P_i does the following:

1. If P_i does not receive a message from some other party (or receives an abort message), she aborts;

2. Otherwise, let $(\mathsf{msg}^3_{j \to i}, \{\widetilde{\mathbf{K}}^b_{j \to i,\alpha}\}_{\alpha \in [\mathsf{L}], b \in \{0,1\}})$ be the third round message received from P_j.

3. Concatenate all received messages $\{\mathsf{msg}^3_{j\to i}\}_{j\in[n]}$ as $(\mu^2_{i,1},\ldots,\mu^2_{i,\mathsf{L}}) \leftarrow (\mathsf{msg}^3_{1\to i},\ldots,\mathsf{msg}^3_{n\to i}) \in \{0,1\}^{\mathsf{L}}$
4. Send to all parties the message $(\widetilde{\mathsf{GC}}_i, \{\widetilde{\mathbf{K}}^{\mu^2_{i,\alpha}}_{j\to i,\alpha}\}_{j\in[n],\alpha\in[\mathsf{L}]})$

Output Computation: Every party P_i does the following:

1. If P_i does not receive a message from some other party (or receives an abort message), she aborts; Otherwise, let $(\widetilde{\mathsf{GC}}_j, \{\widetilde{\mathbf{K}}_{1\to j,\alpha}\}_{\alpha\in[\mathsf{L}]},\ldots,\{\widetilde{\mathbf{K}}_{n\to j,\alpha}\}_{\alpha\in[\mathsf{L}]})$ be the fourth round message received from party P_j.
2. For every $j\in[n]$ and $\alpha\in[\mathsf{L}]$, reconstruct each garbled label by computing $\widetilde{\mathbf{K}}_{j,\alpha} \leftarrow \bigoplus_{k\in[n]} \widetilde{\mathbf{K}}_{j\to k,\alpha}$
3. For every $j\in[n]$, evaluate the garbled circuits as $\mathsf{msg}^4_j \leftarrow \mathsf{eval}(\widetilde{\mathsf{GC}}_j, \{\widetilde{\mathbf{K}}_{j,\alpha}\}_{\alpha\in[\mathsf{L}]})$. If any evaluation fails, aborts.
4. Compute and output $y \leftarrow \mathsf{output}_i(x_i, \{\mathsf{msg}^1_{j\to i}\}_{j\in[n]}, \{\mathsf{msg}^2_j\}_{j\in[n]}, \{\mathsf{msg}^3_{j\to i}\}_{j\in[n]}, \{\mathsf{msg}^4_j\}_{j\in[n]})$

Theorem 1 (*P2P-P2P-P2P-P2P*, **SA, Plain Model**, $n > t$). *Let f be an efficiently computable n-party function, where $n > t$. Let Π_{bc} be a BC-BC-BC-BC protocol that securely computes f with unanimous abort security against $t < n$ corruptions with the additional constraint that a simulator can extract inputs before the last round. Then, assuming secure garbling schemes, the protocol from Fig. 3.1 can compute f with selective-abort security that uses only P2P channels against $t < n$ corruptions.*

$P2P^3$-*BC, UA, Plain Model*, $n > t$. The protocol described in Fig. 3.1 achieves unanimous abort security (against the same corruption threshold) when the last round is executed over the broadcast channel.

The security follows intuitively from the fact that in this case, the honest parties rely on the last round (over broadcast) to recover the output unanimously. In more detail, if any inconsistency is detected in any round before the last round, the honest party aborts signaling to abort to everybody else. Instead, if the last round is executed then the additive shares corresponding to the fourth-round next-message garbled circuits are being broadcast (instead of being sent over peer-to-peer channels), and the adversary can no longer enable only a strict subset of honest parties to evaluate the garbled circuits successfully and obtain the output. Lastly, we point that unlike the case of $P2P^4$, SA protocol in Fig. 3.1, we need not assume that Π_{bc} is such that its simulator can extract inputs before the last round. This is because in this case, the last round of the UA protocol is over broadcast. Therefore any attack in the last round of this protocol directly translates to an attack in the last round of Π_{bc}. More formally, we have the following theorem (we refer the reader to the full version for its formal proof).

Theorem 2 (*P2P-P2P-P2P-BC*, **UA, Plain Model**, $n > t$). *Let f be an efficiently computable n-party function, where $n > t$. Let Π_{bc} be a BC-BC-BC-BC protocol that securely computes f with unanimous abort security against $t < n$ corruptions. Then, assuming secure garbling schemes, the protocol from Fig. 3.1 can compute f with unanimous-abort security by a four-round protocol, where the broadcast channel is used only in the last round (while the first three rounds use peer-to-peer channels).*

BC^3-*P2P, SIA, Plain Model*, $n > t$. Let us consider a protocol Π_{bc} which is a 4-round (where the broadcast channel is available in each round) IA MPC protocol secure against a dishonest majority. Moreover, let us assume that there exists a simulator for Π_{bc} which extracts the inputs of the adversary from the first three rounds. For instance, one can instantiate Π_{bc} using the protocol of [11][13].

Starting from Π_{bc} we can construct a SIA protocol Π in the same setting, where Π is defined exactly as Π_{bc} but where the last round is executed over the peer-to-peer channel. Intuitively, Π achieves SIA security since by our assumptions on Π_{bc} the simulator extracts the inputs of the adversary in the first three rounds, and therefore the adversarial inputs are fixed before the last round. Indeed, in the last round, the adversary can only decide if an honest party gets the output or learns the identity of cheaters (depending on the version of the last round message the adversary sends privately), but two honest parties can not obtain a different output (which is non-$\perp$). It can happen that different honest parties identify different cheaters and others recover (the same) outputs, but this is sufficient for SIA security. Finally, we note that a similar result was shown by [15], but only for the two rounds setting. We prove the following theorem, and refer the reader to the full version for its proof.

Theorem 3 (*BC-BC-BC-P2P*, **SIA, Plain Model**, $n > t$). *Let f be an efficiently computable n-party function, where $n > t$. Let Π_{bc} be a BC-BC-BC-BC protocol that securely computes f with identifiable abort security against $t < n$ corruptions with the additional constraint that a simulator can extract inputs before the last round. Then, f can be computed with selective identifiable-abort security by a four-round protocol, where the first three-rounds use broadcast channels and the last round uses peer-to-peer channels.*

---

[13] The protocol of [11] lifts an UA protocol to achieve IA security (where the simulator of the IA protocol uses the simulator of the UA protocol). If we consider, for instance, the simulator of the UA protocol constructed in [9], this simulator extracts the inputs of the adversary from the first 3 rounds (see page 42 of [8]). Therefore, for instance, by instantiating [11] with [9] we obtain Π_{bc} with the desired property.

4   Negative Results

BC^3-$P2P$, *UA, Plain Model,* $n > t$. At a high-level, we show that any BC^3-$P2P$ protocol achieving UA against dishonest majority implies a three-round oblivious transfer (OT) protocol in the plain model, which is known to be impossible [25]. We prove the following theorem and refer the reader to the full version for the formal proof.

Theorem 4 (BC-BC-BC-$P2P$, **UA,** $n > t$). *There exists function f such that no n-party four-round protocol can compute f with unanimous-abort security against $t < n$ corruptions, such that the first three rounds use broadcast and point-to-point channels and the last round uses only point-to-point channels.*

4.1   SIA Impossibility Results

Theorem 5 (BC-BC-$P2P$-$P2P$, **SIA, Plain Model,** $n > t$). *Assume the existence of pseudorandom functions. There exists function f such that no n-party four-round protocol (in the plain model) can compute with selective identifiable-abort security, against $t < n$ corruptions, while in the protocol, the first two rounds use broadcast channels and the last two rounds use peer-to-peer channels.*

Proof. We start the proof assuming that the four-round protocol Π is run by three parties only, and we extend the proof to the n-party case in the end. By contradiction, assume that there exists a three-party protocol Π that can compute any function f with selective identifiable-abort security where just one party P_{out} gets the output[14] and the broadcast channel is accessible only in the first two rounds. Let us denote the three parties running the protocol Π with P_1, P_2, and P_{out}.

Consider the following adversarial strategy of Fig. 4.1. In summary, in this scenario, corrupted P_1 behaves like an honest party, with the difference that it does not send the third and the fourth message to P_2, and it pretends that it does not receive the third message and the fourth message from P_2.

Figure 4.1: Scenario 1

Setting: P_1 is corrupted party P_2 and P_{out} are honest parties.
Private input: Every party P_i has a private input $x_i \in \{0,1\}^*$.

First round (BC):
Every party P_i samples the randomness r_i from uniform distribution $\mathcal{D}$, computes $\mathsf{msg}_i^1 \leftarrow \mathtt{frst\text{-}msg}_i(x_i; r_i)$, and sends the message over the broadcast channel.

---

[14] We are assuming implicitly this requirement on f thought the rest of the proof.

Second round (BC):
Every party P_i computes $\mathsf{msg}_i^2 \leftarrow \mathtt{nxt\text{-}msg}_i^1(x_i, \{\mathsf{msg}_j^1\}_{j \in \{1,2,\mathsf{out}\}}; r_i)$, and sends it over the broadcast channel.

Third round $(P2P)$:

1. Every party P_i computes $(\{\mathsf{msg}_{i \to j}^3\}_{j \in \{1,2,\mathsf{out}\}}) \leftarrow \mathtt{nxt\text{-}msg}_i^2(x_i, \{\mathsf{msg}_j^k\}_{j \in \{1,2,\mathsf{out}\}, k \in \{1,2\}}; r_i)$.

2. P_1 sends $\mathsf{msg}_{1 \to \mathsf{out}}^3$ to P_{out}. P_{out} sends $\mathsf{msg}_{\mathsf{out} \to 1}^3$ to P_1, and sends $\mathsf{msg}_{\mathsf{out} \to 2}^3$ to P_2. P_2 sends $\mathsf{msg}_{2 \to 1}^3$ to P_1, and sends $\mathsf{msg}_{2 \to \mathsf{out}}^3$ to P_{out}.

Fourth round $(P2P)$:

1. P_1 sets $\mathsf{msg}_{2 \to 1}^3 = \perp$ and computes $(\{\mathsf{msg}_{1 \to j}^4\}_{j \in \{1,2,\mathsf{out}\}}) \leftarrow \mathtt{nxt\text{-}msg}_1^3(x_1, \{\mathsf{msg}_j^k\}_{j \in \{1,2,\mathsf{out}\}, k \in \{1,2\}}, \{\mathsf{msg}_{j \to 1}^3\}_{j \in \{1,2,\mathsf{out}\}}; r_1)$.

2. P_{out} computes $(\{\mathsf{msg}_{2 \to j}^4\}_{j \in \{1,2,\mathsf{out}\}}) \leftarrow \mathtt{nxt\text{-}msg}_{\mathsf{out}}^3(x_{\mathsf{out}}, \{\mathsf{msg}_j^k\}_{j \in \{1,2,\mathsf{out}\}, k \in \{1,2\}}, \{\mathsf{msg}_{j \to \mathsf{out}}^3\}_{j \in \{1,2,\mathsf{out}\}}; r_{\mathsf{out}})$.

3. P_2 computes $(\{\mathsf{msg}_{2 \to j}^4\}_{j \in \{1,2,\mathsf{out}\}}) \leftarrow \mathtt{nxt\text{-}msg}_2^3(x_2, \{\mathsf{msg}_j^k\}_{j \in \{1,2,\mathsf{out}\}, k \in \{1,2\}}, \{\mathsf{msg}_{j \to 2}^3\}_{j \in \{2,\mathsf{out}\}}; r_2)$.

4. P_1 sends $\mathsf{msg}_{1 \to \mathsf{out}}^4$ to P_{out}. P_{out} sends $\mathsf{msg}_{\mathsf{out} \to 1}^4$ to P_1, and sends $\mathsf{msg}_{\mathsf{out} \to 2}^4$ to P_2. P_2 sends $\mathsf{msg}_{2 \to \mathsf{out}}^4$ to P_{out} and $\mathsf{msg}_{2 \to 1}^4$ to P_1.

Given the above adversarial strategy, we proceed now in a series of steps in order to reach a contradiction.

Step 1: P_{out} Can not abort identifying the corrupted party. We prove that, if P_{out} aborts, it can not identify that P_1 aborted. We prove this by contradiction. Consider the scenario of Fig. 4.2. In this, the corrupted P_2 behaves like an honest party, and he does not send the third and the fourth round message to P_1. At the same time, it pretends that it does not receive the third round and fourth message from P_1. P_1 behaves honestly, sending all the messages that the protocol Π prescribes. In summary, P_2 behaves like P_1 behaves in Scenario 1.

Figure 4.2: Scenario 2

Setting: P_2 is corrupted party. P_1 and P_{out} are honest parties.
Private input: Every party P_i has a private input $x_i \in \{0,1\}^*$.

First round (BC):
Every P_i samples the randomness r_i from uniform distribution $\mathcal{D}$, computes $\mathsf{msg}_i^1 \leftarrow \mathtt{frst\text{-}msg}_i(x_i; r_i)$, and sends the message over the broadcast channel.

Second round (BC):
Every party P_i computes $\mathsf{msg}_i^2 \leftarrow \mathtt{nxt\text{-}msg}_i^1(x_i, \{\mathsf{msg}_j^1\}_{j \in \{1,2,\mathsf{out}\}}; r_i)$, and sends it over the broadcast channel.

Third round $(P2P)$:

1. Every party P_i computes $(\{\mathsf{msg}^3_{i \to j}\}_{j \in \{1,2,\mathsf{out}\}})$ ← $\mathsf{nxt\text{-}msg}^2_i(x_i, \{\mathsf{msg}^k_j\}_{j \in \{1,2,\mathsf{out}\}, k \in \{1,2\}}; r_i)$.

2. P_2 sends $\mathsf{msg}^3_{2 \to \mathsf{out}}$ to P_out. P_out sends $\mathsf{msg}^3_{\mathsf{out} \to 1}$ to P_1, and sends $\mathsf{msg}^3_{\mathsf{out} \to 2}$ to P_2. P_1 sends $\mathsf{msg}^3_{1 \to \mathsf{out}}$ to P_out, and sends $\mathsf{msg}^3_{1 \to 2}$ to P_2.

Fourth round ($P2P$):

1. P_1 computes $(\{\mathsf{msg}^4_{1 \to j}\}_{j \in \{1,2,\mathsf{out}\}})$ ← $\mathsf{nxt\text{-}msg}^3_1(x_1, \{\mathsf{msg}^k_j\}_{j \in \{1,2,\mathsf{out}\}, k \in \{1,2\}}, \{\mathsf{msg}^3_{j \to 1}\}_{j \in \{1,\mathsf{out}\}}; r_1)$.

2. P_out computes $(\{\mathsf{msg}^4_{\mathsf{out} \to j}\}_{j \in \{1,2,\mathsf{out}\}})$ ← $\mathsf{nxt\text{-}msg}^3_\mathsf{out}(x_\mathsf{out}, \{\mathsf{msg}^k_j\}_{j \in \{1,2,\mathsf{out}\}, k \in \{1,2\}}, \{\mathsf{msg}^3_{j \to \mathsf{out}}\}_{j \in \{1,2,\mathsf{out}\}}; r_\mathsf{out})$.

3. P_2 sets $\mathsf{msg}^3_{1 \to 2} = \perp$ and computes $(\{\mathsf{msg}^4_{2 \to j}\}_{j \in \{1,2,\mathsf{out}\}})$ ← $\mathsf{nxt\text{-}msg}^3_2(x_2, \{\mathsf{msg}^k_j\}_{j \in \{1,2,\mathsf{out}\}, k \in \{1,2\}}, \{\mathsf{msg}^3_{j \to 2}\}_{j \in \{1,2,\mathsf{out}\}}; r_2)$.

4. P_2 sends $\mathsf{msg}^4_{2 \to \mathsf{out}}$ to P_out. P_out sends $\mathsf{msg}^4_{\mathsf{out} \to 1}$ to P_1, and sends $\mathsf{msg}^4_{\mathsf{out} \to 2}$ to P_2. P_1 sends $\mathsf{msg}^4_{1 \to \mathsf{out}}$ to P_out and $\mathsf{msg}^4_{1 \to 2}$ to P_2.

Intutively, in Scenario 1 (in Fig. 4.1), P_2 can potentially report P_1's misbehaviour to P_out earliest in round 4 (since P_1 behaved honestly in round 1 and round 2). This means that P_out cannot identify the corrupted party (and abort) until all the four rounds are received. However, a corrupted P_1 is pretending that P_2 did not send the third round message. Hence, none of the messages that P_out receives in the fourth round would help him. In particular, P_out sees P_1 and P_2 blaming each other. In addition, P_out can not see what happened on $P2P$ channel between P_1 and P_2, therefore, P_out can not identify the corrupted party correctly.

Formally, if in Scenario 1 P_out aborts, then based on the definition of selective identifiable-abort, P_out identifies P_1 as the corrupted party. However, the view of P_out in the Scenario 1 is identical to the view of P_out in Scenario 2 (in Fig. 4.2). Because the view of P_out is identical in the two scenarios, then P_out has the same behavior in both scenarios. Hence, P_out identifies P_1 as the corrupted party. However, in Scenario 2, P_1 is honest, and this contradicts the SIA security of Π. From the above, we can conclude that P_out does not abort in Scenario 1, hence, it must be able to compute the output.

Step 2: Constructing an SA secure protocol (only for two corruption patterns). We now consider a new protocol, that we denote with Π' (and denote the parties running the protocol with P'_1, P'_2 and P'_out). This protocol works exactly like Π, with the following differences: 1) The honest P'_1 does not send the third message to P'_2. 2) No fourth messages between P'_1 and P'_2. 3) P'_out does not send any fourth round to P'_1 and P'_2.

We prove that this protocol is secure with selective aborts. Informally, this is possible because the honest parties send fewer messages compared to Π, and the party P'_out will still be able to compute the output due to the argument given above. Moreover, given that we just want to obtain SA security, we can remove the messages that P_out sends in the last round. Formally, we prove that if Π is SIA secure, then Π' (that we propose in Fig. 4.3) is secure with selective abort (SA) for two corruption patterns. Namely, we prove that the protocol is secure when either P_1' and P_{out}' are corrupted or when P_{out}' and P_2' are corrupted. Looking ahead, we focus only on these corruption patterns, because proving the security of Π' only in these cases would be enough to reach our final contradiction. Below, we provide a more formal argument.

Figure 4.3: The new protocol Π'

Primitives: A three-party four-round protocol $\Pi = \{(\texttt{frst-msg}_i, \{\texttt{nxt-msg}_i^k\}_{k \in \{1,2,3\}}, \texttt{output}_i)\}_{i \in \{1,2,out\}}$ that securely computes any f with selective identifiable-abort security against $t < n$ corruptions, where the first two rounds use the broadcast channels to exchange messages, and last two rounds use $P2P$ channels.

Private input: Every party P_i' has a private input $x_i \in \{0,1\}^*$.

First round (BC):
Every party P_i' samples the randomness r_i from uniform distribution $\mathcal{D}$, computes $\texttt{msg}_i^1 \leftarrow \texttt{frst-msg}_i(x_i; r_i)$, and sends the message over the broadcast channel.

Second round (BC):
Every party P_i' computes $\texttt{msg}_i^2 \leftarrow \texttt{nxt-msg}_i^1(x_i, \{\texttt{msg}_j^1\}_{j \in \{1,2,out\}}; r_i)$, and sends it over the broadcast channel.

Third round ($P2P$):

1. Every party P_i' computes $(\{\texttt{msg}_{i \to j}^3\}_{j \in \{1,2,out\}}) \leftarrow \texttt{nxt-msg}_i^2(x_i, \{\texttt{msg}_j^k\}_{j \in \{1,2,out\}, k \subset \{1,2\}}; r_i)$.
2. P_1' sends $\texttt{msg}_{1 \to out}^3$ to P_{out}'. P_{out}' sends $\texttt{msg}_{out \to 1}^3$ to P_1', and sends $\texttt{msg}_{out \to 2}^3$ to P_2'. P_2' sends $\texttt{msg}_{2 \to 1}^3$ to P_1', and sends $\texttt{msg}_{2 \to out}^3$ to P_{out}'.

Fourth round ($P2P$):

1. P_1' sets $\texttt{msg}_{2 \to 1}^3 = \bot$ and computes $(\{\texttt{msg}_{1 \to j}^4\}_{j \in \{1,2,out\}}) \leftarrow \texttt{nxt-msg}_1^3(x_1, \{\texttt{msg}_j^k\}_{j \in \{1,2,out\}, k \in \{1,2\}}, \{\texttt{msg}_{j \to 1}^3\}_{j \in \{1,2,out\}}; r_1)$.
2. P_{out}' computes $(\{\texttt{msg}_{out \to j}^4\}_{j \in \{1,2,out\}}) \leftarrow \texttt{nxt-msg}_{out}^3(x_{out}, \{\texttt{msg}_j^k\}_{j \in \{1,2,out\}, k \in \{1,2\}}, \{\texttt{msg}_{j \to out}^3\}_{j \in \{1,2,out\}}; r_{out})$.
3. P_2' computes $(\{\texttt{msg}_{2 \to j}^4\}_{j \in \{1,2,out\}}) \leftarrow \texttt{nxt-msg}_2^3(x_2, \{\texttt{msg}_j^k\}_{j \in \{1,2,out\}, k \in \{1,2\}}, \{\texttt{msg}_{j \to 2}^3\}_{j \in \{2,out\}}; r_2)$.
4. P_1' sends $\texttt{msg}_{1 \to out}^4$ to P_{out}'. P_2' sends $\texttt{msg}_{2 \to out}^4$ to P_{out}'.

Output Computation:

1. P_{out}' compute and output $y \leftarrow \texttt{output}_{out}(x_{out}, \{\texttt{msg}_j^k\}_{j \in \{1,2,out\}, k \in \{1,2\}}, \{\texttt{msg}_{j \to out}^k\}_{j \in \{1,2,out\}, k \in \{3,4\}}; r_{out})$

The security of the SIA protocol Π ensures us that there exist corresponding simulators for (all) the corruption patterns, we will exploit those simulators to construct the simulators for proving the security of Π'. Let $\mathcal{S}_{1,\text{out}}^{\text{SIA}}$ and $\mathcal{S}_{2,\text{out}}^{\text{SIA}}$ be the simulators of Π for, respectively, corrupted P_1 and P_{out} and for corrupted P_2 and P_{out}. We construct two new simulators $\mathcal{S}_{1,\text{out}}^{\text{SA}}$ and $\mathcal{S}_{2,\text{out}}^{\text{SA}}$ which, respectively, make use of $\mathcal{S}_{1,\text{out}}^{\text{SIA}}$ and $\mathcal{S}_{2,\text{out}}^{\text{SIA}}$, and use them to prove the security of Π' in the above-mentioned corruption patterns. To formally do that, we need to transform an adversary $\mathcal{A}^{\text{SA}}$ attacking Π' into an admissible adversary $\mathcal{M}_{\text{intf}}$ of Π (we need to do that since the simulators $\mathcal{S}_{1,\text{out}}^{\text{SIA}}$ and $\mathcal{S}_{2,\text{out}}^{\text{SIA}}$ only work against adversaries attacking the protocol Π). $\mathcal{M}_{\text{intf}}$ runs internally $\mathcal{A}^{\text{SA}}$ and acts as a proxy for the messages between the simulator $\mathcal{S}_{1,\text{out}}^{\text{SIA}}$ (resp. $\mathcal{S}_{2,\text{out}}^{\text{SIA}}$) and $\mathcal{A}^{\text{SA}}$, withholding the messages that honest party P_1' is not supposed to send in Π'. The Fig. 4.4 formally describes $\mathcal{M}_{\text{intf}}$. In this, we denote as the *left interface*, the interface where the adversary sends and receives the protocol messages.

Figure 4.4: The adversary $\mathcal{M}_{\text{intf}}$

Notation: Let $\mathbb{H}$ be the set of indices of the honest parties and $\mathcal{I}$ be the indices of the corrupted parties. $\mathcal{M}_{\text{intf}}$ internally runs the adversary $\mathcal{A}^{\text{SA}}$, and is equipped with a left interface, where it receives the messages computed on behalf of the honest parties and sends the messages computed on the behalf of the corrupted parties.

First round (BC):

1. Upon receiving msg_h^1 on the left interface with $h \in \mathbb{H}$, $\mathcal{M}_{\text{intf}}$ forwards the message to $\mathcal{A}^{\text{SA}}$ in Π'.
2. Upon receiving the messages sent by $\mathcal{A}^{\text{SA}}$, $\mathcal{M}_{\text{intf}}$ forwards them to the left interface, where it is acting as a corrupted party for Π.

Second round (BC):

1. Upon receiving msg_h^2 on the left interface, where $h \in \mathbb{H}$, $\mathcal{M}_{\text{intf}}$ forwards the message to $\mathcal{A}^{\text{SA}}$.
2. Upon receiving the messages sent by $\mathcal{A}^{\text{SA}}$ in Π', $\mathcal{M}_{\text{intf}}$ forwards them, acting as the corrupted parties in Π.

Third round ($P2P$):

1. Upon receiving $\text{msg}_{h \to j}^3$ in the left interface, where $h \in \mathbb{H}$ and $j \in \mathcal{I}$, $\mathcal{M}_{\text{intf}}$ forwards the message $\text{msg}_{h \to \text{out}}^3$ (and the message $\text{msg}_{2 \to 1}^3$ in the case where $2 \in \mathbb{H}$) to $\mathcal{A}^{\text{SA}}$.
2. Upon receiving the messages sent by $\mathcal{A}^{\text{SA}}$, $\mathcal{M}_{\text{intf}}$ forwards them to the left interface acting as the corrupted parties in Π.

Fourth round ($P2P$):

1. Upon receiving $\mathsf{msg}^4_{h \to j}$ on the left interface, where $h \in \mathbb{H}$ and $j \in \mathcal{I}$, $\mathcal{M}_{\mathsf{intf}}$ forwards the message $\mathsf{msg}^4_{h \to \mathsf{out}}$ to $\mathcal{A}^{\mathsf{SA}}$ (if any).
2. Upon receiving the messages sent by $\mathcal{A}^{\mathsf{SA}}$, $\mathcal{M}_{\mathsf{intf}}$ forwards them to its left interface.

We are now ready to show how the simulator $\mathcal{S}^{\mathsf{SA}}_{1,\mathsf{out}}$ of Π' for the case where P'_1 and P'_{out} are corrupted. The simulator $\mathcal{S}^{\mathsf{SA}}_{1,\mathsf{out}}$ is formally described in Fig. 4.5.

Figure 4.5: $\mathcal{S}^{\mathsf{SA}}_{1,\mathsf{out}}$

$\mathcal{S}^{\mathsf{SA}}_{1,\mathsf{out}}$ performs the following steps:

- Invoke $\mathcal{S}^{\mathsf{SIA}}_{1,\mathsf{out}}$ for the adversary $\mathcal{M}_{\mathsf{intf}}$, querying and receiving responses to and from its left interface.
- Work as a proxy between the ideal functionality and $\mathcal{S}^{\mathsf{SIA}}_{1,\mathsf{out}}$.

In the end, $\mathcal{S}^{\mathsf{SA}}_{1,\mathsf{out}}$ output whatever $\mathcal{S}^{\mathsf{SIA}}_{1,\mathsf{out}}$ outputs, and halt.

For the case where P'_2 and P'_{out} are corrupted, we can define the simulator $\mathcal{S}^{\mathsf{SA}}_{2,\mathsf{out}}$ similarly to $\mathcal{S}^{\mathsf{SIA}}_{1,\mathsf{out}}$, but using $\mathcal{S}^{\mathsf{SIA}}_{2,\mathsf{out}}$. If an adversary $\mathcal{A}^{\mathsf{SA}}$ attacking Π' is able to distinguish between when it is receiving messages produced by $\mathcal{S}^{\mathsf{SA}}_{1,\mathsf{out}}$ (resp. $\mathcal{S}^{\mathsf{SA}}_{2,\mathsf{out}}$) from the case when the messages are generated from an honest party running Π', then we can show an adversary that contradicts the SIA security of Π. In the reduction $\mathcal{A}^{\mathsf{SIA}}$ simply runs internally $\mathcal{M}_{\mathsf{intf}}$, which in turn it will run $\mathcal{A}^{\mathsf{SA}}$.

Step 3: Modifying adversary $\mathcal{A}^{\mathsf{SA}}$. As a stepping stone toward proving the final result, we consider first another adversary $\mathcal{A}^{\mathsf{PRF}}_{1,\mathsf{out}}$, which corrupts P'_1 and P'_{out} and acts as follows. The corrupted parties P'_1 and P'_{out} act like the honest parties running Π' would, except that they are rushing in the first round (i.e., they wait to receive the honest party's message before sending their first round), and compute their input and randomness by evaluating a PRF on input the message received from the honest party. More formally, $\mathcal{A}^{\mathsf{PRF}}_{1,\mathsf{out}}$ samples two different keys (k_1, k_2) for a PRF F. Upon receiving the first round msg^1_2 from the honest P'_2, the adversary computes $x_1 \leftarrow \mathsf{F}_{k_1}(\mathsf{msg}^1_2)$, $r_1 \leftarrow \mathsf{F}_{k_2}(\mathsf{msg}^1_2)$. Then $\mathcal{A}^{\mathsf{PRF}}_{1,\mathsf{out}}$ use (x_1, r_1) and original input and randomness of P'_{out} to finish all four round interactions with the honest party P'_2. We define $\mathcal{A}^{\mathsf{PRF}}_{2,\mathsf{out}}$ similarly.

We need to prove even against such an adversary there exists a simulator, that can successfully extract the input from a corrupted P'_1. A simulator for $\mathcal{A}^{\mathsf{PRF}}_{1,\mathsf{out}}$ trivially exists due to the SA security of Π', hence, we need to argue that such a simulator does query the ideal functionality, hence, it extracts the input of the corrupted parties (this will be crucial for the last step of our impossibility proof). To prove that this is indeed the case, we start by observing that, trivially, when all the parties are honest then Π' terminates and P'_{out} computes the output, with no party triggering an abort. Consider now an adversary $\mathcal{A}^{\mathsf{r}}_{1,\mathsf{out}}$, that corrupts the parties with index 1 and out, and instructs these parties to be rushing in the first round, and non-rushing in the remaining rounds, without change behaviors of corrupted parties.

Also in this case, it is easy to see that the honest party will not abort and that P'_{out} will compute the output. What remains to prove is that the view of the honest party stays the same when interacting with $\mathcal{A}^{PRF}_{1,out}$ instead of $\mathcal{A}^r_{1,out}$. To do that, we prove the following lemma, which holds due to the security of the PRF.

Lemma 1. *Let $\mathcal{A}^{PRF}_{1,out}(\text{aux})$ and $\mathcal{A}^r_{1,out}$ be the adversaries described above. Assume that PRFs exist, then, for every auxiliary input aux, for all $x \in (\{0,1\}^*)^3$, for all $\lambda \in \mathbb{N}$, it holds that the probability that the honest party aborts in $REAL_{\Pi,\{1,out\},\mathcal{A}^{PRF}_{1,out}(\text{aux})}(x,1^\lambda)$ is negligible-close to the probability that the honest party aborts in $REAL_{\Pi,\{1,out\},\mathcal{A}^r_{1,out}(\text{aux})}(x,1^\lambda)$.*

We also prove that the same lemma holds for the case where the indices of the corrupted parties are $\{2, out\}$. We refer the reader to the full version for the formal proof. We then prove the following lemma (we refer the reader to the full version for the formal proof), which in summary states that Π remains secure even against such PRF adversaries.

Lemma 2. *Let f be an efficiently computable three-party function. Assume that there exists a three-party protocol Π that securely computes f with selective-abort security when parties P_1 and P_{out} are corrupted, for every PPT real-world adversary $\mathcal{A}^{SA}_{1,out}$ with auxiliary input aux. Then for the same corruption pattern $\mathcal{I}$, for the same auxiliary input aux, for all $x \in (\{0,1\}^*)^3$, for all $\lambda \in \mathbb{N}$, it holds that $\{REAL_{\Pi,\mathcal{I},\mathcal{A}^{PRF}_{1,out}(\text{aux})}(x,1^\lambda)\} \stackrel{c}{\cong} \{IDEAL^{sa\text{-}abort}_{f,\mathcal{I},\mathcal{S}_{1,out}(\text{aux})}(x,1^\lambda)\}$. We also prove that it works for the corruption pattern $\{2, out\}$*

Step 4: Constructing an adversary that breaks the SA security of Π'. We prove that there exists an adversary $\mathcal{A}'_{SA}$ that can use the simulator $\mathcal{S}^{SA}_{1,out}$ to extract the input from an honest P'_1. This would contradict the SA security of Π'. This adversary $\mathcal{A}'_{SA}$ (formally described in Fig. 4.6) controls the parties P'_2 and P'_{out} and runs internally the simulator $\mathcal{S}^{SA}_{1,out}$[15]. Note that $\mathcal{S}^{SA}_{1,out}$ expects to interact with an adversary which corrupts P'_1 and P'_{out} in an execution of Π', hence $\mathcal{A}'_{SA}$ needs to make sure that $\mathcal{S}^{SA}_{1,out}$ can be executed correctly, despite the party P'_1 being honest. In particular, we need to argue that the simulator can work properly (i.e., the simulator extracts the input P'_1) while P'_1 is not rewound.

Figure 4.6: The adversary $\mathcal{A}'_{SA}$

- Define and initialize $j \leftarrow -1$ and sample $k_1, k_2 \leftarrow \{0,1\}^\lambda$. Run $\mathcal{S}^{SA}_{1,out}$, which denotes the simulator of Π' for the case where P'_1 and P'_{out} are

---

[15] Note that the simulator is expected polynomial time, hence we need to cut its running time to make sure that $\mathcal{A}'_{SA}$ remains PPT.

corrupted. $\mathcal{S}_{1,\text{out}}^{\text{SA}}$ is run until it performs up to κ steps (recall that $\mathcal{S}_{1,\text{out}}^{\text{SA}}$ needs $\kappa = \text{poly}(\lambda)$ expected number steps).

- Sample $i \leftarrow [\kappa]$. Any time that $\mathcal{S}_{1,\text{out}}^{\text{SA}}$ opens a new session by sending a new first-round m (m here denotes all the messages received over broadcast in the first round) to the honest P_1' then set $j \leftarrow j + 1$ and do the following.

  - If $j = i$ compute $x_1^i \leftarrow \mathsf{F}_{k_1}(m)$, where x_1^i will denote the input of the honest party P_1' used in the MPC indistinguishability game[a].
  - If $j \neq i$ then reply to all the queries of $\mathcal{S}_{1,\text{out}}^{\text{SA}}$, acting as the honest P_1' would act using the input x_1^j and the randomness r_1^j, where $x_1^j \leftarrow \mathsf{F}_{k_1}(m)$ and $r_1^j \leftarrow \mathsf{F}_{k_2}(m)$.

- In the i-th session act as a proxy between the MPC challenger and $\mathcal{S}_{1,\text{out}}^{\text{SA}}$ with respect to all the messages related to P_1'. Note that the messages from the challenger will either be simulated or generated by running the honest party P_1' with the input x_1^i.

- For every message that $\mathcal{S}_{1,\text{out}}^{\text{SA}}$ sends to P_1' in the session $j \neq i$, reply as the honest party P_1' would using the input x_1^j and the randomness r_1^j.

- Act as an honest P_{out}' would act with the only difference that P_{out}' sends the third round to P_1' in the session i only after that $\mathcal{S}_{1,\text{out}}^{\text{SA}}$ has stopped and it has returned a transcript consistent with the i-th session.

- Whenever $\mathcal{S}_{1,\text{out}}^{\text{SA}}$ tries to send a second round in the i-th session, forward this message only to P_{out}'. When $\mathcal{S}_{1,\text{out}}^{\text{SA}}$ stops and returns its transcript, forward to P_1' the second round message that appears in the transcript.

- When $\mathcal{S}_{1,\text{out}}^{\text{SA}}$ attempts to query the ideal functionality with a value $\tilde{x}_1 = (\tilde{x}^0, \tilde{x}^1)$, $\mathcal{A}_{\text{SA}}'$ records this value, and sends back to the simulator $\tilde{x}^{x_2}$ (here the adversary acts as the ideal functionality would for the simulator $\mathcal{S}_{1,\text{out}}^{\text{SA}}$). When $\mathcal{S}_{1,\text{out}}^{\text{SA}}$ stops, and returns its output, check if the output transcript is consistent with the messages generated in the i-th session. If this is the case then do the following

  - If $\tilde{x}_1 = x_1^i$ then return 1 (this is to denote that the challenger generated a transcript using the honest procedure for P_1').
  - If $\tilde{x}_1 \neq x_1^i$ then return 0 (this is to denote that the messages computed by the challenger on behalf of P_1' were simulated)

  If instead the output transcript of $\mathcal{S}_{1,\text{out}}^{\text{SA}}$ is not consistent with the i-th session, then return a random bit.

---

[a] Note that in the security experiment of MPC protocol must hold for any x_1. In particular, this means that the security must hold for a value x_1 chosen by the adversary prior to the beginning of the experiment.

In other words, we need to prove that any rewind made by the simulator $\mathcal{S}_{1,\text{out}}^{\text{SA}}$ can be emulated by $\mathcal{A}_{\text{SA}}'$ without rewinding the honest P_1'. Finally note that P_{out}' is corrupted, hence $\mathcal{A}_{\text{SA}}'$ can emulate any interaction between $\mathcal{S}_{1,\text{out}}^{\text{SA}}$ and P_{out}'. This means that we can rewind P_{out}', but at the same time need to make sure that any rewind performed on P_{out}', does not implicitly rewind also P_1'. To make sure this does not happen, we instruct $\mathcal{A}'_{\mathsf{SA}}$ to be rushing in the first round and non-rushing in other rounds. We examine now all the possible rewinding patterns, to show that our adversary does not need to rewind P'_1. We do so using different figures (for each pattern), where we use a straight line to denote messages on the $P2P$ channel, a dashed line to denote messages on the broadcast channel and a dotted line to denote rewind messages and corresponding new messages. We also use the number to indicate which round message it is.

We start by considering the scenario where $\mathcal{S}^{\mathsf{SA}}_{1,\mathsf{out}}$ is attempting to rewind (what he sees as a malicious) P'_1 in the first BC round. Because we cut the running time of $\mathcal{S}^{\mathsf{SA}}_{1,\mathsf{out}}$, we can assume that $\mathcal{S}^{\mathsf{SA}}_{1,\mathsf{out}}$ will rewind the first BC round for at most κ times, for some polynomial κ. To deal with this situation, our adversary samples a random index $i \leftarrow [\kappa]$, and forwards to the external challenger only the message generated by $\mathcal{S}^{\mathsf{SA}}_{1,\mathsf{out}}$ related to the i-th session. To define the input x_1 that will be used in the indistinguishability experiment, we evaluate a PRF on input the first round messages received from $\mathcal{S}^{\mathsf{SA}}_{1,\mathsf{out}}$. Note that the security of Π' must hold for any choice of x_1, even for an adversarially chosen one.

For all the other sessions, our adversary will answer the messages generated by $\mathcal{S}^{\mathsf{SA}}_{1,\mathsf{out}}$ acting as the honest P'_1 would, using as input and randomness the output of a PRF evaluated on the messages received from $\mathcal{S}^{\mathsf{SA}}_{1,\mathsf{out}}$. By applying Lemma 2, we can argue that $\mathcal{S}^{\mathsf{SA}}_{1,\mathsf{out}}$ is secure against $\mathcal{A}^{\mathsf{PRF}}$, which means even when the input and randomness are computed by using the PRF, the simulator is still able to extract the input from the corrupted party, with non-negligible probability.

We mentioned that in the i-th session, $\mathcal{A}'_{\mathsf{SA}}$ acts as a proxy between the external challenger and $\mathcal{S}^{\mathsf{SA}}_{1,\mathsf{out}}$ for all the messages related to P'_1. Note that $\mathcal{S}^{\mathsf{SA}}_{1,\mathsf{out}}$ can also rewind the second, third, and fourth rounds in the i-th session. Consider the case where $\mathcal{S}^{\mathsf{SA}}_{1,\mathsf{out}}$ rewinds the second round that goes from P'_2 to P'_{out}. This action, in turn, causes P'_{out} to send multiple third rounds to P'_1. We observe that there is no need to forward all these multiple third rounds to P'_1, as we can just block all of them except the message that will appear in the final simulated session. Note that the simulator must work well even with this modification since the simulator does not see the effect of the rewinds implicitly performed to P'_1 due to the fact that the simulator has no access to the fourth $P2P$ round messages that P'_1 may compute as a consequence of these rewinds (recall that P'_{out} is non-rushing and that it does not send any message to P'_2). We refer to Fig. 4.7.a for a pictorial description.

Figure 4.7.b reflects the scenario where $\mathcal{S}^{\mathsf{SA}}_{1,\mathsf{out}}$ is attempting to rewind (what he sees as a malicious) P'_1 in the third $P2P$ round. By the definition of Π', P'_1 does not react on the third round that comes from P'_1, hence, we can just forward to P'_1 only one message, which corresponds to the message the simulator returns in its final simulated transcript. Figure 4.7.c reflects the scenario where $\mathcal{S}^{\mathsf{SA}}_{1,\mathsf{out}}$ is attempting a rewind to P'_{out} in the third $P2P$ round. By construction of Π', P'_{out} does not send any fourth message. Hence, we can simply allow this rewind as the adversary $\mathcal{A}'_{\mathsf{SA}}$ controls P'_{out}. Figure 4.7.d reflects the scenario where $\mathcal{S}^{\mathsf{SA}}_{1,\mathsf{out}}$ is

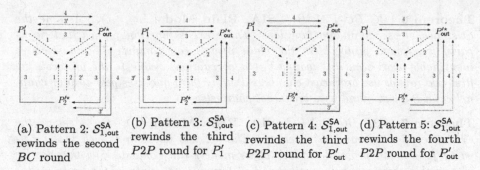

(a) Pattern 2: $\mathcal{S}_{1,\text{out}}^{\text{SA}}$ rewinds the second BC round

(b) Pattern 3: $\mathcal{S}_{1,\text{out}}^{\text{SA}}$ rewinds the third $P2P$ round for P_1'

(c) Pattern 4: $\mathcal{S}_{1,\text{out}}^{\text{SA}}$ rewinds the third $P2P$ round for P_{out}'

(d) Pattern 5: $\mathcal{S}_{1,\text{out}}^{\text{SA}}$ rewinds the fourth $P2P$ round for P_{out}'

Figure 4.7. Rewinding patterns

attempting a rewind P_{out}' in the fourth $P2P$ round. Also in this case, it is easy to see that this action does not implicitly rewind P_1'.

We have argued our adversary can run $\mathcal{S}_{1,\text{out}}^{\text{SA}}$, without perturbing its behavior, while at the same time making sure that P_1' is not rewound. This means that the $\mathcal{S}_{1,\text{out}}^{\text{SA}}$ will, with non-negligible probability, return some value that corresponds to the input of P_1' (when the messages of P_1' are computed accordingly to Π', and are not simulated by the external challenger). Note that $\mathcal{S}_{1,\text{out}}^{\text{SA}}$ may complete a session, where P_1' is fully under the control of the adversary. This happens when the simulated transcript corresponds to some session $i' \neq i$. However, we can argue that with non-negligible probability, the simulated transcript returned by $\mathcal{S}_{1,\text{out}}^{\text{SA}}$ does correspond to the i-th session. Once we have argued that, we can claim that $\mathcal{S}_{1,\text{out}}^{\text{SA}}$ will return the input of P_1', when the MPC challenger computes the messages on behalf of P_1' using the input x_1^i. To reach a contradiction, we need to consider a function that does not implicitly leak the input of P_1' to the adversary. For this, we consider the oblivious transfer functionality, where P_1''s input is $x_1 = (x^0 \in \{0,1\}^\lambda, x^1 \in \{0,1\}^\lambda)$ and P_2''s input is $x_2 \in \{0,1\}$, while P_{out}' does not have any input.: $f(x_1, x_2, \bot) = x^{x_2}$.

Finally, given that the probability that $\mathcal{A}_{\text{SA}}'$ guess the session i correctly is non-negligible, and given that the simulator run internally by $\mathcal{A}_{\text{SA}}'$ will succeed with non-negligible probability, we can claim that our adversary $\mathcal{A}_{\text{SA}}'$ breaks the SA security Π' with non-negligible advantage.

Our theorem can be extended to n-party cases. Assuming there exists a n-party four-round protocol that can compute f with selective identifiable-abort security, against $t < n$ corruptions. We denote the n parties running the protocol with $(P_1, \ldots, P_n)$, then we let P_1 take the input x_1, P_2 take the input x_2, and other parties take no input. If such a protocol would be secure, then we can easily construct a 3-party protocol (where all the parties that have no input are emulated by a single entity) to compute f with selective identifiable-abort security, which would contradict our claim.

We prove the following theorems with similar proofs and refer the reader to the full version for the formal proofs.

Theorem 6 (*BC-BC-P2P-BC*, **SIA, Plain Model**, $n > t$). *Assume the existence of pseudorandom functions. There exists function f such that no n-party four-round protocol (in the plain model) can compute f with selective identifiable-abort security, against $t < n$ corruptions, while in the protocol, the first two rounds use broadcast channels and the third one uses peer-to-peer channels and the last round uses broadcast channels.*

Theorem 7 (*P2P-BC-BC-BC*, **SIA, Plain Model**, $n > t$). *Assume the existence of pseudorandom functions. There exists function f such that no n-party four-round protocol (in the plain model) can compute f with selective identifiable-abort security, against $t < n$ corruptions, while in the protocol, the first round uses the peer-to-peer channels and the remaining three rounds use broadcast channels.*

Theorem 8 (*BC-P2P-BC-BC*, **SIA, Plain Model**, $n > t$). *Assume the existence of pseudorandom functions. There exists function f such that no n-party four-round protocol (in the plain model) can compute f with selective identifiable-abort security, against $t < n$ corruptions, while in the protocol, the first round uses broadcast channels and the second one uses peer-to-peer channels and the last two rounds use broadcast channels.*

References

1. Ananth, P., Choudhuri, A.R., Goel, A., Jain, A.: Round-optimal secure multiparty computation with honest majority. In: Shacham, H., Boldyreva, A. (eds.) CRYPTO 2018, Part II. LNCS, vol. 10992, pp. 395–424. Springer, Cham (2018). https://doi.org/10.1007/978-3-319-96881-0_14
2. Ananth, P., Choudhuri, A.R., Jain, A.: A new approach to round-optimal secure multiparty computation. In: Katz, J., Shacham, H. (eds.) CRYPTO 2017, Part I. LNCS, vol. 10401, pp. 468–499. Springer, Cham (2017). https://doi.org/10.1007/978-3-319-63688-7_16
3. Badrinarayanan, S., Goyal, V., Jain, A., Kalai, Y.T., Khurana, D., Sahai, A.: Promise zero knowledge and its applications to round optimal MPC. In: Shacham, H., Boldyreva, A. (eds.) CRYPTO 2018, Part II. LNCS, vol. 10992, pp. 459–487. Springer, Cham (2018). https://doi.org/10.1007/978-3-319-96881-0_16
4. Badrinarayanan, S., Miao, P., Mukherjee, P., Ravi, D.: On the round complexity of fully secure solitary MPC with honest majority. IACR Cryptol. ePrint Arch., p. 241 (2021)
5. Benhamouda, F., Lin, H.: k-round multiparty computation from k-round oblivious transfer via garbled interactive circuits. In: Nielsen, J.B., Rijmen, V. (eds.) EUROCRYPT 2018, Part II. LNCS, vol. 10821, pp. 500–532. Springer, Cham (2018). https://doi.org/10.1007/978-3-319-78375-8_17
6. Brakerski, Z., Halevi, S., Polychroniadou, A.: Four round secure computation without setup. In: Kalai, Y., Reyzin, L. (eds.) TCC 2017, Part I. LNCS, vol. 10677, pp. 645–677. Springer, Cham (2017). https://doi.org/10.1007/978-3-319-70500-2_22
7. Chaum, D., Damgård, I.B., van de Graaf, J.: Multiparty computations ensuring privacy of each party's input and correctness of the result. In: Pomerance, C. (ed.) CRYPTO 1987. LNCS, vol. 293, pp. 87–119. Springer, Heidelberg (1988). https://doi.org/10.1007/3-540-48184-2_7

8. Choudhuri, A.R., Ciampi, M., Goyal, V., Jain, A., Ostrovsky, R.: Round optimal secure multiparty computation from minimal assumptions. Cryptology ePrint Archive, Paper 2019/216 (2019). https://eprint.iacr.org/2019/216
9. Rai Choudhuri, A., Ciampi, M., Goyal, V., Jain, A., Ostrovsky, R.: Round optimal secure multiparty computation from minimal assumptions. In: Pass, R., Pietrzak, K. (eds.) TCC 2020, Part II. LNCS, vol. 12551, pp. 291–319. Springer, Cham (2020). https://doi.org/10.1007/978-3-030-64378-2_11
10. Ciampi, M., Ostrovsky, R., Waldner, H., Zikas, V.: Round-optimal and communication-efficient multiparty computation. In: Dunkelman, O., Dziembowski, S. (eds.) EUROCRYPT 2022, Part I. LNCS, vol. 13275, pp. 65–95. Springer, Heidelberg (2022). https://doi.org/10.1007/978-3-031-06944-4_3
11. Ciampi, M., Ravi, D., Siniscalchi, L., Waldner, H.: Round-optimal multi-party computation with identifiable abort. In: Dunkelman, O., Dziembowski, S. (eds.) EUROCRYPT 2022, Part I. LNCS, vol. 13275, pp. 335–364. Springer, Heidelberg (2022). https://doi.org/10.1007/978-3-031-06944-4_12
12. Cleve, R.: Limits on the security of coin flips when half the processors are faulty (extended abstract). In: 18th Annual ACM Symposium on Theory of Computing, pp. 364–369. ACM Press (1986). https://doi.org/10.1145/12130.12168
13. Cohen, R., Garay, J., Zikas, V.: Broadcast-optimal two-round MPC. In: Canteaut, A., Ishai, Y. (eds.) EUROCRYPT 2020, Part II. LNCS, vol. 12106, pp. 828–858. Springer, Cham (2020). https://doi.org/10.1007/978-3-030-45724-2_28
14. Damgård, I., Magri, B., Ravi, D., Siniscalchi, L., Yakoubov, S.: Broadcast-optimal two round MPC with an honest majority. In: Malkin, T., Peikert, C. (eds.) CRYPTO 2021, Part II. LNCS, vol. 12826, pp. 155–184. Springer, Cham (2021). https://doi.org/10.1007/978-3-030-84245-1_6
15. Damgård, I., Ravi, D., Siniscalchi, L., Yakoubov, S.: Minimizing setup in broadcast-optimal two round MPC. In: Hazay, C., Stam, M. (eds.) EUROCRYPT 2023, Part II. LNCS, vol. 14005, pp. 129–158. Springer, Heidelberg (2023). https://doi.org/10.1007/978-3-031-30617-4_5
16. Dolev, D., Strong, H.R.: Authenticated algorithms for byzantine agreement. SIAM J. Comput. **12**(4), 656–666 (1983)
17. Fischer, M.J., Lynch, N.A.: A lower bound for the time to assure interactive consistency. Inf. Process. Lett. **14**(4), 183–186 (1982)
18. Garg, S., Mukherjee, P., Pandey, O., Polychroniadou, A.: The exact round complexity of secure computation. In: Fischlin, M., Coron, J.-S. (eds.) EUROCRYPT 2016, Part II. LNCS, vol. 9666, pp. 448–476. Springer, Heidelberg (2016). https://doi.org/10.1007/978-3-662-49896-5_16
19. Garg, S., Srinivasan, A.: Two-round multiparty secure computation from minimal assumptions. In: Nielsen, J.B., Rijmen, V. (eds.) EUROCRYPT 2018, Part II. LNCS, vol. 10821, pp. 468–499. Springer, Cham (2018). https://doi.org/10.1007/978-3-319-78375-8_16
20. Goel, A., Jain, A., Prabhakaran, M., Raghunath, R.: On communication models and best-achievable security in two-round MPC. In: Nissim, K., Waters, B. (eds.) TCC 2021, Part II. LNCS, vol. 13043, pp. 97–128. Springer, Cham (2021). https://doi.org/10.1007/978-3-030-90453-1_4
21. Goldreich, O., Krawczyk, H.: On the composition of zero-knowledge proof systems. SIAM J. Comput. **25**(1), 169–192 (1996). https://doi.org/10.1137/S0097539791220688
22. Goldreich, O., Micali, S., Wigderson, A.: How to play any mental game or A completeness theorem for protocols with honest majority. In: Aho, A. (ed.) 19th

Annual ACM Symposium on Theory of Computing, New York City, NY, USA, 25–27 May 1987, pp. 218–229. ACM Press (1987). https://doi.org/10.1145/28395.28420

23. Goldwasser, S., Lindell, Y.: Secure multi-party computation without agreement. J. Cryptol. **18**(3), 247–287 (2005). https://doi.org/10.1007/s00145-005-0319-z

24. Halevi, S., Hazay, C., Polychroniadou, A., Venkitasubramaniam, M.: Round-optimal secure multi-party computation. In: Shacham, H., Boldyreva, A. (eds.) CRYPTO 2018, Part II. LNCS, vol. 10992, pp. 488–520. Springer, Cham (2018). https://doi.org/10.1007/978-3-319-96881-0_17

25. Hazay, C., Venkitasubramaniam, M.: What security can we achieve within 4 rounds? In: Zikas, V., De Prisco, R. (eds.) SCN 2016. LNCS, vol. 9841, pp. 486–505. Springer, Cham (2016). https://doi.org/10.1007/978-3-319-44618-9_26

26. Katz, J., Ostrovsky, R.: Round-optimal secure two-party computation. In: Franklin, M. (ed.) CRYPTO 2004. LNCS, vol. 3152, pp. 335–354. Springer, Heidelberg (2004). https://doi.org/10.1007/978-3-540-28628-8_21

27. Mukherjee, P., Wichs, D.: Two round multiparty computation via multi-key FHE. In: Fischlin, M., Coron, J.-S. (eds.) EUROCRYPT 2016, Part II. LNCS, vol. 9666, pp. 735–763. Springer, Heidelberg (2016). https://doi.org/10.1007/978-3-662-49896-5_26

28. Yao, A.C.C.: How to generate and exchange secrets (extended abstract). In: 27th Annual Symposium on Foundations of Computer Science, Toronto, Ontario, Canada, 27–29 October 1986, pp. 162–167. IEEE Computer Society Press (1986). https://doi.org/10.1109/SFCS.1986.25

Taming Adaptivity in YOSO Protocols:
The Modular Way

Ran Canetti[1]([⊠]), Sebastian Kolby[2], Divya Ravi[2], Eduardo Soria-Vazquez[3],
and Sophia Yakoubov[2]

[1] Boston University, Boston, USA
canetti@bu.edu
[2] Aarhus University, Aarhus, Denmark
{sk,divya,sophia.yakoubov}@cs.au.dk
[3] Technology Innovation Institute, Abu Dhabi, UAE
eduardo.soria-vazquez@tii.ae

Abstract. YOSO-style MPC protocols (Gentry *et al.*, Crypto'21), are
a promising framework where the overall computation is partitioned into
small, short-lived pieces, delegated to subsets of one-time stateless parties. Such protocols enable gaining from the security benefits provided
by using a large community of participants where "mass corruption"
of a large fraction of participants is considered unlikely, while keeping
the computational and communication costs manageable. However, fully
realizing and analyzing YOSO-style protocols has proven to be challenging: While different components have been defined and realized in various
works, there is a dearth of protocols that have reasonable efficiency and
enjoy full end to end security against adaptive adversaries.

The YOSO model separates the protocol design, specifying the short-
lived responsibilities, from the mechanisms assigning these responsibilities to machines participating in the computation. These protocol designs
must then be translated to run directly on the machines, while preserving security guarantees. We provide a versatile and modular framework
for analyzing the security of YOSO-style protocols, and show how to use
it to compile any protocol design that is secure against *static* corruptions
of t out of c parties, into protocols that withstand *adaptive* corruption
of T out of N machines (where T/N is closely related to t/c, specifically
when $t/c < 0.5$, we tolerate $T/N \leq 0.29$) at overall communication cost
that is comparable to that of the traditional protocol even when $c << N$.

Furthermore, we demonstrate how to minimize the use of costly non-
committing encryption, thereby keeping the computational and communication overhead manageable even in practical terms, while still providing end to end security analysis. Combined with existing approaches for
transforming stateful protocols into stateless ones while preserving static
security (e.g. Gentry et al. 21, Kolby et al. 22), we obtain end to end
security.

© International Association for Cryptologic Research 2023
G. Rothblum and H. Wee (Eds.): TCC 2023, LNCS 14370, pp. 33–62, 2023.
https://doi.org/10.1007/978-3-031-48618-0_2

1   Introduction

Secure multiparty computation (MPC) allows data owners to outsource the processing of their sensitive data to a set of machines, with the guarantee that as long as fewer than a threshold t of those machines are corrupt, no-one will learn more about the data than revealed by the computation output. YOSO MPC [GHK+21] is an emerging new style of MPC where participating machines have very short term roles: they receive messages, performing an internal computation, and send messages in a single communication round to the next set of participating machines. Before sending those messages, the machine erases all other state relevant to the protocol execution.

The advantage of YOSO MPC is that the communication complexity of the protocol can be sublinear in N (the number of available machines), even if the corruption threshold T is linear in N. This might appear impossible, since if the communication complexity is sublinear in N, the set of all machines ever to send a message fits within the adversary's corruption budget; however, the crucial insight is that as long as an adversary cannot predict which machines will "speak", she is unable to target them. One of the challenges of YOSO MPC is choosing participating machines in an unpredictable way, making it harder to locate and adaptively attack those machines while they are active and relevant to the protocol.

YOSO MPC protocols naturally decompose into two tasks. The first of these is *role assignment*, which entails determining which machines will have a role to play and handing them the secret keys they will need in order to do so, while keeping their identities hidden from the adversary. The second task is actually running the MPC by having the chosen machines play their assigned roles.

One can view YOSO MPC protocols through two lenses: In the *natural world*, a protocol must specify instructions for physical machines, including instructions for role assignment; i.e., how the machines should go about determining whether they have a role to play, and if so, which one. In the *abstract world*, a YOSO MPC protocol can be described in terms of the roles alone, without consideration for the machines running them.

Some previous YOSO protocols (e.g. the protocol of Benhamouda *et al.* [BGG+20]) are described in the natural world, running both role assignment and computation in an entwined way. Others (e.g. the protocols of Gentry *et al.* [GHK+21] and Acharya *et al.* [AHKP22]) are described in the abstract world, relying on behind-the-scenes machinery to take care of role assignment.

The second is a more modular approach, resulting in simpler protocol descriptions. However, these descriptions do not suffice for use in the real, natural world. We need a *compiler* to translate them into something machines can run; such a compiler might access an ideal role assignment functionality.

One such role assignment functionality and compiler were introduced by Gentry *et al.* [GHK+21]. However, the role assignment functionality presented by Gentry *et al.* was perhaps too strong, in that it did not allow the adversary to influence the role assignment, instead choosing *all* machines in an ideal, random way. This makes it impossible for the most efficient known role assignment mechanism (that of Benhamouda *et al.* [BGG+20]) to realize this functionality. Furthermore, the compiler of Gentry *et al.* [GHK+21] has two drawbacks: (a) it is inefficient, and (b) it is incompatible with some abstract protocols (e.g. the protocol of Braun *et al.* [BDO22] and Kolby *et al.* [KRY22]).

1.1   Our Contributions

In this paper, we fill the above gaps: we introduce a more realistic role assignment ideal functionality $\mathcal{F}_{RA}$, give a realization of $\mathcal{F}_{RA}$, and present a more efficient, more general compiler that relies on this new functionality. In particular, we use non-committing encryption only for implementing $\mathcal{F}_{RA}$. All the messages of the underlying (statically secure) protocol are encrypted using standard (CCA secure) encryption.

1.1.1   Ideal Role Assignment Functionality In Sect. 3, we introduce our role assignment ideal functionality $\mathcal{F}_{RA}$. Our goal is to capture a more general and broad class of potential and existing role assignment protocols. Towards this, we give a comprehensive design of $\mathcal{F}_{RA}$ that supports modeling various assignment approaches.

At a very high-level $\mathcal{F}_{RA}$ supports two kinds of elections: assignment of a role to a random honest machine, and assignment influenced by the adversary, to a chosen, possibly corrupt machine. The machines are allowed to probe the $\mathcal{F}_{RA}$ to read the public keys of the roles assigned so far, deduce if they themselves have been assigned a role, and retrieve the secret keys in such a case. Furthermore, our design of $\mathcal{F}_{RA}$ supports modeling various scenarios that can occur during its execution, such as (a) when the adaptive adversary manages to corrupt a role that was assigned when it was uncorrupted (before the election of the committee was completed), (b) when a machine wishes to delete its state before it speaks on behalf of a role, and (c) when a machine is unavailable for nomination while it refreshes its secret state.[1] The formal details appear in Sect. 3.

1.1.2   Compiling Abstract Protocols In Sect. 4, we describe how to leverage $\mathcal{F}_{RA}$ to compile an MPC protocol in the abstract world into one that can be run in the natural world. Unlike the compiler of Gentry *et al.* [GHK+21], we only use non-committing encryption within the realization of $\mathcal{F}_{RA}$ (and not within the compiler itself). This has a two-fold advantage: (a) it yields a significant efficiency gain, and (b) it gives compatibility with a broader class of abstract YOSO protocols (e.g. the protocol of Braun *et al.* [BDO22] and Kolby *et al.* [KRY22]).

At a high-level, in our compiled protocol in the natural world, each machine deduces if it has been selected for a role by invoking the $\mathcal{F}_{RA}$. If this is the case, it

---

[1] In our particular use-case, machines are unable to be nominated between deleting their previous secret key and broadcasting a fresh public key. This allows one machine to hold multiple roles, but prevents nominations which overlap with the machine speaking for a role.

reads the bulletin board (in the natural world) to obtain ciphertexts encrypted using that role's public key. It can decrypt these ciphertexts using the secret keys provided by $\mathcal{F}_{RA}$ and proceed to compute the outgoing messages of the role to other roles. These outgoing messages can be encrypted using the other roles' public keys (provided by $\mathcal{F}_{RA}$) and posted on the bulletin board. Just before a machine speaks on behalf of a role, it instructs the $\mathcal{F}_{RA}$ to delete its state. After speaking, it instructs $\mathcal{F}_{RA}$ that it is ready for new nominations.

The main challenge is proving adaptive security of the compiled protocol, assuming that the underlying abstract protocol is only statically secure. The crux of our proof is that the set of corrupt roles can be chosen statically, and then the $\mathcal{F}_{RA}$ may be suitably re-programmed so that adaptive corruption of machines are appropriately matched to the already chosen static corrupt roles. We refer to Sect. 5 for details on the technicalities in our proof.

Compiling Abstract Protocols that Require Message Verification. The above compiler supports abstract protocols that use only ideally private point-to-point and broadcast channels. This does not cover a large class of abstract YOSO protocols where parties are expected to accompany their messages with zero-knowledge proofs that relate their outgoing messages to their secret state and previously received messages. Indeed, in order to compile such protocols to natural ones, such proofs would need to involve both secret state from the abstract protocol and secret keys from the compiler itself. In Sect. 6, we show how our compiler can be extended to abstract protocols that contain such constructs. More specifically, we modify the above compiler to accommodate abstract protocols that leverage the functionality $\mathcal{F}_{VeSPa}$ [KRY22], which is used to enable parties to prove to others that the broadcast and peer-to-peer messages they send within a protocol were derived honestly.

In order to extend our compiler to abstract protocols using $\mathcal{F}_{VeSPa}$, we need to be able to emulate the verifiability of messages in the natural world. For this, we simply rely on augmenting the messages posted on the bulletin board in the compiled protocol with corresponding non-interactive zero-knowledge proofs proving that these messages were computed correctly.

1.1.3 Realizing the Role Assignment Functionality

In Sect. 7, we modify the role assignment protocol of Benhamouda *et al.* [BGG+20] to realize $\mathcal{F}_{RA}$. As shown in [HLH+22], their protocol had problems in addressing the adaptivity of the adversary when it came to realizing the necessary anonymity property. As in [BGG+20], our modified protocol Π_{RA} uses a cryptographic sortition algorithm in order to ensure that an adversary is not able to increase the likelihood of corrupting a role of his choice. Furthermore, Π_{RA} uses Key and Message Non-Commiting Encryption (KM-NCE). This enables the simulator to deal with the different problematic scenarios described above. That is, by creating "fake" ciphertexts, the simulator can deal with the case of honest parties sending messages to recipients who were *a priori* expected to be honest, but then became corrupted by the adversary.

Crucially, our protocol instructs nominated machines to *erase* their private decryption key before making themselves known. As soon as the machine completes its role as a committee member, it chooses a new key pair and registers the new public encryption key with the PKI server. The machine will keep a (truly) long-term signature key in order to authenticate itself to the PKI server.

The much less efficient role assignment protocol of Gentry *et al.* [GHM+21] (which uses any MPC protocol to run random-index PIR) may be modified to trivially realize $\mathcal{F}_{\mathsf{RA}}$, by a similar application of KM-NCE.

2   Preliminaries

2.1   Key and Message Non-commiting Encryption

We recall the notion of a Key and Message Non-Commiting Encryption (KM-NCE) from [HLH+22], which is an extension of receiver non-commiting encryption. Informally, a KM-NCE is a public-key encryption scheme that allows to generate fake ciphertexts *without any public key* in such a way that those fake ciphertexts can later be decrypted to any plaintext for any public key, by generating an appropriate secret key on the fly. We briefly recall the syntax of a KM-NCE scheme, referring the reader to [HLH+22] for a more detailed motivation.

Setup(1^κ) $\rightarrow$ pp: Given security parameter 1^κ, the setup algorithm generates public parameters pp.

Gen(pp) $\rightarrow$ (pk, sk, tk): Given public parameters pp, the key generation algorithm produces a public key pk and secret key sk, as well as a trapdoor key tk. The trapdoor key is not used for encryption or decryption, but instead provides additional information for the purposes of opening simulated ciphertexts.

Enc(pp, pk, m) $\rightarrow$ c: Given public parameters pp, public key pk and a message m, the encryption algorithm produces a ciphertext c.

Dec(pp, sk, c) $\rightarrow$ m: Given public parameters pp, public key pk and a ciphertext c, the decryption algorithm outputs a plaintext m.

Fake(pp) $\rightarrow$ (c, τ): Given only the public parameters pp, the fake algorithm produces a fake ciphertext c and additional trapdoor information τ.

Open$_k$(pp, $tk, pk, sk, (c_\gamma^*, \tau_\gamma^*, m_\gamma^*)_{\gamma \in [k]})$ $\rightarrow$ sk':] Given public parameters pp, keys tk, pk, sk, and k tuples, each containing a ciphertext c_γ, its trapdoor information τ_γ and a desired plaintext m_γ the open algorithm produces a fresh secret key sk' corresponding to pk, such that each ciphertext appropriately decrypts to the desired plaintext.

In the security experiments for KM-NCE the adversary is never given trapdoor keys, implicitly requiring secure erasure of these keys if we wish to achieve adaptive security.

Definition 1 (Security). *A KM-NCE scheme* KM-NCE $=$ (Setup, Gen, Enc, Dec, Fake, Open$_k$) *in the k-challenge setting is* CCA-*secure if for any* PPT *adversary* $\mathcal{A} = (\mathcal{A}_1, \mathcal{A}_2, \mathcal{A}_3)$, *the advantage* $\mathbf{Adv}_{\mathsf{KM\text{-}NCE},\mathcal{A},k}^{\mathsf{KM\text{-}NCE\text{-}CCA}}(\lambda) :=$

$$| \Pr[\mathbf{Exp}_{\mathsf{KM\text{-}NCE},\mathcal{A},k}^{\mathsf{KM\text{-}NCE\text{-}CCA\text{-}real}}(\lambda) = 1] - \Pr[\mathbf{Exp}_{\mathsf{KM\text{-}NCE},\mathcal{A},k}^{\mathsf{KM\text{-}NCE\text{-}CCA\text{-}ideal}}(\lambda) = 1]|$$

is negligible, where $\mathbf{Exp}_{KM\text{-}NCE,\mathcal{A},k}^{KM\text{-}NCE\text{-}CCA\text{-}real}$ *and* $\mathbf{Exp}_{KM\text{-}NCE,\mathcal{A},k}^{KM\text{-}NCE\text{-}CCA\text{-}ideal}$ *are defined in Fig. 1.*

$\mathbf{Exp}_{KM\text{-}NCE,\mathcal{A},k}^{KM\text{-}NCE\text{-}CCA\text{-}real}(\lambda)$:

$pp \leftarrow\!\!\$\ \mathsf{Setup}(1^\lambda)$
$(pk, sk, tk) \leftarrow\!\!\$\ \mathsf{Gen}(pp)$
$((m_\gamma^*)_{\gamma\in[k]}, \mathsf{state}_1) \leftarrow\!\!\$\ \mathcal{A}_1^{\mathcal{O}_{\mathsf{Dec}}}(pp, pk)$
$(c_\gamma^* \leftarrow\!\!\$\ \mathsf{Enc}(pp, pk, m_\gamma^*))_{\gamma\in[k]}$
$\mathsf{state}_2 \leftarrow\!\!\$\ \mathcal{A}_2^{\mathcal{O}_{\mathsf{Dec}}}((c_\gamma^*)_{\gamma\in[k]}, \mathsf{state}_1)$
$b \leftarrow\!\!\$\ \mathcal{A}_3(sk, \mathsf{state}_2)$
Return b

$\mathcal{O}_{\mathsf{Dec}}(c)$:
If $c \in \{c_\gamma^* : \gamma \in [k]\}$: Return $\perp$
$m = \mathsf{Dec}(pp, sk, c)$
Return m

$\mathbf{Exp}_{KM\text{-}NCE,\mathcal{A},k}^{KM\text{-}NCE\text{-}CCA\text{-}ideal}(\lambda)$

$pp \leftarrow\!\!\$\ \mathsf{Setup}(1^\lambda)$
$(pk, sk, tk) \leftarrow\!\!\$\ \mathsf{Gen}(pp)$
$((m_\gamma^*)_{\gamma\in[k]}, \mathsf{state}_1) \leftarrow\!\!\$\ \mathcal{A}_1^{\mathcal{O}_{\mathsf{Dec}}}(pp, pk)$
$((c_\gamma^*, \tau_\gamma^*) \leftarrow\!\!\$\ \mathsf{Fake}(pp))_{\gamma\in[k]}$
$\mathsf{state}_2 \leftarrow\!\!\$\ \mathcal{A}_2^{\mathcal{O}_{\mathsf{Dec}}}((c_\gamma^*)_{\gamma\in[k]}, \mathsf{state}_1)$
$sk' \leftarrow\!\!\$\ \mathsf{Open}_k(pp, tk, pk, sk, (c_\gamma^*,$
$\tau_\gamma^*, m_\gamma^*)_{\gamma\in[k]})$
$b \leftarrow\!\!\$\ \mathcal{A}_3(sk', \mathsf{state}_2)$
Return b

Fig. 1. The experiments for $KM - NCE$-CCA security of a KM-NCE scheme.

Note, KMNC_k-CCA security implies conventional adaptive CCA security, as the fake algorithm does not take a message as input. By a hybrid argument, the encryption of any message m_0 must be indistinguishable from a faked ciphertext, which in turn is itself indistinguishable from the encryption of any other message m_1.

KM-NCE schemes can be constructed from hash proof systems, as shown in [HLH+22].

2.1.1 KM-NCE with a Unique Recipient

We need to define an additional property for KM-NCE, which ensures that the adversary cannot produce (something that looks like) a ciphertext which decrypts under two different honest secret keys.

Definition 2 (Unique recipient). *A KM-NCE scheme* KM-NCE = (Setup, Gen, Enc, Dec, Fake, Open$_k$) *is unique recipients if for any* PPT *adversary* $\mathcal{A}$, $\Pr[\mathbf{Exp}_{KM\text{-}NCE,\mathcal{A}}^{KM\text{-}NCE\text{-}UR}(\lambda) = 1]$ *is negligible, where* $\mathbf{Exp}_{KM\text{-}NCE,\mathcal{A}}^{KM\text{-}NCE\text{-}UR}$ *is defined in Fig. 2.*

2.1.2 A Unique Recipient KM-NCE Construction

We show how to build a unique recipient KM-NCE encryption scheme in the programmable random oracle model. Since this implies the notion of receiver non-committing encryption, we know that random oracles are necessary in order to avoid secret keys that are as long as the messages to be encrypted [Nie02].

Our construction is based on a simple variant of ElGamal, which makes it more efficient than the KM-NCE construction based on hash proof systems

$$\mathbf{Exp}^{\mathsf{KM\text{-}NCE\text{-}UR}}_{\mathsf{KM\text{-}NCE},\mathcal{A}}(\lambda):$$

$\mathsf{pp} \leftarrow\!\!\$ \ \mathsf{Setup}(1^\lambda)$

$((pk_i, sk_i, tk_i) \leftarrow\!\!\$ \ \mathsf{Gen}(\mathsf{pp}))_{i \in [h]}$

$c \leftarrow\!\!\$ \ \mathcal{A}^{\mathcal{O}_{\mathsf{Dec}},\mathsf{RO}}(\mathsf{pp}, \{pk_i\}_{i \in [h]})$

If $\exists i_1, i_2 \in [h] : i_1 \neq i_2 \ \wedge$

$\mathsf{Dec}(\mathsf{pp}, sk_{i_1}, c) \neq \bot \ \wedge$

$\mathsf{Dec}(\mathsf{pp}, sk_{i_2}, c) \neq \bot$, return 1.

Otherwise, return 0.

$\mathcal{O}_{\mathsf{Dec}}(c):$

If $c \in \{c^*_\gamma : \gamma \in [k]\}$: Return $\bot$

$m/\bot \leftarrow \mathsf{Dec}(\mathsf{pp}, sk, c)$

Return $m/\bot$

$\mathsf{RO}(s):$

$\mathcal{S}$ returns a uniformly random t.

Fig. 2. The unique recipient experiment.

(HPS) from [HLH+22, Section 5.3], which relies on a matrix variant of DDH [EHK+13]. Furthermore, that construction does *not* have the unique recipient property that we need. The reason behind this is that, since the projected and unprojected hash need to coincide for elements x of the language, the adversary can use the unprojected hash (in their specific notation, $\widehat{\mathsf{Pub}}$) together with the public keys of honest parties in order to try and find a suitable witness that leads to a collision (in their notation, the same $\widetilde{\pi}$) with several secret keys. Once he has that, it is easy for him to come up with the rest of the elements of the ciphertext (given x, any d can be fixed by varying the message m. Hence, a whole range of values $\tau = H(x, d)$ can be explored by the adversary). It is very easy for the adversary to come up with elements of the language x and their witnesses w, since this is a necessary feature for the practical efficiency of the encryption algorithm. Thus, we cannot rule out maliciously created ciphertexts that decrypt to several recipients. In more detail, for the HPSs from [HLH+22, Section 6], each public key defines a hyperplane, and collisions happen at the intersection of any two such hyperplanes. This gives plenty of candidates for collisions.

Whereas the prior attack to the unique recipient property is specific to the instantiation of construction of [HLH+22, Section 5.3] with the HPSs from [HLH+22, Section 6], it is likely that similar attacks could be mounted for other natural constructions based on HPSs. The necessary relation between the public and private hash functions, together with any nice algebraic description of the public hashing algorithm (e.g. defining hyperplanes as in the attack above) would potentially lead to the same problem.

We define below our candidate construction based on a modification of ElGamal. The algorithms of our scheme are oracle algorithms with query access to the oracle $\mathsf{RO} : \{0,1\}^* \to \{0,1\}^{2\kappa}$, we let this be implicit in our notation.

- $\mathsf{pp} \leftarrow\!\!\$ \ \mathsf{Setup}(1^\kappa)$: Pick a cyclic group $\mathbb{G}$ of order q, where q is a κ-bit prime, and let g be a generator of $\mathbb{G}$. Let the message space of the encryption scheme be $\{0,1\}^\kappa$. Set public parameters $\mathsf{pp} = (\mathbb{G}, g, q)$.

- $(pk, sk, \emptyset) \leftarrow\$ \mathsf{Gen}(\mathsf{pp})$: Sample $a \leftarrow\$ \mathbb{Z}_q$, let $sk = a$. Compute the public key $pk \leftarrow g^a$ and output $(pk, sk, \emptyset)$.
- $c \leftarrow\$ \mathsf{Enc}(\mathsf{pp}, pk, m)$: Sample $r \leftarrow\$ \mathbb{Z}_q$ and compute $\beta \leftarrow g^r$. Query the oracle for a mask $k \leftarrow \mathtt{RO}(pk^r)$ and a MAC $d \leftarrow \mathtt{RO}(r, m)$. Let $e \leftarrow k \oplus (r, m)$, and output $c = (\beta, e, d)$.
- $m \leftarrow \mathsf{Dec}(\mathsf{pp}, sk, c)$: Parse $c = (\beta, e, d)$. Query the oracle $k' \leftarrow \mathtt{RO}(\beta^{sk})$, compute $(r', m') \leftarrow e \oplus k'$. Check if $g^{r'} = \beta$ and $d = \mathtt{RO}(r', m')$, output m' if both conditions are satisfied, otherwise output $\perp$.
- $(c, \tau) \leftarrow\$ \mathsf{Fake}(\mathsf{pp})$: Sample $r \leftarrow\$ \mathbb{Z}_q$ and compute $\beta \leftarrow g^r$. Let $\tau = r$. Sample uniformly random strings $e, d \in \{0, 1\}^{2\kappa}$ and let the fake ciphertext be $c = (\beta, e, d)$. Output (c, τ).
- $sk' \leftarrow \mathsf{Open}_k(\mathsf{pp}, pk, sk, (c^*_\gamma, \tau^*_\gamma, m^*_\gamma)_{\gamma \in [k]})$: To open a fake ciphertext $c^*_\gamma = (\beta, e, d)$ as an encryption a message m^*_γ to a chosen pk. Let $r = \tau^*_\gamma$, program the random oracle such that $\mathtt{RO}(r, m^*_\gamma) = d$ and $\mathtt{RO}(pk^r) = e \oplus (r, m^*_\gamma)$. Output $sk' = sk$.

Intuitively it is possible to replace ciphertexts by fakes as long as the adversary is unable to query either pk^r or (r, m) to the random oracle. We observe that an adversary querying these values it may be used to solve the computational Diffie-Hellman problem. Including $d = \mathtt{RO}(r, m)$ allows the decryption oracle to extract the plaintext and verify the integrity of the ciphertext without use of the secret key. We now formally prove the security of our KM-NCE scheme.

Theorem 1. *The construction above is* KM-NCE$_k$-CCA *and unique recipient secure, in the pROM under the CDH assumption in group* $\mathbb{G}$.

Proof. First, we consider unique recipient security. Assume for contradiction there have been no collisions in random oracle, for a sufficiently large range and bounded adversary this holds with overwhelming probability. A winning adversary outputs a ciphertext $c = (\beta, e, d)$ such that for some sk_i, sk_j: $\mathsf{Dec}(\mathsf{pp}, sk_i, c) \neq \perp$ and $\mathsf{Dec}(\mathsf{pp}, sk_j, c) \neq \perp$. We subscript intermediate values in each decryption with the index of the secret key. For honestly generated keys $sk_i \neq sk_j$ with overwhelming probability, implying $\beta^{sk_i} \neq \beta^{sk_j}$. As a result, $k'_i \neq k'_j$ if there have been no collisions in the random oracle. This in turn implies that $(r'_i, n'_i) \neq (r'_j, n'_j)$. For both outputs to be different from $\perp$, it must be the case that $d = \mathtt{RO}(r'_i, n'_i) = \mathtt{RO}(r'_j, n'_j)$ raising a contradiction.

Now consider KM-NCE$_k$-CCA security. Through a series of hybrids we will replace $c^*_\gamma = (\beta, e, d)$ with a fake ciphertext for each $\gamma \in [k]$. Faking a ciphertext is only different in how c and d are chosen. These two cases are only different in the oracle output on inputs pk^r and (r, m) prior to $\mathcal{A}_3$ receiving the secret key sk.

In the real and ideal worlds the adversary receives the same secret key sk and has access to an identically distributed random oracle. The only input which may differ is state_2, produced by $\mathcal{A}_2$. The views of Adversaries $\mathcal{A}_1$ and $\mathcal{A}_2$ only differ between the real and ideal game when querying pk^r or (r, m) to the random oracle. Thus, if $\mathcal{A}_3$ distinguishes the real and ideal worlds with non-negligible advantage then one of $\mathcal{A}_1, \mathcal{A}_2$ must query pk^r or (r, m) with probability greater than or equal to the advantage. We will argue that such a pair $(\mathcal{A}_1, \mathcal{A}_2)$ may be reduced to an adversary solving the computational Diffie-Hellman problem.

Consider an adversary which queries either pk^r or (r, m) with probability ϵ, while making at most t random oracle queries. Given a computational Diffie-Hellman instance $(g, x = g^a, y = g^r)$, we set $pk = x$ and $\beta = y$. Note, the solution to this instance is $pk^r = \beta^a$. We will address how to provide a decryption oracle without knowing the secret key a later. The reduction chooses a query index $i \leftarrow\$ [t]$. When the adversary makes the ith query, if the input is of the form (r, m), the reduction outputs pk^r, if the input only consists of a single element z the reduction outputs this directly. The reduction aborts before providing $\mathcal{A}_3$ the secret key. Note, the reduction needs $\tau = r$, which it does not have, to open the ciphertexts to $\mathcal{A}_3$, preventing the use of $\mathcal{A}_3$ in the reduction. The reduction yields an adversary solving the Diffie-Hellman problem with probability ϵ/t.

We now return to the issue of providing a suitable decryption oracle during our hybrids. Consider a ciphertext $c^* = (\beta^*, e^*, d^*)$ queried to the decryption oracle, which is not equal to any of the challenge ciphertexts. If d^* is not a random oracle output on an input of the form (r, m) output $\bot$, this includes any d for faked ciphertexts. A ciphertext using d from a challenge with $\beta^* \neq \beta$ or $e^* \neq e$, real decryption would result in $\bot$ with overwhelming probability.

For a given ciphertext, e and $k' = \mathrm{RO}(\beta^{sk})$ uniquely determine (r, m); if this has not yet been queried the probability $\mathrm{RO}(r, m) = d$ is $2^{-2\kappa}$, and we may safely return $\bot$. If d is an output of the random oracle the reduction may retrieve the corresponding input (r, m). We check if $\beta = g^r$, returning $\bot$ if this is not the case. Given r the oracle then computes $k' \leftarrow \mathrm{RO}(pk^r)$; $(r', m') \leftarrow e \oplus k'$. If $(r', m') = (r, m)$ output m, otherwise output $\bot$.

2.2 Cryptographic Sortition

A cryptographic sortition protocol [CM19] allows to provably select a random subset of parties according to some timely and truthful randomness through the use of a Verifiable Random Function (VRF) [MRV99]. Importantly, a party can find out whether it was selected through local computation, given the output from the VRF.

Usual VRF definitions guarantee output unpredictability for adversarially chosen inputs, provided that the keys were honestly generated. In our setting this is insufficient, as it does not preclude an adversary choosing malformed keys which bias its output distribution, causing it to be selected more frequently. To ensure security against rogue key attacks of this form we will use the functionality $\mathcal{F}_{\mathsf{VRF}}$ from [DGKR18], which explicitly allows malicious key generation and VRF evaluation. The key property on which we will rely is "unpredictability under malicious key generation". This property is captured by the functionality always sampling the VRF output regardless of whether the specified key was maliciously generated. For a complete description of $\mathcal{F}_{\mathsf{VRF}}$ with a corresponding realisation we refer the reader to [DGKR18].

2.3   The You-Only-Speak-Once Model

The YOSO model introduced by Gentry *et al.* [GHK+21] formalised a variant of the UC framework enabling the design of protocols focusing only on role execution, and not the mechanisms for role assignment or receiver anonymous communication. We will refer to protocols in this model as *abstract* YOSO protocols. The YOSO model builds on top of the plain UC model. In particular, it uses the following constructs:

- Parties in the UC framework represent *roles,* namely abstract responsibilities. In an actual execution of a YOSO protocol, the roles will would be carried out by machine to which they are assigned to on the fly. The design of a YOSO protocol is indifferent to which actual machines would be executing the role.
- Idealised communication functionalities are provided to the roles executing a protocol, allowing point-to-point messages between roles. This corresponds to the availability of receiver anonymous communication channels, but ignores their realisation.
- Security is proven for "yosoified" versions of the protocol, where all roles are placed within a YOSO wrapper. This wrapper enforces that roles only speak once by killing them once they use a communication functionality. This is modelled by a SPOKE token which the ideal communication functionalities return upon the sending of messages. When receiving SPOKE the wrapper additionally forwards this to any sub-routines and its environment. Killing a role represents the machine running a role erasing any associated state, preventing the adversary from later corrupting the role.
- While we want natural YOSO protocols to be secure against an adaptive adversary, allowing the adversary this power in the abstract world would make protocol design significantly more difficult. Gentry *et al.* [GHK+21] make the observation that an adversary does not know which roles are assigned to a machine before it is corrupted. As a result the adversary may be restricted in the abstract world, while still being able to achieve adaptive security when translated to the natural world. This is enforced through a new "corruption controller" entity which dictates the types of corruptions the environment is allowed to make.

As in [GHK+21], (and following [KMTZ13]) we use a bounded-delay broadcast functionality, along with a global clock, to capture synchronous communication. We recall the ideal functionality allowing point-to-point and broadcast communication as in [GHK+21].

Functionality $\mathcal{F}_{\text{BC\&SPP}}$ [GHK+21]

This ideal functionality has the following behaviour:

- Initially create point-to-point and broadcast maps:
  $y : \mathbb{N} \times \text{Role} \times \text{Role} \to \text{Msg}_\perp$ where $y(r, \text{R}, \text{R}') = \perp$ for all r, R, R'
  $m : \mathbb{N} \times \text{Role} \to \text{Msg}_\perp$ where $m(r, \text{R}) = \perp$ for all r, R.

- On input $(\textsc{Send}, \textsf{S}, ((\textsf{R}_1, x_1), \dots, (\textsf{R}_k, x_k)), x)$ in round r proceed as follows:
  - For $i \in [n]$ update $y(r, \textsf{S}, \textsf{R}_i) = x_i$. *Store point to point messages from the role.*
  - Update $m(r, \textsf{S}) = x$. *Store the broadcast message from the role.*
  - Output $(\textsf{S}, ((\textsf{R}_1, |x_1|), \dots, (\textsf{R}_k, |x_k|)), x)$ to the simulator $\mathcal{S}$.
  - For corrupt roles $\textsf{R}_i$ output x_i to the simulator $\mathcal{S}$. *Leak messages lengths and the broadcast message to the simulator in a rushing fashion.*
  - If $\textsf{S}$ is honest give $\textsc{Spoke}$ to $\textsf{S}$.
- On input $(\textsc{Read}, \textsf{R}, \textsf{S}, r')$ in round r where $r' < r$ for $x = y(r', \textsf{S}, \textsf{R})$ output x to $\textsf{R}$.
- On input $(\textsc{Read}, \textsf{S}, r')$ in round r where $r' < r$ output $x = m(r', \textsf{S})$ to $\textsf{R}$.

The central paradigm of synchronous abstract YOSO protocols is that executions proceeds by a sequence of committees, each permitting a certain corruption threshold. These committees may potentially receive messages concurrently, or even speak in the same round.

2.4   Compiling Abstract YOSO Protocols

By their nature, protocols designed in the abstract YOSO model cannot be run directly on machines, they first have to undergo translation, or *compilation*, to the natural world.

This compilation reraises the issues of role assignment and receiver anonymous communication. Any compiler must provide equivalent guarantees of secure communication between roles in the protocol.

In their presentation of the YOSO model Gentry *et al.* [GHK+21] provide an example of compilation from the abstract to natural world. Their approach used a simplified toy timed ledger with role assignment functionality as a building block. This functionality provided the necessary keys for roles, which were then used to wrap messages in the underlying protocol in encryption. The compiler allowed the compilation of an abstract protocol secure against random adaptive point corruptions (i.e. an adversary only allowed to corrupt random roles), to a natural protocol secure against chosen adaptive point corruptions.

The focus of the compiler of Gentry *et al.* [GHK+21] was demonstrating the feasibility of compilation. As a result the compiler has a number of limitations, such as the role assignment functionality not being realised. Additionally, to achieve adaptive security the compiler uses non-committing encryption for all messages in the underlying protocol, incurring a significant overhead.

3   Role Assignment

In this section we present the ideal functionality $\mathcal{F}_{RA}$[2], which assigns machines
to computation roles while keeping this assignment hidden. (Note that which
machines provide input to the computation—and receive output from the
computation—could be determined in some fixed, external way, depending on
the application; therefore we consider only the assignment of machines to computation roles, and not input and output roles.)

At a high-level, let us consider committee C consisting of c roles. There
are two possible ways in which our $\mathcal{F}_{RA}$ chooses a machine for a role in C:
(a) choosing a machine at random from among the set of honest machines (i.e.
among the machines not corrupted so far), or (b) allowing the adversary to
choose the machine, as long as the number of machines chosen by the adversary
in C so far is within the allowed corruption bound (which is determined as a
function $\mathcal{T}$ on the fraction of corrupt machines). In the former case, $\mathcal{F}_{RA}$ samples
fresh keys, gives the (public) encryption and verification keys to everyone, and
gives the corresponding (secret) decryption and signing keys only to the chosen
machine. In the latter case, all keys are chosen by the adversary. The commands
NOM-HONEST and NOM-CORRUPT capture the above kinds of nominations.

We need to ensure that the fraction of corruptions in a committee remains
within the allowed bound until the nomination is completed. Looking ahead, to
capture adaptive corruptions after the adversary has seen public keys generated
via NOM-HONEST but before FINISH (which finalises the keys for a committee), we introduce an additional command CORRUPT-NOMINEE. This command
allows accounting for the corruptions performed during the nomination process
as needed, rather than always having to generate corrupt keys in proportional
to the worst case threshold.

Once a set of c machines are chosen for the committee C, $\mathcal{F}_{RA}$ picks a random
permutation on $[c]$ to determine which machine plays which role in C. Allowing
$\mathcal{F}_{RA}$ to map nominated machines to roles, instead of having machines assigned
to specific roles in C a priori, prevents the adversary from targeting a specific
role for corruption.

Further, there is a provision for each machine M to:

1. *'Read'*: this allows it to retrieve public keys corresponding to the roles that
   have been assigned, as well as to obtain secret keys if it has been assigned a
   role.
2. *'Delete'*: this command revokes M's ability to perform future reads until the
   point where it inputs *'Ready'*. (This revocation will also enable the implementation protocol to erase any secret keys that allow M to read information
   related to already assigned roles.)
3. *'Ready'*: this allows it to signal that it is available to be assigned a new role.
   We maintain both a global set of ready machines ("ready set"), and a
   committee-specific ready set. The latter keeps track of machines that have
   been ready throughout the nomination process for that committee.

---

[2] Note this is not the same role assignment functionality as presented in [GHK+21].

If a machine that has been assigned a role gets corrupted after it has retrieved its secret keys (which it learns when it inputs 'read') but before it inputs 'delete', its secret keys are leaked to the adversary. However, if it gets corrupted after it inputs 'delete', its secret keys remain hidden. As we will see later, this is crucial for adaptive security, as it allows us to argue that an adversary gets no advantage in corrupting a role after its execution.

The formal description of this ideal functionality $\mathcal{F}_{RA}$ appears below. We assume $\mathcal{F}_{RA}$ to be synchronous, with round switches occurring at the same time as the protocols using it. We present $\mathcal{F}_{RA}$ as a functionality which is reused for multiple committees rather than the perhaps simpler approach of a one time functionality for each committee. We justify this choice by considering how existing constructions update their PKI. Specifically, whenever a machine has held a role and subsequently revealed itself, said machine must refresh its long term keys. This renders the machine unable to decrypt earlier messages pertaining to the revealed role. These key erasures and updates to the PKI impede treating it as a global setup (see [CDPW07]), which would allow consolidating these to just a single PKI. Using a single $\mathcal{F}_{RA}$ for multiple committees thus forces any realisation to deal with this challenge of updates directly.

We divide our role assignment functionality into two parts. The first describes the general setup and commands provided by parties for establishing new committees and reading generated keys. The second describes the powers allowed to the simulator, when populating committees under nomination with keys and the leakage in the case of corruption.

Functionality $\mathcal{F}_{RA}(\mathcal{P}, c, \mathcal{T}, \mathcal{D}, \texttt{delay})$:

This functionality is synchronous, namely it has access to global clock functionality as in the model of Katz *et al.* [KMTZ13]. It has the following parameters:

- $\mathcal{P}$: the set of machines.
- c: the size of a committee.
- $\mathcal{T}$: the function determining the number of allowed corruptions in a committee (based on the current fraction of corrupt machines).
- $\mathcal{D}$ denoting a sampling algorithm, and
- $\texttt{delay}$ denoting the upper bound on the number of rounds required to complete nomination.

Init: The functionality is notified by the adversary whenever a party is corrupted/ restored, and maintains the current partition of $\mathcal{P}$ into the sets $\mathcal{H}$ and $\mathcal{I}$ of all honest and corrupt party identifiers, respectively. It also maintains a global set Ready initially equal to $\mathcal{P}$.

New committee: After receiving (NEW, cid, C) from all honest parties up until the round r specified by the cid [a], store $(cid, C, \mathsf{PKeys} = \emptyset, \mathsf{SKeys} = \emptyset, \texttt{cor} = 0, \texttt{nom} = 0, fin = \bot)$. Ignore the command if any value is already stored for cid.

- The lists PKeys and SKeys are initially empty. The list PKeys would be updated with tuples (ek, vk, R) where (ek, vk) refer to the public keys established for a role R. The list SKeys would be updated with tuples $(\mathsf{pid}, dk, sk, \mathsf{R})$ where (dk, sk) refer to the secret keys corresponding to the role R, which has been assigned to machine with identifier pid.
- The corruption and nomination counters, cor and nom, start at zero.
- A committee-specific ready set $\mathsf{Ready}_{\mathsf{cid}}$ is initialized the same as the global ready set: $\mathsf{Ready}_{\mathsf{cid}} = \mathsf{Ready}$.
- Finally, the flag signaling whether nomination is completed or not is initially false: $fin = \bot$.

Each time an honest party inputs $(\mathrm{NEW}, \mathsf{cid}, C)$, forward this to the simulator $\mathcal{S}$.

---

[a] For simplicity of exposition, we consider the case where all honest parties are expected to take part in each assignment of a role. A natural relaxation would only require some minimal quorum of parties to participate.

The simulator must perform nominations for each committee, but is restricted by the number of nominations it may bias relative to the current fraction of corrupt machines.

Functionality $\mathcal{F}_{\mathsf{RA}}$ (continued):

Nominate honest: On input $(\mathrm{NOM\text{-}HONEST}, \mathsf{cid})$ from the simulator $\mathcal{S}$, retrieve the value $(\mathsf{cid}, C, \mathsf{PKeys}, \mathsf{SKeys}, \mathsf{cor}, \mathsf{nom}, fin)$. If no such value exists do nothing. If $\mathsf{nom} < c$, do the following:

- Update $\mathsf{nom} \leftarrow \mathsf{nom} + 1$.
- Generate fresh encryption and signing keys for the chosen machine: $(ek, dk) \leftarrow \mathsf{PKE.Gen}()$, $(vk, sk) \leftarrow \mathsf{SIG.Gen}()$.
- Append $(ek, vk, \bot)$ to PKeys.
- Add $(\bot, dk, sk, \bot)$ to SKeys.
- If $\mathsf{nom} = c$, go to procedure Finish(cid).
- Output $(\mathrm{NOM\text{-}HONEST}, \mathsf{cid}, ek, vk)$ to the simulator $\mathcal{S}$.

Nominate corrupt: On input $(\mathrm{NOM\text{-}CORRUPT}, \mathsf{cid}, \mathsf{pid}, (ek, vk), (dk, sk))$ from the simulator $\mathcal{S}$, retrieve the value $(\mathsf{cid}, C, \mathsf{PKeys}, \mathsf{SKeys}, \mathsf{cor}, \mathsf{nom}, fin)$. If no such value exists, do nothing. If $\mathsf{nom} < c$ and $\mathsf{cor} + 1 < \mathcal{T}(|\mathcal{I}|/|\mathcal{P}|)$, do the following:

- Update the nominated and corrupt counters $\mathsf{nom} \leftarrow \mathsf{nom} + 1, \mathsf{cor} \leftarrow \mathsf{cor} + 1$.
- Append $(ek, vk, \bot)$ to PKeys and $(\mathsf{pid}, dk, sk, \bot)$ to SKeys.
- If $\mathsf{nom} = c$, go to procedure Finish(cid).

Corrupt nominee: On input (CORRUPT-NOMINEE, cid, pid) from the simulator $\mathcal{S}$, retrieve the value (cid$'$, C, PKeys, SKeys, cor, nom, fin) where cid $=$ cid$'$. If no such value exists, do nothing. If cor $+ 1 < \mathcal{T}(|\mathcal{I}|/|\mathcal{P}|)$ and cor $<$ nom, do the following:

- cor $\leftarrow$ cor $+ 1$
- Choose an element (pid$'$, dk, sk, $\bot$) uniformly at random between the values of SKeys where pid$' = \bot$.
- Update this value to be (pid, dk, sk, $\bot$)
- Output (CORRUPT-NOMINEE, cid, pid, dk, sk) to the simulator $\mathcal{S}$.

Finish (cid): When the procedure Finish(cid) is called, retrieve the value (cid$'$, C, PKeys, SKeys, cor, nom, fin) where cid$' =$ cid and do the following:

- Sample a random permutation ϕ on $[c]$.
- For the ith element of PKeys update $(ek, vk, \bot)$ to $(ek, vk, C_{\phi(i)})$.
- For the ith element of SKeys update (pid, dk, sk, $\bot$) as follows:
  - If pid $= \bot$, choose an honest machine uniformly at random as pid$' \leftarrow\$ \, \mathcal{D}(\mathcal{H}, \mathcal{P})$. If pid$' \in$ Ready$_{\text{cid}}$, update to (pid$'$, dk, sk, $C_{\phi(i)}$).
  - Else, update to (pid, dk, sk, $C_{\phi(i)}$).
- Let r' the current round number (read from the global clock). Set $fin = \top$ for cid if $r' \leq r +$ delay (where r denotes the round number specified by the cid).

Output (FINISH, cid, ϕ, PKeys) to the simulator $\mathcal{S}$ when finished.

Read: On input (READ, cid) from M with identifier pid, retrieve the value (cid*, C, PKeys, SKeys, cor, nom, fin) where cid $=$ cid* and $fin = \top$. If no such value exists, or M has read the output of committee cid before, do nothing.

- Collect all values (pid*, dk, sk, R) in SKeys where pid$^* =$ pid into a list SKeys$'$.
- Output (PKeys, SKeys$'$) to M.

Delete: On input (DELETE) from M with identifier pid, do the following:

- Overwrite all elements of SKeys of the form (pid*, dk, sk, R), where pid$^* =$ pid, with (pid*, $\bot$, $\bot$, R). Disallow any future signing queries by M for role R.
- Set Ready $\leftarrow$ Ready $\setminus \{$pid$\}$.
- Set Ready$_{\text{cid}} \leftarrow$ Ready$_{\text{cid}} \setminus \{pid\}$ for cid with $fin = \bot$.
- Output (DELETE, pid) to $\mathcal{S}$.

Ready: On input (READY) from M with identifier pid, update the global ready set Ready $\leftarrow$ Ready $\cup \{$pid$\}$ in the beginning of the subsequent round. Output (READY, pid) to the simulator $\mathcal{S}$.

Corrupt: Upon receiving (CORRUPT, pid) from $\mathcal{E}$, output all elements (pid*, dk, sk, R) of any stored SKeys, where pid$^* =$ pid to $\mathcal{S}$.

4   Compiling Abstract to Natural YOSO

Consider an abstract YOSO-protocol in the $\mathcal{F}_{\text{BC\&SPP}}$-hybrid model which is maliciously secure against a static adversary. This protocol is run by a set of committees, where each committee is associated with a set of roles. We may assume the execution of any honest role is completed by inputting at most one SEND command to an instance of $\mathcal{F}_{\text{BC\&SPP}}$, this is enforced by the SPOKE token which kills the role.

The goal of our compiler is to transform such a statically-secure YOSO abstract protocol in the $\mathcal{F}_{\text{BC\&SPP}}$-hybrid model into an adaptively-secure natural-world protocol in the $\mathcal{F}_{\text{RA}}$-hybrid model, where $\mathcal{F}_{\text{RA}}$ denotes the ideal functionality for role assignment defined in Sect. 3. We also assume that the natural protocol has access to a bulletin board (formalized as an ideal functionality below) which can be used by anyone to broadcast a message.

Functionality $\mathcal{F}_{\text{BB}}$

- Initially create broadcast maps:
  $m : \mathbb{N} \times \text{Machine} \to \text{Msg}_\perp$ where $m(r, M) = \perp$ for all r, M.
- On input (SEND, sid, msg) from machine M in round r:
  - Update $m(r, M) = \text{msg}$. *Store the broadcast message from the role.*
  - Output (SEND, sid, msg) to the simulator $\mathcal{S}$.
- On input (READ, sid, r') from machine M in round r where $r' < r$ output a set of all elements (M', r', msg) where $\text{msg} = m(r', M') \neq \perp$ to M.

Overview of the Compiler. Suppose we wish to compile an abstract protocol Π. At a high-level, the compiled protocol in the natural world involves the following stages: First, the machines initiate role assignment for committees that need to be nominated, which is determined based on the current round and the public state. Once the nomination process is completed, the machines can retrieve public keys corresponding to all roles in these committees and secret keys for the roles they were chosen for (if any). This can be done by machines inputting READ to $\mathcal{F}_{\text{RA}}$.

Consider a machine M who has been assigned a role for some round of the abstract protocol. Recall that in this case, $\mathcal{F}_{\text{RA}}$ provides M with a decryption key and a signing key. M obtains from $\mathcal{F}_{\text{RA}}$ the signature verification keys of all the roles that are supposed to send messages to the role that's assigned to M, as well as the public encryption keys of the roles that its assigned role is supposed to send messages to. (Note that the latter key may not be available yet.) In this case M keeps asking $\mathcal{F}_{\text{RA}}$ for these keys in each round. As soon as $\mathcal{F}_{\text{RA}}$ provides these keys, the M is ready to execute the role R based on the specifications of the abstract protocol Π. Suppose this role R invokes $\mathcal{F}_{\text{BC\&SPP}}$ in Π with a set of point-to-point and broadcast messages, then the machine does the following to emulate this step on behalf of the role:

- Read the bulletin board to retrieve messages posted by machines emulating sender roles. This includes broadcast messages and ciphertexts encrypting point-to-point messages intended for R as a receiver, accompanied by signatures. Accept the messages only if the signatures are valid (note that the verification key of all roles are made public by $\mathcal{F}_{RA}$).
- To retrieve the point-to-point message, uses the decryption key to decrypt the relevant ciphertexts.
- Proceed to compute the outgoing broadcast and point-to-point messages on behalf of the role R (Note that at this point, the machine has all the information a role holds in Π). Prepare a one-shot message comprising of the following (a) Broadcast messages (b) Ciphertexts encrypting the point-to-point messages using the encryption key of the relevant receiver roles in future committees (made public by $\mathcal{F}_{RA}$) (c) Signature on these messages, computed using the signing key of R received from $\mathcal{F}_{RA}$.
- Once the above one-shot message is computed, invoke $\mathcal{F}_{RA}$ with input DELETE and delete its own entire state, except the one-shot message to be posted. In particular, delete the secret keys, received messages and randomness used on behalf of the role R.
- Post this message to the bulletin board (as an atomic action).

Once the machine M has finished executing the role R, it notifies $\mathcal{F}_{RA}$ that it is READY i.e. available to be assigned a new role.

We point out that in the above informal description, we focused on machines that were assigned computation roles. The compiler easily accommodates actions by input and output roles in Π as well – the only difference is that these roles are carried out by fixed machines and their identity is not secret. Therefore, the public keys of these roles can be established via a PKI and need not be handled by $\mathcal{F}_{RA}$. Further, the messages posted on the bulletin board by machines executing these roles need not be signed.

Protocol Compile(Π)

Notation: The algorithm Nominate(r, $\{\mathsf{Broadcast}_{\mathsf{sid}}\}_{\mathsf{sid}\in\mathsf{SID}}$) denotes a publicly computable function which when given a round number and public state outputs the set of committees $\{\mathsf{cid}_i, C_i\}_{i\in[k]}$ to be nominated in that particular round. We assume that all the cid_i's contains the round number r.

Init: Initialise sets of messages and keys for each role:
- For each R $\in$ Role and sid $\in$ SID define a set R.Rec$_{\mathsf{sid}} \leftarrow \emptyset$ of ciphertexts sent to the role. R.$ek \leftarrow \perp$, R.$vk \leftarrow \perp$, R.$dk \leftarrow \perp$ and R.$sk \leftarrow \perp$.
- If R $\in$ Role$^{\mathrm{IN}} \cup$ Role^{OUT}, set R.ek and R.vk to relevant public keys established by PKI.
- For each sid $\in$ SID: Broadcast$_{\mathsf{sid}} = \emptyset$.

Nominate: In the beginning of round r (i.e. as per the reading of the global clock), compute the (computation) committees to be nominated, $\{\mathsf{cid}_i, C_i\}_{i \in [k]} \leftarrow \mathsf{Nominate}(r, \{\mathsf{Broadcast}_{\mathsf{sid}}\}_{\mathsf{sid} \in \mathsf{SID}})$.
For each committee input $(\mathrm{New}, \mathsf{cid}_i, C_i)$ to $\mathcal{F}_{\mathsf{RA}}$.

Role Keys: Once the machine finishes nominating committees in a round r, it proceeds to read the keys for the committees nominated in the previous round. For each committee, the machine inputs $(\mathrm{Read}, \mathsf{cid})$ to $\mathcal{F}_{\mathsf{RA}}$ receiving lists PKeys and SKeys.

- For each element (ek, vk, R') in PKeys the machine stores the role keys as $\mathsf{R}'.ek \leftarrow ek$ and $\mathsf{R}'.vk \leftarrow vk$.
- For each element $(pid, dk, sk, \mathsf{R})$ in SKeys (where pid corresponds to the machine's identifier) store the keys $\mathsf{R}.dk \leftarrow dk, \mathsf{R}.sk \leftarrow sk$. *We now consider the machine to have been assigned role* R.

Read: After storing new role keys each machine reads the bulletin board to process the next round of messages in the protocol. In round r the machine inputs $(\mathrm{Read}, \mathsf{sid}, r - 1)$ to $\mathcal{F}_{\mathsf{BB}}$, for each output element (M', r', msg') it receives the machine does the following:

- Parse msg' as $((\mathsf{S}, \mathsf{sid}, (\mathsf{R}_1, \overline{x}_1), \ldots, (\mathsf{R}_k, \overline{x}_k), x), \sigma)$
- Verifies the signature $b \leftarrow \mathsf{SIG.Verify}(\mathsf{S}.vk, (\mathsf{S}, \mathsf{sid}, (\mathsf{R}_1, \overline{x}_1), \ldots, (\mathsf{R}_k, \overline{x}_k), x), \sigma)$, ignoring the message if verification does not succeed [a].
- Add (S, x) to $\mathsf{Broadcast}_{\mathsf{sid}}$.
- For $i \in [k]$ add $(\mathsf{S}, \overline{x}_i)$ to $\mathsf{R}_i.\mathsf{Rec}_{\mathsf{sid}}$.

If any role has more than one message with a valid signature, both should be ignored.

Role Execution: When a machine has been assigned a role R, it should run the role in its head and emulate the interaction between the role and its ideal functionality $\mathcal{F}_{\mathsf{BC\&SPP}}$. In a given round a machine should activate each role it has been assigned, until the role signals that it has completed the round.

- If $\mathsf{R} \in \mathsf{Role}^{\mathrm{IN}}$, then this machine (belongs to $\mathsf{Machine}^{\mathrm{IN}}$) must have received command (Input, x) which it passes on to R.
- If R inputs $(\mathrm{Read}, \mathsf{R}, \mathsf{S}, r')$ to $\mathcal{F}^{\mathsf{sid}}_{\mathsf{BC\&SPP}}$, the machine should retrieve the tuple of the form $(\mathsf{S}, \overline{x})$ in $\mathsf{R}.\mathsf{Rec}_{\mathsf{sid}}$, if no such tuple exists $\bot$ should be output directly to the role. The ciphertext should then be decrypted to obtain $x \leftarrow \mathsf{PKE.Dec}^{(\mathsf{sid}, \mathsf{S})}(\mathsf{R}.dk, \overline{x})$ which may be returned to R.
- If R inputs $(\mathrm{Read}, \mathsf{S}, r')$ to $\mathcal{F}^{\mathsf{sid}}_{\mathsf{BC\&SPP}}$, the machine should retrieve the tuple of the form (R, x) in $\mathsf{Broadcast}_{\mathsf{sid}}$, and return x to R, returning $\bot$ if no such value exists.
- If $\mathsf{R} \in \mathsf{Role}^{\mathrm{Out}}$ outputs (Output, y), output the same.

Send $\mathcal{F}_{\mathsf{BC\&SPP}}$: When the role $\mathsf{R} \in \mathsf{Role}^{\mathrm{IN}} \cup \mathsf{Role}^{\mathrm{Comp}}$ assigned to M outputs $(\mathrm{Send}, \mathsf{R}, ((\mathsf{R}_1, x_1), \ldots, (\mathsf{R}_k, x_k)), x)$ to $\mathcal{F}_{\mathsf{BC\&SPP}}$ with session identifier sid do the following:

1. For $j \in [k]$: $\overline{x}_j \leftarrow \mathsf{PKE.Enc}^{(\mathsf{sid},\mathsf{R})}(\mathsf{R}_j.ek, x_j; \rho_j)$.
2. Let $\mathsf{msg} = (\mathsf{R}, r, \mathsf{sid}, (\mathsf{R}_1, \overline{x}_1), \ldots, (\mathsf{R}_k, \overline{x}_k), x)$.
3. Compute $\sigma \leftarrow \mathsf{SIG.Sign}(\mathsf{R}.sk, \mathsf{msg})$ and set $\mathsf{msg}' = (\mathsf{msg}, \sigma)$ [b].
4. If $\mathsf{R} \in \mathsf{Role}^{\mathrm{COMP}}$
   - Input (DELETE) to $\mathcal{F}_{\mathsf{RA}}$.
   - Erase all private local state associated with the role R, excluding $(\mathsf{R}, \mathsf{msg}, \sigma)$. In particular this includes $\mathsf{R}.dk$, $\mathsf{R}.sk$ and the entire state of the copy of R the machine has been running in its head.
5. Post msg' to the bulletin board.
6. Input (READY) to $\mathcal{F}_{\mathsf{RA}}$ if $\mathsf{R} \in \mathsf{Role}^{\mathrm{COMP}}$.

If a machine has been assigned multiple roles it should activate them until they have all sent a message or completed the round, collecting all their messages at Step 6.2 and posting them together.

---

[a] this verification is not needed if $\mathsf{S} \in \mathsf{Role}^{\mathrm{IN}} \cup \mathsf{Role}^{\mathrm{OUT}}$
[b] Here, signatures can be avoided if $\mathsf{R} \in \mathsf{Role}^{\mathrm{IN}}$.

5   Security of the Compiler

In this section, we prove the security of the compiler presented in Sect. 4 which transforms a *static, abstract* YOSO protocol to an *adaptively-secure* natural protocol. The security of our compiled *natural* protocol fundamentally relies on the security of the original *abstract* protocol. The primary challenge arises due to the difference in the adversary's corruption powers between the abstract and natural world. In order to rely on the static security of our abstract protocol, we must be able to translate the adaptive adversary in the natural world to an appropriate static adversary in the abstract world (against which a simulator must exist, due to security of the abstract protocol).

To rely on the static simulator of our abstract protocol it is essential that the natural world adversary cannot influence which roles are revealed through its chosen corruptions of machines. As a starting point, let us consider what goes wrong if a natural simulator is forced to commit to a mapping from roles to machines. An adaptive adversary might then subsequently choose which machines to corrupt based on this commitment. The simulator is essentially forced to guess which machines the adversary will corrupt making it overwhelmingly likely to fail.

To circumvent this issue we may instead consider the possible simulation strategy if our simulator were not committed to this role to machine mapping. Our static abstract simulator must always fix a choice of corrupt roles. The state of these corrupt roles may be simulated, making it acceptable to assign them to corrupt machines. Conversely, we have no way to simulate the state of honest roles, so these must never be revealed to the adversary. During simulation, the simulator presents a role assignment functionality to the natural world adversary.

The natural world adversary expects the roles to be assigned to the machines it has corrupted in proportion to its expended corruptions. This may easily be accounted for by sampling a mapping where an appropriate number of statically corrupt roles are assigned to these machines. Things get more challenging when we start to consider adaptive corruptions, in the real world the adversary will sometimes get lucky and corrupt a machine which has been assigned a role. If we simply fix the mapping from roles to machines at the time of nomination this could cause simulation to fail if the newly corrupted machine had been assigned an honest role. However, if our role assignment functionality does not leak anything to the adversary about the mapping of honest roles we may simply change the assignment of this honest role to a machine which remains honest. This will of course affect the number of roles revealed to the adversary, to account for this we must additionally maintain some budget of statically corrupt roles, which we reveal in place of the honest roles.

As the simulator now controls which roles are revealed to the adversary it may be sure that it never has to open a ciphertext sent between the holders of two honest roles. As a result these ciphertexts need not be non-committing, allowing the use of the much more efficient CCA secure encryption.

We define the class of protocols which are compatible with our compiler.

Definition 3 (Compiler compatible protocol). *We call a protocol Π a compiler compatible secure implementation of $\mathcal{F}$ with threshold c/w, if the following conditions are satisfied:*[6]

- *Let $c = \Omega(\kappa)$ denote the committee size. Then, Π must YOSO securely implement the ideal functionality $\mathcal{F}$ in the presence of c/w static corruptions in the computation committees and an arbitrary number of static corruptions in the input and output roles.*
- *All honest roles in the same committee speak in the same round.*
- *There exists a positive constant* delay, *such that it is publicly computable which committees need to be nominated at least* delay *round(s) in advance.*
- *There exists a constant $R_{max} \geq \kappa$, denoting the upper bound on the concurrently active roles at any point (which refers to roles that are able to receive messages, or currently being nominated).*

Theorem 2. *Consider an abstract protocol Π in the $\mathcal{F}_{BC\&SPP}$-hybrid model, which is a compiler compatible secure implementation of $\mathcal{F}$ with threshold c/w (Definition 3). Let $\mathcal{F}_{RA}$ be shorthand for $\mathcal{F}_{RA}(\mathcal{P}, c, \mathcal{T}, \mathcal{U}, 2)$ where $\mathcal{U}$ samples the uniform distribution and a function $\mathcal{T}(f)$. Further, assume the schemes PKE and SIG used by $\mathcal{F}_{RA}$ are adaptive IND-CCA and EUF-CMA secure respectively.*

Then, assuming a PKI setup, the protocol Compile(Π) UC implements the ideal functionality $\mathcal{F}$ in the $(\mathcal{F}_{BB}, \mathcal{F}_{RA}, \mathcal{F}_{VRF})$-hybrid model, under the presence of $T < N f_t$ adaptive corruptions of the computation machines and any number of static corruptions in the input and output roles, where $N = (R_{max})^{2+\delta}$ for a

---

[6] Note that all existing *abstract* YOSO protocols (such as the protocols in [GHK+21, KRY22]) satisfy these properties.

constant $1 \leq \delta$ *and* f_t *is fixed such that there exists a constant* $\epsilon > 0$ *where for all* $0 < f < f_t$ *it holds that* $\mathcal{T}(f) + (1+\epsilon)(f_t - f)c < c/w$.

If we apply Theorem 2 to the threshold function achieved by our role assignment protocol in Sect. 7 we obtain the following corollary.

Corollary 1. *For* $\mathcal{T}(f) = c\left(1 - (1-\epsilon)(1-f)^2\right)$ *a protocol tolerating* c/w *corruptions may be compiled to a protocol tolerating* $T < Nf_t$ *adaptive corruptions, where* f_t *satisfies* $0 < 1 - 2wf_t + wf_t^2$.[7]

We refer the reader to the full version of this paper for a proof of Theorem 2.

6 Compiling Abstract Protocols Requiring Verification

Our compiler in Sect. 4 supports the class of YOSO protocols in the $\mathcal{F}_{\text{BC\&SPP}}$-hybrid model, such as the information-theoretic protocol of [GHK+21]. However, this notably excludes protocols which assume explicit access to keys for the roles to allow zero-knowledge proofs or any other types of public verifiability for point-to-point messages. A large part of the existing YOSO protocol literature falls under this umbrella, including the protocols presented in [BDO22, KRY22] and the computationally secure protocol of [GHK+21].

Kolby et al. [KRY22] introduced the verifiable state propagation (VeSPa) functionality $\mathcal{F}_{\text{VeSPa}}$ to capture verifiability of point-to-point messages and designed protocols in the $(\mathcal{F}_{\text{VeSPa}}, \mathcal{F}_{\text{BC\&SPP}})$-hybrid model instead. We show how our compiler may be extended to accommodate the compilation of protocols in the $(\mathcal{F}_{\text{VeSPa}}, \mathcal{F}_{\text{BC\&SPP}})$-hybrid model.

Before showing how our compiler may be extended to protocols in the $(\mathcal{F}_{\text{VeSPa}}, \mathcal{F}_{\text{BC\&SPP}})$-hybrid model we will first reflect on the broader role of message verifiability within YOSO protocols. When using $\mathcal{F}_{\text{BC\&SPP}}$ all point-to-point messaging is ideal, making it impossible to directly provide verifiability guarantees for any single message in a single round. Works studying information theoretic YOSO MPC [GHK+21, DKI+23] achieve verifiability by constructing verifiable secret sharing (VSS) protocols in the abstract world. They then make use of VSS to construct their desired MPC protocols. These protocols explicitly handle their need for verifiable message passing in the abstract world, and thus inherit these same guarantees when compiled to the natural world. There are drawbacks to this approach of explicit abstract world verifiability, as existing VSS constructions all introduce an overhead in both rounds and a number of intermediate roles.

An alternative approach follows from the ideas within computationally secure protocols, where verifiability may come from non-interactive zero-knowledge

---

[7] This holds when $f_t < 1 - \frac{\sqrt{w^2 - w}}{w}$. For $w = 2$, namely when the abstract protocol withstands honest minority, this allows $f_t \approx 0.29$. For $w = 1.1$, namely when the abstract protocol withstands corruption of roughly 90% of the parties, this allows $f_t \approx 0.7$.

proofs, rather than additional interaction. In the context of YOSO the restriction to $\mathcal{F}_{BC\&SPP}$ means that we only consider black box communication, and thus cannot directly prove statements about point-to-point messages. To resolve the limitation Kolby *et al.* [KRY22] introduced a new *verifiable state propagation* functionality which enabled enforcing statements for point-to-point messages, giving verifiability. A natural question to consider is whether it is possible to realise $\mathcal{F}_{VeSPa}$ in the abstract world given $\mathcal{F}_{BC\&SPP}$. However, if we recall the cost of achieving VSS in the $\mathcal{F}_{BC\&SPP}$-hybrid model, our hopes of verifying more complex relations, without a significant round and communication complexity overhead are quickly dampened. Conversely, if we do not realise $\mathcal{F}_{VeSPa}$ we are left with a protocol which remains incompatible with compilation. This leaves us with a choice of either realising $\mathcal{F}_{VeSPa}$ in the abstract world, or adapting our compiler to produce protocols which enforce the guarantees of $\mathcal{F}_{VeSPa}$, essentially making verifiability explicit during the translation to the natural world.

We observe that our compiler is actually well suited to the addition of message verifiability, making this a desirable choice. Recall, our modifications have eliminated the need for non-committing encryption for protocol messages, instead simply requiring CCA security. If we extend the few requirements we make of our encryption scheme to additionally permitting efficient proofs of knowledge of plaintext, we may use non-interactive zero-knowledge to prove that the encrypted messages between roles satisfy whatever relations we require.

6.1   Verifiable State Propagation

In this section, we recall the verifiable state propagation (VeSPa) functionality $\mathcal{F}_{VeSPa}$ introduced in Kolby et al. [KRY22]. Informally, this functionality enables both point-to-point and broadcast communication, while allowing the sender to prove that she correctly computed these messages (based on messages she received and possibly other additional inputs).

In more detail, a sender role S in the abstract protocol invokes $\mathcal{F}_{VeSPa}$ with the following information: (a) the point-to-point messages S intends to send to a set of recipient roles (b) the messages S intends to broadcast (c) witness (comprising of the internal state of S such as its private randomness used to compute its outgoing messages).

Consider the statement comprising of these outgoing point-to-point (say, ϕ_{send}) and broadcast messages (say, $\phi_{broadcast}$), the incoming messages that were received by S (say, $\phi_{receive}$) and the public state (containing all the messages broadcast so far, denoted by ϕ_{public}). The role S is associated with a relation $\mathcal{R}(S)$ which basically specifies the correct behaviour of S as per the abstract protocol specifications. The functionality $\mathcal{F}_{VeSPa}$ verifies this relation i.e. checks if the outgoing point-to-point and broadcast messages sent by S are computed correctly based on the incoming messages it received previously, the current public state and its private randomness (given as part of the witness). The messages that are verified are subsequently communicated. The formal description of $\mathcal{F}_{VeSPa}$ appears below.

Functionality $\mathcal{F}_{\mathsf{VeSPa}}$ [KRY22]

This ideal functionality has the following behaviour:

- Define a map $\mathcal{R} : \mathsf{Role} \to \mathsf{Rel}_{\perp}$. *Specify the relations the messages of each role must satisfy.*
- Initially create point-to-point and broadcast maps:
  $y : \mathbb{N} \times \mathsf{Role} \times \mathsf{Role} \to \mathsf{Msg}_{\perp}$ where $y(r, \mathsf{R}, \mathsf{R}') = \perp$ for all $r, \mathsf{R}, \mathsf{R}'$
  $m : \mathbb{N} \times \mathsf{Role} \to \mathsf{Msg}_{\perp}$ where $m(r, \mathsf{R}) = \perp$ for all r, R.
- On input $(\textsc{Send}, \mathsf{S}, ((\mathsf{R}_1, x_1), \dots, (\mathsf{R}_k, x_k)), x, w)$ in round r proceed as follows:
  - Let $\phi_{send} = ((\mathsf{R}_1, x_1), \dots, (\mathsf{R}_k, x_k))$ and $\phi_{broadcast} = x$.
  - Let ϕ_{public} be the current public state, represented by a vector of all elements $(r, \mathsf{R}, \mathsf{msg})$, where $m(r, \mathsf{R}) = \mathsf{msg} \neq \perp$.
  - Collect all $y_k \neq \perp$ for $r' < r, \mathsf{R}' \in \mathsf{Role}$ where $y(r', \mathsf{R}', \mathsf{S}) = y_k$ to produce a vector $\phi_{receive} = ((\mathsf{R}_1', y_1), \dots, (\mathsf{R}_m', y_m))$.
  - If $((\phi_{send}||\phi_{receive}||\phi_{broadcast}||\phi_{public}), w) \notin \mathcal{R}(\mathsf{S})$ ignore the input.
  - Else:
    * For $i \in [n]$ update $y(r, \mathsf{S}, \mathsf{R}_i) = x_i$. *Store point to point messages from the role.*
    * Update $m(r, \mathsf{S}) = x$. *Store the broadcast message from the role.*
    * Output $(\mathsf{S}, ((\mathsf{R}_1, |x_1|), \dots, (\mathsf{R}_k, |x_k|)), x)$ to the simulator $\mathcal{S}$. For corrupt roles R_i output x_i to the simulator $\mathcal{S}$. *Leak messages lengths and the broadcast message to the simulator in a rushing fashion.*

    If S is honest give $\textsc{Spoke}$ to $\mathcal{S}$.
- On input $(\textsc{Read}, \mathsf{R}, \mathsf{S}, r')$ in round r where $r' < r$ for $x = y(r', \mathsf{S}, \mathsf{R})$ output x to R.
- On input $(\textsc{Read}, \mathsf{S}, r')$ in round r where $r' < r$ output $x = m(r', \mathsf{S})$ to R.

6.2 Extending to Verifiable State Propagation

In our extension of the compiler we use the NIZK functionality $\mathcal{F}_{\mathsf{NIZK}}$ introduced by [GOS12]. Looking ahead, the ability to extract witnesses through $\mathcal{F}_{\mathsf{VeSPa}}$ means that we no longer require CCA security for our encryption scheme and may relax this to CPA security.

At a high-level, in order to emulate the invocation of $\mathcal{F}_{\mathsf{VeSPa}}$ by a role R in the abstract protocol, the machine assigned to execute role R does the following (1) first reads the bulletin board to obtain the broadcast messages and incoming point-to-point messages sent to R (by decrypting the relevant ciphertexts). (2) Then, according to the specifications of the underlying abstract protocol (i.e. as per the relation $\mathcal{R}(\mathsf{R})$ required by $\mathcal{F}_{\mathsf{VeSPa}}$ in the underlying protocol), it computes its outgoing point-to-point and broadcast messages based on the incoming messages and internal state. (3) prepares encryptions of these outgoing point-to-point messages using the encryption keys of the recipient roles. (4) Finally, the machine then invokes the $\mathcal{F}_{\mathsf{NIZK}}$ functionality with respect to a relation $\mathcal{R}_{\mathsf{VeSPa}}$ (described below) which essentially checks that the machine did the above actions (1), (2) and (3) correctly.

Accordingly, we define the relation $\mathcal{R}_{\mathsf{VeSPa}}$ which describes what we require of the messages sent by our machines. The requirements may be divided into two categories:

- Encryption and decryption is performed correctly.
- The incoming and outgoing plaintexts, and the public state satisfy the relation $\mathcal{R}(\mathsf{R})$ required by $\mathcal{F}_{\mathsf{VeSPa}}$ in the underlying protocol.

For a message $\mathsf{msg} = (\mathsf{R}, \mathsf{sid}, (\mathsf{R}_1, \overline{x}_1), \ldots, (\mathsf{R}_k, \overline{x}_k), x)$, incoming message set $\mathsf{R.Rec}_{\mathsf{sid}}$, with elements of the form $(\mathsf{S}, \overline{x}_i)$, and past broadcast messages $\mathsf{Broadcast}_{\mathsf{sid}}$, with elements of the form (R, x), we define our relation,[8]

$$
\mathcal{R}_{\mathsf{VeSPa}} = \left\{
\begin{array}{l}
\phi = \begin{pmatrix} \mathsf{R}, \mathsf{sid}, \mathsf{R}.ek, \\ \mathcal{R}_{\mathsf{sid}}(\mathsf{R}), \\ (\mathsf{R}_j.ek)_{j \in [k]}, \\ \mathsf{R.Rec}_{\mathsf{sid}}, \\ \mathsf{msg}, \\ \mathsf{Broadcast}_{\mathsf{sid}} \end{pmatrix} \\[2em]
w = \begin{pmatrix} \mathsf{R}.dk, \\ (x_j, \rho_j)_{j \in [k]}, \\ w' \end{pmatrix}
\end{array}
\;\middle|\;
\begin{array}{l}
\top = \mathsf{KeyMatch}(\mathsf{R}.dk, \mathsf{R}.ek) \\
\text{For } j \in [k] : \\
\quad \overline{x}_j = \mathsf{PKE.Enc}(\mathsf{R}_j.ek, x_j; \rho_j) \\
\text{For } (\mathsf{S}, \overline{y}_j) \in \mathsf{R.Rec}_{\mathsf{sid}} : \\
\quad y_j = \mathsf{PKE.Dec}(\mathsf{R}.dk, \overline{y}_j) \\
\phi_{send} = ((\mathsf{R}_j, x_j))_{j \in [k]} \\
\phi_{rec} = ((\mathsf{R}_j, y_j))_{(\mathsf{S}, \overline{y}_j) \in \mathsf{R.Rec}_{\mathsf{sid}}} \\
\phi_{bc} = x \\
\phi_{pub} = \mathsf{Broadcast}_{\mathsf{sid}} \\
((\phi_{send}, \phi_{rec}, \phi_{bc}, \phi_{pub}), w') \in \mathcal{R}_{\mathsf{sid}}(\mathsf{R})
\end{array}
\right\}.
$$

The only changes we need to allow for this functionality are when dealing with messages sent via $\mathcal{F}_{\mathsf{VeSPa}}$, the role assignment process remains unchanged.

Protocol Extended Compile(Π)

Read: After storing new role keys each machine reads the bulletin board to process the next round of messages in the protocol. In round r the machine inputs $(\textsc{Read}, \mathsf{sid}, r - 1)$ to $\mathcal{F}_{\mathsf{BB}}$, for each output element (M', r', msg') it receives the machine does the following:
- Parse msg' as $((\mathsf{S}, \mathsf{sid}', (\mathsf{R}_1, \overline{x}_1), \ldots, (\mathsf{R}_k, \overline{x}_k), x, \pi), \sigma)$
- If sid' is the session identifier for an instance of $\mathcal{F}_{\mathsf{VeSPa}}$ proceed with these steps, otherwise handle the message as done for $\mathcal{F}_{\mathsf{BC\&SPP}}$ in the original compiler.
- Verifies the signature $b \leftarrow \mathsf{SIG.Verify}(\mathsf{S}.vk, (\mathsf{S}, (\mathsf{S}, \mathsf{sid}', (\mathsf{R}_1, \overline{x}_1), \ldots, (\mathsf{R}_k, \overline{x}_k), x), \pi), \sigma)$, ignoring the message if verification does not succeed.

---

[8] The predicate $\mathsf{KeyMatch}$ is true iff there exists randomness ρ such that $(dk, ek) \leftarrow \mathsf{KGen}(\rho)$.

- Defines the statement $\phi \leftarrow (\mathsf{R}, \mathsf{sid}', \mathsf{R}.ek, \mathcal{R}_{\mathsf{sid}'}(\mathsf{R}), (\mathsf{R}_j.ek)_{j \in [k]}, \mathsf{R}.\mathsf{Rec}_{\mathsf{sid}'},$
  $\mathsf{msg}, \mathsf{Broadcast}_{\mathsf{sid}'})$.
- Inputs $(\textsc{Verify}, \phi, \pi)$ to $\mathcal{F}_{\mathsf{NIZK}}$ with respect to the relation $\mathcal{R}_{\mathsf{VeSPa}}$. and waits for a response $(\textsc{Verification}, , b)$. If $b = 0$ the message is ignored.
- After checks have been made for all the provided messages:
  - Add (S, x) to $\mathsf{Broadcast}_{\mathsf{sid}'}$.
  - For $i \in [k]$ add $(\mathsf{S}, \overline{x}_i)$ to $\mathsf{R}_i.\mathsf{Rec}_{\mathsf{sid}'}$.

If any role has more than one message with a valid signature, both should be ignored.

Execute Role: A machine M nominated for a role R should activate it for each round of the protocol until it speaks.

- If the role inputs $(\textsc{Read}, \mathsf{R}, \mathsf{S}, r')$ to $\mathcal{F}_{\mathsf{VeSPa}}^{\mathsf{sid}}$ the machine should retrieve the tuple of the form $(\mathsf{S}, \overline{x}_i)$ in $\mathsf{R}.\mathsf{Rec}_{\mathsf{sid}}$, if no such tuple exists $\perp$ should be output directly to the role. The ciphertext should then be decrypted to obtain $x_i \leftarrow \mathsf{PKE}.\mathsf{Dec}(\mathsf{R}.dk, \overline{x}_i)$ which may be returned to R.
- If the role inputs $(\textsc{Read}, \mathsf{S}, r')$ to $\mathcal{F}_{\mathsf{VeSPa}}^{\mathsf{sid}}$ the machine should retrieve the tuple of the form (R, x) in $\mathsf{Broadcast}_{\mathsf{sid}}$, and return x to R,

Send $\mathcal{F}_{\mathsf{VeSPa}}$: When the role R assigned to M outputs $(\textsc{Send}, \mathsf{R}, ((\mathsf{R}_1, x_1), \ldots, (\mathsf{R}_k, x_k)), x, w')$ to $\mathcal{F}_{\mathsf{VeSPa}}$ with session identifier sid' do the following:

- For $j \in [k]$: $\overline{x}_j \leftarrow \mathsf{PKE}.\mathsf{Enc}(\mathsf{R}_j.ek, x_j; \rho_j)$.
- Defines the statement $\phi \leftarrow (\mathsf{R}, \mathsf{sid}', \mathsf{R}.ek, \mathcal{R}_{\mathsf{sid}'}(\mathsf{R}), (\mathsf{R}_j.ek)_{j \in [k]}, \mathsf{R}.\mathsf{Rec}_{\mathsf{sid}'},$
  $\mathsf{msg}, \mathsf{Broadcast}_{\mathsf{sid}'})$ and witness $w \leftarrow (\mathsf{R}.dk, (x_j, \rho_j)_{j \in [k]}, w')$
- Inputs $(\textsc{Prove}, \phi, w)$ to $\mathcal{F}_{\mathsf{NIZK}}$ with respect to the relation $\mathcal{R}_{\mathsf{VeSPa}}$. and waits for a response $(\textsc{Proof}, \pi)$.
- Let $\mathsf{msg} = (\mathsf{R}, \mathsf{sid}', (\mathsf{R}_1, \overline{x}_1), \ldots, (\mathsf{R}_k, \overline{x}_k), x, \pi)$.
- $\sigma \leftarrow \mathsf{SIG}.\mathsf{Sign}(\mathsf{R}.sk, (\mathsf{R}, \mathsf{msg}, \pi))$.
- Input $(\textsc{Delete})$ to $\mathcal{F}_{\mathsf{RA}}$.
- Erase all private local state associated with the role R, excluding (msg, σ). In particular this includes $\mathsf{R}.dk, \mathsf{R}.sk$ and the entire state of the copy of R the machine has been running in its head.
- Post (msg, σ) to the bulletin board.
- Input $(\textsc{Ready})$ to $\mathcal{F}_{\mathsf{RA}}$.

6.3 Security of the Extended Compiler

We prove the security of our extended compiler, stated in the formal theorem below.

Theorem 3. *Consider an abstract protocol Π in the $(\mathcal{F}_{\mathsf{VeSPa}}, \mathcal{F}_{\mathsf{BC\&SPP}})$-hybrid model, which is a compiler compatible secure implementation of $\mathcal{F}$ with threshold c/w (Definition 3). Let $\mathcal{F}_{\mathsf{RA}}$ be shorthand for $\mathcal{F}_{\mathsf{RA}}(\mathcal{P}, c, \mathcal{T}, \mathcal{U}, 2)$ where $\mathcal{U}$ samples* the uniform distribution and $\mathcal{T}(f) = c\left(1 - (1 - \epsilon)(1 - f)^2\right)$, for $\epsilon > 0$. Further, assume the schemes PKE and SIG used by $\mathcal{F}_{RA}$ are IND-CPA and EUF-CMA secure respectively.

Then, assuming a PKI setup, the protocol Compile(Π) UC implements the ideal functionality $\mathcal{F}$ in the $(\mathcal{F}_{NIZK}, \mathcal{F}_{BB}, \mathcal{F}_{RA})$-hybrid model, under the presence of $T < Nf_t$ adaptive corruptions of the computation machines and any number of static corruptions in the input and output roles, where $N = (R_{max})^{2+\delta}$ for a constant $\delta \geq 1$ and $0 < 1 - 2wf_t + wf_t^2$.[9]

The proof of Theorem 3 appears in the full version of this paper.

7   Realising Role Assignment

In compilation, we crucially relied on the ability to program the nominations of our role assignment functionality on the fly to mitigate the adaptive corruption powers of the adversary. We will now show how to realise $\mathcal{F}_{RA}$ by modifying the committee selection protocol of Benhamouda et al. [BGG+20] to allow equivocation of the mapping betweeen roles and machines.

We begin by recalling the high level approach of their construction. The task of choosing committee members is delegated to a nomination committee; nominators in this committee do not need to receive any private input and may therefore be self-selecting through cryptographic sortition. For a sufficiently large nomination committee the fraction of corrupt nominators will be close to the fraction of corruptions in the entire system. When a machine is chosen as a nominator it samples fresh ephemeral keys for the role it is nominating, the public key may be broadcast along with an encryption of the secret key under a special form of anonymous PKE. As we consider an adaptive adversary with the capacity to corrupt all members of the nomination committee, were they identified, each nominator must make sure to delete its secret state prior to sending their message. All machines may then observe the broadcast channel, and attempt to decrypt each nomination ciphertext, if the decryption succeeds the machine has been nominated and can decrypt ciphertexts messages sent to the role.

To satisfy our role-assignment functionality we must make some modifications. Recall, in our simulation we want to choose the static corruptions in each committee ahead of time, only ever revealing those chosen corrupt roles. If the role assignment mechanism commits to a mapping between roles and machines a simulator may be forced to corrupt machines which have been assigned honest roles, for which it cannot equivocate. However, if the role assignment mechanism does not commit to the mapping between roles and machines this could conceivably be chosen on the fly to avoid revealing any statically honest roles.

---

[9] This holds when $f_t < 1 - \frac{\sqrt{w^2 - w}}{w}$. For $w = 2$, namely when the abstract protocol withstands honest minority, this allows $f_t \approx 0.29$. For $w = 1.1$, namely when the abstract protocol withstands corruption of roughly 90% of the parties, this allows $f_t \approx 0.7$.

To make the approach compatible with the approach of Benhamouda *et al.* [BGG+20] we replace the encryption scheme used for nomination ciphertexts with key and message non-committing encryption (KM-NCE) [HLH+22]. We additionally introduce the use of a randomness beacon, which provides fresh uniform randomness each round, which we use to ensure the mapping from roles to nominations is uniformly random and not biased by the adversary.

Note, while KM-NCE allows equivocating for both key and message, we will only ever change the key under which ciphertexts decrypt. The committee size must not exceed some fixed size c, to ensure this we must fix the winning probability p such that the expected committee size is smaller than c allowing the application of a tail bound. To this end we let $p = c/((1 + \epsilon')N)$ for some $\epsilon' > 0$.

Protocol Π_{RA}

Each machine M has access to a PKI containing KM-NCE public keys and VRF verification keys for each computation machine. VRF keys are generated by all machines invoking (malicious) key generation on $\mathcal{F}_{\mathsf{VRF}}$. Each machine additionally stores its current long-term KM-NCE secret key as $M.sk$. Let c be the predefined size of a committee.

New Committee: After receiving input $(\mathrm{NEW}, \mathsf{cid}, C)$ in round r, machine M with identifier pid performs the following procedure:
- If there already exists stored value with $\mathsf{cid}^* = \mathsf{cid}$ ignore this command. Otherwise, store the value $(r, \mathsf{cid}, C, \mathsf{PKeys}, \mathsf{SKeys})$, where PKeys and SKeys are empty lists.
- Input (READ, r) to the randomness beacon, to receive randomness ρ.
- Input $(\mathrm{EVALPROVE}, (\rho, \mathsf{cid}))$ to $\mathcal{F}_{\mathsf{VRF}}$ and wait for output $(\mathrm{EVALUTATED}, \mathsf{draw}, \pi)$.
- If draw is a winning draw (i.e. $\mathsf{draw}/2^{\ell_{\mathsf{VRF}}} \leq p$), proceed to nominate a party, otherwise skip the remaining steps.
- Sample a uniformly random machine index $\mathsf{pid}' \leftarrow\$ \mathcal{P}$.
- Generate fresh ephemeral encryption and signing keys for the nominated role, $(ek, dk) \leftarrow \mathsf{PKE.Gen}()$ $(vk, sk) \leftarrow \mathsf{SIG.Gen}()$.
- Encrypt the decryption and signing key to the chosen machine $\mathsf{ctxt} \leftarrow KM-NCE.\mathsf{Enc}(M_{\mathsf{pid}'}.pk, (\mathsf{pid}', dk, sk))$.
- Erase the keys dk, sk and all randomness used for sampling the keys and pid', as well as any encryption randomness.
- Post $(\mathsf{cid}, ek, vk, \mathsf{ctxt}, \mathsf{draw}, \pi)$ to the bulletin board.

Read: On input $(\mathrm{READ}, \mathsf{cid})$ in round r' where $r + 2 \leq r'$
1. Retrieve the value $(r, \mathsf{cid}, C, \mathsf{PKeys}, \mathsf{SKeys})$, stopping if no such value exists.
2. Observe the bulletin board and collect a list of messages for committee identifier cid posted in round r, $(\mathsf{cid}, ek_1, vk_1, \mathsf{ctxt}_1, \mathsf{draw}_1, \pi_1), \ldots, (\mathsf{cid}, ek_k, vk_k, \mathsf{ctxt}_k, \mathsf{draw}_k, \pi_k)$.

3. Remove any elements $(\mathsf{cid}, ek_j, vk_j, \mathsf{ctxt}_j, \mathsf{draw}_j, \pi_j)$ posted by machine M from the list where draw_j is not a winning draw. This may be verified by inputting $(\text{VERIFY}, (\rho, \mathsf{cid}), \mathsf{draw}_j, \pi_j, M_{\mathsf{pid}}.vk^{\mathsf{VRF}})$ to $\mathcal{F}_{\mathsf{VRF}}$ where pid is the identifier of the machine which has posted the message to the bulletin board and ρ is the randomness the beacon has provided for committee cid. Remove the element if $\mathcal{F}_{\mathsf{VRF}}$ returns 0, or $\mathsf{draw}_j/2^{\ell_{\mathsf{VRF}}} > p$.
4. Sort the list lexicographically by encryption key, keeping only the c first elements. If the list does not have exactly c elements pad it with values $(\mathsf{cid}, \bot, \bot, \bot)$.
5. Input $(\text{READ}, r+1)$ to the randomness beacon, to receive randomness ρ.
6. Let σ a uniformly random permutation on $[c]$ defined by the randomness ρ and apply σ to the list.
7. Loop over the list, for the jth element $(\mathsf{cid}, ek_j, vk_j, \mathsf{ctxt}_j)$:
   - Append (ek_j, vk_j, C_j) to PKeys.
   - Attempt to decrypt $(\mathsf{pid}, dk, sk) \leftarrow KM-NCE.\mathsf{Dec}(M_j.sk, \mathsf{ctxt}_j)$. If $(\mathsf{pid}, dk, sk) \neq \bot$ and pid matches the machine which posted the element to the bulletin board, append $(\mathsf{pid}, dk, sk, C_j)$.
8. Output PKeys and SKeys to M.

Delete: When given input DELETE, for each stored value $(r, \mathsf{cid}, C, \mathsf{PKeys}, \mathsf{SKeys})$ delete SKeys overwriting it with the empty list. Finally, delete the long term secret key $M.sk$.

Ready: When given input READY, generate a new key pair $(pk, sk, tk) \leftarrow KM-NCE.\mathsf{Gen}()$, setting $M.sk = sk$ and deleting tk immediately. Finally, post (pid, pk) to the bulletin board.

We now prove the security of our role assignment mechanism. The protocol ensures at most $\mathcal{T}(f) = c\left(1 - (1-\epsilon)(1-f)^2\right)$ of the c roles in a committee are assigned to corrupt machines when the committee is finished being nominated. Here f is the fraction of corruptions at the point where the committee finishes being nominated. Intuitively this corresponds to guaranteeing that the remaining $(1-f)N$ honest machines have nominated other machines which have remained honest at least a fraction $(1-f)$ of the time. The proof of Theorem 4 appears in the full version of this paper.

Theorem 4. *For threshold function $\mathcal{T}(f) = c\left(1 - (1-\epsilon)(1-f)^2\right)$ and the uniform distribution $\mathcal{U}$. If the KM-NCE scheme used has KMNC_k-CCA (for $\mathsf{k} = \mathsf{poly}(\kappa)$[10]) and KM-NCE-UR security and the sortition has winning probability $c/((1+\epsilon')N)$ for $\epsilon' > 0$. Then, assuming a bare PKI setup, the protocol*

---

[10] To weaken this to $\mathsf{k} = O(1)$ would require a bound on the number of honest nominations a machine could receive before refreshing its key.

Π_{RA} *UC realises the functionality* $\mathcal{F}_{\mathsf{RA}}(\mathcal{P}, c, \mathcal{T}, \mathcal{U}, 2)$ *in the presence of* $T \leq N$ *adaptive corruptions in the* $(\mathcal{F}_{\mathsf{Beacon}}, \mathcal{F}_{\mathsf{BB}}, \mathcal{F}_{\mathsf{VRF}})$-*hybrid model.*

8 The Versatility of Our Compiler

The compiler we present allows the compilation of YOSO protocols using both $\mathcal{F}_{\mathsf{BC\&SPP}}$ and $\mathcal{F}_{\mathsf{VeSPa}}$. Of the existing literature only Kolby *et al.* present computationally secure protocols in the $\mathcal{F}_{\mathsf{VeSPa}}$-hybrid model [KRY22], having introduced the functionality. However, existing works which make non-black-box use of the communication between roles may be recast into the $\mathcal{F}_{\mathsf{VeSPa}}$-hybrid model allowing for their efficient compilation. We provide one such example. Braun *et al.* construct a YOSO MPC protocol from class groups, following the circuit based CDN paradigm of [CDN01]. Their protocol proceeds by first performing a distributed key generation to obtain a key for a threshold linearly homomorphic encryption scheme, which is then used for the circuit evaluation.

In the construction of their protocol they assume access to explicit public keys allowing them to prove statements about the ciphertexts and public messages with NIZK. The NIZK proofs are used in three of their functionalities, CreateVSS, CreateTriple and YOSO − ABB. Proving the exact same relations about the messages sent through $\mathcal{F}_{\mathsf{VeSPa}}$ would clearly preserve security, giving the simulator access to the same witnesses it could extract from explicit proofs.

Braun *et al.* [BDO22] specifically tailor their statements to have efficient proofs for the class group encryption scheme they use [CCL+19]. As our extended compiler is secure for any PKE scheme with CPA security, it could in particular be instantiated with the same class group scheme preserving their efficiency.

Acknowledgements. Funded by the European Research Council (ERC) under the European Unions's Horizon 2020 research and innovation programme under grant agreement No 803096 (SPEC), the Danish Independent Research Council under Grant-ID DFF-2064-00016B (YOSO), and the Digital Research Centre Denmark (DIREC).

References

[AHKP22] Acharya, A., Hazay, C., Kolesnikov, V., Prabhakaran, M.: SCALES - MPC with small clients and larger ephemeral servers. In: Kiltz, E., Vaikuntanathan, V. (eds.) TCC 2022. Part II, volume 13748 of LNCS, pp. 502–531. Springer, Heidelberg (2022). https://doi.org/10.1007/978-3-031-22365-5_18

[BDO22] Braun, L., Damgård, I., Orlandi, C.: Secure multiparty computation from threshold encryption based on class groups. Cryptology ePrint Archive, Report 2022/1437 (2022). https://eprint.iacr.org/2022/1437

[BGG+20] Benhamouda, F., et al.: Can a public blockchain keep a secret? In: Pass, R., Pietrzak, K. (eds.) TCC 2020. LNCS, vol. 12550, pp. 260–290. Springer, Cham (2020). https://doi.org/10.1007/978-3-030-64375-1_10

[CCL+19] Castagnos, G., Catalano, D., Laguillaumie, F., Savasta, F., Tucker, I.: Two-party ECDSA from hash proof systems and efficient instantiations. Cryptology ePrint Archive, Report 2019/503 (2019). https://eprint.iacr.org/2019/503

[CDN01] Cramer, R., Damgård, I., Nielsen, J.B.: Multiparty computation from threshold homomorphic encryption. In: Pfitzmann, B. (ed.) EUROCRYPT 2001. LNCS, vol. 2045, pp. 280–300. Springer, Heidelberg (2001). https://doi.org/10.1007/3-540-44987-6_18

[CDPW07] Canetti, R., Dodis, Y., Pass, R., Walfish, S.: Universally composable security with global setup. In: Vadhan, S.P. (ed.) TCC 2007. LNCS, vol. 4392, pp. 61–85. Springer, Heidelberg (2007). https://doi.org/10.1007/978-3-540-70936-7_4

[CM19] Chen, J., Micali, S.: Algorand: a secure and efficient distributed ledger. Theoret. Comput. Sci. **777**, 155–183 (2019)

[DGKR18] David, B., Gaži, P., Kiayias, A., Russell, A.: Ouroboros Praos: an adaptively-secure, semi-synchronous proof-of-stake blockchain. In: Nielsen, J.B., Rijmen, V. (eds.) EUROCRYPT 2018. LNCS, vol. 10821, pp. 66–98. Springer, Cham (2018). https://doi.org/10.1007/978-3-319-78375-8_3

[DKI+23] David, B., Konring, A., Ishai, Y., Kushilevitz, E., Narayanan, V.: Perfect MPC over layered graphs. Cryptology ePrint Archive, Report 2023/330 (2023). https://eprint.iacr.org/2023/330

[EHK+13] Escala, A., Herold, G., Kiltz, E., Ràfols, C., Villar, J.: An algebraic framework for Diffie-Hellman assumptions. In: Canetti, R., Garay, J.A. (eds.) CRYPTO 2013. LNCS, vol. 8043, pp. 129–147. Springer, Heidelberg (2013). https://doi.org/10.1007/978-3-642-40084-1_8

[GHK+21] Gentry, C., et al.: YOSO: you only speak once. In: Malkin, T., Peikert, C. (eds.) CRYPTO 2021. LNCS, vol. 12826, pp. 64–93. Springer, Cham (2021). https://doi.org/10.1007/978-3-030-84245-1_3

[GHM+21] Gentry, C., Halevi, S., Magri, B., Nielsen, J.B., Yakoubov, S.: Random-index PIR and applications. In: Nissim, K., Waters, B. (eds.) TCC 2021. LNCS, vol. 13044, pp. 32–61. Springer, Cham (2021). https://doi.org/10.1007/978-3-030-90456-2_2

[GOS12] Groth, J., Ostrovsky, R., Sahai, A.: New techniques for noninteractive zero-knowledge. J. ACM (JACM) **59**(3), 1–35 (2012)

[HLH+22] Huang, Z., Lai, J., Han, S., Lyu, L., Weng, J.: Anonymous public key encryption under corruptions. In: Agrawal, S., Lin, D. (eds.) ASIACRYPT 2022. Part III, volume 13793 of LNCS, pp. 423–453. Springer, Heidelberg (2022). https://doi.org/10.1007/978-3-031-22969-5_15

[KMTZ13] Katz, J., Maurer, U., Tackmann, B., Zikas, V.: Universally composable synchronous computation. In: Sahai, A. (ed.) TCC 2013. LNCS, vol. 7785, pp. 477–498. Springer, Heidelberg (2013). https://doi.org/10.1007/978-3-642-36594-2_27

[KRY22] Kolby, S., Ravi, D., Yakoubov, S.: Constant-round YOSO MPC without setup. Cryptology ePrint Archive, Paper 2022/187 (2022). https://eprint.iacr.org/2022/187

[MRV99] Micali, S., Rabin, M.O., Vadhan, S.P.: Verifiable random functions. In: 40th FOCS, pp. 120–130. IEEE Computer Society Press, October 1999

[Nie02] Nielsen, J.B.: Separating random oracle proofs from complexity theoretic proofs: the non-committing encryption case. In: Yung, M. (ed.) CRYPTO 2002. LNCS, vol. 2442, pp. 111–126. Springer, Heidelberg (2002). https://doi.org/10.1007/3-540-45708-9_8

Network Agnostic MPC with Statistical Security

Ananya Appan[1](✉) [iD] and Ashish Choudhury[2] [iD]

[1] University of Illinois Urbana Champaign, Champaign, USA
aappan2@illinois.edu
[2] International Institute of Information Technology Bangalore, Bengaluru, India
ashish.choudhury@iiitb.ac.in

Abstract. In this work, we initiate the study of network agnostic MPC protocols with *statistical* security. Network agnostic MPC protocols give the best possible security guarantees, *irrespective* of the behaviour of the underlying network. While network agnostic MPC protocols have been designed earlier with *perfect* and *computational* security, *nothing* is known in the literature regarding their possibility with statistical security. We consider the *general-adversary* model, where the adversary is characterized by an *adversary structure* which enumerates all possible candidate subsets of corrupt parties. Known statistically-secure *synchronous* MPC (SMPC) and *asynchronous* MPC (AMPC) protocols are secure against adversary structures satisfying the $\mathbb{Q}^{(2)}$ and $\mathbb{Q}^{(3)}$ conditions respectively, meaning that the union of *no* two and three subsets from the adversary structure cover the entire set of parties.

Fix adversary structures $\mathcal{Z}_s$ and $\mathcal{Z}_a$, satisfying the $\mathbb{Q}^{(2)}$ and $\mathbb{Q}^{(3)}$ conditions respectively, where $\mathcal{Z}_a \subset \mathcal{Z}_s$. Then given an unconditionally-secure PKI, we ask whether it is possible to design a statistically-secure MPC protocol, which is resilient against $\mathcal{Z}_s$ and $\mathcal{Z}_a$ in a *synchronous* and an *asynchronous* network respectively, even if the parties are *unaware* of the network type. We show that this is possible iff $\mathcal{Z}_s$ and $\mathcal{Z}_a$ satisfy the $\mathbb{Q}^{(2,1)}$ condition, meaning that the union of any two subsets from $\mathcal{Z}_s$ and any one subset from $\mathcal{Z}_a$ is a proper subset of the set of parties. The complexity of our protocol is polynomial in $|\mathcal{Z}_s|$.

Keywords: MPC · Network Agnostic · Statistical Security · VSS

1 Introduction

A secure *multiparty computation* (MPC) protocol [9,26,36,37] allows a set of n mutually distrusting parties $\mathcal{P} = \{P_1, \ldots, P_n\}$ with private inputs to securely

---

A. Appan—Work done as a student at IIIT Bangalore.
A. Choudhury—This research is an outcome of the R&D work undertaken in the project under the Visvesvaraya PhD Scheme of Ministry of Electronics & Information Technology, Government of India, being implemented by Digital India Corporation.

G. Rothblum and H. Wee (Eds.): TCC 2023, LNCS 14370, pp. 63–93, 2023.
https://doi.org/10.1007/978-3-031-48618-0_3

compute any known function f of their inputs. This is achieved even if a subset of the parties are under the control of a centralized *adversary* and behave *maliciously* in a Byzantine fashion during the protocol execution. In any MPC protocol, the parties need to interact over the underlying communication network. Two types of networks have been predominantly considered. The more popular *synchronous* MPC (SMPC) protocols operate over a synchronous network, where every message sent is assumed to be delivered within a *known* Δ time. The synchronous model *does not* capture real-world networks like the Internet appropriately, where messages can be *arbitrarily* delayed. Such networks are better modelled by the *asynchronous* communication model [14]. In any *asynchronous* MPC (AMPC) protocol [8,10], there are *no* timing assumptions on message delays and messages can be arbitrarily, yet finitely delayed. The only guarantee is that every message sent will be *eventually* delivered. The major challenge here is that no participant will know how long it has to wait for an expected message and *cannot* distinguish a "slow" party from a corrupt party. Consequently, in any AMPC protocol, a party *cannot* afford to receive messages from all the parties, to avoid an endless wait. Hence, as soon as a party receives messages from a "subset" of parties, it has to process them as per the protocol, thus ignoring messages from a subset of potentially non-faulty parties.

There is a third category of protocols called *network agnostic* MPC protocols, where the parties *will not* be knowing the network type and the protocol should provide the best possible security guarantees depending upon the network type. Such protocols are practically motivated, since the parties *need not* have to worry about the behaviour of the underlying network.

1.1   Our Motivation and Results

One of the earliest demarcations made in the literature is to categorize MPC protocols based on the computing power of the underlying adversary. The two main categories are *unconditionally-secure* protocols, which remain secure even against *computationally-unbounded* adversaries, and *conditionally-secure* MPC protocols (also called *cryptographically-secure*), which remain secure *only* against *computationally-bounded* adversaries [26,37]. Unconditionally-secure protocols can be further categorized as *perfectly-secure* [8,9] or *statistically-secure* [10,36], depending upon whether the security guarantees are *error-free* or achieved except with a *negligible* probability. The above demarcation carries over even for network agnostic MPC protocols. While perfectly-secure and cryptographically-secure network agnostic MPC protocols have been investigated earlier, *nothing* is known regarding network agnostic statistically-secure MPC protocols. We derive necessary and sufficient conditions for such protocols for the *first* time.

Existing Results for Statistically-Secure MPC. Consider the *threshold* setting, where the maximum number of corrupt parties under the adversary's control is upper bounded by a given threshold. In this model, it is known that statistically-secure SMPC tolerating up to t_s faulty parties is possible iff $t_s < n/2$ [36], provided the parties are given access to an ideal broadcast channel, which can be further instantiated using an *unconditionally-secure* PKI (a.k.a *pseudo-signature*) setup [22,35]. On the other hand, statistically-secure AMPC tolerating up to t_a faulty parties is possible iff $t_a < n/3$ [1,10].

A more generalized form of corruption is the general adversary model (also called *non-threshold* model) [27]. Here, the adversary is specified through a publicly known *adversary structure* $\mathcal{Z} \subset 2^{\mathcal{P}}$, which is the set of all subsets of potentially corruptible parties during the protocol execution. The adversary is allowed to choose any one subset from $\mathcal{Z}$ for corruption. There are several "merits" of studying the general adversary model, especially if the number of parties is small. The downside is that the complexity of the protocols is polynomial in $|\mathcal{Z}|$, which could be $\mathcal{O}(2^n)$ in the *worst* case. In fact, as noted in [27,28], this is *unavoidable*.

Following [27], given a subset of parties $\mathcal{P}' \subseteq \mathcal{P}$ and $\mathcal{Z}$, we say that $\mathcal{Z}$ satisfies the $\mathbb{Q}^{(k)}(\mathcal{P}', \mathcal{Z})$ condition, if for any subsets $Z_{i_1}, \ldots, Z_{i_k} \in \mathcal{Z}$, the condition $(Z_{i_1} \cup \ldots \cup Z_{i_k}) \subset \mathcal{P}'$ holds. In the non-threshold model, statistically-secure SMPC is possible if the underlying adversary structure $\mathcal{Z}_s$ satisfies the $\mathbb{Q}^{(2)}(\mathcal{P}, \mathcal{Z}_s)$ condition, provided the parties have access to an ideal broadcast channel (which can be instantiated using an unconditionally-secure PKI setup) [29], while statistically-secure AMPC requires the underlying adversary structure $\mathcal{Z}_a$ to satisfy the $\mathbb{Q}^{(3)}(\mathcal{P}, \mathcal{Z}_a)$ condition [4,29].

Our Results for Network Agnostic Statistically-Secure MPC. We consider the most generic form of corruption and ask the following question:

Given an unconditionally-secure PKI, a *synchronous adversary structure* $\mathcal{Z}_s$ and an *asynchronous adversary structure* $\mathcal{Z}_a$ satisfying the $\mathbb{Q}^{(2)}(\mathcal{P}, \mathcal{Z}_s)$ and $\mathbb{Q}^{(3)}(\mathcal{P}, \mathcal{Z}_a)$ conditions respectively, where $\mathcal{Z}_a \subset \mathcal{Z}_s$, does there exist a statistically-secure MPC protocol, which remains secure against $\mathcal{Z}_s$ and $\mathcal{Z}_a$ in a synchronous and an asynchronous network respectively?

We answer the above question affirmatively, iff $\mathcal{Z}_s$ and $\mathcal{Z}_a$ satisfy the $\mathbb{Q}^{(2,1)}(\mathcal{P}, \mathcal{Z}_s, \mathcal{Z}_a)$ condition, where by $\mathbb{Q}^{(k,k')}(\mathcal{P}, \mathcal{Z}_s, \mathcal{Z}_a)$ condition, we mean that for any $Z_{i_1}, \ldots, Z_{i_k} \in \mathcal{Z}_s$ and $Z_{j_1}, \ldots, Z_{j_{k'}} \in \mathcal{Z}_a$, the following holds:

$$(Z_{i_1} \cup \ldots \cup Z_{i_k} \cup Z_{j_1} \cup \ldots \cup Z_{j'_k}) \subset \mathcal{P}.$$

Our results when applied against *threshold* adversaries imply that given an unconditionally-secure PKI, and thresholds $0 < t_a < \frac{n}{3} < t_s < \frac{n}{2}$, network agnostic statistically-secure MPC tolerating t_s and t_a corruptions in the *synchronous* and *asynchronous* network is possible, iff $2t_s + t_a < n$ holds. Our results in the context of relevant literature are summarized in Table 1.

1.2   Detailed Technical Overview

We perform shared *circuit-evaluation* [9,36], where f is abstracted as an arithmetic circuit ckt over a finite field $\mathbb{F}$ and the goal is to securely evaluate each gate in ckt in a *secret-shared* fashion. For every value during the circuit-evaluation, each party holds a share, such that the shares of the corrupt parties *do not* reveal any additional information. Once the function output is secret-shared, it is publicly reconstructed. We deploy a *linear* secret-sharing scheme, which enables the

Table 1. Various conditions for MPC in different settings

Network Type	Corruption Scenario	Security	Condition	Reference
Synchronous	Threshold (t)	Perfect	$t < n/3$	[9]
Synchronous	Non-threshold $(\mathcal{Z})$	Perfect	$\mathbb{Q}^{(3)}(\mathcal{P}, \mathcal{Z})$	[27]
Synchronous	Threshold (t)	Statistical	$t < n/2$	[36]
Synchronous	Non-threshold $(\mathcal{Z})$	Statistical	$\mathbb{Q}^{(2)}(\mathcal{P}, \mathcal{Z})$	[29]
Asynchronous	Threshold (t)	Perfect	$t < n/4$	[8]
Asynchronous	Non-threshold $(\mathcal{Z})$	Perfect	$\mathbb{Q}^{(4)}(\mathcal{P}, \mathcal{Z})$	[31]
Asynchronous	Threshold (t)	Statistical	$t < n/3$	[1,10]
Asynchronous	Non-threshold $(\mathcal{Z})$	Statistical	$\mathbb{Q}^{(3)}(\mathcal{P}, \mathcal{Z})$	[4]
Network Agnostic	Threshold (t_s, t_a)	Perfect	$0 < t_a < n/4 < t_s < n/3$ and $3t_s + t_a < n$	[2]
Network Agnostic	Non-threshold $(\mathcal{Z}_s, \mathcal{Z}_a)$	Perfect	$\mathcal{Z}_a \subsetneq \mathcal{Z}_s, \mathbb{Q}^{(3)}(\mathcal{P}, \mathcal{Z}_s), \mathbb{Q}^{(4)}(\mathcal{P}, \mathcal{Z}_a)$ and $\mathbb{Q}^{(3,1)}(\mathcal{P}, \mathcal{Z}_s, \mathcal{Z}_a)$	[3]
Network Agnostic	Threshold (t_s, t_a)	Computational	$0 < t_a < n/3 < t_s < n/2$ and $2t_s + t_a < n$	[13,18]
Network Agnostic	Non-threshold $(\mathcal{Z}_s, \mathcal{Z}_a)$	Statistical	$\mathcal{Z}_a \subset \mathcal{Z}_s, \mathbb{Q}^{(2)}(\mathcal{P}, \mathcal{Z}_s), \mathbb{Q}^{(3)}(\mathcal{P}, \mathcal{Z}_a)$ and $\mathbb{Q}^{(2,1)}(\mathcal{P}, \mathcal{Z}_s, \mathcal{Z}_a)$	This work
Network Agnostic	Threshold (t_s, t_a)	Statistical	$0 < t_a < n/3 < t_s < n/2$ and $2t_s + t_a < n$	This work

parties to evaluate linear gates in ckt in a *non-interactive* fashion. *Non-linear* gates are evaluated using Beaver's method [7] by deploying secret-shared random *multiplication-triples* which are generated *beforehand*.

To instantiate the above approach with *statistical* security, we need the following ingredients: a *Byzantine agreement* (BA) protocol [34], an *information checking protocol* (ICP) [36], a *verifiable secret sharing* (VSS) protocol [15], a *reconstruction* protocol and finally, a secure *multiplication* protocol. However, in a network agnostic setting, we face several challenges to instantiate the above building blocks. We now take the reader through a detailed tour of the technical challenges and how we deal with them.

1.2.1 Network Agnostic BA with $\mathbb{Q}^{(2,1)}(\mathcal{P}, \mathcal{Z}_s, \mathcal{Z}_a)$ Condition

A BA protocol [34] allows the parties in $\mathcal{P}$ with private input bits to agree on a common output bit (*consistency*), which is the input of the non-faulty parties, if they have the *same* input bit (*validity*). Given an unconditionally-secure PKI, *synchronous* BA (SBA) is possible iff the underlying adversary structure $\mathcal{Z}_s$ satisfies the $\mathbb{Q}^{(2)}(\mathcal{P}, \mathcal{Z}_s)$ condition [22,23,35], while *asynchronous* BA (ABA) requires the underlying adversary structure $\mathcal{Z}_a$ to satisfy the $\mathbb{Q}^{(3)}(\mathcal{P}, \mathcal{Z}_a)$ condition [16]. Existing SBA protocols become completely *insecure* in an asynchronous network. On the other hand, any ABA protocol becomes *insecure* when executed in a synchronous network, since $\mathcal{Z}_s$ *need not* satisfy the $\mathbb{Q}^{(3)}(\mathcal{P}, \mathcal{Z}_s)$ condition. Hence, we design a network agnostic BA protocol with $\mathbb{Q}^{(2,1)}(\mathcal{P}, \mathcal{Z}_s, \mathcal{Z}_a)$ condition. The protocol is obtained by generalizing the existing blueprint for network agnostic BA against *threshold* adversaries [2,11].

1.2.2   Network Agnostic ICP with $\mathbb{Q}^{(2,1)}(\mathcal{P}, \mathcal{Z}_s, \mathcal{Z}_a)$ Condition

An ICP [17,36] is used for authenticating data in the presence of a *computationally-unbounded* adversary. In an ICP, there are *four* entities, a *signer* $S \in \mathcal{P}$, an *intermediary* $I \in \mathcal{P}$, a *receiver* $R \in \mathcal{P}$ and all the parties in $\mathcal{P}$ acting as *verifiers* (note that S, I and R also act as verifiers). An ICP has two sub-protocols, one for the *authentication phase* and one for the *revelation phase*.

In the authentication phase, S has an input $s \in \mathbb{F}$, which it distributes to I along with some *authentication information*. Each verifier is provided with some *verification information*, followed by the parties verifying whether S has distributed "consistent" information. If the verification is "successful", then the data held by I is called S's *IC-Signature on s for intermediary I and receiver R*, denoted by $\mathsf{ICSig}(S, I, R, s)$. Later, during the revelation phase, I reveals $\mathsf{ICSig}(S, I, R, s)$ to R, who "verifies" it with respect to the verification information provided by the verifiers and either accepts or rejects s. We require the same security guarantees from IC-signatures as expected from cryptographic signatures, namely *correctness*, *unforgeability* and *non-repudiation*. Additionally, we need *privacy*, meaning if S, I and R are *all* honest, then Adv does not learn s.

The *only known* instantiation of ICP in the *synchronous* network [29] is secure against $\mathbb{Q}^{(2)}$ adversary structures and becomes *insecure* in the *asynchronous* setting. On the other hand, the *only known* instantiation of ICP in the *asynchronous* setting [4] can tolerate *only* $\mathbb{Q}^{(3)}$ adversary structures. Our network agnostic ICP is a careful adaptation of the *asynchronous* ICP of [4]. We first try to *naively* adapt the ICP to deal with the *network agnostic* setting, followed by the technical problems in the naive adaptation and the modifications needed.

During authentication phase, S embeds s in a random t-degree polynomial $F(x)$ at $x = 0$, where t is the cardinality of the maximum-sized subset in $\mathcal{Z}_s$, and gives $F(x)$ to I. In addition, each verifier P_i is given a random *verification-point* (α_i, v_i) on $F(x)$. To let the parties securely verify that it has distributed consistent information, S additionally distributes a random t-degree polynomial $M(x)$ to I, while each verifier P_i is given a point on $M(x)$ at α_i. Each verifier, upon receiving its verification-points, *publicly* confirms the same. Upon receiving these confirmations, I identifies a subset of *supporting verifiers* $\mathcal{SV}$ which have confirmed the receipt of their verification-points. To avoid an endless wait, I waits until $\mathcal{P} \setminus \mathcal{SV} \in \mathcal{Z}_s$. After this, the parties *publicly* check the consistency of the $F(x), M(x)$ polynomials and the points distributed to $\mathcal{SV}$, with respect to a *random* linear combination of these polynomials and points, where the linear combiner is selected by I. This ensures that S has *no* knowledge beforehand about the random combiner and hence, any "inconsistency" will be detected with a high probability. If no inconsistency is detected, the parties proceed to the revelation phase, where I reveals $F(x)$ to R, while each verifier in $\mathcal{SV}$ reveals its verification-point to R, who accepts $F(x)$ (and hence $F(0)$) if it sure that the verification point of at least one *non-faulty* verifier in $\mathcal{SV}$ is "consistent" with the revealed $F(x)$. This would ensure that the revealed $F(x)$ is indeed correct with a high probability, since a *corrupt* I will have no information about the verification-point of any *non-faulty* verifier in $\mathcal{SV}$, provided S is *non-faulty*. To avoid an endless wait, once R finds a subset of verifiers $\mathcal{SV}' \subseteq \mathcal{SV}$, where $\mathcal{SV} \setminus \mathcal{SV}' \in \mathcal{Z}_s$, whose verification-points are found to be "consistent" with $F(x)$, it outputs $F(0)$.

A Technical Problem and Way-Out. The above protocol will achieve all the properties in an *asynchronous* network, due to the $\mathbb{Q}^{(3)}(\mathcal{P}, \mathcal{Z}_a)$ condition. However, it *fails* to satisfy the *unforgeability* property in a *synchronous* network. Namely, a *corrupt* I may *not* include *all* the non-faulty verifiers in $\mathcal{SV}$ and may purposely *exclude* a subset of *non-faulty* verifiers belonging to $\mathcal{Z}_s$. To deal with this, we let S identify and announce $\mathcal{SV}$. This ensures that *all* honest verifiers are present in $\mathcal{SV}$, if S is *honest* and the network is *synchronous*.

Linearity of ICP. Our ICP satisfies the *linearity* property (which will be useful later in our VSS), provided "special care" is taken while generating the IC-signatures. Consider a *fixed* S, I and R and let s_a and s_b be two values, such that I holds $\mathsf{ICSig}(\mathsf{S}, \mathsf{I}, \mathsf{R}, s_a)$ and $\mathsf{ICSig}(\mathsf{S}, \mathsf{I}, \mathsf{R}, s_b)$, where *all* the following conditions are satisfied during the underlying instances of the authentication phase.

- The set of supporting verifiers $\mathcal{SV}$ are the *same* during both the instances.
- For $i = 1, \ldots, n$, corresponding to the verifier P_i, signer S uses the *same* α_i, to compute the verification-points, during both the instances.
- I uses the *same* linear combiner to verify the consistency of the distributed data in both the instances.

Let $s \stackrel{def}{=} c_1 \cdot s_a + c_2 \cdot s_b$, where c_1, c_2 are *publicly known* constants from $\mathbb{F}$. It then follows that if all the above conditions are satisfied, then I can *locally* compute $\mathsf{ICSig}(\mathsf{S}, \mathsf{I}, \mathsf{R}, s)$ from $\mathsf{ICSig}(\mathsf{S}, \mathsf{I}, \mathsf{R}, s_a)$ and $\mathsf{ICSig}(\mathsf{S}, \mathsf{I}, \mathsf{R}, s_b)$, while each verifier in $\mathcal{SV}$ can *locally* compute their corresponding verification-point.

1.2.3   Network Agnostic VSS and Reconstruction

In the network agnostic setting, to ensure privacy, all the values during the circuit evaluation need to be secret-shared "with respect" to $\mathcal{Z}_s$ *irrespective* of the network type. We follow the notion of *additive secret-sharing* [30], also used in the earlier MPC protocols [4,29,32]. Given $\mathcal{Z}_s = \{Z_1, \ldots, Z_{|\mathcal{Z}_s|}\}$, we consider the *sharing specification* $\mathbb{S}_{\mathcal{Z}_s} = \{S_1, \ldots, S_{|\mathcal{Z}_s|}\}$, where each $S_q = \mathcal{P} \setminus Z_q$. Hence there exists at least one subset $S_q \in \mathbb{S}_{|\mathcal{Z}_s|}$ which *does not* contain any faulty party, *irrespective* of the network type (since $\mathcal{Z}_a \subset \mathcal{Z}_s$). A value $s \in \mathbb{F}$ is said to be secret-shared, if there exist shares $s_1, \ldots, s_{|\mathcal{Z}_s|}$ which sum up to s, such that all (non-faulty) parties in S_q have the share s_q. We denote a secret-sharing of s by $[s]$, with $[s]_q$ denoting the share corresponding to S_q. If $[s]_1, \ldots, [s]_{|\mathcal{Z}_s|}$ are randomly chosen, then the probability distribution of the shares learnt by the adversary will be independent of s. We also note that the above secret-sharing is *linear* since, given secret-sharings $[a]$ and $[b]$ and publicly known constants $c_1, c_2 \in \mathbb{F}$, the condition $c_1 \cdot [a] + c_2 \cdot [b] = [c_1 \cdot a + c_2 \cdot b]$ holds. Unfortunately, the above secret-sharing *does not* allow for the *robust* reconstruction of a secret-shared value. This is because the corrupt parties may produce *incorrect* shares at the time of reconstruction. To deal with this, we "augment" the above secret-sharing. As part of secret-sharing of s, we *also* have publicly known *core-sets* $\mathcal{W}_1, \ldots, \mathcal{W}_{|\mathcal{Z}_s|}$, where each $W_q \subseteq S_q$ such that $\mathcal{Z}_s$ satisfies the $\mathbb{Q}^{(1)}(W_q, \mathcal{Z}_s)$ condition (ensuring W_q has at least one *non-faulty* party). Moreover, each (non-faulty) $P_i \in W_q$ will have the IC-signature $\mathsf{ICSig}(P_j, P_i, P_k, [s]_q)$ of every $P_j \in W_q$, for every $P_k \notin S_q$, such that the underlying IC-signatures satisfy the *linearity* property.

We call this augmented secret sharing as *linear secret-sharing with IC-signatures*, which is still denoted as $[s]$. Now to *robustly* reconstruct a secret-shared s, we ask the parties in W_q to make public the share $[s]_q$, along with the IC-signatures of *all* the parties in W_q on $[s]_q$. Any party P_k can then verify whether $[s]_q$ revealed by P_i is *correct* by verifying the IC-signatures.

We design a network agnostic VSS protocol Π_{VSS}, which allows a designated *dealer* $\mathsf{D} \in \mathcal{P}$ with input $s \in \mathbb{F}$ to *verifiably* generate $[s]$, where s remains private for a *non-faulty* s. If D is *faulty* then either no non-faulty party obtains any output (if D *does not* invoke the protocol) or there exists *some* $s^* \in \mathbb{F}$ such that the parties output $[s^*]$. To design Π_{VSS}, we use certain ideas from the statistically-secure *synchronous* VSS (SVSS) and *asynchronous* VSS (AVSS) of [4,29] respectively, along with some new counter-intuitive ideas. In the sequel, we first give a brief outline of the SVSS and AVSS of [4,29], followed by the technical challenges arising in the network agnostic setting and how we deal with them.

Statistically-Secure SVSS of [29] with $\mathbb{Q}^{(2)}(\mathcal{P}, \mathcal{Z}_s)$ Condition. The SVSS of [29] proceeds as a sequence of *synchronized* phases. During the *first* phase, D picks random shares $s_1, \ldots, s_{|\mathcal{Z}_s|}$ for s and sends s_q to the parties in S_q. During the *second* phase, every pair of parties $P_i, P_j \in S_q$ exchange the supposedly common shares received from D, along with their respective IC-signatures. Then during the *third* phase, the parties in S_q *publicly* complain about any "inconsistency", in response to which D makes *public* the share s_q corresponding to S_q during the *fourth* phase. Hence, by the end of *fourth* phase it is ensured that, for every S_q, either the share s_q is *publicly* known (if any complaint was reported for S_q) or all (non-faulty) parties in S_q have the same share (along with the respective IC-signatures of each other on it). The privacy of s is maintained for a *non-faulty* D, since the share s_q corresponding to the set S_q consisting of *only non-faulty* parties is *never* made public.

Statistically-Secure AVSS of [4] with $\mathbb{Q}^{(3)}(\mathcal{P}, \mathcal{Z}_a)$ Condition. Let $\mathcal{Z}_a = \{\mathsf{Z}_1, \ldots, \mathsf{Z}_{|\mathcal{Z}_a|}\}$ and $\mathbb{S}_{\mathcal{Z}_a} = \{\mathsf{S}_1, \ldots, \mathsf{S}_{|\mathcal{Z}_a|}\}$ be the corresponding sharing specification, where each $\mathsf{S}_q = \mathcal{P} \setminus \mathsf{Z}_q$. The AVSS protocol of [4] also follows an idea similar to the SVSS of [29]. However, now the parties *cannot* afford to wait for *all* the parties in S_q to report the statuses of pairwise consistency tests, as the corrupt parties in S_q may *never* turn up. Hence *instead* of looking for *inconsistencies* in S_q, the parties *rather* check how many parties in S_q are reporting the *pairwise consistency* of their supposedly common share. The idea is that if D has *not* cheated, then a subset of parties W_q where $\mathsf{S}_q \setminus W_q \in \mathcal{Z}_a$ should eventually confirm the receipt of a common share from D. Hence, the parties check for *core-sets* $W_1, \ldots, W_{|\mathcal{Z}_a|}$, where each $\mathsf{S}_q \setminus W_q \in \mathcal{Z}_a$, such that the parties in W_q have confirmed the receipt of a common share from D. Note that *irrespective* of

D, each $\mathcal{W}_q$ is bound to have *at least* one non-faulty party, since $\mathcal{Z}_a$ will satisfy the $\mathbb{Q}^{(1)}(\mathcal{W}_q, \mathcal{Z}_a)$ condition.

The existence of $\mathcal{W}_1, \ldots, \mathcal{W}_{|\mathcal{Z}_a|}$ *does not* imply that *all* non-faulty parties in S_q have received a common share, even if D is *non-faulty*, since there *might* be non-faulty parties outside $\mathcal{W}_q$. Hence, after the confirmation of the sets $\mathcal{W}_1, \ldots, \mathcal{W}_{|\mathcal{Z}_a|}$, the goal is to ensure that every (non-faulty) party in $S_q \setminus \mathcal{W}_q$ also gets the common share held by the (non-faulty) parties in $\mathcal{W}_q$. For this, the parties in $\mathcal{W}_q$ reveal their shares to these "outsider" parties, along with the required IC-signatures. The outsider parties then "filter" out the correctly revealed shares. The existence of at least one non-faulty party in each $\mathcal{W}_q$ guarantees that the shares filtered by the outsider parties are indeed correct.

Technical Challenges for Network Agnostic VSS and Way Out. Our approach will be to follow the AVSS of [4], where we look for *pairwise consistency* of supposedly common share in each group. Namely, D picks random shares $s_1, \ldots, s_{|\mathcal{Z}_s|}$ for its input s and distributes s_q to each $S_q \in \mathbb{S}_{|\mathcal{Z}_s|}$. The parties in S_q then exchange IC-signed versions of their supposedly common share. To avoid an endless wait, the parties can only afford to wait till a subset of parties $\mathcal{W}_q \subseteq S_q$ have confirmed the receipt of a common share from D, where $S_q \setminus \mathcal{W}_q \in \mathcal{Z}_s$ holds. Unfortunately, $S_q \setminus \mathcal{W}_q \in \mathcal{Z}_s$ *need not* guarantee that $\mathcal{W}_q$ has at least one *non-faulty* party, since $\mathcal{Z}_s$ *need not* satisfy the $\mathbb{Q}^{(1)}(\mathcal{W}_q, \mathcal{Z}_s)$ condition, which is *desired* as per our semantics of linear secret-sharing with IC-signatures.

To deal with the above problem, we note that if D has distributed the shares consistently, then the subset of parties $\mathbf{S} \in \mathbb{S}_{\mathcal{Z}_s}$ which consists of *only* non-faulty parties will publicly report the pairwise consistency of their supposedly common share. Hence, we now let D search for a candidate set S_p of parties from $\mathbb{S}_{\mathcal{Z}_s}$ which have publicly confirmed the pairwise consistency of their supposedly common share. Once D finds such a candidate S_p, it computes and make public the core-sets $\mathcal{W}_q$ as per the following rules, for $q = 1, \ldots, |\mathcal{Z}_s|$.

- If all the parties in S_q have confirmed the pairwise consistency of their supposedly common share, then set $\mathcal{W}_q = S_q$. **(A)**
- Else if $\mathcal{Z}_s$ satisfies the $\mathbb{Q}^{(1)}(S_p \cap S_q, \mathcal{Z}_s)$ condition *and* the parties in $(S_p \cap S_q)$ have confirmed the consistency of their supposedly common share, then set $\mathcal{W}_q = (S_p \cap S_q)$. **(B)**
- Else set $\mathcal{W}_q = S_q$ and make *public* the share s_q. **(C)**

The parties wait till they see D making public some set $S_p \in \mathbb{S}_{\mathcal{Z}_s}$, along with sets $\mathcal{W}_1, \ldots, \mathcal{W}_{|\mathcal{Z}_s|}$. Upon receiving, the parties verify and "approve" these sets as valid, provided *all* parties in S_p have confirmed the pairwise consistency of their supposedly common share and if each $\mathcal{W}_q$ is computed as per the rule **(A)**, **(B)** or **(C)**. If $\mathcal{W}_1, \ldots, \mathcal{W}_{|\mathcal{Z}_s|}$ are approved, then they indeed *satisfy* the requirements of core-sets as per our semantics of linear secret-sharing with IC-signatures. While this is trivially true if any $\mathcal{W}_q$ is computed either using rule **(A)** or rule **(B)**, the same holds even if $\mathcal{W}_q$ is computed using rule **(C)**. This is because, in this case, the parties publicly set $[s]_q = s_q$. Moreover, the parties take a "default" (linear) IC-signature of s_q on the behalf of S_q, where the IC-signature as well as verification points are *all* set to s_q.

If D is *non-faulty*, then *irrespective* of the network type, it will *always* find a candidate S_p and hence, compute and make public $\mathcal{W}_1, \ldots, \mathcal{W}_{|\mathcal{Z}_s|}$ as per the above rules. This is because the set **S** *always* constitutes a candidate S_p. Surprisingly we can show that even if the core-sets are computed with respect to some *different* candidate $S_p \neq \mathbf{S}$, a *non-faulty* D will *never* make public the share corresponding to **S**, since the rule **(C)** will *not* be applicable over **S**, implying the privacy of s. If the network is *synchronous*, then the parties in S_p *as well as* **S** would report the pairwise consistency of their respective supposedly common share at the *same* time. This is ensured by maintaining sufficient "timeouts" in the protocol to report pairwise consistency of supposedly common shares. Consequently, rule **(A)** will be applied on **S**. For an *asynchronous* network, rule **(B)** will be *applicable* for **S**, as $\mathcal{Z}_s$ will satisfy the $\mathbb{Q}^{(1)}(S_p \cap \mathbf{S}, \mathcal{Z}_s)$ condition, due to the $\mathbb{Q}^{(2,1)}(\mathcal{P}, \mathcal{Z}_s, \mathcal{Z}_a)$ condition and the fact that $\mathbf{S} = \mathcal{P} \setminus Z$ for some $Z \in \mathcal{Z}_a$ in the *asynchronous* network.

1.2.4 Network Agnostic VSS for Multiple Dealers with Linearity

Technical Challenge in Π_{VSS} for Multiple Dealers and Way Out. If *different* dealers invoke instances of Π_{VSS} to secret-share their inputs, then the linearity property of $[\cdot]$-sharing *need not* hold, since the underlying core-sets might be *different*. This implies *failure* of shared circuit-evaluation of ckt, where the inputs for ckt are shared by *different* parties.

To deal with the above problem, we ensure that the core-sets are *common* for *all* the secret-shared values during the circuit-evaluation. Namely, there exist *global* core-sets $\mathcal{GW}_1, \ldots, \mathcal{GW}_{|\mathcal{Z}_s|}$, which constitute the core-sets for *all* the secret-shared values during the circuit-evaluation, where for each $\mathcal{GW}_q$, $\mathcal{Z}_s$ satisfies the $\mathbb{Q}^{(1)}(\mathcal{GW}_q, \mathcal{Z}_s)$ condition. Maintaining common core-sets is challenging, especially in an *asynchronous* network and Π_{VSS} alone is *not sufficient* to achieve this goal. Rather we use a *different* approach. We generate a "bunch" of linearly secret-shared random values with IC-signatures and common core-sets $\mathcal{GW}_1, \ldots, \mathcal{GW}_{|\mathcal{Z}_s|}$ in *advance* through another protocol called Π_{Rand} (discussed in the next section). Later, if any party P_i needs to secret-share some x, then one of these random values is reconstructed *only* towards P_i, which uses it as a one-time pad (OTP) and makes public an OTP-encryption of x. The parties can then take the "default" secret-sharing of the OTP-encryption with IC-signatures and $\mathcal{GW}_1, \ldots, \mathcal{GW}_{|\mathcal{Z}_s|}$ as the core-sets and then non-interactively "remove" the pad from the OTP-encryption. This results in $[x]$, with $\mathcal{GW}_1, \ldots, \mathcal{GW}_{|\mathcal{Z}_s|}$ as core-sets. To ensure privacy, we need to generate L random values through Π_{Rand}, if L is the maximum number of values which need to be secret-shared by different parties during the circuit-evaluation. We show that $L \leq n^3 \cdot c_M + 4n^2 \cdot c_M + n^2 + n$ where c_M is the number of multiplication gates in ckt.

1.2.5 Secret-Shared Random Values with Global Core Sets

Protocol Π_{Rand} generates linearly secret-shared random values with IC-signatures and *common* core-sets. We explain the idea behind the protocol for generating one random value. The "standard" way will be to let each P_i pick a random value $r^{(i)}$ and generate $[r^{(i)}]$ by invoking an instance of Π_{VSS}. To avoid an endless wait, the parties only wait for the completion of Π_{VSS} instances invoked by a set of dealers $\mathcal{P} \setminus Z$ for some $Z \in \mathcal{Z}_s$. To identify the common subset of dealers for which the corresponding Π_{VSS} instances have completed, the parties run an instance of *agreement on a common subset* (ACS) primitive [10,14]. This involves invoking n instances of our network agnostic BA. Let $\mathcal{C}$ be the set of common dealers identified through ACS, where $\mathcal{P} \setminus \mathcal{C} \in \mathcal{Z}_s$. The set $\mathcal{C}$ has at least one *non-faulty* party who has shared a random value. Hence, the sum of the values shared by the dealers in $\mathcal{C}$ will be random for the adversary.

Technical Challenges. The above approach *fails* in our context due to the following two "problems" in the protocol Π_{VSS}, when executed by *different* dealers.

Problem I: The first challenge is to maintain the linearity of underlying IC-signatures. To understand the issue, consider a triplet of parties P_i, P_j, P_k, acting as S, I and R respectively in various instances of Π_{VSS} invoked by *different* dealers. Recall that, to maintain the linearity of IC-signatures, it is *necessary* that P_i selects the *same* set of supporting-verifiers $\mathcal{SV}$ in *all* the instances of authentication phase involving P_j and P_k. This is possible *only if* P_i knows *all* the values on which it wants to generate the IC-signature for P_j and P_k and starts invoking *all* the instances of authentication phase. Instead, if P_i invokes instances of authentication phase *as and when* it has some data to be authenticated for P_j and P_k, then it *may not* be possible to have the *same* $\mathcal{SV}$ in *all* the instances of authentication phase, involving P_i, P_j and P_k in the above roles, especially in an *asynchronous* network. Since, in Π_{VSS}, IC-signatures are generated on the supposedly common shares (after receiving them from the underlying dealer) and multiple instances of Π_{VSS} are invoked (by *different* dealers), this means that P_i should *first* have the data from all the dealers for the various instances of Π_{VSS} and *before* invoking instances of authentication phase to generate IC-signatures on these values for P_j. This *may not* be possible, since P_i *need not* know *beforehand* which dealers it will be receiving shares from as part of Π_{VSS}.

Way Out. To deal with the above issue, we now let the dealers *publicly* commit their shares for the Π_{VSS} instances through *secure verifiable multicast* (SVM). The primitive allows a designated *sender* Sen $\in \mathcal{P}$ with input v to "verifiably" send v to a designated set of *receivers* $\mathcal{R} \subseteq \mathcal{P}$, without leaking any additional information. The verifiability guarantees that even if Sen is *corrupt*, if the non-faulty parties in $\mathcal{R}$ get any value from Sen, then it will be *common* and *all* the (non-faulty) parties in $\mathcal{P}$ will "know" that Sen has sent some value to $\mathcal{R}$. Our instantiation of SVM is very simple: Sen acts as a dealer and generates $[v]$ through Π_{VSS}. Once $[v]$ is generated, the parties know that Sen has "committed" to some *unknown* value. The next step is to let *only* the parties in $\mathcal{R}$ reconstruct v.

Using SVM, we now let the various dealers distribute the shares during the underlying instances of Π_{VSS} (for Π_{Rand}) as follows. Consider the dealer P_ℓ who has invoked an instance of Π_{VSS} with input $r^{(\ell)}$. For this, it picks random shares

$r_1^{(\ell)}, \ldots, r_{|\mathcal{Z}_s|}^{(\ell)}$ which sum up to $r^{(\ell)}$. Now *instead* of directly sending send $r_q^{(\ell)}$ to the parties in S_q, it invokes $|\mathcal{Z}_s|$ instances of SVM with input $r_1^{(\ell)}, \ldots, r_{|\mathcal{Z}_s|}^{(\ell)}$ and $S_1, \ldots, S_{|\mathcal{Z}_s|}$ as the designated set of receivers respectively. This serves *two* purposes. All the parties in $\mathcal{P}$ will now *know* that P_ℓ has distributed shares to each set from $\mathbb{S}_{\mathcal{Z}_s}$. The parties then run an instance of ACS to identify a common subset of *committed dealers* $\mathcal{CD} \subseteq \mathcal{P}$, where $\mathcal{P} \setminus \mathcal{CD} \in \mathcal{Z}_s$, which have invoked the desired instances of SVM and delivered the required shares to each group $S_q \in \mathbb{S}_{|\mathcal{Z}_s|}$. The way timeouts are maintained as part of the ACS, it will be ensured that in a *synchronous* network, all *non-faulty* dealers are present in $\mathcal{CD}$. Once the set $\mathcal{CD}$ is identified, it is guaranteed that every *non-faulty* party P_i will have the shares from *all* the dealers in $\mathcal{CD}$. And once it has the shares from all the dealers in $\mathcal{CD}$, it starts generating the IC-signatures on these shares for the designated parties as part of the Π_{VSS} instances corresponding to the dealers in $\mathcal{CD}$ and ensures that all the pre-requisites are satisfied to guarantee the linearity of the underlying IC-signatures. Now *instead* of selecting the set of dealers $\mathcal{C}$ (for Π_{Rand}) from $\mathcal{P}$, the parties run an instance of ACS over the set of committed dealers $\mathcal{CD}$ to select $\mathcal{C}$ where $\mathcal{CD} \setminus \mathcal{C} \in \mathcal{Z}_s$ holds. We stress that *irrespective* of the network type, the set $\mathcal{C}$ is *still* guaranteed to have at least one non-faulty party. While this is trivially true in an *asynchronous* network where $\mathcal{Z}_a$ satisfies the $\mathbb{Q}^{(1)}(\mathcal{C}, \mathcal{Z}_a)$ condition, the same is true in the *synchronous* network because $\mathcal{CD}$ will have *all* non-faulty dealers.

Problem II: The second problem (in the proposed Π_{Rand}) is that the underlying core-sets might be *different* for the values shared by the dealers in $\mathcal{CD}$ (and hence $\mathcal{C}$). Instead, we require every dealer in $\mathcal{CD}$ to secret-share random values with *common* underlying core-sets. Only then will it be ensured that the random values generated through Π_{Rand} are secret-shared with common core-sets.

Way Out. Getting rid of the above problem is *not* possible if we let every dealer in $\mathcal{CD}$ compute *individual* core-sets during their respective instances of Π_{VSS}, as per the steps of Π_{VSS}. Recall that in Π_{VSS}, the dealer D computes the underlying core-sets with respect to the "first" set of parties S_p from $\mathbb{S}_{|\mathcal{Z}_s|}$ which confirm the pairwise consistency of their supposedly common share after exchanging IC-signatures on these values. As a result, different dealers (in Π_{Rand}) may end up computing *different* core-sets in their instances of Π_{VSS} with respect to *different* candidate S_p sets. To deal with this issue, we *instead* let each dealer in $\mathcal{CD}$ *continue* computing and publishing *different* "legitimate" core-sets with respect to various "eligible" candidate S_p sets from $\mathbb{S}_{\mathcal{Z}_s}$. The parties run an instance of ACS to identify a *common* subset of dealers $\mathcal{C} \in \mathcal{CD}$ where $\mathcal{CD} \setminus \mathcal{C} \in \mathcal{Z}_s$, such that *all* the dealers have computed and published "valid" core-sets, computed with the respect to the *same* $S_p \in \mathbb{S}_{\mathcal{Z}_s}$. The idea here is that there always exists a set $\mathbf{S} \in \mathbb{S}_{\mathcal{Z}_s}$ consisting of *only* non-faulty parties. So if the set of *non-faulty* dealers $\mathcal{H}$ in $\mathcal{CD}$ keep computing and publishing *all possible* candidate core-sets in their Π_{VSS} instances, then they will publish core-sets with respect to $\mathbf{S}$. Hence, $\mathcal{H}$ and $\mathbf{S}$ *always* constitute the candidate $\mathcal{CD}$ and the common S_p set.

Note that identifying $\mathcal{C}$ out of $\mathcal{CD}$ through ACS satisfying the above requirements is *non-trivial* and requires carefully executing the underlying instances of BA in "two-dimensions". We first run $|\mathcal{Z}_s|$ instances of Π_{BA}, one on the behalf of each set in $\mathbb{S}_{\mathcal{Z}_s}$, where the qth instance is executed to decide whether a subset of dealers in $\mathcal{CD} \setminus Z$ for some $Z \in \mathcal{Z}_s$ have published valid core-sets with respect to the set $S_q \in \mathbb{S}_{\mathcal{Z}_s}$. This enables the parties to identify a *common* set $S_{q_{\mathsf{core}}} \in \mathbb{S}_{\mathcal{Z}_s}$, such that it is guaranteed that a subset of dealers in $\mathcal{CD} \setminus Z$ for some $Z \in \mathcal{Z}_s$ have indeed published valid core-sets with respect to the set $S_{q_{\mathsf{core}}}$. Once the set $S_{q_{\mathsf{core}}}$ is identified, the parties then run $|\mathcal{CD}|$ instances of BA to decide which dealers in $\mathcal{CD}$ have published core-sets with respect to $S_{q_{\mathsf{core}}}$.

1.2.6   Network Agnostic Secure Multiplication

To generate secret-shared random multiplication-triples we need a network agnostic secure multiplication protocol which securely generates a secret-sharing of the product of two secret-shared values. The key subprotocol behind our multiplication protocol is a *non-robust* multiplication protocol $\Pi_{\mathsf{BasicMult}}$ (standing for basic multiplication), which takes inputs $[a]$ and $[b]$ and an *existing* set of *globally discarded* parties $\mathcal{GD}$, which contains only *corrupt* parties. The protocol securely generates $[c]$ *without* revealing any additional information about a, b (and c). If *no* party in $\mathcal{P} \setminus \mathcal{GD}$ cheats, then $c = a \cdot b$ holds. The idea behind the protocol is to let each *summand* $[a]_p \cdot [b]_q$ be secret-shared by a *summand-sharing party*. Then $[a \cdot b]$ can be computed from the secret-sharing of each summand, owing to the linearity property. Existing multiplication protocols in the *synchronous* and *asynchronous* setting [4, 29] also use an instantiation of $\Pi_{\mathsf{BasicMult}}$, based on the above idea. In the sequel, we recall them, followed by the technical challenges faced in the network agnostic setting and how we deal with them.

$\Pi_{\mathsf{BasicMult}}$ **in the Synchronous Setting with** $\mathbb{Q}^{(2)}(\mathcal{P}, \mathcal{Z}_s)$ **Condition** [29]. In [29], each summand $[a]_p \cdot [b]_q$ is *statically* assigned to a *designated* summand-sharing party through some *deterministic* assignment, which is possible since $[a]_p$ and $[b]_q$ are held by the parties in $(S_p \cap S_q)$. This is *non-empty*, since the $\mathbb{Q}^{(2)}(\mathcal{P}, \mathcal{Z}_s)$ condition holds. Since the parties in $\mathcal{GD}$ are *already* known to be corrupted, all the shares $[a]_p, [b]_p$ held by the parties in $\mathcal{GD}$ are *publicly reconstructed* and *instead* of letting the parties in $\mathcal{GD}$ secret-share their assigned summands, the parties take the "default" secret-sharing of these summands.

$\Pi_{\mathsf{BasicMult}}$ **in the Asynchronous Setting with** $\mathbb{Q}^{(3)}(\mathcal{P}, \mathcal{Z}_a)$ **Condition** [4]. The idea of *statically* designating each summand $[a]_p \cdot [b]_q$ to a *unique* party in $\mathcal{P} \setminus \mathcal{GD}$ *need not* work in the *asynchronous* setting, since the designated party may be *corrupt* and *need not* secret-share any summand, thus resulting in an *endless* wait. To deal with this challenge, [4] *dynamically* selects the summand-sharing parties for each summand. In more detail, let $\mathcal{Z}_a = \{Z_1, \ldots, Z_{|\mathcal{Z}_a|}\}$ and $\mathbb{S}_{\mathcal{Z}_a} = \{S_1, \ldots, S_{|\mathcal{Z}_a|}\}$, where each $S_r = \mathcal{P} \setminus Z_r$. Since the $\mathbb{Q}^{(3)}(\mathcal{P}, \mathcal{Z}_a)$ condition is satisfied and $\mathcal{GD} \in \mathcal{Z}_a$, it follows that $(S_p \cap S_q) \setminus \mathcal{GD} \neq \emptyset$ and there exists at least one non-faulty party in $(S_p \cap S_q)$, who can secret-share the summand $[a]_p \cdot [b]_q$. Hence, *every* party in $\mathcal{P} \setminus \mathcal{GD}$ is allowed to secret-share *all* the summands it is "capable" of, with special care taken to ensure that each summand $[a]_p \cdot [b]_q$ is considered *exactly once*. For this, the protocol now proceeds in "hops", where in each hop all the parties in $\mathcal{P} \setminus \mathcal{GD}$ secret-share all the summands they are capable of, *but a single* summand sharing party is finally selected for the hop through ACS. Then, all the summands which have been shared by the elected summand-sharing party are "marked" as shared and not considered for sharing in the future hops. Moreover, a party who has already served as a summand-sharing party is *not* selected in the future hops.

Technical Challenges in the Network Agnostic Setting. The *asynchronous* $\Pi_{\mathsf{BasicMult}}$ based on *dynamically* selecting summand-sharing parties will *fail* in the *synchronous* network, since the $\mathbb{Q}^{(3)}$ condition *need not* be satisfied. On the other hand, *synchronous* $\Pi_{\mathsf{BasicMult}}$ based on *statically* selecting summand-sharing parties will *fail* if a designated summand-sharing party *does not* secret-share the required summands, resulting in an endless wait. The way out is to select summand-sharing parties in *three* phases. We *first* select summand-sharing parties dynamically in *hops*, following the approach of [4], till we find a subset of parties from $\mathbb{S}_{Z_s}$ which have shared *all* the summands they are capable of. Then in the *second* phase, the *remaining* summands which are *not* yet secret-shared are *statically* assigned and shared by the respective designated summand-sharing parties. To avoid an endless wait in this phase, the parties wait only for a "fixed" time required for the parties to secret-share the assigned summands (corresponding to the time taken in a *synchronous* network) and run instances of BA to identify which of the designated summand-sharing parties have shared their summands up during the second phase. During the *third* phase, any "leftover" summand which is *not yet* shared is *publicly* reconstructed by reconstructing the corresponding shares and a default sharing is taken for such summands.

The idea here is the following: *all* non-faulty parties will share the summands which are assigned to them, either statically or dynamically, *irrespective* of the network type. Consequently, the first phase will be always over, since the set consisting of *only* non-faulty parties always constitutes a candidate set of summand-sharing parties which the parties look for to complete of the first phase. Once the first phase is over, the second phase is bound to be over since the parties wait *only* for a fixed time. The third phase is always bound to be over, once the first two phases are over, since it involves publicly reconstructing the leftover summands. The way summands are assigned across the three phases, it will be always guaranteed that every summand is considered for sharing once in exactly one of the three phases and no summand will be left out. The crucial point here is that the shares held *only* by the non-faulty parties *never* get publicly reconstructed, thus guaranteeing that the adversary *does not* learn any additional information about a and b. This is obviously true in a *synchronous* network because we always have the *second* phase where every non-faulty party who is *not* selected as a summand-sharing party during the first phase will get the opportunity to secret-share its assigned summands. On the other hand, in an *asynchronous* network, it can be shown that *all* the summands which involve any share held by the non-faulty parties would have been secret-shared during the *first* phase itself. In more detail, let $Z^\star \in \mathcal{Z}_a$ be the set of *corrupt* parties and let $\mathcal{H} = \mathcal{P} \setminus Z^\star$ be the set of *honest* parties. Moreover, let $S_h \in \mathbb{S}_{\mathcal{Z}_s}$ be the group consisting of *only* non-faulty parties which hold the shares $[a]_h$ and $[b]_h$. Consider an *arbitrary* summand $[a]_h \cdot [b]_q$. Suppose the first phase gets over because every party in $S_\ell \in \mathbb{S}_{\mathcal{Z}_s}$ has been selected as a summand-sharing party during the *first* phase. Then consider the set $(S_\ell \cap \mathcal{H} \cap S_q)$, which is *not* empty due to the $\mathbb{Q}^{(2,1)}(\mathcal{P}, \mathcal{Z}_s, \mathcal{Z}_a)$ condition. Hence, there exists *some* $P_j \in (\mathcal{H} \cap S_\ell \cap S_q)$, who would have already shared $[a]_h \cdot [b]_q$ during some hop in the first phase.

1.3   Other Related Works

Almost all the existing works on network agnostic protocols have considered *threshold* adversaries. The work of [12] presents a network agnostic *cryptographically-secure* atomic broadcast protocol. The work of [33] studies state machine replication protocols for multiple thresholds, including t_s and t_a. The work of [24,25] present network agnostic protocols for the task of approximate agreement using the condition $2t_s + t_a < n$. The same condition has been used to design a network agnostic distributed key-generation (DKG) protocol in [6]. A recent work [19] has studied the problem of network agnostic perfectly-secure message transmission (PSMT) [20] over *incomplete* graphs.

1.4   Open Problems

It is *not* known whether the condition $3t_s + t_a < n$ (resp. $\mathbb{Q}^{(3,1)}(\mathcal{P}, \mathcal{Z}_s, \mathcal{Z}_a)$) is *necessary* for the network agnostic MPC with *perfect* security against threshold (resp. non-threshold) adversary. The works of [2,3] and this work just focus on the *possibility* of unconditionally-secure network agnostic MPC. Upgrading the efficiency of these protocols to those of state-of-the-art SMPC and AMPC protocols seems to require a significant research effort. Our MPC protocol when instantiated for *threshold* adversaries may require an *exponential* amount of computation and communication ($|\mathcal{Z}_s|$ will have all subsets of $\mathcal{P}$ of size up to t_s). Hence, designing a network agnostic MPC protocol against *threshold* adversaries with *statistical* security and *polynomial* complexity is left as a challenging open problem. It is also interesting to see whether one can design network-agnostic MPC protocols against general adversaries whose complexity is polynomial in n (and *not* $|\mathcal{Z}_s|$), for specific types of adversary structures.

1.5   Paper Organization

Due to space constraints, we do not provide the details of our network agnostic BA protocol (which is based on existing ideas) and circuit evaluation protocol (which is standard). Also, we skip proofs for the protocols and the impossibility proof. The details of the missing protocols and formal proofs are available in the full version of the article [5].

2 Preliminaries and Definitions

We assume the *pair-wise secure channel* model, where the parties in $\mathcal{P}$ are assumed to be connected by pair-wise secure channels. The underlying communication network can be either synchronous or asynchronous, with parties being *unaware* about the exact network behaviour. If the network behaves *synchronously*, then every message sent is delivered within a *known* time Δ. On the other hand, if the network behaves *asynchronously*, then messages can be delayed arbitrarily, but finitely, with every message sent being delivered *eventually*. The distrust among $\mathcal{P}$ is modelled by a *malicious* (Byzantine) adversary Adv, who can corrupt a subset of the parties in $\mathcal{P}$ and force them to behave in any arbitrary fashion during the execution of a protocol. The parties *not* under the control of Adv are called *honest*. We assume the adversary to be *static*, who decides the set of corrupt parties at the beginning of the protocol execution. Adversary Adv can corrupt any one subset of parties from $\mathcal{Z}_s$ and $\mathcal{Z}_a$ in *synchronous* and *asynchronous* network respectively. The adversary structures are *monotone*, implying that if $Z \in \mathcal{Z}_s$ ($Z \in \mathcal{Z}_a$ resp.), then every subset of Z also belongs to $\mathcal{Z}_s$ (resp. $\mathcal{Z}_a$). We assume that $\mathcal{Z}_s$ and $\mathcal{Z}_a$ satisfy the conditions $\mathbb{Q}^{(2)}(\mathcal{P}, \mathcal{Z}_s)$ and $\mathbb{Q}^{(3)}(\mathcal{P}, \mathcal{Z}_a)$ respectively, which are *necessary* for statistically-secure MPC in the synchronous and asynchronous network respectively. Additionally, we assume that $\mathcal{Z}_a \subset \mathcal{Z}_s$. Moreover, $\mathcal{Z}_s$ and $\mathcal{Z}_a$ satisfy the $\mathbb{Q}^{(2,1)}(\mathcal{P}, \mathcal{Z}_s, \mathcal{Z}_a)$ condition.

In our protocols, all computations are done over a finite field $\mathbb{F}$, where $|\mathbb{F}| > n^5 \cdot 2^{\mathsf{ssec}}$ and ssec is the underlying statistical security parameter. This will ensure that the error probability in our MPC protocol is upper bounded by $2^{-\mathsf{ssec}}$. Without loss of generality, we assume that each P_i has an input $x_i \in \mathbb{F}$, and the parties want to securely compute a function $f : \mathbb{F}^n \to \mathbb{F}$, represented by an arithmetic circuit ckt over $\mathbb{F}$, consisting of linear and non-linear (multiplication) gates, where ckt has c_M multiplication gates and a multiplicative depth of D_M.

We assume the existence of an *unconditionally-secure public-key infrastructure* (PKI), for an unconditionally-secure signature scheme, also called *pseudo-signature* [22,35]. We refer to [22] for complete formal details of such a PKI. We use $|\sigma|$ to denote the size of a pseudo-signature in bits. As done in [2,4], for simplicity, we will *not* be specifying any *termination* criteria for our sub-protocols. The parties will keep on participating in these sub-protocol instances even *after* computing their outputs. The termination criteria of our MPC protocol will ensure the termination of *all* underlying sub-protocol instances. We will be using an existing *randomized* ABA protocol [16] which ensures that the honest parties (eventually) obtain their respective output *almost-surely* with probability 1. The property of *almost-surely* obtaining the output carries over to the "higher" level protocols, where ABA is used as a building block.

3 Network Agnostic Byzantine Agreement

We follow the blueprint of [2,11] to design a network agnostic BA protocol Π_{BA}, which satisfies the requirements of BA, both in a synchronous as well as asynchronous network. If the network behaves asynchronously, then the (honest) parties obtain output within time $T_{\mathsf{BA}} = (t + 33)\Delta$, where t is the cardinality of the maximum-sized subset from the adversary structure $\mathcal{Z}_s$. On the other hand, if the network behaves *asynchronously*, then almost surely, the (honest) parties eventually get their output.

In the process of designing the protocol Π_{BA}, we design a special BA protocol Π_{PW}, by generalizing the classic Dolev-Strong (DS) BA protocol [21] against non-threshold adversaries, based on the pseudo-signature setup [35]. We also design a network agnostic reliable broadcast protocol Π_{BC}, which allows a designated sender party Sen to reliably send its message $m \in \{0,1\}^\ell$ to all the parties. In the protocol, there exists a designated (local) time $T_{\mathsf{BC}} = (t + 4)\Delta$ at which all (honest) parties have an output, such that depending upon the network type and corruption status of Sen, the output satisfies the following conditions:

- *Synchronous Network and Honest* Sen: the output is m for *all* honest parties.
- *Synchronous Network and Corrupt* Sen: the output is a common $m^\star \in \{0,1\}^\ell \cup \{\bot\}$ for *all* honest parties.
- *Asynchronous Network and Honest* Sen: the output is either m or $\bot$ for each honest party.
- *Asynchronous Network and Corrupt* Sen: the output is either a common $m^\star \in \{0,1\}^\ell$ or $\bot$ for each honest party.

Protocol Π_{BC} also gives the parties who output $\bot$ at (local) time T_{BC} an option to switch their output to some ℓ-bit string if the parties keep running the protocol beyond time T_{BC} and if certain "conditions" are satisfied for those parties. We stress that this switching provision is *only* for those who output $\bot$ at time T_{BC}. While this provision is not "useful" and not used while designing Π_{BA}, it comes in handy when Π_{BC} is used to broadcast values in our VSS protocol. Notice that the output-switching provision will *not* lead to a violation of consistency and hence honest parties will *not* end up with different ℓ-bit outputs. Following the terminology of [2], we call the process of computing output at time T_{BC} and beyond time T_{BC} as the *regular mode* and *fallback mode* of Π_{BC} respectively.

In the rest of the paper, we say that P_i *broadcasts* m to mean that P_i invokes an instance of Π_{BC} as Sen with input m, and the parties participate in this instance. Similarly, we say that P_j *receives* m *from the broadcast of* P_i *through regular-mode (resp. fallback-mode)*, to mean that P_j has the output m at (local) time T_{BC} (resp. after time T_{BC}) during the instance of Π_{BC}.

For the details of the BA protocol Π_{BA} and associated sub-protocols, see [5].

4   Network Agnostic Information Checking Protocol

In this section, we present our network agnostic ICP (Fig. 1). The protocol consists of two subprotocols Π_{Auth} and Π_{Reveal}, implementing the authentication and revelation phases respectively. The proof of Theorem 1 is available in [5].

Protocol $\Pi_{\mathsf{ICP}}(\mathcal{P}, \mathcal{Z}_s, \mathcal{Z}_a, \mathsf{S}, \mathsf{I}, \mathsf{R})$

Protocol $\Pi_{\mathsf{Auth}}(\mathcal{P}, \mathcal{Z}_s, \mathcal{Z}_a, \mathsf{S}, \mathsf{I}, \mathsf{R}, s)$: $t \stackrel{def}{=} \max\{|Z| : Z \in \mathcal{Z}_s\}$

- **Distributing Data:** S executes the following steps.
  - Randomly select t-degree *signing-polynomial* $F(x)$ and t-degree *masking-polynomial* $M(x)$, where $F(0) = s$. For $i = 1, \dots, n$, randomly select $\alpha_i \in \mathbb{F} \setminus \{0\}$, and compute $v_i = F(\alpha_i)$ and $m_i = M(\alpha_i)$.
  - Send $(F(x), M(x))$ to I. For $i = 1, \dots, n$, send (α_i, v_i, m_i) to party P_i.
- **Confirming Receipt of Verification Points:** Each party P_i (including S, I and R), upon receiving (α_i, v_i, m_i) from S, broadcasts (Received, i).
- **Announcing Set of Supporting Verifiers:** only S does the following.
  - Initialize the set of *supporting verifiers* $\mathcal{SV}$ to $\emptyset$, and wait till the local time is $\Delta + T_{\mathsf{BC}}$. Upon receiving (Received, i) from the broadcast of P_i, add P_i to $\mathcal{SV}$. Once $\mathcal{P} \setminus \mathcal{SV} \in \mathcal{Z}_s$, broadcast the set $\mathcal{SV}$.
- **Announcing Masked Polynomial:** only I does the following.
  - Wait till the local time is $\Delta + 2T_{\mathsf{BC}}$. Upon receiving $\mathcal{SV}$ from the broadcast of S such that $\mathcal{P} \setminus \mathcal{SV} \in \mathcal{Z}_s$, wait till (Received, i) is received from the broadcast of every $P_i \in \mathcal{SV}$. Then randomly pick $d \in \mathbb{F} \setminus \{0\}$ and broadcast $(d, B(x))$, where $B(x) \stackrel{def}{=} dF(x) + M(x)$.
- **Announcing Validity of Masked Polynomial:** only S does the following.
  - Wait till the local time is $\Delta + 3T_{\mathsf{BC}}$. Upon receiving $(d, B(x))$ from the broadcast of I, broadcast OK, if $B(x)$ is a t-degree polynomial and if $dv_j + m_j = B(\alpha_j)$ holds for every $P_j \in \mathcal{SV}$.
- **Deciding Whether Authentication is Successful:** each $P_i \in \mathcal{P}$ (including S, I and R) waits till the local time is $\Delta + 4T_{\mathsf{BC}}$. Upon receiving $\mathcal{SV}$ and $(d, B(x))$ from the broadcast of S and I respectively, where $\mathcal{P} \setminus \mathcal{SV} \in \mathcal{Z}_s$, it set the variable $\mathsf{authCompleted}_{(\mathsf{S},\mathsf{I},\mathsf{R})}$ to 1 if OK is received from the broadcast of S. Upon setting $\mathsf{authCompleted}_{(\mathsf{S},\mathsf{I},\mathsf{R})}$ to 1, I sets $\mathsf{ICSig}(\mathsf{S}, \mathsf{I}, \mathsf{R}, s) = F(x)$.

Protocol $\Pi_{\mathsf{Reveal}}(\mathcal{P}, \mathcal{Z}_s, \mathcal{Z}_a, \mathsf{S}, \mathsf{I}, \mathsf{R}, s)$

- **Revealing Signing Polynomial and Verification Points:** Each party P_i (including S, I and R) does the following, if $\mathsf{authCompleted}_{(\mathsf{S},\mathsf{I},\mathsf{R})}$ is set to 1.
  - If $P_i = \mathsf{I}$ then send $F(x)$ to R, if $\mathsf{ICSig}(\mathsf{S}, \mathsf{I}, \mathsf{R}, s)$ is set to $F(x)$ during Π_{Auth}.
  - If $P_i \in \mathcal{SV}$, then send (α_i, v_i, m_i) to R.
- **Accepting the IC-Signature:** The following steps are executed only by R, if $\mathsf{authCompleted}_{(\mathsf{S},\mathsf{I},\mathsf{R})}$ is set to 1 during the protocol Π_{Auth}.
  - Wait till the local time becomes a multiple of Δ. Upon receiving $F(x)$ from I, where $F(x)$ is a t-degree polynomial, proceed as follows.
    1. If (α_i, v_i, m_i) is received from $P_i \in \mathcal{SV}$, then *accept* (α_i, v_i, m_i) if either $v_i = F(\alpha_i)$ or $B(\alpha_i) \neq dv_i + m_i$, where $B(x)$ is received from the broadcast of I during Π_{Auth}. Otherwise, *reject* (α_i, v_i, m_i).
    2. Wait till a subset of parties $\mathcal{SV}' \subseteq \mathcal{SV}$ is found, such that $\mathcal{SV} \setminus \mathcal{SV}' \in \mathcal{Z}_s$, and for every $P_i \in \mathcal{SV}'$, the corresponding revealed point (α_i, v_i, m_i) is *accepted*. Then, output $s = F(0)$.

Fig. 1. The network-agnostic ICP

Theorem 1. *Protocols* $(\Pi_{\mathsf{Auth}}, \Pi_{\mathsf{Reveal}})$ *satisfy the following properties, except with probability at most* $\epsilon_{\mathsf{ICP}} \overset{def}{=} \frac{nt}{|\mathbb{F}|-1}$, *where* $t = \max\{|Z| : Z \in \mathcal{Z}_s\}$.

- *If* S, I *and* R *are honest, then the following hold.*
  - $\mathcal{Z}_s$**-Correctness**: *In a synchronous network, each honest party sets* $\mathsf{authCompleted}_{(\mathsf{S},\mathsf{I},\mathsf{R})}$ *to* 1 *during* Π_{Auth} *at time* $T_{\mathsf{Auth}} = \Delta + 4T_{\mathsf{BC}}$. *Moreover* R *outputs* s *during* Π_{Reveal} *which takes* $T_{\mathsf{Reveal}} = \Delta$ *time.*
  - $\mathcal{Z}_a$**-Correctness**: *In an asynchronous network, each honest party eventually sets* $\mathsf{authCompleted}_{(\mathsf{S},\mathsf{I},\mathsf{R})}$ *to* 1 *during* Π_{Auth} *and* R *eventually outputs* s *during* Π_{Reveal}.
  - **Privacy**: *The view of* Adv *is independent of* s, *irrespective of the network.*
- **Unforgeability**: *If* S, R *are honest,* I *is corrupt and if* R *outputs* $s' \in \mathbb{F}$ *during* Π_{Reveal}, *then* $s' = s$ *holds, irrespective of the network type.*
- *If* S *is corrupt,* I, R *are honest and if* I *sets* $\mathsf{ICSig}(\mathsf{S},\mathsf{I},\mathsf{R},s) = F(x)$ *during* Π_{Auth}, *then the following holds.*
  - $\mathcal{Z}_s$**-Non-Repudiation**: *In a synchronous network,* R *outputs* $s = F(0)$ *during* Π_{Reveal}, *which takes* $T_{\mathsf{Reveal}} = \Delta$ *time.*
  - $\mathcal{Z}_a$**-Non-Repudiation**: *In an asynchronous network,* R *eventually outputs* $s = F(0)$ *during* Π_{Reveal}.
- **Communication Complexity**: Π_{Auth} *incurs a communication of* $\mathcal{O}(n^5 \cdot \log|\mathbb{F}| \cdot |\sigma|)$ *bits, while* Π_{Reveal} *incurs a communication of* $\mathcal{O}(n \cdot \log|\mathbb{F}|)$ *bits.*

We use the following notations while invoking instances of ICP.

Notation 2. (for ICP) *While using* $(\Pi_{\mathsf{Auth}}, \Pi_{\mathsf{Reveal}})$, *we say that:*

- "P_i *gives* $\mathsf{ICSig}(P_i, P_j, P_k, s)$ *to* P_j" *to mean that* P_i *acts as* S *and invokes an instance of* Π_{Auth} *with input* s, *where* P_j *and* P_k *play the role of* I *and* R *respectively.*
- "P_j *receives* $\mathsf{ICSig}(P_i, P_j, P_k, s)$ *from* P_i" *to mean that* P_j, *as* I, *has set* $\mathsf{authCompleted}_{(P_i,P_j,P_k)}$ *to* 1 *and* $\mathsf{ICSig}(P_i, P_j, P_k, s)$ *to some* t-*degree polynomial with* s *as the constant term during the instance of* Π_{Auth}, *where* P_i *and* P_k *play the role of* S *and* R *respectively.*
- "P_j *reveals* $\mathsf{ICSig}(P_i, P_j, P_k, s)$ *to* P_k" *to mean* P_j, *as* I, *invokes an instance of* Π_{Reveal}, *with* P_i *and* P_k *playing the role of* S *and* R *respectively.*
- "P_k *accepts* $\mathsf{ICSig}(P_i, P_j, P_k, s)$" *to mean that* P_k, *as* R, *outputs* s *during the instance of* Π_{Reveal}, *invoked by* P_j *as* I, *with* P_i *playing the role of* S.

Linearity of IC Signature and Default IC Signature. We require the linearity property from ICP when used in our VSS protocols, where there will be multiple instances of Π_{Auth} running, involving the *same* $(\mathsf{S},\mathsf{I},\mathsf{R})$ triplet. To achieve this, we ensure that in all the Π_{Auth} instances involving the *same* triplet $(\mathsf{S},\mathsf{I},\mathsf{R})$, the signer uses the same non-zero evaluation point $\alpha_{\mathsf{S},\mathsf{I},\mathsf{R},i}$ for the verifier P_i, while distributing verification information to P_i, as part of the respective Π_{Auth} instances. Similarly, S should find and make public a *common* set of supporting verifiers $\mathcal{SV}$, on behalf of *all* the instances of Π_{Auth}. Finally, I should use the same non-zero random linear combiner d, to compute the masked polynomials for all the instances of Π_{Auth} and once computed, it should *together* make public d and the masked polynomials for *all* the instances of Π_{Auth}. We use the term *"parties follow linearity principle while generating IC-signatures"*, to mean that the underlying instances of Π_{Auth} are invoked as above.

We will also encounter situations where some *publicly known* value s and a triplet $(\mathsf{S}, \mathsf{I}, \mathsf{R})$ exist. Then I can *locally* compute $\mathsf{ICSig}(\mathsf{S}, \mathsf{I}, \mathsf{R}, s)$ by setting $\mathsf{ICSig}(\mathsf{S}, \mathsf{I}, \mathsf{R}, s)$ to the *constant* polynomial $F(x) = s$. Each verifier $P_i \in \mathcal{P}$ *locally* sets $(\alpha_{\mathsf{S},\mathsf{I},\mathsf{R},i}, v_i, m_i)$ as its verification information, where $v_i = m_i = s$. Moreover, the set of supporting verifiers $\mathcal{SV}$ is set as $\mathcal{P}$. We use the term *"parties set $\mathsf{ICSig}(\mathsf{S}, \mathsf{I}, \mathsf{R}, s)$ to the default value"*, to mean the above.

5   Network Agnostic Verifiable Secret Sharing (VSS)

This section presents our network-agnostic VSS protocol Π_{VSS}, which allows a designated dealer to generate a linear secret-sharing with IC-signatures (see the following definition) for its input. For the proof of Theorem 3, see [5].

Definition 1 (Linear Secret Sharing with IC-Signatures). *A value $s \in \mathbb{F}$ is said to be linearly secret-shared with IC-signatures, if there exist shares $s_1, \ldots, s_{|\mathcal{Z}_s|} \in \mathbb{F}$ where $s = s_1 + \ldots + s_{|\mathcal{Z}_s|}$. Moreover, for $q = 1, \ldots, |\mathcal{Z}_s|$, there exists some publicly-known core-set $\mathcal{W}_q \subseteq S_q$, such that all the following holds.*

(a). *$\mathcal{Z}_s$ satisfies the $\mathbb{Q}^{(1)}(\mathcal{W}_q, \mathcal{Z}_s)$ condition and all (honest) parties in the set S_q have the share s_q.* **(b).** *Every honest $P_i \in \mathcal{W}_q$ has the IC-signature $\mathsf{ICSig}(P_j, P_i, P_k, s_q)$ of every $P_j \in \mathcal{W}_q$ for every $P_k \notin S_q$. Moreover, if any corrupt $P_j \in \mathcal{W}_q$ has $\mathsf{ICSig}(P_j, P_i, P_k, s_q')$ of any honest $P_i \in \mathcal{W}_q$ for any $P_k \notin S_q$, then $s_q' = s_q$ holds. Furthermore, all the underlying IC-signatures satisfy the linearity property.*

The vector of information corresponding to a linear secret-sharing with IC-signature of s is denoted by $[s]$.

Theorem 3. *Protocol Π_{VSS} achieves the following, except with a probability of $\mathcal{O}(|\mathbb{S}_{\mathcal{Z}_s}| \cdot n^2 \cdot \epsilon_{\mathsf{ICP}})$, where D has input $s \in \mathbb{F}$ for Π_{VSS} and where $T_{\mathsf{VSS}} = \Delta + T_{\mathsf{Auth}} + 2T_{\mathsf{BC}} + T_{\mathsf{Reveal}}$.*

- *If D is honest, then the following hold.*
  - *$\mathcal{Z}_s$-**correctness**: In a synchronous network, the honest parties output $[s]$ at time T_{VSS}. $\mathcal{Z}_a$-**correctness**: In an asynchronous network, the honest parties eventually output $[s]$.* **Privacy**: *Adversary's view remains independent of s in any network.*

Protocol $\Pi_{\text{VSS}}(\mathsf{D}, \mathcal{Z}_s, \mathcal{Z}_a, s, \mathbb{S}_{\mathcal{Z}_s})$

- **Distribution of Shares:** D, on having input s, randomly chooses $s_1, \ldots, s_{|\mathcal{Z}_s|} \in \mathbb{F}$, such that $s = s_1 + \cdots + s_{|\mathcal{Z}_s|}$. It then sends s_q to all $P_i \in S_q$, for $q = 1, \ldots, |\mathcal{Z}_s|$.
- **Exchanging IC-Signed Values:** Each $P_i \in \mathcal{P}$ (including D), waits till the local time becomes Δ. Then, for each $S_q \in \mathbb{S}_{\mathcal{Z}_s}$ such that $P_i \in S_q$, upon receiving s_{qi} from D, give $\mathsf{ICSig}(P_i, P_j, P_k, s_{qi})$ to every $P_j \in S_q$, for every $P_k \in \mathcal{P}$ such that the parties follow the linearity principle while generating IC-signatures.
- **Announcing Results of Pairwise Consistency Tests:** Each $P_i \in \mathcal{P}$ (including D) waits till the local time becomes $\Delta + T_{\text{Auth}}$ and then does the following.
  - Upon receiving $\mathsf{ICSig}(P_j, P_i, P_k, s_{qj})$ from P_j for each $S_q \in \mathbb{S}$ such that $P_j, P_i \in S_q$, corresponding to every $P_k \in \mathcal{P}$, broadcast $\mathsf{OK}(i, j)$, if $s_{qi} = s_{qj}$ holds.
  - Corresponding to every $P_j \in \mathcal{P}$, participate in any instance of Π_{BC} initiated by P_j as a sender, to broadcast any $\mathsf{OK}(P_j, \star)$ message.
- **Constructing Consistency Graph:** Each $P_i \in \mathcal{P}$ (including D) waits till the local time becomes $\Delta + T_{\text{Auth}} + T_{\text{BC}}$ and then constructs an undirected consistency graph $G^{(i)}$ with $\mathcal{P}$ as the vertex set, where the edge (P_j, P_k) is added to $G^{(i)}$, provided $\mathsf{OK}(j, k)$ and $\mathsf{OK}(k, j)$ is received from the broadcast of P_j and P_k respectively (through any mode).
- **Identification of Core Sets and Public Announcement by the Dealer:** D waits till its local time is $\Delta + T_{\text{Auth}} + T_{\text{BC}}$, and then executes the following steps to compute core sets.
  - Once any $S_p \in \mathbb{S}_{\mathcal{Z}_s}$ forms a clique in the graph $G^{(\mathsf{D})}$, then for $q = 1, \ldots, |\mathcal{Z}_s|$, compute core-set $\mathcal{W}_q$ and broadcast-set $\mathcal{BS}$ with respect to S_p as follows, followed by broadcasting $(\mathsf{CanCS}, \mathsf{D}, S_p, \{\mathcal{W}_q\}_{q=1,\ldots,|\mathcal{Z}_s|}, \mathcal{BS}, \{s_q\}_{q \in \mathcal{BS}})$.[a]
    - If S_q constitutes a clique in the graph $G^{(\mathsf{D})}$, then set $\mathcal{W}_q = S_q$.
    - Else if $(S_p \cap S_q)$ constitutes a clique in $G^{(\mathsf{D})}$ and $\mathcal{Z}_s$ satisfies the $\mathbb{Q}^{(1)}(S_p \cap S_q, \mathcal{Z}_s)$ condition, then set $\mathcal{W}_q = (S_p \cap S_q)$.
    - Else set $\mathcal{W}_q = S_q$ and include q to $\mathcal{BS}$.
- **Identifying Valid Core Sets:** Each $P_i \in \mathcal{P}$ waits till its local time is $\Delta + T_{\text{Auth}} + 2T_{\text{BC}}$ and then initializes a set $\mathcal{C}_i = \emptyset$. For $p = 1, \ldots, |\mathcal{Z}_s|$, party P_i includes (D, S_p) to $\mathcal{C}_i$ (initialized to $\emptyset$), provided *all* the following hold.
  - $(\mathsf{CanCS}, \mathsf{D}, S_p, \{\mathcal{W}_q\}_{q=1,\ldots,|\mathcal{Z}_s|}, \mathcal{BS}, \{s_q\}_{q \in \mathcal{BS}})$ is received from the broadcast of D, such that for $q = 1, \ldots, |\mathcal{Z}_s|$, the following hold.
    - If $q \in \mathcal{BS}$, then the set $\mathcal{W}_q = S_q$.
    - If $(q \notin \mathcal{BS})$, then $\mathcal{W}_q$ is either S_q or $(S_p \cap S_q)$, such that:
      - If $\mathcal{W}_q = S_q$, then S_q constitutes a clique in $G^{(i)}$.
      - Else if $\mathcal{W}_q = (S_p \cap S_q)$, then $(S_p \cap S_q)$ constitutes a clique in $G^{(i)}$ and $\mathcal{Z}_s$ satisfies the $\mathbb{Q}^{(1)}(S_p \cap S_q, \mathcal{Z}_s)$ condition.
- **Computing Output:** Each $P_i \in \mathcal{P}$ does the following, once $\mathcal{C}_i \neq \emptyset$.
  - For every $S_q \in \mathbb{S}_{\mathcal{Z}_s}$ such that $P_i \in \mathcal{W}_q$, corresponding to every $P_j \in \mathcal{W}_q$, reveal $\mathsf{ICSig}(P_j, P_i, P_k, [s]_q)$ to every $P_k \in S_q \setminus \mathcal{W}_q$ upon computing $[s]_q$ and $\mathsf{ICSig}(P_j, P_i, P_k, [s]_q)$ as follows.
    - If $q \in \mathcal{BS}$, then set $[s]_q = s_q$, where s_q is received from the broadcast of D, as part of the message $(\mathsf{CanCS}, \mathsf{D}, S_p, \{\mathcal{W}_q\}_{q=1,\ldots,|\mathcal{Z}_s|}, \mathcal{BS}, \{s_q\}_{q \in \mathcal{BS}})$. Moreover, for every $P_j \in S_q$ and every $P_k \in \mathcal{P}$, set $\mathsf{ICSig}(P_j, P_i, P_k, [s]_q)$ to the default value.
    - Else, set $[s]_q$ to s_{qi}, where s_{qi} was received from D. Moreover, for every $P_j \in \mathcal{W}_q$ and every $P_k \in \mathcal{P}$, set $\mathsf{ICSig}(P_j, P_i, P_k, [s]_q)$ to $\mathsf{ICSig}(P_j, P_i, P_k, s_{qj})$, received from P_j.
  - For every $S_q \in \mathbb{S}_{\mathcal{Z}_s}$ such that $P_i \in S_q \setminus \mathcal{W}_q$, compute $[s]_q$ as follows.
    - Check if there exists any $P_j \in \mathcal{W}_q$ and a value s_{qj}, such that P_i has accepted $\mathsf{ICSig}(P_k, P_j, P_i, s_{qj})$, corresponding to every $P_k \in \mathcal{W}_q$. Upon finding such a P_j, set $[s]_q = s_{qj}$.
  - Wait till the local time becomes $\Delta + T_{\text{Auth}} + 2T_{\text{BC}} + T_{\text{Reveal}}$. Upon setting $\{[s]_q\}_{P_i \in S_q}$ to some value, output $\mathcal{W}_1, \ldots, \mathcal{W}_{|\mathcal{Z}_s|}$, $\{[s]_q\}_{P_i \in S_q}$ and $\mathsf{ICSig}(P_j, P_i, P_k, [s]_q)_{P_j, P_i \in \mathcal{W}_q, P_k \notin S_q}$.

---

[a] If there are multiple S_p from $\mathbb{S}_{\mathcal{Z}_s}$ which constitute a clique in $G^{(\mathsf{D})}$, then consider the one with the smallest index.

Fig. 2. The network agnostic VSS protocol

– *If* D *is corrupt, then the following hold.*
  – $\mathcal{Z}_s$-**commitment**: *In a synchronous network, either no honest party computes any output or there exists some $s^\star \in \mathbb{F}$, such that the honest parties output $[s^\star]$. Moreover, if any honest party computes its output at time T, then all honest parties compute their required output by time $T + \Delta$.*
  – $\mathcal{Z}_a$-**commitment**: *In an asynchronous network, either no honest party computes any output or there exists some $s^\star \in \mathbb{F}$, such that the honest parties eventually output $[s^\star]$.*
– **Communication Complexity**: $\mathcal{O}(|\mathcal{Z}_s| \cdot n^8 \cdot \log |\mathbb{F}| \cdot |\sigma|)$ *bits are communicated by the honest parties.*

5.1   Reconstruction and Secure Multicast Protocol

Let s be a value which is linearly secret-shared with IC-signatures and let $S_q \in \mathbb{S}_{\mathcal{Z}_s}$. Moreover, let $\mathcal{R} \subseteq \mathcal{P}$ be a designated set. Then protocol $\Pi_{\mathsf{RecShare}}([s], S_q, \mathcal{R})$ allows all the (honest) parties in $\mathcal{R}$ to reconstruct the share $[s]_q$. For this, every $P_i \in \mathcal{W}_q$ reveals $[s]_q$ to *all* the parties *outside* $\mathcal{W}_q$, who are in $\mathcal{R}$ (the parties in $\mathcal{W}_q$ who are in $\mathcal{R}$ *already* have $[s]_q$). To ensure that P_i *does not* cheat, P_i actually reveals the IC-signature of *every* party in $\mathcal{W}_q$ on the revealed $[s]_q$. The idea here is that since $\mathcal{W}_q$ has *at least* one *honest* party (irrespective of the network type), a potentially *corrupt* P_i will fail to reveal the signature of an *honest* party from $\mathcal{W}_q$ on an *incorrect* $[s]_q$. On the other hand, an *honest* P_i will be able to reveal the signature of *all* the parties in $\mathcal{W}_q$ on $[s]_q$.

Based on Π_{RecShare}, we design another protocol $\Pi_{\mathsf{Rec}}([s], \mathcal{R})$, which allows all the (honest) parties in $\mathcal{R}$ to reconstruct s. The idea is to run an instance of Π_{RecShare} for *every* $S_q \in \mathbb{S}_{\mathcal{Z}_s}$. We refer to [5] for formal details.

Based on protocols Π_{VSS} and Π_{Rec}, we design a secure verifiable multicast protocol Π_{SVM}, which allows a designed *sender* Sen $\in \mathcal{P}$ to verifiably and securely send its input $v \in \mathbb{F}$ to a designated set of *receivers* $\mathcal{R}$. The idea behind Π_{SVM} is very simple. The parties participate in an instance of Π_{VSS}, where Sen plays the role of the *dealer* with input v. Once any (honest) party computes an output during Π_{VSS} (implying that Sen is committed to some value $v^\star$ which is the same as v for an *honest* Sen), then it turns flag$^{(\mathsf{Sen}, \mathcal{R})}$ to 1. Once flag$^{(\mathsf{Sen}, \mathcal{R})}$ is turned to 1, the parties invoke an instance of Π_{Rec} to let *only* the parties in $\mathcal{R}$ reconstruct the committed value. We refer to [5] for the details.

6   Network Agnostic Protocol for Generating Linearly Secret-Shared Random Values with IC-Signatures

In this section, we present a network agnostic protocol Π_{Rand}, which allows the parties to jointly generate linear secret-sharing of random values with IC-signatures. To design the protocol Π_{Rand}, we first design a subprotocol Π_{MDVSS}.

6.1 Network Agnostic VSS for Multiple Dealers

Protocol Π_{MDVSS} (Fig. 3) is a multi-dealer VSS. In the protocol, each party $P_\ell \in \mathcal{P}$ participates as a dealer with some input $s^{(\ell)}$. Then, *irrespective* of the network type, the protocol outputs a *common* subset of dealers CORE $\subseteq \mathcal{P}$, which is *guaranteed* to have at least one *honest* dealer. Moreover, corresponding to every dealer $P_\ell \in$ CORE, there will be some value, say $s^{\star(\ell)}$, which will be the same as $s^{(\ell)}$ for an *honest* P_ℓ, such that the values $\{s^{\star(\ell)}\}_{P_\ell \in \text{CORE}}$ are linearly secret-shared with IC-signatures. While in a *synchronous* network, $\{[s^{\star(\ell)}]\}_{P_\ell \in \text{CORE}}$ is generated after a "fixed" time, in an *asynchronous* network, $\{[s^{\star(\ell)}]\}_{P_\ell \in \text{CORE}}$ is generated eventually. The high level overview of Π_{MDVSS} has been already discussed in detail in Sect. 1.2.5.[1] The proof of Theorem 4 is available in [5].

Theorem 4. *Protocol Π_{MDVSS} achieves the following where each P_ℓ participates with input $s^{(\ell)}$ and where $T_{\text{MDVSS}} = T_{\text{SVM}} + T_{\text{Auth}} + 2T_{\text{BC}} + 6T_{\text{BA}}$.*

- $\mathcal{Z}_s$**-Correctness & Commitment:** *If the network is synchronous, then except with probability $\mathcal{O}(n^3 \cdot \epsilon_{\text{ICP}})$, at time T_{MDVSS}, all honest parties output a common set* CORE $\subseteq \mathcal{P}$ *such that at least one honest party will be present in* CORE. *Moreover, corresponding to every $P_\ell \in$ CORE, there exists some $s^{\star(\ell)}$, where $s^{\star(\ell)} = s^{(\ell)}$ for an honest P_ℓ, such that the values $\{s^{\star(\ell)}\}_{P_\ell \in \text{CORE}}$ are linearly secret-shared with IC-signatures.*
- $\mathcal{Z}_a$**-Correctness & Commitment:** *If the network is asynchronous, then except with probability $\mathcal{O}(n^3 \cdot \epsilon_{\text{ICP}})$, almost-surely all honest parties output a common set* CORE $\subseteq \mathcal{P}$ *eventually such that at least one honest party will be present in* CORE. *Moreover, corresponding to every $P_\ell \in$ CORE, there exists some $s^{\star(\ell)}$, where $s^{\star(\ell)} = s^{(\ell)}$ for an honest P_ℓ, such that the values $\{s^{\star(\ell)}\}_{P_\ell \in \text{CORE}}$ are eventually linearly secret-shared with IC-signatures.*
- **Privacy:** *Irrespective of the network type, the view of the adversary remains independent of $s^{(\ell)}$, corresponding to every honest $P_\ell \in$ CORE.*
- **Communication Complexity:** $\mathcal{O}(|\mathcal{Z}_s|^2 \cdot n^9 \cdot \log |\mathbb{F}| \cdot |\sigma|)$ *bits are communicated by the honest parties and $\mathcal{O}(|\mathcal{Z}_s| + n)$ instances of Π_{BA} are invoked.*

6.2 Protocol for Generating Secret-Shared Random Values

Protocol Π_{Rand} is presented in Fig. 4. We will refer to the core sets $\mathcal{W}_1, \ldots, \mathcal{W}_{|\mathcal{Z}_s|}$ obtained during Π_{Rand} as *global core-sets* and denote them by $\mathcal{GW}_1, \ldots, \mathcal{GW}_{|\mathcal{Z}_s|}$. From now onwards, all the secret-shared values will be generated with respect to these global core-sets. For the proof of Theorem 5, see [5].

---

[1] Actually, the overview was for Π_{Rand}, but the same idea is also used in Π_{MDVSS}.

Protocol $\Pi_{\mathsf{MDVSS}}(\mathcal{P}, \mathcal{Z}_s, \mathcal{Z}_a, (s^{(1)}, \ldots, s^{(n)}), \mathbb{S}_{\mathcal{Z}_s})$

- **Committing Shares**: Each $P_i \in \mathcal{P}$ executes the following steps.
  - On having input $s^{(i)}$, randomly choose $s_1^{(i)}, \ldots, s_{|\mathcal{Z}_s|}^{(i)}$, such that $s^{(i)} = s_1^{(i)} + \cdots + s_{|\mathcal{Z}_s|}^{(i)}$. Act as Sen and invoke instances $\Pi_{\mathsf{SVM}}(P_i, s_1^{(i)}, S_1), \ldots, \Pi_{\mathsf{SVM}}(P_i, s_{|\mathcal{Z}_s|}^{(i)}, S_{|\mathcal{Z}_s|})$ of Π_{SVM}.
  - Corresponding to every dealer $P_\ell \in \mathcal{P}$, participate in the instances of Π_{SVM}, invoked by P_ℓ as a Sen and wait till the local time becomes T_{SVM}. For $q = 1, \ldots, |\mathcal{Z}_s|$, let $\mathsf{flag}^{(P_\ell, S_q)}$ be the Boolean flag, corresponding to the instance $\Pi_{\mathsf{SVM}}(P_\ell, s_q^{(\ell)}, S_q)$, invoked by P_ℓ.
- **Identifying the Set of Committed Dealers Through ACS**: Each $P_i \in \mathcal{P}$ does the following.
  - For $\ell = 1, \ldots, n$, participate in an instance $\Pi_{\mathsf{BA}}^{(\ell)}$ of Π_{BA} with input 1, provided P_i has set $\mathsf{flag}^{(P_\ell, S_q)} = 1$, for $q = 1, \ldots, |\mathcal{Z}_s|$.
  - Once there exists a subset of dealers $\mathcal{CD}_i$ where $\mathcal{P} \setminus \mathcal{CD}_i \in \mathcal{Z}_s$, such that corresponding to every dealer $P_\ell \in \mathcal{CD}_i$, the instance $\Pi_{\mathsf{BA}}^{(\ell)}$ has produced output 1, then participate with input 0 in all the BA instances $\Pi_{\mathsf{BA}}^{(*)}$, for which no input is provided yet.
  - Once all the n instances of $\Pi_{\mathsf{BA}}^{(*)}$ have produced a binary output, set $\mathcal{CD}$ to be the set of dealers P_ℓ, such that $\Pi_{\mathsf{BA}}^{(\ell)}$ has produced output 1.
- **Exchanging IC-Signed Values**: Each $P_i \in \mathcal{P}$ waits till the local time becomes $T_{\mathsf{SVM}} + 2T_{\mathsf{BA}}$. Then corresponding to each dealer $P_\ell \in \mathcal{CD}$, does the following.
  - For each $S_q \in \mathbb{S}_{\mathcal{Z}_s}$ such that $P_i \in S_q$, upon computing an output $s_{qi}^{(\ell)}$ during $\Pi_{\mathsf{SVM}}(P_\ell, s_q^{(\ell)}, S_q)$, give $\mathsf{ICSig}(P_i, P_j, P_k, s_{qi}^{(\ell)})$ to every $P_j \in S_q$, for every $P_k \in \mathcal{P}$, where the parties follow the linearity principle while generating IC-signatures.
- **Announcing Results of Pairwise Consistency Tests**: Each $P_i \in \mathcal{P}$ waits till the local time becomes $T_{\mathsf{SVM}} + 2T_{\mathsf{BA}} + T_{\mathsf{Auth}}$ and then does the following, corresponding to each dealer $P_\ell \in \mathcal{CD}$.
  - Upon receiving $\mathsf{ICSig}(P_j, P_i, P_k, s_{qj}^{(\ell)})$ from P_j for each $S_q \in \mathbb{S}$ such that $P_j, P_i \in S_q$, corresponding to every $P_k \in \mathcal{P}$, broadcast $\mathsf{OK}^{(\ell)}(i, j)$, if $s_{qi}^{(\ell)} = s_{qj}^{(\ell)}$ holds.

  - Corresponding to every $P_j \in \mathcal{P}$, participate in any instance of Π_{BC} initiated by P_j as a sender, to broadcast any $\mathsf{OK}^{(\ell)}(P_j, \star)$ message.
- **Constructing Consistency Graphs**: Each $P_i \in \mathcal{P}$ waits till the local time becomes $T_{\mathsf{SVM}} + 2T_{\mathsf{BA}} + T_{\mathsf{Auth}} + T_{\mathsf{BC}}$ and then does the following, corresponding to each dealer $P_\ell \in \mathcal{CD}$.
  - Construct an undirected consistency graph $G^{(\ell, i)}$ with $\mathcal{P}$ as the vertex set, where the edge (P_j, P_k) is added to $G^{(\ell, i)}$, provided $\mathsf{OK}^{(\ell)}(j, k)$ and $\mathsf{OK}^{(\ell)}(k, j)$ is received from the broadcast of P_j and P_k respectively.
- **Public Announcement of Core Sets by the Committed Dealers**: Each dealer $P_\ell \in \mathcal{CD}$ waits till its local time is $T_{\mathsf{SVM}} + 2T_{\mathsf{BA}} + T_{\mathsf{Auth}} + T_{\mathsf{BC}}$, and then executes the following steps to compute core sets.
  - $\forall S_p \in \mathbb{S}_{\mathcal{Z}_s}$, once S_p forms a clique in $G^{(\ell, \ell)}$, then for $q = 1, \ldots, |\mathcal{Z}_s|$, compute core-set $\mathcal{W}_{p,q}^{(\ell)}$ and broadcast-set $\mathcal{BS}_p^{(\ell)}$ with respect to S_p as follows, followed by broadcasting $(\mathsf{CanCS}, P_\ell, S_p, \{\mathcal{W}_{p,q}^{(\ell)}\}_{q=1,\ldots,|\mathcal{Z}_s|}, \mathcal{BS}_p^{(\ell)}, \{s_q^{(\ell)}\}_{q \in \mathcal{BS}_p^{(\ell)}})$.
    - If S_q constitutes a clique in the graph $G^{(\ell, \ell)}$, then set $\mathcal{W}_{p,q}^{(\ell)} = S_q$.
    - Else if $(S_p \cap S_q)$ constitutes a clique in $G^{(\ell, \ell)}$ and $\mathcal{Z}_s$ satisfies the $\mathbb{Q}^{(1)}(S_p \cap S_q, \mathcal{Z}_s)$ condition, then set $\mathcal{W}_{p,q}^{(\ell)} = (S_p \cap S_q)$.
    - Else set $\mathcal{W}_{p,q}^{(\ell)} = S_q$ and include q to $\mathcal{BS}_p^{(\ell)}$.

Fig. 3. The statistically-secure VSS protocol for multiple dealers to generate linearly secret-shared values with IC-signatures

- **Identifying Valid Core Sets**: Each $P_i \in \mathcal{P}$ waits for time $T_{\mathsf{SVM}} + 2T_{\mathsf{BA}} + T_{\mathsf{Auth}} + 2T_{\mathsf{BC}}$ and then initializes a set $\mathcal{C}_i = \emptyset$. Corresponding to $P_\ell \in \mathcal{CD}$ and $p = 1, \ldots, |\mathcal{Z}_s|$, party P_i includes (P_ℓ, S_p) to $\mathcal{C}_i$, provided *all* the following hold.
  - $(\mathsf{CanCS}, P_\ell, S_p, \{\mathcal{W}_{p,q}^{(\ell)}\}_{q=1,\ldots,|\mathcal{Z}_s|}, \mathcal{BS}_p^{(\ell)}, \{s_q^{(\ell)}\}_{q \in BS_p^{(\ell)}})$ is received from the broadcast of P_ℓ, such that for $q = 1, \ldots, |\mathcal{Z}_s|$, the following hold.
    - If $q \in \mathcal{BS}_p^{(\ell)}$, then the set $\mathcal{W}_{p,q}^{(\ell)} = S_q$.
    - If $(q \notin \mathcal{BS}_p^{(\ell)})$, then $\mathcal{W}_{p,q}^{(\ell)}$ is either S_q or $(S_p \cap S_q)$, such that:
      - If $\mathcal{W}_{p,q}^{(\ell)} = S_q$, then S_q constitutes a clique in $G^{(\ell,i)}$.
      - Else if $\mathcal{W}_{p,q}^{(\ell)} = (S_p \cap S_q)$, then $(S_p \cap S_q)$ constitutes a clique in $G^{(\ell,i)}$ and $\mathcal{Z}_s$ satisfies the $\mathbb{Q}^{(1)}(S_p \cap S_q, \mathcal{Z}_s)$ condition.
- **Selecting the Common Committed Dealers and Core Sets through ACS**: Each party $P_i \in \mathcal{P}$ does the following.
  - For $p = 1, \ldots, |\mathcal{Z}_s|$, participate in an instance $\Pi_{\mathsf{BA}}^{(1,p)}$ of Π_{BA} with input 1, provided there exists a set of dealers $\mathcal{A}_{p,i} \subseteq \mathcal{CD}$ where $\mathcal{CD} \setminus \mathcal{A}_{p,i} \in \mathcal{Z}_s$ and where $(P_\ell, S_p) \in \mathcal{C}_i$ for every $P_\ell \in \mathcal{A}_{p,i}$.
  - Once any instance of $\Pi_{\mathsf{BA}}^{(1,\star)}$ has produced an output 1, participate with input 0 in all the BA instances $\Pi_{\mathsf{BA}}^{(1,\star)}$, for which no input is provided yet.
  - Once all the $|\mathcal{Z}_s|$ instances of $\Pi_{\mathsf{BA}}^{(1,\star)}$ have produced a binary output, set q_{core} to be the least index among $\{1, \ldots, |\mathcal{Z}_s|\}$, such that $\Pi_{\mathsf{BA}}^{(1,q_{\mathsf{core}})}$ has produced output 1.
  - Once q_{core} is computed, then corresponding to each $P_j \in \mathcal{CD}$, participate in an instance $\Pi_{\mathsf{BA}}^{(2,j)}$ of Π_{BA} with input 1, provided $(P_j, S_{q_{\mathsf{core}}}) \in \mathcal{C}_i$.
  - Once there exists a set of parties $\mathcal{B}_i \subseteq \mathcal{CD}$, such that $\mathcal{CD} \setminus \mathcal{B}_i \in \mathcal{Z}_s$ and $\Pi_{\mathsf{BA}}^{(2,j)}$ has produced output 1, corresponding to each $P_j \in \mathcal{B}_i$, participate with input 0 in all the instances of $\Pi_{\mathsf{BA}}^{(2,\star)}$, for which no input is provided yet.
  - Once all the $|\mathcal{CD}|$ instances of $\Pi_{\mathsf{BA}}^{(2,\star)}$ have produced a binary output, include all the parties P_j from $\mathcal{CD}$ in CORE (initialized to $\emptyset$), such that $\Pi_{\mathsf{BA}}^{(2,j)}$ has produced output 1.
- **Computing Output**: Each $P_i \in \mathcal{P}$ does the following, after computing CORE and q_{core}.
  - If $(\mathsf{CanCS}, P_\ell, S_{q_{\mathsf{core}}}, \{\mathcal{W}_{q_{\mathsf{core}},q}^{(\ell)}\}_{q=1,\ldots,|\mathcal{Z}_s|}, \mathcal{BS}_{q_{\mathsf{core}}}^{(\ell)}, \{s_q^{(\ell)}\}_{q \in BS_{q_{\mathsf{core}}}^{(j)}})$ is not yet received from the broadcast of P_ℓ for for any $P_\ell \in \mathsf{CORE}$, then wait to receive it from the broadcast of P_ℓ through fallback-mode.
  - Once $(\mathsf{CanCS}, P_\ell, S_{q_{\mathsf{core}}}, \{\mathcal{W}_{q_{\mathsf{core}},q}^{(\ell)}\}_{q=1,\ldots,|\mathcal{Z}_s|}, \mathcal{BS}_{q_{\mathsf{core}}}^{(\ell)}, \{s_q^{(\ell)}\}_{q \in BS_{q_{\mathsf{core}}}^{(j)}})$ is available for every $P_\ell \in \mathsf{CORE}$, compute $\mathcal{W}_q$ for $q = 1, \ldots, |\mathcal{Z}_s|$ as follows.
    - If $\mathcal{W}_{q_{\mathsf{core}},q}^{(\ell)} = S_q$ for every $P_\ell \in \mathsf{CORE}$, then set $\mathcal{W}_q = S_q$.
    - Else set $\mathcal{W}_q = (S_{q_{\mathsf{core}}} \cap S_q)$.
  - Corresponding to every $P_\ell \in \mathsf{CORE}$ and every $S_q \in \mathbb{S}_{\mathcal{Z}_s}$ such that $P_i \in S_q$, compute the output as follows.
    - If $q \in \mathcal{BS}_{q_{\mathsf{core}}}^{(\ell)}$, then set $[s^{(\ell)}]_q = s_q^{(\ell)}$, where $s_q^{(\ell)}$ was received from the broadcast of P_ℓ, as part of $(\mathsf{CanCS}, P_\ell, S_{q_{\mathsf{core}}}, \{\mathcal{W}_{q_{\mathsf{core}},q}^{(\ell)}\}_{q=1,\ldots,|\mathcal{Z}_s|}, \mathcal{BS}_{q_{\mathsf{core}}}^{(\ell)}, \{s_q^{(\ell)}\}_{q \in BS_{q_{\mathsf{core}}}^{(j)}})$. Moreover, for every $P_j \in \mathcal{W}_q$ and every $P_k \in \mathcal{P}$, set $\mathsf{ICSig}(P_j, P_i, P_k, [s^{(\ell)}]_q)$ to the default value.
    - Else, set $[s^{(\ell)}]_q$ to $s_{qi}^{(\ell)}$, where $s_{qi}^{(\ell)}$ was computed as output during $\Pi_{\mathsf{SVM}}(P_\ell, s_q^{(\ell)}, S_q)$. Moreover, if $P_i \in \mathcal{W}_q$, then for every $P_j \in \mathcal{W}_q$ and every $P_k \in \mathcal{P}$, set $\mathsf{ICSig}(P_j, P_i, P_k, [s^{(\ell)}]_q)$ to $\mathsf{ICSig}(P_j, P_i, P_k, s_{qj}^{(\ell)})$, received from P_j.

  Output CORE, the core sets $\mathcal{W}_1, \ldots, \mathcal{W}_{|\mathcal{Z}_s|}$, shares $\{[s^{(\ell)}]_q\}_{P_\ell \in \mathsf{CORE} \wedge P_i \in S_q}$ and the IC-signatures $\mathsf{ICSig}(P_j, P_i, P_k, [s^{(\ell)}]_q)_{P_\ell \in \mathsf{CORE} \wedge P_j, P_i \in \mathcal{W}_q, P_k \in \mathcal{P}}$.

Fig. 3. (*continued*)

Protocol $\Pi_{\text{Rand}}(\mathcal{P}, \mathcal{Z}_s, \mathcal{Z}_a, \mathbb{S}_{\mathcal{Z}_s}, L)$

- **Secret-Sharing Random Values**: Each $P_\ell \in \mathcal{P}$ picks L random values $\overrightarrow{R^{(\ell)}} = (r^{(\ell,1)}, \dots, r^{(\ell,L)})$ and participates in an instance of Π_{MDVSS} with input $\overrightarrow{R^{(\ell)}}$ and waits for time T_{MDVSS}.
- **Computing Output**: Let $(\text{CORE}, \mathcal{W}_1, \dots, \mathcal{W}_{|\mathcal{Z}_s|}, \{([r^{\star(\ell,1)}], \dots, [r^{\star(\ell,L)}])\}_{P_\ell \in \text{CORE}})$ be the output from the instance of Π_{MDVSS}. For $\mathsf{I} = 1, \dots, L$, the parties locally compute $[r^{(\mathsf{I})}] = \displaystyle\sum_{P_\ell \in \text{CORE}} [r^{\star(\ell,\mathsf{I})}]$ from $\{[r^{\star(\ell,\mathsf{I})}]\}_{P_\ell \in \text{CORE}}$. The parties then output $(\mathcal{GW}_1, \dots, \mathcal{GW}_{|\mathcal{Z}_s|}, \{[r^{(\mathsf{I})}]\}_{\mathsf{I}=1,\dots,L})$, where $\mathcal{GW}_q = \mathcal{W}_q$ for $q = 1, \dots, |\mathcal{Z}_s|$.

Fig. 4. Protocol for generating linearly secret-shared random values with IC-signatures

Theorem 5. *Protocol* Π_{Rand} *achieves the following where* $T_{\text{Rand}} = T_{\text{MDVSS}} = T_{\text{SVM}} + T_{\text{Auth}} + 2T_{\text{BC}} + 6T_{\text{BA}}$ *and* $L \geq 1$.

- $\mathcal{Z}_s$-*correctness*: *If the network is synchronous, then except with probability* $\mathcal{O}(n^3 \cdot \epsilon_{\text{ICP}})$, *at the time* T_{Rand}, *there exist values* $r^{(1)}, \dots, r^{(L)}$, *which are linearly secret-shared with IC-signatures, where the core-sets are* $\mathcal{GW}_1, \dots, \mathcal{GW}_{|\mathcal{Z}_s|}$.
- $\mathcal{Z}_a$-*correctness*: *If the network is asynchronous, then except with probability* $\mathcal{O}(n^3 \cdot \epsilon_{\text{ICP}})$, *there exist values* $r^{(1)}, \dots, r^{(L)}$, *which are almost-surely linearly secret-shared with IC-signatures, where the core-sets are* $\mathcal{GW}_1, \dots, \mathcal{GW}_{|\mathcal{Z}_s|}$.
- **Privacy**: *Irrespective of the network type, the view of the adversary remains independent of* $r^{(1)}, \dots, r^{(L)}$.
- **Communication Complexity**: *The protocol incurs a communication of* $\mathcal{O}(|\mathcal{Z}_s|^2 \cdot L \cdot n^9 \cdot \log |\mathbb{F}| \cdot |\sigma|)$ *bits, apart from* $\mathcal{O}(|\mathcal{Z}_s| + n)$ *instances of* Π_{BA}.

7 Network Agnostic Protocol for Triple Generation

In this section, we present our network-agnostic triple-generation protocol, which generates random and private multiplication-triples which are linearly secret-shared with IC-signatures. The protocol is based on several sub-protocols which we present next. Throughout this section, we will assume the existence of *global* core-sets $\mathcal{GW}_1, \dots, \mathcal{GW}_{|\mathcal{Z}_s|}$, where $\mathcal{Z}_s$ satisfies the $\mathbb{Q}^{(1)}(\mathcal{GW}_q, \mathcal{Z}_s)$ condition for $q = 1, \dots, |\mathcal{Z}_s|$. Looking ahead, these core-sets will be generated by first running the protocol Π_{Rand}, using an appropriate value of L, which is determined across all the sub-protocols which we will be discussing next. All the secret-shared values in the various sub-protocols have $\mathcal{GW}_1, \dots, \mathcal{GW}_{|\mathcal{Z}_s|}$ as core-sets.

7.1 Generating Linear Secret Sharing of a Value with IC-Signatures

In protocol Π_{LSh}, there exists a designated dealer $\mathsf{D} \in \mathcal{P}$ with private input s. In addition, there is a random value $r \in \mathbb{F}$, which is linearly secret-shared with IC-signatures, such that the underlying core-sets are $\mathcal{GW}_1, \ldots, \mathcal{GW}_{|\mathcal{Z}_s|}$ (the value r will *not* be known to D at the beginning of the protocol). The protocol allows the parties to let D verifiably generate a linear secret-sharing of s with IC-signatures, such that the underlying core-sets are $\mathcal{GW}_1, \ldots, \mathcal{GW}_{|\mathcal{Z}_s|}$, where s remains private for an *honest* D. The protocol idea is very simple. We first let D reconstruct the value r, which is then used as a *one-time pad* (OTP) by D to make public an OTP-encryption of s. Then, using the linearity property of secret-sharing, the parties locally remove the OTP from the OTP-encryption; see [5] for the details.

We will say that "P_i *invokes an instance of* Π_{LSh} *with input* s" to mean that P_i acts as D and invokes an instance $\Pi_{\mathsf{LSh}}(\mathsf{D}, s, \mathcal{Z}_s, \mathcal{Z}_a, \mathbb{S}_{\mathcal{Z}_s}, [r], \mathcal{GW}_1, \ldots, \mathcal{GW}_{|\mathcal{Z}_s|})$ of Π_{LSh}. Here, r will be the corresponding random "pad" for this instance of Π_{LSh}, which will *already* be linearly secret-shared with IC-signatures, with $\mathcal{GW}_1, \ldots, \mathcal{GW}_{|\mathcal{Z}_s|}$ being the underlying core-sets.

7.2 Non-robust Multiplication Protocol

Protocol $\Pi_{\mathsf{BasicMult}}$ (Fig. 5) takes input a and b, which are linearly secret-shared with IC-signatures, with $\mathcal{GW}_1, \ldots, \mathcal{GW}_{|\mathcal{Z}_s|}$ being the underlying core-sets and a *publicly known* subset $\mathcal{GD} \subset \mathcal{P}$, consisting of *only corrupt* parties. The parties output a linear secret-sharing of c with IC-signatures, with $\mathcal{GW}_1, \ldots, \mathcal{GW}_{|\mathcal{Z}_s|}$ being the underlying core-sets. If all the parties in $\mathcal{P} \setminus \mathcal{GD}$ behave *honestly*, then $c = a \cdot b$, else $c = a \cdot b + \delta$, where $\delta \neq 0$. Moreover, the adversary does not learn anything additional about a and b in the protocol. The protocol also takes input an *iteration number* iter and all the sets computed in the protocol are tagged with iter. Looking ahead, our *robust* triple-generation protocol will be executed *iteratively*, with each iteration invoking instances of $\Pi_{\mathsf{BasicMult}}$.

The properties of the protocol $\Pi_{\mathsf{BasicMult}}$ are formally proved in [5].

Protocol $\Pi_{\mathsf{BasicMult}}(\mathcal{Z}_s, \mathcal{Z}_a, \mathbb{S}_{\mathcal{Z}_s}, [a], [b], \mathcal{GW}_1, \ldots, \mathcal{GW}_{|\mathcal{Z}_s|}, \mathcal{GD}, \mathsf{iter})$

- **Initialization:** The parties in $\mathcal{P}$ do the following.
  - Initialize the *summand-index-set* of indices of *all* summands:
  $$\mathsf{SIS}_{\mathsf{iter}} = \{(p, q)\}_{p,q=1,\ldots,|\mathbb{S}_{\mathcal{Z}_s}|}.$$
  - Initialize the *summand-index-set* corresponding to each $P_j \in \mathcal{P} \setminus \mathcal{GD}$:
  $$\mathsf{SIS}_{\mathsf{iter}}^{(j)} = \{(p, q)\}_{P_j \in S_p \cap S_q}.$$
  - Initialize the *summand-index-set* corresponding to each $S_q \in \mathbb{S}_{\mathcal{Z}_s}$:
  $$\mathsf{SIS}_{\mathsf{iter}}^{(S_q)} = \cup_{P_j \in S_q} \mathsf{SIS}_{\mathsf{iter}}^{(j)}.$$
  - Initialize the set of summands-sharing parties:
  $$\mathsf{Selected}_{\mathsf{iter}} = \emptyset.$$
  - Initialize the hop number:
  $$\mathsf{hop} = 1.$$

  Phase I: Sharing Summands Through Dynamic Assignment

- While there exists *no* $S_q \in \mathbb{S}_{\mathcal{Z}_s}$, where $\mathsf{SIS}_{\mathsf{iter}}^{(S_q)} = \emptyset$, the parties do the following:
  - **Sharing Sum of Eligible Summands:** Every $P_i \notin (\mathsf{Selected}_{\mathsf{iter}} \cup \mathcal{GD})$ invokes an instance $\Pi_{\mathsf{LSh}}^{(\mathsf{phl,hop},i)}$ of Π_{LSh} with input $c_{\mathsf{iter}}^{(i)}$, where $c_{\mathsf{iter}}^{(i)} = \sum_{(p,q) \in \mathsf{SIS}_{\mathsf{iter}}^{(i)}} [a]_p [b]_q$.

    Corresponding to every $P_j \notin (\mathsf{Selected}_{\mathsf{iter}} \cup \mathcal{GD})$, the parties in $\mathcal{P}$ participate in the instance $\Pi_{\mathsf{LSh}}^{(\mathsf{phl,hop},j)}$, if invoked by P_j.
  - **Selecting Summand-Sharing Party for the Hop Through ACS:** The parties in $\mathcal{P}$ wait for time T_{LSh} and then do the following.
    - For $j = 1, \ldots, n$, participate in an instance $\Pi_{\mathsf{BA}}^{(\mathsf{phl,hop},j)}$ of Π_{BA} corresponding to $P_j \in \mathcal{P}$ with input 1 if *all* the following holds:
      - $P_j \notin (\mathsf{Selected}_{\mathsf{iter}} \cup \mathcal{GD})$;
      - An output $[c_{\mathsf{iter}}^{(j)}]$ is computed during the instance $\Pi_{\mathsf{LSh}}^{(\mathsf{phl,hop},j)}$.
    - Upon computing an output 1 during the instance $\Pi_{\mathsf{BA}}^{(\mathsf{phl,hop},j)}$ corresponding to some $P_j \in \mathcal{P}$, participate with input 0 in the instances $\Pi_{\mathsf{BA}}^{(\mathsf{phl,hop},k)}$ corresponding to parties $P_k \notin (\mathsf{Selected}_{\mathsf{iter}} \cup \mathcal{GD})$, for which no input has been provided yet.
    - Upon computing outputs during the instances $\Pi_{\mathsf{BA}}^{(\mathsf{phl,hop},i)}$ corresponding to each $P_i \notin (\mathsf{Selected}_{\mathsf{iter}} \cup \mathcal{GD})$, let P_j be the least-indexed party, such that the output 1 is computed during the instance $\Pi_{\mathsf{BA}}^{(\mathsf{phl,hop},j)}$. Then update the following.
      - $\mathsf{Selected}_{\mathsf{iter}} = \mathsf{Selected}_{\mathsf{iter}} \cup \{P_j\}$.
      - $\mathsf{SIS}_{\mathsf{iter}} = \mathsf{SIS}_{\mathsf{iter}} \setminus \mathsf{SIS}_{\mathsf{iter}}^{(j)}$.
      - $\forall P_k \in \mathcal{P} \setminus \{\mathcal{GD} \cup \mathsf{Selected}_{\mathsf{iter}}\}$: $\mathsf{SIS}_{\mathsf{iter}}^{(k)} = \mathsf{SIS}_{\mathsf{iter}}^{(k)} \setminus \mathsf{SIS}_{\mathsf{iter}}^{(j)}$.
      - For each $S_q \in \mathbb{S}_{\mathcal{Z}_s}$, $\mathsf{SIS}_{\mathsf{iter}}^{(S_q)} = \mathsf{SIS}_{\mathsf{iter}}^{(S_q)} \setminus \mathsf{SIS}_{\mathsf{iter}}^{(j)}$.
      - Set $\mathsf{hop} = \mathsf{hop} + 1$.

Fig. 5. Network-agnostic non-robust multiplication protocol

Phase II: Sharing Remaining Summands Through Static Assignment

- **Re-assigning the Summand-Index-Set of Each Party**: Corresponding to each $P_j \in \mathcal{P} \setminus \mathsf{Selected}_{\mathsf{iter}}$, the parties in $\mathcal{P}$ set $\mathsf{SIS}_{\mathsf{iter}}^{(j)}$ as

$$\mathsf{SIS}_{\mathsf{iter}}^{(j)} = \mathsf{SIS}_{\mathsf{iter}} \cap \{(p,q)\}_{P_j = \min(S_p \cap S_q)},$$

  where $\min(S_p \cap S_q)$ denotes the minimum indexed party in $(S_p \cap S_q)$.
- **Sharing Sum of Assigned Summands**: Every party $P_i \notin (\mathsf{Selected}_{\mathsf{iter}} \cup \mathcal{GD})$ invokes an instance $\Pi_{\mathsf{LSh}}^{(\mathsf{phII},i)}$ of Π_{LSh} with input $c_{\mathsf{iter}}^{(i)}$, where $c_{\mathsf{iter}}^{(i)} = \displaystyle\sum_{(p,q) \in \mathsf{SIS}_{\mathsf{iter}}^{(i)}} [a]_p [b]_q$.

  Corresponding to every $P_j \in \mathcal{P} \setminus (\mathsf{Selected}_{\mathsf{iter}} \cup \mathcal{GD})$, the parties in $\mathcal{P}$ participate in the instance $\Pi_{\mathsf{LSh}}^{(\mathsf{phII},j)}$, if invoked by P_j.
- **Agreeing on the Summand-Sharing parties of the Second Phase**: The parties in $\mathcal{P}$ wait for T_{LSh} time after the beginning of the second phase. Then for each $P_j \in \mathcal{P}$, participate in an instance $\Pi_{\mathsf{BA}}^{(\mathsf{phII},j)}$ of Π_{BA} with input 1, if *all* the following hold, otherwise participate with input 0.
  - $P_j \notin (\mathsf{Selected}_{\mathsf{iter}} \cup \mathcal{GD})$;
  - An output $[c_{\mathsf{iter}}^{(j)}]$ is computed during the instance $\Pi_{\mathsf{LSh}}^{(\mathsf{phII},j)}$.
- **Updating the Sets for the Second Phase**: Corresponding to each $P_j \notin (\mathsf{Selected}_{\mathsf{iter}} \cup \mathcal{GD})$, such that 1 is computed as the output during $\Pi_{\mathsf{BA}}^{(\mathsf{phII},j)}$, update
  - $\mathsf{SIS}_{\mathsf{iter}} = \mathsf{SIS}_{\mathsf{iter}} \setminus \mathsf{SIS}_{\mathsf{iter}}^{(j)}$;
  - $\mathsf{Selected}_{\mathsf{iter}} = \mathsf{Selected}_{\mathsf{iter}} \cup \{P_j\}$.

Phase III: Reconstructing the Remaining Summands

- **Reconstructing the Remaining Summands and Taking the Default Sharing**: The parties in $\mathcal{P}$ do the following.
  - Corresponding to each $[a]_p$ such that $(p, \star) \in \mathsf{SIS}_{\mathsf{iter}}$, participate in the instance $\Pi_{\mathsf{RecShare}}([a], S_p, \mathcal{P})$ of Π_{RecShare} to publicly reconstruct $[a]_p$
  - Corresponding to each $[b]_q$ such that $(\star, q) \in \mathsf{SIS}_{\mathsf{iter}}$, participate in the instance $\Pi_{\mathsf{RecShare}}([b], S_q, \mathcal{P})$ of Π_{RecShare} to publicly reconstruct $[b]_q$.
  - Corresponding to every $P_j \in \mathcal{P} \setminus \mathsf{Selected}_{\mathsf{iter}}$, take the *default linear secret-sharing* of the public input $c_{\mathsf{iter}}^{(j)}$ with IC-signatures and core-sets $\mathcal{GW}_1, \ldots, \mathcal{GW}_{|\mathcal{Z}_s|}$, where $c_{\mathsf{iter}}^{(j)} = \displaystyle\sum_{(p,q) \in \mathsf{SIS}_{\mathsf{iter}}^{(j)}} [a]_p [b]_q$.

- **Output Computation**: The parties output $(\mathcal{GW}_1, \ldots, \mathcal{GW}_{|\mathcal{Z}_s|}, [c_{\mathsf{iter}}^{(1)}], \ldots, [c_{\mathsf{iter}}^{(n)}],$ $[c_{\mathsf{iter}}])$, where $c_{\mathsf{iter}} \stackrel{def}{=} c_{\mathsf{iter}}^{(1)} + \ldots + c_{\mathsf{iter}}^{(n)}$.

Fig. 5. (*continued*)

7.3   Random Triple Generation with Cheater Identification

The network-agnostic protocol $\Pi_{\mathsf{RandMultCI}}$ takes an iteration number iter and a publicly known subset of parties $\mathcal{GD}$, who are guaranteed to be *corrupt*. If *all* the parties in $\mathcal{P} \setminus \mathcal{GD}$ behave *honestly*, then the protocol outputs a random linearly secret-shared multiplication-triple with IC-signatures, with $\mathcal{GW}_1, \ldots, \mathcal{GW}_{|\mathcal{Z}_s|}$

being the underlying core sets. Otherwise, with a high probability, the honest parties identify a *new corrupt* party, which is added to $\mathcal{GD}$.

Protocol $\Pi_{\mathsf{RandMultCI}}$ is based on [29] and consists of two stages: during the *first* stage, the parties jointly generate a pair of random values, which are linearly secret-shared with IC-signatures, with $\mathcal{GW}_1, \ldots, \mathcal{GW}_{|\mathcal{Z}_s|}$ being the underlying core sets. During the second stage, the parties run an instance of $\Pi_{\mathsf{BasicMult}}$ to compute the product of the pair of secret-shared random values from the first stage. To check whether any cheating has occurred during the instance of $\Pi_{\mathsf{BasicMult}}$, the parties then run a probabilistic test, namely the "sacrificing trick", for which the parties need *additional* secret-shared random values, which are generated during the first stage itself. We refer to [5] for the details.

7.4 The Multiplication-Triple Generation Protocol

The triple generation protocol Π_{TripGen} is based on [29]. The parties iteratively run instances of $\Pi_{\mathsf{RandMultCI}}$, till they hit upon an instance when *no* cheating is detected. Corresponding to each "failed" instance of $\Pi_{\mathsf{RandMultCI}}$, the parties keep updating the set $\mathcal{GD}$. Since after each failed instance the set $\mathcal{GD}$ is updated with one *new* corrupt party, there will be at most $(t+1)$ iterations, where t is the cardinality of the largest-sized subset in $\mathcal{Z}_s$. We refer to [5] for the details.

References

1. Abraham, I., Dolev, D., Stern, G.: Revisiting asynchronous fault tolerant computation with optimal resilience. In: PODC, pp. 139–148. ACM (2020)
2. Appan, A., Chandramouli, A., Choudhury, A.: Perfectly-secure synchronous MPC with asynchronous fallback guarantees. In: PODC, pp. 92–102. ACM (2022)
3. Appan, A., Chandramouli, A., Choudhury, A.: Perfectly secure synchronous MPC with asynchronous fallback guarantees against general adversaries. IACR Cryptology ePrint Archive, p. 1047 (2022)
4. Appan, A., Chandramouli, A., Choudhury, A.: Revisiting the efficiency of asynchronous MPC with optimal resilience against general adversaries. J. Cryptol. **36**(3), 16 (2023)
5. Appan, A., Choudhury, A.: Network agnostic MPC with statistical security. IACR Cryptology ePrint Archive, p. 820 (2023). https://eprint.iacr.org/2023/820
6. Bacho, R., Collins, D., Liu-Zhang, C., Loss, J.: Network-agnostic security comes for free in DKG and MPC. Cryptology ePrint Archive, Paper 2022/1369 (2022)
7. Beaver, D.: Efficient multiparty protocols using circuit randomization. In: Feigenbaum, J. (ed.) CRYPTO 1991. LNCS, vol. 576, pp. 420–432. Springer, Heidelberg (1992). https://doi.org/10.1007/3-540-46766-1_34
8. Ben-Or, M., Canetti, R., Goldreich, O.: Asynchronous secure computation. In: STOC, pp. 52–61. ACM (1993)
9. Ben-Or, M., Goldwasser, S., Wigderson, A.: Completeness theorems for non-cryptographic fault-tolerant distributed computation (extended abstract). In: STOC, pp. 1–10. ACM (1988)
10. Ben-Or, M., Kelmer, B., Rabin, T.: Asynchronous secure computations with optimal resilience (extended abstract). In: PODC, pp. 183–192. ACM (1994)

11. Blum, E., Katz, J., Loss, J.: Synchronous consensus with optimal asynchronous fallback guarantees. In: Hofheinz, D., Rosen, A. (eds.) TCC 2019. LNCS, vol. 11891, pp. 131–150. Springer, Cham (2019). https://doi.org/10.1007/978-3-030-36030-6_6

12. Blum, E., Katz, J., Loss, J.: TARDIGRADE: an atomic broadcast protocol for arbitrary network conditions. In: Tibouchi, M., Wang, H. (eds.) ASIACRYPT 2021. LNCS, vol. 13091, pp. 547–572. Springer, Cham (2021). https://doi.org/10.1007/978-3-030-92075-3_19

13. Blum, E., Liu-Zhang, C.-D., Loss, J.: Always have a backup plan: fully secure synchronous MPC with asynchronous fallback. In: Micciancio, D., Ristenpart, T. (eds.) CRYPTO 2020. LNCS, vol. 12171, pp. 707–731. Springer, Cham (2020). https://doi.org/10.1007/978-3-030-56880-1_25

14. Canetti, R.: Studies in secure multiparty computation and applications. Ph.D. thesis, Weizmann Institute, Israel (1995)

15. Chor, B., Goldwasser, S., Micali, S., Awerbuch, B.: Verifiable secret sharing and achieving simultaneity in the presence of faults (extended abstract). In: FOCS, pp. 383–395. IEEE (1985)

16. Choudhury, A.: Almost-surely terminating asynchronous Byzantine agreement against general adversaries with optimal resilience. In: ICDCN, pp. 167–176. ACM (2023)

17. Cramer, R., Damgård, I., Dziembowski, S., Hirt, M., Rabin, T.: Efficient multiparty computations secure against an adaptive adversary. In: Stern, J. (ed.) EUROCRYPT 1999. LNCS, vol. 1592, pp. 311–326. Springer, Heidelberg (1999). https://doi.org/10.1007/3-540-48910-X_22

18. Deligios, G., Hirt, M., Liu-Zhang, C.-D.: Round-efficient Byzantine agreement and multi-party computation with asynchronous fallback. In: Nissim, K., Waters, B. (eds.) TCC 2021. LNCS, vol. 13042, pp. 623–653. Springer, Cham (2021). https://doi.org/10.1007/978-3-030-90459-3_21

19. Deligios, G., Liu-Zhang, C.: Synchronous perfectly secure message transmission with optimal asynchronous fallback guarantees. IACR Cryptology ePrint Archive, p. 1397 (2022)

20. Dolev, D., Dwork, C., Waarts, O., Yung, M.: Perfectly secure message transmission. J. ACM **40**(1), 17–47 (1993)

21. Dolev, D., Strong, H.R.: Authenticated algorithms for Byzantine agreement. SIAM J. Comput. **12**(4), 656–666 (1983)

22. Fitzi, M.: Generalized communication and security models in Byzantine agreement. Ph.D. thesis, ETH Zurich, Zürich, Switzerland (2003)

23. Fitzi, M., Maurer, U.: Efficient Byzantine agreement secure against general adversaries. In: Kutten, S. (ed.) DISC 1998. LNCS, vol. 1499, pp. 134–148. Springer, Heidelberg (1998). https://doi.org/10.1007/BFb0056479

24. Ghinea, D., Liu-Zhang, C., Wattenhofer, R.: Optimal synchronous approximate agreement with asynchronous fallback. In: PODC, pp. 70–80. ACM (2022)

25. Ghinea, D., Liu-Zhang, C., Wattenhofer, R.: Multidimensional approximate agreement with asynchronous fallback. In: SPAA, pp. 141–151. ACM (2023)

26. Goldreich, O., Micali, S., Wigderson, A.: How to play any mental game or a completeness theorem for protocols with honest majority. In: STOC, pp. 218–229. ACM (1987)

27. Hirt, M., Maurer, U.: Complete characterization of adversaries tolerable in secure multi-party computation. In: PODC, pp. 25–34. ACM (1997)

28. Hirt, M., Maurer, U.: Player simulation and general adversary structures in perfect multiparty computation. J. Cryptol. **13**(1), 31–60 (2000)

29. Hirt, M., Tschudi, D.: Efficient general-adversary multi-party computation. In: Sako, K., Sarkar, P. (eds.) ASIACRYPT 2013. LNCS, vol. 8270, pp. 181–200. Springer, Heidelberg (2013). https://doi.org/10.1007/978-3-642-42045-0_10

30. Ito, M., Saito, A., Nishizeki, T.: Secret sharing schemes realizing general access structures. In: Globecom, pp. 99–102. IEEE Computer Society (1987)

31. Kumar, M.V.N.A., Srinathan, K., Rangan, C.P.: Asynchronous perfectly secure computation tolerating generalized adversaries. In: Batten, L., Seberry, J. (eds.) ACISP 2002. LNCS, vol. 2384, pp. 497–511. Springer, Heidelberg (2002). https://doi.org/10.1007/3-540-45450-0_37

32. Maurer, U.: Secure multi-party computation made simple. In: Cimato, S., Persiano, G., Galdi, C. (eds.) SCN 2002. LNCS, vol. 2576, pp. 14–28. Springer, Heidelberg (2003). https://doi.org/10.1007/3-540-36413-7_2

33. Momose, A., Ren, L.: Multi-threshold Byzantine fault tolerance. In: CCS, pp. 1686–1699. ACM (2021)

34. Pease, M., Shostak, R., Lamport, L.: Reaching agreement in the presence of faults. J. ACM (JACM) **27**(2), 228–234 (1980)

35. Pfitzmann, B., Waidner, M.: Information-theoretic Pseudosignatures and Byzantine agreement for $t \geq n/3$. Technical report RZ 2882 (#90830), IBM Research (1996)

36. Rabin, T., Ben-Or, M.: Verifiable secret sharing and multiparty protocols with honest majority (extended abstract). In: STOC, pp. 73–85. ACM (1989)

37. Yao, A.C.: Protocols for secure computations (extended abstract). In: FOCS, pp. 160–164. IEEE Computer Society (1982)

On Secure Computation of Solitary Output Functionalities with and Without Broadcast

Bar Alon[1,2]([✉]) [iD] and Eran Omri[2] [iD]

[1] Department of Computer Science, Ben Gurion University, Beersheba, Israel
alonbar08@gmail.com
[2] Department of Computer Science, Ariel University, Ariel Cyber Innovation Center (ACIC), Ariel, Israel
omrier@ariel.ac.il

Abstract. Solitary output secure computation models scenarios, where a single entity wishes to compute a function over an input that is distributed among several mutually distrusting parties. The computation should guarantee some security properties, such as correctness, privacy, and guaranteed output delivery. Full security captures all these properties together. This setting is becoming very important, as it is relevant to many real-world scenarios, such as service providers wishing to learn some statistics on the private data of their users.

In this paper, we study full security for solitary output three-party functionalities in the point-to-point model (without broadcast) assuming at most a single party is corrupted. We give a characterization of the set of three-party Boolean functionalities and functionalities with up to three possible outputs (over a polynomial-size domain) that are computable with full security in the point-to-point model against a single corrupted party. We also characterize the set of three-party functionalities (over a polynomial-size domain) where the output receiving party has no input. Using this characterization, we identify the set of parameters that allow certain functionalities related to private set intersection to be securely computable in this model. Our characterization in particular implies that, even in the solitary output setting, without broadcast not many "interesting" three-party functionalities can be computed with full security.

Our main technical contribution is a reinterpretation of the hexagon argument due to Fischer et al. [Distributed Computing '86]. While the original argument relies on the agreement property (i.e., all parties output the same value) to construct an attack, we extend the argument to the solitary output setting, where there is no agreement. Furthermore, using our techniques, we were also able to advance our understanding of the set of solitary output three-party functionalities that can be computed with full security, assuming broadcast but where two parties may be corrupted. Specifically, we extend the set of such functionalities that were known to be computable, due to Halevi et al. [TCC '19].

© International Association for Cryptologic Research 2023
G. Rothblum and H. Wee (Eds.): TCC 2023, LNCS 14370, pp. 94–123, 2023.
https://doi.org/10.1007/978-3-031-48618-0_4

Keywords: broadcast · point-to-point communication · secure multiparty computation · solitary output · impossibility result

1   Introduction

Solitary output secure computation [24] allows a single entity to compute a function over an input that is distributed among several parties, while guaranteeing security. The two most basic security properties are correctness and privacy. However, in many scenarios, participating parties may also desire the output receiving party to always receive an output (also known as *guaranteed output delivery* or *full security*).[1] Examples include service providers that want to perform some analysis over their client's data, federal regulatory agencies wishing to detect fraudulent users/transactions among banks, researchers looking to collect statistics from users, or a government security agency wishing to detect widespread intrusions on different high-value state agencies. In cryptography, solitary output functionalities have been considered in privacy-preserving federated learning [9,11,12], and in designing minimal communication protocols via Private Simultaneous Messages Protocols [18] and its robust variant [1,8].

Understanding solitary output computations is also of great theoretical value, as it serves as an important and non-trivial special case of secure multiparty computation (MPC). Indeed, [24] initiated the investigation of solitary output computations as a step towards better understanding full security in the general MPC setting. In the late 1980's, it was shown that every function (even non-solitary output) can be computed with full security in the presence of malicious adversaries assuming that a strict minority of the parties are corrupted, and assuming the existence of a *broadcast communication channel* (such a channel allows any party to reliably send the same message to all other parties) and pairwise private channels (which can be established over broadcast using standard cryptographic techniques) [10,21,28].

Conversely, it has been shown that if either a broadcast channel or an honest majority is not assumed, then fully-secure MPC is not possible in general. In the no honest majority setting, most impossibility results, starting with the seminal work of Cleve [13], rely on the impossibility of achieving fairness (requiring that either all parties receive the output or none do) [5,26]. In the no-broadcast setting, most impossibility results rely on the impossibility of achieving agreement (requiring that all parties agree on the same output) [19].

Interestingly, both fairness and agreement are not required in solitary output computations, and thus, cannot be used for proving impossibility results for this setting. Nevertheless, using techniques from the fairness literature (although not using fairness per se) Halevi et al. [24] presented a class of solitary output functionalities that cannot be computed with full security assuming the majority of the parties are corrupted (even assuming a broadcast channel). On the other

---

[1] Formally, full security is defined via the real vs. ideal paradigm, where a (real-world) protocol is required to emulate an ideal setting, in which the adversary is limited to selecting inputs for the corrupted parties and receiving their outputs.

hand, [3,20] presented several examples of three-party solitary output functionalities that cannot be securely computed without a broadcast channel, even when only a single party may be corrupted. Interestingly, the impossibility results of [3] were based on techniques that originally relied on agreement, again, without assuming agreement. However, beside these handful of examples, no general class of solitary output functions was identified to be impossible for fully secure computation without broadcast. This raises the question of identifying the set of functions that can be computed with full security assuming either the availability of a broadcast channel but no honest majority, or vice versa.

In this paper, we investigate the above question for the important, yet already challenging, three-party case. Thus, we aim to study the following question:

Characterize the set of solitary output three-party functionalities that can be computed with full security, assuming either a broadcast channel and two corrupted parties, or assuming no broadcast channel and a single corrupted party.

1.1 Our Contributions

Our main technical contribution is a reinterpretation of the *hexagon argument* due to Fischer et al. [19]. This argument (and its generalization, known as the *ring argument* [15]) uses the agreement property (i.e., that all parties obtain the same output) in order to derive an attack on a given three-party protocol, assuming there is *no* broadcast channel available. As mentioned above, since we consider solitary output functionalities, where only one party receives the output, we cannot rely on agreement. Thus, we cannot use this technique in a straightforward manner. Instead, we derive an attack by leveraging the correlation in the views between the parties.

A Characterization of Interesting Families of Function. Given this new interpretation, we are able to identify a large class of three-party solitary output functionalities that cannot be computed without a broadcast channel. Furthermore, we complement this negative result by showing a non-trivial class of solitary output functionalities that can be computed in this setting. Interestingly, for several important classes of functionalities, our results provide a complete characterization of which solitary output three-party functionality can be computed with full security. Examples include Boolean and even ternary-output functionalities over a domain of polynomial size.

We next describe our positive and negative results, starting with the model where a broadcast channel is not available and only a single party may be corrupted. We consider three-party solitary output functionalities $f : \mathcal{X} \times \mathcal{Y} \times \mathcal{Z} \to \mathcal{W}$, where the first party A holds an input $x \in \mathcal{X}$, the second party B holds an input $y \in \mathcal{Y}$, and the third party C holds an input $z \in \mathcal{Z}$. We let the output receiving party be A. To simplify the presentation, we will limit the following discussion to two families of functionalities, for which our results admit a characterization (a formal statement of the results for a more general class of functionalities appears in Sect. 3). Though this discussion is limited compared to the rest of the paper, all of our techniques and ideas are already present.

The first family we characterize is that of *no-input output-receiving party* (NIORP) functionalities, where the output-receiving party A has no input. We further showcase the usefulness of the result by characterizing which parameters allow for secure computation of various functionalities related to private set intersection. The second family we characterize is the set of ternary-output functionalities, where the output of A is one of three values (with A possibly holding an input). In particular, this yields a characterization of Boolean functionalities. Below are the informal statements of the characterizations for *deterministic* functionalities. We handle randomized functionalities by a reduction to the deterministic case (see Proposition 1 below).

Functionalities with No Input for the Output-receiving Party (NIORP). Before stating the theorem, we define a special partitioning of the inputs of B and C. The partition is derived from an equivalence relation, which we call *common output relation* (CORE), hence, we call the partition the *CORE partition*. To obtain some intuition for the definition, consider the matrix M associated with a NIORP functionality f, defined as $M(y, z) = f(y, z)$ for all $y \in \mathcal{Y}$ and $z \in \mathcal{Z}$.[2]

Before defining the equivalence relation, consider the following relation $\sim$. We say that two inputs $y, y' \in \mathcal{Y}$ satisfy $y \sim y'$ if the rows $M(y, \cdot)$ and $M(y', \cdot)$ contain a common output. Note that this relation is not transitive. The equivalence relation we define is the transitive closure of $\sim$, i.e., y and y' are equivalent if there exists a sequence of inputs starting at y and ending at y' such that every consecutive pair satisfy $\sim$. Formally, we define the relation as follows.

Definition 1 (CORE partition). *Let $f : \{\lambda\} \times \mathcal{Y} \times \mathcal{Z} \to \mathcal{W}$ be a deterministic solitary output three-party NIORP functionality. For inputs $y, y' \in \mathcal{Y}$, we say that $y \sim y'$ if and only if there exist (possibly equal) $z, z' \in \mathcal{Z}$ such that $f(y, z) = f(y', z')$. We define the equivalence relation $\equiv_{\text{rel}}$ to be the transitive closure of $\sim$. That is, $y \equiv_{\text{rel}} y'$ if and only if either $y \sim y'$ or there exist a sequence of inputs $y_1, \ldots, y_k \in \mathcal{Y}$ such that*

$$y \sim y_1 \sim \ldots \sim y_k \sim y'.$$

We partition the set of inputs $\mathcal{Y}$ according to the equivalence classes of $\equiv_{\text{rel}}$, and we write the partition as $\mathcal{Y} = \{\mathcal{Y}_i : i \in [n]\}$. We partition $\mathcal{Z}$ into disjoint sets $\mathcal{Z} = \{\mathcal{Z}_j : j \in [m]\}$ similarly. We also abuse notation and use the relations $\sim$ and $\equiv_{\text{rel}}$ over $\mathcal{Z}$ as well. We refer to these partitions as the CORE partitions of $\mathcal{Y}$ and $\mathcal{Z}$, respectively, with respect to f. When $\mathcal{Y}$, $\mathcal{Z}$, and f are clear from context, we will simply refer to the partitions as CORE partitions.

Observe that given a function f, finding its CORE partition can be done in time that is polynomial in the domain size. As an example, consider the following NIORP solitary output three-party functionality whose associated matrix is

---

[2] We abuse notations and write $f(y, z)$ instead of $f(\lambda, y, z)$ where λ is the empty string (which is the input of A).

given by $\left(\begin{smallmatrix} 0 & 1 & 2 \\ 1 & 3 & 4 \\ 3 & 4 & 5 \end{smallmatrix}\right)$. Here, the CORE partitions of both the rows and the columns result in the trivial partition, i.e., all rows are equivalent and all columns are equivalent. To see this, note that both the first and second rows contain the output 1. Therefore they satisfy the relation $\sim$. Similarly, the second and last row satisfy $\sim$ since 3 (and 4) are a common output. Thus, the first and last rows are equivalent (though they do not satisfy the relation $\sim$). Using a similar reasoning, one can verify that all columns are also equivalent.

We are now ready to state our characterization for NIORP functionalities.

Theorem 1 (Characterization of NIORP functionalities, informal).
Let $f : \{\lambda\} \times \mathcal{Y} \times \mathcal{Z} \to \mathcal{W}$ be a deterministic solitary output three-party NIORP functionality, and let $\mathsf{Y} = \{\mathcal{Y}_i : i \in [n]\}$ and $\mathsf{Z} = \{\mathcal{Z}_j : j \in [m]\}$ be the CORE partitions of $\mathcal{Y}$ and $\mathcal{Z}$, respectively. Then, f can be securely computed against a single corruption in the point-to-point model, if and only if there exist two families of distributions $\{Q_i\}_{i \in [n]}$ and $\{R_j\}_{j \in [m]}$, such that the following holds. For all $i \in [n]$, $j \in [m]$, $y \in \mathcal{Y}_i$, and $z \in \mathcal{Z}_j$, it holds that $f(y^*, z)$ where $y^* \leftarrow Q_i$, and that $f(y, z^*)$ where $z^* \leftarrow R_j$, are computationally indistinguishable.

Stated differently, consider the partition of $\mathcal{Y} \times \mathcal{Z}$ into combinatorial rectangles[3] defined by $\mathcal{R} = \{\mathcal{Y}_i \times \mathcal{Z}_j : i \in [n], j \in [m]\}$, i.e., it is given by all Cartesian products of CORE partitions. Then f can be securely computed if and only if both B and C can each associate a distribution to each set in the partition of their respective set of inputs, such that the output distribution in each combinatorial rectangle in $\mathcal{R}$ looks fixed for any bounded algorithm. That is, if B samples an input $y \leftarrow Q_i$ for some $i \in [n]$, then the only way for C to affect the output of f is by choosing its own equivalence class $\mathcal{Z} \in \mathsf{Z}$, however, choosing a specific input within that class will not change the output distribution.

We briefly describe a few classes of functions that are captured by Theorem 1. Observe that any functionality, where there exists a value $w \in \mathcal{W}$ such that any single party (among B and C) can fix the output of A to be w, regardless of the other party's input, can be securely computed by the above theorem. This includes functionalities such as OR of y and z.[4] In fact, even if there exists a distribution D over $\mathcal{W}$, such that any single party among B and C can fix the output of A to be distributed according to D, can be securely computed. For example, this means that XOR and equality can be securely computed. Theorem 1 essentially refines the latter family of functionalities, by requiring the parties to be able to fix the distributions with respect to the combinatorial rectangles given by the CORE partitions.

In Table 1, we illustrate the usefulness of Theorem 1 by considering various functionalities (which were also considered by [24]) related to private set intersection (PSI), and mark whether each variant can be computed with full

---

[3] A combinatorial rectangle is subset $\mathcal{R} \subseteq \mathcal{Y} \times \mathcal{Z}$ that can be written as $\mathcal{R} = \mathcal{S} \times \mathcal{T}$ where $\mathcal{S} \subseteq \mathcal{Y}$ and $\mathcal{T} \subseteq \mathcal{Z}$.

[4] A similar condition was given by [15] for the symmetric case, where all parties output the same value. There, *every* party must be able to fix the output to be w.

security. Define the NIORP functionality $\mathsf{PSI}_{k_1,k_2,m}^{\ell_1,\ell_2}$ to output to A the intersection of $\mathcal{S}_1$ and $\mathcal{S}_2$, held by B and C, respectively. Here, $\mathcal{S}_i \subseteq \{1,\ldots,m\}$ and $k_i \leq |\mathcal{S}_i| \leq \ell_i$ for every $i \in \{1,2\}$. The variants we consider are those that apply some function g over the output of A, i.e., the functionality the parties compute is $g(\mathsf{PSI}_{k_1,k_2,m}^{\ell_1,\ell_2}(\mathcal{S}_1,\mathcal{S}_2))$. The proofs for which parameters allow each function to be computed are given in the full version of the paper [2]. It is important to note that the domains of the functionalities are *constant* as otherwise some of the claims are provably false (e.g., [3] implicitly showed that $\mathsf{PSI}_{1,1,\kappa}^{1,1}$, where κ is the security parameter, can be securely computed).

Table 1. Summary of our results stated for various versions of the PSI functionality. Each row in the table above corresponds to a different choice of parameters. Each column corresponds to a different function g applied to the output of A. B holds set $\mathcal{S}_1$ and C hold set $\mathcal{S}_1$. We let $\mathcal{S} = \mathcal{S}_1 \cap \mathcal{S}_2$. The parameters k_1, k_2, ℓ_1, ℓ_2 correspond to bounds on the sizes of $\mathcal{S}_1$ and $\mathcal{S}_2$, and m is the size of the universe from which $\mathcal{S}_1$ and $\mathcal{S}_2$ are taken.

Input restriction\Function g	$g(\mathcal{S}) = \mathcal{S}$	$g(\mathcal{S}) = \|\mathcal{S}\|$	$g(\mathcal{S}) = \begin{cases} 1 & \text{if } \mathcal{S} = \emptyset \\ 0 & \text{otherwise} \end{cases}$
$k_1 = k_2 = 0$, or $\ell_1 = 0$, or $\ell_2 = 0$, or $k_1 = m$, or $k_2 = m$	✓	✓	✓
$k_1 = \ell_1 \notin \{0,m\}$ and $k_2 = \ell_2 \notin \{0,m\}$	✗	✓	✓
$0 < k_1 < \ell_1$, $0 < k_2 < \ell_2$, and $\ell_1 + k_2,\, k_1 + \ell_2 > m$	✗	✗	✓
Any other choice	✗	✗	✗

Ternary-output Functionalities. We next give our characterization for ternary-output functionalities. In this setting, party A also has an input, and its output is a value in $\{0,1,2\}$. We stress that this case is far more involved than the NIORP case, in both the analysis and in the description of the characterization. Nevertheless, we later demonstrate the usefulness of this characterization.

Similarly to the NIORP case, we consider partitions over the inputs of B and C. Here, however, each input $x \in \mathcal{X}$ is associated with a different CORE partition. For the characterization, we are interested in the *meet* of all such partitions. Intuitively, the meet of partitions of a is the partition given by using all partitions together. Formally, for partitions $\mathcal{P}_1,\ldots,\mathcal{P}_n$ over a set $\mathcal{S}$, their meet is defined as the collection of all non-empty intersections, i.e.,

$$\bigwedge_{i=1}^{n} \mathcal{P}_i := \left\{ \mathcal{T} \subseteq \mathcal{S} : \mathcal{T} \neq \emptyset, \exists \mathcal{T}_1 \in \mathcal{P}_1,\ldots,\mathcal{T}_n \in \mathcal{P}_n \text{ s.t. } \mathcal{T} = \bigcap_{i=1}^{n} \mathcal{T}_i \right\}.$$

Before stating the theorem, we formalize the meet of the CORE partitions, which we call $\mathsf{CORE}_\wedge$-partition, for a given solitary output functionality.

Definition 2 (CORE$_\wedge$-partition). *Let $f : \mathcal{X} \times \mathcal{Y} \times \mathcal{Z} \to \{0, 1, 2\}$ be a deterministic solitary output three-party ternary-output functionality. For every $x \in \mathcal{X}$, we can view $f(x, \cdot, \cdot)$ as a NIORP functionality, and consider the same CORE partition as in Definition 1. We denote these partitions by $\mathcal{Y}_x = \{\mathcal{Y}_i^x : i \in [n(x)]\}$ and $\mathcal{Z}_x = \{\mathcal{Z}_j^x : j \in [m(x)]\}$. We define the CORE$_\wedge$-partitions of f as the meet of its CORE partitions, that is, we let $\mathcal{Y}_\wedge = \bigwedge_{x \in \mathcal{X}} \mathcal{Y}_x$ and $\mathcal{Z}_\wedge = \bigwedge_{x \in \mathcal{X}} \mathcal{Z}_x$. We denote their sizes as $n_\wedge = |\mathcal{Y}_\wedge|$ and $m_\wedge = |\mathcal{Z}_\wedge|$, and we write them as $\mathcal{Y}_\wedge = \{\mathcal{Y}_i^\wedge : i \in [n_\wedge]\}$ and $\mathcal{Z}_\wedge = \{\mathcal{Z}_j^\wedge : j \in [m_\wedge]\}$.*

As an example, consider the deterministic variant of the convergecast functionality [20], $\mathsf{CC} : (\{0, 1\})^3 \to \{0, 1\}$ defined as[5]

$$\mathsf{CC}(x, y, z) = \begin{cases} y & \text{if } x = 0 \\ z & \text{otherwise} \end{cases} \tag{1}$$

Equivalently, CC can be defined by the two matrices $M_0 = \left(\begin{smallmatrix} 0 & 0 \\ 1 & 1 \end{smallmatrix}\right)$ and $M_1 = \left(\begin{smallmatrix} 0 & 1 \\ 0 & 1 \end{smallmatrix}\right)$. Here, A chooses a matrix, B chooses a row, and C chooses a column. The output of A is the value written in the chosen entry. Observe that in M_0, the rows are not equivalent while the columns are. In M_1, however, the converse holds, namely, the rows are equivalent while the columns are not. Thus, in the CORE$_\wedge$-partitions of CC any two inputs are in *different* sets.

We are now ready to state our characterization for ternary-output functions.

Theorem 2 (Characterization of ternary-output functionalities, informal). *Let $f : \mathcal{X} \times \mathcal{Y} \times \mathcal{Z} \to \{0, 1, 2\}$ be a deterministic solitary output three-party ternary-output functionality, and let $\mathcal{Y}_\wedge = \{\mathcal{Y}_i^\wedge : i \in [n_\wedge]\}$ and $\mathcal{Z}_\wedge = \{\mathcal{Z}_j^\wedge : j \in [m_\wedge]\}$ be its CORE$_\wedge$-partitions. Then f can be securely computed against a single corruption in the point-to-point model, if and only if the following hold.*

1. *Either $\mathcal{Y}_x = \{\mathcal{Y}\}$ for all $x \in \mathcal{X}$, or $\mathcal{Z}_x = \{\mathcal{Z}\}$ for all $x \in \mathcal{X}$. In other words, either all $y \in \mathcal{Y}$ are equivalent for every $x \in \mathcal{X}$, or all $z \in \mathcal{Z}$ are equivalent for every $x \in \mathcal{X}$.*
2. *There exists an algorithm S, and there exist three families of distributions $\{P_x\}_{x \in \mathcal{X}}$, $\{Q_i\}_{i \in [n_\wedge]}$, and $\{R_j\}_{j \in [m_\wedge]}$, such that the following holds. For all $i \in [n_\wedge]$, $j \in [m_\wedge]$, $y \in \mathcal{Y}_i^\wedge$, $z \in \mathcal{Z}_j^\wedge$, and $x \in \mathcal{X}$, it holds that*

$$\mathsf{S}(x, x^*, f(x^*, y, z)), \text{ that } f(x, y^*, z), \text{ and that } f(x, y, z^*),$$

are computationally indistinguishable from each other, where $x^* \leftarrow P_x$, where $y^* \leftarrow Q_i$, and where $z^* \leftarrow R_j$.

In fact, the positive direction holds even for functionalities that are not ternary-output.

---

[5] Fitzi et al. [20] defined the convergecast functionality as the NIORP randomized solitary output functionality, where A outputs y with probability $1/2$, and outputs z with probability $1/2$.

At first sight, it might seem that the characterization is hard to use since it requires the existence of an algorithm S, which in spirit seems like a simulator for a corrupt A. However, note that we only require S to output what would become the output of (an honest) A, and not the entire view of an arbitrary adversary. Arguably, determining whether such an algorithm exists is much simpler than determining whether there exists a simulator for some adversary interacting in some protocol.

We next give two examples for using Theorem 2. As a first example, consider the deterministic convergecast functionality CC. Observe that it does *not* satisfy Item 1 since $\mathcal{Y}_0 \neq \{\mathcal{Y}\}$ and $\mathcal{Z}_1 \neq \{\mathcal{Z}\}$. Therefore it cannot be securely computed. To exemplify Item 2 of Theorem 2, consider the maximum function Max : $\{0,1,2\}^3 \to \{0,1,2\}$. Similarly to CC, it can be defined by the three matrices $M_0 = \left(\begin{smallmatrix} 0 & 1 & 2 \\ 1 & 1 & 2 \\ 2 & 2 & 2 \end{smallmatrix}\right)$, $M_1 = \left(\begin{smallmatrix} 1 & 1 & 2 \\ 1 & 1 & 2 \\ 2 & 2 & 2 \end{smallmatrix}\right)$, and $M_2 = \left(\begin{smallmatrix} 2 & 2 & 2 \\ 2 & 2 & 2 \\ 2 & 2 & 2 \end{smallmatrix}\right)$, where A chooses a matrix, B chooses a row, and C chooses a column. The output of A is the value written in the chosen entry. Clearly, any two y's are equivalent, and any two z's are equivalent as well, for all $x \in \{0,1,2\}$. Therefore, Item 1 holds. As for Item 2, we let Q_1 and R_1 output 2 with probability 1 (recall that $n_\wedge = m_\wedge = 1$). Additionally, we let S ignore its inputs and output 2 with probability 1. It follows that Item 2 holds. Thus, Max can be securely computed. In fact, as the positive direction of Theorem 2 holds for functions that are not ternary-output, the same argument can be made when Max has a domain that is arbitrarily large, i.e., Max : $\{1,\dots,m\}^3 \to \{1,\dots,m\}$ for some natural m.

Randomized Functionalities. So far, we have only dealt with deterministic functionalities. To handle the randomized case, we show how to reduce it to the deterministic case. That is, for any randomized solitary output three-party functionality f, we define a deterministic solitary output three-party functionality f', such that f can be securely computed if and only if f' can be securely computed.

Proposition 1 (Reducing randomized functionalities to deterministic functionalities, informal). *Let $f : \mathcal{X} \times \mathcal{Y} \times \mathcal{Z} \to \mathcal{W}$ be a (randomized) solitary output three-party functionality, and let $\mathcal{R}$ denote the domain of its randomness. Define the deterministic solitary output three-party functionality $f' : (\mathcal{X} \times \mathcal{R}) \times (\mathcal{Y} \times \mathcal{R}) \times (\mathcal{Z} \times \mathcal{R}) \to \mathcal{W}$ as*

$$f'((x,r_1),(y,r_2),(z,r_3)) = f(x,y,z;r_1 + r_2 + r_3),$$

where addition is done over $\mathcal{R}$ when viewed as an additive group. That is, the parties receive a share of the randomness in a 3-out-of-3 secret sharing scheme. Then f can be securely computed if and only if f' can be securely computed.

A New Possibility Result for the With-broadcast Model. Somewhat surprisingly, we are able to show that all functionalities captured by our positive results, can also be securely computed in the face of a dishonest majority (where two parties may be corrupted), assuming a broadcast channel *is available*. In particular, any solitary output three-party ternary-output functionality and any NIORP functionality that can be securely computed without broadcast against a single corruption, can be securely computed with broadcast against two corruptions (in fact, our constructions capture a slightly larger class of functionalities).

We do not know if this is a part of a more general phenomenon (i.e., if the ability to compute a functionality without a broadcast channel against a single corruption implies the ability to compute it with a broadcast channel against two corruptions) and we leave it as an interesting open question. Still, our results do slightly improve the positive results of [24] (see [24, Theorem 4.4]). Indeed, consider the NIORP functionality $f_{special} : \{\lambda\} \times (\{0, 1, 2, 3\})^2 \to \{0, \ldots, 7\}$ defined by the matrix

$$\begin{pmatrix} 0\ 1\ 2\ 3 \\ 1\ 0\ 3\ 2 \\ 4\ 5\ 6\ 7 \\ 5\ 4\ 7\ 6 \end{pmatrix} \tag{2}$$

However, we show that the converse is false, i.e., there exists a solitary output NIORP Boolean three-party functionality that can be securely computed with broadcast against two corruptions, yet it cannot be securely computed without broadcast against a single corruption. As an example, consider the following solitary output three-party variant of the GHKL functionality,[6] denoted soGHKL, defined by the matrix

$$\begin{pmatrix} 0\ 1 \\ 1\ 0 \\ 1\ 1 \end{pmatrix} \tag{3}$$

where B chooses a row, C chooses a column, and the output of A is the value written in the chosen entry. Observe that soGHKL is a NIORP functionality that does not satisfy the necessary conditions given by Theorem 1. Thus, it cannot be securely computed in the point-to-point model. On the other hand, Halevi et al. [24] showed that soGHKL can be computed assuming a broadcast channel.[7] The constructions we use to prove our results use standard techniques. Due to space limitations, we provide them in the full version of the paper.

In Table 2 below, we present several examples of three-party functionalities and compare their status assuming no broadcast channel and one corruption, to the case where such a channel is available with two possible corruptions.

1.2   Our Techniques

We now turn to describe our techniques. In Sect. 1.2.1 we handle NIORP functionalities. Then, in Sect. 1.2.2 we handle ternary-output functionalities. To simplify the proofs in this introduction, we only consider perfect security and functionalities with finite domain and range.

---

[6] Gordon et al. [23] showed that the symmetric two-party variant of this functionality can be computed with full security.

[7] In fact, [24] gave three different protocols for computing soGHKL securely.

Table 2. Comparing the landscape of functionalities that can be computed without broadcast but with an honest majority, to functionalities that can be computed with broadcast but no honest majority. All functions above have a constant domain. It is important that the domain of **EQ** does not include 0.

Function\Model	Without broadcast (honest majority)	With broadcast (no honest majority)
$\mathsf{CC}(x,y,z)$ (see Eq. 1)	✗ Theorem 2	✓ [24]
$\mathsf{soGHKL}(y,z)$ (see Eq. 3)	✗ Theorem 2	✓ [24]
$\mathsf{Max}(x,y,z)$	✓ Theorem 2	✓ [24]
$\mathsf{EQ}(y,z) = \begin{cases} y & \text{if } y = z \\ 0 & \text{otherwise} \end{cases}$	✗ Theorem 2	✗ [24]
f_{special} (see Eq. 2)	✓ Theorem 2	✓ Theorem 2

1.2.1 Characterizing NIORP Functionalities

We start with the negative direction of Theorem 1. Our argument is split into two parts. In the first part, we adapt the hexagon argument, due to Fischer et al. [19], to the MPC setting. Roughly, for every secure three-party protocol we attribute six distributions, all of which are identically distributed by the perfect security of the protocol. The second part of the proof is dedicated to the analysis of these six distributions, resulting in necessary conditions for perfect security.

The Hexagon Argument for NIORP Functionalities. In the following, let f be a solitary output three-party NIORP functionality (no input for the output receiving party), and let π be a three-party protocol computing f securely over point-to-point channels, tolerating a single corrupted party. At a high level, the hexagon argument is as follows.

1. First, we construct a new six-party protocol π'. This is the same hexagon protocol from [19] (see below for a formal definition).
2. Then, we consider six different *semi-honest* adversaries for π' corrupting four parties, and observe that each of them can be emulated by a *malicious* adversary in the original three-party protocol π. In more detail, for each of the semi-honest adversaries we consider for π', we show there exists a malicious adversary corrupting a single party in π satisfying the following: The transcript between the two honest parties and the transcript between each honest party and the adversary, are identically distributed in both protocols. We stress that π' is *not* secure, but rather any attacker for it can be emulated by an attacker for the three-party protocol π.
3. Observe that as the adversaries for π' are semi-honest, the view of each party (both corrupted and honest) is identically distributed across all six scenarios.
4. We then translate the above observation to π using the fact that each of the semi-honest adversaries for π' can be emulated in π. Thus, we obtain a certain correlation between the six malicious adversaries for π.
5. By the assumed security of π, each of the malicious adversaries can be simulated in the ideal world of f. Therefore, we can translate the correlation from

the previous step to the ideal world, and obtain a necessary property f has to satisfy. This results in six distributions with differing definitions, all of which are identically distributed. Looking ahead, the second part of our argument is dedicated to analyzing these distributions.

We next provide a more formal argument. Consider the following six-party protocol π'. For each party $P \in \{A, B, C\}$ in π we have two copies P and P' in π', both use the same code as an honest P does in π. Furthermore, the parties are connected via the following undirected cycle graph: (1) A is connected to B and C, (2) A' is connected to B' and C', (3) B is also connected to C', and (4) C is also connected to B'. See Fig. 1 below for a pictorial definition (alongside the definition of adversarial scenarios). Finally, we let B, B', C, and C' hold inputs y, y', z, and z', respectively.

Now, consider the following 6 attack-scenarios for the six-party protocol, where in each scenario a *semi-honest* adversary corrupts four adjacent parties, as depicted in Fig. 1. Observe that each attacker can be emulated in the original three-party protocol π, by a *malicious* adversary emulating the corresponding four parties in its head. For example, in Scenario 1a, an adversary in π can emulate the attack by corrupting C, and emulating in its head two virtual copies of C, a copy of A, and a copy B.

We now focus on party A in the six-party protocol. First, note that in Scenarios 1a and 1b, where A is honest, its output is identically distributed[8] since the adversaries are semi-honest. Second, in the other four scenarios, where A is corrupted, the adversary's view contains the same view that an honest A has in an honest execution of π'. Therefore, it can compute an output with an identical distribution to the output distribution an honest A has in Scenarios 1a and 1b.

Next, we use the fact that the six semi-honest adversaries in π' can be emulated by malicious adversaries in π. We obtain that there exists a distribution D (that depends on all inputs y, y', z, and z' in the six-party protocol) over the set of possible outputs of A, such that the following hold.

Scenarios 1 and 2: There exist two malicious adversaries for π, one corrupting C and holding (y', z, z'), and one corrupting B and holding (y, y', z'), such that the output of A in both scenarios is distributed according to D.

---

[8] Note that even though f is assumed to be deterministic, it is not guaranteed that the output of an honest A is a fixed value even when interacting with a semi-honest adversary. This is due to the fact that the semi-honest adversaries are emulated in the three-party protocol using malicious adversaries.

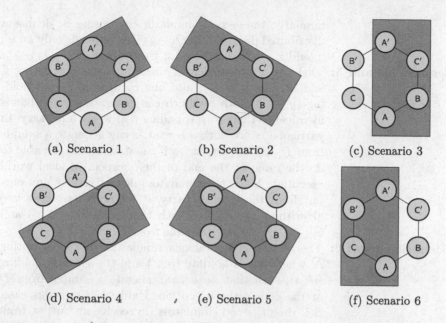

(a) Scenario 1   (b) Scenario 2   (c) Scenario 3

(d) Scenario 4   ,   (e) Scenario 5   (f) Scenario 6

Fig. 1. The six adversaries in the hexagon argument. The shaded yellow areas in each scenario correspond to the (virtual) parties the adversary controls. (Color figure online)

Scenarios 4 and 5: There exist two malicious adversaries for π, one corrupting C and holding (y, z, z'), and one corrupting B and holding (y, y', z), both of which can generate a sample from D at the end of the execution.

Scenarios 3 and 6: There exist two malicious adversaries for π, both corrupting A, where one is holding (y, z') and the other is holding (y', z), such that both can generate a sample from D at the end of the execution.

By the assumed security of π, each of the adversaries can be simulated in the corresponding ideal world of the three-party functionality f. Thus, we obtain six different expressions for the distribution D, representing the output of A. The six expressions are described as follows.

Scenarios 1 and 2: There exist two malicious simulators in the ideal world of f, one corrupting C and holding (y', z, z'), and one corrupting B and holding (y, y', z'), such that the output of A in both ideal world executions is distributed according to D. Recall that the only way for the simulators to affect the output of A is by choosing the input they send to the trusted party. It follows the first simulator corrupting C, defines a distribution $R_{y',z,z'}$ that depends only on y', z, and z', such that $f(y, z^*) \equiv D$, where $z^* \leftarrow R_{y',z,z'}$.

Similarly, the second simulator corrupting B, defines a distributed distribution $Q_{y,y',z'}$ that depends only on y', z, and z', such that $f(y^*, z) \equiv D$, where $y^* \leftarrow Q_{y,y',z'}$.

Scenarios 4 and 5: There exist two malicious simulators, one corrupting C and holding (y, z, z'), and one corrupting B and holding (y, y', z), both of which can generate a view that is identical to their corresponding real world adversary. In particular, since both adversaries can generate a sample from D, it follows that both simulators must be able to do the same at the end of their respective ideal world execution. Since the simulators do not receive any output from the trusted party, it follows there exist two algorithms S_B and S_C, such that both $S_C(y, z, z')$ and $S_B(y, y', z)$ output a sample from D.

Scenarios 3 and 6: There exist two malicious simulators, both corrupting A, where one is holding (y, z') and the other is holding (y', z), such that both can generate a sample from D at the end of the execution. Unlike the previous case, this time the two simulators do receive an output from the trusted party. This implies there exist two algorithms S_3 and S_6, such that both $S_3(y, z', f(y', z))$ and $S_6(y', z, f(y, z'))$ output a sample from D.

We conclude that for all $y, y' \in \mathcal{Y}$ and $z, z' \in \mathcal{Z}$, there exist two efficiently samplable distributions $Q_{y,y',z'}$ and $R_{y',z,z'}$ over $\mathcal{Y}$ and $\mathcal{Z}$, respectively, and four algorithms S_B, S_C, S_3, and S_6, such that

$$
\begin{aligned}
f(y^*, z) &\equiv f(y, z^*) \equiv S_B(y, y', z) \equiv S_C(y, z, z') \\
&\equiv S_3(y, z', f(y', z)) \equiv S_6(y', z, f(y, z')),
\end{aligned} \tag{4}
$$

where $y^* \leftarrow Q_{y,y',z'}$ and where $z^* \leftarrow R_{y',z,z'}$.

Analyzing the Six Distributions Over the Output of A. We now turn to the analysis of Eq. (4), which results in the necessary conditions stated in Theorem 1. Recall that our goal is to show that for all $y \in \mathcal{Y}$ and $z \in \mathcal{Z}$, it holds that

$$
f(y, z^*) \equiv f(y^*, z),
$$

where y^* and z^* are sampled according to specific distributions that depend on the equivalence classes containing y and z, respectively.

First, observe that as S_B is independent of z', it follows that all other distributions are also independent of it. For example, for any $z'' \neq z'$ it holds that

$$
S_3(y, z', f(y', z)) \equiv S_B(y, y', z) \equiv S_3(y, z'', f(y', z)).
$$

Similarly, since S_C is independent of y' it follows that all other distributions are also independent of it as well. From this, we conclude the following: Let y_0

and z_0 be the lexicographically smallest elements of $\mathcal{Y}$ and $\mathcal{Z}$, respectively, and define the distributions $Q'_y := Q_{y,y_0,z_0}$ and $R'_z := R_{y_0,z,z_0}$.[9] Then, the above observation implies that

$$f(y^*, z) \equiv f(y, z^*) \equiv \mathsf{S}_3(y, z', f(y', z)) \equiv \mathsf{S}_6(y', z, f(y, z')), \qquad (5)$$

for all $y' \in \mathcal{Y}$ and $z' \in \mathcal{Z}$, where $y^* \leftarrow Q'_y$ and $z^* \leftarrow R'_z$.

Let us focus on S_3, and fix $\tilde{z} \in \mathcal{Z}$ such that $z \sim \tilde{z}$. Recall that the relation $\sim$ is defined as $z \sim \tilde{z}$ if and only if there exist $\tilde{y}, \tilde{y}' \in \mathcal{Y}$ such that $f(\tilde{y}, z) = f(\tilde{y}', \tilde{z})$. Since S_3 is independent of y', it follows that

$$\mathsf{S}_3(y, z', f(y', z)) \equiv \mathsf{S}_3(y, z', f(\tilde{y}, z)) \equiv \mathsf{S}_3(y, z', f(\tilde{y}', \tilde{z})) \equiv \mathsf{S}_3(y, z', f(y', \tilde{z})),$$

where the first and last transition follows from the previously made observation that the output distribution of S_3 is independent of the value of y', and the second transition follows from the fact that $f(\tilde{y}, z) = f(\tilde{y}', \tilde{z})$, hence S_3 receives the same inputs in both cases. Therefore, changing z to $\tilde{z}$ where $z \sim \tilde{z}$ does not change the output distribution of S_3. Note that the argument can be repeated to show that replacing $\tilde{z}$ with any other $\tilde{z}'$, where $\tilde{z} \sim \tilde{z}'$, does not change the distribution. It follows that changing z to any $\tilde{z}'$ satisfying $z \equiv_{\mathsf{rel}} \tilde{z}'$ does not change the output distribution of S_3. Thus, all distributions in Eq. (5) are not affected by such change.

Plugging this back to Eq. (5), results in the following. For every $j \in [m]$, every $y \in \mathcal{Y}$, and every equivalent $z, \tilde{z}' \in \mathcal{Z}_j$ (recall that $\mathcal{Z}_j$ is the jth equivalence class with respect to the relation $\equiv_{\mathsf{rel}}$), it holds that

$$f(y, z^*) \equiv f(y^*, z) \equiv f(y^*, \tilde{z}') \equiv f(y, \tilde{z}^*),$$

where $y^* \leftarrow Q'_y$, where $z^* \leftarrow R'_z$, and where $\tilde{z}^* \leftarrow R'_{\tilde{z}}$. In particular, the distributions depend only on the index j, and not on the specific choice of input from the equivalence class $\mathcal{Z}_j$. Thus, if for any $j \in [m]$ we define the distribution $R''_j := R'_{z_j}$, where z_j is the lexicographically smallest element in $\mathcal{Z}_j$, it then follows that for every $j \in [m]$, every $y \in \mathcal{Y}$, and every $z \in \mathcal{Z}_j$, that

$$f(y, z^*) \equiv f(y^*, z),$$

where $y^* \leftarrow Q'_y$ and $z^* \leftarrow R'_j$.

Finally, an analogous argument starting by focusing on S_6, implies that the distributions depend only on the equivalence class containing y, rather than depending on y directly. Therefore, for any $i \in [n]$ we can define the distribution $Q''_i := Q'_{y_i}$, where y_i is the lexicographically smallest element in $\mathcal{Y}_i$. It then follows that for every $i \in [n]$, $j \in [m]$, $y \in \mathcal{Y}_i$, and $z \in \mathcal{Z}_j$ it holds that

$$f(y^*, z) \equiv f(y, z^*),$$

where $y^* \leftarrow Q''_i$ and $z^* \leftarrow R''_j$, as claimed.

---

[9] Note that the choice of taking the lexicographically smallest elements of $\mathcal{Y}$ and $\mathcal{Z}$ is arbitrary, and any other element would work.

The Positive Direction for NIORP Functionalities. We now present a protocol for any solitary output three-party NIORP functionality f, satisfying the conditions stated in Theorem 1. Our starting point is the same as that of [3,15], namely, computing f *fairly* (i.e., either all parties obtain the output or none do). This follows from the fact that, by the honest-majority assumption, the protocol of Rabin and Ben-Or [28] computes f assuming a *broadcast channel*; hence by [14] it follows that f can be computed with fairness over a point-to-point network.

We now describe the protocol. The parties start by computing f with fairness. If they receive outputs, then they can terminate, and output what they received.[10] If the protocol aborts, then B finds the unique $i \in [n]$ such that $y \in \mathcal{Y}_i$ and sends i to A. Similarly, C finds the unique $j \in [m]$ such that $z \in \mathcal{Z}_j$ and sends j to A. Observe that this can be done efficiently since the domain of f is of constant size. Party A then samples $y^* \leftarrow Q_i$ and outputs $f(y^*, z_j)$, where z_j is the lexicographically smallest element in $\mathcal{Z}_j$.

Observe that correctness holds since when all parties are honest, the fair protocol will never abort (note that without the fair computation of f the above protocol is not correct since A would always output $f(y^*, z_j)$ instead of $f(y, z)$). Now, consider a corrupt B (the case of a corrupt C is similar). First, note that the adversary does not obtain any information from the fair computation of f. Next, if the adversary sends some i' to A, then the simulator sends $y^* \leftarrow Q_{i'}$ to the trusted party. Then the output of A in the ideal world is $f(y^*, z)$. By our assumption on f, this is identical to $f(y^*, z_j)$ – the output of A in the real world.

Next, consider a corrupt A. Since it does not obtain any information from the (failed) fair computation of f, it suffices to show how a simulator that is given $f(y, z)$ can compute the corresponding i and j. Observe that by our definition for the partition of the inputs, any two distinct combinatorial rectangles $\mathcal{Y}_i \times \mathcal{Z}_j$ and $\mathcal{Y}_{i'} \times \mathcal{Z}_{j'}$, where $(i,j) \neq (i',j')$, have no common output. Indeed, if $f(y, z) = f(y', z')$, where $(y, z) \in \mathcal{Y}_i \times \mathcal{Z}_j$ and $(y', z') \in \mathcal{Y}_{i'} \times \mathcal{Z}_{j'}$, then $y \sim y'$ and $z \sim z'$, hence they belong to the same sets. Therefore, the simulator for the corrupt A can compute the corresponding i and j given the output by simply looking them up (which can be done efficiently since the domain is of constant size).

1.2.2   Characterizing Ternary-Output Functionalities

We now explain our techniques for proving Theorem 2. The positive direction uses the same techniques as in [3] (see the full version for more details), hence we will only show the negative direction. Similarly to the proof of Theorem 1 presented earlier, the argument is comprised of the hexagon argument and the analysis of the six distributions that are obtained. However, since A now has an input, the argument is much more involved.

A Generalized Hexagon Argument. Unlike in the previous proof, here the hexagon argument (as used there) does not suffice. To show where the argu-

---

[10] Although B and C are supposed to receive no output from f, in a fair computation they either receive the empty string indicating that A received its output, or a special symbol $\perp$ indicating abort.

ment falls short, let us first describe the six distributions obtained from the hexagon argument. In this setting, where A now has an input, the six-party protocol described earlier will now have A and A' hold inputs x and x', respectively. The two inputs are then given to the correct adversaries from the six scenarios. Furthermore, observe that the algorithms S_3 and S_6, which came from the two simulators for a corrupt A in the ideal world, can also send to the trusted party an input that is not necessarily the same input that the simulators hold. Let x_3^* and x_6^* denote the inputs used by S_3 and S_6, respectively, each sampled according to a distribution that depends on the simulator's inputs. Thus, to adjust the hexagon argument to this case, Eq. (4) should now be replaced with

$$f(x, y^*, z) \equiv f(x, y, z^*) \equiv S_B(x, y, y', z) \equiv S_C(x, y, z, z') \qquad (6)$$
$$\equiv S_3(x, x', y, z', x_3^*, f(x_3^*, y', z)) \equiv S_6(x, x', y', z, x_6^*, f(x_6^*, y, z')),$$

where $y^* \leftarrow Q_{x',y,y',z'}$, where $z^* \leftarrow R_{x',y',z,z'}$, where $x_3^* \leftarrow P^3_{x,x',y,z'}$, and where $x_6^* \leftarrow P^6_{x,x',y',z}$.

We now show where the argument falls short using an example: recall that we defined the deterministic variant of the convergecast functionality [20], CC : $(\{0,1\})^3 \rightarrow \{0,1\}$ as $CC(x, y, z) = y$ if $x = 0$, and $CC(x, y, z) = z$ otherwise. We claim that there exist distributions and algorithms satisfying Eq. (6), hence the argument is insufficient to show the impossibility of securely computing CC. Indeed, take $Q_{x',y,y',z'}$ to always output $y^* = y$, take $R_{x',y',z,z'}$ to always output $z^* = z$, define $P^3_{x,x',y,z'}$ to always output $x_3^* = 1$ (causing S_3 to obtain z), define $P^6_{x,x',y',z}$ to always output $x_6^* = 0$ (causing S_6 to obtain y), and define S_B and S_C, both of which hold x, y, and z, to compute $CC(x, y, z)$. Then all six distributions always output $CC(x, y, z)$.

However, as we next explain, the functionality CC cannot be computed securely in our setting. Intuitively, this is because the adversary corrupting A as in Scenario 1c using inputs $x = 1$ and $x' = 0$, learns both y' and z. Indeed, in Scenario 1b (where B is corrupted) the output of an *honest* A is z, and in Scenario 1d (where C is corrupted) the output of an *honest* A' is y'. Since the adversaries are semi-honest, the adversary corrupting A as in Scenario 1c can compute both z and y' by computing the output of the honest A and A', respectively. However, in the ideal world, a simulator (for the malicious adversary emulating Scenario 1c) can only learn one of the inputs.

To generalize this intuition, we consider the joint distribution of the outputs of A and A' in the six-party protocol, rather than only the distribution of the output of A. Doing a similar analysis to the NIORP case results in the existence of six distributions $P^3_{x,x',y,z'}$, $P^6_{x,x',y',z}$, $Q_{x,y,y',z}$, $Q'_{x',y,y',z'}$, $R_{x,y,z,z'}$, and $R'_{x',y',z,z'}$, and the existence of six algorithms S_3, S_6, S_B, S'_B, S_C, and S'_C, where S_3 and S_6 output two values (corresponding to the outputs of A and A'), such that the following six distributions are identically distributed:

1. $S_3(x, x', y, z', x_3^*, f(x_3^*, y', z))$, where $x_3^* \leftarrow P^3_{x,x',y,z'}$.
2. $S_6(x, x', y', z, x_6^*, f(x_6^*, y, z'))$, where $x_6^* \leftarrow P^6_{x,x',y',z}$.

3. $(S_B(x, y, y', z, y_1^*), f(x', y_1^*, z'))$, where $y_1^* \leftarrow Q_{x,y,y',z}$.
4. $(f(x, y_2^*, z), S_B'(x', y, y', z', y_2^*))$, where $y_2^* \leftarrow Q'_{x',y,y',z'}$.
5. $(S_C(x, y, z, z', z_1^*), f(x', y', z_1^*))$, where $z_1^* \leftarrow R_{x,y,z,z'}$.
6. $(f(x, y, z_2^*), S_C'(x', y', z, z', z_2^*))$, where $z_2^* \leftarrow R'_{x',y',z,z'}$.

We stress that both S_3 and S_6 output two values from the set of outputs $\{0, 1, 2\}$, while S_B, S_B', S_C, and S_C', each output a single value from $\{0, 1, 2\}$.

Observe that for the function CC, the above distributions and algorithms do not exist for all possible choices of inputs. Indeed, for $x = 1$ and $x' = 0$, it holds that $CC(x, y_2^*, z) = z$ (from the fourth distribution) and that $CC(x', y', z_1^*) = y'$ (from the fifth distribution). Therefore, the marginal distribution of the first value must be z, and the marginal distribution of the second value must be y', both with probability 1. However, note that S_3 is given only one of y' or z, depending on the value of x_3^*, hence it cannot output both of them correctly.

Analyzing the Six Joint Distributions Over the Outputs of A and A'. We now analyze the new six distributions described earlier. First, similarly to the case of NIORP functionalities, we make the observation that the marginal distribution of the first entry is independent of x', y', and z', and the marginal distribution of the second entry is independent of x, y, and z. Let us focus on S_3 and the distribution $P_{x,x',y,z'}^3$.

Our next goal is to analyze the support of $P_{x,x',y,z'}^3$, namely, analyze which inputs x_3^* can be used by S_3. This results in a necessary condition for f to be securely computable, since if the input x_3^* must satisfy some condition, in particular, this implies an input satisfying such condition must exist. We do this analysis by comparing the first (i.e., left) output of S_3 to the distribution in Item 4 above, where the first value is $f(x, y_2^*, z)$, and by comparing the second (i.e., right) output of S_3 to the distribution in Item 5 above, where the second value is $f(x', y', z_1^*)$. In fact, rather than directly comparing the outputs, we compare the *information on the equivalence class* of z and y' with respect to the CORE partitions that can be inferred from the outputs. We next focus on comparing to $f(x, y_2^*, z)$ (comparing to $f(x', y', z_1^*)$ is analogous).

Let us first recall the definition of the CORE partitions. Recall that for every x we can view $f(x, \cdot, \cdot)$ as a NIORP function. Thus, we can partition $\mathcal{Y}$ and $\mathcal{Z}$ according to the CORE partition for the given x. Since we focus on S_3 it suffices, for now, to only consider the partition of $\mathcal{Z}$. Let $M_x \in \{0, 1, 2\}^{|\mathcal{Y}| \times |\mathcal{Z}|}$ be the matrix associated with $f(x, \cdot, \cdot)$, defined as $M_x(y, z) = f(x, y, z)$ for all $y \in \mathcal{Y}$ and $z \in \mathcal{Z}$. Recall that we denote the partition as $\mathcal{Z}_x = \{\mathcal{Z}_j^x : j \in [m(x)]\}$, and we let z and $\tilde{z}$ be in the same equivalence class if and only if there exist $z_1, \ldots, z_k \in \mathcal{Z}$ such that the columns $M_x(\cdot, z)$ and $M_x(\cdot, z_1)$ have a common output, for all $i \in [k-1]$ the columns $M_x(\cdot, z_i)$ and $M_x(\cdot, z_{i+1})$ have a common output, and the columns $M_x(\cdot, z_k)$ and $M_x(\cdot, \tilde{z})$ have a common output. Observe that for any $x \in \mathcal{X}$ and every $y \in \mathcal{Y}$ it holds that if $z \in \mathcal{Z}$ and $\tilde{z} \in \mathcal{Z}$ are in *different* classes, then $f(x, y, z) \neq f(x, y, \tilde{z})$.

Now, consider the distribution in Item 4 above, where the first value is $f(x, y_2^*, z)$. It follows that S_3 must be able to output $f(x, y_2^*, z)$.[11] Next, observe that from $f(x, y_2^*, z)$ it is possible to infer the (unique) $j \in [m(x)]$ satisfying $z \in \mathcal{Z}_j^x$. This is because, as noted earlier, for z and $\tilde{z}$ in different classes, the output of f on each of them (with the same x and y) is always different. Thus, for any fixed value for y_2^*, from the output $f(x, y_2^*, z)$ we can compute the equivalence class of z.

However, the only information that S_3 can obtain on the class $j \in [m(x)]$ can come from the output $f(x_3^*, y', z)$ (which corresponds to the output it receives from the trusted party). That is, the *only* information that S_3 can have is the equivalence class of z with respect to the partition of x_3^* rather than the partition with respect to x. Since the first entry in the output of S_3 must be identically distributed to $f(x, y_2^*, z)$, the value x_3^* it uses must be such that $f(x_3^*, y', z)$ reveals at least the same information on j as $f(x, y_2^*, z)$ does. This implies that x_3^* must be such that if $z \in \mathcal{Z}_{j_3^*}^{x_3^*}$ then $z \in \mathcal{Z}_j^x$, with probability 1. Furthermore, this must hold for all $z \in \mathcal{Z}$ and the distribution $P_{x, x', y, z'}^3$, from which x_3^* is drawn from, is independent of z, it follows that the partition $\mathcal{Z}_{x_3^*}$ must be a *refinement* of $\mathcal{Z}_x$. That is, any $\mathcal{Z} \in \mathcal{Z}_{x_3^*}$ must be a subset of some $\mathcal{Z}' \in \mathcal{Z}_x$. Similarly, since S_3 must also output $f(x', y', z_1^*)$ from the fifth distribution in Item 5, it follows that $\mathcal{Y}_{x_3^*}$ is a refinement of $\mathcal{Y}_{x'}$. As a result, we conclude that for any $x, x' \in \mathcal{X}$ there exists $x_3^* \in \mathcal{X}$ such that $\mathcal{Y}_{x_3^*}$ is a refinement of $\mathcal{Y}_{x'}$ and such that $\mathcal{Z}_{x_3^*}$ is a refinement of $\mathcal{Z}_x$. We stress that so far, we have not used the fact that f is ternary-output, thus the existence of such x_3^* holds for any function that can be securely computed.

We now have all the necessary tools to prove Items 1 and 2 of Theorem 2. Let us start with the former. Recall that we need to show that either $\mathcal{Y}_x = \{\mathcal{Y}\}$ for all x, or $\mathcal{Z}_x = \{\mathcal{Z}\}$ for all x. First, since f is ternary-output, for every x it holds that either $\mathcal{Y}_x = \{\mathcal{Y}\}$ or $\mathcal{Z}_x = \{\mathcal{Z}\}$. Note that this is *weaker* than what we wish to show since for one x it might be the case that $\mathcal{Y}_x = \{\mathcal{Y}\}$, while for another x it might be the case that $\mathcal{Z}_x = \{\mathcal{Z}\}$. Let us assume that Item 1 of Theorem 2 does not hold. Then there exist x and x' such that $\mathcal{Y}_x \neq \{\mathcal{Y}\}$ and $\mathcal{Z}_{x'} \neq \{\mathcal{Z}\}$. Then, as argued above, there exists x^* such that $\mathcal{Y}_{x^*}$ refines $\mathcal{Y}_x$ and $\mathcal{Z}_{x^*}$ refines $\mathcal{Z}_{x'}$. However, this implies that $\mathcal{Y}_{x^*} \neq \{\mathcal{Y}\}$ and $\mathcal{Z}_{x^*} \neq \{\mathcal{Z}\}$, which is impossible for ternary-output functions.

We now prove Item 2 of Theorem 2. From here on, we will only focus on the first (i.e., left) entry in each of the above 6 distributions (there is no need to consider the second entry anymore). The proof follows similar ideas to that of the NIORP case. In more detail, we consider the $\mathrm{CORE}_\wedge$-partition of the inputs $\mathcal{Y}_\wedge$ and $\mathcal{Z}_\wedge$, and we show that changing, say, z to any $\tilde{z}$ that belongs to the same equivalence class $\mathcal{Z}_j^\wedge \in \mathcal{Z}_\wedge$, does not change the distribution. Let us first recall the definition of $\mathrm{CORE}_\wedge$-partition. We define $\mathcal{Z}_\wedge$ to be the meet of the

---

[11] Formally, the marginal distribution of the first value in the output of S_3 is identically distributed to $f(x, y_2^*, z)$.

partitions $\{Z_x\}_{x \in \mathcal{X}}$, defined as

$$Z_\wedge := \left\{ Z^\wedge \subseteq Z : Z^\wedge \neq \emptyset, \text{ and } \forall x \in \mathcal{X} \; \exists Z_x \in Z_x \text{ s.t. } Z^\wedge = \bigcap_{x \in \mathcal{X}} Z_x \right\}.$$

For the sake of brevity, we will abuse notations and let S_3 only output the first entry rather than two values.

First observe that if $z, \tilde{z} \in Z_j^\wedge$ for some $j \in [m_\wedge]$, then for any x there exists $j_x \in [m(x)]$ such that $z, \tilde{z} \in Z_{j_x}^x$. Then, a similar analysis to the NIORP case shows that for any *fixed* $x_3^* \in \mathcal{X}$ satisfying $Z_{x_3^*}$ refines Z_x, it holds that

$$S_3(x, x', y, z', x_3^*, f(x_3^*, y', z)) \equiv S_3(x, x', y, z', x_3^*, f(x_3^*, y', \tilde{z})).$$

As the support of $P_{x,x',y,z'}^3$ is contains only those x_3^* where $Z_{x_3^*}$ refines Z_x, it follows that

$$S_3(x, x', y, z', x_3^*, f(x_3^*, y', z)) \equiv S_3(x, x', y, z', x_3^*, f(x_3^*, y', \tilde{z})),$$

where $x_3^* \leftarrow P_{x,x',z'}^3$. Therefore, the same must hold for all of the six distributions, i.e., they depend on the equivalence classes of y and z with respect to the $CORE_\wedge$-partition, rather than depending on the actual values themselves.

In the following we let x_0, y_0, and z_0 be the lexicographically smallest elements of $\mathcal{X}$, $\mathcal{Y}$, and $\mathcal{Z}$, respectively. For $i \in [n_\wedge]$ let $Q_i'' := Q_{x_0,y_i,y_0,z_0}$, where y_i is the lexicographically smallest elements of $\mathcal{Y}_i^\wedge$. Similarly, for $j \in [m_\wedge]$ we let $R_j'' := R_{x_0,y_0,z_j,z_0}'$, where z_j is the lexicographically smallest element of $\mathcal{Z}_j^\wedge$. Then, similarly to the NIORP case, it follows that for all $i \in [n_\wedge]$, all $j \in [m_\wedge]$, all $x \in \mathcal{X}$, all $y \in \mathcal{Y}_i^\wedge$, and all $z \in \mathcal{Z}^\wedge$, it holds that

$$f(x, y^*, z) \equiv f(x, y, z^*), \tag{7}$$

where $y^* \leftarrow Q_i''$ and $z^* \leftarrow R_j''$. Note that the proof of Eq. (7) did not use the fact that f is ternary-output (see the full version for a formal treatment of the general case).

It is left to show the existence of an algorithm S that given x, x^* sampled from an appropriate distribution P_x, and $f(x, y, z)$ can generate the distribution in Eq. (7). Here we use the fact that we showed that for ternary-output functions, either $\mathcal{Y}_x = \{\mathcal{Y}\}$ for all $x \in \mathcal{X}$, or $Z_x = \{\mathcal{Z}\}$ for all $x \in \mathcal{X}$. Assume first the former. In this case we let $S(x, x^*, w) = S_3(x, x_0, y_0, z_0, x^*, w)$. Then, for $P_x := P_{x,x_0,y_0,z_0}^3$ it holds that

$$S(x, x^*, f(x^*, y, z)) \equiv S_3(x, x_0, y_0, z_0, x^*, f(x^*, y, z)) \equiv f(x, y^*, z) \equiv f(x, y, z^*),$$

where $x^* \leftarrow P_x$, $y^* \leftarrow Q_1''$ (recall we assume that $\mathcal{Y}_x = \{\mathcal{Y}\}$ for all x which implies that $n_\wedge = 1$), and $z^* \leftarrow R_j''$, as claimed. Now, if we assume that $Z_x = \{\mathcal{Z}\}$ for all $x \in \mathcal{X}$, we will define $S(x, x^*, w)$ using S_6 rather than S_3. In more details, we let $S(x, x^*, w) = S_6(x, x_0, y_0, z_0, x^*, w)$. Then, for $P_x := P_{x,x_0,y_0,z_0}^6$ it holds that

$$S(x, x^*, f(x^*, y, z)) \equiv S_6(x, x_0, y_0, z_0, x^*, f(x^*, y, z)) \equiv f(x, y^*, z) \equiv f(x, y, z^*),$$

where $x^* \leftarrow P_x$, $y^* \leftarrow Q_i''$, and $z^* \leftarrow R_1''$ (recall we assume that $Z_x = \{\mathcal{Z}\}$ for all x which implies that $m_\wedge = 1$), as claimed.

1.3   Related Work

For non-solitary output functionalities, Cleve [13] showed that without an honest majority, full security cannot be achieved even for the simple task of fair coin-tossing (even with a broadcast channel). On the other hand, even if two-thirds of the parties are honest, there is no fully secure protocol for computing the broadcast functionality in the plain model (i.e., without setup/proof-of-work assumptions) [19,25,27].[12]

For the two-party setting a characterization was given for the set of two-party, Boolean, symmetric (i.e., where all parties receive the same output) functions over a constant size domain [4,6,23,26]. The cases of asymmetric functions and of multiparty functions assuming broadcast but no honest majority, were also investigated [6,16,17,22,24], but both characterizations are open.

The hexagon argument has been first used in the context of Byzantine agreement to rule out three-party protocols tolerating one corruption [19]. Cohen et al. [15] considered *symmetric* (possibly randomized) functionalities in the point-to-point model, and showed that a symmetric n-party functionality f can be computed against t corruptions, if and only if f is $(n-2t)$-dominated, i.e., there exists y^* such that any $n-2t$ of the inputs can fix the output of f to be y^*. They generalized the hexagon argument to the ring argument to obtain their results.

Recently, Recently, Alon et al. [3] extended the discussion to consider asymmetric functionalities in the point-to-point model. They provided various necessary and sufficient conditions for a functionality to be securely computable. They considered some interesting examples for the special case of solitary-output functionalities, however, provided no characterization for any class of functions.

The investigation of the set of solitary output functionalities that can be securely computed assuming a broadcast channel but no honest majority was initiated in the work of Halevi et al. [24]. They provided various negative and positive results, and further investigated the round complexity required to securely compute solitary output functionalities. Badrinarayanan et al. [7] investigated the round complexity required to compute solitary output functionalities, assuming the availability of a broadcast channel and no PKI, and vice versa.

1.4   Organization

The preliminaries and definition of the model of computation appear in Sect. 2. In Sect. 3 we state our results in the point-to-point model. Due to space considerations, the proofs of our results are deferred to the full version.

---

[12] Note that if strictly more than two-thirds of the parties are honest any functionality can be computed with full security [10].

2   Preliminaries

2.1   Notations

We use calligraphic letters to denote sets, uppercase for random variables and distributions, lowercase for values, and we use bold characters to denote vectors. For $n \in \mathbb{N}$, let $[n] = \{1, 2 \ldots n\}$. For a set $\mathcal{S}$ we write $s \leftarrow \mathcal{S}$ to indicate that s is selected uniformly at random from $\mathcal{S}$. Given a random variable (or a distribution) X, we write $x \leftarrow X$ to indicate that x is selected according to X. A PPT algorithm is probabilistic polynomial time, and a PPTM is a polynomial time (interactive) Turing machine.

A function $\mu \colon \mathbb{N} \to [0, 1]$ is called negligible, if for every positive polynomial $p(\cdot)$ and all sufficiently large n, it holds that $\mu(n) < 1/p(n)$. We write neg for an unspecified negligible function and write poly for an unspecified positive polynomial. For a randomized function (or an algorithm) f we write $f(x)$ to denote the random variable induced by the function on input x, and write $f(x; r)$ to denote the value when the randomness of f is fixed to r.

A *distribution ensemble* $X = \{X_{a,n}\}_{a \in \mathcal{D}_n, n \in \mathbb{N}}$ is an infinite sequence of random variables indexed by $a \in \mathcal{D}_n$ and $n \in \mathbb{N}$, where $\mathcal{D}_n$ is a domain that might depend on n. When the domains are clear, we will sometimes write $\{X_{a,n}\}_{a,n}$ in order to alleviate notations.

The statistical distance between two finite distributions is defined as follows.

Definition 3. *The statistical distance between two finite random variables X and Y is*

$$\mathrm{SD}(X, Y) = \max_{\mathcal{S}} \{\Pr[X \in \mathcal{S}] - \Pr[Y \in \mathcal{S}]\}.$$

For a function $\varepsilon \colon \mathbb{N} \to [0, 1]$, the two ensembles $X = \{X_{a,n}\}_{a \in \mathcal{D}_n, n \in \mathbb{N}}$ and $Y = \{Y_{a,n}\}_{a \in \mathcal{D}_n, n \in \mathbb{N}}$ are said to be ε-close, if for all sufficiently large n and $a \in \mathcal{D}_n$, it holds that

$$\mathrm{SD}(X_{a,n}, Y_{a,n}) \leq \varepsilon(n),$$

and are said to be ε-far otherwise. X and Y are said to be statistically close, denoted $X \overset{S}{\equiv} Y$, if they are ε-close for some negligible function ε. If X and Y are 0-close then they are said to be equivalent, denoted $X \equiv Y$.

Computational indistinguishability is defined as follows.

Definition 4. *Let $X = \{X_{a,n}\}_{a \in \mathcal{D}_n, n \in \mathbb{N}}$ and $Y = \{Y_{a,n}\}_{a \in \mathcal{D}_n, n \in \mathbb{N}}$ be two ensembles. We say that X and Y are computationally indistinguishable, denoted $X \overset{C}{\equiv} Y$, if for every non-uniform PPT distinguisher D, there exists a negligible function $\mu(\cdot)$, such that for all n and $a \in \mathcal{D}_n$, it holds that*

$$|\Pr[\mathsf{D}(X_{a,n}) = 1] - \Pr[\mathsf{D}(Y_{a,n}) = 1]| \leq \mu(n).$$

Definition 5 (Minimal and minimum elements). *Let S be a set and let $\preceq$ be a partial order over S. An element $s \in S$ is called minimal, if no other element is smaller than s, that is, for any $s' \in S$, if $s' \preceq s$ then $s' = s$.*

An element $s \in S$ is called minimum if it is smaller than any other element, that is, for any $s' \in S$ it holds that $s \preceq s'$.

We next define a refinement of a partition of some set.

Definition 6 (Refinement of partitions). *Let $\mathcal{P}_1$ and $\mathcal{P}_2$ be two partitions of some set S. We say that $\mathcal{P}_1$ refines $\mathcal{P}_2$, if for every $S_1 \in \mathcal{P}_1$ there exists $S_2 \in \mathcal{P}_2$ such that $S_1 \subseteq S_2$.*

The meet of two partitions is the partition formed by taking all non-empty intersections. Formally, it is defined as follows.

Definition 7 (Meet of partitions). *Let $\mathcal{P}_1$ and $\mathcal{P}_2$ be two partitions of some set S. The meet of $\mathcal{P}_1$ and $\mathcal{P}_2$, denoted $\mathcal{P}_1 \wedge \mathcal{P}_2$, is defined as*

$$\mathcal{P}_1 \wedge \mathcal{P}_2 := \{S_1 \cap S_2 \mid \forall i \in \{1,2\} : S_i \in \mathcal{P}_i \text{ and } S_1 \cap S_2 \neq \emptyset\}.$$

Observe that $\wedge$ is associative, thus we can naturally extend the definition for several partitions.

Definition 8 (Equivalence class and quotient sets). *For an equivalence relation $\equiv$ over some set S, and an element $s \in S$ we denote by $[s]_\equiv$ the equivalence class of s, $[s]_\equiv := \{s' \in S : s \equiv s'\}$. We let $S/\equiv$ denote the quotient set with respect to $\equiv$ defined as the set of all equivalence classes. Stated differently, it is the partition of S induced by the equivalence relation $\equiv$.*

The Model of Computation. In this paper we consider solitary output three-party functionalities. A functionality is a sequence of function $f = \{f_\kappa\}_{\kappa \in \mathbb{N}}$, where $f_\kappa \colon \mathcal{X}_\kappa \times \mathcal{Y}_\kappa \times \mathcal{Z}_\kappa \to \mathcal{W}_\kappa$ for every $\kappa \in \mathbb{N}$.[13] The functionality is called solitary output if only one party obtains an output. We denote the parties by A, B and C, holding inputs x, y, and z, respectively, and let A receive the output, denoted w. To alleviate notations, we will remove κ from f and its domain and range, and simply write it as $f : \mathcal{X} \times \mathcal{Y} \times \mathcal{Z} \to \mathcal{W}$.

We consider the standard ideal vs. real paradigm for defining security. We mostly consider an ideal computation with *guaranteed output delivery* (also referred to as *full security*), where a trusted party performs the computation on behalf of the parties, and the ideal-model adversary *cannot* abort the computation. We say a protocol admits 1-security if it is fully secure against any single corrupted party.

---

[13] The typical convention in secure computation is to let $f : (\{0,1\}^*)^3 \to \{0,1\}^*$. However, we will mostly be dealing with functionalities whose domain is of polynomial size in κ, which is why we introduce this notation.

3   Our Main Results in the Point-to-Point Model

In this section, we present the statement of our main results in the point-to-point model. We present a necessary condition and two sufficient conditions for solitary output three-party functionalities with polynomial-sized domains, that can be computed with 1-security without broadcast. In Sect. 3.2.1, we present several corollaries of our results. In particular, we show that various interesting families of functionalities, such as deterministic NIORP and (possibly randomized) ternary-output functionalities, our necessary and sufficient conditions are equivalent, thus we obtain a characterization.

3.1   Useful Definitions

Before stating the result, we first present several important definitions. Throughout the entire subsection, we let $f : \mathcal{X} \times \mathcal{Y} \times \mathcal{Z} \to \mathcal{W}$ be a deterministic solitary output three-party functionality.

The first definition introduces an equivalence relation over the domains $\mathcal{Y}$ and $\mathcal{Z}$ with respect to any fixed input $x \in \mathcal{X}$. We call this relation the *common output relation* (CORE). Note that the relation depends on the security parameter κ as well. We will not write κ as part of the notations in order to alleviate them.

Definition 9 (CORE and CORE partition). *For an input $x \in \mathcal{X}$ we define the relation $\sim_x$ over $\mathcal{Y}$ as follows.*

$$y \sim_x y' \text{ if there exist } z, z' \in \mathcal{Z} \text{ such that } f(x, y, z) = f(x, y', z').$$

We define relation $\equiv_x$, called CORE, to be the transitive closure of $\sim_x$, i.e., $y \equiv_x y'$ if either $y \sim_x y'$ or if there exist $y_1, \dots, y_k \in \mathcal{Y}$ such that

$$y \sim_x y_1 \sim_x \cdots \sim_x y_k \sim_x y'.$$

Observe that $\equiv_x$ is an equivalence relation. We let $\mathcal{Y}_x$ denote the set of equivalence classes of $\mathcal{Y}$ formed by $\equiv_x$. We also abuse notations, and define the relations $z \sim_x z'$ and $z \equiv_x z'$ over $\mathcal{Z}$ similarly, and let $\mathcal{Z}_x$ denote the set of equivalence classes over $\mathcal{Z}$ formed by $\equiv_x$.

Additionally, we denote $n(x) = |\mathcal{Y}_x|$, $m(x) = |\mathcal{Z}_x|$, and we write

$$\mathcal{Y}_x = \{\mathcal{Y}_i^x : i \in [n(x)]\} \quad and \quad \mathcal{Z}_x = \{\mathcal{Z}_j^x : j \in [m(x)]\}.$$

Finally, we let

$$\mathcal{R}_x = \{\mathcal{Y}_i^x \times \mathcal{Z}_j^x : i \in [n(x)], j \in [m(x)]\}$$

be the partition of $\mathcal{Y} \times \mathcal{Z}$ into the combinatorial rectangles formed by $\mathcal{Y}_x$ and $\mathcal{Z}_x$. We call $\mathcal{Y}_x$, $\mathcal{Z}_x$, and $\mathcal{R}_x$ the CORE partitions of f with respect to x.

We next introduce equivalence relations over $\mathcal{X}$ that correspond to the CORE partitions formed by the inputs. In addition, we define partial orders over the quotient sets associated with these equivalence relations. Roughly, both the equivalence relations and the partial orders are defined by comparing the corresponding CORE partitions. Similarly to Definition 9, the following definition also depends κ, which is omitted from the notations to alleviate them.

Definition 10 (Equivalence relations and partial orders over $\mathcal{X}$). *We define three equivalence relations $\equiv_B$, $\equiv_C$, and $\equiv$, over $\mathcal{X}$ as follows. We say that $x \equiv_B x'$ if $\mathcal{Y}_x = \mathcal{Y}_{x'}$, we say that $x \equiv_C x'$ if $\mathcal{Z}_x = \mathcal{Z}_{x'}$, and we say that $x \equiv x'$ if $\mathcal{R}_x = \mathcal{R}_{x'}$. Equivalently, $x \equiv x'$ if $x \equiv_B x'$ and $x \equiv_C x'$.*

We define partial orders $\preceq_B$, $\preceq_C$, and $\preceq$ over the quotient sets $\mathcal{X}/\equiv_B$, $\mathcal{X}/\equiv_C$, and $\mathcal{X}/\equiv$, respectively, as follows. We say that $[x]_{\equiv_B} \preceq_B [x']_{\equiv_B}$ if $\mathcal{Y}_x$ refines $\mathcal{Y}_{x'}$, we say that $[x]_{\equiv_C} \preceq_C [x']_{\equiv_C}$ if $\mathcal{Z}_x$ refines $\mathcal{Z}_{x'}$, and we say that $[x]_{\equiv} \preceq [x']_{\equiv}$ if $\mathcal{R}_x$ refines $\mathcal{R}_{x'}$. Equivalently, $[x]_{\equiv} \preceq [x']_{\equiv}$ if $[x]_{\equiv_B} \preceq_B [x']_{\equiv_B}$ and $[x]_{\equiv_C} \preceq_C [x']_{\equiv_C}$.

For brevity, we write the partial orders as if they are over $\mathcal{X}$, e.g., we write $x \preceq_B x'$ instead of $[x]_{\equiv_B} \preceq_B [x']_{\equiv_B}$.[14] Finally, $\chi \in \mathcal{X}$ is called B-minimal if $[\chi]_{\equiv_B}$ is minimal with respect to $\preceq_B$, χ is called C-minimal if $[\chi]_{\equiv_C}$ is minimal with respect to $\preceq_C$, and χ is called R-minimal if $[\chi]_{\equiv}$ is minimal with respect to $\preceq$.

As mentioned in Sect. 1, we are interested in the meet of all CORE partitions. We call this new partition the $\mathrm{CORE}_\wedge$-partition of f. Similarly to previous notations, $\mathrm{CORE}_\wedge$-partition also depends on κ, and we will omit it for brevity.

Definition 11 ($\mathrm{CORE}_\wedge$-partition). *We denote*

$$\mathcal{Y}_\wedge := \bigwedge_{x \in \mathcal{X}} \mathcal{Y}_x = \bigwedge_{\substack{\chi \in \mathcal{X}: \\ \chi \text{ is R-minimal}}} \mathcal{Y}_\chi \quad and \quad \mathcal{Z}_\wedge := \bigwedge_{x \in \mathcal{X}} \mathcal{Z}_x = \bigwedge_{\substack{\chi \in \mathcal{X}: \\ \chi \text{ is R-minimal}}} \mathcal{Z}_\chi,$$

and call these two partitions the $\mathrm{CORE}_\wedge$-partitions of f. We let $n_\wedge = |\mathcal{Y}_\wedge|$ and $m_\wedge = |\mathcal{Z}_\wedge|$, and we write the partitions as

$$\mathcal{Y}_\wedge := \{\mathcal{Y}_i^\wedge : i \in [n_\wedge]\} \quad and \quad \mathcal{Z}_\wedge := \{\mathcal{Z}_j^\wedge : j \in [m_\wedge]\}.$$

Finally, we let

$$\mathcal{R}_\wedge = \{\mathcal{Y}_i^\wedge \times \mathcal{Z}_j^\wedge : i \in [n_\wedge], j \in [m_\wedge]\},$$

be the partition of $\mathcal{Y} \times \mathcal{Z}$ into the combinatorial rectangles formed by $\mathcal{Y}_\wedge$ and $\mathcal{Z}_\wedge$.

The partitions $\mathcal{Y}_\wedge$ and $\mathcal{Z}_\wedge$ are naturally associated with an equivalence relation $\equiv_\wedge$ over $\mathcal{Y}$ and over $\mathcal{Z}$, respectively: We say that $y \equiv_\wedge y'$ if there exists $\mathcal{Y}^\wedge \in \mathcal{Y}_\wedge$ such that $y, y' \in \mathcal{Y}^\wedge$. Equivalently, $y \equiv_\wedge y'$ if $y \equiv_\chi y'$ for all R-minimal $\chi \in \mathcal{X}$. Similarly, $z \equiv_\wedge z'$ if there exists $\mathcal{Z}^\wedge \in \mathcal{Z}_\wedge$ such that $z, z' \in \mathcal{Z}^\wedge$.

We next define an important special property of a functionality f, which we call $\mathrm{CORE}_\wedge$-*forced*. This property plays a central role in both our positive and negative results, and generalizes the forced property defined in [24], which states that any party can fix the distribution of the output, using an appropriate distribution over its input.

Roughly, f is called $\mathrm{CORE}_\wedge$-forced if both B and C can each associate a distribution to each set in the $\mathrm{CORE}_\wedge$-partition of their respective set of inputs,

---

[14] Note that if we had defined $\preceq_B$, $\preceq_C$, and $\preceq$ directly over $\mathcal{X}$, then they would not correspond to partial orders. Indeed, for the relations to be partial orders, it required that they are antisymmetric, i.e., if $x \preceq x'$ and $x' \preceq x$ then $x = x'$. Observe that this is not generally the case, as the only guarantee we have is that $x \equiv x'$.

such that the output distribution of A in each combinatorial rectangle in $\mathcal{R}_\wedge$ is fixed for every input $x \in \mathcal{X}$.

Definition 12 (CORE$_\wedge$-forced). *The function f is said to be CORE$_\wedge$-forced if there exist two ensembles of efficiently samplable distributions $\mathcal{Q} = \{Q_{\kappa,i}\}_{\kappa \in \mathbb{N}, i \in [n_\wedge]}$ and $\mathcal{R} = \{R_{\kappa,j}\}_{\kappa \in \mathbb{N}, j \in [m_\wedge]}$ over $\mathcal{Y}$ and $\mathcal{Z}$, respectively, such that the following holds.*

$$\left\{ f(x, y^*, z_j) \right\}_{\kappa \in \mathbb{N}, x \in \mathcal{X}, i \in [n_\wedge], j \in [m_\wedge], y \in \mathcal{Y}_i^\wedge, z \in \mathcal{Z}_j^\wedge} \overset{S}{\equiv} \left\{ f(x, y^*, z) \right\}_{\kappa \in \mathbb{N}, x \in \mathcal{X}, i \in [n_\wedge], j \in [m_\wedge], y \in \mathcal{Y}_i^\wedge, z \in \mathcal{Z}_j^\wedge}$$

$$\overset{S}{\equiv} \left\{ f(x, y, z^*) \right\}_{\kappa \in \mathbb{N}, x \in \mathcal{X}, i \in [n_\wedge], j \in [m_\wedge], y \in \mathcal{Y}_i^\wedge, z \in \mathcal{Z}_j^\wedge}$$

$$\overset{S}{\equiv} \left\{ f(x, y_i, z^*) \right\}_{\kappa \in \mathbb{N}, x \in \mathcal{X}, i \in [n_\wedge], j \in [m_\wedge], y \in \mathcal{Y}_i^\wedge, z \in \mathcal{Z}_j^\wedge}$$

where $y^* \leftarrow Q_{\kappa,i}$, $z^* \leftarrow R_{\kappa,j}$, and where y_i and z_j are the lexicographically smallest elements in $\mathcal{Y}_i^\wedge$ and $\mathcal{Z}_j^\wedge$, respectively.

3.2 Our Main Results

We are now ready to state our results, providing both sufficient and necessary conditions for a deterministic solitary output three-party functionalities with polynomial-sized domain, to be computable with 1-security over point-to-point channels. The result for randomized functionalities, where the domain of the randomness is polynomial as well, is handled below in Proposition 2 by reducing it to the deterministic case. We start by stating our negative results.

Theorem 3. *Let $f : \mathcal{X} \times \mathcal{Y} \times \mathcal{Z} \to \mathcal{W}$ be a deterministic solitary output three-party functionality. Assume that $|\mathcal{X}|, |\mathcal{Y}|, |\mathcal{Z}| = \mathrm{poly}(\kappa)$. If f can be computed with 1-security, then the following hold.*

1. *For all sufficiently large $\kappa \in \mathbb{N}$, all B-minimal χ_{B} and all C-minimal χ_{C}, there exists an R-minimal $\chi \in \mathcal{X}$ such that $\chi_{\mathsf{B}} \equiv_{\mathsf{B}} \chi \equiv_{\mathsf{C}} \chi_{\mathsf{C}}$.*
2. *f is CORE$_\wedge$-forced.*

Moreover, suppose that f has the property that for all sufficiently large κ, it holds that either $y \equiv_x y'$ for all $x \in \mathcal{X}$ and $y, y' \in \mathcal{Y}$, or $z \equiv_x z'$ for all $x \in \mathcal{X}$ and $z, z' \in \mathcal{Z}$. Then there exists an ensemble of efficiently samplable distributions $\mathcal{P} = \{P_{\kappa,x}\}_{\kappa \in \mathbb{N}, x \in \mathcal{X}}$ and there exists a PPT algorithm S such that

$$\{ \mathsf{S}(1^\kappa, x, x^*, f(x^*, y, z)) \}_{\kappa \in \mathbb{N}, x \in \mathcal{X}, i \in [n_\wedge], j \in [m_\wedge], y \in \mathcal{Y}_i^\wedge, z \in \mathcal{Z}_j^\wedge}$$

$$\overset{S}{\equiv} \{ f(x, y^*, z) \}_{\kappa \in \mathbb{N}, x \in \mathcal{X}, i \in [n_\wedge], j \in [m_\wedge], y \in \mathcal{Y}_i^\wedge, z \in \mathcal{Z}_j^\wedge},$$

where $x^* \leftarrow P_{\kappa,x}$ and $y^* \leftarrow Q_{\kappa,i}$, where $Q_{\kappa,i}$ is the distribution given the CORE$_\wedge$-forced property.

Due to space limitations, the proof is given in the full version of the paper [2]. We now state our two positive results. The first positive result considers functionalities that satisfy the property given in the "moreover" part of Theorem 3. Interestingly, the protocol used in the proof of the theorem below is a slight generalization of the protocol suggested by [3].

Theorem 4. *Let $f : \mathcal{X} \times \mathcal{Y} \times \mathcal{Z} \to \mathcal{W}$ be a deterministic solitary output three-party functionality. Assume that oblivious transfer exists, that $|\mathcal{X}|, |\mathcal{Y}|, |\mathcal{Z}| = \mathrm{poly}(\kappa)$, and that the following hold.*

1. *For all sufficiently large κ, either $y \equiv_x y'$ for all $x \in \mathcal{X}$ and $y, y' \in \mathcal{Y}$, or $z \equiv_x z'$ for all $x \in \mathcal{X}$ and $z, z' \in \mathcal{Z}$.*
2. *f is $\mathrm{CORE}_\wedge$-forced.*
3. *There exists an ensemble of efficiently samplable distributions $\mathcal{P} = \{P_{\kappa,x}\}_{\kappa\in\mathbb{N}, x\in\mathcal{X}}$ and a PPT algorithm S such that*

$$\{\mathsf{S}\left(1^\kappa, x, x^*, f(x^*, y, z)\right)\}_{\kappa\in\mathbb{N}, x\in\mathcal{X}, i\in[n_\wedge], j\in[m_\wedge], y\in\mathcal{Y}_i^\wedge, z\in\mathcal{Z}_j^\wedge}$$

$$\overset{S}{\equiv} \{f(x, y^*, z)\}_{\kappa\in\mathbb{N}, x\in\mathcal{X}, i\in[n_\wedge], j\in[m_\wedge], y\in\mathcal{Y}_i^\wedge, z\in\mathcal{Z}_j^\wedge},$$

where $x^* \leftarrow P_{\kappa,x}$ and $y^* \leftarrow Q_{\kappa,i}$, where $Q_{\kappa,i}$ is the distribution given by the $\mathrm{CORE}_\wedge$-forced property.

Then f can be computed with 1-security.

Due to space limitations, the proof is given in the full version of the paper [2]. The next result gives another sufficient condition. In fact, it characterizes a special class of functionalities, which includes (deterministic) NIORP functionalities, where the output-receiving party A has no input (see Corollary 4 below). Here, instead of assuming the functionality satisfies the property stated in the "moreover" part of Theorem 3, we assume that A has a *minimum input*, i.e., smaller than all other inputs with respect to $\preceq$.

Theorem 5. *Let $f : \mathcal{X} \times \mathcal{Y} \times \mathcal{Z} \to \mathcal{W}$ be a deterministic solitary output three-party functionality. Assume that $|\mathcal{X}|, |\mathcal{Y}|, |\mathcal{Z}| = \mathrm{poly}(\kappa)$, and that for all sufficiently large κ, there exists $\chi \in \mathcal{X}$ such that for all $x \in \mathcal{X}$ it holds that $\chi \preceq x$.[15] Then f can be computed with 1-security if and only if it is $\mathrm{CORE}_\wedge$-forced. Moreover, the protocol in the positive direction admits statistical 1-security.*

Due to space limitations, the proof is given in the full version of the paper [2]. The next proposition reduces the randomized case to the deterministic case. We stress that the reduction holds for general domain sizes, and functionalities where every party obtains an output (in fact, the reduction can be easily generalized to the multiparty setting assuming an honest majority).

Proposition 2 (Reducing randomized functionalities to deterministic functionalities). *Let $f : (\{0,1\}^*)^3 \to \{0,1\}^*$ be a (randomized) three-party functionality. Define the deterministic functionality $f' : (\{0,1\}^*)^2 \times (\{0,1\}^*)^2 \times (\{0,1\}^*)^2 \to \{0,1\}^*$ as follows.*

$$f'((x, r_1), (y, r_2), (z, r_3)) = f(x, y, z; r_1 \oplus r_2 \oplus r_3).$$

Then f can be computed with 1-security if and only if f' can be computed with 1-security.

Due to space limitations, the proof is deferred to the full version [2].

---

[15] Note that there may be several minimum inputs, however, the assumption implies that they are all equivalent.

3.2.1 Interesting Corollaries

Although our necessary and sufficient conditions do not coincide in general, for various interesting families of functionalities the results do form a characterization. In the following section, we consider several such interesting families and present a characterization for them, as can be derived from Theorems 3 to 5.

We first state the characterization for functionalities with at most three possible outputs. For this class of functionalities, we make the observation that for every $x \in \mathcal{X}$, either $y \equiv_x y'$ for all $y, y' \in \mathcal{Y}$, or $z \equiv_x z'$ for all $z, z' \in \mathcal{Z}$.

Corollary 1 (Characterization of ternary-output functionalities). *Let $f : \mathcal{X} \times \mathcal{Y} \times \mathcal{Z} \to \{0, 1, 2\}$ be a deterministic solitary output three-party functionality. Assume that oblivious transfer exists and that $|\mathcal{X}|, |\mathcal{Y}|, |\mathcal{Z}| = \mathrm{poly}(\kappa)$. Then f can be computed with 1-security if and only if the following hold.*

1. *For all sufficiently large $\kappa \in \mathbb{N}$, all B-minimal χ_B and all C-minimal χ_C, there exists an R-minimal $\chi \in \mathcal{X}$ such that $\chi_\mathsf{B} \equiv_\mathsf{B} \chi \equiv_\mathsf{C} \chi_\mathsf{C}$.*
2. *f is $\mathrm{CORE}_\wedge$-forced.*
3. *There exists an ensemble of efficiently samplable distributions $\mathcal{P} = \{P_{\kappa,x}\}_{\kappa \in \mathbb{N}, x \in \mathcal{X}}$ and a PPT algorithm S such that*

$$\{\mathsf{S}(1^\kappa, x, x^*, f(x^*, y, z))\}_{\kappa \in \mathbb{N}, x_\kappa \in \mathcal{X}, i \in [n_\wedge], j \in [m_\wedge], y \in \mathcal{Y}_i^\wedge, z \in \mathcal{Z}_j^\wedge}$$

$$\overset{S}{\equiv} \{f(x, y^*, z)\}_{\kappa \in \mathbb{N}, x_\kappa \in \mathcal{X}, i \in [n_\wedge], j \in [m_\wedge], y \in \mathcal{Y}_i^\wedge, z \in \mathcal{Z}_j^\wedge},$$

where $x^* \leftarrow P_{\kappa,x}$ and $y^* \leftarrow Q_{\kappa,i}$, where $Q_{\kappa,i}$ is the distribution given the $\mathrm{CORE}_\wedge$-forced property.

Proof. It suffices to show that Item 1 from the above statement implies Item 1 from Theorem 4. That is, we show that for all sufficiently large κ, either $y \equiv_x y'$ for all $x \in \mathcal{X}$ and $y, y' \in \mathcal{Y}$, or $z \equiv_x z'$ for all $x \in \mathcal{X}$ and $z, z' \in \mathcal{Z}$. Assume towards contradiction that for infinitely many κ's, there exist $x, x' \in \mathcal{X}$, $y, y' \in \mathcal{Y}$, and $z, z' \in \mathcal{Z}$ such that $y \not\equiv_x y'$ and $z \not\equiv_{x'} z'$. Now, observe that as f is a ternary-output functionality, it holds that x and x' are B-minimal and C-minimal, respectively. Moreover, it holds that $z \equiv_x z'$ and that $y \equiv_{x'} y'$. By (the assumed) Item 1 there exists an R-minimal $\chi \in \mathcal{X}$ satisfying $x \equiv_\mathsf{B} \chi \equiv_\mathsf{C} x'$. However, such χ cannot exists since it satisfies $y \equiv_\chi y'$ and $z \equiv_\chi z'$. $\qquad\square$

We now state a characterization for functionalities that are symmetric with respect to the inputs of B and C, i.e., where $f(x, y, z) = f(x, z, y)$ for all x, y, and z. Here, the characterization follows from the observation all y's are equivalent and z's are equivalent with respect to all x's. In particular, the $\mathrm{CORE}_\wedge$-forced property implies the simpler forced property (i.e., both B and C can fix the distribution of the output).

Corollary 2 (Characterization of (B, C)-symmetric functionalities). *Let $f : \mathcal{X} \times \mathcal{D} \times \mathcal{D} \to \mathcal{W}$ be a deterministic solitary output three-party functionality. Assume that oblivious transfer exists, that $|\mathcal{X}|, |\mathcal{D}| = \mathrm{poly}(\kappa)$, and that for all sufficiently large $\kappa \in \mathbb{N}$, for all $x \in \mathcal{X}$ and for all $y, z \in \mathcal{D}$ it holds that $f(x, y, z) = f(x, z, y)$. Then f can be computed with 1-security if and only if it is forced.*

We next state a characterization for the case where the input of party A is a single bit. The proof follows from the observation that for such functionalities there exists a minimum χ, hence we can apply Theorem 5.

Corollary 3. *Let $f : \{0,1\} \times \mathcal{Y} \times \mathcal{Z} \to \mathcal{W}$ be a deterministic solitary output three-party functionality. Assume that $|\mathcal{Y}|, |\mathcal{Z}| = \mathrm{poly}(\kappa)$. Then f can be computed with 1-security if and only if the following hold.*

1. *For all sufficiently large $\kappa \in \mathbb{N}$, either $0 \preceq 1$ or $1 \preceq 0$.*
2. *f is $\mathrm{CORE}_\wedge$-forced.*

Moreover, the protocol in the positive direction admits statistical 1-security.

Proof. First observe that if $0 \preceq 1$ or $1 \preceq 0$ for all sufficiently large $\kappa \in \mathbb{N}$, then f can be computed due to Theorem 5. For the other direction, we consider two cases. First, if f is not $\mathrm{CORE}_\wedge$-forced then by Theorem 3 it cannot be computed with 1-security. Otherwise, if $0 \npreceq 1$ and $1 \npreceq 0$ infinitely often, then both are R-minimal inputs infinitely often. However, there is no R-minimal χ such that $0 \equiv_{\mathrm{B}} \chi \equiv_{\mathrm{C}} 1$. Therefore, f cannot be computed due to Theorem 3. $\square$

If A has no input, then the first property of Corollary 3 holds vacuously. Thus we have the following.

Corollary 4 (Characterization of NIORP functionalities). *Let $f : \{\lambda\} \times \mathcal{Y} \times \mathcal{Z} \to \mathcal{W}$ be a deterministic solitary output three-party functionality. Assume that $|\mathcal{Y}|, |\mathcal{Z}| = \mathrm{poly}(\kappa)$. Then f can be computed with 1-security if and only if it is $\mathrm{CORE}_\wedge$-forced. Moreover, the protocol in the positive direction admits statistical 1-security.*

Acknowledgments. Research supported in part by grants from the Israel Science Foundation (no.152/17), and by the Ariel Cyber Innovation Center in conjunction with the Israel National Cyber directorate in the Prime Minister's Office. The first author is also supported by Israel Science Foundation grant 391/21.

References

1. Agarwal, N., Anand, S., Prabhakaran, M.: Uncovering algebraic structures in the MPC landscape. In: Ishai, Y., Rijmen, V. (eds.) EUROCRYPT 2019. LNCS, vol. 11477, pp. 381–406. Springer, Cham (2019). https://doi.org/10.1007/978-3-030-17656-3_14
2. Alon, B., Omri, E.: On secure computation of solitary output functionalities with and without broadcast. Cryptology ePrint Archive, Paper 2022/934 (2022). https://eprint.iacr.org/2022/934
3. Alon, B., Cohen, R., Omri, E., Suad, T.: On the power of an honest majority in three-party computation without broadcast. In: Pass, R., Pietrzak, K. (eds.) TCC 2020. LNCS, vol. 12551, pp. 621–651. Springer, Cham (2020). https://doi.org/10.1007/978-3-030-64378-2_22
4. Asharov, G.: Towards characterizing complete fairness in secure two-party computation. In: Lindell, Y. (ed.) TCC 2014. LNCS, vol. 8349, pp. 291–316. Springer, Heidelberg (2014). https://doi.org/10.1007/978-3-642-54242-8_13

5. Asharov, G., Lindell, Y., Rabin, T.: A full characterization of functions that imply fair coin tossing and ramifications to fairness. In: Sahai, A. (ed.) TCC 2013. LNCS, vol. 7785, pp. 243–262. Springer, Heidelberg (2013). https://doi.org/10.1007/978-3-642-36594-2_14

6. Asharov, G., Beimel, A., Makriyannis, N., Omri, E.: Complete characterization of fairness in secure two-party computation of Boolean functions. In: Dodis, Y., Nielsen, J.B. (eds.) TCC 2015. LNCS, vol. 9014, pp. 199–228. Springer, Heidelberg (2015). https://doi.org/10.1007/978-3-662-46494-6_10

7. Badrinarayanan, S., Miao, P., Mukherjee, P., Ravi, D.: On the round complexity of fully secure solitary MPC with honest majority. Cryptology ePrint Archive (2021)

8. Beimel, A., Gabizon, A., Ishai, Y., Kushilevitz, E., Meldgaard, S., Paskin-Cherniavsky, A.: Non-interactive secure multiparty computation. In: Garay, J.A., Gennaro, R. (eds.) CRYPTO 2014. LNCS, vol. 8617, pp. 387–404. Springer, Heidelberg (2014). https://doi.org/10.1007/978-3-662-44381-1_22

9. Bell, J.H., Bonawitz, K.A., Gascón, A., Lepoint, T., Raykova, M.: Secure single-server aggregation with (poly) logarithmic overhead. In: ACM CCS (2020)

10. Ben-Or, M., Goldwasser, S., Wigderson, A.: Completeness theorems for noncryptographic fault-tolerant distributed computations. In: STOC (1988)

11. Bonawitz, K., et al.: Practical secure aggregation for privacy-preserving machine learning. In: Proceedings of the 2017 ACM SIGSAC Conference on Computer and Communications Security, pp. 1175–1191 (2017)

12. Burkhalter, L., Lycklama, H., Viand, A., Kuchler, N., Hithnawi, A.: Rofl: attestable robustness for secure federated learning (2021). arXiv preprint arXiv:2107.03311

13. Cleve, R.: Limits on the security of coin flips when half the processors are faulty (extended abstract). In: STOC (1986)

14. Cohen, R., Lindell, Y.: Fairness versus guaranteed output delivery in secure multiparty computation. J. Cryptol. 30(4), 1157–1186 (2017)

15. Cohen, R., Haitner, I., Omri, E., Rotem, L.: Characterization of secure multiparty computation without broadcast. J. Cryptol. 31(2), 587–609 (2018)

16. Dachman-Soled, D.: Revisiting fairness in MPC: polynomial number of parties and general adversarial structures. In: Pass, R., Pietrzak, K. (eds.) TCC 2020. LNCS, vol. 12551, pp. 595–620. Springer, Cham (2020). https://doi.org/10.1007/978-3-030-64378-2_21

17. Daza, V., Makriyannis, N.: Designing fully secure protocols for secure two-party computation of constant-domain functions. In: Kalai, Y., Reyzin, L. (eds.) TCC 2017. LNCS, vol. 10677, pp. 581–611. Springer, Cham (2017). https://doi.org/10.1007/978-3-319-70500-2_20

18. Feige, U., Killian, J., Naor, M.: A minimal model for secure computation. In: Proceedings of the Twenty-Sixth Annual ACM Symposium on Theory of Computing, pp. 554–563 (1994)

19. Fischer, M.J., Lynch, N.A., Merritt, M.: Easy impossibility proofs for distributed consensus problems. Distrib. Comput. 1(1), 26–39 (1986)

20. Fitzi, M., Garay, J.A., Maurer, U.M., Ostrovsky, R.: Minimal complete primitives for secure multi-party computation. J. Cryptol. 18(1), 37–61 (2005)

21. Goldreich, O., Micali, S., Wigderson, A.: How to play any mental game or a completeness theorem for protocols with honest majority. In: STOC (1987)

22. Gordon, S.D., Katz, J.: Complete fairness in multi-party computation without an honest majority. In: Reingold, O. (ed.) TCC 2009. LNCS, vol. 5444, pp. 19–35. Springer, Heidelberg (2009). https://doi.org/10.1007/978-3-642-00457-5_2

23. Gordon, S.D., Hazay, C., Katz, J., Lindell, Y.: Complete fairness in secure two-party computation. In: STOC (2008)

24. Halevi, S., Ishai, Y., Kushilevitz, E., Makriyannis, N., Rabin, T.: On fully secure MPC with solitary output. In: Hofheinz, D., Rosen, A. (eds.) TCC 2019. LNCS, vol. 11891, pp. 312–340. Springer, Cham (2019). https://doi.org/10.1007/978-3-030-36030-6_13
25. Lamport, L., Shostak, R.E., Pease, M.C.: The byzantine generals problem. ACM Trans. Program. Lang. Syst. (TOPLAS) **4**(3), 382–401 (1982)
26. Makriyannis, N.: On the classification of finite Boolean functions up to fairness. In: Proceedings of the 9th Conference on Security and Cryptography for Networks (SCN), pp. 135–154 (2014)
27. Pease, M.C., Shostak, R.E., Lamport, L.: Reaching agreement in the presence of faults. J. ACM **27**(2), 228–234 (1980)
28. Rabin, T., Ben-Or, M.: Verifiable secret sharing and multiparty protocols with honest majority (extended abstract). In: FOCS, pp. 73–85 (1989)

On the Round Complexity of Fully Secure Solitary MPC with Honest Majority

Saikrishna Badrinarayanan[1]([✉]), Peihan Miao[2], Pratyay Mukherjee[3], and Divya Ravi[4][iD]

[1] LinkedIn, Mountain View, USA
bsaikrishna7393@gmail.com
[2] Brown University, Providence, USA
[3] Supra Research, Kolkata, India
[4] Aarhus University, Aarhus, Denmark

Abstract. We study the problem of secure multiparty computation for functionalities where only *one* party receives the output, to which we refer as *solitary MPC*. Recently, Halevi et al. (TCC 2019) studied fully secure (i.e., with guaranteed output delivery) solitary MPC and showed impossibility of such protocols for certain functionalities when there is no honest majority among the parties.

In this work, we study the round complexity of fully secure solitary MPC in the honest majority setting and with computational security. We note that a broadcast channel or public key infrastructure (PKI) setup is necessary for an n-party protocol against malicious adversaries corrupting up to t parties where $n/3 \leq t < n/2$. Therefore, we study the following settings and ask the question: Can fully secure solitary MPC be achieved in fewer rounds than fully secure standard MPC in which all parties receive the output?

- When there is a broadcast channel and no PKI:
  - We start with a negative answer to the above question. In particular, we show that the exact round complexity of fully secure solitary MPC is 3, which is the same as fully secure standard MPC.
  - We then study the minimal number of broadcast rounds needed to design round-optimal fully secure solitary MPC. We show that both the first and second rounds of broadcast are necessary when $2\lceil n/5 \rceil \leq t < n/2$, whereas pairwise-private channels suffice in the last round. Notably, this result also applies to fully secure standard MPC in which all parties receive the output.
- When there is a PKI and no broadcast channel, nevertheless, we show more positive results:
  - We show an upper bound of 5 rounds for any honest majority. This is superior to the super-constant lower bound for fully secure standard MPC in the exact same setting.
  - We complement this by showing a lower bound of 4 rounds when $3\lceil n/7 \rceil \leq t < n/2$.
  - For the special case of $t = 1, n = 3$, when the output receiving party does not have an input to the function, we show an upper bound of 2 rounds, which is optimal. When the output receiving

ⓒ International Association for Cryptologic Research 2023
G. Rothblum and H. Wee (Eds.): TCC 2023, LNCS 14370, pp. 124–155, 2023.
https://doi.org/10.1007/978-3-031-48618-0_5

party has an input to the function, we show a lower bound of 3, which matches an upper bound from prior work.
- For the special case of $t = 2, n = 5$, we show a lower bound of 3 rounds (an upper bound of 4 follows from prior work).

All our results also assume the existence of a common reference string (CRS) and pairwise-private channels. Our upper bounds use a decentralized threshold fully homomorphic encryption (dTFHE) scheme (which can be built from the learning with errors (LWE) assumption) as the main building block.

1   Introduction

Secure multiparty computation (MPC) [25,39] allows a set of mutually distrusting parties to jointly compute any function on their private data in a way that the participants do not learn anything about the inputs except the output of the function. The strongest possible security notion for MPC is *guaranteed output delivery* (god for short), which states that all honest parties are guaranteed to receive their outputs no matter how the corrupt parties behave. An MPC protocol achieving god is often called a *fully secure* protocol. A seminal work of Cleve [13] showed that there exist functionalities for which it is impossible to construct an MPC protocol with god unless a majority of the parties are honest.

Solitary MPC. Recently, Halevi et al. [29] initiated the study of MPC protocols with god for a special class of functionalities, called *solitary* functionalities, which deliver the output to *exactly one party*. Such functionalities capture many real world applications of MPC in which parties play different roles and only one specific party wishes to learn the output. For example, consider a privacy-preserving machine learning task [35] where several entities provide training data while only one entity wishes to learn a model based on this private aggregated data. As another example, a service provider may want to learn aggregated information about its users while keeping the users' data private [8,9]. In the rest of the paper we refer to such MPC protocols as *solitary MPC*. For clarity of exposition, we refer to protocols where all parties obtain output as *standard MPC*. While the argument of Cleve [13] does not rule out solitary MPC with god in the presence of a dishonest majority,[1] Halevi et al. [29] showed that there exist functionalities for which solitary MPC with god is also impossible with dishonest majority. Hence, the results of [13] and [29] rule out the existence of a generic MPC protocol that can compute *any* standard and solitary functionality respectively with god in dishonest majority (protocols can exist for specific classes of functionalities as shown in [4,27,29]). Both impossibility results hold even when

---

[1] Cleve's argument shows that with dishonest majority, it is impossible for an MPC protocol to achieve *fairness*, which guarantees that malicious parties cannot learn the output while preventing honest parties from learning the output. Since god implies fairness, this impossibility also holds for standard MPC with god. However, it doesn't hold for solitary MPC as fairness is clearly not an issue in the solitary MPC setting.

parties have access to a common reference string (CRS). In this paper, we focus on *solitary MPC with* god in the *honest majority* setting.

Round Complexity. An important efficiency metric of an MPC protocol is its *round complexity*, which quantifies the number of communication rounds required to perform the protocol. The round complexity of standard MPC has been extensively studied over the last four decades (see the full version [7] for a detailed literature survey). In the honest majority setting, *three* rounds are known to be necessary [24,28,36] for *standard MPC with* god, even in the presence of a common reference string (CRS) *and* a broadcast channel (without a PKI setup). Matching upper bounds appear in [3,6,28]. The protocol of Gordon et al. [28] requires a CRS[2], while the other two [3,6] are in the plain model. In this work we focus on the round complexity aspects of solitary MPC protocols.

Necessity of Broadcast or PKI. A closer look at the above protocols reveals that all of them assume the existence of a broadcast channel. For solitary MPC with god, the works of [2,21] show that either a broadcast channel or a public key infrastructure (PKI) setup is indeed necessary assuming an honest majority (in particular, when $n/3 \leq t < n/2$ for an n-party protocol against adversaries corrupting up to t parties) even with a CRS.[3] Note that although PKI setup and broadcast channels are equivalent according to [17] from a feasibility perspective, realizing broadcast under PKI setup with *guaranteed termination* requires super-constant rounds, which we will discuss shortly. In light of this, we study the round complexity of solitary MPC with god when $n/3 \leq t < n/2$ in two settings: (a) there is a broadcast channel and no PKI setup; (b) there is PKI setup and no broadcast channel. When both broadcast channels and PKI are available, we know from prior works [28,30] that the exact round complexity is two.

With Broadcast, No PKI. In this setting we investigate whether we can do better for solitary MPC than standard MPC in terms of round complexity even in the presence of CRS. In particular,

Assuming a broadcast channel and CRS, can we build a solitary MPC protocol with god in fewer than three rounds?

---

[2] This protocol uses a decentralized threshold fully homomorphic encryption (dTFHE) scheme. The public parameter of this dTFHE is assumed to be shared among the parties and viewed as a common reference string (refer to [28] for further details).

[3] Fitzi et al. [21] show that converge-cast cannot be achieved when $n/3 \leq t < n/2$ in the *information theoretic* setting. Alon et al. [2] show a specific solitary functionality that cannot be computed by a 3-party MPC protocol with a single corruption with god in the *plain model* (with no broadcast channel and no PKI), which also extends to $n/3 \leq t < n/2$. Both arguments also work even in the presence of a CRS. We present the proof in the full version [7] for completeness.

Unfortunately, the answer is no! We show that in the presence of a broadcast channel and CRS, the exact round complexity for solitary MPC with god is also *three*, same as standard MPC.

However, broadcast channels are *expensive* to realize in practice – the seminal works of Dolev and Strong [17] and Fischer and Lynch [19] showed that realizing a single round of *deterministic* broadcast requires at least $t + 1$ rounds of communication over pairwise-private channels, where t is the number of corrupt parties, even with a public key infrastructure (PKI) setup.[4] This can be overcome by considering *randomized* broadcast protocols in the honest majority setting [1,18,20,32] requiring expected constant rounds. In particular, the most round-efficient protocol to our knowledge is proposed by Abraham et al. [1], which solves Byzantine agreement for $t < n/2$ in expected 10 rounds. Nevertheless, these protocols do not *guarantee termination* in constant rounds, which is the setting we are interested in.[5] In fact, it is shown that termination cannot be guaranteed in constant rounds [12,31].

Recent works [14–16,22] try to minimize the usage of expensive broadcast channels in the context of round-optimal standard MPC. In particular, they study whether each round of a round-optimal MPC protocol necessarily requires a broadcast channel or pairwise-private channels suffice in some of them. In the context of round-optimal solitary MPC with god, we ask an analogous question:

Is a broadcast channel necessary in every round of a three-round solitary MPC protocol with god?

We show that a broadcast channel is *necessary* in both the *first* and *second* rounds in a three-round solitary MPC protocol with god while pairwise-private channels suffice in the third round.

With PKI, No Broadcast. In this setting a natural question arises: in the absence of a broadcast channel, if we assume a PKI setup, what is the optimal round complexity for solitary MPC with god? In standard MPC, note that since standard MPC with god implies broadcast with guaranteed termination, any protocol without a broadcast channel (only using pairwise-private channels with PKI setup) should *necessarily* require super-constant rounds. In contrast, observe that solitary MPC with god does not imply broadcast with guaranteed termination, so the same lower bound does not hold. This motivates us to ask the following question:

---

[4] Note that PKI setup is in fact necessary for realizing a broadcast channel when $t \geq n/3$ (where n is the total number of parties) [33,37].

[5] In these randomized broadcast protocols, the number of rounds depends on the randomness involved in the protocol. For example, the protocol by Abraham et al. [1] terminates in constant rounds except with constant probability and requires at least super-polylogarithmic rounds (in the security parameter) to terminate with all but negligible probability.

*With a PKI setup and no broadcast channel, can we overcome the above
standard MPC lower bound? Specifically, can we build a constant-round solitary
MPC protocol with god in the honest majority setting?*

We answer this question in the affirmative by constructing a *five-round* solitary MPC protocol that achieves god in the above setting.

1.1 Our Results

1.1.1 With Broadcast, No PKI

When there is a broadcast channel but no PKI setup, we show a lower bound of *three rounds* for achieving solitary MPC with god in the honest majority setting, which is the same as the lower bound for standard MPC.

Informal Theorem 1. *Assume parties have access to CRS, pairwise-private channels and a broadcast channel. Then, there exists a solitary functionality f such that no two-round MPC protocol can compute f with god in the honest majority setting (in particular, when $n/3 \leq t < n/2$) even against a non-rushing adversary.*

This lower bound is tight because we know from prior works [3,6,28] that there are three-round solitary MPC protocols with god in the honest majority setting.

We then study the minimal number of broadcast rounds needed in a round-optimal (three-round) solitary MPC protocol with god. We show that a broadcast channel is necessary in both the first and second rounds.

Informal Theorem 2. *Assume parties have access to CRS and pairwise-private channels. No three-round solitary MPC protocol can compute any solitary functionality f with god in the honest majority setting (in particular, when $2 \lceil n/5 \rceil \leq t < n/2$) even against a non-rushing adversary, unless there are broadcast channels in both Rounds 1 and 2.*

We note that the necessity of a broadcast channel in Round 1 holds for any $n/3 \leq t < n/2$ while the necessity of a broadcast channel in Round 2 only holds for $2 \lceil n/5 \rceil \leq t < n/2$ requiring *at least two parties be corrupted*. In other words, for $t = 1$ and $n = 3$ only the first round broadcast is necessary. This is consistent with and proven tight by the upper bound in the work of Patra and Ravi [36], which constructed a three-round three-party protocol with god tolerating a single corruption, using broadcast only in Round 1.

For the general case when $t \geq 2$, we observe that in the three-round protocols from prior work [3,6,28], only the first two rounds require a broadcast channel while the third-round messages can be sent over pairwise-private channels to the output-receiving party. Thus, our lower bounds are also tight in the general case.

Implications for Standard MPC. The work of Cohen et al. [14] identifies which rounds of broadcast are necessary for achieving round-optimal (two-round) standard MPC with *dishonest majority*. The recent work of [15] studies this question for two-round standard MPC in the honest majority setting, assuming the presence of a correlated randomness setup (or PKI). However, the same question for round-optimal (*three-round*) standard MPC with god in *honest majority* setting and without correlated randomness (or PKI) is not known; which we address in this work. Since standard MPC with god implies solitary MPC with god, our negative results for solitary MPC also apply to standard MPC, namely both the first and second rounds of broadcast are necessary for a three-round standard MPC with god. On the other hand, we observe that the existing three-round protocols [6,28] still work if the third-round messages are sent over pairwise-private channels (we defer the discussion to the full version [7]), thus we fully resolve this problem for standard MPC with god in honest majority setting and without correlated randomness setup (i.e., in the plain and CRS models).

1.1.2 With PKI, No Broadcast

When there is a PKI setup and no broadcast channel, we show that the super-constant lower bound for standard MPC does *not* hold for solitary MPC any more. In particular, we construct a *five-round* protocol that works for any number of parties and achieves god in the honest majority setting. Our protocol builds on the standard MPC protocol with god of Gordon et al. [28] and uses a decentralized threshold fully homomorphic encryption (dTFHE) scheme (defined in [10]) as the main building block, which can be based on the learning with errors (LWE) assumption. Our PKI setup includes a setup for digital signatures as well as one for dTFHE (similarly as in [28])[6].

Informal Theorem 3. *Assuming LWE, there exists a five-round solitary MPC protocol with god in the presence of PKI and pairwise-private channels. The protocol works for any number of parties n, any solitary functionality and is secure against a malicious rushing adversary that can corrupt any $t < n/2$ parties.*

We complement this upper bound by providing a lower bound of *four rounds* in the same setting even in the presence of a non-rushing adversary.

Informal Theorem 4. *Assume a PKI setup and pairwise-private channels. There exists a solitary functionality f such that no three-round MPC can compute f with god in the honest majority setting (in particular, when $3\lceil n/7 \rceil \leq t < n/2$) even against a non-rushing adversary.*

The above lower bound requires $t \geq 3$, namely at least 3 parties are corrupted. Separately we also study the round complexity for scenarios when $t < 3$.

Special Case: $t = 1$. When there is only 1 corrupted party, the only relevant setting is when $n = 3$. We consider two cases: (a) when the function f involves an input from the output-receiving party Q, and (b) when f does not involve

---

[6] We leave it as an interesting open problem to achieve the upper bound using weaker forms of PKI setup and studying the minimal assumption required.

an input from Q. In the first case, we show a lower bound of *three rounds* for achieving solitary MPC with god. That is, there exists a solitary functionality f (involving an input from Q) such that a minimum of three rounds are required to achieve solitary MPC with god. Notably, this lower bound also extends to any $n \geq 3$ and $n/3 \leq t < n/2$. A three-round upper bound for $t = 1$ can be achieved by combining [28] and [17].

In the second case where f does not involve an input from Q, it turns out we can do better than three rounds. In particular, we show a *two-round* protocol to achieve solitary MPC with god. Once again, the main technical tool is decentralized threshold FHE and the protocol can be based on LWE. This upper bound is also tight as we know from prior work [30] that two rounds are necessary.

Special Case: $t = 2$. When the number of corrupted parties is 2, we only consider the case of $n = 5$ and show a lower bound of *three rounds* to compute any function f (with or without input from Q). This lower bound also extends to any $n \geq 5$ and $2 \lceil n/5 \rceil \leq t < n/2$. An upper bound of four rounds for $t = 2$ can also be achieved by combining [28] and [17].

We remark that all our lower bounds above hold not only for PKI, but naturally extend to arbitrary correlated randomness setup model. We summarize all our results along with the known related results for the round complexity of solitary MPC with god in Tables 1 and 2. Note that for certain ranges of (n, t) such as $3 \lceil n/7 \rceil \leq t < n/2$, it is not meaningful for every n (e.g., when $n = 8$, there is no appropriate t in the range). This is an artifact of the partitioning technique used in the proof. Nevertheless, the range is relevant for sufficiently large values of n. All our results also assume the existence of a common reference string (CRS) and pairwise-private channels. Our results are highlighted in red.

Table 1. Round complexity of solitary MPC with god. "—" means it doesn't matter what value to take. Our results are highlighted in red.

broadcast	PKI	(n, t)	Q has input	lower bound	upper bound
yes	yes	$t < n/2$	—	2 [30]	2 [28]
yes	no	$n/3 \leq t < n/2$	—	3 (Theorem 1)	3 [3,6,28]
no	yes	$n = 3, t = 1$	no	2 [30]	2 (full version [7])
no	yes	$n = 3, t = 1$	yes	3 (full version [7])	3 [28] + [17]
no	yes	$n = 5, t = 2$	—	3 (full version [7])	4 [28] + [17]
no	yes	$3 \lceil n/7 \rceil \leq t < n/2$	—	4 (Theorem 4)	5 (Theorem 5)

Table 2. For the setting with broadcast channels and no PKI setup, we study the possibility of achieving a three-round solitary MPC with god with fewer broadcast rounds. "bc in R1" means the parties have access to the broadcast channel in Round 1. All parties have access to pairwise-private channels in all rounds. For all the results, it doesn't matter whether Q has input or not. Our results are highlighted in red.

bc in R1	bc in R2	bc in R3	(n, t)	Possible?
no	yes	yes	$n/3 \leq t < n/2$	No (Theorem 2)
yes	no	yes	$2\lceil n/5 \rceil \leq t < n/2$	No (Theorem 3)
yes	yes	no	$t < n/2$	Yes [3,6,28]
yes	no	no	$n = 3, t = 1$	Yes [36]

1.2 Roadmap

We provide a technical overview in Sect. 2 and preliminaries in Sect. 3. In Sect. 4 we present our lower bound results assuming a broadcast channel but no PKI setup. In Sect. 5 we provide our lower bounds for PKI without broadcast as well as our main five-round protocol as an upper bound. We defer the results for the special cases of $t = 1$ and $t = 2$ to the full version [7].

2 Technical Overview

2.1 Overview of Upper Bounds

In this section, we give a technical overview of the upper bounds. We will mainly focus on the general five-round protocol in the setting with PKI and no broadcast, and briefly discuss other special cases at the end.

Our starting point is the two-round protocol of Gordon et al. [28] which achieves guaranteed output delivery (god) in the presence of an honest majority and delivers output to all parties, assuming the existence of a broadcast channel and PKI setup. The protocol uses a $(t + 1)$-out-of-n decentralized threshold fully homomorphic encryption (dTFHE) scheme, where an FHE public key pk is generated in the setup and the secret key is secret shared among the parties. The encryptions can be homomorphically evaluated and can only be jointly decrypted by at least $(t + 1)$ parties. Their two-round protocol in the broadcast model roughly works as follows. First, the PKI setup generates the dTFHE public key pk and individual secret keys sk_i for each party P_i. In Round 1, each party P_i computes an encryption of its input x_i and broadcasts $[\![x_i]\!]$.[7] Then each party can homomorphically evaluate the function f on $[\![x_1]\!], \ldots, [\![x_n]\!]$ to obtain an encryption of the output $[\![y]\!]$. In Round 2, each party broadcasts a partial decryption of $[\![y]\!]$. At the end of this, every party can individually combine the partial decryptions to learn the output y.

---

[7] We use $[\![x]\!]$ to denote a dTFHE encryption of x.

One immediate observation is that since we only care about one party $P_n(=Q)$ receiving the output, the second round also works without a broadcast channel by requiring every party to only send partial decryptions directly to Q. The main challenge now is to emulate the first round with pairwise-private channels instead of broadcast channels. A naïve approach is to employ a $(t+1)$-round protocol to realize the broadcast functionality over pairwise-private channels [17], but this would result in a $(t+2)$-round protocol.

Even worse, there seems to be a fundamental barrier in this approach to design a constant round protocol. At a high level, to achieve guaranteed output delivery, we want all the honest parties to agree on a set of ciphertexts $[\![x_1]\!], \ldots, [\![x_n]\!]$ so that they can homomorphically evaluate on the same set of ciphertexts and compute partial decryptions on the same $[\![y]\!]$. This already implies Byzantine agreement, which requires at least $(t+1)$ rounds [17].

Circumventing the Lower Bound. A crucial observation here, which also separates solitary MPC from standard MPC, is that we do not need all the honest parties to *always* agree. Instead, we need them to agree *only when Q is honest*. In other words, if the honest parties detect any dishonest behavior of Q, they can simply abort. This does not imply Byzantine agreement now. Hence there is a hope to circumvent the super-constant lower bound.

Relying on Honest Q. First, consider a simple case where honest parties only need to agree on $[\![x_n]\!]$ when Q is honest. This can be done in two rounds (by augmenting the two-round broadcast with abort protocol of [26] with digital signatures). In Round 1, Q sends $[\![x_n]\!]$ to each party (along with its signature). To ensure Q sends the same ciphertext to everyone, in Round 2, parties exchange their received messages in Round 1. If there is any inconsistency, then they detect dishonest behavior of Q, so they can abort; otherwise, all the honest parties will agree on the same $[\![x_n]\!]$ at the end of Round 2 if Q is honest. Unfortunately this simple approach does not work for parties other than Q. If honest parties want to agree on $[\![x_i]\!]$ for $i \neq n$, they cannot simply abort when detecting inconsistent messages from P_i (because they are only allowed to abort when Q is dishonest).

Our next attempt is to crucially rely on Q to send out all the ciphertexts. In Round 1, each party P_i first sends an encryption $[\![x_i]\!]$ to Q. Then in Round 2, Q sends $[\![x_1]\!], \ldots, [\![x_n]\!]$ to each party. In Round 3, parties exchange their messages received from Q. If the honest parties notice any inconsistency in Q's Round-2 messages, they can simply abort. Note that every message is sent along with the sender's signature, so a malicious Q cannot forge an honest P_i's ciphertext $[\![x_i]\!]$; similarly, a malicious P_i cannot forge an honest Q's Round-2 message. Therefore, all the honest parties will agree on the same set of ciphertexts at the end of Round 3 if Q is honest.

Nevertheless, a malicious Q has complete freedom to discard any honest party's input in Round 2 (pretending that these parties did not communicate to him in Round 1) and learn a function excluding these honest parties' inputs, which should not be permitted. The crux of the issue is: Even when Q is malicious, the output of f learned by Q must be either $\bot$ or include every honest party's input. This is implied by the security guarantees of the MPC protocol. In particular, in the real/ideal paradigm, a malicious Q in the ideal world can only obtain an output from the ideal functionality that computes f involving all the honest parties' inputs. Therefore, we need a mechanism to ensure that all the honest parties' ciphertexts are picked by Q. However, the parties do not know the identities of the honest parties. How can they ensure this?

Innocent Until Proven Guilty. Our solution to this problem is for every party P_i to treat other parties with more leniency. That is, unless P_i knows with absolute certainty that another party P_k is malicious, P_i would demand that the ciphertexts picked by Q must also include a ciphertext from P_k. To implement this mechanism, we add another round at the beginning, where each party P_i sends $[\![x_i]\!]$ to every other party. Then in Round 2, each party P_i, besides sending $[\![x_i]\!]$ to Q, also sends all the ciphertexts he has received to Q. In Round 3, Q picks a set of ciphertexts $[\![x_1]\!], \ldots, [\![x_n]\!]$ and sends to each party. In particular, for each party P_k, as long as Q received any valid ciphertext for P_k (either directly from P_k or from other parties), Q must include a ciphertext for P_k. Parties exchange messages in Round 4 to check Q's consistency as before. Finally, we maintain the following invariant for every honest party P_i before sending the partial decryption in Round 5: if P_i received a ciphertext $[\![x_k]\!]$ from party P_k in Round 1, then the ciphertexts picked by Q must also include a ciphertext from P_k. Crucially, this invariant allows Q to pick a different ciphertext $[\![x_k']\!]$ (with a valid signature) if e.g. that was received by Q from P_k. On the other hand, this prevents the attacks discussed earlier as a malicious Q can no longer discard an honest P_k's ciphertext $[\![x_k]\!]$, although P_i is yet to identify the honest parties.

Achieving Fully Malicious Security. To achieve fully malicious security, we still need to ensure that the adversary's messages are correctly generated. The approach taken by [28] is to apply a generic round-preserving compiler [5] that transforms a semi-malicious protocol (where, the semi-malicious adversary needs to follow the protocol specification, but has the liberty to decide the input and random coins in each round) to a malicious protocol using non-interactive zero-knowledge (NIZK) proofs in the CRS model with broadcast channels. In particular, in each round, the adversary must prove (in zero-knowledge) that it is following the protocol consistently with some setting of random coins. However, we cannot directly apply this round-preserving compiler since we do not have broadcast channels. This limitation introduces additional complications in our protocol design to preserve the round complexity while achieving malicious security. We refer the reader to Sect. 5.2 for more details of the protocol and other subtle issues we faced in our protocol design.

Special Cases. As we mentioned above, the two-round protocol of Gordon et al. [28] with broadcast and PKI can be transformed into a $(t+2)$-round protocol if the broadcast in the first round is instantiated by a $(t+1)$-round protocol over pairwise-private channels [17] and parties only send their messages to Q in the second round. For $t = 1$ and 2, we can achieve better than five rounds. For $t = 1$, when Q does not have input, we can design a two-round protocol which crucially relies on the fact that at most one party is corrupted. The details are deferred to the full version [7].

2.2 Overview of Lower Bounds

For each of our lower bound proofs, we design a special solitary function f that cannot be computed with god. At a high level, we assume towards a contradiction that there exists an MPC protocol Π that can compute f with god. Next, we analyze a sequence of scenarios which lead us to the final contradiction regarding the properties that Π must satisfy. Here, we exploit the guarantees of correctness, privacy and full-security (guaranteed output delivery). We carefully design the function f and scenarios for each lower bound proof. For certain proofs, we leverage a delicate *probabilistic argument* technique, which we elaborate below.

With Broadcast and no PKI. For our three-round lower bound with a broadcast channel and no PKI setup, we design a solitary function $f(x_1, x_2, x_3)$ among parties P_1, P_2, and Q (output receiving party) that has an oblivious transfer flavor. The function is defined as $f(x_1 = (m_0, m_1), x_2 = b, x_3 = \bot) := m_b$, where $x_3 = \bot$ denotes that Q has no input; $(m_0, m_1) \in \{0, 1\}^\lambda$ denote a pair of strings and $b \in \{0, 1\}$ denotes a single bit. We assume there exists a two-round protocol Π that computes f with god and consider three scenarios. The first scenario involves a malicious P_2 who drops his private message towards Q in Round 1 and aborts in Round 2. The second scenario involves a passive Q who behaves honestly but recomputes the output by locally emulating Scenario 1 in her head. The security guarantee of god provided by Π allow us to argue that even if P_2 does not communicate privately to Q in Round 1 and aborts in Round 2, Q must still be able to compute the output on x_2 i.e. the input with respect to which it interacted with P_1 in Round 1. Intuitively, this implies that Q relies on the following messages to carry information about x_2 required for output computation (i) P_1's broadcast message in Round 2 and (ii) P_2's broadcast message in Round 1. However, we note that, both of these are also available to P_1 at the end of Round 1 itself. This leads us to a final scenario, in that a passive P_1 can compute the residual function $f(\widetilde{x_1}, x_2, \widetilde{x_3})$ for more than one choices of $(\widetilde{x_1}, \widetilde{x_3})$, while the input of honest P_2 remains fixed – which is the final contradiction. Notably, our specially designed function f allows P_1 to derive P_2's input. We present the full proof in Sect. 4.1.

Necessity of Broadcast in Round 1. To show the necessity of broadcast in Round 1 in a three-round solitary MPC protocol with god (with broadcast and no PKI), we use the same function f as above and assume there exists a three-round protocol Π that computes f with god and uses the broadcast channel only in Round 2 and Round 3 (and uses pairwise-private channels in all rounds). We first consider a scenario with a malicious P_2, who only behaves honestly to P_1 and pretends to have received a maliciously computed message from Q in Round 1. In addition, P_2 aborts in Round 3. We show that an honest Q in this scenario must obtain $f(x_1, x_2, x_3)$ as the output, where x_1, x_2, x_3 are the parties' honest inputs. First of all, Q must learn an output computed on the honest parties' inputs x_1 and x_3 by the god property of Π. The output is also w.r.t. P_2's honest input x_2 because Q's view in this scenario is subsumed by another scenario with a malicious Q, where Q only behaves honestly to P_1 and pretends to have received a maliciously computed message from P_2 in Round 1. Since the first-round messages are only sent via pairwise-private channels, P_1 cannot distinguish whether P_2 is malicious (first scenario) or Q is malicious (second scenario), and P_1's view is identically distributed in both scenarios. Comparing the messages received by Q in the two scenarios, we can conclude Q's view in the first scenario is subsumed by its view in the second scenario. Notice that a malicious Q in the second scenario can only learn an output on the honest parties' input x_1 and x_2, hence Q must learn $f(x_1, x_2, x_3)$ in both scenarios. The key takeaway is that P_2's input can be considered as "committed" in its private message to P_1 in Round 1 and broadcast message in Round 2. This allows a semi-honest P_1 to emulate Q's view in the first scenario and locally compute $f(x_1, x_2, \bot)$. Our specially designed f allows P_1 to derive honest P_2's input, violating the security of Π. A more detailed proof is presented in Sect. 4.2.

Necessity of Broadcast in Round 2. For our result showing necessity of broadcast in Round 2, we design a more sophisticated function f (see Sect. 4.3 for the construction) and leverage a more involved probabilistic argument in our proof. We assume there exists a three-round 5-party solitary MPC Π that computes f with god against 2 corruptions which uses broadcast in only Round 1 and Round 3 (and uses pairwise-private channels in all rounds). The argument involves two crucial observations (1) Π is such that if corrupt P_1 participates honestly using input x_1 only in the broadcast communication and private communication towards $\{P_2, P_5 = Q\}$ in Round 1 (and sends no other messages during Π), then there exists some x_1^* such that the output obtained by Q is *not* computed with respect to x_1^* *with a sufficiently large (constant) probability*. Intuitively, if this does not hold and for all x_1 the output is computed with respect to x_1, then it would mean that Π is such that $\{P_2, Q\}$ obtain sufficient information to compute on x_1 at the end of Round 1 itself. This would make Π susceptible to residual function attack by $\{P_2, Q\}$ which violates security. (2) Π is such that if corrupt $\{P_3, P_4\}$ pretend in Round 2 as if they have not received private communication from P_1 in Round 1, still, the output obtained by Q must be computed on honest P_1's input x_1. This follows from correctness of Π. Next, we design a final scenario building on (1) and (2) where an adversary corrupting $\{P_1, Q\}$ obtains multiple outputs, with respect to both input $x_1' \neq x_1^*$ and x_1^*; which gives the final contradiction. Crucially, due to absence of broadcast in Round 2, the adversary is able to keep the honest parties $\{P_2, P_3, P_4\}$ on different pages with respect to whether P_1 has aborted after Round 1 or not. Specifically, the adversarial strategy in the final scenario exploits the absence of broadcast in Round 2 to ensure the following - (a) view of honest $\{P_3, P_4\}$ is similar to the scenario in **(1)**, where they do not receive any communication from P_1 except its broadcast communication in Round 1 and (b) view of honest P_2 is similar to the scenario in **(2)**. Here, P_2 receives communication from P_1 in both Round 1 and Round 2; but receives communication from $\{P_3, P_4\}$ in Round 2 conveying that they did not receive P_1's private communication in Round 1 (the Round 2 messages from $\{P_3, P_4\}$ could potentially convey this information, depending on protocol design). This inconsistency in the views of honest parties enables the adversary to obtain multiple outputs.

With PKI and no Broadcast. The lower-bound arguments in the setting with a PKI setup and no broadcast tend to be more involved as PKI can be used to allow output obtaining party Q to have some secret useful for output computation (as elaborated in the overview of 3-round lower bound above). For our four-round general lower bound that holds for $3\lceil n/7 \rceil \leq t < n/2$ and $t \geq 3$, we assume there exists a three-round protocol Π with god computing a specially designed 7-party solitary function f (see Sect. 5.1 for the construction of f). We analyze four main scenarios as follows. In Scenarios 1 and 2, $\{P_1, P_6\}$ are corrupt and P_1 does not communicate directly to anyone throughout. The crucial difference between them is in the communication of P_6 in Round 2 to $\{P_2, P_3, P_4, P_5\}$: in Scenario 1, P_6 acts as if he *did not receive* any communication from P_1 in Round 1; in Scenario 2, P_6 pretends to *have received* communication from P_1 in Round 1. We first show that in Scenario 1, there must exist some x_1^* such that the output obtained by Q is *not* computed with respect to x_1^* *with a sufficiently large (constant) probability*. Intuitively, this holds because the communication in Scenario 1 is independent of P_1's input. Next, we prove via a sequence of hybrids that in Scenario 2, there also exists x_1^* such that the output is *not* computed on x_1^* *with a sufficiently large probability*. This lets us infer a critical property satisfied by Π - if $\{P_3, P_4, P_5\}$ do not receive any communication *directly* from P_1 throughout Π and only potentially receive information regarding P_1 *indirectly* via P_6 (say P_6 claims to have received authenticated information from P_1 which can be verified by $\{P_3, P_4, P_5\}$ due to availability of PKI), then Q obtains an output on some $x_1'(\neq x_1^*)$ *with a sufficiently large probability*.

Next, we consider an orthogonal scenario (Scenario 3) where $\{P_3, P_4, P_5\}$ are corrupt and pretend as if they received no information from P_1 directly. Correctness of Π ensures that Q must obtain output on honest input of P_1 using the messages from $\{P_1, P_2, P_6\}$. Roughly speaking, the above observations enable us to partition the parties $\{P_1, \ldots, P_6\}$ into two sets $\{P_1, P_2, P_6\}$ and $\{P_3, P_4, P_5\}$. Combining the above inferences, we design the final scenario where adversary corrupts $\{P_1, P_2, Q\}$ and participates with x_1^*. Here, P_1 behaves honestly only to P_6 (among the honest parties). The communication of corrupt parties is carefully defined so that the following holds: (a) the views of $\{P_3, P_4, P_5\}$ are identically distributed to their views in Scenario 2, and (b) the views of $\{P_1, P_2, P_6\}$ are identically distributed to their views in Scenario 3. We then demonstrate that

Q can obtain an output computed on x_1^* as well as another output computed on some $x_1' \neq x_1^*$ by using the communication from $\{P_1, P_2, P_6\}$ and $\{P_3, P_4, P_5\}$ *selectively*, violating the security of Π.

Finally, we observe that the above approach inherently demands the presence of 3 or more corruptions. The main bottleneck in extending it to $t = 2$ arises from the sequence of hybrids between Scenario 1 and 2, which requires the presence of an additional corruption besides $\{P_1, P_6\}$. This shows hope for better upper bounds (less than four rounds) for lower corruption thresholds. In this direction, we investigated the cases of $t = 1$ and $t = 2$ separately. We showed the necessity of three rounds for $t = 1$ when Q has input and for $t = 2$ (irrespective of whether Q has input). These lower bounds also employ the common approach outlined above but differ significantly in terms of the associated scenarios. We refer to the full version [7] for details. Notably, all the lower bounds also extend to arbitrary correlated randomness setup.

3 Preliminaries

3.1 Notation and Setting

We use λ to denote the security parameter. By $\mathsf{poly}(\lambda)$ we denote a polynomial function in λ. By $\mathsf{negl}(\lambda)$ we denote a negligible function, that is, a function f such that $f(\lambda) < 1/p(\lambda)$ holds for any polynomial $p(\cdot)$ and sufficiently large λ. We use $[\![x]\!]$ to denote an encryption of x.

We consider a set of parties $\{P_1 \ldots, P_n\}$. Each party is modelled as a probabilistic polynomial-time (PPT) Turing machine. We assume that there exists a PPT adversary who can corrupt up to t parties where $n/3 \leq t < n/2$. We assume throughout that the parties are connected by pairwise-secure and authentic channels and have access to a common reference string (CRS). Additional setup or network assumption is explicitly mentioned in the respective sections.

The security definition of solitary MPC with guaranteed output delivery is deferred to the full version.

3.2 Cryptographic Primitives

In our constructions, we need to use digital signatures, simulation-extractable non-interactive zero-knowledge (NIZK) arguments, and decentralized threshold fully homomorphic encryption (dTFHE). In this section, we only define the syntax of dTFHE and the NIZK languages used in our constructions, and defer their security definitions to the full version.

Syntax of dTFHE. We define a t-out-of-n decentralized threshold fully homomorphic encryption scheme with the following syntax as in [10].

Definition 1 (*Decentralized Threshold Fully Homomorphic Encryption (dTFHE)*). *Let* $\mathcal{P} = \{P_1, \ldots, P_n\}$ *be a set of parties. A dTFHE scheme is a tuple of PPT algorithms* $\mathsf{dTFHE} = (\mathsf{dTFHE.DistGen}, \mathsf{dTFHE.Enc}, \mathsf{dTFHE.PartialDec}, \mathsf{dTFHE.Eval}, \mathsf{dTFHE.Combine})$ *with the following syntax:*

- $(\mathsf{pk}_i, \mathsf{sk}_i) \leftarrow \mathsf{dTFHE.DistGen}(1^\lambda, 1^d, i; r_i)$: *On input the security parameter λ, a depth bound d, party index i and randomness r_i, the distributed setup outputs a public-secret key pair $(\mathsf{pk}_i, \mathsf{sk}_i)$ for party P_i. We denote the public key of the scheme as $\mathsf{pk} = (\mathsf{pk}_1 \| \ldots \| \mathsf{pk}_n)$.*
- $[\![m]\!] \leftarrow \mathsf{dTFHE.Enc}(\mathsf{pk}, m)$: *On input a public key pk, and a plaintext m in the message space $\mathcal{M}$, it outputs a ciphertext $[\![m]\!]$.*
- $[\![y]\!] \leftarrow \mathsf{dTFHE.Eval}(\mathsf{pk}, C, [\![m_1]\!], \ldots, [\![m_k]\!])$: *On input a public key pk, a circuit C of depth at most d that takes k inputs each from the message space and outputs one value in the message space, and a set of ciphertexts $[\![m_1]\!], \ldots, [\![m_k]\!]$ where $k = \mathsf{poly}(\lambda)$, the evaluation algorithm outputs a ciphertext $[\![y]\!]$.*
- $[\![m : \mathsf{sk}_i]\!] \leftarrow \mathsf{dTFHE.PartialDec}(\mathsf{sk}_i, [\![m]\!])$: *On input a secret key share sk_i and a ciphertext $[\![m]\!]$, it outputs a partial decryption $[\![m : \mathsf{sk}_i]\!]$.*
- $m/\bot \leftarrow \mathsf{dTFHE.Combine}(\mathsf{pk}, \{[\![m : \mathsf{sk}_i]\!]\}_{i \in S})$: *On input a public key pk and a set of partial decryptions $\{[\![m : \mathsf{sk}_i]\!]\}_{i \in S}$ where $S \subseteq [n]$, the combination algorithm either outputs a plaintext m or the symbol $\bot$.*

NIZK Languages Used. In our solitary MPC protocols, we will consider two NP languages L_1, L_2 for the NIZK described below.

- **NP Language L_1:**
  Statement $\mathsf{st} = ([\![x]\!], \mathsf{pk})$ Witness $\mathsf{wit} = (x, \rho)$
  $R_1(\mathsf{st}, \mathsf{wit}) = 1$ iff $[\![x]\!] = \mathsf{dTFHE.Enc}(\mathsf{pk}, x; \rho)$.
- **NP Language L_2:**
  Statement $\mathsf{st} = ([\![x : \mathsf{sk}]\!], [\![x]\!], \mathsf{pk}, i)$ Witness $\mathsf{wit} = (\mathsf{sk}, r)$
  $R_2(\mathsf{st}, \mathsf{wit}) = 1$ iff $[\![x : \mathsf{sk}]\!] = \mathsf{dTFHE.PartialDec}(\mathsf{sk}, [\![x]\!])$ and $(\mathsf{pk}, \mathsf{sk}) = \mathsf{dTFHE.DistGen}(1^\lambda, 1^d, i; r)$.

4   With Broadcast and No PKI

In this section, we assume a network setting where the parties have access to a broadcast channel in addition to pairwise-private channels. In terms of setup, we assume that all parties have access to a common reference string (CRS). First, we present a new lower bound of *three* rounds for solitary MPC with god in Sect. 4.1. Then we study whether it is possible to use fewer rounds of broadcast and show in Sect. 4.2 and Sect. 4.3 that broadcast is necessary in both the first and second rounds. The above negative results are tight given the existing results of [3,6,28,36], which we discuss in the full version [7].

4.1   Necessity of Three Rounds

We show that it is impossible to design a two-round solitary MPC with god in the honest majority setting (in particular, $n/3 \le t < n/2$), assuming the presence of pairwise-private channels and a broadcast channel. Our result holds in the presence of any common public setup such as CRS, even against non-rushing adversaries and irrespective of whether the output-obtaining party Q provides an input or not. We discuss in the full version why the existing proofs of lower bounds (three rounds) for standard MPC with god in the presence of an honest majority [24,28,36] do not hold for solitary functionalities.

Theorem 1. *Assume parties have access to CRS, pairwise-private channels and a broadcast channel. Let n and t be positive integers such that $n \geq 3$ and $n/3 \leq t < n/2$. Then, there exists a solitary functionality f such that no two-round n-party MPC protocol tolerating t corruptions can compute f with god, even when the adversary is assumed to be non-rushing.*

Proof. For simplicity, we present the argument for the setting $n = 3$ and $t = 1$ below and elaborate on how to extend the proof to $n/3 \leq t < n/2$ later. Consider a solitary function $f(x_1, x_2, x_3)$ among $\{P_1, P_2, P_3\}$ where $Q = P_3$ denotes the output receiving party. We define f as $f(x_1 = (m_0, m_1), x_2 = b, x_3 = \bot) := m_b$, where $x_3 = \bot$ denotes that Q has no input; $(m_0, m_1) \in \{0,1\}^\lambda$ denote a pair of strings and $b \in \{0,1\}$ denotes a single bit. For the sake of contradiction, suppose there exists a two-round 3-party solitary MPC with god, say Π which can compute f. Note that at most the adversary corrupts at most one party.

We consider three different scenarios of the execution of Π. For simplicity, we assume the following about the structure of Π: **(a)** Round 2 involves only broadcast messages while Round 1 involves messages sent via both pairwise-private and broadcast channels. This holds without loss of generality since the parties can perform pairwise-private communication by exchanging random pads in the first round and then using these random pads to unmask later broadcasts [23]. **(b)** In Round 1, each pair of parties communicate via their pairwise-private channels (any protocol where a pair of parties does not communicate privately in Round 1 can be transformed to one where dummy messages are exchanged between them). **(c)** Round 2 does not involve any outgoing communication from Q (as Q is the only party to receive the output at the end of Round 2).

Next, we define some useful notation: Let $\mathsf{pc}_{i \to j}$ denote the pairwise-private communication from P_i to P_j in Round 1 and $\mathsf{b}_{i \to}^r$ denote the message broadcast by P_i in round r, where $r \in [2], \{i, j\} \in [3]$. These messages may be a function of the crs as per protocol specifications. Let View_i denotes the view of party P_i which consists of crs, its input x_i, randomness r_i and all incoming messages.

Following is a description of the scenarios. In each of these scenarios, we assume that the adversary uses the honest input on behalf of the corrupt parties and its malicious behaviour is limited to dropping some of the messages supposed to be sent by the corrupt party. The views of the parties for all the scenarios are shown in Table 3.

Scenario 1: The adversary actively corrupts P_2 who behaves honestly in Round 1 towards P_1 but doesn't communicate privately to Q in Round 1. In more detail, P_2 sends messages $\mathsf{pc}_{2 \to 1}, \mathsf{b}_{2 \to}^1$ according to the protocol specification but drops the message $\mathsf{pc}_{2 \to 3}$. In Round 2, P_2 aborts.

Scenario 2: The adversary passively corrupts Q who behaves honestly throughout and learns output $f(x_1, x_2, x_3)$. Additionally, Q locally re-computes the output by emulating Scenario 1, namely when P_2 does not communicate privately to Q in Round 1 and aborts in Round 2. Specifically, Q can locally emulate this by discarding $\mathsf{pc}_{2\to3}$ (private communication from P_2 to Q in Round 1) and $\mathsf{b}_{2\to}^2$ (broadcast communication from P_2 in Round 2).

Scenario 3: The adversary corrupts P_1 passively who behaves honestly throughout. P_1 also does the following local computation: Locally emulate the view of Q as per Scenario 1 (from which the output can be derived) for various choices of inputs of $\{P_1, P_3\}$ while the input of P_2 i.e. x_2 remains fixed. In more detail, P_1 does the following - Let $(\mathsf{pc}_{2\to1}, \mathsf{b}_{2\to}^1)$ be fixed to what was received by P_1 in the execution. Choose various combinations of inputs and randomness on behalf of P_1 and P_3. Consider a particular combination, say $\{(\widetilde{x_1}, \widetilde{r_1}), (\widetilde{x_3}, \widetilde{r_3})\}$. Use it to locally compute $\widetilde{\mathsf{b}_{1\to}^1}, \widetilde{\mathsf{b}_{3\to}^1}, \widetilde{\mathsf{pc}_{1\to3}}, \widetilde{\mathsf{pc}_{3\to1}}$. Next, locally compute $\widetilde{\mathsf{b}_{1\to}^2}$ using the Round 1 emulated messages which results in the complete view $\widetilde{\mathsf{View}_3}$ of Q analogous to Scenario 1, where $\widetilde{\mathsf{View}_3} = \{\mathsf{crs}, \widetilde{x_3}, \widetilde{r_3}, \widetilde{\mathsf{b}_{1\to}^1}, \mathsf{b}_{2\to}^1, \widetilde{\mathsf{pc}_{1\to3}}, \widetilde{\mathsf{b}_{1\to}^2}\}$ corresponds to the inputs $(\widetilde{x_1}, x_2, \widetilde{x_3})$.

Table 3. Views of P_1, P_2, P_3 in Scenarios 1 – 3.

	Scenario 1			Scenario 2 & 3		
	View$_1$	View$_2$	View$_3$	View$_1$	View$_2$	View$_3$
Initial Input	(x_1, r_1, crs)	(x_2, r_2, crs)	(x_3, r_3, crs)	(x_1, r_1, crs)	(x_2, r_2, crs)	(x_3, r_3, crs)
Round 1	$\mathsf{pc}_{2\to1}, \mathsf{pc}_{3\to1}, \mathsf{b}_{2\to}^1, \mathsf{b}_{3\to}^1$	$\mathsf{pc}_{1\to2}, \mathsf{pc}_{3\to2}, \mathsf{b}_{1\to}^1, \mathsf{b}_{3\to}^1$	$\mathsf{pc}_{1\to3}, -, \mathsf{b}_{1\to}^1, \mathsf{b}_{2\to}^1$	$\mathsf{pc}_{2\to1}, \mathsf{pc}_{3\to1}, \mathsf{b}_{2\to}^1, \mathsf{b}_{3\to}^1$	$\mathsf{pc}_{1\to2}, \mathsf{pc}_{3\to2}, \mathsf{b}_{1\to}^1, \mathsf{b}_{3\to}^1$	$\mathsf{pc}_{1\to3}, \mathsf{pc}_{2\to3}, \mathsf{b}_{1\to}^1, \mathsf{b}_{2\to}^1$
Round 2	–	$\mathsf{b}_{1\to}^2$	$\mathsf{b}_{1\to}^2$	$\mathsf{b}_{2\to}^2$	$\mathsf{b}_{1\to}^2$	$\mathsf{b}_{1\to}^2, \mathsf{b}_{2\to}^2$

The proof skeleton is as follows. First, we claim that if Scenario 1 occurs, then Q must obtain $f(x_1, x_2, x_3)$ with overwhelming probability. If not, then Π is vulnerable to a potential attack by semi-honest Q (that is captured in Scenario 2) which enables Q to learn information that he is not supposed to learn; which violates security. Intuitively, this inference captures Q's reliance on P_1's messages in Round 2 and P_2's broadcast in Round 1 to carry information about x_2 required for output computation. Note that this information is available to P_1 at the end of Round 1 itself. Building on this intuition, we show that Π is such that an adversary corrupting P_1 passively (as in Scenario 3) can compute $f(\widetilde{x_1}, x_2, \widetilde{x_3})$ for any choice of $(\widetilde{x_1}, \widetilde{x_3})$, which is the final contradiction. We present the formal proof and show how the proof can be extended for $n \geq 3$ and $n/3 \leq t < n/2$ (using player partitioning technique [34]) in the full version [7].

4.2 Necessity of Broadcast in Round 1

Now we show that any three-round n-party solitary MPC with god against t corruptions must use broadcast channel in Round 1, where $n/3 \leq t < n/2$.

Theorem 2. *Assume parties have access to CRS and pairwise-private channels. Let n and t be positive integers such that $n \geq 3$ and $n/3 \leq t < n/2$. There exists a solitary functionality f such that no three-round n-party solitary MPC protocol securely computes f with **god** against t corruptions, while making use of the broadcast channel only in Round 2 and Round 3 (pairwise-private channels can be used in all the rounds).*

Proof. For simplicity, we present the argument for the setting $n = 3$ and $t = 1$ below. The proof can be extended for $n/3 \leq t < n/2$ using player partitioning technique. Consider the function $f(x_1, x_2, x_3)$ defined as in the proof of Theorem 1, i.e. $f(x_1 = (m_0, m_1), x_2 = b, x_3 = \bot) := m_b$. Suppose for the sake of contradiction that there exists a three-round solitary MPC protocol with **god**, say Π that computes f and utilizes broadcast channel only in Rounds 2 and 3 (i.e., Π uses only pairwise-private channels in Round 1, and uses both broadcast and pairwise-private channels in Rounds 2 and 3).

Without loss of generality, we can assume that Π has the following structure: **(a)** No broadcast messages are sent during Round 3, and Round 3 only involves private messages sent to Q. This is without loss of generality as any solitary MPC that uses broadcast in the last round can be transformed into one where the messages sent via broadcast are sent privately only to Q (as Q is the only party supposed to receive output at the end of Round 3). **(b)** Round 2 only involves broadcast messages. This is also without loss of generality since the parties can perform pairwise-private communication by exchanging random pads in the first round and then using these random pads to unmask later broadcasts [23].

We analyze three different scenarios of the execution of Π. Before describing the scenarios, we define some useful notation. We assume (r_1, r_2, r_3) are the randomness used by the three parties if they behave honestly during the protocol execution. Let $\mathsf{pc}_{i \to j}$ where $i, j \in [3]$ denote the pairwise-private communication from P_i to P_j in Round 1 if P_i behaves honestly using input x_i and randomness r_i. Similarly, let $\widetilde{\mathsf{pc}_{i \to j}}$ denote the pairwise-private communication from P_i to P_j in Round 1 if P_i follows the protocol but uses some other input $\widetilde{x_i}$ and randomness $\widetilde{r_i}$. Let $\mathsf{b}_i^{x, r, \mathsf{pc}_{i-1}, \mathsf{pc}_{i+1}}$ where $i \in [3]$ denote the broadcast communication by P_i in Round 2 if P_i behaves honestly using input x and randomness r, and received pc_{i-1} from P_{i-1} and pc_{i+1} from P_{i+1} in Round 1 (let $P_0 := P_3$ and $P_4 := P_1$). Lastly, let $\mathsf{pc}_{i \to 3}^{\ell}$ where $i \in [2], \ell \in [3]$ denote the pairwise-private communication from P_i to Q in Round 3 in Scenario ℓ. A party's view consists of crs, its input, randomness and incoming messages. Following is a description of the three scenarios. The views of the parties are described in Tables 4 – 5.

Scenario 1: Adversary corrupts P_2. In Round 1, P_2 behaves honestly to P_1 using input x_2 and randomness r_2 while behaving dishonestly to Q using $(\widetilde{x_2}, \widetilde{r_2})$. In other words, P_2 sends $\mathsf{pc}_{2 \to 1}$ to P_1 and $\widetilde{\mathsf{pc}_{2 \to 3}}$ to Q.
In Round 2, P_2 broadcasts a message as if he behaved honestly in Round 1 to both parties (using (x_2, r_2)) and received a message from Q computed using $(\widetilde{x_3} = \bot, \widetilde{r_3})$ in Round 1. Formally, P_2 broadcasts $\mathsf{b}_2^{x_2, r_2, \mathsf{pc}_{1 \to 2}, \widetilde{\mathsf{pc}_{3 \to 2}}}$.
In Round 3, P_2 aborts.

Scenario 2: Adversary corrupts Q. In Round 1, Q behaves towards P_1 using $(x_3 = \bot, r_3)$ while behaving towards P_2 using $(\widetilde{x_3} = \bot, \widetilde{r_3})$. In other words, Q sends $\mathsf{pc}_{3\to1}$ to P_1 and $\widetilde{\mathsf{pc}_{3\to2}}$ to P_2.

In Round 2, Q broadcasts a message as if he behaved honestly in Round 1 to both parties (using $(x_3 = \bot, r_3)$) and received a message from P_2 in Round 1 using $(\widetilde{x_2}, \widetilde{r_2})$. Formally, Q broadcasts $\mathsf{b}_3^{x_3,r_3,\mathsf{pc}_{1\to3},\widetilde{\mathsf{pc}_{2\to3}}}$.

Scenario 3: Adversary passively corrupts P_1 behaving honestly using (x_1, r_1) in all rounds.

Table 4. Views of $\{P_1, P_2, Q\}$ in Scenarios 1 and 2.

	Scenario 1			Scenario 2		
	View$_1$	View$_2$	View$_3$	View$_1$	View$_2$	View$_3$
Initial Input	(x_1, r_1, crs)	(x_2, r_2, crs)	$(x_3 = \bot, r_3, \mathsf{crs})$	(x_1, r_1, crs)	(x_2, r_2, crs)	$(x_3 = \bot, r_3, \mathsf{crs})$
Round 1	$\mathsf{pc}_{2\to1}, \mathsf{pc}_{3\to1}$	$\mathsf{pc}_{1\to2}, \mathsf{pc}_{3\to2}$	$\mathsf{pc}_{1\to3}, \widetilde{\mathsf{pc}_{2\to3}}$	$\mathsf{pc}_{2\to1}, \widetilde{\mathsf{pc}_{3\to1}}$	$\mathsf{pc}_{1\to2}, \widetilde{\mathsf{pc}_{3\to2}}$	$\mathsf{pc}_{1\to3}, \mathsf{pc}_{2\to3}$
Round 2	$\mathsf{b}_2^{x_2,r_2,\mathsf{pc}_{1\to2},\widetilde{\mathsf{pc}_{3\to2}}}$ $\mathsf{b}_3^{x_3,r_3,\mathsf{pc}_{1\to3},\widetilde{\mathsf{pc}_{2\to3}}}$	$\mathsf{b}_1^{x_1,r_1,\mathsf{pc}_{2\to1},\mathsf{pc}_{3\to1}}$ $\mathsf{b}_3^{x_3,r_3,\mathsf{pc}_{1\to3},\mathsf{pc}_{2\to3}}$	$\mathsf{b}_1^{x_1,r_1,\mathsf{pc}_{2\to1},\mathsf{pc}_{3\to1}}$ $\mathsf{b}_2^{x_2,r_2,\mathsf{pc}_{1\to2},\widetilde{\mathsf{pc}_{3\to2}}}$	$\mathsf{b}_2^{x_2,r_2,\mathsf{pc}_{1\to2},\widetilde{\mathsf{pc}_{3\to2}}}$ $\mathsf{b}_3^{x_3,r_3,\mathsf{pc}_{1\to3},\widetilde{\mathsf{pc}_{2\to3}}}$	$\mathsf{b}_1^{x_1,r_1,\mathsf{pc}_{2\to1},\mathsf{pc}_{3\to1}}$ $\mathsf{b}_3^{x_3,r_3,\mathsf{pc}_{1\to3},\widetilde{\mathsf{pc}_{2\to3}}}$	$\mathsf{b}_1^{x_1,r_1,\mathsf{pc}_{2\to1},\mathsf{pc}_{3\to1}}$ $\mathsf{b}_2^{x_2,r_2,\mathsf{pc}_{1\to2},\widetilde{\mathsf{pc}_{3\to2}}}$
Round 3	–	–	$\mathsf{pc}^1_{1\to3}$	–	–	$\mathsf{pc}^2_{1\to3}, \mathsf{pc}^2_{2\to3}$

Table 5. Views of $\{P_1, P_2, Q\}$ in Scenario 3.

	View$_1$	View$_2$	View$_3$
Initial Input	(x_1, r_1, crs)	(x_2, r_2, crs)	$(x_3 = \bot, r_3, \mathsf{crs})$
Round 1	$\mathsf{pc}_{2\to1}, \mathsf{pc}_{3\to1}$	$\mathsf{pc}_{1\to2}, \mathsf{pc}_{3\to2}$	$\mathsf{pc}_{1\to3}, \mathsf{pc}_{2\to3}$
Round 2	$\mathsf{b}_2^{x_2,r_2,\mathsf{pc}_{1\to2},\mathsf{pc}_{3\to2}}$ $\mathsf{b}_3^{x_3,r_3,\mathsf{pc}_{1\to3},\mathsf{pc}_{2\to3}}$	$\mathsf{b}_1^{x_1,r_1,\mathsf{pc}_{2\to1},\mathsf{pc}_{3\to1}}$ $\mathsf{b}_3^{x_3,r_3,\mathsf{pc}_{1\to3},\mathsf{pc}_{2\to3}}$	$\mathsf{b}_1^{x_1,r_1,\mathsf{pc}_{2\to1},\mathsf{pc}_{3\to1}}$ $\mathsf{b}_2^{x_2,r_2,\mathsf{pc}_{1\to2},\mathsf{pc}_{3\to2}}$
Round 3	–	–	$\mathsf{pc}^3_{1\to3}, \mathsf{pc}^3_{2\to3}$

The proof skeleton is as follows. First, we claim if Scenario 1 occurs, then Q must obtain $f(x_1, x_2, \bot)$ with overwhelming probability. Due to the god property of Π, the honest Q in Scenario 1 must learn an output on the honest P_1's input, namely x_1. The output should also be computed on P_2's honest input x_2 because Q's view is Scenario 1 is subsumed by its view in Scenario 2, where the malicious Q can only learn an output computed on the honest P_2's input. Intuitively, P_2's input is "committed" in its private communication to P_1 in Round 1 and broadcast message in Round 2. This allows a semi-honest P_1 in Scenario 3 to emulate Q's view in Scenario 1 and learn $f(x_1, x_2, \bot)$, which compromises the security of Π. We defer the formal proof to the full version [7].

4.3   Necessity of Broadcast in Round 2

In this section, we show that any three-round n-party solitary MPC with god against t corruptions must use broadcast channel in Round 2 when $2\lceil n/5\rceil \le t < n/2$ (note that $t \ge 2$). Interestingly, the use of broadcast in Round 2 is not necessary for the special case of single corruption (refer full version [7]).

Theorem 3. *Assume parties have access to CRS. Let n and t be positive integers such that $n \ge 5$ and $2\lceil n/5\rceil \le t < n/2$. Then, there exists a solitary functionality f such that no three-round n-party solitary MPC protocol tolerating t corruptions securely computes f with god, while making use of the broadcast channel only in Round 1 and Round 3 (pairwise-private channels can be used in all the rounds).*

Proof. We present the argument for the setting of $n = 5$ and $t = 2$ below, and elaborate later on how to extend to $2\lceil n/5\rceil \le t < n/2$. Consider the solitary function $f(x_1,\ldots,x_5)$ among $\{P_1,\ldots,P_5\}$ where $Q = P_5$ denotes the output receiving party. We clarify that our argument holds irrespective of whether f involves an input from Q or not. First, set $k = 10$ (looking ahead, we set k to be sufficiently large for the probability arguments to go through). Let $f(x_1 = (x_c, x_r), x_2 = (x_2^0, x_2^1), x_3 = (x_3^0, x_3^1), x_4 = \bot, x_5 = \bot)$ be defined as follows, where $x_c \in \{0,1\}$, $x_r, x_2^0, x_2^1, x_3^0, x_3^1 \in \{0,1\}^k$ and $x_2^0 \ne x_2^1, x_3^0 \ne x_3^1$:

$$f(x_1,\ldots,x_5) = \begin{cases} (x_r \oplus x_2^0,\ x_3^0) \text{ if } x_c = 0 \\ (x_r \oplus x_2^1,\ x_3^1) \text{ if } x_c = 1 \end{cases}.$$

Suppose for the sake of contradiction that there exists a three-round 5-party solitary MPC protocol with god against two corruptions, say Π that computes f and utilizes broadcast channel only in Round 1 and Round 3 (i.e. Π uses broadcast and pairwise-private channels in Round 1 and Round 3; and only pairwise-private channels in Round 2).

Without loss of generality, we assume for simplicity the following structure for Π: **(a)** Round 3 involves only private messages sent to Q - no broadcast messages. This is w.l.o.g as any solitary MPC that uses broadcast in last round can be transformed to one where the messages sent via broadcast are sent privately only to Q (as Q is the only party supposed to receive output). **(b)** Round 2 does not involve messages from P_i ($i \in [4]$) to Q (such a message is meaningful only if Q communicates to P_i in Round 3, which is not the case as per **(a)**).

We consider an execution of Π with inputs $(x_1,\ldots,x_5)$ where x_i denotes the input of P_i. In the above definition of f, $x_4 = x_5 = \bot$ indicates that P_4 and P_5 do not have any inputs. Next, we analyze four different scenarios. Before describing the scenarios, we define some useful notation. Let b_i^1 denote the broadcast communication by P_i in Round 1 when P_i behaves honestly. In Rounds 1 and 2, let $\mathsf{pc}_{i \to j}^r$ where $r \in [2], i, j \in [5]$ denote the pairwise-private communication from P_i to P_j in Round r, as per an execution where everyone behaves honestly. Next, we use $\widetilde{\mathsf{pc}_{i \to j}^2}$ to denote the messages that P_i ($i \in [5]$) is supposed to send in Round 2 to P_j ($j \in [4] \setminus i$) incase P_i did not receive Round 1 message from

P_1. Note that this communication could be potentially different from what P_i would send in an honest execution. Lastly, since Round 3 messages to Q could potentially be different for each of the four scenarios, we index them additionally with ℓ indicating the scenario i.e. $pc_{j\to5}^{3,\ell}$ denotes P_j's Round 3 message to Q in Scenario ℓ ($j \in [4], \ell \in [4]$). These messages may be a function of the common reference string (denoted by crs). A party's view comprises of crs, its input, randomness and incoming messages.

Following is a description of the scenarios. In each of these scenarios, we assume that the adversary uses the honest input on behalf of the corrupt parties and its malicious behaviour is limited to dropping some of the messages that were received or supposed to be sent by the actively corrupt parties. The views of the parties are described in Tables 6, 7, 8 and 9.

[**Scenario 1**: Adversary corrupts P_1. In Round 1, P_1 behaves honestly w.r.t his broadcast communication and private message towards P_2 and Q, but drops his private message towards P_3 and P_4. Further, P_1 remains silent after Round 1 (i.e. does not communicate at all in Round 2 and Round 3). In other words, in Scenario 1, P_1 computes and sends only the following messages honestly : b_1^1, $pc_{1\to2}^1$ and $pc_{1\to5}^1$.

Scenario 2: Adversary corrupts $\{P_1, P_2\}$. P_1 behaves identical to Scenario 1. P_2 behaves honestly except that he drops his Round 3 message towards Q.

Scenario 3: Adversary corrupts $\{P_3, P_4\}$. In Round 1, $\{P_3, P_4\}$ behave honestly as per protocol steps. In Round 2, $\{P_3, P_4\}$ only communicate to P_2, towards whom they pretend that they did not receive Round 1 message from P_1 (i.e. P_i sends $\widetilde{pc_{i\to2}^2}$ to P_2 where $i \in \{3, 4\}$). Lastly, $\{P_3, P_4\}$ remain silent in Round 3 i.e. do not communicate towards Q.

Scenario 4: Adversary corrupts $\{P_1, Q\}$. Q behaves honestly throughout the protocol. P_1 behaves as follows: In Round 1, P_1 behaves identical to Scenario 1 (i.e. behaves honestly w.r.t its broadcast communication and private message to P_2 and Q; but drops his private message to P_3 and P_4). In Round 2, P_1 behaves honestly only to P_2 (but does not communicate to others). Lastly, P_1 sends its Round 3 message to Q as per Scenario 3 (i.e. as per protocol specifications when P_1 does not receive Round 2 message from P_3 and P_4). The communication in Round 3 among the corrupt parties is mentioned only for clarity.

Table 6. Views of $\{P_1, \ldots, P_5\}$ in Scenario 1.

	View$_1$	View$_2$	View$_3$	View$_4$	View$_5$
Initial Input	(x_1, r_1, crs)	(x_2, r_2, crs)	(x_3, r_3, crs)	(x_4, r_4, crs)	(x_5, r_5, crs)
Round 1	$\{b_j^1\}_{j\in[5]\setminus\{1\}}$, $\{pc_{j\to1}^1\}_{j\in[5]\setminus\{1\}}$	$\{b_j^1\}_{j\in[5]\setminus\{2\}}$, $\{pc_{j\to2}^1\}_{j\in[5]\setminus\{2\}}$	$\{b_j^1\}_{j\in[5]\setminus\{3\}}$, $\{pc_{j\to3}^1\}_{j\in[5]\setminus\{1,3\}}$	$\{b_j^1\}_{j\in[5]\setminus\{4\}}$, $\{pc_{j\to4}^1\}_{j\in[5]\setminus\{1,4\}}$	$\{b_j^1\}_{j\in[5]\setminus\{5\}}$, $\{pc_{j\to5}^1\}_{j\in[5]\setminus\{5\}}$
Round 2	$\{pc_{j\to1}^2\}_{j\in\{2,5\}}$, $\{pc_{j\to1}^2\}_{j\in\{3,4\}}$	$\{pc_{j\to2}^2\}_{j\in\{5\}}$, $\{pc_{j\to2}^2\}_{j\in\{3,4\}}$	$\{pc_{j\to3}^2\}_{j\in\{2,5\}}$, $\{pc_{j\to3}^2\}_{j\in\{4\}}$	$\{pc_{j\to4}^2\}_{j\in\{2,5\}}$, $\{pc_{j\to4}^2\}_{j\in\{3\}}$	– –
Round 3	–	–	–	–	$\{pc_{j\to5}^{3,1}\}_{j\in\{2,3,4\}}$

Table 7. Views of $\{P_1, \ldots, P_5\}$ in Scenario 2.

	View$_1$	View$_2$	View$_3$	View$_4$	View$_5$
Initial Input	(x_1, r_1, crs)	(x_2, r_2, crs)	(x_3, r_3, crs)	(x_4, r_4, crs)	(x_5, r_5, crs)
Round 1	$\{\mathsf{b}_j^1\}_{j \in [5]\setminus\{1\}}$, $\{\mathsf{pc}_{j\to 1}^1\}_{j \in [5]\setminus\{1\}}$	$\{\mathsf{b}_j^1\}_{j \in [5]\setminus\{2\}}$, $\{\mathsf{pc}_{j\to 2}^1\}_{j \in [5]\setminus\{2\}}$	$\{\mathsf{b}_j^1\}_{j \in [5]\setminus\{3\}}$, $\{\mathsf{pc}_{j\to 3}^1\}_{j \in [5]\setminus\{1,3\}}$	$\{\mathsf{b}_j^1\}_{j \in [5]\setminus\{4\}}$, $\{\mathsf{pc}_{j\to 4}^1\}_{j \in [5]\setminus\{1,4\}}$	$\{\mathsf{b}_j^1\}_{j \in [5]\setminus\{5\}}$, $\{\mathsf{pc}_{j\to 5}^1\}_{j \in [5]\setminus\{5\}}$
Round 2	$\{\mathsf{pc}_{j\to 1}^2\}_{j \in \{2,5\}}$ $\{\mathsf{pc}_{j\to 1}^2\}_{j \in \{3,4\}}$	$\{\mathsf{pc}_{j\to 2}^2\}_{j \in \{5\}}$ $\{\mathsf{pc}_{j\to 2}^2\}_{j \in \{3,4\}}$	$\{\mathsf{pc}_{j\to 3}^2\}_{j \in \{2,5\}}$ $\{\mathsf{pc}_{j\to 3}^2\}_{j \in \{4\}}$	$\{\mathsf{pc}_{j\to 4}^2\}_{j \in \{2,5\}}$ $\{\mathsf{pc}_{j\to 4}^2\}_{j \in \{3\}}$	– –
Round 3	–	–	–	–	$\{\mathsf{pc}_{j\to 5}^{3,2}\}_{j \in \{3,4\}}$

Table 8. Views of $\{P_1, \ldots, P_5\}$ in Scenario 3.

	View$_1$	View$_2$	View$_3$	View$_4$	View$_5$
Initial Input	(x_1, r_1, crs)	(x_2, r_2, crs)	(x_3, r_3, crs)	(x_4, r_4, crs)	(x_5, r_5, crs)
Round 1	$\{\mathsf{b}_j^1\}_{j \in [5]\setminus\{1\}}$, $\{\mathsf{pc}_{j\to 1}^1\}_{j \in [5]\setminus\{1\}}$	$\{\mathsf{b}_j^1\}_{j \in [5]\setminus\{2\}}$, $\{\mathsf{pc}_{j\to 2}^1\}_{j \in [5]\setminus\{2\}}$	$\{\mathsf{b}_j^1\}_{j \in [5]\setminus\{3\}}$, $\{\mathsf{pc}_{j\to 3}^1\}_{j \in [5]\setminus\{3\}}$	$\{\mathsf{b}_j^1\}_{j \in [5]\setminus\{4\}}$, $\{\mathsf{pc}_{j\to 4}^1\}_{j \in [5]\setminus\{4\}}$	$\{\mathsf{b}_j^1\}_{j \in [5]\setminus\{5\}}$, $\{\mathsf{pc}_{j\to 5}^1\}_{j \in [5]\setminus\{5\}}$
Round 2	$\{\mathsf{pc}_{j\to 1}^2\}_{j \in \{2,5\}}$	$\{\mathsf{pc}_{j\to 2}^2\}_{j \in \{1,5\}}, \{\mathsf{pc}_{j\to 2}^2\}_{j \in \{3,4\}}$	$\{\mathsf{pc}_{j\to 3}^2\}_{j \in \{1,2,5\}}$	$\{\mathsf{pc}_{j\to 4}^2\}_{j \in \{1,2,5\}}$	–
Round 3	–	–	–	–	$\{\mathsf{pc}_{j\to 5}^{3,3}\}_{j \in \{1,2\}}$

Table 9. Views of $\{P_1, \ldots, P_5\}$ in Scenario 4.

	View$_1$	View$_2$	View$_3$	View$_4$	View$_5$
Initial Input	(x_1, r_1, crs)	(x_2, r_2, crs)	(x_3, r_3, crs)	(x_4, r_4, crs)	(x_5, r_5, crs)
Round 1	$\{\mathsf{b}_j^1\}_{j \in [5]\setminus\{1\}}$, $\{\mathsf{pc}_{j\to 1}^1\}_{j \in [5]\setminus\{1\}}$	$\{\mathsf{b}_j^1\}_{j \in [5]\setminus\{2\}}$, $\{\mathsf{pc}_{j\to 2}^1\}_{j \in [5]\setminus\{2\}}$	$\{\mathsf{b}_j^1\}_{j \in [5]\setminus\{3\}}$, $\{\mathsf{pc}_{j\to 3}^1\}_{j \in [5]\setminus\{1,3\}}$	$\{\mathsf{b}_j^1\}_{j \in [5]\setminus\{4\}}$, $\{\mathsf{pc}_{j\to 4}^1\}_{j \in [5]\setminus\{1,4\}}$	$\{\mathsf{b}_j^1\}_{j \in [5]\setminus\{5\}}$, $\{\mathsf{pc}_{j\to 5}^1\}_{j \in [5]\setminus\{5\}}$
Round 2	$\{\mathsf{pc}_{j\to 1}^2\}_{j \in \{2,5\}}$ $\{\mathsf{pc}_{j\to 1}^2\}_{j \in \{3,4\}}$	$\{\mathsf{pc}_{j\to 2}^2\}_{j \in \{1,5\}}$ $\{\mathsf{pc}_{j\to 2}^2\}_{j \in \{3,4\}}$	$\{\mathsf{pc}_{j\to 3}^2\}_{j \in \{2,5\}}$ $\{\mathsf{pc}_{j\to 3}^2\}_{j \in \{4\}}$	$\{\mathsf{pc}_{j\to 4}^2\}_{j \in \{2,5\}}$ $\{\mathsf{pc}_{j\to 4}^2\}_{j \in \{3\}}$	–
Round 3	– –	– –	– –	– –	$\{\mathsf{pc}_{j\to 5}^{3,4}\}_{j \in \{1,2\}} = \{\mathsf{pc}_{j\to 5}^{3,3}\}_{j \in \{1,2\}}$ $\{\mathsf{pc}_{j\to 5}^{3,4}\}_{j \in \{3,4\}} = \{\mathsf{pc}_{j\to 5}^{3,2}\}_{j \in \{3,4\}}$

The proof skeleton is as follows. First, we claim that there exists an $x_c^* \in \{0,1\}$ and $x_r^* \in \{0,1\}^k$ such that if Scenario 1 occurs with respect to $x_1 = (x_c^*, x_r^*)$ and uniformly randomly sampled x_2 and x_3, then the output obtained by Q must be computed with respect to $\neg x_c^*$ with a sufficiently large (constant) probability. Intuitively, if for all x_c and x_r, the output of Scenario 1 was computed on x_c, then it would mean that $\{P_2, Q\}$ have sufficient information about x_c at the end of Round 1 itself. This would make Π vulnerable to a residual function attack by $\{P_2, Q\}$. Next, we claim the same statement also holds for Scenario 2 (with a different probability). Regarding Scenario 3, correctness of Π lets us infer that Q must compute output on the input $x_1 = (x_r, x_c)$ of honest P_1. Lastly, we argue that Q's view in Scenario 4 subsumes its views in Scenario 2 and Scenario 3. This would allow corrupt $\{P_1, Q\}$ (who participate with $x_c = x_c^*$) in Scenario 4 to obtain multiple outputs i.e. output with respect to both $\neg x_c^*$ (as in Scenario 2) and x_c^* (as in Scenario 3), which contradicts security of Π. This completes the proof sketch. We present the formal proof and show its extension to $2\lceil n/5 \rceil \le t < n/2$ in the full version [7]. Note that for certain cases, such as

$n = 6$, this range of values of (n, t) is not meaningful. However, this is relevant for sufficiently large values of n.

5   With PKI and No Broadcast

In this section, we consider the setting where the parties only have access to pairwise-private channels. In terms of setup, we assume that all parties have access to a pubic-key infrastructure (PKI) and a common reference string (CRS). We first present a lower bound of four rounds for solitary MPC with god. Then we present a five-round construction that works for any n and $t < n/2$. Next, we elaborate on a non-constant round protocol (i.e. $(t + 2)$ rounds) that can be derived from the protocol of [28]. While the former upper bound significantly improves over the latter for most values of (n, t), the latter achieves better round complexity for special cases of $t \leq 2$.

5.1   Necessity of Four Rounds

In this section, we assume a network setting where the parties have access to pairwise-private channels and PKI. We show that when $3 \lceil n/7 \rceil \leq t < n/2$, four rounds are necessary for n-party solitary MPC with god against t corruptions. This holds irrespective of whether Q has input or not and even if the adversary is non-rushing. However, the argument crucially relies on the fact that $t \geq 3$ (details appear at the end of this section) which leads us to conjecture that there is a potential separation between the cases of $t \leq 2$ and $t \geq 3$ for solitary MPC. We investigate the special cases of $t \leq 2$ in the full version [7]. The impossibility for the general case is formally stated below.

Theorem 4. *Assume parties have access to CRS, PKI and pairwise-private channels. Let n, t be positive integers such that $n \geq 7$ and $3 \lceil n/7 \rceil \leq t < n/2$. Then, there exists a solitary functionality f such that no three-round n-party MPC protocol tolerating t corruptions can compute f with god, even if the adversary is assumed to be non-rushing.*

Proof. For simplicity, we consider the setting of $n = 7$ and $t = 3$ (extension to any $3 \lceil n/7 \rceil \leq t < n/2$ appears in the full version). Consider the solitary function $f(x_1, , \ldots, x_7)$ among $\{P_1, \ldots, P_7\}$ where $Q = P_7$ denotes the output receiving party. We clarify that our lower bound argument holds irrespective of whether f involves an input from Q. First, set $k = 10$ (looking ahead, we set k to be sufficiently large for the probability arguments to go through). Let $f(x_1, x_2 = \bot, x_3 = (x_3^0, x_3^1), x_4 = (x_4^0, x_4^1), x_5 = \bot, x_6 = (x_6^0, x_6^1), x_7 = \bot)$ be defined as follows, where $x_1 \in \{0, 1\}$, $x_3^0, x_3^1, x_4^0, x_4^1, x_6^0, x_6^1 \in \{0, 1\}^k$ and $x_3^0 \neq x_3^1, x_4^0 \neq x_4^1, x_6^0 \neq x_6^1$:

$$f(x_1, \ldots, x_7) = \begin{cases} (x_3^0, x_4^0, x_6^0) & \text{if } x_1 = 0 \\ (x_3^1, x_4^1, x_6^1) & \text{if } x_1 = 1 \end{cases}.$$

In the definition, $x_2 = x_5 = x_7 = \perp$ indicates that P_2, P_5, P_7 do not have any inputs. Suppose for the sake of contradiction that there exists a three-round solitary MPC protocol with god, say Π that computes f.

Without loss of generality, we assume that Π has the following structure: **(a)** Round 3 involves only messages sent to Q; **(b)** Round 2 does not involve messages from P_i ($i \in [6]$) to Q (such a message is meaningful only if Q communicates to P_i in Round 3, which is not the case as per **(a)**).

We consider an execution of Π with inputs $(x_1, \ldots, x_7)$ where x_i denotes the input of P_i and analyze four different scenarios. Before describing the scenarios, we define some useful notation. In Rounds 1 and 2, let $\mathsf{pc}^r_{i \to j}$ where $r \in [2], \{i, j\} \in [7]$ denote the pairwise-private communication from P_i to P_j in Round r, as per an execution where everyone behaves honestly. Next, we use $\widetilde{\mathsf{pc}^2_{i \to j}}$ to denote the messages that P_i ($i \in [7]$) is supposed to send in Round 2 to P_j ($j \in [6] \setminus i$) incase P_i did not receive Round 1 message from P_1. Note that this communication could be potentially different from what P_i would send in an honest execution. Lastly, since Round 3 messages to Q could potentially be different for each of the four scenarios, we index them additionally with ℓ indicating the scenario i.e. $\mathsf{pc}^{3,\ell}_{j \to 7}$ denotes P_j's Round 3 message to Q in Scenario ℓ ($j \in [6], \ell \in [4]$). These messages may be a function of the common reference string (denoted by crs) and the PKI setup. Let α_i denote the output of the PKI setup (or more generally, the output of an arbitrary correlated randomness setup) to party P_i. A party's view comprises of crs, α_i, its input, randomness and incoming messages.

Due to the involved nature of the scenarios, we begin with an intuitive description. Broadly speaking, this argument involves partitioning the parties $\{P_1, \ldots, P_6\}$ into two sets $\{P_1, P_2, P_6\}$ and $\{P_3, P_4, P_5\}$. Looking ahead, the final scenario is designed in a manner that allows a corrupt Q to obtain: (i) output with respect to some input of P_1 using the communication from $\{P_1, P_2, P_6\}$ and (ii) output with respect to a different input of P_1 using the communication from $\{P_3, P_4, P_5\}$. Tracing back, we carefully design the other scenarios such that Scenarios 1 and 2 let us conclude that if P_1 behaves honestly only in its messages to P_6, then there must exist some $x_1^* \in \{0, 1\}$ such that the communication from $\{P_3, P_4, P_5\}$ to Q enables Q to obtain output with respect $\neg x_1^*$ with a sufficiently large probability. On the other hand, Scenario 3 involves corrupt $\{P_3, P_4, P_5\}$ who pretend to have received no message from P_1, which lets us conclude that the messages from $\{P_1, P_2, P_6\}$ in such a case must enable Q to obtain output with respect to honest input x_1 of P_1. Combining the above two inferences in the final scenario lets us reach the final contradiction.

Following is a description of the scenarios. In each scenario, on behalf of the corrupt parties, we assume that the adversary uses the honest input and its malicious behaviour is limited to dropping some of the messages that were received or supposed to be sent. The views of the parties across various scenarios are described in Tables 10, 11, 12 and 13.

Scenario 1: Adversary corrupts $\{P_1, P_6\}$. P_1 does not communicate throughout the protocol. P_6 behaves honestly in Round 1 and Round 2 (thereby would send $\widetilde{\mathsf{pc}^2_{6\to j}}$ for $j \in [5]$) and aborts (does not communicate) in Round 3.

Scenario 2: Adversary corrupts $\{P_1, P_6\}$. P_1 does not communicate throughout the protocol. P_6 behaves honestly in Round 1 and Round 2, except that P_6 pretends to have received Round 1 message from P_1 (thereby would send $\mathsf{pc}^2_{6\to j}$ for $j \in [5]$). Note that it is possible for P_6 to pretend in such a manner as adversary corrupts both P_1, P_6. Lastly, P_6 aborts in Round 3.

Scenario 3: Adversary corrupts $\{P_3, P_4, P_5\}$. All corrupt parties behave honestly in Round 1. In Round 2, $\{P_3, P_4, P_5\}$ only communicate towards P_6, towards whom they pretend that they did not receive Round 1 message from P_1 (i.e. P_i sends $\widetilde{\mathsf{pc}^2_{i\to 6}}$ to P_6 for $i \in \{3,4,5\}$). Lastly, $\{P_3, P_4, P_5\}$ abort in Round 3.

Scenario 4: Adversary corrupts $\{P_1, P_2, Q\}$ who do the following:[8]

Round 1: P_1 behaves honestly only to $\{P_2, P_6, Q\}$ (only P_6 among the honest parties). P_2 and Q behave honestly.

Round 2: P_1 behaves honestly only to $\{P_2, P_6, Q\}$. P_2 and Q pretend towards $\{P_3, P_4, P_5\}$ as if they did not receive Round 1 message from P_1 (i.e. send $\widetilde{\mathsf{pc}^2_{i\to j}}$ to P_j for $i \in \{2,7\}$, $j \in \{3,4,5\}$). Towards $\{P_1, P_2, P_6\}$ (only P_6 among honest parties), P_2 and Q act as if Round 1 message had been received from P_1 (i.e. send $\mathsf{pc}^2_{i\to j}$ to P_j for $i \in \{2,7\}$, $j \in \{1,2,6\} \setminus i$).

Round 3: P_1 and P_2 drop the Round 2 messages obtained from $\{P_3, P_4, P_5\}$ (to emulate Scenario 3) and communicate to Q accordingly.

Table 10. Views of $\{P_1 \ldots P_7\}$ in Scenario 1.

	View₁	View₂	View₃	View₄	View₅	View₆	View₇
Initial Input	$(x_1, z_1, \mathsf{crs}, \alpha_1)$	$(x_2, r_2, \mathsf{crs}, \alpha_2)$	$(x_3, r_3, \mathsf{crs}, \alpha_3)$	$(x_4, r_4, \mathsf{crs}, \alpha_4)$	$(x_5, r_5, \mathsf{crs}, \alpha_5)$	$(x_6, r_6, \mathsf{crs}, \alpha_6)$	$(x_7, r_7, \mathsf{crs}, \alpha_7)$
Round 1	$\{\mathsf{pc}^j_{\to 1}\}_{j\in[7]\setminus\{1\}}$	$\{\mathsf{pc}^j_{\to 2}\}_{j\in[7]\setminus\{1,2\}}$	$\{\mathsf{pc}^j_{\to 3}\}_{j\in[7]\setminus\{1,3\}}$	$\{\mathsf{pc}^j_{\to 4}\}_{j\in[7]\setminus\{1,4\}}$	$\{\mathsf{pc}^j_{\to 5}\}_{j\in[7]\setminus\{1,5\}}$	$\{\mathsf{pc}^j_{\to 6}\}_{j\in[7]\setminus\{1,6\}}$	$\{\mathsf{pc}^j_{\to 7}\}_{j\in[7]\setminus\{1,7\}}$
Round 2	$\{\mathsf{pc}^2_{\to 1}\}_{j\in[7]\setminus\{1\}}$	$\{\mathsf{pc}^2_{\to 2}\}_{j\in[7]\setminus\{1,2\}}$	$\{\mathsf{pc}^2_{\to 3}\}_{j\in[7]\setminus\{1,3\}}$	$\{\mathsf{pc}^2_{\to 4}\}_{j\in[7]\setminus\{1,4\}}$	$\{\mathsf{pc}^2_{\to 5}\}_{j\in[7]\setminus\{1,5\}}$	$\{\mathsf{pc}^2_{\to 6}\}_{j\in[7]\setminus\{1,6\}}$	–
Round 3	–	–	–	–	–	–	$\{\mathsf{pc}^{3,1}_{j\to 7}\}_{j\in\{2,3,4,5\}}$

Table 11. Views of $\{P_1 \ldots P_7\}$ in Scenario 2.

	View₁	View₂	View₃	View₄	View₅	View₆	View₇
Initial Input	$(x_1, r_1, \mathsf{crs}, \alpha_1)$	$(x_2, r_2, \mathsf{crs}, \alpha_2)$	$(x_3, r_3, \mathsf{crs}, \alpha_3)$	$(x_4, r_4, \mathsf{crs}, \alpha_4)$	$(x_5, r_5, \mathsf{crs}, \alpha_5)$	$(x_6, r_6, \mathsf{crs}, \alpha_6)$	$(x_7, r_7, \mathsf{crs}, \alpha_7)$
Round 1	$\{\mathsf{pc}^j_{\to 1}\}_{j\in[7]\setminus\{1\}}$	$\{\mathsf{pc}^j_{\to 2}\}_{j\in[7]\setminus\{1,2\}}$	$\{\mathsf{pc}^j_{\to 3}\}_{j\in[7]\setminus\{1,3\}}$	$\{\mathsf{pc}^j_{\to 4}\}_{j\in[7]\setminus\{1,4\}}$	$\{\mathsf{pc}^j_{\to 5}\}_{j\in[7]\setminus\{1,5\}}$	$\{\mathsf{pc}^j_{\to 6}\}_{j\in[7]\setminus\{1,6\}}$	$\{\mathsf{pc}^j_{\to 7}\}_{j\in[7]\setminus\{1,7\}}$
Round 2	$\{\mathsf{pc}^j_{\to 1}\}_{j\in\{2,3,4,5,7\}}$ $\mathsf{pc}^2_{6\to 1}$	$\{\mathsf{pc}^j_{\to 2}\}_{j\in\{3,4,5,7\}}$ $\mathsf{pc}^2_{6\to 2}$	$\{\mathsf{pc}^j_{\to 3}\}_{j\in\{2,4,5,7\}}$ $\mathsf{pc}^2_{6\to 3}$	$\{\mathsf{pc}^j_{\to 4}\}_{j\in\{2,3,5,7\}}$ $\mathsf{pc}^2_{6\to 4}$	$\{\mathsf{pc}^j_{\to 5}\}_{j\in\{2,3,4,7\}}$ $\mathsf{pc}^2_{6\to 5}$	$\{\mathsf{pc}^j_{\to 6}\}_{j\in\{2,3,4,5,7\}}$	–
Round 3	–	–	–	–	–	–	$\{\mathsf{pc}^{3,2}_{j\to 7}\}_{j\in\{2,3,4,5\}}$

---

[8] Generally, communication between corrupt parties need not be specified but we include it here for easier understanding of Table 13.

Table 12. Views of $\{P_1 \ldots P_7\}$ in Scenario 3.

	View$_1$	View$_2$	View$_3$	View$_4$	View$_5$	View$_6$	View$_7$
Initial Input	$(x_1, r_1, \text{crs}, \alpha_1)$	$(x_2, r_2, \text{crs}, \alpha_2)$	$(x_3, r_3, \text{crs}, \alpha_3)$	$(x_4, r_4, \text{crs}, \alpha_4)$	$(x_5, r_5, \text{crs}, \alpha_5)$	$(x_6, r_6, \text{crs}, \alpha_6)$	$(x_7, r_7, \text{crs}, \alpha_7)$
Round 1	$\{pc^1_{j\to1}\}_{j\in[7]\setminus\{1\}}$	$\{pc^1_{j\to2}\}_{j\in[7]\setminus\{2\}}$	$\{pc^1_{j\to3}\}_{j\in[7]\setminus\{3\}}$	$\{pc^1_{j\to4}\}_{j\in[7]\setminus\{4\}}$	$\{pc^1_{j\to5}\}_{j\in[7]\setminus\{5\}}$	$\{pc^1_{j\to6}\}_{j\in[7]\setminus\{6\}}$	$\{pc^1_{j\to7}\}_{j\in[7]\setminus\{7\}}$
Round 2	$\{pc^2_{j\to1}\}_{j\in\{2,6,7\}}$	$\{pc^2_{j\to2}\}_{j\in\{1,6,7\}}$	$\{pc^2_{j\to3}\}_{j\in\{1,2,6,7\}}$	$\{pc^2_{j\to4}\}_{j\in\{1,2,6,7\}}$	$\{pc^2_{j\to5}\}_{j\in\{1,2,6,7\}}$	$\{pc^2_{j\to6}\}_{j\in\{1,2,7\}}$ $\{pc^2_{j\to6}\}_{j\in\{3,4,5\}}$	–
Round 3	–	–	–	–	–	–	$\{pc^{3,3}_{j\to7}\}_{j\in\{1,2,6\}}$

Table 13. Views of $\{P_1 \ldots P_7\}$ in Scenario 4.

	View$_1$	View$_2$	View$_3$	View$_4$	View$_5$	View$_6$	View$_7$
Initial Input	$(x_1, r_1, \text{crs}, \alpha_1)$	$(x_2, r_2, \text{crs}, \alpha_2)$	$(x_3, r_3, \text{crs}, \alpha_3)$	$(x_4, r_4, \text{crs}, \alpha_4)$	$(x_5, r_5, \text{crs}, \alpha_5)$	$(x_6, r_6, \text{crs}, \alpha_6)$	$(x_7, r_7, \text{crs}, \alpha_7)$
Round 1	$\{pc^1_{j\to1}\}_{j\in[7]\setminus\{1\}}$	$\{pc^1_{j\to2}\}_{j\in[7]\setminus\{2\}}$	$\{pc^1_{j\to3}\}_{j\in[7]\setminus\{1,3\}}$	$\{pc^1_{j\to4}\}_{j\in[7]\setminus\{1,4\}}$	$\{pc^1_{j\to5}\}_{j\in[7]\setminus\{1,5\}}$	$\{pc^1_{j\to6}\}_{j\in[7]\setminus\{6\}}$	$\{pc^1_{j\to7}\}_{j\in[7]\setminus\{7\}}$
Round 2	$\{pc^2_{j\to1}\}_{j\in\{3,4,5\}}$ $\{pc^2_{j\to1}\}_{j\in\{2,6,7\}}$	$\{pc^2_{j\to2}\}_{j\in\{3,4,5\}}$ $\{pc^2_{j\to2}\}_{j\in\{1,6,7\}}$	$\{pc^2_{j\to3}\}_{j\in\{2,4,5,7\}}$ $pc^2_{6\to3}$	$\{pc^2_{j\to4}\}_{j\in\{2,3,5,7\}}$ $pc^2_{6\to4}$	$\{pc^2_{j\to5}\}_{\{2,3,4,7\}}$ $pc^2_{6\to5}$	$\{pc^2_{j\to6}\}_{j\in\{3,4,5\}}$ $\{pc^2_{j\to6}\}_{j\in\{1,2,7\}}$	–
Round 3	–	–	–	–	–	–	$\{pc^{3,4}_{j\to7} \equiv pc^{3,3}_{j\to7}\}_{j\in\{1,2,6\}}$ $\{pc^{3,4}_{j\to7} \equiv pc^{3,2}_{j\to6}\}_{j\in\{3,4,5\}}$

The proof outline is as follows. First, we show that there exits $x_1^* \in \{0,1\}$ such that if Scenario 1 occurs with respect to x_1^* and uniformly randomly sampled x_3, x_4, x_6, then the output obtained by Q is computed on $\neg x_1^*$ with a sufficiently large (constant) probability. Next, we show this is also the case for Scenario 2 (with a different probability). Since this inference may appear counter-intuitive, we elaborate the argument in some detail below. Note that the difference between Scenario 1 and 2 lies in the communication from P_6 to honest parties $\{P_2, P_3, P_4, P_5\}$ in Round 2. While in the former, P_6 acts as if he did not receive Round 1 message from P_1; in the latter he pretends as if he did receive Round 1 message from P_1. We define a sequence of hybrids $\text{hyb}_0, \ldots, \text{hyb}_4$. Specifically, hyb_0 and hyb_4 refer to Scenario 1 and 2 respectively and hyb_i is same as hyb_{i-1} $(i \in \{1, \ldots, 4\})$ except that P_6 acts towards P_{i+1} that he did receive Round 1 message from P_1. We show that in each hybrid, the output obtained by Q is w.r.t. $\neg x_1^*$ with a sufficiently large (but slightly different) probability. Next, if Scenario 3 occurs, then the output obtained by Q must be computed on x_1 (honest input of P_1) due to correctness of Π. Lastly, we show that such a protocol Π is susceptible to an attack by $\{P_1, P_2, Q\}$ which allows Q to obtain both the above evaluations of f (i.e., on both x_1^* and $\neg x_1^*$), which is a contradiction to security of Π. We defer the formal proof to the full version [7].

5.2 General Five-Round Protocol

In this section, we present a five-round solitary output MPC protocol with guaranteed output delivery that works for any n in the presence of an honest majority - that is, any $t < n/2$ where n is the number of parties and t is the number of corrupt parties. Our protocol uses the following primitives: a $(\frac{n}{2}+1)$-out-of-n decentralized threshold FHE scheme dTFHE = (dTFHE.DistGen, dTFHE.Enc, dTFHE.PartialDec, dTFHE.Eval, dTFHE.Combine), a digital signature scheme (Gen, Sign, Verify), and a simulation-extractible NIZK argument

(NIZK.Setup, NIZK.Prove, NIZK.Verify). We use the NIZK argument for two NP languages L_1, L_2 defined in Sect. 3.2. All of them can be built assuming LWE [10,11,38]. Formally, we show the following theorem:

Theorem 5. *Assuming LWE, protocol $\Pi_{5-\text{round}}$ described below is a five-round secure solitary output MPC protocol with god with a PKI setup and pairwise-private channels. The protocol works for any n, any function and is secure against a malicious rushing adversary that can corrupt any $t < n/2$ parties.*

Overview. Consider n parties $P_1, \ldots, P_n$ who wish to evaluate function $f : (\{0,1\}^\lambda)^{n-1} \to \{0,1\}^\lambda$. We also denote P_n as the output receiving party Q. In some places, we use the notation $\text{msg}^{i \to j}$ to indicate that the message was sent by party P_i to P_j. At a high level, our protocol works as follows. In Round 1, each party P_i sends to every other party a dTFHE encryption $[\![x_i]\!]$ along with a NIZK argument π_i proving that the encryption is well formed. On top of that, P_i also attaches its signature $\sigma_i \leftarrow \text{Sign}(\text{skey}_i, ([\![x_i]\!], \pi_i))$. In Round 2, each party sends all the messages it received in Round 1 to Q. In Round 3, Q first initializes a string $\text{msg} = \bot$ and does the following for each $i \in [n]$: if it received a *valid* message from P_i in Round 1, (where *valid* means the signature σ_i and the NIZK π_i verify successfully) it includes the message in msg and sets a value $\text{ct}_i = [\![x_i]\!]$. Else, in Round 2, if a different party P_{i_1}, forwards a *valid* message $([\![x_i]\!]^{i_1 \to n}, \pi^{i_1 \to n}, \sigma^{i_1 \to n})$ received from P_i in Round 1, include that in msg and set ct_i to be $[\![x_i]\!]^{i_1 \to n}$. If no such i_1 exists, set $\text{ct}_i = \bot$ and append $\bot$ to msg. Then, Q sends msg and a signature on it σ_{msg} to all parties. In Round 4, each party sends the tuple received from Q in Round 3 to every other party. Finally, in Round 5, each party P_i sends its partial decryption (along with a NIZK) on the homomorphically evaluated ciphertext $[\![y]\!] = \text{dTFHE.Eval}(f, \text{ct}_1, \ldots, \text{ct}_n)$ if: (i) in Round 3, Q sent $(\text{msg}, \sigma_{\text{msg}})$ such that σ_{msg} verifies, (ii) it did not receive a different tuple $(\text{msg}', \sigma_{\text{msg}'})$ from another party in Round 4 such that $\sigma_{\text{msg}'}$ verifies, (iii) in the string msg, every tuple of the form $([\![x_j]\!], \pi_j, \sigma_j)$ is *valid*, (iv) for every party P_k, if P_i received a *valid* message from P_k in Round 1, then in Q's Round 3 message msg, there must exist *some valid* tuple of the form $([\![x'_k]\!], \pi'_k, \sigma'_k)$ on behalf of P_k (not necessarily the one P_i received in Round 1). After Round 5, Q combines all the partial decryptions (if the NIZK verifies) to recover the output. Our protocol is formally described below. We defer the security proof to the full version [7].

CRS: Send $\text{crs} \leftarrow \text{NIZK.Setup}(1^\lambda)$ to every party.

PKI Setup:

- For each $i \in [n]$: sample $(\text{pk}_i, \text{sk}_i) \leftarrow \text{dTFHE.DistGen}(1^\lambda, 1^d, i; r_i)$ and $(\text{vkey}_i, \text{skey}_i) \leftarrow \text{Gen}(1^\lambda)$.
- Public key: $\text{pk} = \text{pk}_1 \| \ldots \| \text{pk}_n$ and $\{\text{vkey}_i\}_{i \in [n]}$.
- Secret keys: $(\text{sk}_i, r_i, \text{skey}_i)$ to party P_i for each $i \in [n]$.

Inputs: For each $i \in [n]$, party P_i has an input $x_i \in \{0,1\}^\lambda$.

Protocol:

1. **Round 1:** For each $i \in [n]$:
   - P_i computes $[\![x_i]\!] \leftarrow$ dTFHE.Enc$(\mathsf{pk}, x_i; \rho_i)$ using randomness ρ_i, $\pi_i \leftarrow$ NIZK.Prove$(\mathsf{crs}, \mathsf{st}_i, \mathsf{wit}_i)$ for $\mathsf{st}_i \in \mathsf{L}_1$ where $\mathsf{st}_i = ([\![x_i]\!], \mathsf{pk})$ and $\mathsf{wit}_i = (x_i, \rho_i)$.
   - Then, compute $\sigma_i \leftarrow$ Sign$(\mathsf{skey}_i, ([\![x_i]\!], \pi_i))$ and send $([\![x_i]\!], \pi_i, \sigma_i)$ to every party.
2. **Round 2:** For each $i \in [n]$, P_i sends all the messages it received in Round 1 to party $P_n(= Q)$.
3. **Round 3:** Party $P_n(= Q)$ does the following:
   - Define strings $\mathsf{msg}, \mathsf{ct}_1, \ldots, \mathsf{ct}_n$ as $\bot$.
   - For each $i \in [n]$, let $\{([\![x_j]\!]^{i \to n}, \pi_j^{i \to n}, \sigma_j^{i \to n})\}_{j \in [n] \setminus \{i\}}$ denote the message received from P_i in Round 2 and $([\![x_i]\!]^{i \to n}, \pi_i^{i \to n}, \sigma_i^{i \to n})$ denote the message received from P_i in Round 1.
   - For each $j \in [n]$, do the following:
     - Let $\{([\![x_j]\!]^{1 \to n}, \pi_j^{1 \to n}, \sigma_j^{1 \to n}), \ldots, ([\![x_j]\!]^{n \to n}, \pi_j^{n \to n}, \sigma_j^{n \to n})\}$ be the messages received across both rounds on behalf of party P_j.
     - Pick the lowest i_1 such that Verify$(\mathsf{vkey}_j, ([\![x_j]\!]^{i_1 \to n}, \pi_j^{i_1 \to n}), \sigma_j^{i_1 \to n}) = 1$ and NIZK.Verify$(\mathsf{crs}, \pi_j^{i_1 \to n}, \mathsf{st}_j) = 1$ for $\mathsf{st}_j \in \mathsf{L}_1$ where $\mathsf{st}_j = ([\![x_j]\!]^{i_1 \to n}, \mathsf{pk})$. Set $\mathsf{ct}_j := [\![x_j]\!]^{i_1 \to n}$ and $\mathsf{msg} := \mathsf{msg} \| \text{``Party j ''} \| ([\![x_j]\!]^{i_1 \to n}, \pi_j^{i_1 \to n}, \sigma_j^{i_1 \to n})$.
     - If no such i_1 exists, set $\mathsf{msg} = \mathsf{msg} \| \text{``Party j ''} \| \bot$.
   - Compute $\sigma_{\mathsf{msg}} \leftarrow$ Sign$(\mathsf{skey}_n, \mathsf{msg})$. Send $(\mathsf{msg}, \sigma_{\mathsf{msg}})$ to all parties.
   - Set $[\![y]\!] =$ dTFHE.Eval$(\mathsf{pk}, f, \mathsf{ct}_1, \ldots, \mathsf{ct}_n)$.[9]
4. **Round 4:** For each $i \in [n-1]$, P_i sends the message received from Q in Round 3 to every party.
5. **Round 5:** For each $i \in [n-1]$, P_i does the following:
   - Let $\{(\mathsf{msg}^{j \to i}, \sigma_{\mathsf{msg}}^{j \to i})\}_{j \in [n-1] \setminus \{i\}}$ be the messages received in Round 4 and $(\mathsf{msg}^{n \to i}, \sigma_{\mathsf{msg}}^{n \to i})$ be the message from Q in Round 3.
   - If Verify$(\mathsf{vkey}_n, \mathsf{msg}^{n \to i}, \sigma_{\mathsf{msg}}^{n \to i}) \neq 1$ (OR) $\mathsf{msg}^{n \to i}$ is not of the form $(\text{``Party 1 ''} \| m_1 \| \ldots \| \text{``Party n ''} \| m_n)$, send $\bot$ to Q and end the round.
   - Output $\bot$ to Q and end the round if there exists $j \neq n$ such that:
     - $\mathsf{msg}^{j \to i} \neq \mathsf{msg}^{n \to i}$ (AND)
     - Verify$(\mathsf{vkey}_n, \mathsf{msg}^{j \to i}, \sigma_{\mathsf{msg}}^{j \to i}) = 1$ (AND)
     - $\mathsf{msg}^{j \to i}$ is of the form $(\text{``Party 1 ''} \| m_1, \ldots, \| \text{``Party n ''} \| m_n)$. This third check is to ensure that a corrupt P_j doesn't re-use a valid signature sent by Q in the first round as its message in Round 4.
   - Define strings $\mathsf{ct}_1, \ldots, \mathsf{ct}_n$.
   - Parse $\mathsf{msg}^{n \to i}$ as $(\text{``Party 1 ''} \| m_1, \ldots, \| \text{``Party n ''} \| m_n)$.
   - For each $j \in [n]$, do the following:

---

[9] Let $\mathcal{S} = \{i | \mathsf{ct}_i = \bot\}$. Here, we actually homomorphically evaluate the residual function $f_{\mathcal{S}}(\cdot)$ that only takes as input $\{x_j\}_{j \notin \mathcal{S}}$ and uses the default values for all indices in the set $\mathcal{S}$. For ease of exposition, we skip this notation in the rest of the protocol and proof.

- If in Round 1, P_i received $(\llbracket x_j \rrbracket, \pi_j, \sigma_j)$ from P_j such that $\mathsf{Verify}(\mathsf{vkey}_j, (\llbracket x_j \rrbracket, \pi_j), \sigma_j) = 1$ and $\mathsf{NIZK.Verify}(\pi_j, \mathsf{st}_j) = 1$ for $\mathsf{st}_j \in \mathsf{L}_1$ where $\mathsf{st}_j = (\llbracket x_j \rrbracket, \mathsf{pk})$, set $\mathsf{bit}_j = 1$. Else, set $\mathsf{bit}_j = 0$.
- If $m_j = \perp$:
  * If $\mathsf{bit}_j = 1$, send $\perp$ to Q and end the round.
  * Else, set $\mathsf{ct}_j = \perp$.
- If $m_j = (\llbracket x_j \rrbracket^{i_1 \to n}, \pi_j^{i_1 \to n}, \sigma_j^{i_1 \to n})$:
  * If $\mathsf{Verify}(\mathsf{vkey}_j, (\llbracket x_j \rrbracket^{i_1 \to n}, \pi_j^{i_1 \to n}), \sigma_j^{i_1 \to n}) = 1$ and $\mathsf{NIZK.Verify}(\mathsf{crs}, \pi_j^{i_1 \to n}, \mathsf{st}_j) = 1$ for $\mathsf{st}_j \in \mathsf{L}_1$ where $\mathsf{st}_j = (\llbracket x_j \rrbracket^{i_1 \to n}, \mathsf{pk})$, set $\mathsf{ct}_j = \llbracket x_j \rrbracket^{i_1 \to n}$.
  * Else, send $\perp$ to Q and end the round.
- Compute $\llbracket y \rrbracket \leftarrow \mathsf{dTFHE.Eval}(\mathsf{pk}, f, \mathsf{ct}_1, \ldots, \mathsf{ct}_n)$.
- Compute $\llbracket y : \mathsf{sk}_i \rrbracket \leftarrow \mathsf{dTFHE.PartialDec}(\mathsf{sk}_i, \llbracket y \rrbracket)$ and $\pi_i^{\mathsf{dec}} \leftarrow \mathsf{NIZK.Prove}(\mathsf{crs}, \mathsf{st}_i^{\mathsf{dec}}, \mathsf{wit}_i^{\mathsf{dec}})$ for $\mathsf{st}_i^{\mathsf{dec}} \in \mathsf{L}_2$ where $\mathsf{st}_i^{\mathsf{dec}} = (\llbracket y : \mathsf{sk}_i \rrbracket, \llbracket y \rrbracket, \mathsf{pk}_i, i)$ and $\mathsf{wit}_i^{\mathsf{dec}} = (\mathsf{sk}_i, r_i)$.
- Send $(\llbracket y : \mathsf{sk}_i \rrbracket, \pi_i^{\mathsf{dec}})$ to Q.

6. **Output Computation:** Q does the following:
   - Recall the value $\llbracket y \rrbracket$ computed in Round 3.
   - For each $i \in [n]$, if $\mathsf{NIZK.Verify}(\mathsf{crs}, \pi_i^{\mathsf{dec}}, \mathsf{st}_i^{\mathsf{dec}}) \neq 1$ for $\mathsf{st}_i^{\mathsf{dec}} \in \mathsf{L}_2$ where $\mathsf{st}_i^{\mathsf{dec}} = (\llbracket y : \mathsf{sk}_i \rrbracket, \llbracket y \rrbracket, \mathsf{pk}_i, i)$, discard $\llbracket y : \mathsf{sk}_i \rrbracket$.
   - Output $y \leftarrow \mathsf{dTFHE.Combine}(\mathsf{pk}, \{\llbracket y : \mathsf{sk}_i \rrbracket\}_{i \in S})$ where S contains the set of non-discarded values from the previous step.

5.3 $(t + 2)$ Round Protocol

We now describe how to transform the two-round protocol (say Π) of [28] into a $(t + 2)$-round protocol Π' for solitary MPC with god. Recall that protocol Π (that assumes a PKI setup) achieves god for standard MPC and involves communication only via broadcast channels in both rounds. We propose the following changes to Π. First, we employ a $(t + 1)$-round protocol over pairwise-private channels that realizes the broadcast functionality [17] to execute Round 1 of Π. Next, the messages communicated via broadcast in Round 2 of Π are instead sent privately only to Q (as only Q is supposed to obtain output) in Round $(t + 2)$ of Π'. This completes the high-level description of Π' whose security follows directly from security of Π. This approach achieves better round complexity than our general five-round construction (Sect. 5.2) when $t \leq 2$.

Acknowledgments. We would like to thank the anonymous reviewers for their helpful and constructive comments on the manuscript. P. Miao is supported in part by the NSF CNS Award 2247352, a DPI Science Team Seed Grant, a Meta Award, and a DSI Seed Grant. All the authors did part of the work while at Visa Research.

References

1. Abraham, I., Devadas, S., Dolev, D., Nayak, K., Ren, L.: Synchronous byzantine agreement with expected $O(1)$ rounds, expected $o(n^2)$ communication, and optimal resilience. In: FC (2019)
2. Alon, B., Cohen, R., Omri, E., Suad, T.: On the power of an honest majority in three-party computation without broadcast. In: TCC (2020)
3. Ananth, P., Choudhuri, A.R., Goel, A., Jain, A.: Round-optimal secure multiparty computation with honest majority. In: Shacham, H., Boldyreva, A. (eds.) CRYPTO 2018. LNCS, vol. 10992, pp. 395–424. Springer, Cham (2018). https://doi.org/10.1007/978-3-319-96881-0_14
4. Asharov, G., Beimel, A., Makriyannis, N., Omri, E.: Complete characterization of fairness in secure two-party computation of Boolean functions. In: Dodis, Y., Nielsen, J.B. (eds.) TCC 2015. LNCS, vol. 9014, pp. 199–228. Springer, Heidelberg (2015). https://doi.org/10.1007/978-3-662-46494-6_10
5. Asharov, G., Jain, A., López-Alt, A., Tromer, E., Vaikuntanathan, V., Wichs, D.: Multiparty computation with low communication, computation and interaction via threshold FHE. In: Pointcheval, D., Johansson, T. (eds.) EUROCRYPT 2012. LNCS, vol. 7237, pp. 483–501. Springer, Heidelberg (2012). https://doi.org/10.1007/978-3-642-29011-4_29
6. Badrinarayanan, S., Jain, A., Manohar, N., Sahai, A.: Threshold multi-key FHE and applications to round-optimal MPC. In: ASIACRYPT (2020)
7. Badrinarayanan, S., Miao, P., Mukherjee, P., Ravi, D.: On the round complexity of fully secure solitary mpc with honest majority. Cryptology ePrint Archive, Paper 2021/241 (2021). https://eprint.iacr.org/2021/241
8. Bell, J.H., Bonawitz, K.A., Gascón, A., Lepoint, T., Raykova, M.: Secure single-server aggregation with (poly)logarithmic overhead. In: CCS, pp. 1253–1269. ACM (2020)
9. Bonawitz, K., et al. Practical secure aggregation for privacy-preserving machine learning. In: CCS (2017)
10. Boneh, D., Gennaro, R., Goldfeder, S., Jain, A., Kim, S., Rasmussen, P.M.R., Sahai, A.: Threshold cryptosystems from threshold fully homomorphic encryption. In: Shacham, H., Boldyreva, A. (eds.) CRYPTO 2018. LNCS, vol. 10991, pp. 565–596. Springer, Cham (2018). https://doi.org/10.1007/978-3-319-96884-1_19
11. Canetti, R., et al.: Fiat-shamir: from practice to theory. In: STOC (2019)
12. Chor, B., Merritt, M., Shmoys, D.B.: Simple constant-time consensus protocols in realistic failure models. J. ACM (JACM) **36**(3), 591–614 (1989)
13. Cleve, R.: Limits on the security of coin flips when half the processors are faulty (extended abstract). In: STOC (1986)
14. Cohen, R., Garay, J., Zikas, V.: Broadcast-optimal two-round MPC. In: Canteaut, A., Ishai, Y. (eds.) EUROCRYPT 2020. LNCS, vol. 12106, pp. 828–858. Springer, Cham (2020). https://doi.org/10.1007/978-3-030-45724-2_28
15. Damgård, I., Magri, B., Ravi, D., Siniscalchi, L., Yakoubov, S.: Broadcast-optimal two round MPC with an honest majority. In: Malkin, T., Peikert, C. (eds.) CRYPTO 2021. LNCS, vol. 12826, pp. 155–184. Springer, Cham (2021). https://doi.org/10.1007/978-3-030-84245-1_6
16. Damgård, I., Ravi, D., Siniscalchi, L., Yakoubov, S.: Minimizing setup in broadcast-optimal two round MPC. In: Hazay, C., Stam, M. (eds.) EUROCRYPT 2023. LNCS, vol. 14005, pp. 129–158. Springer, Heidelberg (2023). https://doi.org/10.1007/978-3-031-30617-4_5

17. Dolev, D., Strong, H.R.: Authenticated algorithms for Byzantine agreement. SIAM J. Comput. **12**(4), 656–666 (1983)
18. Feldman, P., Micali, S.: An optimal probabilistic algorithm for synchronous Byzantine agreement. In: Ausiello, G., Dezani-Ciancaglini, M., Della Rocca, S.R. (eds.) ICALP 1989. LNCS, vol. 372, pp. 341–378. Springer, Heidelberg (1989). https://doi.org/10.1007/BFb0035770
19. Fischer, M.J., Lynch, N.A.: A lower bound for the time to assure interactive consistency. Inf. Process. Lett. **14**(4), 183–186 (1982)
20. Fitzi, M., Garay, J.A.: Efficient player-optimal protocols for strong and differential consensus. In: Borowsky, E., Rajsbaum, S. (eds.) 22nd ACM PODC, pp. 211–220. ACM (2003)
21. Fitzi, M., Garay, J.A., Maurer, U., Ostrovsky, R.: Minimal complete primitives for secure multi-party computation. In: Kilian, J. (ed.) CRYPTO 2001. LNCS, vol. 2139, pp. 80–100. Springer, Heidelberg (2001). https://doi.org/10.1007/3-540-44647-8_5
22. Garg, S., Goel, A., Jain, A.: The broadcast message complexity of secure multiparty computation. In: Galbraith, S.D., Moriai, S. (eds.) ASIACRYPT 2019. LNCS, vol. 11921, pp. 426–455. Springer, Cham (2019). https://doi.org/10.1007/978-3-030-34578-5_16
23. Gennaro, R., Ishai, Y., Kushilevitz, E., Rabin, T.: The round complexity of verifiable secret sharing and secure multicast. In: STOC (2001)
24. Gennaro, R., Ishai, Y., Kushilevitz, E., Rabin, T.: On 2-round secure multiparty computation. In: Yung, M. (ed.) CRYPTO 2002. LNCS, vol. 2442, pp. 178–193. Springer, Heidelberg (2002). https://doi.org/10.1007/3-540-45708-9_12
25. Goldreich, O., Micali, S., Wigderson, A.: How to play any mental game or a completeness theorem for protocols with honest majority. In: STOC (1987)
26. Goldwasser, S., Lindell, Y.: Secure multi-party computation without agreement. J. Cryptol. **18**, 247–287 (2005)
27. Gordon, S.D., Hazay, C., Katz, J., Lindell, Y.: Complete fairness in secure two-party computation. J. ACM **58**(6), 24:1–24:37 (2011)
28. Dov Gordon, S., Liu, F.-H., Shi, E.: Constant-round MPC with fairness and guarantee of output delivery. In: Gennaro, R., Robshaw, M. (eds.) CRYPTO 2015. LNCS, vol. 9216, pp. 63–82. Springer, Heidelberg (2015). https://doi.org/10.1007/978-3-662-48000-7_4
29. Halevi, S., Ishai, Y., Kushilevitz, E., Makriyannis, N., Rabin, T.: On fully secure MPC with solitary output. In: Hofheinz, D., Rosen, A. (eds.) TCC 2019. LNCS, vol. 11891, pp. 312–340. Springer, Cham (2019). https://doi.org/10.1007/978-3-030-36030-6_13
30. Halevi, S., Lindell, Y., Pinkas, B.: Secure computation on the web: computing without simultaneous interaction. In: Rogaway, P. (ed.) CRYPTO 2011. LNCS, vol. 6841, pp. 132–150. Springer, Heidelberg (2011). https://doi.org/10.1007/978-3-642-22792-9_8
31. Karlin, A., Yao, A.: Probabilistic lower bounds for byzantine agreement. Unpublished document (1986)
32. Katz, J., Koo, C.Y.: On expected constant-round protocols for byzantine agreement. J. Comput. Syst. Sci. **75**(2), 91–112 (2009)
33. Lamport, L., Shostak, R.E., Pease, M.C.: The byzantine generals problem. ACM Trans. Program. Lang. Syst. (1982)
34. Lynch, N.A.: Distributed Algorithms. Morgan Kaufmann, Burlington (1996)
35. Mohassel, A., Zhang, Y.: Secureml: a system for scalable privacy-preserving machine learning. In: IEEE S & P (2017)

36. Patra, A., Ravi, D.: On the exact round complexity of secure three-party computation. In: Shacham, H., Boldyreva, A. (eds.) CRYPTO 2018. LNCS, vol. 10992, pp. 425–458. Springer, Cham (2018). https://doi.org/10.1007/978-3-319-96881-0_15
37. Pease, M., Shostak, R., Lamport, L.: Reaching agreement in the presence of faults. J. ACM **27**(2), 228–234 (1980)
38. Peikert, C., Shiehian, S.: Noninteractive zero knowledge for NP from (plain) learning with errors. In: Boldyreva, A., Micciancio, D. (eds.) CRYPTO 2019. LNCS, vol. 11692, pp. 89–114. Springer, Cham (2019). https://doi.org/10.1007/978-3-030-26948-7_4
39. Yao, A.C.C.: How to generate and exchange secrets (extended abstract). In: FOCS (1986)

Three Party Secure Computation with Friends and Foes

Bar Alon[1,2]($\boxtimes$) , Amos Beimel[1] , and Eran Omri[2]

[1] Department of Computer Science, Ben Gurion University, Beer Sheva, Israel
alonbar08@gmail.com
[2] Department of Computer Science, Ariel University, Ariel Cyber Innovation Center (ACIC), Ariel, Israel
omrier@ariel.ac.il

Abstract. In secure multiparty computation (MPC), the goal is to allow a set of mutually distrustful parties to compute some function of their private inputs in a way that preserves security properties, even in the face of adversarial behavior by some of the parties. However, classical security definitions do not pose any privacy restrictions on the view of honest parties. Thus, if an attacker adversarially leaks private information to *honest* parties, it does not count as a violation of privacy. This is arguably undesirable, and in real-life scenarios, it is hard to imagine that possible users would agree to have their private information revealed, even if only to other honest parties.

To address this issue, Alon et al. [CRYPTO 20] introduced the notion of *security with friends and foes* (FaF security). In essence, (t, h)-FaF security requires that a malicious adversary corrupting up to t parties cannot help a coalition of h semi-honest parties to learn anything beyond what they can learn from their inputs and outputs (combined with the input and outputs of the malicious parties). They further showed that (t, h)-FaF security with n parties is achievable for any functionality if $2t + h < n$, and for some functionality, (t, h)-FaF security is impossible assuming $2t + h \geq n$. A remaining important open problem is to characterize the set of n-party functionalities that can be computed with (t, h)-FaF security assuming $2t + h \geq n$.

In this paper, we focus on the special, yet already challenging, case of $(1, 1)$-FaF security for three-party, 2-ary (two inputs), symmetric (all parties output the same value) functionalities. We provide several positive results, a lower bound on the round complexity, and an impossibility result. In particular, we prove the following. (1) we identify a large class of three-party Boolean symmetric 2-ary functionalities that can be computed with $(1, 1)$-FaF full security, and (2) We identify a large class of three-party (possibly non-Boolean) symmetric 2-ary functionalities, for which no $O(\log \kappa)$-round protocol computes them with $(1, 1)$-FaF full security. This matches the round complexity of our positive results for various interesting functionalities, such as equality of strings.

Keywords: MPC with friends and foes · full security · lower bounds · protocols

© International Association for Cryptologic Research 2023
G. Rothblum and H. Wee (Eds.): TCC 2023, LNCS 14370, pp. 156–185, 2023.
https://doi.org/10.1007/978-3-031-48618-0_6

1   Introduction

In secure multiparty computation (MPC), the goal is to allow a set of mutually distrustful parties to compute some function of their private inputs in a way that preserves security properties, even despite adversarial behavior by some of the parties. Some of the most basic security properties that may be desired are correctness, privacy, independence of inputs, fairness, and guaranteed output delivery. The notion of full security captures all of the above security properties.[1] Classical security definitions (cf., [12]) assume the existence of a single adversarial entity controlling the set of corrupted parties. A malicious adversary may deviate from the protocol in any way. In particular, it may send non-prescribed messages to honest parties. Such messages could potentially leak private information to *honest* parties, e.g., the secret input of some other honest party. Since the classical definitions pose *no* restrictions on the view of honest parties in the protocol, they do not count this as a violation of privacy. Moreover, even the protocol itself may instruct all parties to send their inputs to other honest parties, if say, all possible corrupted parties have been previously revealed (e.g., in the protocol of [19]). Again, this would still not count as a violation of privacy according to the classical security definition. This is arguably undesirable in many situations that fall into the MPC framework. Furthermore, when considering MPC solutions for real-life scenarios, it is hard to imagine that possible users would agree to have their private inputs revealed to honest parties (albeit not to malicious ones).

To address this issue, Alon et al. [1] introduced a new security definition called *security with friends and foes* (FaF security) that, in addition to standard security requirement, poses a privacy requirement on the view of subsets of honest parties. In essence, (t, h)-FaF security requires that for every malicious adversary $\mathcal{A}$ corrupting t parties, and for any disjoint subset of h parties, both the view of the adversary and the joint view of the additional h parties can be simulated (separately) in the ideal model. The security of the protocol should hold even if the malicious adversary sends to some h (semi-)honest parties non-prescribed messages. In fact, the adversary is allowed to send messages after the protocol is terminated.

Alon et al. [1] accompanied the new security notion with several feasibility and impossibility results. They showed that achieving (t, h)-FaF security with n parties against computational adversaries is achievable for any functionality if and only if $2t + h < n$. That is, if $2t + h < n$ then for any n-party functionality there exists a (t, h)-FaF secure protocol computing it, and conversely, if $2t + h \geq n$, then there exists a functionality that cannot be computed with (t, h)-FaF security. Note that this does not rule out the existence of n-party functionalities that can still be computed with (t, h)-FaF security, even when $2t + h \geq n$. Indeed, Alon et al. [1] also presented interesting examples of such functionalities. This

---

[1] Formally, security is defined via the real vs. ideal paradigm, where a (real-world) protocol is required to emulate an ideal setting, in which the adversary is limited to selecting inputs for the corrupted parties and receiving their outputs.

includes n-party coin tossing with (t, h)-FaF security assuming $t < n/2$ and $h \leq n - t$, and three-party XOR with $(1, 1)$-FaF security, both of which are known to be impossible to securely compute without an honest majority (with standard security requirements) [9]. This raises the following natural question:

> *Which n-party functionalities can be computed with*
> *(t, h)-FaF security assuming $2t + h \geq n$?*

1.1   Our Results

In this paper, we are interested in the special, yet already challenging, three-party setting where all parties output the same value and are interested in achieving $(1, 1)$-FaF security[2]. We show several positive results, a lower bound on the round complexity required for achieving FaF security, and an impossibility result. We next review our results, starting with describing the positive results. Before doing so, we introduce a *dealer model*, which simplifies the proofs and descriptions of our protocols.

The Dealer Model. The following dealer model serves as a middle ground between the ideal world for FaF security and real-world protocols. It is useful for constructing protocols as it abstracts away technical implementation issues. In particular, this allows our protocols to admit information-theoretic security in the dealer model. Furthermore, in the dealer model we define, the adversary receives no messages, and the only attacks it can perform are to change its input and abort prematurely. This makes the security analysis of such protocols much simpler. Importantly, we show a general compilation from protocols in the dealer model to protocols in the real world and vice versa. The second direction, where we compile a real-world FaF secure protocol into a FaF secure protocol in the dealer model, helps us describe impossibility results in a clear way. It additionally gives more intuition into the impossibility result of Alon et al. [1], where the attacker aborts by selecting a round independently from its view in the protocol. The above compilation shows that indeed an attack cannot rely on the view of the adversary, apart from the round number.

In this dealer model, parties interact in rounds via a trusted dealer, and the malicious adversary is only allowed to abort in each round. In more detail, the interaction proceeds as follows. First, the parties send their inputs to the dealer. The dealer then computes *backup values* for each pair of parties for each round. These values will later be used as the output of two parties in case the remaining third party aborts. Then, in each round, the dealer approaches the parties in a certain order, without revealing any information to the approached party, besides the round number. The party being approached responds with either continue or abort. If it sends abort, then the dealer sends to the remaining pair of parties a backup value (that depends on the round number). The two parties output this value and halt. Additionally, the dealer also sends to each

---

[2] The security notion was called FaF full security in [1].

honest party the appropriate backup values corresponding to the honest party and the aborting party (this models FaF security where the malicious adversary may send its real world view to the other parties). If no abort occurred then the dealer sends the output of the function to all parties.

Theorem 1.1 (Informal). *Assume that secure protocols for oblivious transfer exist. Let $f : \mathcal{X} \times \mathcal{Y} \times \mathcal{Z} \to \mathcal{W}$ be a three-party functionality. Then f can be computed with $(1,1)$-FaF security if and only if it can be computed with $(1,1)$-FaF security in the dealer model.*

Possibility Results for $(1,1)$-FaF Security. We focus on $(1,1)$-FaF security in the three-party setting, assuming that only two parties hold inputs, and that all parties receive the same output (i.e., symmetric functionalities). We provide several positive results in this setting.

In our first result, we show that if a 2-ary function (two inputs) f has a two-party protocol that computes it with both (standard) malicious security and with (standard) semi-honest security, then f can be computed as a three-party functionality with $(1,1)$-FaF security, with all three parties obtaining the output. It is instructive to note that even if a two-party protocol is secure against malicious adversaries, it may still *not* be secure against semi-honest adversaries [5].

Theorem 1.2 (Informal). *Assume that secure protocols for oblivious transfer exist. Let $f : \mathcal{X} \times \mathcal{Y} \to \mathcal{W}$ be a 2-ary function. Assume that there exists a protocol π for computing f as a symmetric two-party functionality, providing both (standard) malicious and semi-honest security. Then f can be computed as a symmetric three-party functionality with $(1,1)$-FaF security.*

Note that simply letting the two parties holding inputs run the secure protocol between themselves, and then having them send the output to the remaining third party does not work. This is due to the fact that a corrupt party can lie about the outcome, and then the third party has no way of detecting who is lying.

As an application, consider Boolean functionalities, namely, the output of the parties is a single bit. Asharov et al. [3] characterized all two-party symmetric Boolean functionalities that can be securely computed. We observe that the protocol they constructed also admits semi-honest security. Thus, we may apply Theorem 1.2 to the class of functionalities captured by the (positive) result of [3], and obtain the following result for three-party FaF-secure computation. First, for a deterministic function $f : \mathcal{X} \times \mathcal{Y} \times \{\lambda\} \to \{0,1\}$ we associate with it a matrix $M_f \in \{0,1\}^{|\mathcal{X}| \times |\mathcal{Y}|}$ defined as $M_f(x,y) = f(x,y)$ for all $x \in \mathcal{X}$ and $y \in \mathcal{Y}$. Then we have the following.

Corollary 1.3. *Assume that secure protocols for oblivious transfer exist. Let $f : \mathcal{X} \times \mathcal{Y} \times \{\lambda\} \to \{0,1\}$ be a three-party Boolean symmetric functionality. Assume that either the all-one vector or the all-zero vector is an affine combination[3] of either the rows or the columns of M_f. Then f can be computed with $(1,1)$-FaF security.*

---

[3] A affine combination is a linear combination where the sum of the coefficients is 1.

160 B. Alon et al.

We now turn to our second positive result, providing several sufficient conditions for the existence of $(1, 1)$-FaF secure 3-party protocols for Boolean functionalities. For a Boolean function f we let $\overline{M}_f$ be the negated matrix, defined as $\overline{M}_f(x, y) = 1 - f(x, y)$ for all $x \in \mathcal{X}$ and $y \in \mathcal{Y}$.

Theorem 1.4 (Informal). *Assume that secure protocols for oblivious transfer exist. Let $f : \mathcal{X} \times \mathcal{Y} \times \{\lambda\} \to \{0, 1\}$ be a three-party Boolean symmetric functionality. Assume that at least one of the following holds.*

1. *Both M_f and $\overline{M}_f$ have a trivial kernel, or both M_f^T and $\overline{M}_f^T$ have a trivial kernel, i.e., the kernel contains only the all-zero vector.*
2. *The all-one vector is a linear combination of either the rows or columns of M_f, where all coefficients are strictly positive.*

Then f can be computed with $(1, 1)$-FaF security.

The round complexity of the protocol we construct is $\omega(\log \kappa)$, where κ is the security parameter. Below we present a lower bound on the round complexity that matches the upper bound for several functionalities.

Observe that the class of functionalities captured by Theorem 1.4 is different from the class of functionalities captured by Corollary 1.3. Indeed, for an integer $m \geq 2$, consider the equality function $\mathsf{EQ} : [m]^2 \times \{\lambda\} \to \{0, 1\}$, defined as $\mathsf{EQ}(x, y) = 1$ if $x = y$, and $\mathsf{EQ}(x, y) = 0$ if $x \neq y$. Then the associated matrix M_{EQ} is the $m \times m$ identity matrix, which clearly satisfies Item 1, hence it can be computed with $(1, 1)$-FaF security. However, it cannot be computed as a two-party functionality as it implies coin tossing. We provide a more general theorem alongside its proof in Sect. 4.2.

Negative Results. We now turn to our negative results. Our first result is a lower bound on the number of rounds required for FaF security. We identify a class of functionalities such that, in order to compute any of them with $(1, 1)$-FaF security, would require many rounds of interactions. To simplify the presentation in this introduction, we limit the statement to Boolean functions (see Theorem 5.2 for the generalization to non-Boolean functions).

Theorem 1.5 (Informal). *Let $f : \mathcal{X} \times \mathcal{Y} \times \{\lambda\} \to \{0, 1\}$ be a deterministic three-party Boolean functionality. Assuming that the matrix M_f has no constant rows, no constant columns, and that no row or column has its negation appearing in M_f. Then there is no $O(\log \kappa)$-round protocol computing f with $(1, 1)$-FaF security.*

Observe that the equality function $\mathsf{EQ} : [m]^2 \times \{\lambda\} \to \{0, 1\}$, where $m \geq 3$, satisfies the conditions in Theorem 1.5. Note that this matches the round complexity of the protocol from Theorem 1.4.

Our final result states there exists a three-party non-Boolean functionality that depends on two inputs, which cannot be computed with FaF security.

Theorem 1.6 (Informal). *Assume the existence of one-way permutations. Then there exists a three-party 2-ary symmetric functionality that cannot be computed with $(1,1)$-FaF security.*

We do not know if such impossibility results hold for a Boolean functionality, and we leave it as an interesting open question.

1.2   Our Techniques

In this section, we provide an overview of our techniques. Let us first recall the definition of $(1,1)$-FaF security. We say that a protocol computes a functionality f with $(1,1)$-FaF security, if for any adversary $\mathcal{A}$ (statically) corrupting a party P the following holds: (i) there exists a simulator Sim that can simulate (in the ideal-world[4]) $\mathcal{A}$'s view in the real-world (so far, this is standard security), and (ii) for any uncorrupted party $Q \neq P$, there exists a "semi-honest" simulator $\mathrm{Sim_Q}$, such that, given the parties' inputs and Sim's ideal-world view (i.e., its randomness, inputs, auxiliary input, and output received from the trusted party), can generate a view that is indistinguishable form the real-world view of Q, i.e., $(\mathrm{VIEW_Q^{real}}, \mathrm{OUT^{real}})$ is indistinguishable from $(\mathrm{VIEW_{Sim_Q}^{ideal}}, \mathrm{OUT^{ideal}})$.

We now proceed to describe our techniques. Throughout the rest of the section, we denote the parties by A, B, and C, holding inputs x, y, and z, respectively.

Proof of Theorem 1.1. We show that a functionality can be computed with $(1,1)$-FaF security if and only if it can be computed with in an appropriate dealer model. Let us begin with a more detailed description of a dealer-model protocol. An r-round protocol in the dealer model for $(1,1)$-FaF security is described as follows. First, the parties send their inputs to the dealer. The dealer then computes *backup value* $\mathsf{ab}_0, \ldots, \mathsf{ab}_r$, $\mathsf{ac}_0, \ldots, \mathsf{ac}_r$, and $\mathsf{bc}_0, \ldots, \mathsf{bc}_r$. Then, for $i = 1$ to r, the dealer does the following.

1. If no abort was ever sent, approach party A, which responds with either continue or abort.
2. If A responds with abort, then send x and bc_{i-1} to B and C, sends $\mathsf{ab}_0, \ldots, \mathsf{ab}_{i-1}$ to B and $\mathsf{ac}_0, \ldots, \mathsf{ac}_{i-1}$ to C, and halts. Parties B and C then output bc_{i-1}.
3. If A responds with continue, approach party B, which responds with either continue or abort.
4. If B responds with abort, then sends y and ac_{i-1} to A and C, sends $\mathsf{ab}_0, \ldots, \mathsf{ab}_{i-1}$ to A and $\mathsf{bc}_0, \ldots, \mathsf{bc}_i$ to C, and halts. Parties A and C then output ac_{i-1}.
5. If B responds with continue, approach party C, which responds with either continue or abort.

---

[4] All the adversary can do in the ideal-world is to select its input for the computation and receive the output. Specifically, it cannot prevent the output from other parties or learn anything other than the output.

6. If C responds with abort, then sends z and ab_{i-1} to A and B, sends $ac_0, \ldots, ac_i$ to A and $bc_0, \ldots, bc_i$ to B, and halts. Parties A and B then output ab_{i-1}.

If no abort was ever sent, then the dealer sends the last backup values (which must equal to $f(x,y,z)$ with high probability to ensure correctness), and the parties output the value they received. Showing that the protocol in the dealer model can be emulated by a real world protocol (without the dealer) is done using standard techniques. Specifically, the parties compute a 3-out-of-3 secret sharing of the backup values, each signed using a signature scheme. This computation is done using a FaF secure-with-identifiable-abort protocol. That is, the malicious and semi-honest adversaries may learn the output first, and may prevent the honest party from receiving the output at the cost of revealing the identity of the malicious party. Then, in every round, the parties send their shares for the backup value of the other two parties. If a party changes its share (which is captured with overwhelming probability using the signature scheme) or does not send any message at all, then the remaining two parties reconstruct and output the last backup value that they can reconstruct. See Sect. 3 for more details.

As for the other direction, we compile a real-world FaF secure protocol into a FaF secure protocol in the dealer model. Here, the dealer samples randomness for the parties and executes the protocol in its head. For each round i, it computes the value that a pair of parties output in case the remaining third party aborts after sending i messages (honestly). It then uses these values to define the backup values that it gives to the parties in the protocol.

Proof of Theorem 1.2. Recall that we are given a function f, for which there is a two-party protocol π_2 that computes f with both malicious security and with semi-honest security. We show that f can be computed with $(1,1)$-FaF security in the three-party setting when all parties receive the output. Let r denote the number of rounds in π_2. We assume without loss of generality that the interaction in π_2 is as follows. Each round $i \in [r]$ is composed of two messages, the first sent by A and the second sent by B.[5] A malicious party may send any message that it wants, or send no message at all. In the latter case, the honest party must output some value from the range of the function (recall that π is fully secure). These values are called *backup values*. We denote by $a_0, \ldots, a_r$ and $b_0, \ldots, b_r$ the backup values of the parties A and B, respectively. Specifically, we let a_i be the output of A assuming that B sent the messages of the first i rounds honestly but did not send the $(i+1)^{\text{th}}$ message, and we let b_i be the output of B assuming that A sent the messages of the first i rounds honestly but did not send the $(i+1)^{\text{th}}$ message.

We next construct a FaF secure three-party protocol π_3. By Theorem 1.1, it suffices to do so in the dealer model, i.e., it suffices to describe how the dealer computes the backup values. For every $i \in [r]$, the dealer sets $ab_i = f(x,y)$, $ac_i = a_i$, and $bc_i = b_i$. Intuitively, a corrupt C cannot affect the output of A and B. Moreover, as π_2 admits semi-honest security, the backup values they receive

---

[5] Note that transforming a protocol into one with this structure might double the number of rounds.

reveal no information to them.[6] As for a malicious A (a malicious B is completely symmetric), note that A has no view. Therefore, to simulate an adversary $\mathcal{A}_3$ corrupting A, we only need to define an appropriate distribution over the inputs (sent by the simulator to the trusted party), so that the output in both the real and ideal world are indistinguishable. To do this, we emulate $\mathcal{A}_3$ using an adversary $\mathcal{A}_2$ for the two-party protocol π_2. The adversary $\mathcal{A}_2$ behaves honestly until the round where $\mathcal{A}_3$ aborts, and aborts at the same round. By the assumed security of π_2, this attack can be simulated in the two-party ideal world. This defines a distribution over the inputs of A. Using the same distribution in the three-party ideal world results in the same distribution for the output. Now, consider a semi-honest party Q in the three-party protocol; the challenge in the FaF model is to construct a view consistent with the input chosen by the malicious adversary controlling A, and the messages B gets from the dealer. Let i denote the round where $\mathcal{A}$ aborts. If Q = B, then the only information it receives in the real world is $ab_0, \ldots, ab_{i-1}$ and the output $bc_{i-1} = b_{i-1}$. Since $ab_j = f(x, y)$ for all j, this can be simulated in the ideal world, since the simulator for the semi-honest B receives the input of the malicious party A. On the other hand, if Q = C, then in the real world it receives $ac_0 = a_0, \ldots, ac_{i-1} = a_{i-1}$. These values are generated by the simulator for $\mathcal{A}_2$ in the two-party setting. Moreover, they are generated consistently with the output $bc_{i-1} = b_{i-1}$. Therefore, this simulator can be used to simulate the view of C.

Proof of Theorem 1.4. We now turn to our second positive result. Here we are given a three-party Boolean symmetric functionality $f : \mathcal{X} \times \mathcal{Y} \times \{\lambda\} \rightarrow \{0, 1\}$ satisfying one of two conditions. We show that it can be computed with $(1, 1)$-FaF security. Similarly to the previous result, we may describe only the backup values for the protocol in the dealer model. We construct a protocol inspired by the protocols of [3,13], which follow the special round paradigm, however, the proof of security follows a new construction for the simulator.

Roughly, a special round i^* (whose value is unknown to all parties) is sampled at random according to a geometric distribution with a sufficiently small parameter $\alpha > 0$. Before round i^* is reached, the backup values ac_i of A and C, and bc_i of B and C, are random and independent. After i^* the backup values are equal to $f(x, y)$. In more detail, for every $i < i^*$ we let $ac_i = f(x, \tilde{y}_i)$, where $\tilde{y}_i \leftarrow \mathcal{Y}$ is sampled uniformly at random, and for every $i < i^* + 1$ we let $bc_i = f(\tilde{x}_i, y)$, where $\tilde{x}_i$ is chosen according to some distribution that depends on the function. All other backup values are equal to $f(x, y)$. Finally, the backup values for A and B are all equal to $f(x, y)$.[7]

First, observe that a corrupt C cannot attack the protocol, since it cannot prevent A and B from outputting $f(x, y)$, nor can it provide them with any

---

[6] Note that here are using the fact that π_2 is secure against semi-honest adversaries. Indeed, since A and B are semi-honest, to properly simulate them in the ideal world we need to use a simulator that does not change its input.

[7] The choice of setting bc_i to equal $f(x, y)$ only from round $i^* + 1$ is so that A and C learn the output before B and C. Another approach could be to modify the dealer model so that the dealer approaches B before A.

new information. Next, similarly to [3,13], a corrupt B cannot attack since C learns the backup value ac_i before it learns bc_i. Thus, if B aborts at round i^* or afterwards, then A and C output $f(x,y)$. Otherwise, if B aborts before i^*, then A and C output an independent random value. Additionally, B cannot help either of the other parties to obtain any additional information. We are left with the case where A is malicious, which can generate an advantage for C by guessing i^*+1 and aborting in this round. This causes B and C to output $\mathsf{bc}_{i^*} = f(\tilde{x}_{i^*}, y)$, which is a random value. However, C receives $\mathsf{ac}_{i^*} = f(x,y)$ from the dealer.

We show that a simulator exists; we do so by constructing a different simulator than the one constructed by [3,13]. There, the malicious simulator generates the view exactly the same as in the real world, and the advantage of the adversary is simulated by sending to the trusted party an input sampled according to a carefully chosen distribution. For our protocol, we let the malicious simulator send an input according to the "expected" distribution, i.e., the one used in the real world, which is either a random input before $i^* + 1$ or the real input from $i^* + 1$ onward.

We are now left with simulating the advantage that a semi-honest C has over the honest party B. We define its simulator by sampling the backup values *differently* from the real world. In more detail, let i denote the round where the malicious adversary aborted (set to $r + 1$ if no such round exists). For every round $j < i$ the simulator generates a backup value ac_j according to the same distribution used in the real world, that is, ac_j is a random value if $j < i^*$, and $\mathsf{ac}_j = f(x,y)$ if $j \geq i^*$ (note that since $i > j$ it follows that $i \geq i^* + 1$ in this case, hence the simulator received $f(x,y)$ from the trusted party). At round i, if $i > i^*$ we let the simulator set $\mathsf{ac}_i = f(x,y)$. Otherwise, if $i \leq i^*$ then the simulator samples the backup value according to a carefully chosen distribution. We show that under our assumptions on f, there exists a distribution such that the joint distribution of the view generated by the simulator and the output of honest parties is indistinguishable from the real world. We refer the reader to Sect. 4.2 for more details.

Proof of Theorem 1.5. We now sketch the proof of our lower bound on the round complexity required for FaF secure computation. Recall that we fix a three-party functionality $f : \mathcal{X} \times \mathcal{Y} \times \{\lambda\} \rightarrow \{0,1\}$, for which the matrix M_f has no constant rows, no constant columns, and that no row or column has its negation appearing in M_f. We show there is no $O(\log \kappa)$-round protocol computing f with $(1,1)$-FaF security. We assume that f is such that M_f has no duplicated rows and columns. This is without loss of generality since duplicating rows and columns, and removing duplications, does not compromise the FaF security of the protocol.

Assume towards contradiction there exists an $r = O(\log \kappa)$-round protocol computing f with $(1,1)$-FaF security. We assume without loss of generality that the protocol is in the dealer model (note that the transformation from a real world FaF secure protocol to a FaF secure protocol in the dealer model preserves the number of rounds). To gain some intuition, let us first consider a malicious adversary $\mathcal{B}$ corrupting B that sends continue to the dealer until round r. The adversary then aborts, causing A and C to output ac_{r-1}, and causing the dealer to send $\mathsf{bc}_r = f(x,y)$ to C.

First, we claim that in order to simulate the attack, the malicious simulator $\mathsf{Sim}_\mathcal{B}$ must send y to the trusted party, except with negligible probability. Intuitively, this follows from the following observation. Since $M_f(\cdot, y)$ is not constant, does not appear as duplication, and since the negation of $M_f(\cdot, y)$ does not appear anywhere else in M_f, for any $y' \neq y$ there exists $x_1, x_2 \in \mathcal{X}$ such that $M_f(x_1, y) \neq M_f(x_2, y)$ and $M_f(x_1, y') = M_f(x_2, y')$. Pictorially, the 2×2 matrix

$$\begin{array}{c} \\ x_1 \\ x_2 \end{array} \overset{\displaystyle y \ \ y'}{\begin{pmatrix} a & b \\ b & b \end{pmatrix}}$$

where $a \neq b \in \{0,1\}$, is embedded in M_f restricted to y and y' (in particular M_f contains an embedded OR). Now, suppose that the malicious simulator $\mathsf{Sim}_\mathcal{B}$ sends y' to the trusted party. Consider the semi-honest simulator $\mathsf{Sim}_{\mathcal{B},\mathcal{C}}$ for a semi-honest C. Note that it will not be able to distinguish between the case where A has input x_1 from the case it has input x_2. However, in the real world C is able to distinguish between them since it receives the output $f(x,y)$.

Next, given that $\mathsf{Sim}_\mathcal{B}$ does send y to the trusted party, this implies that in the ideal world the output of the honest party A is $f(x,y)$. Therefore, the same must hold in the real world, except with negligible probability. Recall that the malicious B aborted after receiving r messages from A, thus the output of A is ac_{r-1}. This implies that $\mathsf{ac}_{r-1} = f(x,y)$ except with negligible probability.

We can now continue with the same argument as before, this time applied to a malicious adversary corrupting A and aborting after receiving $r-1$ messages from B. We then apply this argument inductively for all r rounds, each time accumulating another error (from when comparing the real and ideal world). Similarly to the lower bound due to [13], we note that when formalizing this argument, the error that is being accumulated each round is multiplicative, with the error each time being $O(|\mathcal{X}| \cdot |\mathcal{Y}|)$. Therefore, after applying the argument $r = O(\frac{\log \kappa}{\log |\mathcal{X}| + \log |\mathcal{Y}|})$ times, we conclude that with constant probability the parties can compute f without any interaction at all, which is a clear contradiction. We stress that our overall strategy is substantially different from [13] in that we analyze what the simulator can send to the trusted party. We refer the reader to Sect. 5 for a formal analysis.

Proof of Theorem 1.6. We now show there exists a three-party functionality that depends on two inputs and cannot be computed with $(1,1)$-FaF security. The functionality we consider and the proof of impossibility are nearly identical to that of [1]. Let f be a one-way permutation. We consider the following functionality. Party A holds two strings a and y_B, and party B holds two string b and y_A. Party C holds no input. The output of all parties is (a,b) if $f(a) = y_\mathsf{A}$ and $f(b) = y_\mathsf{B}$, and $\perp$ otherwise.

Assume towards contradiction there exists a $(1,1)$-FaF secure protocol computing the function. We may assume the protocol to be in the dealer model.

Consider an execution where the strings a and b are sampled uniformly and independently, and that $y_A = f(a), y_B = f(b)$. An averaging argument yields that there must exist a round i, where two parties, say A together with C, can recover (a, b) with significantly higher probability than B together with C. Our attacker corrupts A, sends its original inputs a and y_B to the dealer, and sends continue until round $i + 1$. At round $i + 1$ it sends abort.

Intuitively, in order to have the output of the honest party B in the ideal world distributed as in the real world (where it is $\perp$ with noticeable probability), the malicious simulator has to change its input (sent to the trusted party) with high enough probability. However, in this case, the semi-honest simulator for C, receives $\perp$ from the trusted party. Since the only information it has on b is $f(b)$, by the assumed security of f, the simulator for B will not be able to recover b with non-negligible probability. Hence, B's simulator will fail to generate a valid view for B. The detailed proof appears in Sect. 6.

1.3   Related Work

Understanding which functionalities can be computed with full security is the subject of many papers in the standard setting. This started with the seminal result of Cleve [9], who showed that fair two-party coin tossing is impossible. Surprisingly, Gordon et al. [13] showed that many two-party functionalities can be computed with full security. In particular, they showed a functionality containing an embedded XOR that can be computed with full security. This led to a series of works trying to characterize which two-party functionalities can be computed with full security [2,3,11,21,22]. In particular, [3] characterized the set of symmetric Boolean functionalities that are computable with full security.

In the multiparty setting much less is known. In the honest majority setting, if the parties are given secure point-to-point channels and a broadcast channel, then any functionality can be computed with full security without any cryptographic assumptions [23]. The dishonest majority setting was first considered by [14]. They showed that the three-party majority functionality, and n-party OR can be computed securely, for any number of corruptions. The case where exactly half of the parties can be corrupted was considered by Asharov et al. [3]. The setting of a non-constant number of parties was considered in Dachman-Soled [10]. The "Best-of-both-worlds security" definition [17,18,20] requires full security to hold in case of an honest majority, however, if at least half of the parties are corrupted, then the same protocol should be secure-with-abort. Finally, Halevi et al. [15] were the first to consider the solitary output setting, where only one party obtains the output.

1.4   Organization

We present the preliminaries in Sect. 2. We describe the dealer model in Sect. 3. Then, in Sect. 4 we present our positive results. In Sect. 5 we show our lower bound on the round complexity of $(1, 1)$-FaF secure protocols. Finally, in Sect. 6 we show an impossibility for a 2-ary three-party functionality.

2 Preliminaries

2.1 Notations

We use calligraphic letters to denote sets, uppercase for random variables and distributions, lowercase for values, and we use bold characters to denote vectors. For $n \in \mathbb{N}$, let $[n] = \{1, 2 \ldots n\}$. For a set $\mathcal{S}$ we write $s \leftarrow \mathcal{S}$ to indicate that s is selected uniformly at random from $\mathcal{S}$. Given a random variable (or a distribution) X, we write $x \leftarrow X$ to indicate that x is selected according to X. We let λ be the empty string. For a randomized function (or an algorithm) f we write $f(x)$ to denote the random variable induced by the function on input x, and write $f(x; \text{rnd})$ to denote its value when the randomness of f is fixed to rnd.

To define security of protocols, we need to define computational indistinguishability between two distribution ensembles (i.e., the distributions of the real and ideal world). A *distribution ensemble* $X = (X_{a,n})_{a \in \mathcal{D}_n, n \in \mathbb{N}}$ is an infinite sequence of random variables indexed by $a \in \mathcal{D}_n$ and $n \in \mathbb{N}$, where $\mathcal{D}_n$ is a domain that might depend on n. A PPT algorithm is probabilistic polynomial time, and a PPTM is a polynomial time (interactive) Turing machine. A PPT algorithm is non-uniform if it receives an advice as an additional input. A function $\mu \colon \mathbb{N} \to [0, 1]$ is called negligible, if for every positive polynomial $p(\cdot)$ and all sufficiently large n, it holds that $\mu(n) < 1/p(n)$. We let $\text{neg}(n)$ denote an unspecified negligible function. Computational indistinguishability is defined as follows.

Definition 2.1. *Let* $X = (X_{a,n})_{a \in \mathcal{D}_n, n \in \mathbb{N}}$ *and* $Y = (Y_{a,n})_{a \in \mathcal{D}_n, n \in \mathbb{N}}$ *be two ensembles, and let* $\varepsilon = \varepsilon(\cdot)$. *We say that* X *and* Y *are* ε-*computationally indistinguishable, denoted* $X \overset{c}{\equiv}_\varepsilon Y$, *if for every non-uniform* PPT *distinguisher* D *such that for all sufficiently large* n *and for all* $a \in \mathcal{D}_n$, *it holds that*

$$|\Pr[D(X_{a,n}) = 1] - \Pr[D(Y_{a,n}) = 1]| < \varepsilon(n).$$

We say that X *and* Y *are* computationally indistinguishable, *denoted* $X \overset{c}{\equiv} Y$, *if they are* n^{-c}-*computationally indistinguishable for all* $c \in \mathbb{N}$.

Secret Sharing Schemes. A (threshold) secret-sharing scheme [7, 25] is a method in which a dealer distributes shares of some secret to n parties such that t colluding parties do not learn anything about the secret, and any subset of $t + 1$ parties can fully reconstruct the secret. We let $\mathcal{P} = \{P_1, \ldots, P_n\}$ denote the set of participating parties. As a convention, for a secret s and a party $P_i \in \mathcal{P}$, we let $s[i]$ be the share received by P_i. For a subset $\mathcal{S} \subseteq \mathcal{P}$ we denote $s[\mathcal{S}] = (s[i])_{i \in \mathcal{S}}$.

Definition 2.2 (Secret sharing). *A* $(t + 1)$-*out-of-*n *secret-sharing scheme over a message space* $\mathcal{M}$ *consists of a pair of algorithms* (Share, Recon) *satisfying the following properties:*

1. $(t+1)$-**reconstructability:** *For every secret* $s \in \mathcal{M}$ *and every subset* $\mathcal{I} \subseteq [n]$ *of size* $|\mathcal{I}| \geq t + 1$, *if* $(s[1], \ldots, s[n]) \leftarrow$ Share(s) *then* $s =$ Recon$(s[\mathcal{I}])$.

2. t-**privacy:** *For every two secrets $s_1, s_2 \in \mathcal{M}$, and every subset $\mathcal{I} \subseteq [n]$ of size $|\mathcal{I}| \leq t$, the distribution of the shares $s_1[\mathcal{I}]$ of s_1 is identical to that of $s_2[\mathcal{I}]$ of s_2, where $(s_1[1], \ldots, s_1[n]) \leftarrow \mathsf{Share}(s_1)$ and $(s_2[1], \ldots, s_2[n]) \leftarrow \mathsf{Share}(s_2)$.*

In this work, we only consider 3-out-of-3 additive secret sharing schemes. Here, the message space $\mathcal{M}$ is an additive group $\mathbb{G}$, and $\mathsf{Share}(s)$ samples $s[1], s[2] \leftarrow \mathbb{G}$ independently, and sets $s[3] = s - s[1] - s[2]$. The reconstruction algorithm simply adds all shares.

2.2   The Model of Computation

We follow the standard *ideal vs. real* paradigm for defining security [8,12]. Intuitively, security is defined by describing an ideal functionality, in which both the corrupted and non-corrupted parties interact with a trusted entity. A real-world protocol is secure if an adversary in the real world cannot cause more harm than an adversary in the ideal world. In the classical definition, this is captured by showing that an ideal-world adversary (simulator) can simulate the full view of the real world malicious adversary. For FaF security, we further require that the view of a subset of the uncorrupted parties can be simulated in the ideal world (including the interaction with the adversary). We next give a more detailed definition, tailored to the three-party setting.

The FaF Real Model

A three-party protocol π is defined by a set of three PPT interactive Turing machines $\{\mathsf{A}, \mathsf{B}, \mathsf{C}\}$. Each Turing machine (party) holds at the beginning of the execution the common security parameter 1^κ, a private input, and random coins.

Throughout the entire work, we will assume the parties execute the protocol over a synchronous network. That is, the execution proceeds in rounds: each round consists of a *send phase* (where parties send their messages for this round) followed by a *receive phase* (where they receive messages from other parties). We consider a fully connected point-to-point network, where every pair of parties is connected by a communication line. We will consider the *secure-channels* model, where the communication lines are assumed to be ideally private (and thus the adversary cannot read or modify messages sent between two honest parties). Additionally, we assume the parties have access to a broadcast channel, allowing each party to faithfully send the same message to all other parties.

An adversary is a *non-uniform* PPT interactive Turing machine. It starts the execution with an input that contains the identity of the corrupted party, its input, and an additional auxiliary input $\mathsf{aux} \in \{0,1\}^*$. We will only consider static adversaries that can choose the subset of parties to corrupt prior to the execution of the protocol. At the end of the protocol's execution, the adversary outputs some function of its view (which consists of its random coins, its auxiliary input, the input of the corrupted party, and the messages it sees during the execution of the protocol, and specifically, including possibly non-prescribed messages sent to it by a malicious adversary).

We consider two adversaries. The first adversary we consider is a malicious adversary $\mathcal{A}$ that controls a single party $P \in \{A, B, C\}$. We will refer to P as the malicious party. The adversary has access to the full view of the corrupted party. Additionally, the adversary may instruct the corrupted party to deviate from the protocol in any way it chooses. The adversary can send messages (even if not prescribed by the protocol) to any uncorrupted party – in every round of the protocol, and can do so after all messages for this round were sent. The adversary can also send messages to the uncorrupted parties *after* the protocol is terminated. The adversary is also given an auxiliary input $\mathsf{aux}_{\mathcal{A}}$.

The second adversary is a semi-honest adversary $\mathcal{A}_Q$ that controls a party $Q \in \{A, B, C\} \setminus \{P\}$ of the remaining parties (for the sake of clarity, we will only refer to P as corrupted). Similarly to $\mathcal{A}$, this adversary also has access to the full view of its party. However, $\mathcal{A}_Q$ *cannot* instruct the party to deviate from the prescribed protocol in any way, but may try to infer information about the remaining non-corrupted party, given its view in the protocol (which includes the joint view of P and Q). This adversary is given an auxiliary input aux_Q. We will refer to Q as the semi-honest party.

We next define the real-world global view for security parameter $\kappa \in \mathbb{N}$, an input tuple (x, y, z), and auxiliary inputs $\mathsf{aux}_{\mathcal{A}}, \mathsf{aux}_Q \in \{0, 1\}^*$ with respect to adversaries $\mathcal{A}$ and $\mathcal{A}_Q$ controlling the parties P and Q respectively. Let $\mathrm{OUT}^{\mathrm{real}}_{\pi, \mathcal{A}}(\kappa, (x, y, z))$ denote the outputs of the uncorrupted parties (i.e., those in $\{A, B, C\} \setminus \{P\}$) in a random execution of π, with $\mathcal{A}$ corrupting the party P. Further let $\mathrm{VIEW}^{\mathrm{real}}_{\pi, \mathcal{A}}(\kappa, (x, y, z))$ be the output of the malicious adversary $\mathcal{A}$ during an execution of π. In addition, we let $\mathrm{VIEW}^{\mathrm{real}}_{\pi, \mathcal{A}, \mathcal{A}_Q}(\kappa, (x, y, z))$ be the output of $\mathcal{A}_Q$ during an execution of π when running alongside $\mathcal{A}$.

We let

$$\mathrm{REAL}_{\pi, \mathcal{A}(\mathsf{aux}_{\mathcal{A}})}, (\kappa, (x, y, z)) = \left(\mathrm{VIEW}^{\mathrm{real}}_{\pi, \mathcal{A}}(\kappa, (x, y, z)), \ \mathrm{OUT}^{\mathrm{real}}_{\pi, \mathcal{A}}(\kappa, (x, y, z)) \right),$$

denote the view of the malicious adversary and the output of the uncorrupted parties, and we let

$$\mathrm{REAL}_{\pi, \mathcal{A}(\mathsf{aux}_{\mathcal{A}}), \mathcal{A}_Q(\mathsf{aux}_Q)}(\kappa, (x, y, z))$$
$$= \left(\mathrm{VIEW}^{\mathrm{real}}_{\pi, \mathcal{A}, \mathcal{A}_Q}(\kappa, (x, y, z)), \ \mathrm{OUT}^{\mathrm{real}}_{\pi, \mathcal{A}}(\kappa, (x, y, z)) \right),$$

denote the view of the semi-honest adversary and the output of the uncorrupted parties.

The FaF Ideal Model

We next describe the interaction in the *FaF security ideal model*, which specifies the requirements for fully secure FaF computation of the function f with security parameter κ. Let $\mathcal{A}$ be an adversary in the ideal world, which is given an auxiliary input $\mathsf{aux}_{\mathcal{A}}$ and corrupts a party P called *corrupted*. Further let $\mathcal{A}_Q$ be a semi-honest adversary, which controls a party $Q \in \{A, B, C\} \setminus \{P\}$ and is given an auxiliary input $\mathsf{aux_Q}$. We stress that the classical formulation of the ideal model does not contain the second adversary.

The ideal model roughly follows the standard ideal model, where the parties send their inputs to a trusted party that does the computation and sends them the output. Additionally, we give the semi-honest adversary $\mathcal{A_Q}$ the ideal-world view of $\mathcal{A}$ (i.e., its input, randomness, auxiliary input, and output received from the trusted party). This is done due to the fact that in the real world, we cannot prevent the adversary from sending its entire view to the uncorrupted parties. Formally, the ideal world is described as follows.

The FaF Ideal Model – Full Security.

Inputs: Party A holds 1^κ and $x \in \{0,1\}^*$, party B holds 1^κ and $y \in \{0,1\}^*$, and party C holds 1^κ and $z \in \{0,1\}^*$. The adversaries $\mathcal{A}$ and $\mathcal{A_Q}$ are given each an auxiliary input $\mathsf{aux}_\mathcal{A}, \mathsf{aux_Q} \in \{0,1\}^*$ respectively, and the inputs of the party controlled by them. The trusted party T holds 1^κ.

Parties send inputs: Each uncorrupted party (including the semi-honest party) sends its input to T. The malicious adversary $\mathcal{A}$ sends a value v' as the input for corrupted party P. If the adversary does not send any input, the trusted party replaces its input with a default value. Write (x', y', z') for the tuple of inputs received by the trusted party.

The trusted party performs computation: The trusted party T selects a random string rnd and computes $(w_\mathsf{A}, w_\mathsf{B}, w_\mathsf{C}) = f(x', y', z'; \mathsf{rnd})$, and sends w_A to A, sends w_B to B, and sends w_C to C.

The malicious adversary sends its (ideal-world) view: $\mathcal{A}$ sends to $\mathcal{A_Q}$ its randomness, inputs, auxiliary input, and the output received from T.

Outputs: Each uncorrupted party (i.e., not P) outputs whatever output it received from T, party P output nothing. $\mathcal{A}$ and $\mathcal{A_Q}$ output some function of their respective views.

We next define the ideal-world global view for security parameter $\kappa \in \mathbb{N}$, an input tuple (x, y, z), and auxiliary inputs $\mathsf{aux}_\mathcal{A}, \mathsf{aux_Q} \in \{0,1\}^*$ with respect to adversaries $\mathcal{A}$ and $\mathcal{A_Q}$ controlling the parties P and Q respectively. Let $\mathrm{OUT}_{f,\mathcal{A}}^{\mathsf{ideal}}(\kappa, (x, y, z))$ denote the output of the uncorrupted parties (those in $\{\mathsf{A}, \mathsf{B}, \mathsf{C}\} \setminus \{\mathsf{P}\}$) in a random execution of the above ideal-world process, with $\mathcal{A}$ corrupting P. Further let $\mathrm{VIEW}_{f,\mathcal{A}}^{\mathsf{ideal}}(\kappa, (x, y, z))$ be the *output* of $\mathcal{A}$ in such a process (this output should simulate the real world view of P). In addition, we let $\mathrm{VIEW}_{f,\mathcal{A},\mathcal{A_Q}}^{\mathsf{ideal}}(\kappa, (x, y, z))$ be the view description being the *output* of $\mathcal{A_Q}$ in such a process, when running alongside $\mathcal{A}$. We let

$$\mathrm{IDEAL}_{f,\mathcal{A}(\mathsf{aux}_\mathcal{A})}(\kappa, (x, y, z)) = \left(\mathrm{VIEW}_{f,\mathcal{A}}^{\mathsf{ideal}}(\kappa, (x, y, z)),\ \mathrm{OUT}_{f,\mathcal{A}}^{\mathsf{ideal}}(\kappa, (x, y, z))\right),$$

and we let

$$\mathrm{IDEAL}_{f,\mathcal{A}(\mathsf{aux}_\mathcal{A}),\mathcal{A_Q}(\mathsf{aux_Q})}(\kappa, (x, y, z), \mathcal{A_Q})$$
$$= \left(\mathrm{VIEW}_{f,\mathcal{A},\mathcal{A_Q}}^{\mathsf{ideal}}(\kappa, (x, y, z)),\ \mathrm{OUT}_{f,\mathcal{A}}^{\mathsf{ideal}}(\kappa, (x, y, z))\right).$$

Having defined the real and ideal models, we can now define FaF full security of protocols according to the real/ideal paradigm. For brevity, we will refer to it simply as FaF security. We define a more general security notion, where the distinguishing advantage between the real and ideal worlds, is required to be bounded by a function $\varepsilon(\kappa)$ (we use this in Sect. 5 to state a more general lower bound on the round complexity required for FaF secure computations).

Definition 2.3 (FaF security). *Let π be a protocol for computing f, and let $\varepsilon = \varepsilon(\cdot)$ be a function of the security parameter. We say that π computes f with $(1,1)$-FaF ε-security, if the following holds. For every non-uniform* PPT *adversary $\mathcal{A}$, controlling at most one party $\mathsf{P} \in \{\mathsf{A}, \mathsf{B}, \mathsf{C}\}$ in the real world, there exists a non-uniform* PPT *adversary $\mathsf{Sim}_{\mathcal{A}}$ controlling the same party (if there is any) in the ideal model and for every non-uniform semi-honest* PPT *adversary $\mathcal{A}_{\mathsf{Q}}$ controlling at most one party $\mathsf{Q} \in \{\mathsf{A}, \mathsf{B}, \mathsf{C}\} \setminus \{\mathsf{P}\}$ among the remaining parties, there exists a non-uniform* PPT *adversary $\mathsf{Sim}_{\mathcal{A},\mathsf{Q}}$, controlling the same party (if there is any) in the ideal-world, such that*

$$\left\{ \mathrm{IDEAL}_{f,\mathsf{Sim}(\mathsf{aux}_{\mathcal{A}})}\left(\kappa, (x,y,z)\right) \right\}_{\kappa \in \mathbb{N}, x,y,z \in \{0,1\}^*, \mathsf{aux}_{\mathcal{A}} \in \{0,1\}^*}$$
$$\overset{\mathrm{C}}{\equiv}_\varepsilon \left\{ \mathrm{REAL}_{\pi,\mathcal{A}(\mathsf{aux}_{\mathcal{A}})}\left(\kappa, (x,y,z)\right) \right\}_{\kappa \in \mathbb{N}, x,y,z \in \{0,1\}^*, \mathsf{aux}_{\mathcal{A}} \in \{0,1\}^*}.$$

and

$$\left\{ \mathrm{IDEAL}_{f,\mathsf{Sim}_{\mathcal{A}}(\mathsf{aux}_{\mathcal{A}}),\mathsf{Sim}_{\mathcal{A},\mathsf{Q}}(\mathsf{aux}_{\mathsf{Q}})}\left(\kappa, (x,y,z), \mathsf{Sim}_{\mathcal{A},\mathsf{Q}}\right) \right\}_{\kappa \in \mathbb{N}, x,y,z \in \{0,1\}^*, \mathsf{aux}_{\mathcal{A}}, \mathsf{aux}_{\mathsf{Q}} \in \{0,1\}^*}$$
$$\overset{\mathrm{C}}{\equiv}_\varepsilon \left\{ \mathrm{REAL}_{\pi,\mathcal{A}(\mathsf{aux}_{\mathcal{A}}),\mathcal{A}_{\mathsf{Q}}(\mathsf{aux}_{\mathsf{Q}})}\left(\kappa, (x,y,z), \mathcal{A}_{\mathsf{Q}}\right) \right\}_{\kappa \in \mathbb{N}, x,y,z \in \{0,1\}^*, \mathsf{aux}_{\mathcal{A}}, \mathsf{aux}_{\mathsf{Q}} \in \{0,1\}^*}.$$

We say that π computed f with $(1,1)$-FaF security if for all $c \in \mathbb{N}$, π computes f with $(1,1)$-FaF κ^{-c}-security.

Observe that the correctness of the computation (in an honest execution) is implicitly required by the above definition. Indeed, as we allow the adversary to corrupt at most one party, by considering adversaries that corrupt no party, the definition requires the output of all parties in the real world to be indistinguishable from $f(x,y,z)$.

We next define the notion of backup values, which are the values that honest parties output in case the third party aborts (after sending messages honestly). Note that the notions of backup values are well-defined for any $(1,1)$-FaF secure protocol.

Definition 2.4 (Backup values). *Let $f : \mathcal{X} \times \mathcal{Y} \times \mathcal{Z} \to \mathcal{W}$ be a three-party functionality, and let π be an r-round protocol computing f with $(1,1)$-FaF security. Let $i \in \{0, \ldots, r\}$, sample the randomness of the parties, and consider an honest execution of π with the sampled randomness until all parties sent i messages. For two distinct parties $\mathsf{P}, \mathsf{Q} \in \{\mathsf{A}, \mathsf{B}, \mathsf{C}\}$, the ith backup value of the pair $\{\mathsf{P}, \mathsf{Q}\}$ is the value that an honest P and Q output if the third party aborts after sending i messages honestly.*

2.3 FaF Security-With-Identifiable-Abort

Although the focus of this work is on full security, in some of our constructions
we use protocols admitting *security-with-identifiable-abort*. In terms of the definition, the only requirement that is changed is that the ideal-world simulator
operates in a *different ideal model*. We next describe the interaction in the *FaF-
secure-with-identifiable-abort ideal model* for the computation of the function f
with security parameter κ.

Unlike the full security ideal model, here the malicious adversary can instruct
the trusted party not to send the output to the honest parties, however, in this
case, the adversary must publish the identity of a corrupted party. In addition,
since there is no guarantee that in the real world the semi-honest parties will
not learn the output, we always let the them receive their output in the ideal
execution. This allows us to simulate unfair protocols, where in addition to the
malicious adversary learning the output, it can decide whether the semi-honest
parties can learn the output as well.

Let $\mathcal{A}$ be a malicious adversary in the ideal world, which is given an auxiliary
input $\mathsf{aux}_{\mathcal{A}}$ and corrupts a party $P \in \{A, B, C\}$. Furthermore, let $\mathcal{A}_Q$ be a semi-
honest adversary, which controls a party $Q \neq P$ and is given an auxiliary input
aux_Q.

The FaF Ideal Model – Security-with-Identifiable-Abort.

Inputs: Party A holds 1^κ and $x \in \{0,1\}^*$, party B holds 1^κ and $y \in \{0,1\}^*$,
  and party C holds 1^κ and $z \in \{0,1\}^*$. The adversaries $\mathcal{A}$ and $\mathcal{A}_Q$ are given
  each an auxiliary input $\mathsf{aux}_{\mathcal{A}}, \mathsf{aux}_Q \in \{0,1\}^*$ respectively, and the inputs of
  the party controlled by them. The trusted party T holds 1^κ.
Parties send inputs: Each uncorrupted party sends its input to T. The malicious adversary $\mathcal{A}$ sends a value v' as the input for corrupted party P. If the
  adversary does not send any input, the trusted party replaces its input with a
  default value. Write (x', y', z') for the tuple of inputs received by the trusted
  party.
The trusted party performs computation: The trusted party T selects a
  random string rnd and computes $(w_A, w_B, w_C) = f(x', y', z'; \mathsf{rnd})$, and sends
  w_P to $\mathcal{A}$ and sends w_Q to $\mathcal{A}_Q$.
The malicious adversary sends its (ideal-world) view: $\mathcal{A}$ sends to $\mathcal{A}_Q$ its
  randomness, inputs, auxiliary input, and the output received from T.
Malicious adversary instructs trusted party to continue or halt: The
  adversary $\mathcal{A}$ sends either continue or (abort, P) to T. If it sent continue, then
  for every uncorrupted party $P' \neq P$ the trusted party sends it $w_{P'}$. Otherwise,
  if $\mathcal{A}$ sent (abort, P), then T sends (abort, P) to the all honest parties.
Outputs: Each uncorrupted party (i.e., not P) outputs whatever output it
  received from T, party P output nothing. $\mathcal{A}$ and $\mathcal{A}_Q$ output some function of
  their respective views.

2.4   The Two-Party Model

In one of our results, we will be interested in the two-party setting with (standard) security against both a malicious adversary and a semi-honest adversary, corrupting one party. In terms of definition, both the real and ideal world in the two-party setting are defined analogously to the three-party setting. That is, in the real world, two parties A and B interact, and each holds a private input, the security parameter, and random coins. In the ideal world, the computation is done via a trusted party in a similar way to the three-party definition. In this paper, we consider both security against a malicious adversary, and security against a semi-honest adversary. We say that a two-party protocol is fully secure if it is secure against any malicious adversary, and we say that the protocol if it has semi-honest security if it is secure against any semi-honest adversary.

3   The Dealer Model

In the description of our positive results, it will be convenient to consider a model with a dealer. Here, the real world is augmented with a trusted dealer, which is a PPTM that can interact with the parties in a limited way. Furthermore, the adversary is also limited when compared to a real world adversary: the adversary is assumed to be fail-stop, namely, it acts honestly, however, it may decide to abort prematurely. Additionally, it may change the input it sends to the dealer. This model, which we show below to be equivalent to $(1,1)$-FaF security, offers a much simpler way to analyze the security of protocols. Moreover, our constructions will achieve information-theoretic security in the dealer model. A similar model was already considered for standard security with a dishonest majority [2–4,6].

We next describe a blueprint for an r-round protocol in the dealer model for the $(1,1)$-FaF security model. That is, the blueprint instructs the dealer to compute $3r+3$ backup values and does not specify how to compute these backup values. A protocol in the dealer model is obtained from the blueprint by defining $3r+3$ functions computing these backup values. We will show that such $(1,1)$-FaF secure protocols exist if and only if a $(1,1)$-FaF secure protocol exists in the real world (assuming secure protocols for OT). For simplicity, we assume the function to be symmetric, i.e., all parties obtain the same output.

Protocol 3.1.
Inputs: *Parties A, B, and C hold inputs x, y, and z, respectively.*
Common input: *All parties hold the security parameter 1^κ.*

1. *The honest parties send their inputs to the dealer. The malicious adversary sends a value as the input for the corrupted party. If the adversary does not send any input, the dealer replaces it with a default value.*
2. *The dealer computes backup values $ab_0,\dots,ab_r$, $ac_0,\dots,ac_r$, and $bc_0,\dots,bc_r$. It is required that ab_0, ac_0, and bc_0, do not depend on the inputs of C, B, and A, respectively.*

3. *For $i = 1$ to r:*
    (a) *The dealer approaches party* A, *which responds with either* continue *or* abort.
    (b) *If* A *responds with* abort, *then the dealer sends x and bc_{i-1} to* B *and* C, *sends* $ab_0, \ldots, ab_{i-1}$ *to* B *and* $ac_0, \ldots, ac_{i-1}$ *to* C, *and halts. Parties* B *and* C *then output* bc_{i-1}.
    (c) *The dealer approaches party* B, *which responds with either* continue *or* abort.
    (d) *If* B *responds with* abort, *then the dealer sends y and ac_{i-1} to* A *and* C, *sends* $ab_0, \ldots, ab_{i-1}$ *to* A *and* $bc_0, \ldots, bc_i$ *to* C, *and halts. Parties* A *and* C *then output* ac_{i-1}.
    (e) *The dealer approaches party* C, *which responds with either* continue *or* abort.
    (f) *If* C *responds with* abort, *then the dealer sends z and ab_{i-1} to* A *and* B, *sends* $ac_0, \ldots, ac_i$ *to* A *and* $bc_0, \ldots, bc_i$ *to* B, *and halts. Parties* A *and* B *then output* ab_{i-1}.
4. *If no party aborted, the dealer sends ab_r to* A, *sends bc_r to* B, *and sends ac_r to* C.
5. *Party* A *output* ab_r, *party* B *output* bc_r, *and party* C *output* ac_r.

....

We stress that the dealer is always honest in the above execution. The security of the protocol is defined by comparing the above execution to the ideal world defined previously. However, unlike the real world, here the malicious adversary is only fail-stop. Thus, we say the protocol in the dealer model is $(1, 1)$-FaF security if it is $(1, 1)$-FaF secure against fail-stop adversaries. Furthermore, note that if the protocol is correct, then it is secure against semi-honest adversaries. This is because the only information the adversary receives is the last backup value, which equals to the output. Therefore, when proving security, it suffices to always consider the case where there is a malicious adversary corrupting a party. Removing the dealer (i.e., constructing a $(1, 1)$-FaF secure protocol without the dealer) can be done using standard techniques. We next provide an intuitive description of the real-world protocol without the dealer. The formal protocol appears below.

At the beginning of the interaction, the parties compute a secret sharing of all the backup values computed by the dealer, using a 3-out-of-3 secret sharing scheme, and all shares are signed.[8] This computation is done using a $(1, 1)$-FaF secure-with-identifiable-abort protocol. Then, in each round i, party C broadcasts its share of ab_i, then B broadcasts its share of ac_i, and finally, party A broadcasts its share of bc_i. If a party does not send its share or it sends a different share (which is caught using the signature scheme, except with negligible probability), then the remaining two parties reconstruct the last backup value for which they hold the aborting party's share.

Observe that the view of a corrupted party consists of only random independent shares. Thus, it aborts (or sends an incorrect share) in the real world if

---

[8] The signature key can be replaced with a one-time MAC for every share.

and only if it aborts in the dealer model. Additionally, the view of a semi-honest party consists of random shares, the backup value it computes with the remaining honest party, and the shares it can reconstruct if given the malicious party's view. Thus, any attack in the real world can be emulated in the dealer model.

Additionally, the converse is also true. That is, if there is a $(1,1)$-FaF secure protocol computing f in the real world, there is a $(1,1)$-FaF secure protocol computing f in the dealer model. Indeed, the dealer simply computes the backup values of every pair of parties and interacts with the parties as described in the above model. Thus, as the real world and the ideal model are essentially equivalent, we will sometimes refer to the dealer model as the real world. We next formalize the statement and its proof.

Theorem 3.2. *Let* $f : \mathcal{X} \times \mathcal{Y} \times \mathcal{Z} \to \mathcal{W}$ *be a three-party functionality. Then, assuming secure protocols for* OT *exist,* f *can be computed with* $(1,1)$-*FaF security in the real world if and only if it can be computed with* $(1,1)$-*FaF security in the dealer model.*

We next prove that any FaF-secure protocol in the dealer model can be transformed into a FaF-secure protocol in the real world. The other direction is given in the full version.

Lemma 3.3. *Let* $f : \mathcal{X} \times \mathcal{Y} \times \mathcal{Z} \to \mathcal{W}$ *be a three-party functionality. Then, if secure protocols for* OT *exist and* f *can be computed with* $(1,1)$-*FaF security in the dealer model, then* f *can be computed with* $(1,1)$-*FaF security in the real world.*

Proof. Assume there is a protocol π^D computing f in the dealer model that is $(1,1)$-FaF secure against fail-stop adversaries. We construct a protocol π^R computing f with $(1,1)$-FaF security in the real world.

Fix a signature scheme $\mathsf{Sig} = (\mathsf{Gen}, \mathsf{Sign}, \mathsf{Ver})$ (since OT implies one-way functions [16] and one-way functions imply signature scheme [24], the assumption of the lemma implies signature schemes). Let ShrGen denote the three-party functionality that, given the parties' inputs, outputs a 3-out-of-3 secret sharing for each of the backup values computed by the dealer, each signed using the signature scheme. Formally, we define ShrGen as follows.

Algorithm 3.4 (ShrGen).
Inputs: *Parties* A, B, *and* C *hold inputs* x, y, *and* z, *respectively.*
Common input: *The parties hold the security parameter* 1^κ.

1. *Sample a signature scheme keys* $(\mathsf{pk}, \mathsf{sk}) \leftarrow \mathsf{Gen}(1^\kappa)$.
2. *For every* $i \in \{0, \dots, r\}$ *do the following:*
   (a) *Compute the backup values* ab_i, ac_i, *and* bc_i, *as the dealer computes them.*
   (b) *If* $i = 0$, *then share each backup value in a 2-out-of-2 additive sharing scheme. Otherwise, share each backup value in a 3-out-of-3 additive secret-sharing scheme.*
   (c) *If* $i \geq 1$, *then for each backup value of two parties, sign the share of the third party. That is, for every* $i \in [r]$ *compute the following values:*

- $\sigma_{i,\mathsf{C}} \leftarrow \mathsf{Sign}_{\mathsf{sk}}(\mathsf{ab}_i[\mathsf{C}])$.
- $\sigma_{i,\mathsf{B}} \leftarrow \mathsf{Sign}_{\mathsf{sk}}(\mathsf{ac}_i[\mathsf{B}])$.
- $\sigma_{i,\mathsf{A}} \leftarrow \mathsf{Sign}_{\mathsf{sk}}(\mathsf{bc}_i[\mathsf{A}])$.

3. *Compute the following signatures:*
   - $\sigma_{\mathsf{ab},\mathsf{A}} \leftarrow \mathsf{Sign}_{\mathsf{sk}}(\mathsf{ab}_r[\mathsf{A}])$ *and* $\sigma_{\mathsf{ac},\mathsf{A}} \leftarrow \mathsf{Sign}_{\mathsf{sk}}(\mathsf{ac}_r[\mathsf{A}])$.
   - $\sigma_{\mathsf{ab},\mathsf{B}} \leftarrow \mathsf{Sign}_{\mathsf{sk}}(\mathsf{ab}_r[\mathsf{B}])$ *and* $\sigma_{\mathsf{bc},\mathsf{B}} \leftarrow \mathsf{Sign}_{\mathsf{sk}}(\mathsf{bc}_r[\mathsf{B}])$.
   - $\sigma_{\mathsf{ac},\mathsf{C}} \leftarrow \mathsf{Sign}_{\mathsf{sk}}(\mathsf{ac}_r[\mathsf{C}])$ *and* $\sigma_{\mathsf{bc},\mathsf{C}} \leftarrow \mathsf{Sign}_{\mathsf{sk}}(\mathsf{bc}_r[\mathsf{C}])$.

4. *The parties obtain the following output.*
   - A *receives the public key* pk, *the shares of the backup value* $(\mathsf{ab}_i[\mathsf{A}], \mathsf{ac}_i[\mathsf{A}])_{i=0}^{r}$ *and* $(\mathsf{bc}_i[\mathsf{A}])_{i=1}^{r}$, *and the signatures* $(\sigma_{i,\mathsf{A}})_{i=1}^{r}$, $\sigma_{\mathsf{ab},\mathsf{A}}$, *and* $\sigma_{\mathsf{ac},\mathsf{A}}$.
   - B *receives the public key* pk, *the shares of the backup value* $(\mathsf{ab}_i[\mathsf{B}], \mathsf{bc}_i[\mathsf{B}])_{i=0}^{r}$ *and* $(\mathsf{ac}_i[\mathsf{B}])_{i=1}^{r}$, *and the signatures* $(\sigma_{i,\mathsf{B}})_{i=1}^{r}$, $\sigma_{\mathsf{ab},\mathsf{B}}$, *and* $\sigma_{\mathsf{bc},\mathsf{B}}$.
   - C *receives the public key* pk, *the shares of the backup value* $(\mathsf{ac}_i[\mathsf{C}], \mathsf{bc}_i[\mathsf{C}])_{i=0}^{r}$ *and* $(\mathsf{ab}_i[\mathsf{C}])_{i=1}^{r}$, *and the signatures* $(\sigma_{i,\mathsf{C}})_{i=1}^{r}$, $\sigma_{\mathsf{ac},\mathsf{C}}$, *and* $\sigma_{\mathsf{bc},\mathsf{C}}$.

Additionally, for each party P, we let $f_{\text{-}\mathsf{P}}$ denote the two-party functionality between the other two parties, obtained from f by fixing the input of P to a default value (x_0 if P = A, y_0 if P = B, and z_0 if P = C). We consider the following three-party protocol π^R for computing f, described in the $\{\mathsf{ShrGen}, f_{\text{-}\mathsf{A}}, f_{\text{-}\mathsf{B}}, f_{\text{-}\mathsf{C}}\}$-hybrid model. By [1, Theorem 4.2] there exists a protocol computing ShrGen with $(1,1)$-FaF security-with-identifiable-abort. Moreover, each $f_{\text{-}\mathsf{P}}$ can be computed with semi-honest security [26]. Thus, by the composition theorem, this implies the existence of a $(1,1)$-FaF secure protocol for computing f in the real world.[9]

Protocol 3.5.
Inputs: *Parties* A, B, *and* C *hold inputs* x, y, *and* z, *respectively.*
Common input: *The parties hold the security parameter* 1^κ.

1. *The parties call* ShrGen *with* $(1,1)$-*FaF security-with-identifiable-abort, with their inputs.*
2. *If* P *aborts the execution, then the remaining two parties call* $f_{\text{-}\mathsf{P}}$ *with their inputs and output the result.*
3. *Otherwise, the parties do the following. For* $i = 1$ *to* r:
   (a) *Party* A *broadcasts* $(\mathsf{bc}_i[\mathsf{A}], \sigma_{i,\mathsf{A}})$.
   (b) *If* A *did not send any message or* $\mathsf{Ver}_{\mathsf{pk}}(\mathsf{bc}_i[\mathsf{A}], \sigma_{i,\mathsf{A}}) = \mathsf{Fail}$, *then* B *and* C *reconstruct and output* bc_{i-1}.
   (c) *Otherwise, party* B *broadcasts* $(\mathsf{ac}_i[\mathsf{B}], \sigma_{i,\mathsf{B}})$.

---

[9] Technically, the composition theorem in [1] doesn't handle a subprotocol with semi-honest security after an abort occurred. However, we note that since the aborting party receives no messages at all after it aborts, the proof of the composition theorem can be easily extended to our setting.

(d) *If* B *did not send any message or* $\text{Ver}_{\text{pk}}(\text{ac}_i[\text{B}], \sigma_{i,\text{B}}) = \text{Fail}$, *then* A *and* C *reconstruct and output* ac_{i-1}.

(e) *Otherwise, party* C *broadcasts* $(\text{ab}_i[\text{C}], \sigma_{i,\text{C}})$.

(f) *If* C *did not send any message or* $\text{Ver}_{\text{pk}}(\text{ab}_i[\text{C}], \sigma_{i,\text{C}}) = \text{Fail}$, *then* A *and* B *reconstruct and output* ab_{i-1}.

4. *If no abort occurred, then*
   - A *broadcasts* $(\text{ab}_r, \sigma_{\text{ab},\text{A}})$ *and* $(\text{ac}_r, \sigma_{\text{ac},\text{A}})$.
   - B *broadcasts* $(\text{ab}_r, \sigma_{\text{ab},\text{B}})$ *and* $(\text{bc}_r, \sigma_{\text{bc},\text{B}})$.
   - C *broadcasts* $(\text{ac}_r, \sigma_{\text{ac},\text{C}})$ *and* $(\text{bc}_r, \sigma_{\text{bc},\text{C}})$.

5. *Since there is at most a single malicious party, each uncorrupted party received 3 shares for at least one of the backup values (one from round r, one from the other honest party, and one that they hold). Each party outputs the lexicographically first one.*

Note that correctness is immediately implied from the correctness of the protocol in the dealer model, stating that $\text{ab}_r = \text{bc}_r = \text{ac}_r$. The proof of security is deferred to the full version due to space limitations. $\square$

4   Feasibility Results for Three-Party FaF Security

In this section, we present our positive results. In Sect. 4.1, we show that if a function can be computed by a secure *two-party* protocol, then it can be computed by a three-party $(1,1)$-FaF secure protocol. Then, in Sect. 4.2 we provide feasibility results for symmetric Boolean functions, where all parties output the same bit as output.

4.1   A Compiler from 2-Party Standard Security to 3-Party FaF-Security

The next theorem states that if a function can be computed as a two-party symmetric functionality (i.e., both parties receive the same output) with security against a single malicious adversary and with security against a single semi-honest adversary (and might be also $(1,1)$-FaF secure), then it can be computed with $(1,1)$-FaF security as a three-party symmetric functionality. Note that simply letting the two parties A and B run the secure protocol between themselves, and then having them send the output to C does not work (since the original protocol might not be $(1,1)$-FaF secure). Furthermore, even if the original two-party protocol is $(1,1)$-FaF secure, a corrupt party can lie about the outcome, and then C has no way of detecting whether A is lying or B is.

Theorem 4.1. *Let $g : \mathcal{X} \times \mathcal{Y} \to \mathcal{W}$ be a symmetric 2-party functionality, and let $f : \mathcal{X} \times \mathcal{Y} \times \{\lambda\} \to \mathcal{W}$ be the 3-party functionality symmetric variant of g, i.e., it is defined as $f(x,y,\lambda) = g(x,y)$ for all $x \in \mathcal{X}$ and $y \in \mathcal{Y}$. Suppose that there exists a two-party protocol computing g that is both fully secure and has semi-honest security. Then, assuming secure protocols for OT exist, f can be computed with $(1,1)$-FaF security.*

Proof. Let π_2 be the secure protocol for computing g that is assumed to exist, and let r denote its number of rounds. We construct a three-party protocol π_3 in the dealer model, computing f with $(1,1)$-FaF security. By Theorem 3.2 this implies the existence of a $(1,1)$-FaF secure protocol in the real world (assuming secure protocols for OT). Further let $a_0, \ldots, a_r$ and $b_0, \ldots, b_r$ denote the backup values of A and B, respectively (obtained by sampling randomness for A and B and simulating them in π_2). We assume without loss of generality that in each round, B is the first to send a message. Thus, A obtains a_i before B obtains b_i. We next construct the three-party protocol π_3. Recall that a protocol in the dealer model is given by $3r + 3$ functions for computing the backup values for each pair of parties in each round. We define these backup values as follows. Given inputs x and y of A and B, respectively, for every $i \in \{0, 1, \ldots, r\}$ let $\mathsf{ab}_i = f(x, y, \lambda)$, let $\mathsf{ac}_i = \mathsf{a}_i$, and let $\mathsf{bc}_i = \mathsf{b}_i$. Recall, a_0 is the output of A in π_2 if B sent no message, and thus is independent of y. Similarly, b_0 is independent of x. Thus, the 0th backup value does not depend on the third party's input.

Correctness of π_3 follows from the correctness of π_2, which implies that $\mathsf{a}_r = \mathsf{b}_r = g(x, y) = f(x, y, \lambda)$, except with negligible probability. The proof of security of π_3 is deferred to the full version. □

4.2   FaF Secure Protocols for Boolean Functionalities

In this section, we consider a Boolean three-party functionality that depends only on two inputs. We provide three classes of such functions that can be computed with FaF security. Before stating the theorem, we first introduce some notations.

Notations. For a 2-ary three-party functionality $f : \mathcal{X} \times \mathcal{Y} \times \{\lambda\} \to \{0,1\}$, we will write $f(x, y)$ instead of $f(x, y, \lambda)$ for brevity. Additionally, we associate a matrix $M_f \in \{0,1\}^{|\mathcal{X}| \times |\mathcal{Y}|}$, whose rows are indexed by elements $x \in \mathcal{X}$, whose columns are indexed by elements $y \in \mathcal{Y}$, and is defined as $M_f(x, y) = f(x, y)$. We further define the negated matrix $\overline{M}_f$ as $\overline{M}_f(x, y) = 1 - M_f(x, y)$ for all $x \in \mathcal{X}$ and $y \in \mathcal{Y}$.

Definition 4.2. *The* affine span *of a collection of vectors over $\mathbb{R}$ is the set of all their linear combinations where the sum of coefficients is exactly 1.*

As a corollary of Theorem 4.1, we apply the characterization from [3] of the 2-party symmetric Boolean functionalities that can be computed with full security. We obtain the following result.

Corollary 4.3. *Let $f : \mathcal{X} \times \mathcal{Y} \times \{\lambda\} \to \{0,1\}$ be a Boolean 3-party functionality. Suppose that the all-one vector or the all-zero vector is in the affine span of either the rows or the columns of M_f. Then, assuming secure protocols for OT exist, f can be computed with $(1,1)$-FaF security in the dealer model.*

We next state the main result of this section. We consider a collection of systems of linear equations (that depend on the function f). The theorem roughly states that if any single one of them has a solution, then there exists a FaF secure protocol computing f.

Theorem 4.4. *Let $f : \mathcal{X} \times \mathcal{Y} \times \{\lambda\} \to \{0, 1\}$ be a Boolean 3-party functionality. Suppose there exists a probability vector $\mathbf{p} \in \mathbb{R}^{|\mathcal{X}|}$ with no 0 entries, i.e., $\mathbf{p} = (p_x)_{x \in \mathcal{X}}$ satisfies $p_x > 0$ for all $x \in \mathcal{X}$ and $\sum_{x \in \mathcal{X}} p_x = 1$, such that for all $x \in \mathcal{X}$ it holds that $\mathrm{Im}(M_f^T)$ contains the vector*

$$\mathbf{v}_x = \left(M_f(x, y) \cdot \left(\mathbf{p}^T \cdot M_f(\cdot, y)\right)\right)_{y \in \mathcal{Y}}^T,$$

and such that $\mathrm{Im}(\overline{M}_f^T)$ contains the vector

$$\widetilde{\mathbf{v}}_x = \left(\overline{M}_f(x, y) \cdot \left(\mathbf{p}^T \cdot \overline{M}_f(\cdot, y)\right)\right)_{y \in \mathcal{Y}}^T.$$

Then, assuming secure protocols for OT exist, f can be computed with $(1, 1)$-FaF security in the dealer model.

Proof. We present a protocol that $(1, 1)$-FaF securely computes f in the dealer model. By Theorem 3.2 this implies the existence of a $(1, 1)$-FaF secure protocol in the real world (assuming secure protocols for OT). The protocol follows the special round paradigm of Gordon et al. [13], where until a special (random and unknown) round i^* the parties' backup values are independent, and from i^* the backup values equal to the output of f. We next present the protocol. Recall that in the dealer model, we may only describe the distribution of the backup values computed by the dealer.

First, we denote the *geometric distribution with parameter* $\alpha > 0$ as $\mathsf{Geom}(\alpha)$, and it is defined as $\Pr_{i \leftarrow \mathsf{Geom}(\alpha)}[i = n] = (1 - \alpha)^{n-1} \cdot \alpha$, for all integers $n \geq 1$. We further fix $r(\kappa) = r = \omega(\log \kappa)$ to be the number of rounds. We are now ready to describe the distribution of the backup values, given inputs x and y of A and B, respectively. The dealer samples $i^* \leftarrow \mathsf{Geom}(\alpha)$, where $\alpha > 0$ is sufficiently small that will be chosen below. Then, for every $i \in \{0, \ldots, r\}$, the dealer computes backup values as follows. For every $i \in \{0, \ldots, i^*\}$ sample $\tilde{x}_i \leftarrow \mathbf{p}$ and for every $i \in \{0, \ldots, i^* + 1\}$ sample $\tilde{y}_i \leftarrow \mathcal{Y}$ (i.e., $\tilde{y}_i$ is uniformly distributed over $\mathcal{Y}$), independently. Then for every $i \in \{0, \ldots, r\}$ the dealer sets $\mathsf{ab}_i = f(x, y)$ and sets

$$\mathsf{ac}_i = \begin{cases} f(x, \tilde{y}_i) & \text{if } i < i^* \\ f(x, y) & \text{otherwise} \end{cases} \quad ; \quad \mathsf{bc}_i = \begin{cases} f(\tilde{x}_i, y) & \text{if } i < i^* + 1 \\ f(x, y) & \text{otherwise} \end{cases}$$

The choice of setting bc_i to equal $f(x, y)$ only from round $i^* + 1$ is so that A and C learn the output before B and C. Since $r = \omega(\log \kappa)$ it follows that $i^* + 1 \leq r$ except with negligible probability. Therefore $\mathsf{ab}_r = \mathsf{bc}_r = \mathsf{ac}_r = f(x, y)$ except with negligible probability, and thus the protocol is correct. Due to space considerations, the proof of security is deferred in the full version. □

Theorem 4.4 identifies a set of functionalities that can be computed with $(1, 1)$-FaF security. We do not know if there are functionalities that are not captured by Theorem 4.4, and we leave their existence as an open question. Corollary 4.6 below provides two simple classes of functionalities captured by

Theorem 4.4 (though Corollary 4.6 is less general than Theorem 4.4, see the full version for more details).

The following lemma, states that for certain families of functionalities, there exists a solution to one of the system of equations considered in Theorem 4.4.

Lemma 4.5. *Let $f : \mathcal{X} \times \mathcal{Y} \times \{\lambda\} \to \{0,1\}$ be a three-party 2-ary Boolean functionality. Suppose that one of the following holds.*

1. *Both M_f and $\overline{M}_f$ have a trivial kernel.*
2. *The all-one vector is a linear combination of the rows of M_f, where all coefficients are strictly positive.*

Then there exists a probability vector $\mathbf{p} \in \mathbb{R}^{|\mathcal{X}|}$ with no 0 entries, such that for all $x \in \mathcal{X}$ it holds that $\mathrm{Im}(M_f^T)$ contains the vector

$$\mathbf{v}_x = \left(M_f(x,y) \cdot \left(\mathbf{p}^T \cdot M_f(\cdot,y)\right)\right)_{y \in \mathcal{Y}}^T$$

and $\mathrm{Im}(\overline{M}_f^T)$ contains the vector

$$\widetilde{\mathbf{v}}_x = \left(\overline{M}_f(x,y) \cdot \left(\mathbf{p}^T \cdot \overline{M}_f(\cdot,y)\right)\right)_{y \in \mathcal{Y}}^T.$$

Proof. Let us first assume that both M_f and $\overline{M}_f$ have a trivial kernel. Here, any choice of $\mathbf{p}$ with no zero entries works (e.g., the uniform probability vector). Indeed, $\mathbf{v}_x \in \mathrm{Im}(M_f^T)$ if and only if it is orthogonal to the kernel of M. By assumption, $\ker(M_f) = \{\mathbf{0}\}$ hence any vector is orthogonal to it. Similarly, $\widetilde{\mathbf{v}}_x \in \mathrm{Im}(\overline{M}_f^T)$.

We now assume there exists a vector $\mathbf{u} \in \mathbb{R}^{|\mathcal{X}|}$ with strictly positive entries, such that $\mathbf{u}^T \cdot M_f = \mathbf{1}^T$. Here we take $\mathbf{p} = \mathbf{u}/\|\mathbf{u}\|_1$, where $\|\mathbf{u}\|_1 = \sum_{x \in \mathcal{X}} u_x$ is the ℓ_1 norm of $\mathbf{u}$. Let $\delta > 0$ be such that

$$\mathbf{p}^T \cdot M_f = \delta \cdot \mathbf{1}^T. \tag{1}$$

Then

$$\mathbf{v}_x = \left(M_f(x,y) \cdot \left(\mathbf{p}^T \cdot M_f(\cdot,y)\right)\right)_{y \in \mathcal{Y}} = \left(M_f(x,y) \cdot \delta\right)_{y \in \mathcal{Y}} = (\delta \cdot \mathbf{e}_x) \cdot M_f,$$

where $\mathbf{e}_x$ is the xth standard basis vector. Thus, $\mathbf{v}_x \in \mathrm{Im}(M_f^T)$. It is left to show that $\widetilde{\mathbf{v}}_x \in \mathrm{Im}(\overline{M}_f^T)$. We assume that M_f is not the all-one matrix, as otherwise, the claim is trivial since $\widetilde{\mathbf{v}}_x = \mathbf{0}$ and $\overline{M}_f$ is the all-zero matrix. Let J denote the $|\mathcal{X}| \times |\mathcal{Y}|$ all-one matrix. Observe that by Equation (1) and since $\mathbf{p}$ is a probability vector

$$\mathbf{p}^T \cdot \overline{M}_f = \mathbf{p}^T \cdot (J - M_f) = \mathbf{p}^T \cdot J - \delta \cdot \mathbf{1}_{|\mathcal{Y}|}^T = (\mathbf{p}^T \cdot \mathbf{1}_{|\mathcal{X}|} - \delta) \cdot \mathbf{1}_{|\mathcal{Y}|}^T = (1 - \delta) \cdot \mathbf{1}^T.$$

Since M_f is Boolean and $\mathbf{p}$ is a probability vector, for every $y \in \mathcal{Y}$ it follows that

$$\delta = \mathbf{p}^T \cdot M(\cdot,y) \le \mathbf{p}^T \cdot \mathbf{1} = 1,$$

with equality if and only if for every $x \in \mathcal{X}$ such that $p_x > 0$ it holds that $M(x,y) = 1$. Since $\mathbf{p}$ has no zero entries and M is not the all-one matrix, we conclude that the inequality is strict; i.e., $\delta < 1$. Therefore, a similar analysis to the previous case shows that

$$\tilde{\mathbf{v}}_x^T = ((1 - \delta) \cdot \mathbf{e}_x) \cdot \overline{M}_f.$$

$\square$

Note that if M_f^T satisfies the conditions in Lemma 4.5, then a secure protocol can be obtained by switching the roles of A and B. Thus, we obtain the following corollary. Although less general than Theorem 4.4 (see the full version for a functionality that is captured by Theorem 4.4 but not by Corollary 4.6), it is conceptually simpler.

Corollary 4.6. *Let $f : \mathcal{X} \times \mathcal{Y} \times \{\lambda\} \to \{0,1\}$ be a three-party 2-ary Boolean functionality. Suppose that one of the following holds.*

1. *Both M_f and $\overline{M}_f$ have a trivial kernel, or both M_f^T and $\overline{M}_f^T$ have a trivial kernel, i.e., it contains only the all-zero vector.*
2. *The all-one vector is a linear combination of either the rows or columns of M_f, where all coefficients are strictly positive.*

Then, assuming secure protocols for OT exist, f can be computed with $(1,1)$-FaF security in the dealer model.

As an example of Corollary 4.6, consider the equality function $\mathsf{EQ}_m : [m]^2 \times \{\lambda\} \to \{0,1\}$, where $m \geq 1$ is an integer. It is defined as $\mathsf{EQ}_m(x,y) = 1$ if $x = y$ and $\mathsf{EQ}_m(x,y) = 0$ otherwise. Then, M_{EQ_m} is the $m \times m$ identity matrix. Therefore, it satisfies Item 1 of Corollary 4.6, hence it can be computed with $(1,1)$-FaF security. To exemplify Item 2, consider the functionality f given by the following matrix

$$M_f = \begin{pmatrix} 0 & 1 & 0 & 1 \\ 1 & 0 & 1 & 0 \\ 0 & 1 & 1 & 0 \\ 1 & 0 & 0 & 1 \end{pmatrix}$$

Observe that the kernel of both M_f and M_f^T contain $(1,1,-1,-1)^T$, hence Item 1 does not hold for f. However, note that

$$M_f \cdot (1/4, 1/4, 1/4, 1/4)^T = (1/2, 1/2, 1/2, 1/2)^T.$$

Therefore f satisfies Item 2, hence it can be computed with $(1,1)$-FaF security.

Remark 4.7. Although only proved for deterministic functionalities, Corollary 4.6 (and the more general Theorem 4.4) can be easily generalized to randomized functionalities by defining $M_f(x,y) = \Pr[f(x,y) = 1]$ for all $x \in \mathcal{X}$ and $y \in \mathcal{Y}$.

5   Lower Bound on the Round Complexity of FaF Secure Protocols

In this section, we present a lower bound on the round complexity required for certain FaF secure computations. Specifically, we focus on deterministic three-party functionalities that depend on two inputs. Before stating the result, we first define the notion of *maximally informative input*. Roughly, an input $x \in \mathcal{X}$ for party A is said to be maximally informative if for any other input x' the input-output pair $(x', f(x', y))$ does not give to A more information about the input y of B than the input-output pair $(x, f(x, y))$. We formalize this by requiring that for any x' there exists $y_0, y_1 \in \mathcal{Y}$ such that the input x can distinguish y_0 from y_1, while x' cannot distinguish them. Formally we define it as follows.

Definition 5.1 (Maximally informative input). *Let $f : \mathcal{X} \times \mathcal{Y} \times \{\lambda\} \to \mathcal{W}$ be a deterministic three-party functionality. We say that an input $x \in \mathcal{X}$ is maximally informative if for every $x' \in \mathcal{X} \setminus \{x\}$ there exists $y_0, y_1 \in \mathcal{Y}$ such that $f(x, y_0) \neq f(x, y_1)$ and $f(x', y_0) = f(x', y_1)$. A maximally informative input $y \in \mathcal{Y}$ is defined analogously.*

We are now ready to state our theorem. Roughly, it states that for any deterministic 2-ary functionalities, if all inputs do not fix the output and are maximally informative, then for any ε, the function cannot be computed with an $O(\frac{\log \varepsilon^{-1}}{\log |\mathcal{X}| + \log |\mathcal{Y}|})$-round FaF secure protocol.

Theorem 5.2. *Let $f : \mathcal{X} \times \mathcal{Y} \times \{\lambda\} \to \mathcal{W}$ be a deterministic three-party functionality. For every $x \in \mathcal{X}$ let $p_x := \max_{w \in \mathcal{W}} \Pr[f(x, y) = w]$ where $y \leftarrow \mathcal{Y}$, and let $p_1 := \max_{x \in \mathcal{X}} p_x$. Similarly, for every $y \in \mathcal{Y}$ let $p_y := \max_{w \in \mathcal{W}} \Pr[f(x, y) = w]$ where $x \leftarrow \mathcal{X}$, and let $p_2 := \max_{y \in \mathcal{Y}} p_y$. Finally, denote $p = \max\{p_1, p_2\}$. Assume that there is no input that fixes the output of f and that all $x \in \mathcal{X}$ and $y \in \mathcal{Y}$ are maximally informative (observe that this implies that $p < 1$). Then for any $\varepsilon = \varepsilon(\kappa)$ and any r-round protocol π computing f with $(1,1)$-FaF ε-security, it holds that*

$$r \geq \frac{\log \left(\frac{1}{4\varepsilon} \right) - \log \left(\frac{1}{1-p} \right)}{\log(9 \cdot |\mathcal{X}| \cdot |\mathcal{Y}|)}.$$

Due to space limitations, the proof of Theorem 5.2 is deferred to the full version. As a corollary, we get that for any f satisfying the conditions in Theorem 5.2 there is no $O(\log \kappa)$-round protocol computing f with $(1,1)$-FaF security.

Corollary 5.3. *Let $f : \mathcal{X} \times \mathcal{Y} \times \{\lambda\} \to \mathcal{W}$ be a deterministic three-party functionality. Assume that there is no input that fixes the output of f and that all $x \in \mathcal{X}$ and $y \in \mathcal{Y}$ are maximally informative. Then there is no $O(\log \kappa)$-round protocol computing f with $(1,1)$-FaF security.*

Proof. Fix a constant $c \in \mathbb{N}$ and let $\varepsilon(\kappa) = \kappa^{-c'}$, where $c' = 2c \cdot \log(9 \cdot |\mathcal{X}| \cdot |\mathcal{Y}|)$. Since p, $|\mathcal{X}|$, and $|\mathcal{Y}|$ are constant, it holds that

$$c' \geq \frac{c \cdot \log \kappa \cdot \log(9 \cdot |\mathcal{X}| \cdot |\mathcal{Y}|) + \log\left(\frac{1}{1-p}\right)}{\log\left(\frac{\kappa}{4}\right)},$$

for all sufficiently large κ. By Theorem 5.2 it follows that $r \geq c \cdot \log \kappa$.   □

Below we show an example of a Boolean functionality that can be computed with $(1,1)$-FaF security and satisfies the conditions of Theorem 5.2.

For Boolean functions, the result can be stated in simpler terms using the associated matrix M_f of the function. Observe that an input $x \in \mathcal{X}$ is maximally informative if and only if the row $M_f(x, \cdot)$ is either constant or the negation of the row, namely $\overline{M}_f(x, \cdot)$, does not appear in M_f. Additionally, note that duplicating rows and columns, and removing duplications does not compromise the FaF security of the protocol. Thus, we have the following corollary.

Corollary 5.4. *Let $f : \mathcal{X} \times \mathcal{Y} \times \{\lambda\} \rightarrow \{0,1\}$ be a deterministic three-party Boolean functionality. Assuming that the matrix M_f has no constant rows, no constant columns, and that no row or column has its negation appearing in M_f. Then there is no $O(\log \kappa)$-round protocol computing f with $(1,1)$-FaF security.*

As an example, for an integer $m \geq 3$, consider the equality function $\mathsf{EQ}_m : [m]^2 \times \{\lambda\} \rightarrow \{0,1\}$ defined as $\mathsf{EQ}_m(x,y) = 1$ if $x = y$, and $\mathsf{EQ}_m(x,y) = 0$ otherwise. Then M_{EQ_m} is the $m \times m$ identity matrix. It has no constant rows and columns, and since $m \geq 3$ no row or column has its negation appearing in M_{EQ_m}. Therefore, by Corollary 5.4 any protocol computing it must have round complexity of $\omega(\log \kappa)$. Note that this matches the round complexity of the protocol given by Corollary 4.6.

6 Impossibility for a Two-Input Three-Party Functionality

In this section, we show that there is a function with inputs from two parties that gives the same output to 3 parties and cannot be computed with a $(1,1)$-FaF secure protocol. We prove the following.

Theorem 6.1. *Assume the existence of one-way permutations. Then there exists a three-party symmetric 2-ary functionality for which there is no protocol computing it with $(1,1)$-FaF security.*

The functionality we consider and the proof that no protocol computes it with FaF security is nearly identical to that of [1]. Let $f = \{f_\kappa : \{0,1\}^\kappa \mapsto \{0,1\}^\kappa\}_{\kappa \in \mathbb{N}}$ be a one-way permutation. Define the symmetric 3-party functionality $\mathsf{Swap} = \{\mathsf{Swap}_\kappa : \{0,1\}^{2\kappa} \times \{0,1\}^{2\kappa} \times \{\lambda\} \mapsto \{0,1\}^{2\kappa}\}_{\kappa \in \mathbb{N}}$ as follows. Parties A and B each hold two strings $(a, y_\mathsf{B}), (b, y_\mathsf{A}) \in \{0,1\}^{2\kappa}$ respectively, and party C holds no input. The output is defined as: if $f_\kappa(a) = y_A$ and $f_\kappa(b) = y_B$, then $\mathsf{Swap}_\kappa\left((a, y_B), (b, y_A), \lambda\right) = (a, b)$, otherwise $\mathsf{Swap}_\kappa\left((a, y_B), (b, y_A), \lambda\right) = \bot$.

Due to space limitations, the proof that Swap cannot be computed with $(1,1)$-FaF security is deferred to the full version.

Acknowledgments. The first and third author are partially supported by Israel Science Foundation grant 152/17 and by a grant from the Ariel Cyber Innovation Center in conjunction with the Israel National Cyber directorate in the Prime Minister's Office. The first author is also supported by Israel Science Foundation grant 391/21. The third author is also supported by the Robert L. McDevitt, K.S.G., K.C.H.S. and Catherine H. McDevitt L.C.H.S. endowment at Georgetown University. Part of this work was done when he was hosted by Georgetown University. The second author is supported by Israel Science Foundation grant 391/21 and by ERC grant 742754 (project NTSC).

References

1. Alon, B., Omri, E., Paskin-Cherniavsky, A.: MPC with friends and foes. In: Micciancio, D., Ristenpart, T. (eds.) CRYPTO 2020. LNCS, vol. 12171, pp. 677–706. Springer, Cham (2020). https://doi.org/10.1007/978-3-030-56880-1_24

2. Asharov, G.: Towards characterizing complete fairness in secure two-party computation. In: Lindell, Y. (ed.) TCC 2014. LNCS, vol. 8349, pp. 291–316. Springer, Heidelberg (2014). https://doi.org/10.1007/978-3-642-54242-8_13

3. Asharov, G., Beimel, A., Makriyannis, N., Omri, E.: Complete characterization of fairness in secure two-party computation of Boolean functions. In: Dodis, Y., Nielsen, J.B. (eds.) TCC 2015. LNCS, vol. 9014, pp. 199–228. Springer, Heidelberg (2015). https://doi.org/10.1007/978-3-662-46494-6_10

4. Beimel, A., Lindell, Y., Omri, E., Orlov, I.: 1/p-secure multiparty computation without an honest majority and the best of both worlds. J. Cryptol. **33**(4), 1659–1731 (2020)

5. Beimel, A., Malkin, T., Micali, S.: The all-or-nothing nature of two-party secure computation. In: Wiener, M. (ed.) CRYPTO 1999. LNCS, vol. 1666, pp. 80–97. Springer, Heidelberg (1999). https://doi.org/10.1007/3-540-48405-1_6

6. Beimel, A., Omri, E., Orlov, I.: Protocols for multiparty coin toss with a dishonest majority. J. Cryptol. **28**(3), 551–600 (2015)

7. Blakley, G.R.: Safeguarding cryptographic keys. In: International Workshop on Managing Requirements Knowledge, p. 313. IEEE Computer Society (1979)

8. Canetti, R.: Security and composition of multiparty cryptographic protocols. J. Cryptol. **13**(1), 143–202 (2000)

9. Cleve, R.: Limits on the security of coin flips when half the processors are faulty (extended abstract). In: Proceedings of the 18th Annual ACM Symposium on Theory of Computing (STOC), pp. 364–369 (1986)

10. Dachman-Soled, D.: Revisiting fairness in MPC: polynomial number of parties and general adversarial structures. In: Pass, R., Pietrzak, K. (eds.) TCC 2020. LNCS, vol. 12551, pp. 595–620. Springer, Cham (2020). https://doi.org/10.1007/978-3-030-64378-2_21

11. Daza, V., Makriyannis, N.: Designing fully secure protocols for secure two-party computation of constant-domain functions. In: Proceedings of the 15th Theory of Cryptography Conference (TCC), part I, pp. 581–611 (2017)

12. Goldreich, O.: Foundations of Cryptography - Volume 2: basic applications. Cambridge University Press (2004)
13. Gordon, S.D., Hazay, C., Katz, J., Lindell, Y.: Complete fairness in secure two-party computation. In: Proceedings of the 40th Annual ACM Symposium on Theory of Computing (STOC), pp. 413–422 (2008)
14. Gordon, S.D., Katz, J.: Complete fairness in multi-party computation without an honest majority. In: Reingold, O. (ed.) TCC 2009. LNCS, vol. 5444, pp. 19–35. Springer, Heidelberg (2009). https://doi.org/10.1007/978-3-642-00457-5_2
15. Halevi, S., Ishai, Y., Kushilevitz, E., Makriyannis, N., Rabin, T.: On fully secure MPC with solitary output. In: Hofheinz, D., Rosen, A. (eds.) TCC 2019. LNCS, vol. 11891, pp. 312–340. Springer, Cham (2019). https://doi.org/10.1007/978-3-030-36030-6_13
16. Impagliazzo, R., Luby, M.: One-way functions are essential for complexity based cryptography. In: 30th Annual Symposium on Foundations of Computer Science, pp. 230–235. IEEE Computer Society (1989)
17. Ishai, Y., Katz, J., Kushilevitz, E., Lindell, Y., Petrank, E.: On achieving the "best of both worlds" in secure multiparty computation. SIAM J. Comput. **40**(1), 122–141 (2011)
18. Ishai, Y., Kushilevitz, E., Lindell, Y., Petrank, E.: On combining privacy with guaranteed output delivery in secure multiparty computation. In: Dwork, C. (ed.) CRYPTO 2006. LNCS, vol. 4117, pp. 483–500. Springer, Heidelberg (2006). https://doi.org/10.1007/11818175_29
19. Ishai, Y., Kushilevitz, E., Paskin, A.: Secure multiparty computation with minimal interaction. In: Rabin, T. (ed.) CRYPTO 2010. LNCS, vol. 6223, pp. 577–594. Springer, Heidelberg (2010). https://doi.org/10.1007/978-3-642-14623-7_31
20. Katz, J.: On achieving the "best of both worlds" in secure multiparty computation. In: Proceedings of the 39th Annual ACM Symposium on Theory of Computing, San Diego, California, USA, 11–13 June 2007, pp. 11–20. ACM (2007)
21. Makriyannis, N.: On the classification of finite Boolean functions up to fairness. In: Abdalla, M., De Prisco, R. (eds.) SCN 2014. LNCS, vol. 8642, pp. 135–154. Springer, Cham (2014). https://doi.org/10.1007/978-3-319-10879-7_9
22. Makriyannis, N.: Fairness in two-party computation: characterizing fair functions, Ph. D. thesis, Universitat Pompeu Fabra (2016)
23. Rabin, T., Ben-Or, M.: Verifiable secret sharing and multiparty protocols with honest majority. In: Proceedings of the 30th Annual Symposium on Foundations of Computer Science (FOCS), pp. 73–85 (1989)
24. Rompel, J.: One-way functions are necessary and sufficient for secure signatures. In: Proceedings of the 22nd Annual ACM Symposium on Theory of Computing, 13–17 May 1990, Baltimore, Maryland, USA, pp. 387–394. ACM (1990)
25. Shamir, A.: How to share a secret. Commun. ACM **22**(11), 612–613 (1979)
26. Yao, A.C.: Protocols for secure computations. In: Proceedings of the 23rd Annual Symposium on Foundations of Computer Science (FOCS), pp. 160–164 (1982)

Encryption

CASE: A New Frontier in Public-Key Authenticated Encryption

Shashank Agrawal[1]([✉]), Shweta Agrawal[2], Manoj Prabhakaran[3], Rajeev Raghunath[3], and Jayesh Singla[3]

[1] Coinbase, San Francisco, USA
sagrawal@protonmail.ch
[2] IIT Madras, Chennai, India
[3] IIT Bombay, Mumbai, India
{mp,mrrajeev,jayeshs}@cse.iitb.ac.in

Abstract. We introduce a new cryptographic primitive, called Completely Anonymous Signed Encryption (CASE). CASE is a public-key authenticated encryption primitive, that offers anonymity for senders as well as receivers. A "case-packet" should appear, without a (decryption) key for opening it, to be a blackbox that reveals no information at all about its contents. To *decase* a case-packet fully–so that the message is retrieved and authenticated–a verification key is also required.

Defining security for this primitive is subtle. We present a relatively simple *Chosen Objects Attack* (COA) security definition. Validating this definition, we show that it implies a comprehensive indistinguishability-preservation definition in the real-ideal paradigm. To obtain the latter definition, we extend the Cryptographic Agents framework of [2,3] to allow maliciously created objects.

We also provide a novel and practical construction for COA-secure CASE under standard assumptions in public-key cryptography, and in the standard model.

We believe CASE can be a staple in future cryptographic libraries, thanks to its robust security guarantees and efficient instantiations based on standard assumptions.

1 Introduction

In this work, we introduce a new cryptographic primitive, called Completely Anonymous Signed Encryption (CASE). CASE is a public-key authenticated encryption primitive, that offers anonymity for senders as well as receivers. CASE captures the intuition that once a message is "encased"–resulting in a case-packet–it should appear, to someone without a (decryption) key for opening the case-packet, to be a blackbox that reveals no information at all about its contents.[1] To *decase* a case-packet fully–so that the message is retrieved and authenticated–a verification key is also required.

---

[1] For simplicity, we consider a finite message space. If messages of arbitrary length are to be allowed, we will let a case-packet reveal the length of the message (possibly after padding). All our definitions and results can be readily generalized to this setting.

© International Association for Cryptologic Research 2023
G. Rothblum and H. Wee (Eds.): TCC 2023, LNCS 14370, pp. 189–219, 2023.
https://doi.org/10.1007/978-3-031-48618-0_7

The significance of such a primitive stems from its *fundamental nature* as well as its potential as a *practical tool*. For instance, in blockchain-like systems where data packets can be publicly posted, for privacy, not only the contents of the packet should be hidden, but also the originator and the intended recipient of the data should remain anonymous. Further, we may require that even the recipient of a packet should not learn about its sender unless they have acquired a verification key that allows them to authenticate packets from the sender (this is what we call *complete* anonymity).

CASE, while fundamental in nature, is still a fairly complex primitive, and formally defining security for it is a non-trivial task. It involves two pairs of keys (public and secret keys, for encryption and signature), used in different combinations (e.g., a decryption key is enough to open the case-packet for reading a message, but a verification key is also needed for authentication), and multiple security requirements based on which keys are available to the adversary and which are not.

Public-key authenticated encryption has been well-explored in the literature (see Sect. 1.1) and has also been making its way into standards (e.g., [4, 11]). However, these notions do not incorporate anonymity as we do here. Further, we seek and achieve *significantly more comprehensive security guarantees and strong key-hiding properties*. In particular, we seek security against active adversaries who can access oracles that combine honest objects with adversarial objects, where "objects" refer to both keys as well as case-packets. For instance, the adversary can query a decasing oracle with its own decryption key and case-packet, but requesting to use one of two verification keys picked by the experiment. We term such attacks **Chosen Objects Attack** (COA), as a generalization of Chosen Ciphertext Attack. We present a relatively simple definition of COA-secure CASE consisting of three elegant experiments (Total-Hiding, Sender-Anonymity, Unforgeability),[2] correctness conditions, an unpredictability condition, and a set of natural –but new–*existential consistency* requirements.

Is COA Security Comprehensive? (Yes!) At first glance, our COA security definition for CASE may appear as an incomplete list of desirable properties. Indeed, given the subtleties of defining security for a complex primitive, it is not possible to appeal to intuition to argue that all vulnerabilities have been covered by this definition. Instead, one should use a comprehensive definition in the *real-ideal* paradigm, where the ideal model is intuitively convincing. This approach has formed the foundation for general frameworks like Universally Composable security [15] and Constructive Cryptography [29]. However, using a simulation based security definition for modeling *objects that can be passed around* (rather than functionalities implemented using protocols wherein parties never transfer their secret keys) quickly leads to impossibility results in the standard model without random oracles (see the full version). To avoid such outright impossibility results, we consider a definition in the real-ideal paradigm that uses **indistinguishability-preservation** [2,3] as the security notion, rather than simulation. In the process, we extend the Cryptographic Agents framework of [2,3] to allow maliciously created objects, which is an *important additional contribution of this work*.

---

[2] These distinct experiments can be combined to give an equivalent unified experiment in which the adversary is allowed to adaptively attack any of the above security properties over a collection of keys and case-packets. Such a definition is presented as an intermediate step to showing the comprehensiveness of this definition (see below).

Once the definitions are in place, our main results, are a novel construction of a COA-secure CASE from standard assumptions in public-key cryptography, and also showing that COA-secure CASE meets the real-ideal security definition for CASE.

Our Contributions. We summarize our contributions here.

- We introduce CASE as a practical and powerful cryptographic primitive.
- We present a strong security definition for CASE, called COA security (Sect. 3).
- We give a construction for COA-secure CASE under standard assumptions in the standard model (Sect. 4). We also show how to leverage the efficiency of any symmetric-key encryption scheme to get a correspondingly efficient COA-secure CASE (Sect. 4.4).
- We present the Active Agents Framework as an extension of the Cryptographic Agents model, to capture comprehensive security guarantees for complex primitives like CASE under the real-ideal paradigm (Sect. 5).
- We show that COA secure CASE yields a secure implementation of CASE in the active agents framework (Sect. 6).

While we present the COA security definition upfront, it is important to point out that this definition was arrived at starting from the security definition in the active agents framework, and working through the demands of satisfying that definition.

1.1 Related Work

Public-key authenticated encryption has been extensively studied since signcryption was introduced by Zheng [41]. Despite being a fundamental primitive studied for over two decades, it has proved challenging to find the right definitions of security for this notion. Indeed, the original scheme by Zheng was proven secure several years after its introduction [8]. A sequence of works [5,6,8,34,40] formalized security in the so called "outsider security model" and "insider security model" where the former is used to model network attacks while the latter is used to model (a priori) legitimate users whose keys have been compromised. Even as these basic security definitions remained ad hoc, a significant number of works have constructed concrete schemes based on different assumptions [25,26,38,41,42], and gone on to realize advanced properties [9,13,14,17–19,22,25,27,28,36,37,39].

An early attempt by Gjøsteen and Kråkmo [23] modelled unforgeability and confidentiality in the outsider security model by using an ideal functionality. More recently, [7] provided a constructive cryptography perspective of the basic security notions of signcryption. This work modelled the goal of authenticated public-key encryption as a secure communication network, with static corruption of nodes. As it used a simulation-based definition for the communication functionality, it does not account (and could not have accounted) for secret key transfers, or more generally, the use of the scheme's objects in non-standard ways outside of the prescribed communication protocols (e.g., posting ciphertexts on a bulletin board or forwarding them, using signatures to prove the possession of a signing key, etc.).

Recently, Bellare and Stepanovs studied signcryption from a quantitative perspective due to its use in various practical systems and standards [11]. More recently, Alwen et al. [4] conducted a thorough study of the "authenticated mode" of the Hybrid Public Key Encryption (HPKE) standard, which combines a Key Encapsulation Mechanism and an Authenticated Encryption. They abstract this notion using a new primitive which they call Authenticated Public Key Encryption. However, their study is tailored to the HPKE standard, and primarily studies weaker variants of security. Another recent work by Maurer et al. [30] studied the related notion of "Multi-Designated Receiver Signed Public Key Encryption" which allows a sender to select a set of designated receivers and both encrypt and sign a message that only these receivers will be able to read and authenticate.

While the aforementioned works make important progress towards the goal of finding the right formalization for public-key authenticated encryption, *none of them consider anonymity* of the sender and intended receiver. They also work with *relatively weak or ad hoc security definitions* and do not comprehensively model an adversary that can combine honest and adversarial objects via oracles.

2   Technical Overview

We proceed to provide a technical overview of our definitions, constructions and proofs of security.

2.1   Defining COA-Secure CASE

CASE is a fairly complex primitive. For instance, in contrast to symmetric-key authenticated encryption, encasing and decasing a message involves four keys. Further, in comparison to signcryption, which itself has been the subject of an extensive body of work, CASE requires strong *key-hiding* properties. We also require that even if one of the two keys used to create a case-packet, or used to decase a possibly malicious case-packet, is maliciously crafted, the residual hiding assurances for the honestly created key should hold.

We start off by presenting a fairly intuitive set of security games and correctness properties. We term our definition security against *Chosen Objects Attack*, or **COA-security** (Sect. 3), since the adversary needs to be provided with oracles which take not only malicious "ciphertexts" (or case-packets), but also malicious keys; both encasing and decasing oracles need to be provided to the adversary. There are standard correctness requirements and three security games–**total hiding** and **sender anonymity** games with a flavor of CCA security, and an **unforgeability** game paralleling a standard signature unforgeability requirement. In addition, there is an **unpredictability** requirement and a set of **existential consistency** requirements, which are crucial for security against malicious keys. The former requires that encasing a message with any encryption key and signing key results in a case-packet with high min-entropy (or results in an error); while this is implied by the above security experiments for honestly generated keys, the additional requirement is that it holds for *all* keys in the key-space. The existential consistency conditions require that a case-packet should have at most one set of keys and message that can be associated with it, and similarly a verification key should have at most one signing key, and an encryption key should have at most one decryption key.

Like the unpredictability requirement, the consistency requirements are also remarkably unremarkable in nature–indeed, one may feel that they are to be expected in any reasonable scheme–but, they are non-trivial to enforce.

2.2 Constructing a COA-Secure CASE

We start with a sign-then-encrypt strategy. Indeed, in the setting of (non-anonymous) signcryption, sign-then-encrypt is a generic composition that is known to yield a secure signcryption [5], but only with the weakened form of "replayable CCA" security (introduced in [5] as *generalized CCA* or gCCA). The main drawback of this construction is replayability: suppose Eve receives a case-packet CP signed by Alice and encrypted using Eve's encryption key; then, Eve can decrypt it and reencrypt using any encryption key of its choice (without needing to modify the underlying signature of Alice). This is clearly problematic because, if Bob receives a case-packet that he can decase and authenticate to be from Alice, he still cannot be sure if Alice had actually sent it to him, or to someone like Eve (who then carried out the above attack). An immediate solution to this is to include in the signed message the encryption key to be used as well; this would prevent Eve from passing off the signed message with her encryption key in it as a message intended for Bob. However, this still leaves some non-ideal behavior: On receiving one case-packet from Alice, Eve can construct many *distinct* case-packets by decrypting and reencrypting it with its encryption key many times. Each of these case-packets would verify as coming from Alice by someone with Eve's decryption key. Whether this translates to concrete harm or not is application dependent–but this a behavior that is not possible in the ideal setting.

We thus want to authenticate the entire case-packet (rather than just the message and the encryption key) in the signature. However, this leads to a circularity as the case-packet is determined only after the signature is computed. It turns out that one can circumvent this circularity by exposing a little more structure from the underlying PKE scheme. The idea is as follows, instead of signing the case-packet itself, it is enough to sign everything that goes into the case-packet other than the signature itself–i.e., the message, the encryption key, and the *randomness that will be used to create the encryption*. This idea should be implemented with some care, so that the security of the encryption scheme (which is not designed to support message-dependent-randomness) remains un-affected.

We call an encryption scheme **quasi-deterministic** if any ciphertext generated by it includes a part τ that is independent of the message, but is a perfectly binding encoding of all the randomness r used in the encryption. As a simple example, El Gamal encryption is quasi-deterministic, since $\mathrm{Enc}_{\mathrm{ElGamal}}((g, h), m; r) = (g^r, m \cdot h^r)$ where (g, h) is the public-key, m the message and r the randomness, and g^r is a binding encoding of r. The same is true for Cramer-Shoup encryption [16].

This gives us the structure of our final scheme: we need a signature scheme (with sufficiently short signatures) and a quasi-deterministic PKE scheme (with sufficiently long messages). To encase m, we first pick the randomness r for the PKE scheme and compute the first component τ of the ciphertext (without needing the message). Then, we set the case-packet to be $\mathrm{pkeEnc}(EK, m\|\sigma; r)$ where $\sigma =$

sigSign($SK, m||EK||\tau$). Note that, the ciphertext produced by pkeEnc using randomness r will contain τ as a part, and during decasing, the signature σ can be verified.

To make this construction work, we need the right kind of PKE and signature schemes, with their own anonymity and existential consistency in addition to the standard security guarantees (CCA and strong unforgeability, resp.). We capture these security requirements as *COA-secure Quasi-Deterministic PKE* (COA-QD-PKE) and *Existentially Consistent Anonymous Signatures* (ECAS).

COA Secure Quasi-Deterministic PKE. The definition of COA security of PKE consists of a single indistinguishability requirement–Anonymous-CCA-QD security (adapted from Anonymous-CCA security [1, 12])–plus a set of existential consistency requirements.

To be able to exploit the quasi-determinism (described above), we need to modify the CCA security game slightly into a CCA-QD game as follows. The adversary receives the first part τ of the challenge ciphertext (which does not depend on the message) upfront along with the public-key; it receives the rest of the ciphertext after it submits a pair of challenge messages.

To construct a COA-QD-PKE scheme, we start from an Anonymous-CCA-QD secure scheme. As it turns out, we already have a construction in the literature that is Anonymous-CCA-QD secure: [1] showed that with a slight modification, the Cramer-Shoup encryption scheme [16] becomes Anonymous-CCA secure; we reanalyze this scheme to show that it is Anonymous-CCA-QD secure as well.[3]

We also require existential consistency s.t. if a ciphertext decrypts successfully, it can only decrypt to at most a single message with at most a single decryption key. We now show how a given Anonymous-CCA-QD-PKE with perfect correctness (such as the modified Cramer-Shoup scheme [1]) can be modified to be existentially consistent while retaining its original security. Note that, perfect correctness only refers to honestly generated keys and ciphertexts, and does not entail existential consistency.

A helpful first step in preventing invalid secret-keys is to redefine it to be the randomness used to generate the original secret-key. Further towards enforcing existential consistency, we augment the public-key to include a perfectly binding commitment to the secret-key, and the ciphertext is augmented to include one to the public-key. That is, the ciphertext has the form (α, β), where α is a commitment to the public-key and β is a ciphertext in the original scheme. To preserve anonymous-CCA security, we need to tie α and β together: it turns out to be enough to let β be the encryption of $m||d$ where d is the canonical decommitment information for α (from which α also can be computed).

Here we point out one subtlety in the above construction. Note that the public-key is required to include a binding commitment of the secret-key. But we in fact require that the public-key can be *deterministically* computed from the secret-key (since this property will be required of our CASE scheme). Hence the randomness needed to

---

[3] We note that, CCA-QD security is not implied by CCA security and the QD structure alone. E.g., one can modify a CCA-QD secure PKE scheme such that, if the encoding of the randomness (the pre-computed component of the ciphertext) happens to equal the message, it simply sets the second component to $\perp$, thereby revealing the message; while this remains CCA secure, an adversary in the CCA-QD game can set one of the challenge messages to be equal to the encoding of the randomness and break CCA-QD security.

compute this commitment must already be part of the secret-key, leading to a circularity. This circularity can be avoided by using a commitment scheme that is "fully binding"–i.e., the output of the commitment is perfectly binding not only for the message, but also for the randomness used. An example of such a scheme, under the DDH assumption, is obtained from the El Gamal encryption scheme mentioned above: $\mathrm{Com}(m; g, h, r) = (g, h, g^r, mh^r)$.

Existentially Consistent Anonymous Signature. We require ECAS to be a (strongly unforgeable) signature scheme with an anonymity guarantee: without knowing a verification key, one cannot tell if two signatures are signed using the same key or not. We shall also require existential consistency guarantees of ECAS.

To construct an ECAS scheme, we start with a plain (strongly unforgeable) signature scheme, which w.l.o.g., has uniformly random signing keys from which verification keys are deterministically derived (by considering the randomness of the key-generation process as the signing key). We first augment this scheme to support anonymity by adding a layer of encryption, and include the decryption key in the signing and verification keys of the ECAS scheme. To obtain existential consistency, we make the following modifications:

- The signing key SK includes the underlying scheme's signing key, the decryption key for the encryption layer, and additional randomness for making the commitment below.
- The verification key VK includes the underlying verification key, the decryption key for the encryption layer and a commitment to the underlying signing key (using a fully binding commitment scheme as above).
- The signature includes a commitment to VK (but to the encryption key in it) using fresh randomness $\hat{r}$, and a *quasi-deterministic* encryption of $(\hat{r}||\sigma)$ where σ is a signature on $m||\hat{r}||\tau$ using the underlying signature scheme, where τ is the first component of the quasi-deterministic ciphertext.
- Verification corresponds to decrypting the ciphertext, verifying the signature according to the underlying signature scheme and then verifying the consistency of the commitment.

For existential consistency, as well as (strong) unforgeability, we will rely on the encryption scheme to be a COA-QD-PKE. Note that we have rely on the quasi-deterministic nature of the encryption scheme to prevent forgeries which simply refresh the encryption layer (decrypt and re-encrypt).

We point out one subtlety in the above construction. We have defined the signature above to include a commitment to (SK^*, c, EK^*) rather than the actual verification key $VK = (SK^*, c, DK^*)$. This is to avoid the following circularity: the commitment would have the decryption key in it while the encryption would have the randomness used for this commitment. This would prevent us from arguing the properties of ECAS.

Please refer to the full version for the full details. Note that this construction shares several similarities with our CASE construction. If one unrolls our CASE construction, there are two layers of COA-QD-PKE, but using two different keys.

Improving the Efficiency. As described in Sect. 4.4, CASE admits an analogue of "hybrid encryption," whereby long messages can be encased at the cost of applying symmetric-key encryption (SKE) and collision-resistant hashing to the original message, plus the cost of encasing a fixed size message (consisting of the keys for SKE and hashing, and the hash of the message). This makes our CASE construction quite practical.

2.3   A Real-Ideal Definition

A major concern with game-based security definitions is that they may leave out several subtler aspects of security. For instance, even for the simpler (and heavily studied) setting of public-key encryption, the security definition has been strengthened incrementally through a sequence of notions that emerged over the decades: Semantic security or IND-CPA [24], IND-CCA (1 and 2) [20,32,35], anonymity [12] and robustness [1,21,31]. With CASE, this is clearly an even more pressing concern, given its complexity. In particular, our definition of COA-secure CASE has several games and conditions as part of it, and one may suspect that more such components could be added in the future.

To address this concern, we seek a definition following the *real-ideal paradigm*, where by inspecting the ideal world, one can be easily convinced about the meaningfulness of the definition. However, a *simulation-based definition* quickly leads us to impossibility results. Even for PKE with adaptive security (when decryption keys may be revealed adaptively–a situation we do intend to cover), as observed by Nielsen [33], a simulation based definition is impossible to achieve in the standard model.

In this work, we develop a new definition in the real-ideal paradigm that avoids simulation, but is nevertheless powerful enough to subsume game-based definitions like IND-CCA security. Our definition is based on the *indistinguishability-preserving* security notion of the Cryptographic Agents framework [2,3]. The original framework of [2,3] did not allow an adversary to send (possibly maliciously created) objects to an honest party, and as such was not powerful to capture even IND-CCA security. We remove this restriction from the framework and extend it with other useful features. Then, we model CASE in this framework using a natural idealized version, and seek an indistinguishability-preserving implementation for it.

Our main result in this model, informally, is that a COA-secure CASE scheme is in fact, an indistinguishability-preserving implementation of ideal CASE. This validates our COA security definition for CASE.

Active Agents Framework. We briefly discuss the active agents framework (with more technical details in Sect. 5). The framework is minimalistic and conceptually simple, and consists of the following:

- *Two arbitrary entities.* Test models the honest party, and User models the adversary.
- *The ideal model* has a trusted party $\mathcal{B}$ which hands out *handles* to Test and User for manipulating data stored with it via an idealized interface called "schema"(akin to a functionality in the UC security model).
- *The real model* has Test and User interact with each other using cryptographic objects, in place of ideal handles.

⋆ *Indistinguishability Preservation:* The security requirement in this model is as follows. For any predicate on Test's inputs that is hidden from User in the ideal world, it should be hidden in the real world as well.

An ideal world schema will have an interface corresponding to each algorithm of an application (such as key generation, encasing and decasing for CASE) and an agent corresponding to each cryptographic object (such as keys and ciphertexts). Both Test and User only get handle numbers to agents. Constructing objects via algorithms is modelled as invoking the corresponding schema command and getting a handle for a new agent. Sending cryptographic objects is modelled via a special command called **Transfer**. Test (respectively User) can transfer its agents (via handles) to User (respectively Test), which gets a new handle number to the transferred agent.

Δ-s-**IND-PRE Security.** To obtain our full definition, we need to further qualify indistinguishability-preservation by specifying the class of Tests and Users in the ideal model. We denote s-IND-PRE as the class of all PPT Test that are hiding against *even unbounded* Users in the *ideal world* (as in [3]).[4]

The strongest possible s-IND-PRE definition one can ask for in the active agents framework is for the test-family of all PPT programs, which results in a definition that is impossible to realize (even for symmetric key encryption and even in the original framework of [2]–see the full version). However, a more restricted test-family called Δ suffices to subsume all possible IND-style (a.k.a. "real-or-random") definitions. Informally, a Test $\in \Delta$ reveals everything about the handles for agents it uses in its interaction with User except for a test-bit b corresponding to some arbitrary predicate. When transferring an agent to User, Test chooses two handles h_0, h_1 and communicates these to the user but *transfers only agent for h_b*. Thus, User knows that Test has transferred one of two known agents to her, but does not know which. User may proceed to perform any idealized operation with this newly transferred agent.

In intuitive terms, Δ-s-IND-PRE formalizes the following guarantee: *as long as Test does not reveal a secret in the ideal world, the real world will also keep it hidden.* It *subsumes essentially all meaningful IND security definitions* for a given interface of the primitive: for any such IND security game, there is Test $\in \Delta$ which carries out this game, such that it statistically hides the test-bit when an ideal encryption scheme is used (e.g., in the case of IND-CCA security this formulation corresponds to a game that never decrypts a ciphertext that is identical to the ciphertext that was earlier given as the challenge, called IND-CCA-SE in [10]), and Δ-s-IND-PRE security applied to this Test translates to the security guarantee in the IND security game.

In particular, Δ-s-IND-PRE security directly addresses the chosen object attacks of interest, as they can all be captured using specific tests.

Beyond CASE. We point out that the active agents framework developed here is quite general and can be used to model security for other schemas in the presence of adversarially created objects. The original frameworks of [2,3] modeled security notions for more advanced primitives like indistinguishability obfuscation, differing-inputs obfus-

---

[4] So that, it is statistical indistinguishability in the ideal model that is required to be preserved as computational indistinguishability in the real model.

cation and VGB obfuscation by using different test families. Transferring these definitions to our new model would yield stronger notions with additional non-malleability guarantees; the resulting primitives remain to be explored. Indeed, as the basic security definitions for obfuscation and functional encryption are increasingly considered to be realizable, the achievability of stronger definitions emerges as an important question.

Limits of Δ-s-IND-PRE. Even though Δ-s-IND-PRE security is based on an ideal world model, and subsumes *all possible* IND definitions, we advise caution against interpreting Δ-s-IND-PRE security on par with a simulation-based security definition (which is indeed unrealizable). For instance, Δ-s-IND-PRE does not require preserving non-negligible advantages: e.g., a distinguishing advantage of 0.1 in the ideal world could translate to an advantage of 0.2 in the real world. Note that this is usually not a concern, since it corresponds to an ideal world that is already "insecure".

Another issue is that, while an ideal encryption scheme could be used as a non-malleable commitment scheme, Δ-s-IND-PRE security makes no such assurances. This is because, in the ideal world, if a commitment is to be opened such that indistinguishability ceases, then IND-PRE security makes no more guarantees. We leave it as an intriguing question whether Δ-s-IND-PRE secure encryption could be leveraged in an indirect way to obtain a non-malleable commitment scheme.

Δ-s-IND-PRE definition also does not cover side-channel attacks. One can extend the definition to allow the interface of an implementation to have more commands (corresponding to leakage) than in the ideal interface of the schema. We defer this to future work.

Finally, the idealized model in the Agents framework excludes certain kinds of usages that a simulation-based idealization would permit. Specifically, since the ideal interface provides honest users only with handles (serial numbers) for the cryptographic objects they create or receive, they cannot use a cryptographic object as input to another algorithm, or even to an algorithm in the same scheme (e.g., a key cannot be used as a message that is encased). We remark that this restriction is, in fact, a *desirable feature* in a programming interface for a cryptographic library; violating this interface should not be up to the programmer, but should be carefully designed, analyzed and exposed as a new schema by the creators of the cryptographic library.

2.4 Proving COA Security $\Rightarrow$ Δ-s-IND-PRE Secure CASE

Implementing the schema Σ_{case} is a challenging task because it is highly idealized and implies numerous security guarantees that may not be immediately apparent. (For instance, in the ideal world, to produce a case-packet, not only is the signing key needed, but so is the encryption key; hence an adversary with the signing key who gets oracle access to encasing and decasing, should not be able to create a new valid case-packet.) These guarantees are not explicit in the definition of COA security. Nevertheless, we show the following:

Theorem 1. *A Δ-s-IND-PRE secure implementation of Σ_{case} exists if a COA secure CASE scheme exists.*

The construction itself is direct, syntactically translating the elements of a CASE scheme into those of an implementation of Σ_{case}. However, the proof of security is quite non-trivial. This should not be surprising given the simplicity of the COA security definition vis-à-vis the generality of Δ-s-IND-PRE security. We use a careful sequence of hybrids to argue indistinguishability preservation, where some of the hybrids involve the use of an "extended schema" (which is partly ideal and partly real). To switch between these hybrids, we use both PPT simulators (which rely on the indistinguishability and unforgeability guarantees in the COA security) and computationally unbounded simulators (which rely on existential consistency). As we shall see, the simulators heavily rely on the fact that Test $\in \Delta$, and hence the only uncertainty regarding agents transferred by Test is the choice between one of two known agents, determined by the test-bit b given as input to Test. The essential ingredients of these simulators are summarized below.[5]

- First, we move from the real execution to a hybrid execution in which objects originating from Test are replaced with ideal agents, while the objects originating from the adversary are replaced–by an efficient simulator $\mathcal{S}_b^\dagger$ (which knows the test bit b)–with ideal agents only when their structure can be deduced efficiently based on the objects already in the transcript; otherwise $\mathcal{S}_b^\dagger$ prepares non-ideal agents which internally contain cryptographic objects and transfers them.

  In this hybrid, an "extended" schema which allows both ideal and non-ideal agents is used. The extended schema is carefully designed to allow sessions to run correctly, even when non-ideal agents (prepared by $\mathcal{S}_b^\dagger$) and ideal agents interact with each other.

  A detailed analysis, using a graph $\mathbb{G}_b^\dagger$ which encodes the combined view of Test and $\mathcal{A}$, is used to argue that the modifications in this hybrid will cause the execution to deviate only if certain "bad events" occur (see the full version). The bad events mainly correspond to the violation of conditions explicitly included in the COA security definition (like correctness, unforgeability and unpredictability) or other consequences of the definition (like encasing resistance, in Sect. 3.1). Since these bad events can all shown to have negligible probability, making this modification keeps the experiment's outcome indistinguishable.[6]

- The next step is to show that there is a simulator $\mathcal{S}^\ddagger$ which does not need to know the bit b to carry out the above simulation. This is perhaps the most delicate part of the proof. The high-level idea is to argue that the executions for $b = 0$ and $b = 1$ should proceed identically from the point of view of the adversary (as Test hides the bit b in the ideal world), and hence a joint simulation should be possible. $\mathcal{S}^\ddagger$ will abort when it cannot assign a single simulated object for the two possible choices of a transferred agent, corresponding to $b = 0$ and $b = 1$. Intuitively, this event corresponds to revealing the test-bit b in the ideal execution. This argument crucially relies on the hiding properties that are part of COA security. These hiding properties are used to first show indistinguishability in an augmented security game (Sect. 3.2) which resembles the over all system conditioned on Test keeping the bit b hidden statistically in the ideeal execution. Then it is argued that if Test hides the test bit in

---

[5] To facilitate keeping track of the arguments being made, we describe the corresponding hybrids from Sect. 6. The goal is to show $H_0 \approx H_7$, for hybrids corresponding to real executions with $b = 0$ and $b = 1$ respectively.

[6] This corresponds to $H_0 \approx H_1$ (with $b = 0$) and $H_6 \approx H_7$ (with $b = 1$).

this execution, then the simulation is good, unless the augmented security guarantee can be broken.

The execution of $S^{\ddagger}$ involves assigning "tentative" objects to handles when they are needed to compute objects that are being transferred to the adversary, but they are finalized only they themselves are transferred. The conditions corresponding to the simulator $S^{\ddagger}$ failing are carefully restricted to only those cases which reveal the test-bit. For example, suppose Test transfers a case-packet agent such that it has different messages in the two executions corresponding to $b = 0$ and $b = 1$. Then there is no consistent assignment of that agent to an object that works for both $b = 0$ and $b = 1$. Nevertheless this may still keep b hidden, as long as the corresponding decryption keys are not transferred. So $S^{\ddagger}$ can assign a random case-packet to this agent, provided that a decryption key which can decase the case-packet will be never transferred.

Here, b not being hidden does not yield a contradiction yet.[7]

- The next simulator S^* is computationally unbounded, and helps us move from the ideal world with the extended schema to the ideal world involving only the schema Σ_{case}. The key to this step is existential consistency: S^* will use unbounded computational power to break open objects sent by the adversary and map them to ideal agents. It replaces the non-ideal agents from before with ideal agents. S^* can be thought of as simulating the interface of the extended schema to $S^{\ddagger}$, while itself interacting with the ideal schema. Existential consistency guarantees help ensure that the view of Test and $\mathcal{A}$ remains the same.[8]

- To prove Δ-s-IND-PRE security we need only consider Test $\in \Delta$ such that the bit b remains hidden against a *computationally unbounded* adversary. For such a Test, the above two hybrids are indistinguishable from each other.[9]

Together these steps establish that if b is statistically hidden in the ideal execution, then that it is (computationally) hidden in the real execution. Section 6 and the full version together present the complete argument.

3 COA Security for CASE

A CASE scheme involves four keys: a signing key (denoted as SK, typically), a verification key (VK), a decryption key (DK) and an encryption key (EK). Two key generation processes sample the signing and decryption keys, and each of them can be deterministically transformed into corresponding verification and encryption keys. Analogous to encryption and decryption, the two operations in CASE are termed ***encasing*** and ***decasing***. We refer to the output of encasing as a ***case-packet*** (denoted as CP). Below we present the syntax and the COA security definition of a CASE scheme.

Definition 1 (COA-secure CASE). A COA-secure CASE scheme with efficiently recognizable key-spaces $(\mathcal{SK}, \mathcal{VK}, \mathcal{DK}, \mathcal{EK})$ and message space $\mathcal{M}$ consists of the following efficient (polynomial in κ) algorithms.

---

[7] This corresponds to showing that *if* $H_2 \approx H_5$, *then* $H_1 \approx H_2$ and $H_5 \approx H_6$.
[8] This shows $H_2 \approx H_3$ and $H_4 \approx H_5$.
[9] That is, $H_3 \approx H_4$.

- skGen: takes security parameter as input, outputs a signing key $SK \in \mathcal{SK}$.
- dkGen: takes security parameter as input, outputs a decryption key $DK \in \mathcal{DK}$.
- vkGen: converts $SK \in \mathcal{SK}$ to a verification key $VK \in \mathcal{VK} \cup \{\perp\}$.
- ekGen: converts $DK \in \mathcal{DK}$ to an encryption key $EK \in \mathcal{EK} \cup \{\perp\}$.
- encase: takes $(SK, EK, m) \in \mathcal{SK} \times \mathcal{DK} \times \mathcal{M}$, outputs $CP \in \mathcal{CP} \cup \{\perp\}$.
- decase: takes $(VK, DK, CP) \in \mathcal{VK} \times \mathcal{DK} \times \mathcal{CP}$ and outputs (m, b) where $m \in \mathcal{M} \cup \{\perp\}$ and $b \in \{0, 1\}$.
- acc: takes any string $obj \in \{0,1\}^{poly(\kappa)}$ as input and outputs a token $t \in \{\text{SK}, \text{VK}, \text{DK}, \text{EK}, \text{CP}, \perp\}$.

Of these, vkGen, ekGen, decase and acc are deterministic algorithms. Below we refer to algorithms decase-msg and decase-verify derived from decase as follows:

- decase-msg$(DK, CP) = m$ where $(m, b) = $ decase$(\perp, DK, CP)$
- decase-verify$(VK, DK, CP) = m$ if decase$(VK, DK, CP) = (m, 1)$, and $\perp$ otherwise.

We require the algorithms of a CASE scheme to satisfy the following:

1. **Correctness (of Accept and Accepted Objects)**: $\forall SK \in \mathcal{SK}$, $\forall DK \in \mathcal{DK}$, acc$(SK) = $ SK $\Rightarrow$ acc$($vkGen$(SK)) = $ VK and acc$(DK) = $ DK $\Rightarrow$ acc$($ekGen$(DK)) = $ EK. Further, there exists a negligible function negl s.t. $\forall \kappa$, $\forall SK \in \mathcal{SK}$, $DK \in \mathcal{DK}$, $EK \in \mathcal{EK}$, $m \in \mathcal{M}$, the following probabilities are at most negl(κ):

$$\Pr\left[\text{acc}(\text{skGen}(1^{\kappa})) \neq \text{SK}\right] \qquad \Pr\left[\text{acc}(\text{dkGen}(1^{\kappa})) \neq \text{DK}\right]$$

$$\Pr\left[\text{acc}(SK) = \text{SK} \wedge \text{acc}(EK) = \text{EK} \wedge \text{acc}\big(\text{encase}(SK, EK, m)\big) \neq \text{CP}\right]$$

$$\Pr\Big[\text{acc}(SK) = \text{SK} \wedge \text{acc}(DK) = \text{DK}$$
$$\wedge \ \text{decase-msg}\big(DK, \text{encase}(SK, \text{ekGen}(DK), m)\big) \neq m\Big]$$

$$\Pr\Big[\text{acc}(SK) = \text{SK} \wedge \text{acc}(DK) = \text{DK}$$
$$\wedge \ \text{decase-verify}\big(\text{vkGen}(SK), DK, \text{encase}(SK, \text{ekGen}(DK), m)\big) \neq m\Big]$$

2. **Total Hiding**: For any PPT adversary $\mathcal{A} = (A_0, A_1)$, there exists a negligible function negl such that, for distinguish-sans-DK as in Fig. 1, $\Pr\left[\text{distinguish-sans-DK}(\mathcal{A}, \kappa) = 1\right] \leq \frac{1}{2} + \text{negl}(\kappa)$.

3. **Sender Anonymity**: For any PPT adversary $\mathcal{A} = (A_0, A_1)$, there exists a negligible function negl such that, for distinguish-sans-VK as in Fig. 1:

$$\Pr\left[\text{distinguish-sans-VK}(\mathcal{A}, \kappa) = 1\right] \leq \frac{1}{2} + \text{negl}(\kappa).$$

4. **Strong-Unforgeability**: For any PPT adversary $\mathcal{A}$, there exists a negligible function negl such that, for forge as in Fig. 1, $\Pr\left[\text{forge}(\mathcal{A}, \kappa) = 1\right] \leq \text{negl}(\kappa)$.

5. **Unpredictability**: For all $SK \in \mathcal{SK}, EK \in \mathcal{EK}, CP \in \mathcal{CP}$ ($CP \neq \perp$) and $m \in \mathcal{M}$, there exists a negligible function negl such that $\Pr\left[\text{encase}(SK, EK, m) = CP\right] \leq \text{negl}(\kappa)$.

6. **Existential Consistency**: There exist functions (not required to be computationally efficient) $\mathsf{skId} : \mathcal{VK} \to \mathcal{SK} \cup \{\bot\}$, $\mathsf{vkId} : \mathcal{CP} \to \mathcal{VK} \cup \{\bot\}$, $\mathsf{dkId} : \mathcal{EK} \to \mathcal{DK} \cup \{\bot\}$, $\mathsf{ekId} : \mathcal{CP} \to \mathcal{EK} \cup \{\bot\}$, $\mathsf{msgId} : \mathcal{CP} \to \mathcal{M} \cup \{\bot\}$ such that,

$$\mathsf{vkGen}(SK) = VK \Rightarrow \mathsf{skId}(VK) = SK \qquad \forall VK, SK$$

$$\mathsf{ekGen}(DK) = EK \Rightarrow \mathsf{dkId}(EK) = DK \qquad \forall EK, DK$$

$$\mathsf{decase\text{-}msg}(DK, CP) = m \neq \bot \Rightarrow \mathsf{dkId}(CP) = DK,$$
$$\mathsf{msgId}(CP) = m \qquad \forall DK, CP$$

$$\mathsf{decase\text{-}verify}(VK, DK, CP) = m \neq \bot \Rightarrow \mathsf{vkId}(CP) = VK,$$
$$\mathsf{dkId}(\mathsf{ekId}(CP)) = DK,$$
$$\mathsf{msgId}(CP) = m \qquad \forall VK, DK, CP$$

Total Hiding Experiment distinguish-sans-DK$(\mathcal{A}, \kappa)$ where $\mathcal{A} = (A_0, A_1)$ is a 2-stage adversary

- For each $b \in \{0, 1\}$, sample $DK_b \leftarrow \mathsf{dkGen}(1^\kappa)$ and let $EK_b \leftarrow \mathsf{ekGen}(DK_b)$
- ▷ Let $\mathcal{D}$ be s.t. $\mathcal{D}(b, VK, CP) = \mathsf{decase}(VK, DK_b, CP)$.
- $(\mathsf{st}_{A_0}, SK_0, SK_1, m_0, m_1) \leftarrow A_0^{\mathcal{D}}(EK_0, EK_1)$
- $b^* \leftarrow \{0, 1\}$, $CP^* \leftarrow \mathsf{encase}(SK_{b^*}, EK_{b^*}, m_{b^*})$
- ▷ Let $\mathcal{D}'$ be s.t. $\mathcal{D}'(b, VK, CP) = \bot$ if $CP = CP^*$, and $\mathcal{D}(b, VK, CP)$ otherwise.
- $b' \leftarrow A_1^{\mathcal{D}'}(\mathsf{st}_{A_0}, CP^*)$
- Output 1 iff $b^* = b'$

Sender Anonymity Experiment distinguish-sans-VK$(\mathcal{A}, \kappa)$ where $\mathcal{A} = (A_0, A_1)$ is a 2-stage adversary

- For each $b \in \{0, 1\}$, sample $SK_b \leftarrow \mathsf{skGen}(1^\kappa)$ and let $VK_b \leftarrow \mathsf{vkGen}(SK_b)$
- ▷ Let $\mathcal{E}$ be s.t. $\mathcal{E}(b, EK, m)$ returns $\mathsf{encase}(SK_b, EK, m)$
- ▷ Let $\mathcal{D}$ be s.t. $\mathcal{D}(b, DK, CP) = \mathsf{decase}(VK_b, DK, CP)$
- $(\mathsf{st}_{A_0}, EK, m) \leftarrow A_0^{\mathcal{E}, \mathcal{D}}(\mathsf{st}_{A_0})$
- $b^* \leftarrow \{0, 1\}$, $CP^* \leftarrow \mathsf{encase}(SK_{b^*}, EK, m)$
- ▷ Let $\mathcal{D}'$ be s.t. $\mathcal{D}'(b, DK, CP) = \bot$ if $CP = CP^*$, and $\mathcal{D}(b, DK, CP)$ otherwise.
- $b' \leftarrow A_1^{\mathcal{E}, \mathcal{D}'}(\mathsf{st}_{A_1}, CP^*)$
- Output 1 iff $b^* = b'$

Strong-Unforgeability Experiment forge$(\mathcal{A}, \kappa)$

- Sample $SK \leftarrow \mathsf{skGen}(1^\kappa)$, $VK \leftarrow \mathsf{vkGen}(SK)$
- ▷ Let $\mathcal{E}$ be such that $\mathcal{E}(m, EK)$ returns $\mathsf{encase}(SK, EK, m)$
- $(DK, CP) \leftarrow \mathcal{A}^{\mathcal{E}}(VK)$
- Output 1 iff $\mathsf{decase\text{-}verify}(VK, DK, CP) \neq \bot$ and CP was not response of any query to $\mathcal{E}$.

Fig. 1. Experiments for defining COA security of CASE

Remark 1. *Minor variations of the above definition are also acceptable. For example, one may allow* decase *and* acc *to be randomized and all our results can be extended to this definition too. However, for the sake of convenience, and since our construction allows it, we have required them to be deterministic. Also, one may include an additional* perfect correctness *condition, which our construction meets; but since our results do not rely on this, we leave this out of the definition.*

3.1 Encasing Resistance

We point out an implication of COA security–called "encasing resistance"–that will be useful later. Encasing resistance requires that any PPT adversary who is given access to an honestly generated encryption/decryption key-pair only via oracles for encasing (w.r.t. any signing key) and decasing using those keys, has negligible probability of generating a "new" valid case-packet for these keys (i.e., a case-packet that is different from the ones returned by the encasing oracle queries, and which on feeding to the decasing oracle returns a non-$\perp$ output).

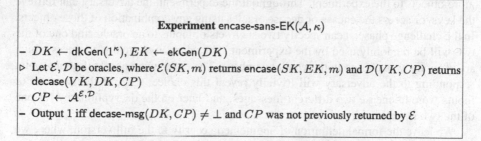

Experiment encase-sans-EK$(\mathcal{A}, \kappa)$

- $DK \leftarrow \mathsf{dkGen}(1^\kappa)$, $EK \leftarrow \mathsf{ekGen}(DK)$
- ▷ Let $\mathcal{E}, \mathcal{D}$ be oracles, where $\mathcal{E}(SK, m)$ returns encase(SK, EK, m) and $\mathcal{D}(VK, CP)$ returns decase(VK, DK, CP)
- $CP \leftarrow \mathcal{A}^{\mathcal{E}, \mathcal{D}}$
- Output 1 iff decase-msg$(DK, CP) \neq \perp$ and CP was not previously returned by $\mathcal{E}$

Fig. 2. Encasing-Resistance Experiment for CASE

Definition 2 (Encasing-Resistance). A CASE scheme satisfies encasing-resistance if, for all PPT adversaries $\mathcal{A}$, there exists a negligible function negl s.t. for encase-sans-EK as in Fig. 2:

$$\Pr\left[\text{encase-sans-EK}(\mathcal{A}, \kappa) = 1\right] \leq \mathsf{negl}(\kappa) \qquad \triangleleft$$

Lemma 1. *Any COA-secure CASE scheme satisfies encasing-resistance.*

Proof sketch 1: The idea behind the proof is that in the encasing-resistance experiment, the adversary has access to the pair (DK, EK) only through an oracle, and thanks to the total hiding property, it cannot distinguish if the keys used in the oracle are replaced with an independent pair (but the experiment's output is still defined w.r.t. original key pair). Now, in this modified experiment, the adversary's goal is to produce a case-packet that can be decased with a freshly sampled decryption key. This in turn is not feasible, because by existential consistency, a case-packet can be decased by at most one decryption key, and the probability that a freshly sampled decryption key equals the one associated with the the case-packet is negligible. The formal argument is given in the full version.   □

We point out that the proof crucially relies on existential consistency as well as the hiding guarantees. Indeed, a CASE scheme modified to include a "dummy" case-packet for which decase-msg yields a non-$\bot$ message for every decryption key continues to satisfy all the other properties; and this dummy case-packet can be used to violate encasing resistance of the modified scheme.

3.2 Augmented Security

It would be convenient for us to capture the consequences of the total hiding and sender anonymity conditions in COA security in an "augmented" hiding experiment. This experiment allows an adversary $\mathcal{A}$ to adaptively choose the kind of hiding property it wants to attack. The experiment maintains n decryption/encryption key pairs and n signing/verification key pairs (where n is specified by $\mathcal{A}$), and also allows $\mathcal{A}$ to send more objects to the experiment. Throughout the experiment, the adversary can retrieve the keys, or access the encase or decase oracles using any combination of these objects. In the challenge phase, it can specify two such sets of inputs to an oracle, and one of the two will be randomly used by the experiment. The adversary's goal is to guess which set of inputs was chosen in the challenge phase. The experiment aborts if at any point responding to the adversary will trivially reveal this choice. (E.g., if the two sets of inputs were to encase two different messages, and later on the decryption key for one of the two is requested.)

We leave the formal definition of augmented security to the full version, where we also show that any COA-secure CASE scheme satisfies this definition.

4   Constructing a COA-Secure CASE scheme

In this section, we instantiate a COA-secure CASE scheme. We first describe the building blocks that will be needed.

4.1 Building Block: COA-Secure QD-PKE

Definition 3: (COA-secure Quasi-Deterministic PKE). A PKE scheme (pkeSKGen, pkePKGen, pkeEnc, pkeDec) is quasi-deterministic and COA-secure if it has the following additional algorithm

– pkeAcc: takes any string $obj \in \{0,1\}^{poly(\kappa)}$ and outputs a token $t \in \{\text{EK}, \text{DK}, \text{CT}, \bot\}$.

Where, pkeAcc is a deterministic algorithm. We require the algorithms to satisfy the following:

1. **Correctness**: $\forall m \in \mathcal{M}, \forall SK \in \mathcal{SK}, \forall EK \in \mathcal{PK}$, the following probabilities are negligible in κ

$$\Pr\left[\mathsf{pkeAcc}(\mathsf{pkeSKGen}(1^\kappa)) \neq \mathrm{DK}\right]$$

$$\Pr\left[\mathsf{pkeAcc}(EK) = \mathrm{EK} \ \wedge \ \mathsf{pkeAcc}(\mathsf{pkeEnc}(EK, m)) \neq \mathrm{CT}\right]$$

$$\Pr\left[\mathsf{pkeAcc}(DK) = \mathrm{DK} \ \wedge \ \mathsf{pkeAcc}(\mathsf{pkePKGen}(DK)) \neq \mathrm{EK}\right]$$

$$\Pr\left[\mathsf{pkeAcc}(DK) = \mathrm{DK} \ \wedge \ \mathsf{pkeDec}\Big(DK, \mathsf{pkeEnc}(\mathsf{pkePKGen}(DK), m)\Big) \neq m\right]$$

2. **Quasi-Deterministic**: There exists an efficient randomized algorithm pkeEnc_1 and an inefficient deterministic algorithm pkeEnc_2 such that $\forall \kappa, \forall x \in \mathcal{M} \ \forall EK \in \mathcal{PK}$, $\forall r \in \{0,1\}^{poly(\kappa)}$, it holds that:

$$\mathsf{pkeEnc}(EK, x; r) = \Big(\mathsf{pkeEnc}_1(EK; r), \ \mathsf{pkeEnc}_2\big(EK, \mathsf{pkeEnc}_1(EK; r), x\big)\Big)$$

3. **Quasi-Deterministic Anonymous IND-CCA security**: For any PPT adversary $\mathcal{A} = (A_0, A_1, A_2)$, there exists a negligible function $\mathsf{negl}(.)$ such that for $\mathsf{pkeQDAnonCCAExp}$ as in Fig. 3:

$$\Pr\left[\mathsf{pkeQDAnonCCAExp}(\mathcal{A}) = 1\right] \leq \frac{1}{2} + \mathsf{negl}(\kappa)$$

QD Anon-CCA Experiment $\mathsf{pkeQDAnonCCAExp}$

Parameters: $\mathcal{A} = (A_0, A_1)$ is a 2-stage adversary and κ is the security parameter.

- for each $b \in \{0,1\}$, sample $(DK_b, EK_b) \leftarrow \mathsf{pkeGen}(1^\kappa)$.
- $b^* \leftarrow \{0,1\}, r \leftarrow \{0,1\}^\kappa, \tau \leftarrow \mathsf{pkeEnc}_1(EK_{b^*}; r)$ using randomness r.
▷ Let $\mathcal{D}$ be s.t. $\mathcal{D}(b, CP) = \mathsf{pkeDec}(DK_b, CP)$
- $(\mathsf{st}_0, m_0, m_1) \leftarrow A_0^{\mathcal{D}}(EK_0, EK_1, \tau)$
- $CP^* \leftarrow \mathsf{pkeEnc}(EK_{b^*}, m_{b^*}; r)$ using randomness r.
▷ Let $\mathcal{D}'$ be s.t. $\mathcal{D}'(b, CP) = \bot$ if $CP = CP^*$ else $\mathsf{pkeDec}(DK_b, CP)$
- $b' \leftarrow A_1^{\mathcal{D}'}(\mathsf{st}_0, CP^*)$
- Output 1 if $b^* = b'$, else output 0.

Fig. 3. Experiment for COA-secure QD-PKE.

4. **Existential Consistency**: There exist *computationally inefficient* deterministic extractor algorithms $\mathsf{pkeSKId} : \mathcal{PK} \rightarrow \mathcal{SK} \cup \{\bot\}$, $\mathsf{pkePKId} : \mathcal{CP} \rightarrow \mathcal{PK} \cup \{\bot\}$,

pkeMsgId : $\mathcal{CP} \to \mathcal{M} \cup \{\bot\}$ such that, $\forall m \in \mathcal{M}, \forall EK \in \mathcal{PK}, \forall CP \in \mathcal{CP}, \forall DK \in \mathcal{SK}$:

$$pkePKGen(DK) = EK \quad\quad \Rightarrow pkeSKId(EK) = DK$$
$$pkeEnc(EK, m) = CP \quad\quad \Rightarrow pkePKId(CP) = EK$$
$$pkeDec(DK, CP) = m \neq \bot \Rightarrow pkeSKId(pkePKId(CP)) = DK$$
$$pkeDec(DK, CP) = m \neq \bot \Rightarrow pkeMsgId(CP) = m \quad\quad \triangleleft$$

$\square$

Following the description in Sect. 2.2, we obtain the following construction of a COA-secure QD-PKE (proven in the full version).

Lemma 2. *Assuming the Decisional Diffie-Hellman assumption (DDH), there exists a COA-secure Quasi-Deterministic PKE scheme.*

4.2 Building Block: Existentially Consistent Anonymous Signature

Definition 4 (Existentially Consistent Anonymous Signature). A signature scheme (sigSKGen, sigVKGen, sigSign, sigVerify) is Existentially Consistent Anonymous Signature if it has the following additional algorithm

– sigAcc: takes any string $obj \in \{0,1\}^{poly(\kappa)}$ and outputs a token $t \in \{\textsc{sk}, \textsc{vk}, \textsc{sig}, \bot\}$.

Where, sigAcc is a deterministic algorithm. We require the algorithms to satisfy the following:

1. **Correctness**: $\forall \kappa$, there exists a negligible function negl(.) such that, $\forall SK \in \mathcal{SK}$, $\forall m \in \mathcal{M}$, the following probabilities are negligible in κ

$$\Pr\left[sigAcc(sigSKGen(1^\kappa)) \neq \textsc{sk}\right]$$
$$\Pr\left[sigAcc(SK) = \textsc{sk} \wedge sigAcc\Big(sigVKGen(SK)\Big) \neq \textsc{vk}\right]$$
$$\Pr\left[sigAcc(SK) = \textsc{sk} \wedge sigAcc\Big(sigSign(SK, m)\Big) \neq \textsc{sig}\right]$$
$$\Pr\left[sigAcc(SK) = \textsc{sk} \wedge sigVerify\Big(sigVKGen(SK), m, sigSign(SK, m)\Big) \neq 1\right]$$

2. **Strong-Unforgeability**: For any PPT adversary $\mathcal{A}$, there exists a negligible function negl(.) such that for SigForgeExp in Fig. 4:

$$\Pr\left[SigForgeExp(\mathcal{A}) = 1\right] \leq negl(\kappa)$$

3. **(Signer) Anonymity**: For any PPT adversary $\mathcal{A} = (A_0, A_1)$, there exists a negligible function negl(.) such that tfor SigAnonExp as in Fig. 4:

$$\Pr\left[SigAnonExp(\mathcal{A}) = 1\right] \leq \frac{1}{2} + negl(\kappa)$$

4. **Existential Consistency**: There exist *computationally inefficient* deterministic extractor algorithms sigVKId : $\Sigma \rightarrow \mathcal{VK} \cup \{\bot\}$, sigSKId : $\mathcal{VK} \rightarrow \mathcal{SK} \cup \{\bot\}$ s.t. $\forall SK \in \mathcal{SK}, \forall VK \in \mathcal{VK}, \forall \sigma \in \Sigma$, the following probabilities are negligible in κ:

$$\text{sigVKGen}(SK) = VK \quad \Rightarrow \text{sigSKId}(VK) = SK$$
$$\text{sigSign}(SK, x) = \sigma \quad \Rightarrow \text{sigSKId}(\text{sigVKId}(\sigma) = SK$$
$$\text{sigVerify}(VK, x, \sigma) = 1 \quad \Rightarrow \text{sigVKId}(\sigma)) = VK \qquad \triangleleft$$

Experiment SigAnonExp

Parameter: $\mathcal{A} = (A_0, A_1)$ is a 2-stage adversary and κ is the security parameter.

– for each $b \in \{0,1\}$, sample $(SK_b, VK_b) \leftarrow \text{sigGen}(1^\kappa)$.
▷ Let $\mathcal{S}$ be s.t. $\mathcal{S}(b', m') = \text{sigSign}(SK_{b'}, m')$
– $(\text{st}_{A_0}, m) \leftarrow A_0^{\mathcal{S}}(1^\kappa)$
– $b^* \leftarrow \{0,1\}, \sigma \leftarrow \text{sigSign}(SK_{b^*}, m),$
– $b^* \leftarrow A_1^{\mathcal{S}}(\text{st}_{A_0}, \sigma)$
– Output 1 iff $b = b^*$.

Fig. 4. Experiment for Existentially Consistent Anonymous Signature.

Following the description in Sect. 2.2, we obtain the following result (proven in the full version).

Lemma 3. *If there exists a signature scheme, a COA-secure QD-PKE scheme and a perfectly binding commitment scheme; then there exists a Existentially Consistent Anonymous Signature scheme.*

Compactness. Without loss of generality, we assume that our signature schemes have fixed length signatures independent of the size of the message (beyond the security parameter). To achieve compactness, we can start with any plain signature scheme and define a new scheme where the signature is actually on a hash of the message computed using a full-domain collision-resistant hash function.

4.3 Main Construction: COA-Secure CASE

We now describe the main construction.

Lemma 4. *If there exists a COA-secure QD-PKE scheme and an Existentially Consistent Anonymous Signature scheme, then there exists a COA-secure CASE scheme.*

Parameter: Let κ be the security parameter.

Let $S = $ (sigGen, sigSign, sigVerify, sigAcc, sigSKId, sigVKId) be a Existentially Consistent Anonymous Signature scheme.

Let $E = $ (pkeGen, pkeEnc$_1$, pkeEnc, pkeDec, pkeAcc, pkeSKId, pkePKId, pkeMsgId) be a COA-secure QD-PKE scheme.

COA-secure CASE Scheme SE:

- skGen(1^κ):
    output $SK \leftarrow$ sigSKGen(1^κ)

- vkGen(SK):
    output $VK \leftarrow$ sigVKGen(SK)

- encase(SK, EK, m):
    $\tau \leftarrow$ pkeEnc$_1$($EK; r$)
    $\sigma \leftarrow$ sigSign($SK, m\|EK\|\tau$)
    $CP \leftarrow$ pkeEnc($EK, m\|\sigma; r$)
    output CP

- acc(obj):
    if $obj \in SK \cup VK$, output
    sigAcc(obj)
    else if $obj \in DK \cup EK \cup CP$, output
    pkeAcc(obj)
    else output $\perp$

- dkGen(1^κ):
    output $DK \leftarrow$ pkeSKGen(1^κ)

- ekGen(DK):
    output $EK \leftarrow$ pkePKGen(DK)

- decase-msg(DK, CP):
    if pkeDec(DK, CP) = $\perp$, output $\perp$
    $m\|\sigma \leftarrow$ pkeDec(DK, CP)
    output m

- decase(VK, DK, CP):
    if pkeDec(DK, CP) = $\perp$, output $\perp$
    $m\|\sigma \leftarrow$ pkeDec(DK, CP)
    $EK \leftarrow$ pkePKGen(DK)
    parse CP as (τ, c)
    output $(m,$ sigVerify($VK, \sigma, m\|EK\|\tau$))

Existential Consistency:

- skId(VK):
    output sigSKId(VK)

- vkId(CP):
    $m\|\sigma \leftarrow$ pkeMsgId(CP)
    output sigVKId(σ)

- msgId(CP):
    $m\|\sigma \leftarrow$ pkeMsgId(CP)
    output m

- dkId(EK):
    output pkeSKId(EK)

- ekId(CP):
    output pkePKId(CP)

Fig. 5. COA secure CASE

Proof: Let E be a COA-secure QD-PKE scheme (Definition 3) and S be a ECAS scheme (Definition 4). We prove that the scheme in Fig. 5 is a COA-secure CASE scheme (Definition 1).

- **Total Hiding:** we prove this via a reduction to the quasi-deterministic anon IND-CCA security of the underlying PKE scheme. Let A be an adversary with advantage α in the distinguish-sans-DK experiment. We build an adversary A^* for the pkeQDAnonCCAExp experiment as follows. It accepts (EK_0, EK_1, τ) from the experiment and forwards (EK_0, EK_1) to $\mathcal{A}$. For any polynomial oracle query of the form (VK', b', CP') from $\mathcal{A}$, it queries the experiment on (b', CP'), receives the decryption $m'||\sigma'$, checks if the signature is valid w.r.t. VK' and returns m' to $\mathcal{A}$. It receives the challenge messages (SK_0, SK_1, m_0, m_1) from $\mathcal{A}$, constructs each m_b^* as $m_b^* = m_b||\sigma_b$, where $\sigma_b = \mathsf{sigSign}(SK_b, m||PK_b||\tau)$. It sends (m_0^*, m_1^*) to the experiment, receives the challenge ciphertext and forwards it to $\mathcal{A}$. Finally, it outputs $\mathcal{A}$'s output. Thus, $\mathcal{A}^*$ has advantage α, which from our assumption that E is a secure quasi-deterministic anon-PKE scheme, must be negligible.

- **Sender Anonymity:** we prove this via a reduction to the anonymity of the underlying signature scheme. Let $\mathcal{A}$ be an adversary with advantage α in the distinguish-sans-VK experiment. We build an adversary $\mathcal{A}^*$ for the SigAnonExp experiment as follows. For any polynomial oracle query of the form (b', EK', m') that it receives from $\mathcal{A}$, it samples randomness r', constructs $\tau' \leftarrow \mathsf{pkeEnc}_1(EK'; r')$, queries the oracle on $(b', m'||EK'||\tau')$, gets back σ' and sends $CP' = \mathsf{pkeEnc}(EK', m'||\sigma'; r')$ to $\mathcal{A}$. When $\mathcal{A}$ outputs the challenge (EK, m), it samples randomness r, constructs $\tau \leftarrow \mathsf{pkeEnc}_1(EK; r)$, sends $m||EK||\tau$ as the challenge message to the experiment, receives σ as the challenge signature, sends $CP = \mathsf{pkeEnc}(EK, m||\sigma; r)$ as the challenge ciphertext to $\mathcal{A}$ and outputs $\mathcal{A}$'s output. Thus, $\mathcal{A}^*$ has advantage α, which from our assumption that S is a COA-secure signature scheme, must be negligible.

- **Strong-Unforgeability:** we prove this via a reduction to the unforgeability of the underlying signature scheme. Let $\mathcal{A}$ be an adversary with advantage α in the forge experiment. We build an adversary $\mathcal{A}^*$ for the SigForgeExp experiment as follows. It receives VK from the experiment and forwards it to $\mathcal{A}$. For any polynomial oracle query of the form (m', EK') that it receives from $\mathcal{A}$, it samples randomness r', constructs $\tau' \leftarrow \mathsf{pkeEnc}_1(EK'; r')$, queries the oracle on $m'||EK'||\tau'$, gets back σ' and sends $CP' = \mathsf{pkeEnc}(EK', m'||\sigma'; r')$ to $\mathcal{A}$. When $\mathcal{A}$ outputs the forgery (DK, CP), it gets $EK \leftarrow \mathsf{ekGen}(DK)$, parses CP as (τ, c), decrypts CP to get $m||\sigma \leftarrow \mathsf{decase\text{-}verify}(VK, DK, CP)$ and outputs $(m||EK||\tau, \sigma)$ as its forgery. Thus, $\mathcal{A}^*$ has advantage α, which from our assumption that S is a COA-secure signature scheme, must be negligible.

- **Unpredictability:** this follows trivially from the Quasi-Deterministic property of the PKE scheme. The PKE ciphertext is of the form (τ, CP'), but τ must have enough entropy so that IND-CCA holds.

- **Correctness and Existential Consistency:** $\forall SK \in \mathcal{SK}, DK \in \mathcal{DK}, m \in \mathcal{M}$, let $VK \leftarrow \mathsf{vkGen}(SK)$, $EK \leftarrow \mathsf{ekGen}(DK)$, $CP \leftarrow \mathsf{encase}(SK, EK, m)$.
  - From the correctness of the underlying primitives, it holds that the objects are accepted with probability $1 - \mathsf{negl}(\kappa)$. Further, $\mathsf{pkeDec}(DK, CP)$ outputs $m||\sigma$ and $\mathsf{sigVerify}(VK, \sigma, m||EK||\tau)$ outputs 1 with probability $1 - \mathsf{negl}(\kappa)$.
  - From the existential consistency of the underlying primitives, it holds that $\mathsf{skId}(VK) = SK$, $\mathsf{dkId}(EK) = DK$. Further, for any $CP \in \mathcal{CP}$ s.t. $\mathsf{acc}(CP) = 1$, it holds that if $\mathsf{decase\text{-}msg}(DK, CP) \neq \bot$, then $\mathsf{ekId}(CP) = EK$. Similarly, if $\mathsf{decase\text{-}verify}(VK, DK, CP) \neq \bot$, it holds that $\mathsf{vkId}(CP) = VK$.

□

4.4 Improving the Efficiency of COA-Secure CASE

We now show how to improve the efficiency of a COA-secure CASE scheme like the one above, by leveraging the efficiency of a CPA-secure SKE and a collision-resistant hash scheme, analogous to hybrid encryption.

Parameter: Let κ be the security parameter.

Let $S = (\text{skeGen}, \text{skeEnc}, \text{skeDec})$ be a CPA-secure symmetric-key encryption scheme.

Let H be a collision-resistant hash function family.

Let case $= (\text{skGen}, \text{vkGen}, \text{dkGen}, \text{ekGen}, \text{encase}, \text{decase})$ be a COA-secure CASE scheme.

COA-secure CASE Scheme case*:

- case*.skGen(1^κ):
    output $SK \leftarrow$ case.skGen(1^κ)

- case*.vkGen(SK):
    output $VK \leftarrow$ case.vkGen(SK)

- case*.encase(SK, EK, m):
    sample $k_1 \leftarrow$ skeGen(1^κ), $k_2 \leftarrow \{0,1\}^\kappa$
    $c_1 \leftarrow$ skeEnc(k_1, m)
    $c_0 \leftarrow$ case.encase($SK, EK, k_1\|k_2\|H(k_2, c_1)$)
    output (c_0, c_1)

- case*.acc(obj):
    output case.acc(obj)

- case*.dkGen(1^κ):
    output $DK \leftarrow$ case.dkGen(1^κ)

- case*.ekGen(DK):
    output $EK \leftarrow$ case.ekGen(DK)

- case*.decase(VK, DK, CP):
    parse CP as (c_0, c_1)
    $(m', b) \leftarrow$ case.decase(VK, DK, c_0)
    parse m' as $k_1\|k_2\|h$
    $m \leftarrow$ skeDec(k_1, c_1)
    If $H(k_2, c_1) = h$, output (m, b); else output $\perp$

Existential Consistency:

- case*.dkId(EK):
    output case.dkId(EK)

- case*.skId(VK):
    output case.skId(VK)

- case*.vkId(CP):
    parse CP as (c_0, c_1)
    output case.vkId(c_0)

- case*.msgId(CP):
    parse CP as (c_0, c_1)
    $k_1\|k_2\|h \leftarrow$ case.msgId(c_0), $m \leftarrow$ skeDec(k_1, c_1)
    output m

- case*.ekId(CP):
    parse CP as (c_0, c_1)
    output case.ekId(c_0)

Fig. 6. Efficient COA secure CASE via hybrid encryption

Lemma 5. *The scheme* case* *in Fig. 6 is a COA-secure CASE scheme (Definition 1), if S is a CPA-secure SKE scheme, H is a CRHF scheme and* case *is a COA-secure CASE scheme.*

Please refer to the full version for the proof.

5   Active Agents Framework

Cryptographic Agents [2] provides a framework that naturally models all cryptographic objects (keys as well as ciphertexts, in our case) as transferable agents, which the users can manipulate only via an idealized interface. But the original framework of [2] does not capture attacks involving maliciously created objects, as only the honest user (Test) is allowed to create objects. Hence in the case of encryption, even CCA security could not be modeled in this framework. Here we present the technical details of the active agents framework which we develop and use. the full version gives a summary of the substantial differences between the new model and the original model of [2]. Note that this framework itself is not specialized for CASE; that is carried out in Sect. 6.

5.1   The Model

Agents and Sessions. *Agents* are interactive Turing machines with tapes for input, output, incoming communication, outgoing communication, randomness and work-space. A *schema* defines the behavior of agents corresponding to a cryptographic functionality. Multiple agents of a schema can interact with one another in a *session* (as detailed in the full version).

Ideal World Model. Formally, a schema Σ is described by an agent; it is a program that will behave differently depending on the contents of its work-tape. (Jumping ahead, the CASE schema Σ_{case} in Fig. 8 has an agent that can behave as an decryption-key, encryption-key, signing-key, verification-key or a case-packet.) The ideal system for a schema Σ consists of two parties Test and User and a fixed third party $\mathcal{B}[\Sigma]$ (for "blackbox"). All three parties are probabilistic polynomial time (PPT) ITMs, have a security parameter κ built-in. Test and User may be non-uniform. Test receives a *test-bit* b as input and User produces an output bit b'.

$\mathcal{B}[\Sigma]$ maintains two lists of handles $<^{\text{Test}}$ and $<^{\text{User}}$, which contain the set of handles belonging to Test and User respectively. Each handle in these lists is mapped to an agent. At the beginning of an execution, both the lists are empty. While Test and User can arbitrarily talk to each other, their interaction with $\mathcal{B}[\Sigma]$ can be summarized as follows:

- **Creating agents.** Test and User can, at any point, request $\mathcal{B}[\Sigma]$ for creating a new agent. More precisely, they can send a command (init, string) to $\mathcal{B}[\Sigma]$, where string is an initial input for the agent of the schema. Then, $\mathcal{B}[\Sigma]$ will instantiate the agent (with an empty work-tape) and run it with string and security parameter as inputs. It then stores (h, config) in the list of the party who sent the command ($<^{\text{Test}}$ or $<^{\text{User}}$) where config is the agent's configuration after the execution and h is a new handle (say, simply, the number of handles stored so far in the list); h is returned to the relevant party (Test or User).
- **Request for Session Execution.** At any point in time, Test or User may request an execution of a session. We describe the process when Test requests a session execution; the process for User is symmetric.

Test can send a command $(\mathrm{run}, (h_1, x_1) \ldots, (h_t, x_t))$, where h_i are handles obtained in the list $<^{\mathsf{Test}}$, and x_i are input strings for the corresponding agents.[10] $\mathcal{B}[\Sigma]$ executes a session with the agents with starting configurations in $<^{\mathsf{Test}}$, corresponding to the specified handles, with their respective inputs, till it terminates. It obtains a collection of outputs $(y_1, \ldots, y_t)$ and updated configurations of agents. It generates new handles $h_1', \ldots, h_t'$ corresponding to the updated configurations, adds them to $<^{\mathsf{Test}}$, and returns $(h_1', \ldots, h_t', y_1, \ldots, y_t)$ to Test. If an agent halts in a session, no new handle h_i' is given out for that agent. After a session, the old handles for the agents are not invalidated; so a party can access a configuration of an agent any number of times, by using the same handle.

- **Transferring agents.** Test can send a command $(\mathsf{transfer}, h)$ to $\mathcal{B}[\Sigma]$ upon which it looks up the entry (h, config) from $<^{\mathsf{Test}}$ (if such an entry exists) and adds an entry (h', config) to $<^{\mathsf{User}}$, where h' is a new handle, and sends the handle h' to User. Symmetrically, User can transfer an agent to Test using the transfer command.

We define the random variable $\mathrm{IDEAL}\langle \mathsf{Test}(b) \mid \Sigma \mid \mathsf{User}\rangle$ to be the output of User in an execution of the above system, when Test gets b as the test-bit. We write $\mathrm{IDEAL}\langle \mathsf{Test} \mid \Sigma \mid \mathsf{User}\rangle$ to denote the output when the test-bit is a uniformly random bit. We also define $\mathrm{TIME}\langle \mathsf{Test} \mid \Sigma \mid \mathsf{User}\rangle$ as the maximum number of steps taken by Test (with a random input), $\mathcal{B}[\Sigma]$ and User in total.

In this work, we use the notion of *statistical* hiding in the ideal world as introduced in [3], rather than the original notion used in [2]. (This still results in a security definition that subsumes the traditional definitions, as they involve tests that are statistically hiding.)

Definition 5 ((Statistical) Ideal world hiding). A Test is *s-hiding w.r.t. a schema Σ* if, for all unbounded users User who make at most a polynomial number of queries,

$$\mathrm{IDEAL}\langle \mathsf{Test}(0) \mid \Sigma \mid \mathsf{User}\rangle \approx \mathrm{IDEAL}\langle \mathsf{Test}(1) \mid \Sigma \mid \mathsf{User}\rangle. \qquad \triangleleft$$

Real World Model. The real world for a schema Σ consists of two parties Test and User that interact with each other arbitrarily, as in the ideal world. However, the third party $\mathcal{B}[\Sigma]$ in the ideal world is replaced by two other parties $\mathcal{I}[\Pi, \mathsf{Repo}_{\mathsf{Test}}]$ and $\mathcal{I}[\Pi, \mathsf{Repo}_{\mathsf{User}}]$ (when User is honest), which run the algorithms specified by a *cryptographic scheme* Π. A cryptographic scheme (or simply scheme) Π is a collection of stateless (possibly randomized) algorithms $\Pi.\mathsf{init}$, $\Pi.\mathsf{run}$ and $\Pi.\mathsf{receive}$, which use a repository Repo to store a mapping from handles to objects. More precisely, the repository is a table with entries of the form (h, obj), where h is a unique handle (say, a non-negative integer) and obj is a cryptographic object (represented, for instance, as a binary string). At the start of an execution, Repo is empty.

If a scheme implementation ($\mathcal{I}[\Pi, \mathsf{Repo}_{\mathsf{Test}}]$ or $\mathcal{I}[\Pi, \mathsf{Repo}_{\mathsf{User}}]$) receives input (init, string), then it runs $\Pi.\mathsf{init}(\mathtt{string})$ to obtain an object obj which is added to Repo and a handle is returned. If it receives the command $(\mathrm{run}, (h_1, x_1), \cdots, (h_t, x_t))$, then

---

[10] If a handle appears more than once among $h_1, \ldots, h_t$, it is interpreted as separate agents with the same configuration (but possibly different inputs). In our use-case of CASE, this scenario is not relevant.

objects $(obj_1, \ldots, obj_t)$ corresponding to $(h_1, \ldots, h_t)$ are retrieved from Repo and $\Pi.\text{run}((obj_1, x_1), \ldots, (obj_t, x_t))$ is evaluated to obtain $((obj'_1, y_1), \ldots, (obj'_t, y_t))$ where obj'_i are new objects and y_i are output strings; the objects are added to Repo, with a new handle for each, and the new handles, along with the outputs, are returned. (If an obj'_i is empty, then no new handle is added; this corresponds to an agent having halted.)

$\mathcal{I}[\Pi, \text{Repo}_{\text{Test}}]$ and $\mathcal{I}[\Pi, \text{Repo}_{\text{User}}]$ do not interact with each other, except when one of them receives a transfer command. If Test sends a command $(\text{transfer}, h)$ to $\mathcal{I}[\Pi, \text{Repo}_{\text{Test}}]$, it looks for an entry (h, obj) in $\text{Repo}_{\text{Test}}$ and sends obj to $\mathcal{I}[\Pi, \text{Repo}_{\text{User}}]$; on receiving obj from $\mathcal{I}[\Pi, \text{Repo}_{\text{Test}}]$, $\mathcal{I}[\Pi, \text{Repo}_{\text{User}}]$ will run $\Pi.\text{receive}(obj)$ which outputs (a possibly modified) object obj' and if $obj' \neq \bot$, $\mathcal{I}[\Pi, \text{Repo}_{\text{User}}]$ will add (h', obj') to $\text{Repo}_{\text{User}}$, where h' is a new handle, and outputs h' to User. The process of User transferring an object to Test is symmetric.

When an object is transferred to $\mathcal{I}[\Pi, \text{Repo}_{\text{User}}]$, the receive algorithm can be used to accept or reject the object. This check is performed only once, rather than each time the object is used: aside from the inefficiency of repeating this operation, note that the check may be probabilistic and an object may pass sometimes and fail at other times. Since this is not captured in the ideal world, an object is tested and received once and for all.

Note that we *do not* allow Test direct access to the cryptographic objects stored in its repository. In particular, it cannot look up the object associated with a handle in $\text{Repo}_{\text{Test}}$. Also observe that if User is corrupt, which we denote by $\mathcal{A}$, it may not run the scheme it is supposed to. It can run any arbitrary algorithm and send any object of its choice directly to $\mathcal{I}[\Pi, \text{Repo}_{\text{Test}}]$.

We define the random variable $\text{REAL}\langle \text{Test}(b) \mid \Pi \mid \mathcal{A} \rangle$ to be the output of $\mathcal{A}$ in an execution of the above system involving Test with test-bit b, $\mathcal{I}[\Pi, \text{Repo}_{\text{User}}]$ and $\mathcal{A}$; as before, we omit b from the notation to indicate a random bit. Also, as before, $\text{TIME}\langle \text{Test} \mid \Pi \mid \mathcal{A} \rangle$ is the maximum number of steps taken by Test (with a random input), $\mathcal{I}[\Pi, \text{Repo}_{\text{User}}]$ and $\mathcal{A}$ in total.

Definition 6. Test is said to be *hiding w.r.t.* Π if $\forall$ PPT party $\mathcal{A}$,

$$\text{REAL}\langle \text{Test}(0) \mid \Pi \mid \mathcal{A} \rangle \approx \text{REAL}\langle \text{Test}(1) \mid \Pi \mid \mathcal{A} \rangle. \qquad \lhd$$

Security Definition. We are ready to present the security definition of a cryptographic agent scheme Π implementing a schema Σ. Below, the *honest real-world user*, corresponding to an ideal-world user User, is defined as the composite program $\mathcal{I}[\Pi, \text{Repo}_{\text{User}}] \circ \text{User}$ as shown in Fig. 7.

Test Families. We write Γ_{ppt} to denote the family of all PPT Test. We also define a test-family Δ as follows: Test $\in \Delta$ iff it behaves as follows: every init and run command it sends to $\mathcal{B}[\Sigma]$ is also reported to User. For transfer commands, it picks two handles h_0, h_1 and sends a message $(\text{transfer}, h_0, h_1)$ to User and sends transfer$[h_b]$ to $\mathcal{B}[\Sigma]$, where b is the test-bit.

Now we define our security notion, $\Delta\text{-}s\text{-IND-PRE}$. Note that below the correctness and efficiency requirements are w.r.t. all PPT Test, but indistinguishability-preservation is only for Test $\in \Delta$.

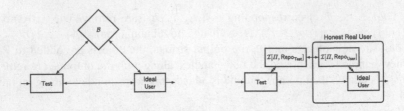

Fig. 7. IDEAL world (left) and REAL world with an honest user.

Definition 7. A cryptographic agent scheme Π is said to be a Δ-s-IND-PRE-*secure scheme* for a schema Σ if the following conditions hold.

– *Correctness.* $\forall$ PPT User, $\forall$ Test $\in \Gamma_{\mathsf{ppt}}$,

$$\text{IDEAL}\langle \text{Test} \mid \Sigma \mid \text{User}\rangle \approx \text{REAL}\langle \text{Test} \mid \Pi \mid \mathcal{I}[\Pi, \text{Repo}_{\mathsf{User}}] \circ \text{User}\rangle.$$

– *Efficiency.* There exists a polynomial poly s.t. $\forall$ PPT User, $\forall$ Test $\in \Gamma_{\mathsf{ppt}}$,
$\text{TIME}\langle \text{Test} \mid \Pi \mid \mathcal{I}[\Pi, \text{Repo}_{\mathsf{User}}] \circ \text{User}\rangle \leq \text{poly}(\text{TIME}\langle \text{Test} \mid \Sigma \mid \text{User}\rangle, \kappa)$.

– *(Statistical) Indistinguishability Preservation.* $\forall$ Test $\in \Delta$,

$$\text{Test is } s\text{-hiding w.r.t. } \Sigma \Rightarrow \text{Test is hiding w.r.t. } \Pi. \qquad \lhd$$

6   CASE in the Active Agents Framework

We now prove Theorem 1, i.e., that a COA secure CASE scheme implies a Δ-s-IND-PRE secure implementation of Σ_{case}. We first define the schema Σ_{case}, and then describe the (syntactic) transformation from any COA secure CASE scheme to Π_{case}.

Proof of Security: An Overview

We show that the Π_{case} in Fig. 9 is a Δ-s-IND-PRE secure implementation of Σ_{case}. Given any Test $\in \Delta$ that is hiding w.r.t. Σ_{case}, we need to argue that for all PPT adversary $\mathcal{A}$,

$$\text{REAL}\langle \text{Test}(0) \mid \Pi \mid \mathcal{A}\rangle \approx \text{REAL}\langle \text{Test}(1) \mid \Pi \mid \mathcal{A}\rangle.$$

The proof uses guarantees such as unforgeability, total hiding and encasing resistance from the underlying COA-Secure CASE scheme case, along with the statistical guarantees of existential consistency, given in terms of computationally unbounded algorithms like case.skld, case.ekld and case.msgld. The argument uses a sequence of hybrid random variables to prove Δ-s-IND-PRE security, H_i for $i = 0$ to 7:

H_0: $\text{REAL}\langle \text{Test}(0) \mid \Pi_{\mathsf{case}} \mid \mathcal{A}\rangle$ H_7: $\text{REAL}\langle \text{Test}(1) \mid \Pi_{\mathsf{case}} \mid \mathcal{A}\rangle$

H_1: $\text{IDEAL}\langle \text{Test}(0) \mid \Sigma_{\Pi_{\mathsf{case}}}^{\ddagger} \mid \mathcal{S}_0^{\dagger} \circ \mathcal{A}\rangle$ H_6: $\text{IDEAL}\langle \text{Test}(1) \mid \Sigma_{\Pi_{\mathsf{case}}}^{\ddagger} \mid \mathcal{S}_1^{\dagger} \circ \mathcal{A}\rangle$

H_2: $\text{IDEAL}\langle \text{Test}(0) \mid \Sigma_{\Pi_{\mathsf{case}}}^{\ddagger} \mid \mathcal{S}^{\ddagger} \circ \mathcal{A}\rangle$ H_5: $\text{IDEAL}\langle \text{Test}(1) \mid \Sigma_{\Pi_{\mathsf{case}}}^{\ddagger} \mid \mathcal{S}^{\ddagger} \circ \mathcal{A}\rangle$

H_3: $\text{IDEAL}\langle \text{Test}(0) \mid \Sigma_{\mathsf{case}} \mid \mathcal{S}^* \circ \mathcal{S}^{\ddagger} \circ \mathcal{A}\rangle$ H_4: $\text{IDEAL}\langle \text{Test}(1) \mid \Sigma_{\mathsf{case}} \mid \mathcal{S}^* \circ \mathcal{S}^{\ddagger} \circ \mathcal{A}\rangle$

CASE: A New Frontier in Public-Key Authenticated Encryption   215

Schema Σ_{case}:

Σ_{case} consists of an agent which behaves as follows.

- **Initialization.** When run with an empty work-tape and input (key-type, κ):
  - if key-type = SK, it samples $sk\text{-}tag \leftarrow \{0,1\}^\kappa$ and records (sk, $sk\text{-}tag$) on its work-tape
  - if key-type = DK, it samples $dk\text{-}tag \leftarrow \{0,1\}^\kappa$ and records (dk, $dk\text{-}tag$) on its work-tape

- **Deriving a verification-key.** When run with (sk, $sk\text{-}tag$) on its work-tape and input vkGen, it updates its work-tape as (vk, $sk\text{-}tag$)

- **Deriving an encryption-key.** When run with (dk, $dk\text{-}tag$) on its work-tape and input ekGen, it updates its work-tape as (ek, $dk\text{-}tag$)

- **Encasing a message.** When two agents are run in a session with input (encase, m):
  - if work-tape of agent has (sk, $sk\text{-}tag$), it receives (ek, $dk\text{-}tag$) from the other agent, samples $cp\text{-}tag \leftarrow \{0,1\}^\kappa$ and updates its work-tape as (cp, m, $sk\text{-}tag$, $dk\text{-}tag$, $cp\text{-}tag$)
  - if work-tape of agent has (ek, $dk\text{-}tag$), it sends it's work-tape contents to the first agent

- **Decasing a message.** When three agents are run in a session with input decase-verify:
  - if work-tape of agent has (dk, $dk\text{-}tag$), it accepts (vk, $sk\text{-}tag^*$) and (cp, m, $sk\text{-}tag$, $dk\text{-}tag^*$, $cp\text{-}tag$) from the other agents. It outputs $\perp$ if $dk\text{-}tag \neq dk\text{-}tag^*$, outputs $(m,1)$ if $sk\text{-}tag = sk\text{-}tag^*$ and $(m,0)$ else.
  - if work-tape of agent has (vk, $sk\text{-}tag$), it sends it to first agent
  - if work-tape of agent has (cp, m, $sk\text{-}tag$, $dk\text{-}tag$, $cp\text{-}tag$), it sends it to first agent.

- **Extracting the message.** When two agents are run in a session with input decase-msg:
  - if work-tape of agent has (dk, $dk\text{-}tag$), it accepts (cp, m, $sk\text{-}tag$, $dk\text{-}tag^*$, $cp\text{-}tag$) from the other agent. It outputs $\perp$ if $dk\text{-}tag \neq dk\text{-}tag^*$, else outputs m.
  - if work-tape of agent has (cp, m, $sk\text{-}tag$, $dk\text{-}tag$, $cp\text{-}tag$), it sends it to first agent.

- **Type of agent:** When run with input type, it behaves as follows:
  - if the work-tape has (sk, $sk\text{-}tag$), output SK.
  - if the work-tape has (vk, $sk\text{-}tag$), output VK.
  - if the work-tape has (dk, $dk\text{-}tag$), output DK.
  - if the work-tape has (ek, $dk\text{-}tag$), output EK.
  - if the work-tape has (cp, m, $sk\text{-}tag$, $dk\text{-}tag$, $cp\text{-}tag$), output CP.

- **Comparing agents:** When two agents are run in a session with input compare, the second agent sends the contents of it's work tape to the first agent. The first agent waits for a message from the other agent in the session and if the message is identical to its own tape's contents, it outputs true, otherwise it outputs false.

Fig. 8. Schema Σ_{case} for CASE.

Hybrids H_0 and H_7 correspond to the output of $\mathcal{A}$ in the real world with test bits $b = 0$ and $b = 1$ respectively. The simulators $\mathcal{S}_b^\dagger$ (for $b \in \{0,1\}$), $\mathcal{S}^\ddagger$ are computationally bounded while $\mathcal{S}^* \circ \mathcal{S}^\ddagger$ is a computationally unbounded simulator due to $\mathcal{S}^*$.

When Test $\in \Delta$ is s-hiding w.r.t. Σ_{case}, we show:

1. Firstly, $H_3 \approx H_4$, even though they involve a computationally unbounded simulator $\mathcal{S}^*$ (by definition of s-hiding of Test).

Scheme Π_{case}:

Let case = (skGen, vkGen, dkGen, ekGen, encase, decase, acc) be a COA-secure CASE scheme.

- **Initialization.** Π_{case}.init (key-type, κ)
  - if key-type = SK: sample $SK \leftarrow$ case.skGen(1^κ) and output SK
  - if key-type = DK: sample $DK \leftarrow$ case.dkGen(1^κ) and output DK

- **Deriving a verification key.** Π_{case}.run (obj,vkGen) outputs (case.vkGen(obj), $\perp$).

- **Deriving an encryption key.** Π_{case}.run (obj,ekGen) outputs (case.ekGen(obj), $\perp$).

- **Encasing a message.** Π_{case}.run ((obj_{sk},(encase,m)),(obj_{pk},(encase,m))) outputs (((case.encase(obj_{sk}, obj_{pk}, m), $\perp$), ($\perp$, $\perp$)).

- **Decasing a message.** Π_{case}.run ((obj_{dk},decase-verify),(obj_{vk},decase-verify), (obj,decase-verify)) outputs (($\perp$, case.decase(obj_{dk}, obj_{vk}, obj)), ($\perp$, $\perp$), ($\perp$, $\perp$)).

- **Extracting a message.** Π_{case}.run ((obj_{dk},decase-msg), (obj,decase-msg)) outputs (($\perp$, case.decase-msg(obj_{dk}, obj)), ($\perp$, $\perp$), ($\perp$, $\perp$)).

- **Type of agent.** Π_{case}.run (obj, type) outputs ($\perp$, case.acc(obj)).

- **Comparing agents:** Π_{case}.run ((obj_1,compare),(obj_2,compare)) outputs (($\perp$, true), ($\perp$, $\perp$)) if $obj_1 = obj_2$ and (($\perp$, false), ($\perp$, $\perp$)) otherwise.

- **Receiving agents:** Π_{case}.receive (obj) outputs obj if case.acc(obj) $\neq \perp$ else outputs $\perp$.

Fig. 9. Schema Π_{case} for CASE.

2. We rely on the existential consistency of the underlying signature scheme to show that $H_2 \approx H_3$ and (symmetrically) $H_4 \approx H_5$.
3. We use the augmented security guarantees of the underlying CASE scheme to establish that $H_1 \approx H_2$ and (symmetrically) $H_5 \approx H_6$.
4. Finally, we argue that $H_0 \approx H_1$ and $H_6 \approx H_7$. This follows from the construction of $\mathcal{S}_0^\dagger$ and $\mathcal{S}_1^\dagger$, conditioned on some "bad events" not occurring. We prove that these bad events occur with negligible probability using the guarantees - strong-unforgeability, total hiding, sender anonymity, unpredictability and encasing resistance from the underlying COA-Secure CASE scheme case (see Lemma ??) and statistical guarantees of sampling from a uniform distribution (sampling of tags in Σ_{case} and $\Sigma_{\Pi_{\text{case}}}^\ddagger$).

Together, these steps show that any Test $\in \Delta$ that is s-hiding w.r.t. Σ_{case} is also hiding w.r.t. Σ_{case}. Please refer to the full version for the full proof.

References

1. Abdalla, M., Bellare, M., Neven, G.: Robust encryption. In: Micciancio, D., (ed.) TCC (2010)
2. Agrawal, S., Agrawal, S., Prabhakaran, M.: Cryptographic agents: towards a unified theory of computing on encrypted data. In: Oswald, E., Fischlin, M. (eds.) EUROCRYPT 2015. LNCS, vol. 9057, pp. 501–531. Springer, Heidelberg (2015). https://doi.org/10.1007/978-3-662-46803-6_17

3. Agrawal, S., Prabhakaran, M., Yu, C.-H.: Virtual grey-boxes beyond obfuscation: a statistical security notion for cryptographic agents. In: TCC 2016-B (2016)
4. Alwen, J., Blanchet, B., Hauck, E., Kiltz, E., Lipp, B., Riepel, D.: Analysing the HPKE standard. In: Canteaut, A., Standaert, F.-X. (eds.) EUROCRYPT 2021. LNCS, vol. 12696, pp. 87–116. Springer, Cham (2021). https://doi.org/10.1007/978-3-030-77870-5_4
5. An, J.H., Dodis, Y., Rabin, T.: On the security of joint signature and encryption. In: Knudsen, L.R. (ed.) EUROCRYPT 2002. LNCS, vol. 2332, pp. 83–107. Springer, Heidelberg (2002). https://doi.org/10.1007/3-540-46035-7_6
6. An, J.H., Dodis, Y., Rabin, T.: On the security of joint signature and encryption. In: Knudsen, L.R. (ed.) EUROCRYPT 2002. LNCS, vol. 2332, pp. 83–107. Springer, Heidelberg (2002). https://doi.org/10.1007/3-540-46035-7_6
7. Badertscher, C., Banfi, F., Maurer, U.: A constructive perspective on signcryption security. In: Catalano, D., De Prisco, R. (eds.) SCN 2018. LNCS, vol. 11035, pp. 102–120. Springer, Cham (2018). https://doi.org/10.1007/978-3-319-98113-0_6
8. Baek, J., Steinfeld, R., Zheng, Y.: Formal proofs for the security of signcryption. In: Naccache, D., Paillier, P. (eds.) PKC 2002. LNCS, vol. 2274, pp. 80–98. Springer, Heidelberg (2002). https://doi.org/10.1007/3-540-45664-3_6
9. Barbosa, M., Farshim, P.: Certificateless signcryption. In: Proceedings of the 2008 ACM Symposium on Information, Computer and Communications Security, pp. 369–372 (2008)
10. Bellare, M., Hofheinz, D., Kiltz, E.: Subtleties in the definition of IND-CCA: when and how should challenge decryption be disallowed? J. Cryptol. **28**(1), 29–48 (2015). https://doi.org/10.1007/s00145-013-9167-4
11. Bellare, M., Stepanovs, I.: Security under message-derived keys: Signcryption in iMessage. In: Canteaut, A., Ishai, Y. (eds.) EUROCRYPT 2020. LNCS, vol. 12107, pp. 507–537. Springer, Cham (2020). https://doi.org/10.1007/978-3-030-45727-3_17
12. Bellare, M., Boldyreva, A., Desai, A., Pointcheval, D.: Key-privacy in public-key encryption. In: Boyd, C. (ed.) ASIACRYPT 2001. LNCS, vol. 2248, pp. 566–582. Springer, Heidelberg (2001). https://doi.org/10.1007/3-540-45682-1_33
13. Bjørstad, T.E., Dent, A.W.: Building better signcryption schemes with Tag-KEMs. In: Yung, M., Dodis, Y., Kiayias, A., Malkin, T. (eds.) PKC 2006. LNCS, vol. 3958, pp. 491–507. Springer, Heidelberg (2006). https://doi.org/10.1007/11745853_32
14. Boyen, X.: Multipurpose identity-based signcryption. In: Boneh, D. (ed.) CRYPTO 2003. LNCS, vol. 2729, pp. 383–399. Springer, Heidelberg (2003). https://doi.org/10.1007/978-3-540-45146-4_23
15. Canetti, R.: Universally composable security: A new paradigm for cryptographic protocols. In: Proceedings of the 42nd IEEE Symposium on Foundations of Computer Science, FOCS 2001 (2001)
16. Cramer, R., Shoup, V.: A practical public key cryptosystem provably secure against adaptive chosen ciphertext attack. In: Krawczyk, H. (ed.) CRYPTO 1998. LNCS, vol. 1462, pp. 13–25. Springer, Heidelberg (1998). https://doi.org/10.1007/BFb0055717
17. Datta, P., Dutta, R., Mukhopadhyay, S.: Compact attribute-based encryption and signcryption for general circuits from multilinear maps. In: Biryukov, A., Goyal, V. (eds.) INDOCRYPT 2015. LNCS, vol. 9462, pp. 3–24. Springer, Cham (2015). https://doi.org/10.1007/978-3-319-26617-6_1
18. Datta, P., Dutta, R., Mukhopadhyay, S.: Functional signcryption: notion, construction, and applications. In: Au, M.-H., Miyaji, A. (eds.) ProvSec 2015. LNCS, vol. 9451, pp. 268–288. Springer, Cham (2015). https://doi.org/10.1007/978-3-319-26059-4_15
19. Dent, A.W.: Hybrid signcryption schemes with insider security. In: Boyd, C., González Nieto, J.M. (eds.) ACISP 2005. LNCS, vol. 3574, pp. 253–266. Springer, Heidelberg (2005). https://doi.org/10.1007/11506157_22

20. Dolev, D., Dwork, C., Naor, M.: Nonmalleable cryptography. SICOMP **30**(2), 391–437 (2000)

21. Farshim, P., Libert, B., Paterson, K.G., Quaglia, E.A.: Robust encryption, revisited. In: Kurosawa, K., Hanaoka, G., (eds.) PKC (2013)

22. Gagné, M., Narayan, S., Safavi-Naini, R.: Threshold attribute-based signcryption. In: Garay, J.A., De Prisco, R. (eds.) SCN 2010. LNCS, vol. 6280, pp. 154–171. Springer, Heidelberg (2010). https://doi.org/10.1007/978-3-642-15317-4_11

23. Gjøsteen, K., Kråkmo, L.: Universally Composable Signcryption. In: Lopez, J., Samarati, P., Ferrer, J.L. (eds.) EuroPKI 2007. LNCS, vol. 4582, pp. 346–353. Springer, Heidelberg (2007). https://doi.org/10.1007/978-3-540-73408-6_26

24. Goldwasser, S., Micali, S.: Probabilistic encryption. JCSS **28**(2), 270–299 (1984)

25. Libert, B., Quisquater, J.-J.: A new identity based signcryption scheme from pairings. In: Proceedings 2003 IEEE Information Theory Workshop (Cat. No. 03EX674), pp. 155–158. IEEE (2003)

26. Libert, B., Quisquater, J.-J.: Efficient signcryption with key privacy from gap Diffie-Hellman groups. In: Bao, F., Deng, R., Zhou, J. (eds.) PKC 2004. LNCS, vol. 2947, pp. 187–200. Springer, Heidelberg (2004). https://doi.org/10.1007/978-3-540-24632-9_14

27. Liu, J.K., Baek, J., Zhou, J.: Online/offline identity-based signcryption revisited. In: Lai, X., Yung, M., Lin, D. (eds.) Inscrypt 2010. LNCS, vol. 6584, pp. 36–51. Springer, Heidelberg (2011). https://doi.org/10.1007/978-3-642-21518-6_3

28. Malone-Lee, J.: Identity-based signcryption. Cryptology ePrint Archive (2002)

29. Maurer, U.: Constructive cryptography - a new paradigm for security definitions and proofs. In: Theory of Security and Applications - Joint Workshop, TOSCA 2011, pp. 33–56 (2011). https://doi.org/10.1007/978-3-642-27375-9

30. Maurer, U., Portmann, C., Rito, G.: Multi-designated receiver signed public key encryption. In: Dunkelman, O., Dziembowski, S. (eds.) Advances in Cryptology. EUROCRYPT 2022. LNCS, vol. 13276, pp. 644–673. Springer, Cham (2022). https://doi.org/10.1007/978-3-031-07085-3_22

31. Mohassel, P.: A closer look at anonymity and robustness in encryption schemes. In: Abe, M. (ed.) ASIACRYPT 2010. LNCS, vol. 6477, pp. 501–518. Springer, Heidelberg (2010). https://doi.org/10.1007/978-3-642-17373-8_29

32. Naor, M., Yung, M.: Public-key cryptosystems provably secure against chosen ciphertext attacks. In: STOC, pp. 427–437 (1990)

33. Nielsen, J.B.: Separating random oracle proofs from complexity theoretic proofs: the non-committing encryption case. In: Yung, M. (ed.) CRYPTO 2002. LNCS, vol. 2442, pp. 111–126. Springer, Heidelberg (2002). https://doi.org/10.1007/3-540-45708-9_8

34. Paterson, K.G., Schuldt, J.C.N., Stam, M., Thomson, S.: On the joint security of encryption and signature, revisited. In: Lee, D.H., Wang, X. (eds.) ASIACRYPT 2011. LNCS, vol. 7073, pp. 161–178. Springer, Heidelberg (2011). https://doi.org/10.1007/978-3-642-25385-0_9

35. Rackoff, C., Simon, D.R.: Non-interactive zero-knowledge proof of knowledge and chosen ciphertext attack. In: Feigenbaum, J. (ed.) CRYPTO 1991. LNCS, vol. 576, pp. 433–444. Springer, Heidelberg (1992). https://doi.org/10.1007/3-540-46766-1_35

36. Selvi, S.S.D., Sree Vivek, S., Pandu Rangan, C.: Identity based public verifiable signcryption scheme. In: Heng, S.-H., Kurosawa, K. (eds.) ProvSec 2010. LNCS, vol. 6402, pp. 244–260. Springer, Heidelberg (2010). https://doi.org/10.1007/978-3-642-16280-0_17

37. Selvi, S.S.D., Vivek, S.S., Vinayagamurthy, D., Rangan, C.P.: ID based signcryption scheme in standard model. In: Takagi, T., Wang, G., Qin, Z., Jiang, S., Yu, Y. (eds.) ProvSec 2012. LNCS, vol. 7496, pp. 35–52. Springer, Heidelberg (2012). https://doi.org/10.1007/978-3-642-33272-2_4

38. Steinfeld, R., Zheng, Y.: A signcryption scheme based on integer factorization. ISW **1975**, 308–322 (2000)

39. Wang, Yang, Manulis, Mark, Au, Man Ho, Susilo, Willy: Relations among privacy notions for signcryption and key invisible "Sign-then-Encrypt". In: Boyd, Colin, Simpson, Leonie (eds.) ACISP 2013. LNCS, vol. 7959, pp. 187–202. Springer, Heidelberg (2013). https://doi.org/10.1007/978-3-642-39059-3_13

40. Yung, M., Dent, A., Zheng, Y.: Practical Signcryption. Springer Science & Business Media, Heidelberg (2010). https://doi.org/10.1007/978-3-540-89411-7

41. Zheng, Y.: Digital signcryption or how to achieve cost (signature & encryption) cost (signature) + cost(encryption). In: Kaliski, B.S. (eds.) Advances in Cryptology–CRYPTO 1997. LNCS, vol. 1294, pp. 165–179. Springer, Heidelberg (1997). https://doi.org/10.1007/BFb0052234

42. Zheng, Y., Imai, H.: How to construct efficient signcryption schemes on elliptic curves. Inf. Process. Lett. **68**(5), 227–233 (1998)

Revisiting Updatable Encryption: Controlled Forward Security, Constructions and a Puncturable Perspective

Daniel Slamanig[iD] and Christoph Striecks[✉][iD]

AIT Austrian Institute of Technology, Vienna, Austria
{daniel.slamanig,christoph.striecks}@ait.ac.at

Abstract. Updatable encryption (UE) allows a third party to periodically rotate encryption keys from one epoch to another without the need to download, decrypt, re-encrypt and upload already encrypted data by a client. Updating those outsourced ciphertexts is carried out via the use of so-called update tokens which in turn are generated during key rotation and can be sent (publicly) to the third party. The arguably most efficient variant of UE is *ciphertext-independent* UE as the key rotation does not depend on the outsourced ciphertexts which makes it particularly interesting in scenarios where access to (information of the) ciphertexts is not possible during key rotation.

Available security notions for UE cannot guarantee any form of *forward security* (i.e., old ciphertexts are in danger after key leakage). Counter-intuitively, forward security would violate correctness, as ciphertexts should be updatable ad-infinitum given the update token. In this work, we investigate if we can have at least some form of "controlled" forward security to mitigate the following shortcoming: an adversary would record available information (i.e., some ciphertexts, all update tokens) and simply would wait for a *single* key leakage to decrypt all data ever encrypted. Our threefold contribution is as follows:

a) First, we introduce an epoch-based UE CPA security notion to allow fine-grained updatability. It covers the concept of *expiry epochs*, i.e., ciphertexts can lose the ability of being updatable via a token after a certain epoch has passed. This captures the above mentioned shortcoming as the encrypting party can decide how long a ciphertext can be updatable (and, hence, decryptable).

b) Second, we introduce a novel approach of constructing UE which significantly departs from previous ones and in particular views UE from the perspective of puncturable encryption (Green and Miers, S&P'15). We define *tag-inverse* puncturable encryption as a new variant that generalizes UE and may be of independent interest.

c) Lastly, we present and prove secure the first UE scheme with the aforementioned properties. It is constructed via tag-inverse puncturable encryption and instantiated from standard assumptions. As it turned out, constructing such puncturing schemes is not straightforward and we require adapted proof techniques. Surprisingly, as a special case, this yields the first backwards-leak UE scheme with

G. Rothblum and H. Wee (Eds.): TCC 2023, LNCS 14370, pp. 220–250, 2023.
https://doi.org/10.1007/978-3-031-48618-0_8

sub-linear ciphertexts from standard assumptions (an open problem posted in two recent works by Jiang Galteland and Pan & Miao et al., PKC'23).

Keywords: Updatable Encryption · Puncturable Encryption · Dual-System Groups

1   Introduction

When outsourcing the storage of data, the primary measure to protect its confidentiality is encryption. However, a compromise of the respective encryption key(s) will potentially expose the entire data to unauthorized parties and may cause severe damage. Consequently, it is widely considered a good practice to periodically rotate encryption keys. Major providers of cloud-storage services such as Google[1], Microsoft[2] or Amazon[3] recommend this practice and sometimes it is even mandated by regulations [1,2]. This raises the immediate question of how to efficiently update already outsourced encrypted data to new keys. An obvious solution for key rotation is to download the data, decrypt it locally under the old key, re-encrypt it under a new key and upload it again. Unfortunately, this imposes a significant overhead and soon becomes impractical.

UPDATABLE ENCRYPTION. At CRYPTO 2013, Boneh, Lewi, Montgomery, and Raghunathan [3] proposed the concept of updatable encryption (UE). UE is a symmetric encryption primitive that addresses the above problem by allowing to update ciphertexts to new keys without the requirement for decryption by means of a so-called update token. UE schemes can be *ciphertext-dependent* [3–6] where the key rotation depends on the specific ciphertext to be updated and, thus, to compute the update token, a part of every ciphertext needs to be downloaded. Or, and from an efficiency point more desirable, quite a number of recent works deal with UE schemes that are *ciphertext-independent* [7–13] such that the key rotation is independent of any information of the ciphertexts in the system.

Particularly, we strive for scenarios where the key-rotating party may not have access to ciphertexts directly.[4] Hence, to be as generic as possible, in the remainder of this work, we focus on UE schemes with ciphertext-independent updates and will simply call them UE schemes. Such a UE scheme consists of the usual algorithms (Gen, Enc, Dec) for key generation, encryption and decryption. Time is discretized in so-called epochs and Gen produces an initial secret key

---

[1] https://cloud.google.com/kms/docs/keyrotation.

[2] https://docs.microsoft.com/en-us/azure/storage/blobs/security-recommendations.

[3] https://docs.aws.amazon.com/kms/latest/developerguide/rotate-keys.html.

[4] One can think of a user that holds encrypted sensitive data with a current key from some key management system and gets offline for some time before the ciphertexts should be decrypted again. However, during the user's offline time, key rotations might be executed. This issue was also mentioned during a talk at RWC 2023 on Google's crypto agility concerning key rotation [14].

K_1 (for epoch 1). Additionally, there is an algorithm RotKey which takes a key K_e and outputs a next-epoch key K_{e+1} along with a so-called update token Δ_{e+1}. This update token can be used by a (semi-trusted) third party to update ciphertexts under key K_e for epoch e to ciphertexts for epoch $e + 1$ under key K_{e+1} via an algorithm Upd.

MOTIVATING STRONGER GUARANTEES. When looking at state-of-the-art UE security models[5] [11–13], it can be observed that they do not capture the following shortcoming. Namely, an adversary would record available information (i.e., ciphertexts $(C_e)_e$, all update tokens $(\Delta_{e+1})_e$) in the lifetime of the system and simply would wait for a *single* key leakage $K_{e'}$ in epoch e' with $e' > e$. Such single key leakage allows to completely break confidentiality of all ciphertexts captured before.

While such a behavior is demanded by the correctness of current UE definitions (i.e., ciphertexts should always be updatable by a token to the current epoch and decryptable), it is a natural question if such a coarse-grained approach is necessary. Indeed, if we want to mitigate such type of shortcoming, we must introduce a more fine-grained adjustment of the updatability of ciphertexts. However, since we do not want to allow access to any (information of the) ciphertexts during key rotation, the token cannot carry the information needed which ciphertext should be updated and which not. Hence, the only possibility we see is via the encryption phase where information to limit the updatability can be embedded.

While post-compromise security for UE (i.e., leaking the current key does not endanger new ciphertexts) is already well understood and constructions in the currently strongest security model are available [10–13]. Unfortunately, even having strong guarantees such as the ones provided by Nishimaki [11], the orthogonal security property of *forward security* (i.e., leaking the current key does not endanger old ciphertexts) cannot be met by any of the known UE models and constructions.

EXTENDED UE SECURITY WITH EXPIRY EPOCHS. As an important security feature, forward security was already considered in cryptographic areas such as interactive key-exchange protocols (e.g., TLS 1.3, QUIC, hybrid KE, or ratcheting) [17–21], public-key encryption [22,23], digital signatures [24,25], search on encrypted data [26], mobile Cloud backups [27], proxy cryptography [28], new approaches to Tor [29], and distributed key management [30], among others.

We believe that forward security yields an important feature for UE in practice as well and should be inherently considered in full in the UE regime.[6] Google's key management system for instance sets the maximum age for key-

---

[5] Our focus is on the established game-based security models. However, we want to note that recent works also study UE in composable frameworks and in particular the framework of constructive cryptography [15,16].

[6] Prior work offers only a very weak form of forward security by restricting access to tokens artificially.

wrapping ciphertexts to 90 days[7], which shows that ciphertexts *should not* be made available forever in real-world systems to mitigate the risk after key leakages. While forward security can be achieved in *ciphertext-dependent* UE in a fine-grained way (as access to parts of the ciphertexts is allowed during key rotation), we want to stress that the situation for ciphertext-independent UE is precarious as the key rotation does not have access to any ciphertext information.

As we show in this work, restricting the update capabilities during the encryption phase yields fine-grained updatability. In particular, we introduce the concept of expiry epochs such that for every ciphertext, one can decide during encryption time how long updates should yield decryptable ciphertexts, i.e., encryption in epoch e is performed as $C_{e,e_{exp}} \leftarrow \mathsf{Enc}(K_e, M, e_{exp})$ and when epoch e_{exp} is reached, a ciphertext cannot longer be updated into a decryptable ciphertext. Note that an update token should still work for all ciphertexts that have an expiry epoch in the future. Also, by virtually never letting ciphertexts expire, i.e., using $e_{exp} = 2^\lambda$ for all encryptions with security-parameter values $\lambda \in \mathbb{N}$, we are essentially back in the currently strongest models [11–13].

This conceptually simple modification has an interesting effect. Namely, to meet our proposed UE security notion, we at least require the UE scheme to solely allow ciphertext updates via the token in the forward direction. So far, such UE schemes are only known to exist by relying on indistinguishability obfuscation [11]. Our notion even requires more and is particularly not implied by [11] which makes the task of constructing such a UE scheme non-trivial (there exists no such UE scheme so far). Moreover, since UE is inspired mainly by practice, we want constructions from standard assumptions and where key, ciphertext and token sizes are as compact as possible, but certainly sub-linear in the maximum number of possible epochs. While compactness can be achieved in weaker models or from non-standard assumptions [9–11], this important feature turned out to be non-trivial in our model. Notably, the strongest UE schemes from standard assumptions [12,13] have linear-size ciphertexts and constructing schemes with sub-linear ciphertext expansion was posted as a significant open problem in the aforementioned works.

UE FROM A PUNCTURABLE PERSPECTIVE. We offer a novel view of UE from the perspective of Puncturable Encryption (PE). We recall that PE, introduced by Green and Miers in [31], is a tag-based public-key (or secret-key [32–34]) encryption primitive with an additional puncturing algorithm that takes a secret key and a tag t as input, and produces an updated (punctured) secret key. This key is able to decrypt all ciphertexts *except* those tagged with t and (updated) secret keys can be iteratively punctured on distinct tags. PE is a versatile primitive that has already found numerous applications and in particular where forward security is required [26,28,30,31,35–39].

In UE, rotating keys from one epoch to the next is abstractly reminiscent of puncturing when viewing tags as epochs. Loosely speaking, puncturing a key on an epoch e would make all ciphertexts in epoch e inaccessible (if all ciphertexts

---

[7] https://cloud.google.com/docs/security/key-management-deep-dive/resources/google-cloud-kms-deep-dive.pdf, Sec. 4.2.

are "tagged" on e). However, this would not yield a useful UE scheme and one needs a mechanism to transform ciphertexts to the next epoch $e + 1$.

From a forward-security point of view, we want that for some ciphertexts, the punctured key should not work while for some other ciphertexts, the punctured key should indeed work. Interestingly, we can make the puncturing more fine-grained by tagging ciphertexts not only on the current epoch e but allow also each ciphertext to be associated with a unique tag.

Such a view has an interesting effect. Namely, the crucial point is that puncturing would take the current epoch key as input, but also tags for ciphertexts for which the key should *not* be punctured. Notably, see that such a feature partly *inverts* the view of plain PE. The output of such a puncturing algorithm would be the punctured key (as in plain PE), but also some information which ciphertext should be excluded from puncturing (see that we do not want to allow access to any ciphertext during puncturing).

To transport such information, the concept of update tokens for ciphertexts must be introduced. Consequently, via such tokens, only ciphertexts that are not intended to be punctured in the key or are not expired[8] yet will be decryptable after key puncturing while for all other ciphertexts, the key will be punctured and, hence, decryption will fail. Indeed, such a puncturing view abstractly yields a UE scheme with "controlled" forward-security guarantees.

1.1 Our Contribution

Briefly summarized, our contribution is as follows:

a) First, we simplify and extend the state-of-the-art UE chosen-plaintext security models [11–13] to capture the guarantees provided by UE schemes that restrict the function of update tokens to ciphertext updates in the forward direction only. Importantly, we introduce *expiry epochs* as a fine-grained updatability feature. By letting ciphertexts expire, we can mitigate the "record now, leak later" attack discussed above. Moreover, we show that our notion implies the most recent chosen-plaintext UE notion due to [11,12].
b) Second, we introduce a novel primitive dubbed Tag-Inverse Puncturable Encryption (TIPE) which we believe provides an easier intuition towards UE with "controlled" forward-security guarantees. We prove that the TIPE notion implies our UE notion. In particular, we believe that the tag-inverse puncturing in TIPE will further increase the applicability of the already very useful concept of puncturable encryption [31] and might be of independent interest.
c) Lastly, we construct a TIPE scheme that is secure in our model and thus yields the first UE scheme with such strong properties. Moreover, its security is based on the standard d-Lin assumption (where for $d = 1$ we get SXDH) in prime-order bilinear groups using the well-known dual-system paradigm [40–43]. Indeed, to overcome the hurdles towards TIPE with such strong properties, we require novel construction and adapted proof techniques. Noteworthy,

---

[8] We introduce expiry epoch analogously to our UE model.

our UE scheme enjoys sub-linear key and ciphertext sizes (yielding the first backward-leak UE scheme with such properties as a special case and answering an open problem from [12,13] in the affirmative).

MODELLING KEY SECURITY FEATURES WITH EXPIRY EPOCHS. Post-compromise security (PCS) is an essential security guarantee in UE and the currently strongest schemes under standard assumptions are known to achieve it [11–13]. PCS loosely speaking means: once an old key leaks, future ciphertexts are not in danger even in the presence of tokens. This is due to the fact that tokens cannot be used to update keys in the forward direction as well for updating ciphertexts in the backward direction. We achieve PCS as we are building on the strongest prior (game-based) chosen-plaintext-secure model.

Moreover, the introduction of expiry epochs allows us to achieve forward security (FS) when keys are leaked beyond that expiry epoch of a ciphertext—where by FS we mean, again loosely speaking: once a key leaks, expired ciphertexts are not in danger even in presence of tokens. Recall that by correctness of UE schemes *without* expiry epochs, such strong form of FS *cannot* be met and is indeed not foreseen in any prior model (i.e., once a key leaks, old ciphertexts are immediately in danger when access to all tokens is granted).

In contrast to prior models, we particularly consider the attack that an adversary can use a token Δ_e to update a key K_e to K_{e-1} in the backward direction (i.e., yielding a key that is consistent with epoch-$(e-1)$ ciphertexts and which would break FS). Indeed, the currently strongest UE schemes [11–13] allow for such an attack. In contrast, in our model, we aim for mitigating such a leakage. Say, we have a ciphertext that expires in epoch e^*. The token in the expiry epoch Δ_{e^*+1} should not be of help to update a key K_{e^*+1} to an expiry-epoch key K_{e^*} in the backward direction and we explicitly provide the adversary with capabilities to query such a token.

Noteworthy, when setting the expiry epochs of each ciphertext to 2^λ (for security parameter λ), we achieve the same security guarantees as [11–13] which we formally show. Moreover, we can even show that our notion implies a simple and natural "ciphertext indistinguishability" notion where challenge ciphertexts with different expiry epochs are indistinguishable in the same challenge epoch.

TAG-INVERSE PUNCTURABLE ENCRYPTION AS AN ABSTRACTION OF UE. In a nutshell, TIPE that can be viewed ·as a symmetric PE scheme (Gen, KPunc, Enc, Dec) with an additional algorithm ExPunc to control which ciphertexts are excluded for key puncturing. Such a scheme is associated to a polynomial sized set of epochs, i.e., $(1, \ldots, n)$, as well as an unbounded ciphertext-tag space $\mathcal{T}$. KPunc sequentially punctures keys on epochs, i.e., removes the ability to decrypt ciphertexts tagged under them step by step. In addition, KPunc can take a set of tags $\mathcal{S} \subseteq \mathcal{T}$ (or a special "for-all" tag $\forall$) and outputs an update token, which can then be used to exclude ciphertexts carrying tags in $\mathcal{S}$ from puncturing (in case of $\forall$, all ciphertext can be excluded). In TIPE, ciphertexts are not only computed w.r.t. a tag $t \in \mathcal{T}$, but additionally take an "expiry-tag" $e_{\exp} \in [n]$. If epoch $e_{\exp}$ is reached, then for ciphertexts carrying such a tag, the key is implicitly punctured and such a ciphertext cannot be excluded from puncturing anymore.

As a key feature, update tokens can also be associated to such tags or not. Only ciphertexts with tags in tokens can be excluded from being punctured. However, there is one exception, a token can be constructed to be working for all ciphertexts denoted by the symbol $\forall$ in the token. Moreover, because of tags, TIPE is stronger than our UE definition as it allows the adversary to even query more tokens (since those can be crafted in a more fine-grained way via tags now). Noteworthy, keys are agnostic of tags and, hence, the restriction of querying keys are the same in UE and TIPE. As a consequence, TIPE yields an even more fine-grained primitive compared to what our UE notion offers.

Indeed, we can see that UE is essentially a special variant of TIPE. For UE, it is sufficient to set $\forall$ as input to key puncturing KPunc and fix the ciphertext-tag set of TIPE to a singleton $\mathcal{T} = \{t\}$ for any arbitrary tag t. Particularly, we use key puncturing for rotating to the next UE key (i.e., "puncturing" on the TIPE epoch e) and exclude puncturing for ciphertexts via a token, i.e., ciphertexts can be updated to the next epoch (where ciphertexts with expired epochs are punctured implicitly). Encryption and decryption directly map to UE's encryption and decryption functionality, respectively. Moreover, we believe that TIPE provides an interesting abstraction for protected outsourced file storage with forward security and fine-grained secure shredding of files (in the vein of puncturable key wrapping [44], but augmented with efficient key rotation).

IDEA OF INSTANTIATING TIPE. The main construction idea is the following. The first ingredient is a special encoding mapping epochs to encoded binary epochs. See that such binary epochs have only a length of λ while allowing 2^λ epochs. One can think of it as a binary-tree encoding as discussed in detail in [25, Sec. 4.2] where nodes are labeled as epochs, e.g., epochs $e_0 = (0,0,0), e_1 = (0,0,1), \ldots, e_7 = (1,1,1)$ encoding 2^3 epochs. However, this is not sufficient and we need a second ingredient, namely, group elements from the dual-system groups [42,45,46], to support such an encoding in the final TIPE scheme.

We use a special variant of dual-system groups (DSGs) due to Gong et al. [43] (which is based on [42]) and that was used to build an unbounded hierarchical identity-based encryption (HIBE) scheme [47]. Indeed, our is scheme is closely related to unbounded HIBEs, but we need more features which an HIBE cannot guarantee. (Particularly, ciphertext updates are not foreseen in HIBEs.) Fortunately, we observe that the above DSG from [43] has more to offer than implying unbounded HIBEs, which was not known before. Interestingly, we can even use a relaxed version of their DSG and leave out unnecessary features whereby we did not add anything to their syntax, correctness or security. As a consequence, we can safely assume that our relaxed DSG variant is implied by the full DSG variant from [43] and we give a concrete prime-order instantiation from the standard d-Lin assumption in the standard model in the extended version of this work [48].

Starting from the initial work by Waters [40], the richness of the dual-system paradigm was demonstrated in several prior works already (e.g., [42,43,45,46,49–55]). The abstraction concept of [43] is particularly useful as it provides us with functionalities that are also essential in the TIPE (and, hence, UE) paradigm where ciphertext updates only work in the forward direction. This connection is new and enriches the applications of the dual-system paradigm. We will now use such a connection for our TIPE construction.

To construct a TIPE scheme from DSGs with the encoding from [25], we implicitly encode epochs in keys in a complete binary tree, i.e., the nodes represent a prefix bit representation of the epoch and, hence, the root of the tree is associated with key K^ε (an initial key used to bootstrap *all* epoch keys). In its basic form, this is not new and reminiscent of prior works, e.g., work on forward secure public-key encryption [22,28,37,38]. However, we need to add ciphertext updates as well and enhance it to incorporate tokens.

Fortunately, the DSG approach allows us to also encode epochs in ciphertexts in a complete binary tree similarly to keys, i.e., the nodes represent a prefix bit representation of epochs and, hence, the root of the tree is associated with ciphertext $C_{t,e_{\exp}}^\varepsilon$ (an initial ciphertext). The more the epochs advance, depending on the configuration of the tree, the more ciphertext elements are required. See Fig. 1 for an illustrative example how keys and ciphertext are constructed on the intuitive level.

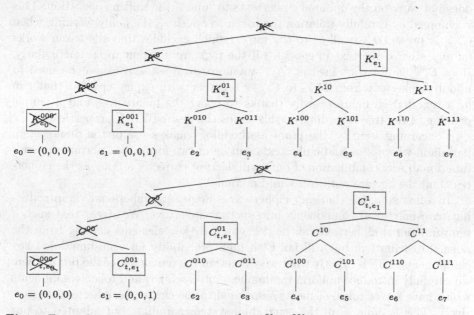

Fig. 1. Example of a TIPE key $K_{e_1} = (K_{e_1}^1, K_{e_1}^{01}, K_{e_1}^{001})$ that has been punctured on epoch $e_0 = (0,0,0)$. Moreover, a token tailored to t and epoch e_0 is generated during puncturing and can be used to update the ciphertext C_{t,e_0} to $C_{t,e_1} = (C_{e_1}^1, C_{e_1}^{01}, C_{e_1}^{001})$. Only the $\boxed{\text{boxed}}$ elements have to be stored and the remaining elements lower in the tree can be derived from those.

As a ciphertext can have many elements, the main hurdle is the common randomness that blinds the message part where such a randomness has to be "associated" to all ciphertext parts (otherwise decryption will not work). Surprisingly, we can use techniques from [43] where ciphertexts have "local" randomnesses and one "global" randomness, where the latter is used to hide the message part and the local randomness are required to mitigate mix-and-match attacks.

The correctness guarantees are now that a ciphertext for epoch $e_0 = (0, 0, 0)$ (encoded using [25]) can be decrypted by a key in epoch e_0, but not with keys in later epochs.[9] When a key is updated to $e_1 = (0, 0, 1)$, the node containing key elements from $K_{e_1}^{000}$ is discarded and all other key elements will have a uniform "linear shift" in their group elements. (Such a shift can be seen as switching the master secret key in an HIBE and we use the same shift for all key elements.)

Moreover, an update token is generated and incorporates the linear shift (as we have to transport this information to the ciphertexts). Such a token will not work on any key components, but can be used to "lift" a ciphertext in epoch e_0 to a valid ciphertext in epoch e_1. The tokens work only on ciphertext element C_{t,e_0}^{000} which results in a "shifting" element that can be used to all other ciphertext elements. The shift operation ensures that the secret key and the ciphertext are in sync again. After the shifting is done, C_{t,e_0}^{000} is discarded. This results in a ciphertext that cannot be decrypted by prior-epoch key elements as the token does not work on the updated ciphertexts to "undo" the shifting operation. This is enforced by carefully tailoring the token to epoch e_0 (i.e., only working when C_{t,e_0}^{000} is present), as well as to the tag t (which excludes that the token works on any other ciphertext in epoch e_0 if the tags are different to t). Particularly, since C_{t,e_0}^{000} is not contained in C_{t,e_1} anymore, such a token cannot be used to update ciphertext from C_{t,e_1} to C_{t,e_0}. Together with expiry epochs (that can be integrated straightforwardly thanks to using the binary tree and a simple pruning of the tree accordingly), this yields the desired TIPE properties.

Concerning security, the proof methodology makes use of the dual-system paradigm where keys and ciphertexts can be of two forms, i.e., normal or semi-functional. Any combination of both will decrypt correctly as long as the ciphertext and the key are not both semi-functional.

In a first step, the challenge ciphertext is made semi-functional via introducing semi-functional components into such a ciphertext. We stress that such a semi-functional ciphertext can be decrypted by key elements coming from the normal distribution, but will fail with high probability for semi-functional key components. This is exactly what we will use in the remainder of the proof where we carefully introduce uniform randomness into each key and token components which have key or token elements associated to the challenge ciphertext, respectively. This is done as in the usual dual-system paradigm but adapted to our setting where we can embed uniform randomness into such components and their associated tags or epochs encodings are not "prefixes" of the challenge ciphertext tag or epoch encoding.

---

[9] Also later-epochs keys cannot decrypt prior-epoch ciphertexts.

1.2   Preliminaries and Outline

NOTATION. For $n \in \mathbb{N}$, let $[n] := \{1, \ldots, n\}$, and let $\lambda \in \mathbb{N}$ be the security parameter. For a finite set $\mathcal{S}$, we denote by $s \leftarrow \mathcal{S}$ the process of sampling s uniformly from $\mathcal{S}$. For an algorithm A, let $y \leftarrow A(\lambda, x)$ be the process of running A on input (λ, x) with access to uniformly random coins and assigning the result to y. (We may omit to mention the λ-input explicitly and assume that all algorithms take λ as input.) To make the random coins r explicit, we write $A(\lambda, x; r)$. We say an algorithm A is probabilistic polynomial time (PPT) if the running time of A is polynomial in λ. A function f is negligible if its absolute value is smaller than the inverse of any polynomial (i.e., if $\forall c \in \mathbb{N} \; \exists k_0 \; \forall \lambda \geq k_0 :$ $|f(\lambda)| < 1/\lambda^c$). We write $\mathbf{v} = (v_i)_{i \in [n]}$, for $n \in \mathbb{N}$.

PAIRINGS. Let $\mathbb{G}, \mathbb{H}, G_T$ be cyclic groups. A *pairing* $e : \mathbb{G} \times \mathbb{H} \to G_T$ is a map that is *bilinear* (i.e., for all $g, g' \in \mathbb{G}$ and $h, h' \in \mathbb{H}$, we have $e(g \cdot g', h) = e(g, h) \cdot e(g', h)$ and $e(g, h \cdot h') = e(g, h) \cdot e(g, h')$), *non-degenerate* (i.e., for generators $g \in \mathbb{G}, h \in \mathbb{H}$, we have that $e(g, h) \in G_T$ is a generator), and *efficiently computable*.

GROUP GENERATOR. Let $\mathsf{G}(\lambda, n')$ be a group generator that generates the tuple $(\mathbb{G}, \mathbb{H}, G_T, N, g, h, (g_{p_i})_{i \in [n']}, e)$, for a pairing $e : \mathbb{G} \times \mathbb{H} \to G_T$, for composite-order groups $\mathbb{G}, \mathbb{H}, G_T$, all of known group order $N = p_1 \cdots p_{n'}$, generators $g, h, (g_{p_i})_{i \in [n']}$, and for $\Theta(\lambda)$-bit primes $(p_i)_i$.

OUTLINE OF THE PAPER. In Sect. 2, we present our security model with expiry epochs and discuss relations to previous models. In Sect. 3, we introduce Tag-Inverse Puncturable Encryption (TIPE), show how we can instantiate UE from TIPE and present a concrete TIPE construction. Moreover, we briefly discuss other applications of TIPE.

2   Updatable Encryption with Expiry Epochs

We define UE with expiry epochs in ciphertexts which allow ciphertexts to being excluded from updates. We build on the recent UE models [11–13]. The main idea of UE with expiry epochs is the following. On the very high level, all operations are bound to discrete epochs $1, 2, \ldots$ where keys and ciphertexts as well as so-called update tokens are associated to. System setup Gen creates a first-epoch symmetric key K_1. As an illustration, with this key, one can create a first-epoch ciphertext $C_{1,e_{\exp}} \leftarrow \mathsf{Enc}(K_1, M, e_{\exp})$, for some message M and expiry epoch $e_{\exp} > 1$, and, e.g., outsource $C_{1,e_{\exp}}$ to some semi-trusted third-party. With probabilistic algorithm RotKey, K_1 can be updated (or, rotated) to K_2 while also an update token Δ_2 is generated. With Δ_2, a semi-trusted third-party can update $C_{1,e_{\exp}}$ to $C_{2,e_{\exp}} \leftarrow \mathsf{Upd}(\Delta_2, C_{1,e_{\exp}})$ such that $C_{2,e_{\exp}}$ is "consistent" with K_2. Correctness guarantees that decryption of $C_{2,e_{\exp}}$ yields $M = \mathsf{Dec}(K_2, C_{2,e_{\exp}})$ as intended (and so on, if the ciphertext is not expired already). More formally:

Definition 1. *A UE scheme* UE *with message space* $\mathcal{M}$ *consist of the PPT algorithms* (Gen, RotKey, Enc, Upd, Dec):

$\mathsf{Gen}(\lambda)$: *on input security parameter* λ, *key generation outputs an initial (symmetric) key* K_1.

$\mathsf{RotKey}(K_e)$: *on input key* K_e, *key rotation outputs an updated key* K_{e+1} *for the next epoch together with an update token* Δ_{e+1}.

$\mathsf{Enc}(K_e, M, e_{\exp})$: *on input key* K_e, *a message* $M \in \mathcal{M}$, *and expiry epoch* $e_{\exp}$, *encryption outputs a ciphertext* $C_{e,e_{\exp}}$ *or* $\bot$.

$\mathsf{Upd}(\Delta_{e+1}, C_{e,e_{\exp}})$: *on input an update token* Δ_{e+1} *and a ciphertext* $C_{e,e_{\exp}}$, *update outputs an updated ciphertext* $C_{e+1,e_{\exp}}$ *or* $\bot$.

$\mathsf{Dec}(K_e, C_{e,e_{\exp}})$: *on input key* K_e *and a ciphertext* $C_{e,e_{\exp}}$, *decryption outputs* $M \in \mathcal{M} \cup \{\bot\}$.

Correctness. We require that an honestly generated epoch-j ciphertext $C_{j,e_{\exp}}$ (obtained via $\mathsf{Enc}(K_j, M, e_{\exp})$) is decryptable to M if the expiry epoch is not reached yet. Moreover, an honest update of a valid ciphertext $C_{j,e_{\exp}}$ (via Δ_{j+1}) from epoch j to $j+1$ yields a valid ciphertext $C_{j+1,e_{\exp}}$ that can be decrypted under the epoch key K_{j+1} (obtained via $\mathsf{RotKey}(K_j)$) if the ciphertext is not already expired. (See that we do not give any correctness guarantees beyond the expiry epochs.)

More formally, for all $\lambda \in \mathbb{N}$, for all $e \in [\lfloor \mathsf{poly}(\lambda) \rfloor]$, for $K_1 \leftarrow \mathsf{Gen}(\lambda)$, for all $i \in \{1, \ldots, e\}$, for all $(K_{i+1}, \Delta_{i+1}) \leftarrow \mathsf{RotKey}(K_i)$, for all $M \in \mathcal{M}$, for all $e_{\exp} \in \mathbb{N}$, for all $j \in \{1, \ldots, e+1\}$, for all $C_{j,e_{\exp}} \leftarrow \mathsf{Enc}(K_j, M, e_{\exp})$, we require that $M = \mathsf{Dec}(K_j, C_{j,e_{\exp}})$ holds if $e_{\exp} \geq j$. Moreover, for all $j \in \{1, \ldots, e\}$, for all $C_{j,e_{\exp}} \leftarrow \mathsf{Enc}(K_j, M, e_{\exp})$, for all $i \in \{j, \ldots, e\}$, for $C'_{j,e_{\exp}} := C_{j,e_{\exp}}$, for all $C'_{i+1,e_{\exp}} \leftarrow \mathsf{Upd}(\Delta_{i+1}, C'_{i,e_{\exp}})$, we require that $M = \mathsf{Dec}(K_{e+1}, C'_{e+1,e_{\exp}})$ holds if $e_{\exp} \geq e+1$.

Intuition of Our Security Notion. The notion is an extension of prior-work notions [11,12] which we augment with the introduction of expiry epochs. (We later show that our notion implies such prior-work notions.) The distinguishing feature of our model is that we allow the adversary to query the update token in an epoch which corresponds to the challenge-ciphertext expiry epoch $e_{\exp}$ *and* allow that the key in $e_{\exp} + 1$ can be retrieved. In models without expiry epochs, leaking the epoch-e challenge ciphertext and an epoch-e token together with a key in epoch $e + 1$ would yield a trivial win (per definition of correctness).

More concretely, in each epoch, the adversary has access to several oracles as given in Fig. 2. Thereby, we assume that any (expiry-)epoch information is explicitly retrievable from the keys, tokens, and ciphertexts. The adversary is allowed to query honestly generated ciphertexts (with chosen expiry epoch) via Enc'. RotKey' triggers rotation of the current key to the next epoch. Upd' is an oracle that updates chosen but honestly generated ciphertexts to the current epoch (depending on the expiry epoch). $\mathsf{Corrupt}$ lets the adversary retrieve either the token or the key for a specific epoch. Chall takes a chosen message and a chosen but honestly generated ciphertext, and outputs a challenge ciphertext (depending on a uniform bit b). $\mathsf{GetUpdC}^*$ returns the current challenge ciphertext. At the end of the experiment, we require that the adversary did not retrieve keys to trivially decrypt the challenge ciphertext or retrieves an update token to update the challenge ciphertext to an epoch where it has a key. If such validity checks pass and the adversary guessed b correctly, then the adversary wins the experiment. Otherwise, we say that a UE scheme is EE-IND-UE-CPA secure as such a notion essentially ensures that fresh and updated ciphertexts are indistinguishable even if the adversary has access the aforementioned oracles adaptively. We define:

Definition 2. *A UE scheme* UE *is* EE-IND-UE-CPA-*secure iff for any PPT adversary A, the advantage function*

$$\mathsf{Adv}_{\mathsf{UE},A}^{\mathsf{ee\text{-}ind\text{-}ue\text{-}cpa}}(\lambda) := \left| \Pr\left[\mathsf{Exp}_{\mathsf{UE},A}^{\mathsf{ee\text{-}ind\text{-}ue\text{-}cpa}}(\lambda) = 1 \right] - 1/2 \right|$$

is negligible in λ, *where* $\mathsf{Exp}_{\mathsf{UE},A}^{\mathsf{ee\text{-}ind\text{-}ue\text{-}cpa}}$ *is defined as in Fig. 2.*

Experiment $\mathsf{Exp}_{\mathsf{UE},A}^{\mathsf{ee\text{-}ind\text{-}ue\text{-}cpa}}(\lambda)$
  $K_1 \leftarrow \mathsf{Gen}(\lambda), \mathsf{phase} = 0, e = 1, c = 0, \Delta_1 = \bot$
  $\mathcal{L}^* := \emptyset, \mathcal{C}^* := \emptyset, \mathcal{K}^* := \emptyset, \mathcal{D}^* := \emptyset, b \leftarrow \{0,1\}$
  $b' \leftarrow A^{\mathsf{Enc}',\mathsf{RotKey}',\mathsf{Upd}',\mathsf{Corrupt},\mathsf{Chall},\mathsf{GetUpdC}^*}(\lambda)$
  if A is not valid, then return $b'' \leftarrow \{0,1\}$
  if $b = b'$, then return 1 else return 0

Oracles
$\mathsf{Enc}'(M, e_{\mathsf{exp}})$: run $C_{e,e_{\mathsf{exp}}} \leftarrow \mathsf{Enc}(K_e, M, e_{\mathsf{exp}})$ and set $\mathcal{L}^* := \mathcal{L}^* \cup (c, e, C_{e,e_{\mathsf{exp}}}), c = c+1$. Return $C_{e,e_{\mathsf{exp}}}$.
RotKey' : run $(K_{e+1}, \Delta_{e+1}) \leftarrow \mathsf{RotKey}(K_e)$. If $\mathsf{phase} = 1$, run $C_{e+1,b}^* \leftarrow \mathsf{Upd}(\Delta_{e+1}, C_{e,b}^*)$. Set $e = e+1$.
$\mathsf{Upd}'(C_{e-1,e_{\mathsf{exp}}})$: if $(\cdot, e-1, C_{e-1,e_{\mathsf{exp}}}) \notin \mathcal{L}^*$, return $\bot$. Run $C_{e,e_{\mathsf{exp}}} \leftarrow \mathsf{Upd}(\Delta_e, C_{e-1,e_{\mathsf{exp}}})$ and set $\mathcal{L}^* := \mathcal{L}^* \cup (c, e, C_{e,e_{\mathsf{exp}}}), c = c+1$. Return $C_{e,e_{\mathsf{exp}}}$.
$\mathsf{Corrupt}(\mathsf{inp}, e')$: if $e' > e$, return $\bot$. If $\mathsf{inp} = \mathsf{key}$, set $\mathcal{K}^* = \mathcal{K}^* \cup \{e'\}$ and return $K_{e'}$. If $\mathsf{inp} = \mathsf{token}$, set $\mathcal{D}^* = \mathcal{D}^* \cup \{e'\}$ and return $\Delta_{e'}$.
$\mathsf{Chall}(M, C_{e-1,e_{\mathsf{exp}}})$: if $\mathsf{phase} = 1$, return $\bot$. Set $\mathsf{phase} = 1$. If $(\cdot, e-1, C_{e-1,e_{\mathsf{exp}}}) \notin \mathcal{L}^*$, return $\bot$. If $b = 0$, set $C_{e,0}^* \leftarrow \mathsf{Enc}(K_e, M, e_{\mathsf{exp}})$, else $C_{e,1}^* \leftarrow \mathsf{Upd}(\Delta_e, C_{e-1,e_{\mathsf{exp}}})$. Set $\mathcal{C}^* = \mathcal{C}^* \cup (e, C_{e,b}^*)$, $e^* = e$, $e_{\mathsf{exp}}^* = e_{\mathsf{exp}}$, and return $C_{e,b}^*$.
$\mathsf{GetUpdC}^*$: If $\mathsf{phase} = 0$, return $\bot$. Set $\mathcal{C}^* := \mathcal{C}^* \cup (e, C_{e,b}^*)$ and return $C_{e,b}^*$.

A **is valid iff**:
1) For all $e' \in \mathcal{K}^*$, $(e', C_{e',b}^*) \notin \mathcal{C}^*$ holds. (No trivial win via retrieved keys.)
2) For all $e' \in \mathcal{K}^*$ with $e^* < e' \le e_{\mathsf{exp}}^*$ and $(e'-1, C_{e'-1,b}^*) \in \mathcal{C}^*$, $e'-1 \notin \mathcal{D}^*$ holds. (No trivial win via retrieved update token.)

Fig. 2. Our EE-IND-UE-CPA security notion for UE schemes with expiry epochs.

2.1   Relation to Other UE Security Notions

Our security notions implies IND-UE-CPA security as defined in [11,12]. Moreover, we can even show that our notion implies a simple and natural ciphertext indistinguishability notion for chosen messages and (public) expiry epochs where challenge ciphertexts with different expiry epochs are indistinguishable in the same challenge epoch. Due to space constraints, we show in the extended version of this work [48]:

Corollary 1. *EE-IND-UE-CPA security implies IND-UE-CPA security with expiry epochs set to $e_{\exp} = 2^\lambda$.*

Corollary 2. *EE-IND-UE-CPA security implies ciphertext indistinguishability for chosen messages and (public) expiry epochs in the same challenge epoch.*

3 UE from a Puncturable-Encryption Perspective

We introduce a novel primitive dubbed Tag-Inverse Puncturable Encryption (TIPE), provide a TIPE security model and show how to construct UE with expiry epochs from TIPE. Finally, we give an instantiation of TIPE under standard assumptions. TIPE essentially views UE from the perspective of puncturable encryption [31] and generalizes UE. We believe that TIPE has application beyond UE.

3.1 Tag-Inverse Puncturable Encryption

The main intuition of TIPE is the following. On the very high level, all operations are bound to discrete epochs $1, 2, \ldots$ where keys and ciphertexts as well as update tokens are associated to. Moreover, as in plain PE, ciphertexts are attached with a tag coming from an exponentially large tag space $\mathcal{T}$. System setup Gen creates a first-epoch symmetric key K_1. To show the idea, with such a key, one can create a first-epoch ciphertext $C_{1,t,e_{\exp}} \leftarrow \mathsf{Enc}(K_1, t, M, e_{\exp})$, for some message M, tag $t \in \mathcal{T}$, and expiry epoch $e_{\exp} > 1$. With probabilistic algorithm KPunc, K_1 can be updated to K_2 depending on a tag set $\mathcal{S} \subseteq \mathcal{T}$ (i.e., for which ciphertexts the key should *not* be punctured) while also update tokens $(\Delta_{2,t})_{t \in \mathcal{S} \cup \{\forall\}}$ are generated. (We allow even a special symbol $\forall$ in the token $\Delta_{2,\forall}$ which indicates that the key is not punctured on *any* ciphertext.) With $(\Delta_{2,t})_{t \in \mathcal{S} \cup \{\forall\}}$, a semi-trusted third-party can update $C_{1,t,e_{\exp}}$ to $C_{2,t,e_{\exp}} \leftarrow \mathsf{ExPunc}(\Delta_{2,t'}, C_{1,t,e_{\exp}})$ if $t \in \{t', \forall\}$ such that $C_{2,t,e_{\exp}}$ is "consistent" with K_2. Correctness guarantees that decryption of $C_{2,t,e_{\exp}}$ yields $M = \mathsf{Dec}(K_2, C_{2,t,e_{\exp}})$ as intended (and so on, if the ciphertext is not expired already). More formally:

Definition 3. *A Tag-Inverse Puncturable Encryption (TIPE) scheme* TIPE *for epochs $(1, \ldots, \mathsf{poly}(\lambda))$, ciphertext-tag space $\mathcal{T}$, and message space $\mathcal{M}$ consists of the PPT algorithms* (Gen, KPunc, Enc, ExPunc, Dec):

$\mathsf{Gen}(\lambda)$: on input security parameter λ, key generation outputs initial key K_1.
$\mathsf{KPunc}(K_e, \mathcal{S})$: on input key K_e for epoch e and ciphertext tags $\mathcal{S} \subseteq \mathcal{T}$ or $\mathcal{S} = \forall$, if $\mathcal{S} \subseteq \mathcal{T}$, key puncturing outputs a punctured key K_{e+1} and tag-specific tokens $(\Delta_{e+1,t})_{t \in \mathcal{S}}$; otherwise, if $\mathcal{S} = \forall$, outputs a punctured key K_{e+1} and (universal) token $\Delta_{e+1,\forall}$.
$\mathsf{Enc}(K_e, t, M, e_{\exp})$: on input key K_e, ciphertext tag $t \in \mathcal{T}$, message $M \in \mathcal{M}$, and expiry epoch $e_{\exp}$, encryption outputs a ciphertext $C_{e,t,e_{\exp}}$ or $\bot$.

$\mathsf{ExPunc}(\Delta_{e+1,t'}, C_{e,t,e_{\exp}})$: on input token $\Delta_{e+1,t'}$ and ciphertext $C_{e,t,e_{\exp}}$, the exclude-from-puncturing algorithm outputs a ciphertext $C_{e+1,t,e_{\exp}}$ if $t' \in \{t, \forall\}$ and $e < e_{\exp}$; otherwise outputs $\bot$.

$\mathsf{Dec}(K_e, C_{e',t,e_{\exp}})$: on input key K_e and ciphertext $C_{e,t,e_{\exp}}$, decryption outputs message $M \in \mathcal{M}$ if $e = e'$; otherwise outputs $\bot$.

Correctness. We require that an honestly generated epoch-j ciphertext $C_{j,t,e_{\exp}}$ (obtained via $\mathsf{Enc}(K_j, t, M, e_{\exp})$) is decryptable to M if the expiry epoch is not reached yet. Moreover, an honest exclusion from being punctured for a valid ciphertext $C_{j,t,e_{\exp}}$ (via $\Delta_{j+1,\mathcal{S}}$ with $t \in \mathcal{S}$ or $\mathcal{S} = \forall$) from epoch j to $j+1$ yields a valid ciphertext $C_{j+1,t,e_{\exp}}$ that can be decrypted under the epoch key K_{j+1} (obtained via $\mathsf{KPunc}(K_j, \mathcal{S})$) if the ciphertext is not already expired. (See that we do not give any correctness guarantees beyond the expiry epochs.)

More formally, for all $\lambda \in \mathbb{N}$, for all $e \in [\lfloor \mathsf{poly}(\lambda) \rfloor]$, for $K_1 \leftarrow \mathsf{Gen}(\lambda)$, for all $i \in \{1, \dots, e\}$, for any $\mathcal{S} \in \mathcal{T} \cup \{\forall\}$, for all $(K_{i+1}, \Delta_{i+1,\mathcal{S}}) \leftarrow \mathsf{KPunc}(K_i, \mathcal{S})$, for all $M \in \mathcal{M}$, for all expiry epochs $e_{\exp} \in \mathbb{N}$, for all $t \in \mathcal{T}$, for all $j \in \{1, \dots, e+1\}$, for all $C_{j,t,e_{\exp}} \leftarrow \mathsf{Enc}(K_j, t, M, e_{\exp})$, we require that $M = \mathsf{Dec}(K_j, C_{j,t,e_{\exp}})$ holds if $e_{\exp} \geq j$. Moreover, for all $j \in \{1, \dots, e\}$, for all $C_{j,t,e_{\exp}} \leftarrow \mathsf{Enc}(K_j, t, M, e_{\exp})$, for all $i \in \{j, \dots, e\}$, for $C'_{j,t,e_{\exp}} := C_{j,t,e_{\exp}}$, for all $C'_{i+1,t,e_{\exp}} \leftarrow \mathsf{ExPunc}(\Delta_{i+1,t'}, C'_{i,t,e_{\exp}})$ with $t' \in \{t, \forall\}$, we require that $M = \mathsf{Dec}(K_{e+1}, C'_{e+1,t,e_{\exp}})$ holds if $e_{\exp} \geq e+1$.

Intuition of Our Security Notion. We define IND-TIPE-CPA which guarantees that freshly generated ciphertexts cannot be distinguished from ones that are excluded from puncturing similarly to UE, but we give more power to the adversary as it is allowed to even query more tokens. Thereby, we assume that any (expiry-)epoch information is explicitly retrievable from the keys, tokens, and ciphertexts. Similarly, we assume that any tag information is explicitly retrievable from the tokens and ciphertexts.

To emphasize the main difference to our UE model, consider some epoch e' after the challenge epoch where the adversary queried a key $K_{e'}$ and the challenge ciphertext is not expired, i.e., $e' \leq e_{\exp}$. In our UE definition, the adversary is not allowed to query a token $\Delta_{e'}$ while in TIPE, we allow querying tokens $(\Delta_{e',t})_{t\in\mathcal{S}}$ that do not incorporate update capabilities for the challenge tag t^*, i.e., $t^* \notin \mathcal{S}$. Moreover, a token $\Delta_{e',\forall}$ is obviously not allowed to be queried in epoch e'. Those are the essential differences to our UE notion.

Moreover, similarly to our UE notion, we assume that any (expiry-)epoch and tag information is explicitly retrievable from the keys, tokens, and ciphertexts. We define:

Definition 4. *A TIPE scheme* TIPE *is* IND-TIPE-CPA-*secure iff for any PPT adversary A, the advantage function*

$$\mathsf{Adv}_{\mathsf{TIPE},A}^{\mathsf{ind\text{-}tipe\text{-}cpa}}(\lambda) := \left| \Pr\left[\mathsf{Exp}_{\mathsf{TIPE},A}^{\mathsf{ind\text{-}tipe\text{-}cpa}}(\lambda) = 1 \right] - 1/2 \right|$$

is negligible in λ*, where* $\mathsf{Exp}_{\mathsf{TIPE},A}^{\mathsf{ind\text{-}tipe\text{-}cpa}}$ *is defined as in Fig. 3.*

Experiment $\mathsf{Exp}_{\mathsf{TIPE},A}^{\mathsf{ind\text{-}tipe\text{-}cpa}}(\lambda)$

$K_1 \leftarrow \mathsf{Gen}(\lambda)$, $\mathsf{phase} = 0, e = 0, \mathcal{S} = \emptyset, c = 0, \Delta_{1,\forall} = \bot$

$\mathcal{L}^* := \emptyset, \mathcal{C}^* := \emptyset, \mathcal{K}^* := \emptyset, \mathcal{D}^* := \emptyset, b \leftarrow \{0,1\}$

$b' \leftarrow A^{\mathsf{Enc}',\mathsf{KPunc}',\mathsf{ExPunc}',\mathsf{Corrupt},\mathsf{Chall},\mathsf{GetUnpuncC}^*}(\lambda)$

if A is not valid, then return $b'' \leftarrow \{0,1\}$

if $b = b'$, then return 1 else return 0

Oracles

$\mathsf{Enc}'(t, M, e_{\mathsf{exp}})$: run $C_{e,t,e_{\mathsf{exp}}} \leftarrow \mathsf{Enc}(K_e, t, M, e_{\mathsf{exp}})$ and set $\mathcal{L}^* := \mathcal{L}^* \cup (c, e, C_{e,t,e_{\mathsf{exp}}}), c = c+1$. Return $C_{e,t,e_{\mathsf{exp}}}$.

$\mathsf{KPunc}'(\mathcal{S}')$: run $(K_{e+1}, (\Delta_{e+1,t})_{t \in \mathcal{S}'}) \leftarrow \mathsf{KPunc}(K_e, \mathcal{S}')$. If $\mathsf{phase} = 1$ and $t^* \in \mathcal{S}'$ or $\mathcal{S}' = \forall$, run $C^*_{e+1,t^*,b} \leftarrow \mathsf{ExPunc}(\Delta_{e+1,t^*}, C^*_{e,t^*,b})$ (if $t^* \in \mathcal{S}'$) or $C^*_{e+1,t^*,b} \leftarrow \mathsf{ExPunc}(\Delta_{e+1,\forall}, C^*_{e,t^*,b})$ (if $\mathcal{S}' = \forall$). Set $e = e+1$ and $\mathcal{S} = \mathcal{S}'$.

$\mathsf{ExPunc}'(C_{e-1,t,e_{\mathsf{exp}}})$: if $(\cdot, e-1, C_{e-1,t,e_{\mathsf{exp}}}) \notin \mathcal{L}^*$, or if $t \notin \mathcal{S}$ and $\mathcal{S} \neq \forall$, return $\bot$. Run $C_{e,t,e_{\mathsf{exp}}} \leftarrow \mathsf{ExPunc}(\Delta_{e,t}, C_{e-1,t,e_{\mathsf{exp}}})$ (if $t \in \mathcal{S}$) or $C_{e,t,e_{\mathsf{exp}}} \leftarrow \mathsf{ExPunc}(\Delta_{e,\forall}, C_{e-1,t,e_{\mathsf{exp}}})$ (if $\mathcal{S} = \forall$) and set $\mathcal{L}^* := \mathcal{L}^* \cup (c, e, C_{e,t,e_{\mathsf{exp}}}), c = c+1$. Return $C_{e,t,e_{\mathsf{exp}}}$.

$\mathsf{Corrupt}(\mathsf{inp}, e')$: if $e' > e$, return $\bot$. If $\mathsf{inp} = \mathsf{key}$, set $\mathcal{K}^* = \mathcal{K}^* \cup \{e'\}$ and return $K_{e'}$. If $\mathsf{inp} = \mathsf{token}$, set $\mathcal{D}^* = \mathcal{D}^* \cup \{e', \mathcal{S}\}$ and return $(\Delta_{e',t})_{t \in \mathcal{S}}$.

$\mathsf{Chall}(M, C_{e-1,t,e_{\mathsf{exp}}})$: if $\mathsf{phase} = 1$, or if $t \notin \mathcal{S}$ and $\mathcal{S} \neq \forall$, return $\bot$. Set $\mathsf{phase} = 1$. If $(\cdot, e-1, C_{e-1,t,e_{\mathsf{exp}}}) \notin \mathcal{L}^*$, return $\bot$. If $b = 0$, set $C^*_{e,t,0} \leftarrow \mathsf{Enc}(K_e, t, M, e_{\mathsf{exp}})$, else $C^*_{e,t,1} \leftarrow \mathsf{ExPunc}(\Delta_{e,t}, C_{e-1,t,e_{\mathsf{exp}}})$ (if $t \in \mathcal{S}$) or $C^*_{e,t,1} \leftarrow \mathsf{ExPunc}(\Delta_{e,\forall}, C_{e-1,t,e_{\mathsf{exp}}})$ (if $\mathcal{S} = \forall$). Set $\mathcal{C}^* = \mathcal{C}^* \cup (e, C^*_{e,t,b})$, $e^* = e$, $t^* = t$, $e^*_{\mathsf{exp}} = e_{\mathsf{exp}}$, and return $C^*_{e,t,b}$.

$\mathsf{GetUnpuncC}^*$: If $\mathsf{phase} = 0$, return $\bot$. Set $\mathcal{C}^* := \mathcal{C}^* \cup (e, C^*_{e,t,b})$ and return $C^*_{e,t,b}$.

A **is valid iff**:

1) For all $e' \in \mathcal{K}^*$, $(e', C^*_{e',b}) \notin \mathcal{C}^*$ holds. (No trivial win via retrieved keys.)
2) For all $e' \in \mathcal{K}^*$ with $e^* < e' \leq e^*_{\mathsf{exp}}$ and $(e'-1, C^*_{e'-1,t^*,b}) \in \mathcal{C}^*$, $(e'-1, \mathcal{S}') \notin \mathcal{D}^*$ for $\mathcal{S}' = \forall$ or $t^* \in \mathcal{S}'$ holds. (No trivial win via retrieved update token.)

Fig. 3. Our IND-TIPE-CPA security notion for TIPE.

3.2 Generic UE Construction from TIPE

In the following, let $\mathsf{TIPE} = (\mathsf{TIPE.Gen}, \mathsf{TIPE.KPunc}, \mathsf{TIPE.Enc}, \mathsf{TIPE.ExPunc}, \mathsf{TIPE.Dec})$ be a TIPE with tag space $\mathcal{T} = \{t\}$ and message space $\mathcal{M}_{\mathsf{TIPE}}$. We construct a UE scheme $\mathsf{UE} = (\mathsf{Gen}, \mathsf{RotKey}, \mathsf{Enc}, \mathsf{Upd}, \mathsf{Dec})$ with message space $\mathcal{M} := \mathcal{M}_{\mathsf{TIPE}}$. The main intuition here is that we only need a single tag in $\mathcal{T}$ and each ciphertext is generated with such a tag. Moreover, the key rotation in UE generates the next UE key and a token that works for *any* tag, particularly for the single tag in $\mathcal{T}$. We construct:

$\mathsf{Gen}(\lambda)$: return $K_1 \leftarrow \mathsf{TIPE.Gen}(\lambda)$.

$\overline{\mathsf{RotKey}(K_e)}$: return $(K_{e+1}, \Delta_{e+1}) \leftarrow \mathsf{TIPE.KPunc}(K_e, \forall)$.

$\overline{\mathsf{Enc}(K_e, M, e_{\mathsf{exp}})}$: return $C_{e,e_{\mathsf{exp}}} \leftarrow \mathsf{TIPE.Enc}(K_e, t, M, e_{\mathsf{exp}})$, for $t \in \mathcal{T}$.

$\overline{\mathsf{Upd}(\Delta_{e+1}, C_{e,e_{\mathsf{exp}}})}$ return $C_{e+1,e_{\mathsf{exp}}} \leftarrow \mathsf{TIPE.ExPunc}(C_{e,e_{\mathsf{exp}}}, \Delta_{e+1})$.

$\overline{\mathsf{Dec}(K_e, C_{e,e_{\mathsf{exp}}})}$: return $M := \mathsf{TIPE.Dec}(K_e, C_{e,e_{\mathsf{exp}}})$.

Correctness. See that this directly translates from the TIPE scheme, i.e., the ciphertexts that were computed by Enc and/or updated via Upd can be decrypted by Dec if the keys are in the same epoch and the ciphertext is not expired.

Theorem 1. *If* TIPE *is* IND-TIPE-CPA *secure, then* UE *is* EE-IND-UE-CPA *secure. Concretely, for any PPT adversary A there is a distinguisher D in the* IND-TIPE-CPA *security experiment, such that* $\mathsf{Adv}_{\mathsf{TIPE},D}^{\mathsf{ind\text{-}tipe\text{-}cpa}}(\lambda) \geq \mathsf{Adv}_{\mathsf{UE},A}^{\mathsf{ind\text{-}ue\text{-}cpa}}(\lambda)$.

Proof. We show the theorem by constructing a PPT distinguisher D in the IND-TIPE-CPA security experiment with TIPE from any successful PPT adversary A in the EE-IND-UE-CPA security with UE. D runs $A(\lambda)$. Let TIPE.Enc′, KPunc, ExPunc, TIPE.Corrupt, TIPE.Chall, TIPE.GetUnpuncC* be the TIPE oracles. Let A's oracles be as follows:

Enc′(M, e_{exp}) : return $C_{e,e_{\mathsf{exp}}} \leftarrow$ TIPE.Enc′(M, t, e_{exp}), for $t \in \mathcal{T}$.
RotKey′ : run KPunc$(\forall)$.
Upd′$(C_{e-1,e_{\mathsf{exp}}})$: return $C_{e,e_{\mathsf{exp}}} \leftarrow$ ExPunc$(C_{e-1,e_{\mathsf{exp}}})$.
Corrupt(inp, e') : return the result of TIPE.Corrupt(inp, e'). (This is either a key or a token depending on inp.)
Chall$(M, C_{e-1,e_{\mathsf{exp}}})$: return $C_{e,b}^* \leftarrow$ TIPE.Chall$(M, C_{e-1,e_{\mathsf{exp}}})$.
GetUpdC* : return $C_{e,b}^* \leftarrow$ TIPE.GetUnpuncC*.

We conclude that D provides a consistent view for A. If A is a successful PPT adversary in the EE-IND-UE-CPA security experiment with UE (see that also the validity conditions of TIPE subsumes the validity conditions of UE), then D is a successful PPT adversary in the IND-TIPE-CPA security experiment with TIPE. □

3.3 TIPE from Standard Assumptions

We show how to construct TIPE from standard assumption. Before that, we introduce encoding of epochs and the dual-system group paradigm. Both are important ingredients to our construction and discussed in the introduction on the high-level. In the following, we formally provide such ingredients and give a proof from standard assumptions.

Encoding of Epochs. We use the encoding function of the recent work due to Drijvers, Gorbunov, Neven, and Wee [25, Sec. 4.2]. They give a function e that maps tags $\mathbf{t} = (t_1, \ldots) \in \{1,2\}^{\leq \lambda-1}$, for $\lambda = \lfloor \log_2 n \rfloor$, to epochs $[n]$:[10]

$$e(\mathbf{t}) = 1 + \sum_{i=1}^{|\mathbf{t}|}(1 + (2^{\lambda-i}-1)(t_i-1)).^{10}$$

---

[10] In the introduction, we used the tag set $\{0,1\}^\lambda$ for illustrating purposes; due to technical reasons, the tag set $\{1,2\}^\lambda$ is actually required.

Moreover, $\mathbf{t}$ is the inverse function that maps epochs $e \in [n]$ to tags $\{1,2\}^{\leq \lambda - 1}$:

$$t(e) = \begin{cases} \varepsilon & \text{if } e = 1 \\ \mathbf{t}(e-1)||1 & \text{if } |\mathbf{t}(e-1)| < \lambda - 1 \\ \bar{\mathbf{t}}||2 & \text{if } |\mathbf{t}(e-1)| = \lambda - 1, \end{cases}$$

for longest string $\bar{\mathbf{t}}$ such that $\bar{\mathbf{t}}||1$ is a prefix of $t(e-1)$. Furthermore, they define sets $\Gamma_{\mathbf{t}} \subset \{1,2\}^{\leq \lambda - 1}$ for each $\mathbf{t}$ such that:

$$\Gamma_{\mathbf{t}} = \{\mathbf{t}\} \cup \{\bar{\mathbf{t}}||2 : \bar{\mathbf{t}}||1 \text{ prefix of } \mathbf{t}\}.$$

The properties of $\Gamma_{\mathbf{t}}$ are: (1) $\mathbf{t} \preceq \mathbf{t}' \Leftrightarrow \exists \mathbf{u} \in \Gamma_{\mathbf{t}}$ such that $\mathbf{u}$ is a prefix of $\mathbf{t}'$, (2) $\forall \mathbf{t}$, it holds $\Gamma_{\mathbf{t}(e(\mathbf{t})+1)} = \Gamma_{\mathbf{t}} \backslash \{\mathbf{t}\}$ if $|\mathbf{t}| = \lambda - 1$ or $\Gamma_{\mathbf{t}(e(\mathbf{t})+1)} = (\Gamma_{\mathbf{t}} \backslash \{\mathbf{t}\}) \cup \{\mathbf{t}||1, \mathbf{t}||2\}$ otherwise, (3) $\forall \mathbf{t}' \succ \mathbf{t}$, it holds $\forall \mathbf{u}' \in \Gamma_{\mathbf{t}'}, \exists \mathbf{u} \in \Gamma_{\mathbf{t}}$ such that $\mathbf{u}$ is a prefix of $\mathbf{u}'$.

Dual System Groups. Our (relaxed) DSG DSG based on [43] consists of the PPT algorithms (SampP, SampG, SampH, SampS, SampK, $\widehat{\mathsf{SampG}}$, $\widehat{\mathsf{SampH}}$):

SampP(λ, n) : sample $(\mathbb{G}, \mathbb{H}, G_T, N, (g_{p_i})_{i \in [n']}, e) \leftarrow \mathsf{G}(\lambda, n')$, for fixed integer n'.

Define $m : \mathbb{H} \rightarrow \mathbb{G}_T$ to be linear map, let $\hat{g}$ and $\hat{h}$ be group elements generated by g_s and h_s, respectively (see below). Further, $pars, \widehat{pars}$ may contain arbitrary information. Output public parameters $pp = (\mathbb{G}, \mathbb{H}, G_T, N, e, m, pars)$ and secret parameters $sp = (\hat{g}, \hat{h}, \widehat{pars})$

SampG(pp) : output $\mathbf{g} = (g_0, \dots, g_n) \in \mathbb{G}^{n+1}$.

SampS(pp) : output $S \in \mathbb{G}$.

SampH(pp) : output $\mathbf{h} = (h_0, \dots, h_n) \in \mathbb{H}^{n+1}$.

SampK(pp) : output $K \in \mathbb{H}$.

$\widehat{\mathsf{SampG}}(pp, sp)$: output $\hat{\mathbf{g}} = (\hat{g}_0, \dots, \hat{g}_n) \in \mathbb{G}^{n+1}$ and $g_s \in \mathbb{G}$.

$\widehat{\mathsf{SampH}}(pp, sp)$: output $\hat{\mathbf{h}} = (\hat{h}_0, \dots, \hat{h}_n) \in \mathbb{H}^{n+1}$ and $h_s, h_a \in \mathbb{H}$.

SampG, SampS, SampH and SampK sample from a "normal" distribution (used for correctness) while $\widehat{\mathsf{SampG}}$ and $\widehat{\mathsf{SampH}}$ sample from a "semi-functional" distribution (used in the security proof). When proving UE security, we can switch UE ciphertexts and keys to semi-functional ones. The essence of dual system is then carried out, namely, semi-functional ciphertexts and keys are incompatible meaning that we can derive at a stage where the UE ciphertexts carry a uniformly random group element and indistinguishability can be shown.

Correctness. For all $\lambda, n \in \mathbb{N}$, for all pp (generated via SampP(λ, n)):

Projectiveness. $m(h)^s = e(\mathsf{SampS}(pp; s), h)$, for all $s \in \mathbb{Z}_N^*$ and $h \in \mathbb{H}$.

Orthogonality. $e(S, h_i) = 1$ and $e(g_0, K) = 1$, for all $i \in [n]$, $(h_0, \dots, h_n) \leftarrow$ SampH(pp), $S \leftarrow$ SampS(pp), $(g_0, \dots) \leftarrow$ SampH(pp), and $K \leftarrow$ SampK(pp).

Associativity. $e(g_0, h_i) = e(g_i, h_0)$, for all $i \in [n]$, $(g_0, \dots, g_n) \leftarrow$ SampG(pp) and $(h_0, \dots, h_n) \leftarrow$ SampH(pp).

$\mathbb{G}$-$\mathbb{H}$-*subgroups.* The outputs of SampG(pp) and SampS(pp) are uniformly distributed over the generators of non-trivial subgroups of $\mathbb{G}^{n+1}$ and $\mathbb{G}$, respectively. The outputs of SampH(pp) and SampK(pp) are uniformly distributed over the generators of non-trivial subgroups of $\mathbb{H}^{n+1}$ and $\mathbb{H}$, respectively.

Security. For all $\lambda, n \in \mathbb{N}$, for all $(pp, sp) \leftarrow \mathsf{SampP}(\lambda, n)$:

Orthogonality. $m(\widehat{h}) = 1$.

Non-degeneracy. h lies in a subgroup of h_s, g_s lies in a subgroup of $\widehat{g}$.

Left-subgroup indistinguishability (LS). For any PPT D, $\mathsf{Adv}^{\mathsf{ls}}_{\mathsf{DSG},D}(\lambda, n) :=$

$$|\Pr\left[D(pp, \mathbf{g}) = 1\right] - \Pr\left[D(pp, \mathbf{g}\widehat{\mathbf{g}}) = 1\right]|$$

is negligible in λ, for $\mathbf{g} \leftarrow \mathsf{SampG}(pp)$ and $(\widehat{\mathbf{g}}, \cdot) \leftarrow \widehat{\mathsf{SampG}}(pp, sp)$.

Right-subgroup indistinguishability (RS). For any PPT D, $\mathsf{Adv}^{\mathsf{rs}}_{\mathsf{DSG},D}(\lambda, n) :=$

$$\left|\Pr\left[D(pp, \widehat{h}, \mathbf{g}\widehat{\mathbf{g}}, \mathbf{h}) = 1\right] - \Pr\left[D(pp, \widehat{h}, \mathbf{g}\widehat{\mathbf{g}}, \mathbf{h}\widehat{\mathbf{h}}) = 1\right]\right|$$

is negligible in λ, for $\mathbf{g} \leftarrow \mathsf{SampG}(pp)$, $(\widehat{\mathbf{g}}, \cdot) \leftarrow \widehat{\mathsf{SampG}}(pp, sp)$, $\mathbf{h} \leftarrow \mathsf{SampH}(pp)$, and $(\widehat{\mathbf{h}}, \cdot, \cdot) \leftarrow \widehat{\mathsf{SampH}}(pp, sp)$.

Parameter-hiding. The distributions

$$\{pp, \widehat{g}, \widehat{h}, \widehat{\mathbf{g}}, \widehat{\mathbf{h}}\} \text{ and } \{pp, \widehat{g}, \widehat{h}, \widehat{\mathbf{g}}\mathbf{g}', \widehat{\mathbf{h}}\mathbf{h}'\}$$

are identically distributed, for $(\widehat{\mathbf{g}} = (\widehat{g}_0, \ldots, \widehat{g}_n), g_s) \leftarrow \widehat{\mathsf{SampG}}(pp, sp)$, $(\widehat{\mathbf{h}} = (\widehat{h}_0, \ldots, \widehat{h}_n), h_s, h_a) \leftarrow \widehat{\mathsf{SampH}}(pp, sp)$, $\widehat{\mathbf{g}}' = (1, g_s^{\gamma_1}, \ldots, g_s^{\gamma_n})$, and $\widehat{\mathbf{h}}' = (1, h_s^{\gamma_1}, \ldots, h_s^{\gamma_n})$, for $\gamma_1, \ldots, \gamma_n \leftarrow \mathbb{Z}_N$.

Computational non-degeneracy (ND). For any PPT D, $\mathsf{Adv}^{\mathsf{nd}}_{\mathsf{DSG},D}(\lambda, n) :=$

$$\left|\Pr\left[D(pp, \mathbf{S} \cdot \mathbf{g}\widehat{\mathbf{g}}, K \cdot \widehat{h}^\alpha, e(S, K)) = 1\right] - \Pr\left[D(pp, \mathbf{S} \cdot \mathbf{g}\widehat{\mathbf{g}}, K \cdot \widehat{h}^\alpha, R = 1\right]\right|$$

is negligible in λ, for $\mathbf{S} = (S, 1, \ldots)$, $S \leftarrow \mathsf{SampS}(pp)$, $\mathbf{g} \leftarrow \mathsf{SampG}(pp)$, $(\widehat{\mathbf{g}}, \cdot) \leftarrow \widehat{\mathsf{SampG}}(pp, sp)$, $K \leftarrow \mathsf{SampK}(pp)$, $\alpha \leftarrow \mathbb{Z}_N$, and $R \leftarrow G_T$.

Remark. The properties have the following implications which we will need later on. From orthogonality and projectiveness, we retrieve $e(S, \widehat{h}) = 1$. By projectiveness, it holds $m(K)^s \cdot m(K')^s = e(\mathsf{SampS}(pp; s), K) \cdot e(\mathsf{SampS}(pp; s), K') = m(K \cdot K')^s$, for $s \in \mathbb{Z}_N^*$, and $K, K' \in \mathbb{H}$. Moreover, by projectiveness and $\mathbb{G}$-subgroups, we have $m(K)^s \cdot m(K)^{s'} = e(\mathsf{SampS}(pp; s), K) \cdot e(\mathsf{SampS}(pp; s'), K) = e(g^{s+s'}, K) = m(K)^{s+s'}$, for $K \in \mathbb{H}$ and suitable generator $g \in \mathbb{G}$.

Intuition of Our Construction. Beyond what is already discussed in the introduction on the intuition of our construction, we give some more technical details in the following. We assume that tags in the tag set $\mathcal{T}$ are integers in $\mathbb{Z}_N^*$ for simplicity. During key generation, we use $\lambda + 1$ as input to the DSG parameter-sampling algorithm SampP as this will give us one additional element for embedding the ciphertext tag during encryption. The initial key K_1 consists of DSG group elements (that are sampled from the normal distribution) with a distinguished element k_1 that can be seen as acting similarly to a master secret key in an (unbounded) HIBE [43]. (K_1 corresponds essentially to the root of the binary tree for the key.)

Key puncturing KPunc prunes the tree as follows: if a node corresponding to the current epoch is not a leaf node, then it computes the children of such a node. One child gets associated with 1 and the other one with 2 which maps directly to the encoding. Then, the key material of the parent node is discarded; otherwise, if such a node is a leaf node, then the key material for this node is discarded. A re-randomization step for all elements forms the resulting key for epoch $e + 1$. The corresponding token is computed around a distinguished element δ (depending on $\mathcal{S}$) which is blinded with epoch (and tag) dependent group elements from the DSG's normal distribution; it acts a linear shift for k_e.

Encryption Enc, depending on the current tree configuration and the expiry epoch, computes the ciphertext material depending on such a configuration where each group element is similarly computed to a simple form of an unbounded HIBE ciphertext in [43] but enhanced with further DSG group elements. Those elements are crucial and used in ExPunc. The message itself is blinded by $m(k_e)^s$, where the uniform s is also embedded as "global" randomness in ciphertext elements corresponding to the tree configuration (see element $\mathcal{S}$).

During ExPunc, the linear shift $m(\delta)^s$ is computed only if ciphertext material corresponding to the token is available (i.e., if such a token—potentially depending also on the tag—matches ciphertext material in the current epoch). Such a shift can then be used to update the blinding group element for the message to the next epoch. Moreover, the ciphertext tree is pruned analogously to how key material is delegated and discarded in KPunc. Particularly, ciphertext material for the node associated to the then-old epoch is discarded. Decryption recovers the message if the epochs of the key and unexpired ciphertext match.

Our Construction. Let DSG $=$ (SampP, SampG, SampH, SampS, SampK, $\widehat{\mathsf{SampG}}, \widehat{\mathsf{SampH}}$) be DSG. We construct a TIPE scheme TIPE $=$ (Gen, KPunc, Enc, ExPunc, Dec) with tag space $\mathcal{T} = \mathbb{Z}_N^*$ (determined during Gen) and message space $\mathcal{M}$:

Gen(λ) : compute $(pp, sp) \leftarrow$ SampP($\lambda + 1$), set $\mathcal{T} = \mathbb{Z}_N^*$, sample $(h_0, \ldots, h_{\lambda+1}) \leftarrow$ SampH(pp), $k_1 \leftarrow$ SampK(pp) and return $K_1 = (\{K_1'\}, m(k_1), pp)$, with $K_1' = (h_0, k_1 \cdot h_1, \ldots, h_\lambda)$.

KPunc($K_e, \mathcal{S}$) : for $K_e = (\{K_{\mathbf{u}}' : \mathbf{u} \in \Gamma_{\mathbf{t}(e)}\}, m(k_e), pp)$, if $|\mathbf{t}(e)| < \lambda - 1$, then find $K_{\mathbf{t}(e)}' = (T_0, T_1, T_{|\mathbf{t}(e)|+1}, \ldots, T_\lambda)$, compute

$$K_{\mathbf{t}(e+1)}' = (T_0, T_1 \cdot T_{|\mathbf{t}(e)|+1}, T_{|\mathbf{t}(e)|+2}, \ldots, T_\lambda),$$
$$K_{\mathbf{t}(e+2)}' = (T_0, T_1 \cdot T_{|\mathbf{t}(e)|+1}^2, T_{|\mathbf{t}(e)|+2}, \ldots, T_\lambda).$$

Sample elements $\delta \leftarrow$ SampK(pp) and $(h_0, \ldots, h_{\lambda+1}), (h_{\mathbf{u},0}, \ldots, h_{\mathbf{u},\lambda+1})_{\mathbf{u} \in [|\Gamma_{\mathbf{t}(e+1)}|]} \leftarrow$ SampH(pp), for $\mathbf{t}(e + 1) = (\mathbf{t}(e+1)_1, \ldots, \mathbf{t}(e+1)_{|\mathbf{t}(e+1)|})$, compute

$$\Delta_{e+1} = \begin{cases} (\Delta_{e+1,t})_{t\in\mathcal{S}} = (h_0, \delta \cdot h_{\lambda+1}^t \prod_{i=1}^{|\mathbf{t}(e+1)|} h_i^{\mathbf{t}(e+1)_i}, m(k_e \cdot \delta))_{t\in\mathcal{S}} & (\text{if } \mathcal{S} \neq \forall) \\ (h_0, \delta \cdot \prod_{i=1}^{|\mathbf{t}(e+1)|} h_i^{\mathbf{t}(e+1)_i}, m(k_e \cdot \delta)) & (\text{if } \mathcal{S} = \forall) \end{cases}$$

$$K_{\mathbf{u}}'' = (T_{\mathbf{u},0}' h_{\mathbf{u},0}, T_{\mathbf{u},1}' \cdot \delta \cdot \prod_{i=1}^{|\mathbf{u}|} h_{\mathbf{u},i}^{\mathbf{u}_i}, T_{\mathbf{u},|\mathbf{u}|+1}' h_{\mathbf{u},|\mathbf{u}|+1}, \ldots, T_{\mathbf{u},\lambda}' h_{\mathbf{u},\lambda}),$$

for $\{K_{\mathbf{u}}' = (T_{\mathbf{u},0}', \ldots, T_{\mathbf{u},\lambda}') : \mathbf{u} = (\mathbf{u}_1, \ldots) \in \Gamma_{\mathbf{t}(e+1)}\}$. Set $K_{e+1} = (\{K_{\mathbf{u}}'' : \mathbf{u} \in \Gamma_{\mathbf{t}(e+1)}\}, m(k_e \cdot \delta), pp)$ and return (Δ_{e+1}, K_{e+1}).

$\underline{\mathsf{Enc}(K_e, t, M, e_{\mathsf{exp}})}$: if $e > e_{\mathsf{exp}}$, return $\bot$. For $K_e = (\ldots, m(k_e), pp)$, sample $(g_{\mathbf{u},0}, \ldots, g_{\mathbf{u},\lambda+1})_{\mathbf{u}\in\Gamma_{\mathbf{t}(e)}\backslash\Gamma_{\mathbf{t}(e_{\mathsf{exp}}+1)}} \leftarrow \mathsf{SampG}(pp)$, $S \leftarrow \mathsf{SampS}(pp; s)$, for $s \leftarrow \mathbb{Z}_N^*$, and for all $\mathbf{u} = (\mathbf{u}_1, \ldots) \in \Gamma_{\mathbf{t}(e)} \backslash \Gamma_{\mathbf{t}(e_{\mathsf{exp}}+1)}$, return

$$C_{e,t,e_{\mathsf{exp}}} = (\{(Sg_{\mathbf{u},0}, \prod_{i=1}^{|\mathbf{u}|} g_{\mathbf{u},i}^{\mathbf{u}_i}, g_{\mathbf{u},|\mathbf{u}|+1}, \ldots, g_{\mathbf{u},\lambda}, g_{\mathbf{u},\lambda+1}^t)\}, m(k_e)^s \cdot M).$$

$\underline{\mathsf{ExPunc}(\Delta_{e+1,t'}, C_{e,t,e_{\mathsf{exp}}})}$: if $e \geq e_{\mathsf{exp}}$ or $t' \notin \{t, \forall\}$, return $\bot$. For $\Delta_{e+1,t} = (D_0, D_1, m(k_{e+1}))$ and $C_{e,t,e_{\mathsf{exp}}} = (\{C_{\mathbf{u}}' : \mathbf{u} \in \Gamma_{\mathbf{t}(e)}\}, m(k_e)^s \cdot M)$, if $|\mathbf{t}(e)| < \lambda - 1$, then find $C_{\mathbf{t}(e)}' = (S_0, S_1, S_{|\mathbf{t}(e)|+1}, \ldots, S_\lambda)$, compute

$$C_{\mathbf{t}(e+1)}' = (S_0, S_1 \cdot S_{|\mathbf{t}(e)|+1}, S_{|\mathbf{t}(e)|+2}, \ldots, S_{\lambda+1}),$$
$$C_{\mathbf{t}(e+2)}' = (S_0, S_1 \cdot S_{|\mathbf{t}(e)|+1}^2, S_{|\mathbf{t}(e)|+2}, \ldots, S_{\lambda+1}).$$

Sample $S \leftarrow \mathsf{SampS}(pp; s')$, for $s' \leftarrow \mathbb{Z}_N^*$, $(g_{\mathbf{u},0}, \ldots, g_{\mathbf{u},\lambda+1})_{\mathbf{u}\in\Gamma_{\mathbf{t}(e+1)}} \leftarrow \mathsf{SampG}(pp)$, compute $m(\delta)^s = \frac{e(S_0, D_1)}{e(D_0, S_1 S_{\lambda+1})}$ (where $S_{\lambda+1}$ is only present if $t' \neq \forall$) and

$$C_{\mathbf{u}}'' = (S_{\mathbf{u},0} Sg_{\mathbf{u},0}, S_{\mathbf{u},1} \prod_{i=1}^{|\mathbf{u}|} g_{\mathbf{u},i}^{\mathbf{u}_i}, S_{\mathbf{u},|\mathbf{u}|+1} g_{\mathbf{u},|\mathbf{u}|+1}, \ldots, S_{\mathbf{u},\lambda} g_{\mathbf{u},\lambda}, S_{\mathbf{u},\lambda+1} g_{\mathbf{u},\lambda+1}^t),$$

for $\{C_{\mathbf{u}}' = (S_{\mathbf{u},0}, \ldots, S_{\mathbf{u},\lambda}) : \mathbf{u} = (\mathbf{u}_1, \ldots) \in \Gamma_{\mathbf{t}(e)} \backslash \Gamma_{\mathbf{t}(e_{\mathsf{exp}}+1)}\}$. Return $C_{e+1,t,e_{\mathsf{exp}}} = (\{C_{\mathbf{u}}'' : \mathbf{u} \in \Gamma_{\mathbf{t}(e+1)}\}, m(k_e \cdot \delta)^{s+s'} \cdot M)$.

$\underline{\mathsf{Dec}(K_e, C_{e,t,e_{\mathsf{exp}}})}$: if $e > e_{\mathsf{exp}}$, return $\bot$. For $K_e = (\{K_{\mathbf{u}}' : \mathbf{u} \in \Gamma_{\mathbf{t}(e)}\}, m(k_e), pp)$ and $C_{e,t,e_{\mathsf{exp}}} = (\{C_{\mathbf{u}}' : \mathbf{u} \in \Gamma_{\mathbf{t}(e)}\}, S_T)$, find $K_{\mathbf{t}(e)}' = (T_0, T_1, \ldots)$ and $C_{\mathbf{t}(e)}' = (S_0, S_1, \ldots)$, and return

$$M = S_T \cdot \frac{e(T_0, S_1)}{e(S_0, T_1)}.$$

Correctness. We show:

1) Correct decryption of ciphertexts:

$$M = S_T \cdot \frac{e(T_0, S_1)}{e(S_0, T_1)} = m(k_e)^s \cdot M \cdot \frac{e(h_0, \prod_{i=1}^e g_i)}{e(Sg_0, k_e \prod_{i=1}^e h_i)} = \frac{m(k_e)^s}{e(S, k_e)} \cdot M = M,$$

where $m(k_e)^s = e(S, k_e)$, for some $s \in \mathbb{Z}_N^*$, $e(S, h_i) = 1$, for all $i \in [e]$, and $e(g_0, k_e) = 1$ due to projectiveness, orthogonality, and associativity.

2) Correctness for excluding ciphertexts $C_{e+1,t,e_{\exp}} = (\{C''_{\mathbf{u}} : \mathbf{u} = (u_1, \ldots) \in \Gamma_{\mathbf{t}(e+1)}\}, m(k_{e+1})^{s+s'} \cdot M)$ from puncturing:

$$C''_{\mathbf{u}} = (S_{\mathbf{u},0} S g_{\mathbf{u},0}, S_{\mathbf{u},1} \prod_{i=1}^{|\mathbf{u}|} g_{\mathbf{u},i}^{\mathbf{u}_i}, S_{\mathbf{u},|\mathbf{u}|+1} g_{\mathbf{u},|\mathbf{u}|+1}, \ldots, S_{\mathbf{u},\lambda} g_{\mathbf{u},\lambda+1}^t),$$

where $S \leftarrow \mathsf{SampS}(pp; s')$, for $s' \leftarrow \mathbb{Z}_N^*$, $(g_{\mathbf{u},0}, \ldots, g_{\mathbf{u},\lambda})_{\mathbf{u} \in \Gamma_{\mathbf{t}(e+1)}} \leftarrow \mathsf{SampG}(pp)$, $m(k_{e+1})^{s+s'} = m(k_e)^s \cdot m(\delta)^s \cdot m(k_{e+1})^{s'}$, for $m(\delta)^s = \frac{e(S_{\mathbf{t}(e+1),0}, D_1)}{e(D_0, S_{\mathbf{t}(e+1),1})}$, due to projectiveness, orthogonality, associativity, and $\mathbb{G}$-$\mathbb{H}$-subgroups.

Theorem 2. *If DSG is a DSG scheme, then* TIPE *is IND-TIPE-CPA-secure. Concretely, for any PPT adversary A, it holds:*

$$\mathsf{Adv}_{\mathsf{TIPE},A}^{\mathsf{ind\text{-}tipe\text{-}cpa}}(\lambda) \leq \mathsf{Adv}_{\mathsf{DSG},D_1}^{\mathsf{ls}}(\lambda, \lambda+1) + 2 \cdot (|\Gamma_{\mathbf{t}(e_{\exp}^*)}| + q) \cdot \mathsf{poly}(\lambda) \cdot$$
$$\mathsf{Adv}_{\mathsf{DSG},D_2}^{\mathsf{rs}}(\lambda, \lambda+1) + \mathsf{poly}(\lambda) \cdot \mathsf{Adv}_{\mathsf{DSG},D_3}^{\mathsf{nd}}(\lambda, \lambda+1),$$

with q number of tag-based token queries.

Proof. Let $S_{A,j}$ be the event that A succeeds in Game j. We map the symbol $\forall$ to the integer 0 for ease of proof exposition. Let $S_{A,j}$ be the event that A succeeds in Game j. We highlight changes boxed.

Lemma 1 (Game 0 to Game 1). *For any PPT adversary A, it holds:*

$$|\Pr[S_{A,0}] - \Pr[S_{A,1}]| = 0.$$

Proof. We change the behavior of the challenge oracle such that we use a fresh encryption instead of updating the ciphertext provided by A. The change is agnostic of the tag (and independent of the tokens) and the Chall oracle in Game 1 is as follows:

Chall$(M, C_{e-1,t,e_{\exp}})$: if phase $= 1$, or if $t \notin \mathcal{S}$ and $\mathcal{S} \neq \forall$, return $\bot$. Set phase $= 1$. If $(\cdot, e-1, C_{e-1,t,e_{\exp}}) \notin \mathcal{L}^*$, return $\bot$. If $b = 0$, set $C_{e,t,0}^* \leftarrow \mathsf{Enc}(K_e, t, M, e_{\exp})$, else $\boxed{M := \mathsf{Dec}(K_{e-1}, C_{e-1,t,e_{\exp}})}$ and $\boxed{C_{e,t,1}^* \leftarrow \mathsf{Enc}(K_e, t, M, e_{\exp})}$. Set $\mathcal{C}^* = \mathcal{C}^* \cup (e, C_{e,t,b}^*)$, $e^* = e$, $t^* = t$, $e_{\exp}^* = e_{\exp}$, and return $C_{e,t,b}^*$.

Due to correctness (i.e., via perfect re-randomization), the ciphertexts derived from Enc and ExPunc for an epoch e and tag t yield the same distribution. Hence, such a change cannot be detected by A.

Lemma 2 (Game 1 to Game 2). *For any PPT adversary A there is a distinguisher D on LS such that*

$$|\Pr[S_{A,1}] - \Pr[S_{A,2}]| \leq \mathsf{Adv}_{\mathsf{DSG},D}^{\mathsf{ls}}(\lambda, \lambda+1).$$

Proof. The input is provided as $(pp, \mathbf{T})$, where $\mathbf{T} = (T_0, \ldots, T_{\lambda+1})$ is either $\mathbf{g}$ or $\mathbf{g}\widehat{\mathbf{g}}$, for $\mathbf{g} = (g_0, \ldots, g_{\lambda+1}) \leftarrow \mathsf{SampG}(pp)$ and $(\widehat{\mathbf{g}} = (\widehat{g}_0, \ldots, \widehat{g}_{\lambda+1}), \cdot) \leftarrow \widehat{\mathsf{SampG}}(pp, sp)$. The Chall oracle in Game 2 is as follows:
$\underline{\mathsf{Chall}(M, C_{e-1,t,e_{\exp}})}$: if phase $= 1$, or if $t \notin S$ and $S \neq \forall$, return $\bot$. Set phase $= 1$. If $(\cdot, e-1, C_{e-1,t,e_{\exp}}) \notin \mathcal{L}^*$, return $\bot$. With $\mathbf{u} = (\mathbf{u}_1, \ldots) \in \Gamma_{\mathbf{t}(e)} \setminus \Gamma_{\mathbf{t}(e_{\exp}+1)}$, set

$$C^*_{e,t,0} = (\{(ST_0 g_{\mathbf{u},0}, \prod_{i=1}^{|\mathbf{u}|} T_i^{\mathbf{u}_i} g_{\mathbf{u},i}, T_{|\mathbf{u}|+1} g_{\mathbf{u},|\mathbf{u}|+1}, \ldots, T_{\lambda+1}^t g_{\mathbf{u},\lambda+1})\}_{\mathbf{u}}, m(k_e)^s \cdot M)$$

$$C^*_{e,t,1} = (\{(ST_0 g_{\mathbf{u},0}, \prod_{i=1}^{|\mathbf{u}|} T_i^{\mathbf{u}_i} g_{\mathbf{u},i}, T_{|\mathbf{u}|+1} g_{\mathbf{u},|\mathbf{u}|+1}, \ldots, T_{\lambda+1}^t g_{\mathbf{u},\lambda+1})\}_{\mathbf{u}}, m(k_e)^s \cdot M'),$$

for $M' \leftarrow \mathsf{Dec}(K_{e^*-1}, C_{e^*-1,t,e_{\exp}})$, for $(g_{\mathbf{u},0}, \ldots, g_{\mathbf{u},\lambda+1})_{\mathbf{u}=(\mathbf{u}_1,\ldots) \in \Gamma_{\mathbf{t}(e)} \setminus \Gamma_{\mathbf{t}(e_{\exp}+1)}} \leftarrow \mathsf{SampG}(pp)$, $S \leftarrow \mathsf{SampS}(pp; s)$, for $s \leftarrow \mathbb{Z}_N^*$. Set $\mathcal{C}^* = \mathcal{C}^* \cup (e, C^*_{e,t,b})$, $e^* = e$, $t^* = t$, $e^*_{\exp} = e_{\exp}$, and return $C^*_{e,t,b}$.
If $\mathbf{T} = \mathbf{g}$, then the challenge ciphertext(s) are distributed as in Game 1. If $\mathbf{T} = \mathbf{g}\widehat{\mathbf{g}}$, then the challenge ciphertext(s) are distributed as in Game 2. $\square$

Lemma 3 (Game 2 to Game 3.1.0). *For any PPT adversary A, it holds:*

$$|\Pr[S_{A,2}] - \Pr[S_{A,3.1.0}]| = 0.$$

Proof. This is a conceptional change. Essentially we consistently re-randomize the token and key elements. The KPunc′-oracle in Game 3.0.0 is as follows (where we alter K'_{e+1} after calling KPunc):
$\underline{\mathsf{KPunc}'(S')}$: run $(K'_{e+1}, \Delta'_{e+1}) \leftarrow \mathsf{KPunc}(K_e, S')$. For $K'_{e+1} = (\{(T_{\mathbf{u},0}, T_{\mathbf{u},1}, T_{\mathbf{u},|\mathbf{u}|+1}, \ldots, T_{\mathbf{u},\lambda}) : \mathbf{u} \in \Gamma_{\mathbf{t}(e+1)}\}, m(K_e), pp)$ and $\Delta'_{e+1} = (D_{t,0}, D_{t,1}, D_{t,2})_{t \in S' \cup \{\forall\}}$, sample $(h_{t,0}, \ldots, h_{t,\lambda+1})_{t \in S' \cup \{\forall\}}, (h_{\mathbf{u},0}, \ldots, h_{\mathbf{u},\lambda+1})_{\mathbf{u} \in \Gamma_{\mathbf{t}(e+1)}} \leftarrow \mathsf{SampH}(pp)$, and compute

$$\Delta_{e+1} = (D_{t,0} \boxed{h_{t,0}}, D_{t,1} \cdot \boxed{h_{t,\lambda+1}^t \cdot \prod_{i=1}^{|\mathbf{t}(e+1)|} h_{t,i}^{\mathbf{t}(e+1)_i}}, D_{t,2})_{t \in S'},$$

$$K'_{\mathbf{u}} = (T_{\mathbf{u},0} \boxed{h_{\mathbf{u},0}}, T_{\mathbf{u},1} \boxed{\prod_{i=1}^{|\mathbf{u}|} h_{\mathbf{u},i}^{\mathbf{u}_i}}, T_{\mathbf{u},|\mathbf{u}|+1} \boxed{h_{\mathbf{u},|\mathbf{u}|+1}}, \ldots, T_{\mathbf{u},\lambda} \boxed{h_{\mathbf{u},\lambda}}),$$

for all $\mathbf{u} \in \Gamma_{\mathbf{t}(e+1)}$. Set $K_{e+1} = (\{K'_{\mathbf{u}} : \mathbf{u} \in \Gamma_{\mathbf{t}(e+1)}\}, m(K_e), pp)$. If phase $= 1$, and $t^* \in S'$ or $S' = \forall$, run $C^*_{e+1,t^*,b} \leftarrow \mathsf{ExPunc}(\Delta_{e+1,t^*}, C^*_{e,t^*,b})$ or $C^*_{e+1,t^*,b} \leftarrow \mathsf{ExPunc}(\Delta_{e+1,\forall}, C^*_{e,t^*,b})$, respectively. Set $e = e + 1$ and $S = S'$.

Lemma 4 (Game 3.i.0 to Game 3.i.1). *For any PPT adversary A there is a distinguisher D on RS such that*

$$|\Pr[S_{A,3.i.0}] - \Pr[S_{A,3.i.1}]| \leq \mathsf{poly}(\lambda) \cdot \mathsf{Adv}^{\mathsf{rs}}_{\mathsf{DSG},D}(\lambda, \lambda+1),$$

for $i \in [|\Gamma_{\mathbf{t}(e^*_{\exp})}| + q]$ *and* q *the number of tag-based tokens queried in epochs* $e^* - 1$ *and* $\hat{e}'$.

Proof. The input is provided as $(pp, \widehat{h}, \mathbf{g}\widehat{\mathbf{g}}, \mathbf{T})$, where $\mathbf{T} = (T_0, \dots, T_{\lambda+1})$ is either $\mathbf{h}$ or $\mathbf{h}\widehat{\mathbf{h}}$, for $\mathbf{h} = (h_0, \dots, h_{\lambda+1}) \leftarrow \mathsf{SampH}(pp)$, $(\widehat{\mathbf{h}} = (\widehat{h}_0, \dots, \widehat{h}_{\lambda+1}), \cdot, \cdot) \leftarrow \widehat{\mathsf{SampH}}(pp, sp)$, and $\mathbf{g}\widehat{\mathbf{g}} = (g_0\widehat{g}_0, \dots, g_{\lambda+1}\widehat{g}_{\lambda+1})$. We guess the challenge, expiry, and "window" epoch elements $\hat{e}^*, \hat{e}^*_{\exp}, \hat{e}' \leftarrow [\lfloor \mathsf{poly}(\lambda) \rfloor]$ and abort if $e^* \neq \hat{e}^*$ or $e^*_{\exp} \neq \hat{e}^*_{\exp}$, $\hat{e}' \leq \hat{e}^*$ or $\hat{e}' > \hat{e}^*_{\exp}$. The KPunc' and Chall oracles are as follows:
$\mathsf{KPunc}'(\mathcal{S}')$: run $(K'_{e+1}, \Delta'_{e+1}) \leftarrow \mathsf{KPunc}(K_e, \mathcal{S}')$. For $K'_{e+1} = (\{(T_{\mathbf{u},j'',0}, \overline{T_{\mathbf{u},j'',1}, T_{\mathbf{u},j'',|\mathbf{u}|+1}, \dots, T_{\mathbf{u},j'',\lambda}) : \mathbf{u} \in \Gamma_{\mathbf{t}(e+1)}, j'' \in [|\Gamma_{\mathbf{t}(e+1)}|]\}, m(K_e), pp)$ (we can assume a natural order in K'_{e+1}) and $\Delta'_{e+1} = (D_{t,0}, D_{t,1}, D_{t,2})_{t \in \mathcal{S}' \cup \{\forall\}}$, sample $(h_{t,0}, \dots, h_{t,\lambda+1})_{t \in \mathcal{S} \cup \{\forall\}}, (h_{\mathbf{u},0}, \dots, h_{\mathbf{u},\lambda+1})_{\mathbf{u} \in \Gamma_{\mathbf{t}(e+1)}} \leftarrow \mathsf{SampH}(pp)$, and for the (j, j')-th query (j-th token with its j'-th tag-based part, $(j, j') \in [q'] \times [q_t]$ with $q = q' + q_t$) compute token Δ'_{e+1} as follows:

if $j + j' < i + 1 \wedge (e = \hat{e}^* - 1 \vee e = \hat{e}' - 1)$:

$$(D_{t_{j'},0}h_{t_{j'},0}, D_{t_{j'},1} \cdot h_{t_{j'},\lambda+1}^{t_{j'}} \cdot (\widehat{h})^\alpha \cdot \prod_{i=1}^{|\mathbf{t}(e+1)|} h_{t_{j'},i}^{\mathbf{t}(e+1)_i}, D_{t_{j'},2})_{t_{j'} \in \mathcal{S}' \cup \{\forall\}}$$

if $j + j' = i + 1 \wedge (e = \hat{e}^* - 1 \vee e = \hat{e}' - 1)$:

$$(D_{t_{j'},0} \boxed{T_0}, D_{t_{j'},1} \boxed{T_{\lambda+1}^{t_{j'}}} \cdot \prod_{i=1}^{|\mathbf{t}(e+1)|} \boxed{T_i^{\mathbf{t}(e+1)_i}}, D_{t_{j'},2})_{t_{j'} \in \mathcal{S}' \cup \{\forall\}}$$

else:

$$(D_{t_{j'},0}h_{t_{j'},0}, D_{t_{j'},1} \cdot h_{t_{j'},\lambda+1}^{t_{j'}} \cdot \prod_{i=1}^{|\mathbf{t}(e+1)|} h_i^{\mathbf{t}(e+1)_i}, D_{t_{j'},2})_{t_{j'} \in \mathcal{S}' \cup \{\forall\}}.$$

Moreover, compute key $K'_{\mathbf{u}}$ as follows:

if $q + j'' = i \wedge e = e^*_{\exp}$:

$$(T_{\mathbf{u},j'',0} \boxed{T_0}, T_{\mathbf{u},j'',1} \cdot \prod_{i=1}^{|\mathbf{u}|} \boxed{T_i^{\mathbf{u}_i}}, T_{\mathbf{u},j'',|\mathbf{u}|+1} \boxed{T_{|\mathbf{u}|+1}}, \dots, T_{\mathbf{u},j'',\lambda} \boxed{T_\lambda})$$

else:

$$(T_{\mathbf{u},j,0}h_{\mathbf{u},0}, T_{\mathbf{u},j,1} \cdot \prod_{i=1}^{|\mathbf{u}|} h_{\mathbf{u},i}^{\mathbf{u}_i}, T_{\mathbf{u},j,|\mathbf{u}|+1}h_{\mathbf{u},|\mathbf{u}|+1}, \dots, T_{\mathbf{u},j,\lambda}h_{\mathbf{u},\lambda}),$$

for all $\mathbf{u} \in \Gamma_{\mathbf{t}(e+1)}$, and $\alpha \leftarrow \mathbb{Z}_N$. Set $K_{e+1} = (\{K'_{\mathbf{u}} : \mathbf{u} \in \Gamma_{\mathbf{t}(e+1)}\}, m(K_e), pp)$. If phase = 1, and $t^* \in \mathcal{S}'$ or $\mathcal{S}' = \forall$, run $C^*_{e+1,t^*,b} \leftarrow \mathsf{ExPunc}(\Delta_{e+1,t^*}, C^*_{e,t^*,b})$ or $C^*_{e+1,t^*,b} \leftarrow \mathsf{ExPunc}(\Delta_{e+1,\forall}, C^*_{e,t^*,b})$, respectively. Set $e = e + 1$ and $\mathcal{S} = \mathcal{S}'$.

$\underline{\mathsf{Chall}(M, C_{\hat{e}^*-1, t^*, \hat{e}^*_{\exp}})}$: if phase $= 1$, or if $t^* \notin \mathcal{S}$ and $\mathcal{S} \neq \forall$, return $\bot$. Set phase $= 1$. If $(\cdot, \hat{e}^* - 1, C_{\hat{e}^*-1, t^*, \hat{e}^*_{\exp}}) \notin \mathcal{L}^*$, return $\bot$. Set

$$C^*_{\hat{e}^*, t^*, 0} = (\{(S\boxed{g_0\widehat{g_0}}g_{\mathbf{u},0}, \prod_{i=1}^{|\mathbf{u}|}\boxed{(g_i\widehat{g_i})^{\mathbf{u}_i}}g^{\mathbf{u}_i}_{\mathbf{u},i}, \boxed{g_{|\mathbf{u}|+1}\widehat{g}_{|\mathbf{u}|+1}}g_{\mathbf{u},|\mathbf{u}|+1}, \ldots,$$

$$\boxed{(g_{\lambda+1}\widehat{g}_{\lambda+1})^{t^*}}g^{t^*}_{\mathbf{u}, \lambda+1}) : \mathbf{u} = (u_1, \ldots) \in \Gamma_{\mathbf{t}(\hat{e}^*)} \setminus \Gamma_{\mathbf{t}(\hat{e}^*_{\exp}+1)}\}, m(k_{\hat{e}^*})^s \cdot M),$$

$$C^*_{\hat{e}^*, t^*, 1} = (\{(S\boxed{g_0\widehat{g_0}}g_{\mathbf{u},0}, \prod_{i=1}^{|\mathbf{u}|}\boxed{(g_i\widehat{g_i})^{\mathbf{u}_i}}g^{\mathbf{u}_i}_{\mathbf{u},i}, \boxed{g_{|\mathbf{u}|+1}\widehat{g}_{|\mathbf{u}|+1}}g_{\mathbf{u},|\mathbf{u}|+1}, \ldots,$$

$$\boxed{(g_{\lambda+1}\widehat{g}_{\lambda+1})^{t^*}}g^{t^*}_{\mathbf{u}, \lambda+1}) : \mathbf{u} = (u_1, \ldots) \in \Gamma_{\mathbf{t}(\hat{e}^*)} \setminus \Gamma_{\mathbf{t}(\hat{e}^*_{\exp}+1)}\}, m(k_{\hat{e}^*})^s \cdot M'),$$

for $M' \leftarrow \mathsf{Dec}(K_{e^*-1}, C_{e^*-1, t^*, e_{\exp}})$, for $(g_{\mathbf{u},0}, \ldots, g_{\mathbf{u},\lambda+1})_{\mathbf{u}=(u_1,\ldots)\in \Gamma_{\mathbf{t}(\hat{e}^*)}}$ $\setminus \Gamma_{\mathbf{t}(\hat{e}^*_{\exp}+1)} \leftarrow \mathsf{SampG}(pp)$, $S \leftarrow \mathsf{SampS}(pp; s)$, for $s \leftarrow \mathbb{Z}^*_N$. Set $\mathcal{C}^* = \mathcal{C}^* \cup (\hat{e}^*, C^*_{\hat{e}^*, t^*, b})$, $e^* = \hat{e}^*$, $e^*_{\exp} = \hat{e}^*_{\exp}$, and return $C^*_{\hat{e}^*, t^*, b}$.

If $\mathbf{T} = \mathbf{h}$, then the token $\Delta_{e^*, t}$ with $t \in \{t^*, \forall\}$, the token $\Delta_{e', t}$ with $t \notin \{t^*, \forall\}$, and the key $K_{e'}$ (if $K_{e'}$ is queried) or the key $K_{e^*_{\exp}+1}$ (if $K_{e'}$ is not queried) are distributed as in Game 3.i.0. If $\mathbf{T} = \mathbf{h}\hat{\mathbf{h}}$, then those are distributed as in Game 3.i.1. This reduction loses a polynomial factor.

Lemma 5 (Game 3.i.1 to Game 3.i.2). *For any PPT adversary A, it holds:*

$$|\Pr[S_{A,3.i.1}] - \Pr[S_{A,3.i.2}]| = 0,$$

for $i \in [|\Gamma_{\mathbf{t}(e^*_{\exp})}| + q]$ and a large-enough $e(\lambda)$ polynomial in λ and q the number of tag-based token queries.

Proof. This is reminiscent of Lemma 11 in [43] and results in a pseudo-normal semi-functional token and keys. For all key elements in the set $\Gamma_{\mathbf{t}(e')}$ (if $K_{e'}$ is queried) or in $\Gamma_{\mathbf{t}(e^*_{\exp})}$ (if $K_{e'}$ is not queried) and for all tag-based token queries, we information-theoretically embed $(\widehat{h})^\alpha$ in the i-th (key or token) query step-by-step for each i. This can be only be done if the key or token queries have no epoch or tag prefixes with the challenge ciphertext.

For the tokens $(\Delta_{e^*, t})_{t \in \mathcal{S} \cup \{\forall\}}$ before the challenge epoch, see that such a token has no prefix with the challenge ciphertexts (as the epochs do not match, i.e., such tokens have the epoch $e^* - 1$ encoded and the challenge ciphertext are in epochs $\geq e^*$). We can use this fact to embed a $(\widehat{h})^\alpha$ in $(\Delta_{e^*, t})_{t \in \mathcal{S} \cup \{\forall\}}$ due to [43]. Moreover, see that by validity condition 2), A is not allowed to query a token $\Delta_{e', t}$ with $e^* < e' \leq e^*_{\exp}$ and $t = t^*$ or $t = \forall$ when it has queried a key $K_{e'}$. Hence, we can use such a fact here to embed an $(\widehat{h})^\alpha$-element in $K_{e'}$ as the tokens $(\Delta_{e', t})_t$ do not share prefixes with the challenge ciphertext. (Otherwise the token can be used to update the challenge ciphertext which would raise the validity to fail.) Moreover, no information on $\widehat{h}$ is given out in any $\Delta_{e', t}$ due to orthogonality (i.e., $m(\widehat{h}) = 1$). For the key $K_{e^*_{\exp}+1}$ see that it does not have any prefixes of the challenge ciphertext and we can safely embed $(\widehat{h})^\alpha$ (if $K_{e'}$ was not queried; otherwise, $(\widehat{h})^\alpha$ has already been embedded in such a key). As shown in [43], due to non-degeneracy, we have that $(h_s)^{\alpha'}$ can be replaced by some suitable $(\widehat{h})^\alpha$, for suitable $\alpha, \alpha' \in \mathbb{Z}_N$.

Lemma 6 (Game 3.i.2 to Game 3.i.3). *For any PPT adversary A there is a distinguisher D on RS such that*

$$|\Pr[S_{A,3.i.2}] - \Pr[S_{A,3.i.3}]| \leq \mathsf{poly}(\lambda) \cdot \mathsf{Adv}^{\mathrm{rs}}_{\mathsf{DSG},D}(\lambda, \lambda+1),$$

for $i \in [|\Gamma_{\mathbf{t}(e^*_{\exp})}| + q]$ and q number of tag-based token queries.

Proof. In this step, we undo the game hop from Lemma 4. As a result, we now have a uniform element $(\widehat{h})^\alpha$ embedded in the key and in the token queries for $K_{e'}, K_{e^*_{\exp}+1}$ and $\Delta_{e^*}, \Delta_{e'}$. If $\mathbf{T} = h\widehat{h}$, then the tokens $\Delta_{e^*}, \Delta_{e'}$ and the keys $K_{e'}, K_{e^*_{\exp}+1}$, are distributed as in Game 3.i.2. If $\mathbf{T} = h$, then those are distributed as in Game 3.i.3. This reduction loses a polynomial factor.

Lemma 7 (Game 3.$|\Gamma_{\mathbf{t}(e^*_{\exp})}| + q$.3 to Game 4). *For any PPT adversary A there is a distinguisher D on ND such that*

$$\left|\Pr\left[S_{A,3.|\Gamma_{\mathbf{t}(e^*_{\exp})}|+q.3}\right] - \Pr[S_{A,4}]\right| \leq \mathsf{poly}(\lambda) \cdot \mathsf{Adv}^{\mathrm{nd}}_{\mathsf{DSG},D}(\lambda, \lambda+1),$$

for $i \in [|\Gamma_{\mathbf{t}(e^*_{\exp})}| + 1]$ and q number of tag-based token queries.

Proof. The input is provided as $(pp, \mathbf{Sg}\widehat{\mathbf{g}}, K \cdot (\widehat{h})^\alpha, \mathbf{T})$, where $\mathbf{T}$ is either $e(S, K)$ or $R \leftarrow G_T$, for $\mathbf{g} \leftarrow \mathsf{SampG}(pp)$, $(\widehat{\mathbf{g}}, \cdot) \leftarrow \widehat{\mathsf{SampG}}(pp, sp)$, and $\mathbf{h} \leftarrow \mathsf{SampH}(pp)$, $S \leftarrow \mathsf{SampS}(pp)$, $\mathbf{S} = (S, 1, 0, \ldots)$, $K \leftarrow \mathsf{SampK}(pp)$. We guess the challenge, expiry, and "window" epochs elements $\hat{e}^*, \hat{e}^*_{\exp}, \hat{e}' \leftarrow [\lfloor e(\lambda) \rfloor]$ and abort if $e^* \neq \hat{e}^*$ or $e^*_{\exp} \neq \hat{e}^*_{\exp}$ or $\hat{e}^* < \hat{e}' \leq \hat{e}^*_{\exp}$. The RotKey$'$ and Chall oracles are as follows: KPunc$'(\mathcal{S}')$: run $(K'_{e+1}, \Delta'_{e+1}) \leftarrow \mathsf{KPunc}(K_e, \mathcal{S}')$. (We additionally assume that δ which is sampled in KPunc is available in KPunc$'$ as well as k_1 sampled in Gen in the beginning of the experiment.) For $K'_{e+1} = (\{(T_{\mathbf{u},j'',0}, T_{\mathbf{u},j'',1}, T_{\mathbf{u},j'',|\mathbf{u}|+1}, \ldots, T_{\mathbf{u},j'',\lambda}) : \mathbf{u} \in \Gamma_{\mathbf{t}(e+1)}, j'' \in [|\Gamma_{\mathbf{t}(e+1)}|]\}, m(K_e), pp)$ (we can assume a natural order in K'_{e+1}) and $\Delta'_{e+1} = (D_{t,0}, D_{t,1}, D_{t,2})_{t \in \mathcal{S}' \cup \{\forall\}}$, store $\delta_{e+1} = \delta$, $k_{e+1} = \delta \cdot k_e$ (for $e = \hat{e}^* - 1$, we set $K \cdot k^{-1}_{\hat{e}^*-1}$ as "delta" and K as key in epoch e^*, implicitly), sample $(h_{t,0}, \ldots, h_{t,\lambda+1})_{t \in \mathcal{S} \cup \{\forall\}}, (h_{\mathbf{u},0}, \ldots, h_{\mathbf{u},\lambda+1})_{\mathbf{u} \in \Gamma_{\mathbf{t}(e+1)}} \leftarrow \mathsf{SampH}(pp)$, and for the (j, j')-th token (j-th token with its j'-th tag-based part) query compute token Δ'_{e+1} as follows

if $e = \hat{e}^* - 1$:

$$(D_{t_{j'},0} h_{t_{j'},0}, D_{t_{j'},1} \cdot h_{t_{j'},\lambda+1}^{t_{j'}^{j'}}, \boxed{K \cdot (\widehat{h})^\alpha \cdot k_e^{-1} \cdot \delta_{e+1}^{-1}} \cdot \prod_{i=1}^{|\mathbf{t}(e+1)|} h_{t_{j'},i}^{\mathbf{t}(e+1)_i}, m(\boxed{K \cdot (\widehat{h})^\alpha}))_{t_{j'} \in \mathcal{S}' \cup \{\forall\}}$$

if $e = \hat{e}' - 1$:

$$(D_{t_{j'},0}h_{t_{j'},0}, D_{t_{j'},1} \cdot h_{t_{j'},\lambda+1}^{t_{j'}} \cdot \boxed{(K \cdot (\hat{h})^\alpha \cdot \prod_{e^*}^{e'} \delta_i^{-1} \cdot k_{e'})} \cdot \prod_{i=1}^{|\mathbf{t}(e+1)|} h_{t_{j'},i}^{\mathbf{t}(e+1)_i},$$

$$m\boxed{\left(K \cdot (\hat{h})^\alpha \cdot \prod_{e^*}^{e'} \delta_i^{-1}\right)})_{t_{j'} \in S' \cup \{\forall\}}$$

else:

$$(D_{t_{j'},0}h_{t_{j'},0}, D_{t_{j'},1} \cdot h_{t_{j'},\lambda+1}^{t_{j'}} \cdot \prod_{i=1}^{|\mathbf{t}(e+1)|} h_i^{\mathbf{t}(e+1)_i}, D_{t_{j'},2})_{t_{j'} \in S' \cup \{\forall\}}.$$

Moreover, compute key $K'_{\mathbf{u}}$ as follows:

if $e = e^*_{\exp}$:

$$(T_{\mathbf{u},j'',0}h_{\mathbf{u},0}, T_{\mathbf{u},j'',1} \cdot \boxed{K \cdot (\hat{h})^\alpha \cdot \prod_{i=e^*+1}^{e^*_{\exp}+1} \delta_i} \cdot \prod_{i=1}^{|\mathbf{u}|} h_{\mathbf{u},i}^{\mathbf{u}_i}, T_{\mathbf{u},j'',|\mathbf{u}|+1}h_{\mathbf{u},|\mathbf{u}|+1}, \ldots, T_{\mathbf{u},j'',\lambda}h_{\mathbf{u},\lambda})$$

else:

$$(T_{\mathbf{u},j,0}h_{\mathbf{u},0}, T_{\mathbf{u},j,1} \cdot \prod_{i=1}^{|\mathbf{u}|} h_{\mathbf{u},i}^{\mathbf{u}_i}, T_{\mathbf{u},j,|\mathbf{u}|+1}h_{\mathbf{u},|\mathbf{u}|+1}, \ldots, T_{\mathbf{u},j,\lambda}h_{\mathbf{u},\lambda}),$$

for all $\mathbf{u} \in \Gamma_{\mathbf{t}(e+1)}$, and $\alpha \leftarrow \mathbb{Z}_N$. Set $K_{e+1} = (\{K'_{\mathbf{u}} : \mathbf{u} \in \Gamma_{\mathbf{t}(e+1)}\}, m(K_e), pp)$. If phase $= 1$, and $t^* \in S'$ or $S' = \forall$, run $C^*_{e+1,t^*,b} \leftarrow$ ExPunc$(\Delta_{e+1,t^*}, C^*_{e,t^*,b})$ or $C^*_{e+1,t^*,b} \leftarrow$ ExPunc$(\Delta_{e+1,\forall}, C^*_{e,t^*,b})$, respectively. Set $e = e + 1$ and $S = S'$.

Chall$(M, C_{\hat{e}^*-1,t^*,\hat{e}^*_{\exp}})$: if phase $= 1$, or if $t^* \notin S$ and $S \neq \forall$, return $\bot$. Set phase $= 1$. If $(\cdot, \hat{e}^* - 1, C_{\hat{e}^*-1,t^*,\hat{e}^*_{\exp}}) \notin \mathcal{L}^*$, return $\bot$. Set

$$C^*_{\hat{e}^*,t^*,0} = (\{(\boxed{Sg_0\hat{g}_0} g_{\mathbf{u},0}, \prod_{i=1}^{|\mathbf{u}|} \boxed{(g_i\hat{g}_i)^{\mathbf{u}_i}} g_{\mathbf{u},i}^{\mathbf{u}_i}, \boxed{g_{|\mathbf{u}|+1}\hat{g}_{|\mathbf{u}|+1}} g_{\mathbf{u},|\mathbf{u}|+1}, \ldots,$$

$$\boxed{(g_\lambda \hat{g}_{\lambda+1}} g_{\mathbf{u},\lambda+1})^{t^*}) : \mathbf{u} = (u_1, \ldots) \in \Gamma_{\mathbf{t}(\hat{e}^*)} \setminus \Gamma_{\mathbf{t}(\hat{e}^*_{\exp}+1)}\}, \mathbf{T} \cdot M)$$

$$C^*_{\hat{e}^*,t^*,1} = (\{(\boxed{Sg_0\hat{g}_0} g_{\mathbf{u},0}, \prod_{i=1}^{|\mathbf{u}|} \boxed{(g_i\hat{g}_i)^{\mathbf{u}_i}} g_{\mathbf{u},i}^{\mathbf{u}_i}, \boxed{g_{|\mathbf{u}|+1}\hat{g}_{|\mathbf{u}|+1}} g_{\mathbf{u},|\mathbf{u}|+1}, \ldots,$$

$$\boxed{(g_{\lambda+1}\hat{g}_{\lambda+1}} g_{\mathbf{u},\lambda+1})^{t^*}) : \mathbf{u} = (u_1, \ldots) \in \Gamma_{\mathbf{t}(\hat{e}^*)} \setminus \Gamma_{\mathbf{t}(\hat{e}^*_{\exp}+1)}\}, \mathbf{T} \cdot M'),$$

for $M' \leftarrow$ Dec$(K_{\hat{e}^*-1}, C_{\hat{e}^*-1,t^*,\hat{e}^*_{\exp}})$, for $(g_{\mathbf{u},0}, \ldots, g_{\mathbf{u},\lambda+1})_{\mathbf{u}=(u_1,\ldots) \in \Gamma_{\mathbf{t}(\hat{e}^*)} \setminus \Gamma_{\mathbf{t}(\hat{e}^*_{\exp}+1)}} \leftarrow$ SampG(pp), $S \leftarrow$ SampS$(pp; s)$, for $s \leftarrow \mathbb{Z}_N^*$. Set $\mathcal{C}^* = \mathcal{C}^* \cup (\hat{e}^*, C^*_{\hat{e}^*,t^*,b})$, $e^* = \hat{e}^*$, $e^*_{\exp} = \hat{e}^*_{\exp}$, and return $C^*_{\hat{e}^*,t^*,b}$.

See that $m(K \cdot (\hat{h})^\alpha) = m(K)$ holds. Hence, no information on $(\hat{h})^\alpha$ is given out via m in Δ_{e^*}. Moreover, if the adversary queried $K_{e'}$ (by validity, it is not allowed to have queried $\Delta_{e'-1,t}$ with $t \in \{t^*, \forall\}$), then $(\widehat{h})^\alpha$ hides all key elements in $K_{e'}$. Otherwise, if the adversary did not query $K_{e'}$, then $(\widehat{h})^\alpha$ blinds the key elements in $K_{e^*_{\exp}}$. Now, if $\mathbf{T} = e(S, K)$, then the challenge ciphertext(s) are distributed as in Game $3.|\Gamma_{t(e^*_{\exp})}| + q.3$. If $\mathbf{T} = R$, then the challenge ciphertext(s) are distributed as in Game 4.

Lemma 8 (Game 4). *For any PPT adversary A, $\Pr[S_{A,4}] = 1/2$ holds.*

Proof. In Game 4, for (uniform) $b \in \{0, 1\}$, we provide A with challenge ciphertext(s) that include a uniform G_T-element instead of a A-chosen b-dependent message. Hence, b is completely hidden from A's view.

Taking Lemmata 1, 2, 3, 4, 5, 6, 7, and 8 together, shows Theorem 2.   □

Applications of TIPE beyond UE. TIPE provides an interesting abstraction for outsourced file storage with forward-security and fine-grained secure shredding of files. In a recent work, Backendal, Günther and Paterson [44] introduced such a so-called protected file storage setting and show how this can be instantiated via puncturable key wrapping (introduced in the same work). Loosely speaking, Backendal et al. achieve forward-security via key-rotation (but this requires to download, decrypt and re-encrypt of all file encryption keys) and the shredding of files is achieved via key-puncturing.

We observe that the concept of epochs in TIPE (used as expiry epochs when instantiating UE from TIPE) allows to implement the fine-grained forward-security aspect via efficient key-rotation (though in contrast to [44] via help of the server). Moreover, the ciphertext-tag space in TIPE provides an additional dimension for granularity which allows to implement a secure fine-grained shredding of files, i.e., via puncturing of the ciphertext (by excluding them from updates). We hope that TIPE will find additional applications in this and beyond this context and leave a more detailed study to future work.

Acknowledgements. We thank the anonymous reviewers for valuable feedback. This project has received funding from the European Union's Horizon 2020 ECSEL Joint Undertaking project under grant agreement No 783119 (SECREDAS) and No 826610 (COMP4DRONES), from the Austrian Science Fund (FWF) and netidee SCIENCE grant P31621-N38 (PROFET), and from the European Union's Horizon 2020 Research and Innovation Programme project under grant agreement No 101019808 (TeamAware).

References

1. Barker, E.: Recommendation for key management. NIST Special Publication 800-57 Part 1, Revision 4 (2016). https://doi.org/10.6028/NIST.SP.800-57pt1r4
2. PCI SSC: Ci security standards council. payment card industry data security standard: requirements and testing procedures, v4.0 (2022). https://listings.pcisecuritystandards.org/documents/PCI-DSS-v4-0.pdf

3. Boneh, D., Lewi, K., Montgomery, H., Raghunathan, A.: Key homomorphic PRFs and their applications. In: Canetti, R., Garay, J.A. (eds.) CRYPTO 2013, Part I. LNCS, vol. 8042, pp. 410–428. Springer, Heidelberg (2013). https://doi.org/10.1007/978-3-642-40041-4_23

4. Everspaugh, A., Paterson, K., Ristenpart, T., Scott, S.: Key rotation for authenticated encryption. In: Katz, J., Shacham, H. (eds.) CRYPTO 2017, Part III. LNCS, vol. 10403, pp. 98–129. Springer, Cham (2017). https://doi.org/10.1007/978-3-319-63697-9_4

5. Boneh, D., Eskandarian, S., Kim, S., Shih, M.: Improving speed and security in updatable encryption schemes. In: Moriai, S., Wang, H. (eds.) ASIACRYPT 2020, Part III. LNCS, vol. 12493, pp. 559–589. Springer, Cham (2020). https://doi.org/10.1007/978-3-030-64840-4_19

6. Chen, L., Li, Y., Tang, Q.: CCA updatable encryption against malicious re-encryption attacks. In: Moriai, S., Wang, H. (eds.) ASIACRYPT 2020, Part III. LNCS, vol. 12493, pp. 590–620. Springer, Cham (2020). https://doi.org/10.1007/978-3-030-64840-4_20

7. Lehmann, A., Tackmann, B.: Updatable encryption with post-compromise security. In: Nielsen, J.B., Rijmen, V. (eds.) EUROCRYPT 2018, Part III. LNCS, vol. 10822, pp. 685–716. Springer, Cham (2018). https://doi.org/10.1007/978-3-319-78372-7_22

8. Klooß, M., Lehmann, A., Rupp, A.: (R)CCA secure updatable encryption with integrity protection. In: Ishai, Y., Rijmen, V. (eds.) EUROCRYPT 2019, Part I. LNCS, vol. 11476, pp. 68–99. Springer, Cham (2019). https://doi.org/10.1007/978-3-030-17653-2_3

9. Boyd, C., Davies, G.T., Gjøsteen, K., Jiang, Y.: Fast and secure updatable encryption. In: Micciancio, D., Ristenpart, T. (eds.) CRYPTO 2020, Part I. LNCS, vol. 12170, pp. 464–493. Springer, Cham (2020). https://doi.org/10.1007/978-3-030-56784-2_16

10. Jiang, Y.: The direction of updatable encryption does not matter much. In: Moriai, S., Wang, H. (eds.) ASIACRYPT 2020, Part III. LNCS, vol. 12493, pp. 529–558. Springer, Cham (2020). https://doi.org/10.1007/978-3-030-64840-4_18

11. Nishimaki, R.: The direction of updatable encryption does matter. In: Hanaoka, G., Shikata, J., Watanabe, Y. (eds.) PKC 2022, Part II. LNCS, vol. 13178, pp. 194–224. Springer, Heidelberg (2022). https://doi.org/10.1007/978-3-030-97131-1_7

12. Galteland, Y.J., Pan, J.: Backward-leak uni-directional updatable encryption from (homomorphic) public key encryption. In: Boldyreva, A., Kolesnikov, V. (eds.) PKC 2023, Part II. LNCS, vol. 13941, pp. 399–428. Springer, Heidelberg (2023). https://doi.org/10.1007/978-3-031-31371-4_14

13. Miao, P., Patranabis, S., Watson, G.J.: Unidirectional updatable encryption and proxy re-encryption from DDH. In: Boldyreva, A., Kolesnikov, V. (eds.) PKC 2023, Part II. LNCS, vol. 13941, pp. 368–398. Springer, Heidelberg (2023). https://doi.org/10.1007/978-3-031-31371-4_13

14. Kölbl, S., Pandit, A., Misoczki, R., Schmieg, S.: Crypto agility and post-quantum cryptography at google. Real-World Crypto Symposium (2023)

15. Levy-dit-Vehel, F., Roméas, M.: A composable look at updatable encryption. Cryptology ePrint Archive, Report 2021/538 (2021). https://eprint.iacr.org/2021/538

16. Fabrega, A., Maurer, U., Mularczyk, M.: A fresh approach to updatable symmetric encryption. Cryptology ePrint Archive, Report 2021/559 (2021). https://eprint.iacr.org/2021/559

17. Günther, C.G.: An identity-based key-exchange protocol. In: Quisquater, J.-J., Vandewalle, J. (eds.) EUROCRYPT 1989. LNCS, vol. 434, pp. 29–37. Springer, Heidelberg (1990). https://doi.org/10.1007/3-540-46885-4_5

18. Diffie, W., van Oorschot, P.C., Wiener, M.J.: Authentication and authenticated key exchanges. Des. Codes Cryptogr. **2**(2), 107–125 (1992)

19. Dallmeier, F., et al.: Forward-secure 0-RTT goes live: implementation and performance analysis in QUIC. In: Krenn, S., Shulman, H., Vaudenay, S. (eds.) CANS 2020. LNCS, vol. 12579, pp. 211–231. Springer, Cham (2020). https://doi.org/10.1007/978-3-030-65411-5_11

20. Bruckner, S., Ramacher, S., Striecks, C.: Muckle+: end-to-end hybrid authenticated key exchanges. In: Johansson, T., Smith-Tone, D. (eds.) PQCrypto 2023. LNCS, vol. 14154, pp. 601–633. Springer, Cham (2023). https://doi.org/10.1007/978-3-031-40003-2_22

21. Rösler, P., Slamanig, D., Striecks, C.: Unique-path identity based encryption with applications to strongly secure messaging. In: Hazay, C., Stam, M. (eds.) EUROCRYPT 2023, Part V. LNCS, vol. 14008, pp. 3–34. Springer, Heidelberg (2023). https://doi.org/10.1007/978-3-031-30589-4_1

22. Canetti, R., Halevi, S., Katz, J.: A forward-secure public-key encryption scheme. In: Biham, E. (ed.) EUROCRYPT 2003. LNCS, vol. 2656, pp. 255–271. Springer, Heidelberg (2003). https://doi.org/10.1007/3-540-39200-9_16

23. Groth, J.: Non-interactive distributed key generation and key resharing. Cryptology ePrint Archive, Report 2021/339 (2021). https://eprint.iacr.org/2021/339

24. Bellare, M., Miner, S.K.: A forward-secure digital signature scheme. In: Wiener, M. (ed.) CRYPTO 1999. LNCS, vol. 1666, pp. 431–448. Springer, Heidelberg (1999). https://doi.org/10.1007/3-540-48405-1_28

25. Drijvers, M., Gorbunov, S., Neven, G., Wee, H.: Pixel: multi-signatures for consensus. In Capkun, S., Roesner, F. (eds.) USENIX Security 2020, pp. 2093–2110. USENIX Association (2020)

26. Bost, R., Minaud, B., Ohrimenko, O.: Forward and backward private searchable encryption from constrained cryptographic primitives. In: Thuraisingham, B.M., Evans, D., Malkin, T., Xu, D. (eds.) ACM CCS 2017, pp. 1465–1482. ACM Press (2017)

27. Dauterman, E., Corrigan-Gibbs, H., Mazières, D.: Safetypin: encrypted backups with human-memorable secrets. In: 14th USENIX Symposium on Operating Systems Design and Implementation (2020)

28. Derler, D., Krenn, S., Lorünser, T., Ramacher, S., Slamanig, D., Striecks, C.: Revisiting proxy re-encryption: forward secrecy, improved security, and applications. In: Abdalla, M., Dahab, R. (eds.) PKC 2018, Part I. LNCS, vol. 10769, pp. 219–250. Springer, Cham (2018). https://doi.org/10.1007/978-3-319-76578-5_8

29. Lauer, S., Gellert, K., Merget, R., Handirk, T., Schwenk, J.: T0RTT: Non-interactive immediate forward-secret single-pass circuit construction. PoPETs **2020**(2), 336–357 (2020)

30. Derler, D., Ramacher, S., Slamanig, D., Striecks, C.: Fine-grained forward secrecy: allow-list/deny-list encryption and applications. In: FC (2021)

31. Green, M.D., Miers, I.: Forward secure asynchronous messaging from puncturable encryption. In: 2015 IEEE Symposium on Security and Privacy, pp. 305–320. IEEE Computer Society Press (2015)

32. Sun, S., et al.: Practical backward-secure searchable encryption from symmetric puncturable encryption. In Lie, D., Mannan, M., Backes, M., Wang, X. (eds.) ACM CCS 2018, pp. 763–780. ACM Press (2018)

33. Aviram, N., Gellert, K., Jager, T.: Session resumption protocols and efficient forward security for TLS 1.3 0-RTT. J. Cryptol. **34**(3), 20 (2021)

34. Boyd, C., Davies, G.T., de Kock, B., Gellert, K., Jager, T., Millerjord, L.: Symmetric key exchange with full forward security and robust synchronization. In: Tibouchi, M., Wang, H. (eds.) ASIACRYPT 2021 (2021)

35. Cohen, A., Holmgren, J., Nishimaki, R., Vaikuntanathan, V., Wichs, D.: Watermarking cryptographic capabilities. In: Wichs, D., Mansour, Y. (eds.) 48th ACM STOC, pp. 1115–1127. ACM Press (2016)

36. Canetti, R., Raghuraman, S., Richelson, S., Vaikuntanathan, V.: Chosen-ciphertext secure fully homomorphic encryption. In: Fehr, S. (ed.) PKC 2017, Part II. LNCS, vol. 10175, pp. 213–240. Springer, Heidelberg (2017). https://doi.org/10.1007/978-3-662-54388-7_8

37. Günther, F., Hale, B., Jager, T., Lauer, S.: 0-RTT key exchange with full forward secrecy. In: Coron, J.-S., Nielsen, J.B. (eds.) EUROCRYPT 2017, Part III. LNCS, vol. 10212, pp. 519–548. Springer, Cham (2017). https://doi.org/10.1007/978-3-319-56617-7_18

38. Derler, D., Jager, T., Slamanig, D., Striecks, C.: Bloom filter encryption and applications to efficient forward-secret 0-RTT key exchange. In: Nielsen, J.B., Rijmen, V. (eds.) EUROCRYPT 2018, Part III. LNCS, vol. 10822, pp. 425–455. Springer, Cham (2018). https://doi.org/10.1007/978-3-319-78372-7_14

39. Derler, D., Gellert, K., Jager, T., Slamanig, D., Striecks, C.: Bloom filter encryption and applications to efficient forward-secret 0-RTT key exchange. J. Cryptol. **34**, 1–59 (2021)

40. Waters, B.: Dual system encryption: realizing fully secure IBE and HIBE under simple assumptions. In: Halevi, S. (ed.) CRYPTO 2009. LNCS, vol. 5677, pp. 619–636. Springer, Heidelberg (2009). https://doi.org/10.1007/978-3-642-03356-8_36

41. Lewko, A.: Tools for simulating features of composite order bilinear groups in the prime order setting. In: Pointcheval, D., Johansson, T. (eds.) EUROCRYPT 2012. LNCS, vol. 7237, pp. 318–335. Springer, Heidelberg (2012). https://doi.org/10.1007/978-3-642-29011-4_20

42. Chen, J., Wee, H.: Fully, (almost) tightly secure IBE and dual system groups. In: Canetti, R., Garay, J.A. (eds.) CRYPTO 2013, Part II. LNCS, vol. 8043, pp. 435–460. Springer, Heidelberg (2013). https://doi.org/10.1007/978-3-642-40084-1_25

43. Gong, J., Cao, Z., Tang, S., Chen, J.: Extended dual system group and shorter unbounded hierarchical identity based encryption. Des. Codes Cryptogr. **80**(3), 525–559 (2016)

44. Backendal, M., Günther, F., Paterson, K.G.: Puncturable key wrapping and its applications. In: Agrawal, S., Lin, D. (eds.) ASIACRYPT 2022, Part II. LNCS, vol. 13792, pp. 651–681. Springer, Heidelberg (2022). https://doi.org/10.1007/978-3-031-22966-4_22

45. Lewko, A., Waters, B.: New techniques for dual system encryption and fully secure HIBE with short ciphertexts. In: Micciancio, D. (ed.) TCC 2010. LNCS, vol. 5978, pp. 455–479. Springer, Heidelberg (2010). https://doi.org/10.1007/978-3-642-11799-2_27

46. Lewko, A., Waters, B.: Unbounded HIBE and attribute-based encryption. In: Paterson, K.G. (ed.) EUROCRYPT 2011. LNCS, vol. 6632, pp. 547–567. Springer, Heidelberg (2011). https://doi.org/10.1007/978-3-642-20465-4_30

47. Lewko, A.: Tools for simulating features of composite order bilinear groups in the prime order setting. Cryptology ePrint Archive, Report 2011/490 (2011). https://eprint.iacr.org/2011/490

48. Slamanig, D., Striecks, C.: Puncture 'EM all: updatable encryption with no-directional key updates and expiring ciphertexts. Cryptology ePrint Archive, Report 2021/268 (2021). https://eprint.iacr.org/2021/268

49. Okamoto, T., Takashima, K.: Fully secure unbounded inner-product and attribute-based encryption. In: Wang, X., Sako, K. (eds.) ASIACRYPT 2012. LNCS, vol. 7658, pp. 349–366. Springer, Heidelberg (2012). https://doi.org/10.1007/978-3-642-34961-4_22

50. Hofheinz, D., Koch, J., Striecks, C.: Identity-based encryption with (almost) tight security in the multi-instance, multi-ciphertext setting. In: Katz, J. (ed.) PKC 2015. LNCS, vol. 9020, pp. 799–822. Springer, Heidelberg (2015). https://doi.org/10.1007/978-3-662-46447-2_36

51. Attrapadung, N., Hanaoka, G., Yamada, S.: A framework for identity-based encryption with almost tight security. In: Iwata, T., Cheon, J.H. (eds.) ASIACRYPT 2015, Part I. LNCS, vol. 9452, pp. 521–549. Springer, Heidelberg (2015). https://doi.org/10.1007/978-3-662-48797-6_22

52. Gong, J., Chen, J., Dong, X., Cao, Z., Tang, S.: Extended nested dual system groups, revisited. In: Cheng, C.-M., Chung, K.-M., Persiano, G., Yang, B.-Y. (eds.) PKC 2016, Part I. LNCS, vol. 9614, pp. 133–163. Springer, Heidelberg (2016). https://doi.org/10.1007/978-3-662-49384-7_6

53. Gong, J., Waters, B., Wee, H.: ABE for DFA from k-Lin. In: Boldyreva, A., Micciancio, D. (eds.) CRYPTO 2019, Part II. LNCS, vol. 11693, pp. 732–764. Springer, Cham (2019). https://doi.org/10.1007/978-3-030-26951-7_25

54. Gong, J., Wee, H.: Adaptively secure ABE for DFA from k-Lin and more. In: Canteaut, A., Ishai, Y. (eds.) EUROCRYPT 2020, Part III. LNCS, vol. 12107, pp. 278–308. Springer, Cham (2020). https://doi.org/10.1007/978-3-030-45727-3_10

55. Datta, P., Komargodski, I., Waters, B.: Fully adaptive decentralized multi-authority ABE. In: Hazay, C., Stam, M. (eds.) EUROCRYPT 2023, Part III. LNCS, vol. 14006, pp. 447–478. Springer, Heidelberg (2023). https://doi.org/10.1007/978-3-031-30620-4_15

Combinatorially Homomorphic Encryption

Yuval Ishai$^{(\boxtimes)}$ ⒾⒹ, Eyal Kushnir ⒾⒹ, and Ron D. Rothblum ⒾⒹ

Technion, Haifa, Israel
{yuvali,eyal.kushnir,rothblum}@cs.technion.ac.il

Abstract. Homomorphic encryption enables public computation over encrypted data. In the past few decades, homomorphic encryption has become a staple of both the theory and practice of cryptography. Nevertheless, while there is a general loose understanding of what it means for a scheme to be homomorphic, to date there is no single unifying minimal definition that captures all schemes. In this work, we propose a new definition, which we refer to as *combinatorially homomorphic encryption*, which attempts to give a broad base that captures the intuitive meaning of homomorphic encryption.

Our notion relates the ability to accomplish some task when given a ciphertext, to accomplishing the same task without the ciphertext, in the context of *communication complexity*. Thus, we say that a scheme is combinatorially homomorphic if there exists a communication complexity problem $f(x, y)$ (where x is Alice's input and y is Bob's input) which requires communication c, but can be solved with communication less than c when Alice is given in addition also an encryption $E_k(y)$ of Bob's input (using Bob's key k).

We show that this definition indeed captures pre-existing notions of homomorphic encryption and (suitable variants are) sufficiently strong to derive prior known implications of homomorphic encryption in a conceptually appealing way. These include constructions of (lossy) public-key encryption from homomorphic private-key encryption, as well as collision-resistant hash functions and private information retrieval schemes.

1 Introduction

Homomorphic encryption, originally proposed by Rivest, Adleman, and Dertouzos [39], is one of the cornerstones of modern cryptography. Roughly speaking, an encryption scheme is homomorphic wrt to a function f if given an encryption of a message m, it is possible to generate an encryption of $f(m)$, without knowing the secret key. Homomorphic encryption is used extensively in cryptography, whether explicitly, or implicitly via homomorphisms offered by concrete schemes (e.g., based on factoring, discrete log, or lattices). Until 2009, the default interpretation of homomorphic encryption was for f to be a linear function; this is still a commonly used special case today both in theory and in practice. However, since then, we have seen the development of *fully* homomorphic encryption schemes [11,18], which are homomorphic wrt to *all* functions f.

© International Association for Cryptologic Research 2023
G. Rothblum and H. Wee (Eds.): TCC 2023, LNCS 14370, pp. 251–278, 2023.
https://doi.org/10.1007/978-3-031-48618-0_9

There are many different candidates for homomorphic encryption from the literature (Goldwasser-Micali [22], Benaloh [6], ElGamal [17], Paillier [34], Damgård-Jurik [15], Regev [38] and more) and many different interpretations and precise definitions for what exact form of homomorphism they achieve. However, all definitions that we are aware of (and are discussed in detail next) are either too strict, in the sense that they only capture a few of the candidates, or are too broad, in the sense that they do not draw a clear line between "trivial" and "nontrivial" homomorphism.

Thus, despite being a central notion in cryptography, there is no canonical definition of what it means for an encryption scheme to be homomorphic. The main goal of this work is to introduce such a broad notion (or rather several variants following one theme) that captures and abstracts the intuition underlying the concept of homomorphic encryption and may serve as a default "minimal" interpretation of what homomorphic encryption means.

Let (Gen, Enc, Dec) be a (private-key or public-key) encryption scheme. We proceed to discuss several takes on the notion of homomorphic encryption, and what we find lacking in each.

Ideal Homomorphism: A very simple and strong definition of homomorphic encryption may require that a homomorphically evaluated ciphertext, generated by an evaluation of the function f on the ciphertext $E_{pk}(m)$, is distributed similarly[1] to $E_{pk}(f(m))$.

This notion is extremely strong (and useful) and is satisfied by a few number theoretic based schemes such as Goldwasser-Micali [22] and Benaloh [6] (ElGamal [17] and Paillier/Damgård-Jurik [15,34] also offer some form of ideal homomorphism but suffer from caveats that are discussed below). Unfortunately, many other schemes, especially lattice-based ones, do not satisfy it. Moreover, this strong notion is an overkill for many applications.

Algebraic Homomorphism: (a.k.a. Linear Homomorphism or Additive Homomorphism) An algebraic perspective taken earlier on (and inspired by the number-theory based schemes available at the time), is to view the plaintext and ciphertexts spaces as groups, so that the encryption function is a homomorphism from the former to the latter.[2] Thus, running the group operation on the ciphertexts has the effect of implementing the corresponding group operation on the plaintexts.

Unfortunately, this definition is quite restrictive. In particular, it does not capture homomorphisms that are non-linear such as [9,20,28] let alone fully-homomorphic schemes (e.g., [11,18,21]). ElGamal with plaintexts implemented as group elements is only homomorphic wrt the underlying cryptographic group, whereas ElGamal with plaintexts in the exponent only supports decryption of small plaintext values. Lattice-based encryption schemes

---

[1] Several variants of the definition are possible depending on whether the similarity should be perfect, statistical or computational, and also whether it should hold even given additional information such as $E_{pk}(m)$, or even given the corresponding secret-key. We ignore these subtleties here.

[2] Indeed, this is the source of the term homomorphic encryption.

such as Regev [38] only support a bounded number of operations that depend on the modulus-to-noise ratio.

Functional Homomorphism: A typical modern definition of (public-key) homomorphic encryption states that an encryption scheme (Gen, Enc, Dec) is homomorphic wrt to a function f, or (more generally) a class $\mathcal{F}$ of functions, if there exists a poly-time Eval algorithm such that $\mathsf{Dec}_{sk}\Big(\mathsf{Eval}_{pk}\big(\mathsf{Enc}_{pk}(m), f\big)\Big) = f(m)$ for all messages m, key-pairs (pk, sk), and $f \in \mathcal{F}$. To avoid trivial solutions, the homomorphic evaluation algorithm is further assumed to be "compact." This is typically defined to mean that the size of the generated ciphertext or the decryption circuit is smaller than the circuit size of f.[3] The precise notion of compactness varies both quantitatively (Should the size of the evaluated ciphertext be independent of the circuit? Is a poly-logarithmic or even sub-linear dependence allowed?) and qualitatively (Why circuits? How exactly is circuit complexity measured? What about redundancies in the representation?). In particular, it is unclear what a minimal notion of compactness that suffices for applications should be. Beyond the difficulty with formalizing the common notion of compactness, we point out several additional difficulties with existing definitions of functional homomorphism:

1. Usually, lattice-based schemes only satisfy an approximate notion of this definition as there is a noise associated with each ciphertext, and this noise grows as the homomorphic evaluation is performed, until a point in which the ciphertext is undecryptable.

   This can sometimes be avoided by using a large modulus-to-noise ratio, but that is merely hiding the problem under the rug—we do think of the schemes as homomorphic even when the modulus-to-noise ratio is small, but the definition is not flexible enough to capture this.

2. Discrete-log based schemes such as ElGamal, over a cyclic plaintext group of order q, are often thought of as linearly homomorphic with addition in the group $\mathbb{Z}_q$. As briefly mentioned above though, one can only decrypt ciphertexts whose messages are polynomially small as decryption involves a discrete-log operation.

   Despite this well-known fact, ElGamal is considered to be additively homomorphic but capturing it within the existing framework is quite messy.

3. Lastly, if one wishes to define homomorphic encryption in general, that is, not specifically wrt some function f, this approach becomes problematic. For example, simply assuming the existence of *some* function f such that

---

[3] If compactness is not required, then the homomorphic evaluation can be trivially delegated to the decryptor (e.g., by appending the description of the circuit the ciphertext). Nevertheless, some homomorphic schemes such as [41] or constructions based on garbled circuits [12,19,25,27] are not compact but are circuit private, meaning that the ciphertext does not reveal the evaluated circuit. In this work, we focus on compact homomorphic encryption, which is meaningful even without circuit privacy.

the scheme is functionally homomorphic wrt f is not very meaningful if f is the identity function or a constant function. More generally, it is not entirely clear what non-triviality constraints f needs to satisfy for this notion to be meaningful or useful.

1.1   Combinatorially Homomorphic Encryption

Our main contribution is proposing a new definition for homomorphic encryption. Our goal in this definition is threefold: (1) we wish to find a notion that is consistent and truly formalizes the intuitive meaning of homomorphic encryption, drawing precise lines between "trivial" and "nontrivial" homomorphism; (2) for the definition to be sufficiently broad to capture all schemes that are currently thought of as homomorphic (including both number-theory and lattice-based schemes) and (3) for the definition to be sufficiently strong to preserve the known implications of existing notions of homomorphic encryption such as public-key encryption (PKE), collision-resistant hashing (CRH) and private information retrieval (PIR). We believe that positioning homomorphic encryption as a true cryptographic primitive, similarly to "one-way function" or "public-key encryption", will facilitate a systematic study of its relation with other cryptographic primitives.

We call this new framework *combinatorially homomorphic encryption*, of which we describe several variants. The first variant refers to *communication complexity* [43], which we briefly review. Recall that in *distributional communication complexity* there are two parties, Alice and Bob, who respectively get inputs x and y, drawn from some joint distribution. Their goal is to compute some function $f(x, y)$ while minimizing the number of bits exchanged between them to the extent possible. In our most basic definition (which is sufficient for most of the goals listed above), we focus specifically on *one-way* communication complexity—that is when communication is only allowed from Alice to Bob (and not in the other direction). In other words, the minimal number of bits that Alice needs to send to Bob so that he can compute $f(x, y)$. See [29,36] for a detailed introduction to communication complexity.

The first instantiation of our framework for homomorphic encryption takes the following operational perspective. We say that a scheme is *communication-complexity (CC) homomorphic* if there exists some one-way communication complexity problem f, which requires communication c, such that if Alice is given, in addition to x, a ciphertext $\mathsf{Enc}_k(y)$ of Bob's input using Bob's key k, then the communication problem can be solved using less than c bits (and where Alice and Bob both run in polynomial-time). Note that while it is possible to talk about CC-homomorphic encryption with respect to a specific communication complexity problem, our main definition refers to the *existence* of a communication complexity problem for which the notion is non-trivial.

Definition 1 (Informally Stated, see Sect. *3*). *We say that an encryption scheme* (Gen, Enc, Dec) *is* CC homomorphic *if there exists a communication complexity problem f which requires communication c, but there exists a polynomial-*

time one-way protocol for solving the problem $f'((x, \mathsf{Enc}_k(y)), (y, k))$, *defined as* $f'((x, \mathsf{Enc}_k(y)), (y, k)) = f(x, y)$, *with communication less than* c.

The definition can be adapted to the public-key setting in the natural way (i.e., y is encrypted under the public key and Bob gets the corresponding private key).

CC homomorphic encryption captures the basic intuitive understanding that homomorphic encryption should enable *useful* computation on encrypted data. Here, Alice can perform such a computation in a way that helps Bob derive the output more efficiently than if Alice had not been given the ciphertext.

We also consider generalizations of this notion in two ways. First, we consider an interactive variant (presented in the full version), in which the homomorphic communication game is allowed to be interactive and the communication complexity lower bound holds in the interactive setting (which is the standard model for communication complexity). Motivated by applications described below, we also consider comparing the "homomorphic communication complexity" to other combinatorial measures of the function f such as its VC dimension.[4] Lastly, while our basic definition considers distributional communication complexity over efficiently sampleable *product* distributions, it suffices for our results that the conditional marginal distributions are efficiently sampleable.

Existing Schemes in the Lens of Combinatorially Homomorphic Encryption. To see that CC homomorphic encryption indeed captures existing schemes, consider an encryption scheme that is linearly homomorphic mod 2, in the standard functional sense. To see that such a scheme is combinatorially homomorphic, consider the inner product communication complexity game in which Alice and Bob get as input random vectors $x, y \in \{0, 1\}^n$ and Bob's goal is to compute their inner product $\langle x, y \rangle = \bigoplus_{i \in [n]} x_i y_i$. It is well-known that this task requires communication complexity $\Omega(n)$ (in fact, in the one-way version, this follows directly from the leftover hash lemma). However, if Alice is given in addition to x, also a bit-by-bit encryption $\mathsf{Enc}_k(y_1), \ldots, \mathsf{Enc}_k(y_n)$ of Bob's input, then using the linear homomorphism she can compute an encryption of $\langle x, y \rangle$ and send it to Bob, who can decrypt and retrieve the result. The compactness property of functional homomorphic encryption guarantees that the communication in this new protocol is smaller than the $\Omega(n)$ lower bound that holds when Alice is not given the encryption of Bob's input.

The above idea can be generalized to linear homomorphisms over any group, as stated in the following theorem. A simple unifying explanation is that traditional homomorphic schemes from the literature imply PIR, which can be thought of as being CC-homomorphic with respect to the "index" function. In particular, it shows that Goldwasser-Micali [22], Benaloh [6] and Regev [38] fall within our framework.

Theorem 1 (Informally Stated, see the full version). *Any linearly homomorphic private-key encryption scheme is combinatorially homomorphic.*

---

[4] More precisely, we consider the VC dimension of the function family $\{f_x : \{0, 1\}^n \rightarrow \{0, 1\}\}_x$, where $f_x(y) = f(x, y)$.

To illustrate a concrete instantiation, we show a simple private-key scheme based on Learning with Errors (LWE) that satisfies our definition. The secret key is a random vector $\mathbf{s} \leftarrow \mathbb{Z}_q^\lambda$. To encrypt a bit $b \in \{0,1\}$, sample a random $\mathbf{a} \leftarrow \mathbb{Z}_q^\lambda$ and output $(\mathbf{a}, \langle \mathbf{a}, \mathbf{s} \rangle + e + \lfloor q/2 \rfloor \cdot b)$ as the ciphertext, where $e \in \mathbb{Z}_q$ comes from a B-bounded noise distribution. The security of this private-key scheme follows almost tautologically from decisional LWE.

Now consider the communication complexity game in which Alice and Bob get as their respective inputs $x, y \in \{0,1\}^n$ and their goal is to compute the inner product. As mentioned above, it is well known that this problem requires communication complexity $\Omega(n)$. Suppose however that Alice is given a bit-by-bit encryption of Bob's input. Namely, ciphertexts $c_1, \ldots, c_n$ such that $c_i = (\mathbf{a}_i, \langle \mathbf{a}_i, \mathbf{s} \rangle + e_i + \lfloor q/2 \rfloor \cdot y_i)$. Alice can now compute a new ciphertext $(\mathbf{a}', \sigma')$, where $\mathbf{a}' = \sum_i x_i \cdot \mathbf{a}_i$ and $\sigma' = \sum_i x_i \cdot (\langle \mathbf{a}_i, \mathbf{s} \rangle + e_i + \lfloor q/2 \rfloor \cdot y_i) = \langle \mathbf{a}', \mathbf{s} \rangle + \sum_i x_i e_i + \lfloor q/2 \rfloor \cdot \langle x, y \rangle$ (and all arithmetic is mod q). Alice sends this ciphertext to Bob who computes $\sigma' - \langle \mathbf{a}', \mathbf{s} \rangle = \sum_i x_i e_i + \lfloor q/2 \rfloor \cdot \langle x, y \rangle$. As long as $\sum_i x_i e_i < q/4$ (which holds if $B \cdot n < q/4$), then Bob can now correctly round and obtain $\langle x, y \rangle$. If the communication in this game (which is $(\lambda + 1) \cdot \log(q)$) is smaller than the communication complexity lower bound of $\Omega(n)$, then this basic private-key scheme is CC homomorphic.[5]

Jumping ahead, one of our main applications is a construction of *public-key encryption* from any CC homomorphic *private-key* encryption (which extends the [40] construction of public-key encryption from linearly homomorphic encryption). Thus, the above construction yields a public-key encryption scheme from LWE which, we believe, cleanly abstracts Regev's [38] celebrated public-key scheme. Furthermore, our work is the first one to offer a qualitative notion of homomorphism, where each choice of parameters (including secret distribution and noise distribution) can be classified as either being combinatorially homomorphic or not.

Note that the definition of CC homomorphic encryption is sufficiently flexible to allow for variations of linear homomorphisms, and even for non-linear homomorphisms, that may be difficult to capture otherwise. All one needs to do is to adapt the communication complexity game to capture the specific functionality that is offered by the scheme and show the corresponding communication complexity lower bound (which is usually not difficult).

Consider, for example, the ElGamal cryptosystem [17] with plaintexts in the exponent, which is widely considered to be homomorphic, yet is not captured by the standard linearly homomorphic encryption definition (since decryption involves a discrete-log operation). The scheme works over a cyclic group $\mathbb{G}$ of order q with generator g. The secret key is a random $s \leftarrow \mathbb{Z}_q$. To encrypt a bit $b \in \{0,1\}$, sample a random $r \leftarrow \mathbb{Z}_q$ and output $(g^r, g^{s \cdot r + b})$. To decrypt a ciphertext (c_0, c_1), compute $z = c_1 \cdot c_0^{-s}$ and output 0 if $z = 1$ and 1 otherwise.

---

[5] The homomorphic private-key to public-key transformation of Rothblum [40] can also be viewed as morally giving an abstraction of Regev's scheme, but the actual formal definition of homomorphic encryption used in [40] is not technically achieved by the above private-key scheme.

The security of this private-key scheme follows from the decisional Diffie-Hellman assumption.

To show that the above encryption scheme is CC-homomorphic we will use the well-known Disjointness communication complexity problem, where Alice and Bob are given sets $x, y \subseteq [n]$ respectively, and need to determine whether their sets are disjoint. Babai *et al.* [4] showed that the disjointness problem has communication complexity $\Omega(\sqrt{n})$ (on a specific product distribution[6]). Suppose however that Alice is given bit-by-bit encryptions $c_1, ..., c_n$ of Bob's input (the input sets x and y can be represented as indicator vectors so that $c_i = (g^{r_i}, g^{r_i \cdot s + y_i})$. Alice can then compute $\left(\prod_{i \in \mathcal{I}(x)} g^{r_i}, \prod_{i \in \mathcal{I}(x)} g^{r_i \cdot s + y_i} \right) = (g^{r'}, g^{r' \cdot s + \sum_{i \in \mathcal{I}(x)} y_i})$, where $\mathcal{I}(x) = \{i : x_i = 1\}$. Alice can send this ciphertext to Bob who can compute $z = g^{r' \cdot s + \sum_{i \in \mathcal{I}(x)} y_i} \cdot (g^{r'})^{-s} = g^{\sum_{i \in \mathcal{I}(x)} y_i}$. It holds that $z = 1$ if and only if the sets are disjoint. Therefore, if the communication complexity of this protocol (which is $2\log(q)$) is smaller than the communication complexity lower bound (which is $\sqrt{n}$), then the private-key scheme is CC-homomorphic.

The above idea can be generalized to capture any encryption scheme that is homomorphic with respect to the OR operation, as stated in the following theorem.

Theorem 2 (Informally Stated, see the full version). *Any OR-homomorphic private-key encryption scheme is combinatorially homomorphic.*

We also show a specific instantiation of our scheme using low-noise LPN (i.e., when the absolute noise is roughly $\log^2(\lambda)$). Using our framework in combination with the applications listed below, we can re-derive recent results on LPN (due to [7,10]) in a way that we find to be conceptually simpler.

Applications. As our main technical results, we show that suitable variations of our basic notion of combinatorially homomorphic encryption suffice to derive some of the key applications that are known from (say) standard linearly homomorphic encryption.

Our first main result shows how to transform any combinatorially homomorphic *private-key* encryption into a public-key one. This generalizes the work of Rothblum [40], who gave such a transformation for linearly homomorphic private-key encryption. As a matter of fact, we obtain the stronger notion of *lossy* public-key encryption [5,35] (which is equivalent to semi-honest two-message statistical oblivious transfer [23]).

Theorem 3 (Informally Stated, see Theorem 8). *If there exists a combinatorially homomorphic private-key encryption scheme then there exists a lossy public-key encryption scheme.*

---

[6] In fact, Razborov [37] showed an input distribution on which the communication complexity of disjointness is $\Omega(n)$. However, since this input distribution is not a *product* distribution, using involves slightly more involved techniques (see further discussion in Sect. 3.1).

We remark that the security property required from the private-key scheme is very mild (and in particular is weaker than CPA security). Specifically, we merely need a weak notion of "entropic security" (see Definition 7) which, loosely speaking, requires that the distributions $(y, \mathsf{Enc}_k(y))$ and $(y, \mathsf{Enc}_k(y'))$ are computationally indistinguishable, where y, y' are independent samples drawn from Bob's input distribution in the communication game.

As it is instructive to understanding the power of CC homomorphic encryption, we briefly sketch a simplified proof of Theorem 3 next. The public key of the scheme is $(y, \mathsf{Enc}_k(y))$, where y is a random input for Bob in the communication game, and k is the private key of the private-key scheme. To encrypt a bit b, a random input x for Alice is sampled, and the ciphertext is Alice's message in the "homomorphic" protocol m_A, as well as $f(x, y) \oplus b$. To decrypt, we run Bob on input $((y, k), m_A)$ to compute $f(x, y)$, and then we can retrieve the message bit b. Correctness follows from the correctness of the homomorphic protocol. As for security, using the entropic security of the private-key scheme, we can switch the public key $(y, \mathsf{Enc}_k(y))$ to the lossy public key $(y, \mathsf{Enc}_k(y'))$. Thus, the adversary's goal now is essentially to compute $f(x, y)$ given $(y, \mathsf{Enc}_k(y'))$ and m_A.

Assume that this is possible. Then we can derive a more efficient communication complexity protocol for computing f in the standard setting, in which Alice gets only x and Bob gets only y. Alice and Bob sample a key k and a ciphertext $\mathsf{Enc}_k(y')$ using shared randomness.[7] Then, Alice generates a message m_A from the homomorphic protocol and sends it to Bob, who can then run the adversary on input $((y, c), m_A)$ to compute $f(x, y)$. Since we required that Alice's message in the homomorphic protocol is shorter than the communication complexity of f, we derive a contradiction. Note that this argument immediately gives the stronger notion of *lossy* encryption.

This basic result can be generalized to interactive combinatorially homomorphic encryption in which case we derive a key agreement protocol (which can be thought of as an interactive analog of public-key encryption).

Theorem 4 (Informally Stated, see the full version). *If there exists an interactive combinatorially homomorphic encryption scheme then there exists a key agreement protocol.*

Ishai, Kushilevitz and Ostrovsky [26] showed how to construct a *collision-resistant hash function* (CRH) from any linearly homomorphic encryption scheme. Recall that a CRH is a collection of shrinking hash functions so that no polynomial-time adversary can find a collision, given the description of a random function from the collection. We generalize the [26] result and construct CRH from any CC homomorphic encryption.

Theorem 5 (Informally Stated, see Theorem 9). *If there exists a combinatorially homomorphic encryption scheme (satisfying a mild non-triviality constraint) then there exists a collision-resistant hash function.*

---

[7] As usual in distributional communication complexity, this shared randomness can be eliminated by non-uniformly fixing the best choice.

(The mild non-triviality constraint that we require is that the communication complexity problem is defined wrt a function f such that the function family $\{f_y : \{0,1\}^n \to \{0,1\}\}_y$, where $f_y(x) = f(x,y)$, is a universal hash function family).

As in [26], for this application, we do not need the decryption algorithm to be efficient, and a more general notion of "CC homomorphic commitment" (in which Bob can be inefficient in the communication game) suffices.

Next, we revisit the Kushilevitz-Ostrovsky [30] construction of *private information retrieval* (PIR) scheme from a linearly homomorphic encryption scheme.[8] Recall that a PIR scheme is a two-party protocol between a server, which is given a database $x \in \{0,1\}^n$, and a client who is given as input an index $i \in [n]$. The goal is for the client to reconstruct x_i whereas the index i is computationally hidden from the server (both parties are assumed to be polynomial-time). We say that the PIR scheme is non-trivial if the communication complexity is less than n.[9]

We generalize the [30] construction and derive PIR from combinatorially homomorphic encryption. For this result, we need the communication in the homomorphic variant of the communication game to be shorter than before. Specifically, rather than beating the communication complexity lower bound for the game, it should beat its *VC dimension*. We refer to schemes satisfying this (intuitively stronger) notion as *VC homomorphic*.

Theorem 6 (Informally Stated, see the full version). *Assume that there exists a VC homomorphic encryption scheme then there exists a non-trivial PIR scheme.*

Applications from Learning Parity with Noise. As noted above, we can capture a low noise variant of LPN (specifically with an absolute noise level of roughly $\log^2(n)$) in our framework, via a simple construction. Using Theorem 5, we can use LPN with this noise level to obtain CRH, thereby giving a conceptually simple derivation of recent results [10,44]. Similarly, using Theorem 3 we get a simple construction of semi-honest 2-message statistical OT from LPN. This can be viewed as an abstraction of a recent result of Bitansky and Freizeit [7]. We emphasize though that [7] use the semi-honest construction only as a stepping stone towards a construction that achieves security against malicious receivers (but additionally requires a Nisan-Wigderson style derandomization assumption).

---

[8] The [30] construction is based on the Quadratic Residuosity assumption, but is easy to generalize to compact linearly homomorphic encryption (for a suitable notion of compactness), see [31,42].

[9] While a PIR scheme with communication, say, $n-1$ does not seem directly useful, it is sufficient for deriving some important consequences of PIR such as CRH [26], oblivious transfer [14], lossy encryption [23] and SZK hardness [32].

1.2 Related Work

As previously mentioned, Rothblum [40] showed that any linearly homomorphic encryption that satisfies a mild compactness property can be used to construct a public-key encryption scheme. His proof relies on the Leftover Hash Lemma and can be streamlined using our framework (see discussion in Sect. 1.1).

Alamati et al. [1,2] study the possibility of constructing Cryptomania primitives (such as CRH and PKE) based on Minicrypt primitives that are equipped with certain algebraic structures. Their work is limited to primitives with group homomorphism over the input or output spaces. In particular, like [40], their work does not consider non-linear homomorphisms.

Bogdanov and Lee [8] study the limits of security for homomorphic encryption. Along the way, they introduce a notion of sensitivity for homomorphically evaluated functions. While this notion suffices for their applications, it does not seem to be a minimal notion of non-triviality for functional homomorphisms.

Cohen and Naor [13] study a different connection between communication complexity and cryptography, and in particular, show that the existence of non-trivial communication complexity protocols in which the inputs are drawn from efficiently sampleable distributions imply cryptographic primitives (such as distribution collision-resistant hash functions).

2 Preliminaries

For a distribution D, we denote by $x \leftarrow D$ the process of sampling from D. For any joint distribution (X,Y) we will denote by $x \leftarrow \mathsf{Proj}_1(X,Y)$ or $y \leftarrow \mathsf{Proj}_2(X,Y)$ sampling from (X,Y) and keeping only the first or the second element of the pair, respectively. A function $\mu : \mathbb{N} \rightarrow [0,1]$ is *negligible* if for every polynomial p and sufficiently large λ it holds that $\mu(\lambda) \leq 1/p(\lambda)$. All logarithms considered in this paper are in base 2.

Definition 2 (Statistical Distance). *Let X and Y be two distributions over a finite domain U. The statistical distance between X and Y is defined as follows.*

$$\mathsf{SD}(X,Y) = \max_{f:U \rightarrow \{0,1\}} \left| \Pr\left[f(X) = 1\right] - \Pr\left[f(Y) = 1\right] \right|.$$

If $\mathsf{SD}(X,Y) \leq \epsilon$ we say that X is ϵ-close to Y.

Next, we define computational indistinguishability, which can be thought of as a computational analog of the statistical distance.

Definition 3 (Computational Indistinguishability). *We say that two distribution ensembles $X = (X_\lambda)_{\lambda \in \mathbb{N}}$ and $Y = (Y_\lambda)_{\lambda \in \mathbb{N}}$ are computationally indistinguishable, and denote it by $X \approx_c Y$, if for every probabilistic polynomial-size distinguisher $\mathcal{D}$ there exists a negligible function μ such that for every $\lambda \in \mathbb{N}$,*

$$\left| \Pr\left[\mathcal{D}(X_\lambda) = 1\right] - \Pr\left[\mathcal{D}(Y_\lambda) = 1\right] \right| \leq \mu(\lambda).$$

2.1 Communication Complexity

Communication complexity (CC), introduced by Yao [43], provides a mathematical model for the study of communication between two or more parties. It has proven to be a powerful tool in a surprising variety of fields such as circuit complexity, streaming, and quantum computing. We refer to the books by Kushilevitz and Nisan [29] and by Rao and Yehudayoff [36] for a comprehensive introduction. We now turn to recall several CC-related definitions that will be used in this paper.

Let f be a 2-argument function. Consider the setting of two communicating parties, Alice and Bob, who are given inputs x and y respectively, and wish to *cooperatively* compute the value of $f(x, y)$ (without loss of generality we will require that only Bob outputs this value). The communication between them is conducted according to some fixed deterministic protocol π. The output of the protocol (i.e., Bob's output) on inputs x and y is denoted by $\pi(x, y)$.

Distributional Communication Complexity. We allow the protocol to err with a small probability on some input distribution. Namely,

Definition 4 (Protocol Correctness). *Given a function $f : \mathcal{X} \times \mathcal{Y} \rightarrow \{0, 1\}$ and a joint input distribution (X, Y), we say that a deterministic protocol π computes f with error ϵ on (X, Y) if*

$$\Pr\left[\pi(x, y) \neq f(x, y) : (x, y) \leftarrow (X, Y)\right] \leq \epsilon.$$

Interchangeably, we can say that the protocol π computes f with correctness $1 - \epsilon$ *on (X, Y).*

The communication complexity of a protocol π on inputs x and y is defined to be the number of bits exchanged by the parties while running the protocol on these inputs. The length of a protocol π on input distribution (X, Y), denoted by $\mathsf{CC}[\pi, (X, Y)]$, is defined to be the maximal communication complexity of the protocol on any input in the support of the distribution (notice that this measure is well-defined since these sets are finite).

The ϵ-error distributional communication complexity of f on (X, Y) is the minimal length of any deterministic protocol computing f with error ϵ with respect to (X, Y). That is,

Definition 5 (Distributional Communication Complexity). *Given a function f and a joint input distribution (X, Y) we define the ϵ-error (X, Y)-distributional communication complexity of f as follows.*

$$\mathcal{D}^{A \leftrightarrow B}\big(f, (X, Y), \epsilon\big) := \min_{\substack{\pi \text{ computes } f \\ \text{with error } \epsilon \\ \text{on } (X, Y)}} \mathsf{CC}[\pi, (X, Y)].$$

The *one-way ϵ-error (X, Y)-distributional communication complexity* of f, denoted by $\mathcal{D}^{A \rightarrow B}\big(f, (X, Y), \epsilon\big)$, is defined similarly but limited to one-round protocols that consist of only one message - from Alice to Bob.

Discrepancy. The discrepancy method is a common technique for proving lower bounds on distributional communication complexity. We now define the discrepancy of a function with respect to an input distribution.

Definition 6 (Discrepancy). *Given a function $f : \mathcal{X} \times \mathcal{Y} \to \{0,1\}$ and a joint input distribution (X, Y) we define the discrepancy of f on a rectangle $R = S \times T \subseteq (X, Y)$, denoted here by $\mathsf{Disc}(f, (X, Y); R)$, as follows.*

$$\mathsf{Disc}(f, (X, Y); R) := \left| \Pr\Big[(x,y) \in R \wedge f(x,y) = 1\Big] - \Pr\Big[(x,y) \in R \wedge f(x,y) = 0\Big] \right|,$$

where $(x, y) \leftarrow (X, Y)$. The discrepancy of f on (X, Y) is defined as

$$\mathsf{Disc}(f, (X, Y)) := \max_R \mathsf{Disc}(f, (X, Y); R).$$

A well-known theorem (see, e.g., [36, Theorem 5.2]) shows that the discrepancy can be used to lower bound distributional communication complexity.

Theorem 7. *For any function $f : \mathcal{X} \times \mathcal{Y} \to \{0,1\}$, a joint input distribution (X, Y) and an error rate $\epsilon \in (0, \frac{1}{2})$ we have that*

$$\mathcal{D}^{A \to B}(f, (X, Y), \epsilon) \geq \log\left(\frac{1 - 2\epsilon}{\mathsf{Disc}(f, (X, Y))}\right)$$

2.2 Encryption

In this subsection, we describe the various notions of encryption that will be used throughout this work.

Definition 7 ($\mathcal{M}$-Entropic Secure Private-Key Encryption). *Let $\mathcal{M} = (\mathcal{M}_\lambda)_{\lambda \in \mathbb{N}}$ be a message space. An $\mathcal{M}$-entropic secure private-key encryption scheme $\mathcal{E} = (\mathsf{Gen}, \mathsf{Enc}, \mathsf{Dec})$, with correctness error $\epsilon = \epsilon(\lambda)$, is a triplet of probabilistic polynomial-time algorithms with the following syntax.*

- ***Key generation.** Given a security parameter 1^λ, the algorithm Gen outputs a key k.*
- ***Encryption.** Given a message $m \in \mathcal{M}_\lambda$ and a key k, the algorithm Enc outputs a ciphertext c.*
- ***Decryption.** Given a ciphertext c and a key k, the algorithm Dec outputs a message m.*

We require $\mathcal{E}$ to satisfy the following properties.

- ***Correctness.** For any $\lambda \in \mathbb{N}$ and message $m \in \mathcal{M}_\lambda$ it holds that $\Pr[\mathsf{Dec}_k(c) = m] \geq 1 - \epsilon(\lambda)$, where $k \leftarrow \mathsf{Gen}(1^\lambda)$ and $c \leftarrow \mathsf{Enc}_k(m)$.*
- ***$\mathcal{M}$-entropic security.** $(m, \mathsf{Enc}_k(m))_{\lambda \in \mathbb{N}} \approx_c (m, \mathsf{Enc}_k(m'))_{\lambda \in \mathbb{N}}$, where m and m' are two independent messages sampled from $\mathcal{M}$.*

We remark that the notion of entropic security defined above is morally weaker than notions such as CPA security since (1) the adversary is not given access to an encryption oracle and (2) security needs to hold only wrt messages arising from the given distribution (rather than "worst-case" messages).

Definition 8 (CPA-Secure Private-Key Encryption). *A chosen-plaintext attack (CPA) secure private-key encryption scheme* $\mathcal{E} = (\mathsf{Gen}, \mathsf{Enc}, \mathsf{Dec})$ *with message length* $\ell = \ell(\lambda)$ *and correctness error* $\epsilon = \epsilon(\lambda)$, *is defined similarly to Definition 7 but the entropic security requirement is replaced with the following:*

- **CPA Security.** *Consider the following security game.*
  1. *The challenger samples a key* $k \leftarrow \mathsf{Gen}(1^\lambda)$.
  2. *The adversary chooses a message* m *of length* $\ell(\lambda)$ *and receives* $\mathsf{Enc}_k(m)$ *from the challenger. This step is repeated for a polynomial number of times.*
  3. *The adversary chooses two challenge message* m_0, m_1 *of length* $\ell(\lambda)$ *and receives from the challenger* $\mathsf{Enc}_k(m_b)$.
  4. *The adversary outputs a bit* $b' \in \{0, 1\}$.

  For any probabilistic polynomial-size adversary $\mathcal{A}$, *we denote by* $\mathsf{CPA}_\mathcal{A}^b(1^\lambda)$ *the output of* $\mathcal{A}$ *in the game above, and we require that there exists a negligible function* μ *such that for any* $\lambda \in \mathbb{N}$,

$$\left| \Pr\left[\mathsf{CPA}_\mathcal{A}^0(1^\lambda) = 1 \right] - \Pr\left[\mathsf{CPA}_\mathcal{A}^1(1^\lambda) = 1 \right] \right| \leq \mu(\lambda).$$

We will next define a variant of lossy encryption [5,35], which is equivalent to a 2-message (semi-honest) statistical OT [35].

Definition 9 (Lossy Encryption). *Let* $\nu = \nu(\lambda)$ *and* $\epsilon = \epsilon(\lambda)$. *A* ν-*lossy bit-encryption scheme* $\mathcal{E} = (\mathsf{Gen}, \mathsf{Enc}, \mathsf{Dec}, \mathsf{LossyGen})$ *with correctness error* ϵ, *is a quadruple of polynomial-time algorithms with the following syntax,*

- **Key generation.** *Given a security parameter* 1^λ, *the algorithm* Gen *outputs a secret key* sk *and a public key* pk.
- **Encryption.** *Given a bit* b *and a public key* pk, *the algorithm* Enc *outputs a ciphertext* c.
- **Decryption.** *Given a ciphertext* c *and a secret key* sk, *the algorithm* Dec *outputs a bit* b.
- **Lossy key generation.** *Given a security parameter* 1^λ, *the algorithm* $\mathsf{LossyGen}$ *outputs a lossy key* lk.

We require $\mathcal{E}$ *to satisfy the following properties.*

- **Correctness.** *For any* $\lambda \in \mathbb{N}$ *and bit* b *it holds that* $\Pr\left[\mathsf{Dec}_{sk}(c) = b\right] \geq 1 - \epsilon(\lambda)$, *where* $(sk, pk) \leftarrow \mathsf{Gen}(1^\lambda)$ *and* $c \leftarrow \mathsf{Enc}_{pk}(b)$.
- **Key indistinguishability.** $\left(\mathsf{Proj}_2\left(\mathsf{Gen}(1^\lambda)\right)\right)_{\lambda \in \mathbb{N}} \approx_c \left(\mathsf{LossyGen}(1^\lambda)\right)_{\lambda \in \mathbb{N}}$.
- **Lossiness of lossy keys.** *For any* $\lambda \in \mathbb{N}$, *we have that* $\left(lk, \mathsf{Enc}_{lk}(0)\right)$ *is* $\nu(\lambda)$-*close in statistical distance to* $\left(lk, \mathsf{Enc}_{lk}(1)\right)$, *where* $lk \leftarrow \mathsf{LossyGen}(1^\lambda)$.

If not otherwise specified, by default, we take the parameters ν and ϵ to be negligible in parameter λ. One can also consider relaxed notions of lossy encryption, where either the correctness error is high—namely, $\epsilon(\lambda) = \frac{1}{2} - \frac{1}{p(\lambda)}$, for some polynomial p—or the statistical distance between encryptions under a lossy key is large—namely, $\nu(\lambda) = 1 - \frac{1}{p(\lambda)}$, for some polynomial p. Next, we will show that both variants are equivalent to the standard definition. We note however that if both the correctness *and* lossiness are close to $1/2$, then amplification is not known (see [16,24] for further discussion and relation to the circuit polarization problem).

Claim (Weak-Correctness Lossy Encryption implies Lossy Encryption). Assume there exists a lossy encryption scheme with correctness error $\frac{1}{2} - \frac{1}{p(\lambda)}$, for some polynomial p, then there exists a lossy encryption scheme (Definition 9).

Claim (Weak-Lossiness Lossy Encryption implies Lossy Encryption). Assume there exists a $(1 - \frac{1}{p(\lambda)})$-lossy encryption scheme, for some polynomial p, then there exists a lossy encryption scheme (Definition 9).

The proofs of Sect. 2.2 and Sect. 2.2 are given in the full version.

2.3   Collision Resistant Hash Function

Definition 10 (Collision Resistant Hash Function). *A collision resistant function with input length $\ell(n)$ and output length $\ell'(n) < \ell(n)$ is defined by a pair of algorithms (Gen, Eval) with the following syntax,*

- **Key generation.** *Given 1^λ the probabilistic polynomial-time algorithm Gen outputs an index s.*
- **Evaluation.** *Given index s and input x of length $\ell(\lambda)$, the polynomial-time algorithm Eval outputs $y \in \{0,1\}^{\ell'(\lambda)}$.*

For any $\lambda \in \mathbb{N}$, $s \leftarrow \mathsf{Gen}(1^\lambda)$ and $x \in \{0,1\}^{\ell(\lambda)}$ we define $h_s(x) := \mathsf{Eval}(s, x)$.
   We require the scheme to satisfy the following collision resistance property.

- **Collision resistance.** *for every probabilistic polynomial-size adversary $\mathcal{A}$ there exists a negligible function μ such that for any $\lambda \in \mathbb{N}$,*

$$\Pr\left[x \neq x' \wedge h_s(x) = h_s(x') : \begin{array}{l} s \leftarrow \mathsf{Gen}(1^\lambda), \\ (x, x') \leftarrow \mathcal{A}(s) \end{array}\right] \leq \mu(\lambda).$$

3   Combinatorially Homomorphic Encryption

First, we define an extension of a function ensemble and an input distribution ensemble with respect to a private key encryption scheme. These will be used throughout the following sections.
   Let f be an ensemble of 2-argument functions. Let (X, Y) be an ensemble of input distributions, where $X = (X_\lambda)_{\lambda \in \mathbb{N}}$ and $Y = (Y_\lambda)_{\lambda \in \mathbb{N}}$. Let $\mathcal{E} =$

$(\mathsf{Gen}, \mathsf{Enc}, \mathsf{Dec})$ be a private-key encryption scheme (see Definition 7). We extend f and (X, Y) by defining for every $\lambda \in \mathbb{N}$,

$$\mathsf{Ext}_{\mathcal{E}}(X_\lambda, Y_\lambda) := \left\{ ((x,c),(y,k)) : \begin{array}{c} (x,y) \leftarrow (X_\lambda, Y_\lambda) \\ k \leftarrow \mathsf{Gen}(1^\lambda) \\ c \leftarrow \mathsf{Enc}_k(y) \end{array} \right\},$$

$$\mathsf{Ext}_{\mathcal{E}}(f_\lambda) : ((x,c),(y,k)) \mapsto f_\lambda(x,y).$$

We denote $\mathsf{Ext}_{\mathcal{E}}(X, Y) := \big(\mathsf{Ext}_{\mathcal{E}}(X_\lambda, Y_\lambda)\big)_{\lambda \in \mathbb{N}}$ and $\mathsf{Ext}_{\mathcal{E}}(f) := \big(\mathsf{Ext}_{\mathcal{E}}(f_\lambda)\big)_{\lambda \in \mathbb{N}}$.

3.1   CC-Homomorphic Encryption

We now introduce our new homomorphic encryption definition. Informally, an encryption scheme $\mathcal{E}$ is combinatorially homomorphic if there exists a polynomial-time communication protocol for $\mathsf{Ext}_{\mathcal{E}}(f)$ that utilizes the homomorphic properties of $\mathcal{E}$ to achieve communication cost that is lower than the standard communication complexity of f, on a specific input distribution.

We put forward two variants of the definition. Namely, CC-homomorphism in the *perfect correctness regime*, where we require the "homomorphic protocol" for $\mathsf{Ext}_{\mathcal{E}}(f)$ to have perfect correctness, and CC-homomorphism in the *balanced regime*, where we allow imperfect correctness, but require that the function f be *balanced*, that is, that $\Pr[f(x,y) = 0 : (x,y) \leftarrow (X,Y)] = \frac{1}{2}$. In addition to these two variants, we present an even more general setting in the full version, based on an average-case adaptation of the distributional communication complexity definition.

Our definitions will require the input distribution to be *efficiently sampleable*, defined as follows.

Definition 11 (Efficiently Sampleable Distribution). *We say that a distribution ensemble (X, Y) is* efficiently sampleable *if there exists a probabilistic polynomial-time sampling algorithm that given 1^λ outputs a random element from (X_λ, Y_λ).*

Definition 12 (Communication Complexity Homomorphic Encryption in the Perfect Correctness Regime). *A private-key encryption scheme $\mathcal{E}$ (Definition 7) is* communication-complexity homomorphic *(or CC-homomorphic) in the* perfect correctness regime, *if there exists a function ensemble f, an efficiently sampleable* product *distribution ensemble (X, Y) and a function $c = c(\lambda)$ such that,*

– *There exists a polynomial-time one-way protocol that computes $\mathsf{Ext}_{\mathcal{E}}(f)$ with perfect correctness on input distribution $\mathsf{Ext}_{\mathcal{E}}(X, Y)$, using $c(\lambda)$ bits of communication,*
– *Any unbounded one-way protocol that computes f on (X, Y), using $c(\lambda)$ bits of communication has correctness at most $1 - \frac{1}{p(\lambda)}$, for some polynomial p.*

Remark 1. A natural relaxation of the definition allows a negligible failure probability in the homomorphic communication protocol. However, jumping ahead, having perfect correctness here will be useful as it will also lead to perfect correctness in some of our applications (e.g., lossy encryption, see Theorem 8).

Remark 2. Instead of requiring that (X, Y) is an ensemble of *product* distributions, it is sufficient to require it to be an ensemble of joint distributions such that the conditional distributions $X|Y$ are efficiently sampleable.

Definition 13 (Communication Complexity Homomorphic Encryption in the Balanced Regime). *A private-key encryption scheme $\mathcal{E}$ (Definition 7) is* communication-complexity homomorphic *(or CC-homomorphic) in the balanced regime, if there exists a function ensemble f, an efficiently sampleable product distribution ensemble (X, Y) and a function $c = c(\lambda)$ such that,*

- $\Pr[f(x, y) = 0 : (x, y) \leftarrow (X, Y)] = \frac{1}{2}$,
- *There exists a polynomial-time one-way protocol that computes $\text{Ext}_{\mathcal{E}}(f)$ with correctness at least $\frac{1}{2} + \frac{1}{p(\lambda)}$, for some polynomial p, on $\text{Ext}_{\mathcal{E}}(X, Y)$ using c bits of communication,*
- *There exists a negligible function μ such that any unbounded one-way protocol that computes f on input distribution (X, Y) using c bits of communication has correctness at most $\frac{1}{2} + \mu(\lambda)$, for any sufficiently large λ.*

4   Applications

In this section, we demonstrate applications of our new notions of homomorphic encryption. In Sect. 4.1 we construct Lossy Encryption. In Sect. 4.2 we construct a Collision Resistant Hash function.

4.1   Lossy Encryption

In this section, we show how to use CC-homomorphic encryption to construct lossy public-key encryption.

Theorem 8 (CC-homomorphic Encryption Implies Lossy Encryption). *Assume there exists a CC-homomorphic encryption scheme in either the perfect correctness regime (see Definition 12) or the balanced regime (see Definition 13), then there exists a lossy encryption scheme.*

We will prove Theorem 8 in the balanced regime (Definition 13). The proof in the perfect correctness regime (Definition 12) is similar, but produces a $(1 - \frac{1}{p(\lambda)})$-lossy encryption, for some polynomial p, with perfect correctness that can be amplified to full-fledged lossy encryption scheme using Sect. 2.2.

Proof (Proof of Theorem 8.) Let $\mathcal{E} = (\text{Gen}, \text{Enc}, \text{Dec})$ be a Y-entropic secure CC-homomorphic encryption scheme with respect to function ensemble f and input product distribution ensemble (X, Y) such that $\Pr[f(x, y) = 0 : (x, y) \leftarrow (X, Y)]$

$= \frac{1}{2}$. Let π be a polynomial-time one-way protocol computing the extended function ensemble $\mathsf{Ext}_{\mathcal{E}}(f)$ with error less than $\frac{1}{2} - \frac{1}{\tau(\lambda)}$ on $\mathsf{Ext}_{\mathcal{E}}(X, Y)$, for some polynomial τ, with communication cost $c = c(\lambda)$, such that any unbounded protocol for f with error $\frac{1}{2} - \frac{1}{p(\lambda)}$ on (X, Y), for some polynomial p, requires strictly more than c bits of communication.

For the following, given input $((x, c), (y, k))$ from $\mathsf{Ext}_{\mathcal{E}}(X, Y)$, we denote by $\mathsf{Alice}(x, c)$ the message Alice generates in the protocol and we denote by $\mathsf{Bob}(y, k, m_A)$ the output of Bob after receiving a message m_A from Alice. Consider the following scheme $(\mathsf{Gen}^*, \mathsf{Enc}^*, \mathsf{Dec}^*, \mathsf{LossyGen}^*)$.

- **Key generation.** Given a security parameter 1^λ the probabilistic polynomial-time algorithm Gen^* samples a key $k \leftarrow \mathsf{Gen}(1^\lambda)$ and an element $y \leftarrow Y$, and outputs the public key $pk = \big(y, \mathsf{Enc}_k(y)\big)$ and the secret key $sk = (y, k)$.
- **Encryption.** Given the public key $pk = (y, c)$ and a bit b, the probabilistic polynomial-time algorithm Enc^* samples $x \leftarrow X$ that satisfies $f(x, y) = b$ (by rejection sampling) and outputs $m_A = \mathsf{Alice}(x, c)$.
- **Decryption.** Given the secret key $sk = (y, k)$ and a ciphertext m_A, the deterministic polynomial-time algorithm Dec^* outputs $\mathsf{Bob}(y, k, m_A)$.
- **Lossy Key generation.** Given a security parameter 1^λ the probabilistic polynomial-time algorithm $\mathsf{LossyGen}^*$ samples a key $k \leftarrow \mathsf{Gen}(1^\lambda)$ and elements $y, y' \leftarrow Y$, and outputs the lossy key $lk = \big(y, \mathsf{Enc}_k(y')\big)$.

Claim. The scheme satisfies correctness (see Definition 9).

Proof. For any $\lambda \in \mathbb{N}$,

$$\Pr\Big[\mathsf{Dec}^*_{sk}\big(\mathsf{Enc}^*_{pk}(b)\big) \neq b\Big] \underset{(1)}{=} \Pr\left[\mathsf{Bob}(y, k, \mathsf{Alice}(x, c)) \neq f(x, y) : \begin{array}{l}(x, y) \leftarrow (X, Y) \\ \text{s.t. } f(x, y) = b\end{array}\right]$$

$$\underset{(2)}{=} \Pr\Big[\mathsf{Bob}(y, k, \mathsf{Alice}(x, c)) \neq f(x, y) : (x, y) \leftarrow (X, Y)\Big]$$

$$\underset{(3)}{\leq} \frac{1}{2} - \frac{1}{\tau(\lambda)},$$

where $b \leftarrow \{0, 1\}$, $(sk, pk) \leftarrow \mathsf{Gen}^*(1^\lambda)$, $k \leftarrow \mathsf{Gen}(1^\lambda)$ and $c \leftarrow \mathsf{Enc}_k(y)$, and where (1) is by the definition of the scheme, (2) is since $\Pr[f(x, y) = 0 : (x, y) \leftarrow (X, Y)] = \frac{1}{2}$, and therefore sampling $b \leftarrow \{0, 1\}$ and then sampling from (X, Y) conditioned on $f(x, y) = b$ is the same as sampling directly from (X, Y), and (3) is since the protocol π computes $\mathsf{Ext}_{\mathcal{E}}(f)$ on $\mathsf{Ext}_{\mathcal{E}}(X, Y)$ with error less than $B - \frac{1}{\tau(\lambda)}$, and since $((x, c), (y, k))$ is sampled similarly to a random sample from $\mathsf{Ext}_{\mathcal{E}}(X, Y)$.

Claim. The scheme satisfies key indistinguishability (see Definition 9).

Proof. We have that for any fixed y and y' sampled from Y,

$$\Big(\mathsf{Proj}_2(\mathsf{Gen}^*(1^\lambda))\Big)_{\lambda \in \mathbb{N}} = (y, c)_{\lambda \in \mathbb{N}} \approx_c (y, c')_{\lambda \in \mathbb{N}} = \big(\mathsf{LossyGen}^*(1^\lambda)\big)_{\lambda \in \mathbb{N}},$$

where $k \leftarrow \mathsf{Gen}(1^\lambda)$, $c \leftarrow \mathsf{Enc}_k(y)$ and $c' \leftarrow \mathsf{Enc}_k(y')$, and where the equalities are by the definition of the scheme and the computational indistinguishability is by the Y-entropic security of $\mathcal{E}$.

Claim. The scheme satisfies lossiness of lossy keys (see Definition 9).

Proof. We will show that given an unbounded distinguisher for encryptions under a lossy key, with non-negligible distinguishing advantage, one can construct a one-way protocol in the standard distributional communication complexity model (Sect. 2.1) that computes f with correctness $\frac{1}{2} + \frac{1}{p(\lambda)}$ on (X, Y), for some polynomial p, with communication cost c. Such a protocol cannot exist by our assumption that $\mathcal{E}$ is CC-homomorphic in the balanced regime with respect to f and (X, Y) (see Definition 13).

Assume towards a contradiction that there exists a (computationally unbounded) distinguisher $\mathcal{D}$ and a polynomial p such that for infinitely many $\lambda \in \mathbb{N}$,

$$\Pr\left[\mathcal{D}(lk, \mathsf{Enc}_{lk}^*(b)) = b : b \leftarrow \{0,1\}, \, lk \leftarrow \mathsf{LossyGen}^*(1^\lambda)\right] \geq \frac{1}{2} + \frac{1}{p(\lambda)}.$$

By the definitions of $\mathsf{LossyGen}^*$ and Enc^* we have that for infinitely many $\lambda \in \mathbb{N}$,

$$\Pr\left[\mathcal{D}(y, c, \mathsf{Alice}(x, c)) = f(x, y)\right] \geq \frac{1}{2} + \frac{1}{p(\lambda)},$$

where $x \leftarrow X$, $y, y' \leftarrow Y$, $k \leftarrow \mathsf{Gen}(1^\lambda)$ and $c \leftarrow \mathsf{Enc}_k(y')$.

We start by constructing a protocol in the standard distributional communication complexity model (Sect. 2.1) that uses shared randomness which we will eliminate later. Consider the following unbounded one-way protocol π^* between parties Alice^* and Bob^* who are given inputs x and y sampled from (X, Y) and have access to shared random coins.

1. Alice^* and Bob^* sample a key $k \leftarrow \mathsf{Gen}(1^\lambda)$, an element $y' \leftarrow Y$ and an encryption $c \leftarrow \mathsf{Enc}_k(y')$ using the shared random coins.
2. Alice^* sends $m_A = \mathsf{Alice}(x, c)$ to Bob^*.
3. Bob^* runs $\mathcal{D}$ on (y, c, m_A) and outputs its answer.

We denote by $\pi^*(x, y; r)$ the output of the protocol on inputs (x, y) and random coins r. infinitely many $\lambda \in \mathbb{N}$,

$$\Pr\left[\pi^*(x, y; r) = f(x, y) : \begin{matrix} (x, y) \leftarrow (X, Y) \\ r \leftarrow \{0,1\}^* \end{matrix}\right] = \Pr\left[\mathcal{D}(y, c, \mathsf{Alice}(x, c)) = f(x, y)\right] \geq \frac{1}{2} + \frac{1}{p(\lambda)},$$

where $x \leftarrow X$, $y, y' \leftarrow Y$, $k \leftarrow \mathsf{Gen}(1^\lambda)$ and $c \leftarrow \mathsf{Enc}_k(y')$.

The above statement holds over a random choice of r. However, by an averaging argument, for infinitely many $\lambda \in \mathbb{N}$ there exists a fixed randomness r^* such that

$$\Pr\left[\pi^*(x, y; r^*) = f(x, y) : (x, y) \leftarrow (X, Y)\right] \geq \frac{1}{2} + \frac{1}{p(\lambda)}.$$

To conclude, we have that π^* with fixed random coins r^* is an unbounded one-way protocol that computes f with error less than $\frac{1}{2} - \frac{1}{p(\lambda)}$ on (X,Y) with communication cost $|\mathsf{Alice}(x,c)| = c$, which is a contradiction to the assumption that such a protocol cannot exist.

4.2   Collision Resistant Hash Function

Next, we use a variant of CC-homomorphic encryption to construct a collision resistant hash function. First, we define an *efficient encoding* algorithm for a set X.

Definition 14 (Efficient Encoding). *Let* $X = (X_\lambda)_{\lambda \in \mathbb{N}}$ *be an ensemble of finite sets. We say that X supports an* efficient encoding *with input length $\ell = \ell(\lambda)$ if there exists an efficiently computable (polynomial-time) injective function* $\mathsf{Encode} : \{0,1\}^\ell \to X_\lambda$.

Our CRH construction will require a function f and input distribution (X,Y) such that the ensemble $f_Y = (f_\lambda)_{\lambda \in \mathbb{N}}$, where $f_\lambda := \{f(\cdot, y) : y \in Y_\lambda\}$, is a universal hash function family. We put forward the definition.

Definition 15 (Universal Hash Function Family). *A set H of functions from X to $\{0,1\}$ is a universal hash function family if for every distinct $x_1, x_2 \in X$ the hash function family H satisfies the following constraint.*

$$\Pr\left[h(x_1) = h(x_2) : h \leftarrow H\right] \leq \frac{1}{2}.$$

Theorem 9 (CC-Homomorphic Encryption Implies CRH). *Assume there exists a CC-homomorphic encryption scheme (Definitions 12 and 13) with respect to function f, input distribution (X,Y) and parameter c that satisfies the following conditions.*

- *The function ensemble $\left(\{f(\cdot, y) : y \in Y_\lambda\}\right)_{\lambda \in \mathbb{N}}$ is a universal hash function family.*
- *The polynomial-time protocol for $\mathsf{Ext}_\mathcal{E}(f)$ is correct on any input from $\mathsf{Ext}_\mathcal{E}(X,Y)$ w.p. $\frac{1}{2} + \frac{1}{p(\lambda)}$, for some polynomial p,*
- *The ensemble X supports an efficient encoding with input length $\ell(\lambda) \geq c(\lambda)$ for any sufficiently large λ.*

Then, there exists a collision resistant hash function (Definition 10).

Remark 3. As a matter of fact, similarly to [26], a relaxed notion of encryption with an inefficient decryption algorithm (in other words, a commitment scheme) is sufficient.

We will prove Theorem 9 in the balanced regime (Definition 13), but it can also be adapted to the perfect correctness regime (Definition 12).

Proof (Proof of Theorem 9). Let f be a function ensemble and (X, Y) be an input distribution ensemble such that $\left(\{ f(\cdot, y) : y \in Y_\lambda \} \right)_{\lambda \in \mathbb{N}}$ is a universal hash function family and such that X supports an efficient encoding with input length $\ell = \ell(\lambda)$. Let $\mathcal{E} = (\mathsf{Gen}, \mathsf{Enc}, \mathsf{Dec})$ be a Y-entropic secure encryption scheme. Let π be a polynomial-time one-way protocol computing the extended function ensemble $\mathsf{Ext}_{\mathcal{E}}(f)$ with correctness $\frac{1}{2} + \frac{1}{p(\lambda)}$ on any input from $\mathsf{Ext}_{\mathcal{E}}(X, Y)$, for some polynomial p, with communication cost $\ell'(\lambda) < \ell(\lambda)$.

Consider the following scheme $(\mathsf{Gen}^*, \mathsf{Eval}^*)$.

- **Key generation.** Given security parameter 1^λ, the probabilistic polynomial-time algorithm Gen^* samples $y \leftarrow Y$, $k \leftarrow \mathsf{Gen}(1^\lambda)$ and $s \leftarrow \mathsf{Enc}_k(y)$ and outputs s.
- **Evaluation.** Given index s and input $m \in \{0,1\}^{\ell(\lambda)}$, the polynomial-time algorithm Eval^* outputs $\mathsf{Alice}(\mathsf{Encode}(m), s)$.

We first show that the scheme indeed compresses. Indeed, for any $\lambda \in \mathbb{N}$, $s \leftarrow \mathsf{Gen}^*(1^\lambda)$ and $m \in \{0,1\}^{\ell(\lambda)}$,

$$\left| h_s(m) \right| = \left| \mathsf{Alice}(\mathsf{Encode}(m), s) \right| \leq \ell'(\lambda) < \ell(\lambda).$$

Assume towards a contradiction that the scheme is not collision resistant. Therefore, there exists a probabilistic polynomial-size adversary $\mathcal{A}$ and a polynomial q such that for infinitely many $\lambda \in \mathbb{N}$,

$$\Pr\left[m \neq m' \wedge h_s(m) = h_s(m') : \begin{matrix} s \leftarrow \mathsf{Gen}^*(1^\lambda), \\ (m, m') \leftarrow \mathcal{A}(s) \end{matrix} \right] = \frac{1}{q(\lambda)}.$$

Consider the distinguisher $\mathcal{D}$ for the Y-entropic security of $\mathcal{E}$. Given (y_0, c), where $k \leftarrow \mathsf{Gen}(1^\lambda)$, $y_0, y_1 \leftarrow Y$, $b \leftarrow \{0,1\}$ and $c \leftarrow \mathsf{Enc}_k(y_b)$, the distinguisher $\mathcal{D}$ computes $(m, m') \leftarrow \mathcal{A}(c_b)$. It then checks that $m \neq m'$, that $h_c(m) = h_c(m')$ and that $f(\mathsf{Encode}(m), y_0) = f(\mathsf{Encode}(m'), y_0)$. If all checks pass, it outputs 1. Otherwise, it outputs a random bit. For the following, we denote $x := \mathsf{Encode}(m)$, $x' := \mathsf{Encode}(m')$.

We first consider the case where $b = 0$. Given $k \leftarrow \mathsf{Gen}(1^\lambda)$, $y_0 \leftarrow Y$, $c \leftarrow \mathsf{Enc}_k(y_0)$ and $(m, m') \leftarrow \mathcal{A}(c)$, we define the following events,

1. The event E_1 where $f(x, y_0) = f(x', y_0)$.
2. The event E_2 where $m \neq m'$ and $h_c(m) = h_c(m')$.
3. The event E_3 where $\pi((x, c), (y_0, k)) = \pi((x', c), (y_0, k))$.
4. The event E_4 where the protocol π is correct on both $((x, c), (y_0, k))$ and $((x', c), (y_0, k))$, or is wrong on both of them.

First, since π is correct on any input w.p. at least $\frac{1}{2} + \frac{1}{p(\lambda)}$, there exists a function $\tau : \mathbb{N} \to \mathbb{N}$ such that π is correct on any input w.p. exactly $\frac{1}{2} + \frac{1}{\tau(\lambda)}$, and $\tau(\lambda) \leq p(\lambda)$ for any $\lambda \in \mathbb{N}$. Therefore,

$$\Pr[E_4] = \left(\frac{1}{2} + \frac{1}{\tau(\lambda)} \right)^2 + \left(\frac{1}{2} - \frac{1}{\tau(\lambda)} \right)^2 = \frac{1}{2} + \frac{2}{\tau^2(\lambda)} \geq \frac{1}{2} + \frac{2}{p^2(\lambda)}. \tag{1}$$

Furthermore, we have that,

$$
\begin{aligned}
\Pr\left[E_1|E_2\right] &\underset{(1)}{=} \Pr\left[E_1|E_2 \wedge E_3\right] \\
&\geq \Pr\left[E_1 \wedge E_4|E_2 \wedge E_3\right] \\
&\underset{(2)}{=} \Pr\left[E_1|E_2 \wedge E_3 \wedge E_4\right] \cdot \Pr\left[E_4\right] \\
&\underset{(3)}{=} \Pr\left[E_4\right],
\end{aligned}
\tag{2}
$$

where (1) is since assuming E_2 happened, we have that $\mathsf{Alice}(x,c) = h_c(m) = h_c(m') = \mathsf{Alice}(x',c)$, and therefore, since π is a deterministic one-way protocol, we have that $\pi\big((x,c),(y_0,k)\big) = \pi\big((x',c),(y_0,k)\big)$, (2) is by conditional probability, and (3) is since if the protocol outputs the same output on both inputs and is correct on both of them or wrong on both of them, then $f(x,y_0) = f(x',y_0)$.

Finally, for infinitely many $\lambda \in \mathbb{N}$ we have that,

$$
\begin{aligned}
\Pr\left[\mathcal{D}(y_0,c) = 1\right] &\underset{(1)}{=} \Pr\left[E_1 \wedge E_2\right] + \frac{1}{2} \cdot \left(1 - \Pr\left[E_1 \wedge E_2\right]\right) \\
&= \frac{1}{2} + \frac{1}{2} \cdot \Pr\left[E_1 \wedge E_2\right] \\
&= \frac{1}{2} + \frac{1}{2}\Pr\left[E_1|E_2\right] \cdot \Pr\left[E_2\right] \\
&\underset{(2)}{=} \frac{1}{2} + \frac{1}{2q(\lambda)}\Pr\left[E_1|E_2\right] \\
&\underset{(3)}{\geq} \frac{1}{2} + \frac{1}{2q(\lambda)} \cdot \left(\frac{1}{2} + \frac{2}{p^2(\lambda)}\right),
\end{aligned}
$$

where $k \leftarrow \mathsf{Gen}(1^\lambda)$, $y_0 \leftarrow Y$, $c \leftarrow \mathsf{Enc}_k(y_0)$ and $(m,m') \leftarrow \mathcal{A}(c)$, and where (1) is by the definition of $\mathcal{D}$, (2) is since $\mathcal{D}$ simulates for the adversary $\mathcal{A}$ a proper collision resistant game, and event E_2 is the event where $\mathcal{A}$ wins in this game, which happens w.p. $1/q(\lambda)$, and (3) is by Eqs. (1) and (2).

On the other hand, for the case where $b = 1$, we have that for any $\lambda \in \mathbb{N}$,

$$
\begin{aligned}
\Pr\left[\mathcal{D}(y_0,c) = 1\right] &\underset{(1)}{=} \frac{1}{2} + \frac{1}{2q(\lambda)}\Pr\left[f(x,y_0) = f(x',y_0)|m \neq m' \wedge h_s(m) = h_s(m')\right] \\
&\leq \frac{1}{2} + \frac{1}{2q(\lambda)}\Pr\left[f(x,y_0) = f(x',y_0)\right] \\
&\underset{(2)}{=} \frac{1}{2} + \frac{1}{2q(\lambda)} \cdot \frac{1}{2},
\end{aligned}
$$

where $k \leftarrow \mathsf{Gen}(1^\lambda)$, $y_0, y_1 \leftarrow Y$, $c \leftarrow \mathsf{Enc}_k(y_1)$ and $(m,m') \leftarrow \mathcal{A}(c)$, and where (1) follows by similar reasoning as in the case where $b = 0$ and (2) is since x and x' are independent of y_0 and since f_Y is a universal hash family, and therefore the probability that $f(x,y_0) = f(x',y_0)$ is $1/2$.

Therefore, for infinitely many $\lambda \in \mathbb{N}$,

$$
\begin{aligned}
\Big|\Pr\left[\mathcal{D}(y_0,c_0) = 1\right] - \Pr\left[\mathcal{D}(y_0,c_1) = 1\right]\Big| &\geq \left(\frac{1}{2} + \frac{1}{2q(\lambda)} \cdot \left(\frac{1}{2} + \frac{2}{p^2(\lambda)}\right)\right) - \left(\frac{1}{2} + \frac{1}{2q(\lambda)} \cdot \frac{1}{2}\right) \\
&= \frac{2}{2q(\lambda) \cdot p^2(\lambda)},
\end{aligned}
$$

where $k \leftarrow \mathsf{Gen}(1^\lambda)$, $y_0, y_1 \leftarrow Y$ and $c_b \leftarrow \mathsf{Enc}_k(y_b)$ for $b \in \{0, 1\}$, in contradiction to the assumption that $\mathcal{E}$ is Y-entropic secure.

5 Instantiations

5.1 Low Noise LPN

In this section we will construct a CC-homomorphic encryption scheme from low noise LPN, thereby giving a conceptually simple derivation of recent results [7,10,44]. We first present the learning parity with noise assumption. For $\mu \in [0, 1]$ we denote by Ber_μ the Bernoulli distribution with mean μ.

Definition 16 (Learning Parity with Noise Assumption). *For noise rate* $\mu = \mu(\lambda) \in (0, \frac{1}{2})$, *the* LPN_μ *assumption is that for any* $m(\lambda) = \lambda^{O(1)}$,

$$(A, As + e)_{\lambda \in \mathbb{N}} \approx_c (A, u)_{\lambda \in \mathbb{N}},$$

where $A \leftarrow \mathbb{F}_2^{m \times \lambda}$, $s \leftarrow \mathbb{F}_2^\lambda$, $e \leftarrow \mathsf{Ber}_\mu^m$ *and* $u \leftarrow \mathbb{F}_2^m$.

Theorem 10 (CC-homomorphic Encryption from Low Noise LPN).
Assuming $\mathsf{LPN}_{\frac{\log^2 \lambda}{\lambda}}$ *(Definition 16) there exists a CC-homomorphic encryption scheme in the balanced regime (Definition 13).*

In fact, we will construct a CC-homomorphic encryption scheme that satisfies the conditions of Theorem 9, thus deriving the following two theorems.

Theorem 11 (Lossy Encryption from Low Noise LPN). *Assuming* $\mathsf{LPN}_{\frac{\log^2 \lambda}{\lambda}}$ *(Definition 16) there exists a lossy encryption scheme (Definition 9).*

Theorem 12 (CRH from Low Noise LPN). *Assuming* $\mathsf{LPN}_{\frac{\log^2 \lambda}{\lambda}}$ *(Definition 16) there exists a collision resistant hash function (Definition 10).*

Theorems 11 and 12 follows directly from Theorems 8 to 10. We note however that we do not know how to use LPN to derive a similar result to Alekhnovich's scheme [3] via our framework. Indeed, the stronger conclusions implied by our framework (lossy encryption, CRH) are not known from the flavor of LPN used by Alekhnovich.

We now describe a private-key encryption scheme $\mathcal{E} = (\mathsf{Gen}, \mathsf{Enc}, \mathsf{Dec})$ based on low noise LPN.

- **Key generation.** Given a security parameter 1^λ, the probabilistic algorithm Gen outputs a private key $s \leftarrow \mathbb{F}_2^\lambda$.
- **Encryption.** Given a message $y \in \mathbb{F}_2^{\lambda^2}$ and a private key s, the probabilistic algorithm Enc samples a random matrix $A \leftarrow \mathbb{F}_2^{\lambda^2 \times \lambda}$ and a random noise $e \leftarrow \mathsf{Ber}_{\frac{\log^2 \lambda}{\lambda}}^{\lambda^2}$, and outputs a ciphertext $(A, A \cdot s + e + y)$.
- **Decryption.** Given a ciphertext (A, b), the deterministic algorithm Dec outputs $b - A \cdot s$.

We define the following homomorphic operation that supports ciphertext-plaintext multiplication.

- **Ciphertext-plaintext multiplication.** Given a plaintext $x \in \mathbb{F}_2^{\lambda^2}$ and a ciphertext (A, b), where $A \in \mathbb{F}_2^{\lambda^2 \times \lambda}$ and $b \in \mathbb{F}_2^{\lambda^2}$, the deterministic algorithm PlainMult outputs $(x^\top \cdot A, x^\top \cdot b)$.

We will show that $\mathcal{E}$ is CC-homomorphic with respect to the inner product functionality $f = \left(f_\lambda(x, y) = x^\top y\right)_{\lambda \in \mathbb{N}}$ over the uniform input distribution (X, Y) where X and Y contain vectors in $\mathbb{F}_2^{\lambda^2}$, while X_λ is restricted to vectors with Hamming weight $\frac{2\lambda}{\log \lambda}$. Looking ahead, we will construct a polynomial-time protocol for $\mathsf{Ext}_{\mathcal{E}}(f)$ with correctness $\frac{1}{2} + \frac{1}{p(\lambda)}$ on $\mathsf{Ext}_{\mathcal{E}}(X, Y)$, for some polynomial p, that uses $c = c(\lambda) = \lambda + 1$ bits of communication. Furthermore, we will show that there exists a negligible function μ such that any unbounded one-way protocol that computes f on (X, Y) using c bits of communication has correctness at most $\frac{1}{2} + \mu(\lambda)$, for any sufficiently large λ.

Notice that

$$\Pr\left[f(x, y) = 0 : (x, y) \leftarrow (X, Y)\right] = \frac{1}{2},$$

and that $\left(\{f(\cdot, y) : y \in Y_\lambda\}\right)_{\lambda \in \mathbb{N}}$ is a universal hash function family. Furthermore, the ensemble X supports an efficient encoding with input length $2\lambda \geq c$, for any sufficiently large λ. Namely, given a vector $m \in \mathbb{F}_2^{2\lambda}$ we map every $\log \lambda$ bits of m to a unit vector in $\mathbb{F}_2^\lambda$. Then, we concatenate these unit vectors to a vector in $\mathbb{F}_2^{\lambda^2}$ with Hamming weight $\frac{2\lambda}{\log \lambda}$.

First, we will show that the private-key encryption scheme $\mathcal{E}$ is Y-entropic secure (Definition 7).

Claim (Y-Entropic Security of $\mathcal{E}$). Assuming $\mathsf{LPN}_{\frac{\log^2 \lambda}{\lambda}}$ (Definition 16), for every $\lambda \in \mathbb{N}$ and $y, y' \leftarrow \mathbb{F}_2^{\lambda^2}$ we have that,

$$\left(y, \mathsf{Enc}_s(y)\right)_{\lambda \in \mathbb{N}} \approx_c \left(y, \mathsf{Enc}_s(y')\right)_{\lambda \in \mathbb{N}},$$

where $s \leftarrow \mathsf{Gen}(1^\lambda)$.

Proof. For any fixed $y, y' \in \mathbb{F}_2^{\lambda^2}$,

$$\left(y, \mathsf{Enc}_s(y')\right)_{\lambda \in \mathbb{N}} = \left(y, (A, A \cdot s + e + y')\right)_{\lambda \in \mathbb{N}} \underset{(*)}{\approx_c} \left(y, (A, u + y')\right)_{\lambda \in \mathbb{N}} = \left(y, (A, u)\right)_{\lambda \in \mathbb{N}}$$

where $u \leftarrow \mathbb{F}_2^{\lambda^2}$, $s \leftarrow \mathbb{F}_2^\lambda$, $A \leftarrow \mathbb{F}_2^{\lambda^2 \times \lambda}$ and $e \leftarrow \mathsf{Ber}_{\frac{\log^2 \lambda}{\lambda}}^{\lambda^2}$, and where $(*)$ holds by the $\mathsf{LPN}_{\frac{\log^2 \lambda}{\lambda}}$ assumption.

Now, consider the following polynomial-time one-way protocol for the extended function ensemble $\mathsf{Ext}_{\mathcal{E}}(f)$. Given inputs x and $c = \mathsf{Enc}_k(y)$, Alice computes $m_A = \mathsf{PlainMult}(x, c)$ and sends it to Bob, who outputs $\mathsf{Dec}_k(m_A)$.

The communication cost of this protocol is $c(\lambda) = |m_A| = \lambda + 1$. We show the correctness probability of the protocol using the Piling-Up Lemma.

Lemma 1 (The Piling-Up Lemma [33]). *Let $e_1, ..., e_k \in \mathbb{F}_2$ be i.i.d. random variables such that $\Pr[e_i = 1] = \epsilon$, then*

$$\Pr\left[\bigoplus_{i=1}^{k} e_i = 0\right] = \frac{1}{2} + \frac{1}{2}(1 - 2\epsilon)^k.$$

Claim (Protocol Correctness). For every $\lambda \in \mathbb{N}$, $x \in X$ and $y \in Y$ we have that

$$\Pr\left[\mathsf{Dec}_s\Big(\mathsf{PlainMult}(x, \mathsf{Enc}_s(y))\Big) = x^\top \cdot y : s \leftarrow \mathsf{Gen}(1^\lambda)\right] > \frac{1}{2} + \frac{1}{2\lambda^8}.$$

Proof. By the definition of $\mathcal{E}$ it's enough to show that $\Pr\left[x^\top \cdot e = 0\right] > \frac{1}{2} + \frac{1}{2\lambda^8}$. By Lemma 1 we have that

$$\Pr\left[x^\top \cdot e = 0\right] = \Pr\left[\bigoplus_{i=1}^{\frac{2\lambda}{\log \lambda}} e_i = 0\right] \geq \frac{1}{2} + \frac{1}{2}(1 - 2\frac{\log^2 \lambda}{\lambda})^{\frac{2\lambda}{\log \lambda}} \geq \frac{1}{2} + \frac{1}{2} \cdot 2^{-4\frac{\log^2 \lambda}{\lambda} \frac{2\lambda}{\log \lambda}} = \frac{1}{2} + \frac{1}{2\lambda^8},$$

where the second inequality holds since $1 - x \geq 2^{-2x}$ for $x \leq \frac{1}{2}$.

Finally, we will show that for the negligible function $\mu = 2^{-\lambda}$ we have that any unbounded one-way protocol that computes f on input distribution (X, Y) using $c(\lambda) = \lambda + 1$ bits of communication has correctness at most $\frac{1}{2} + \mu(\lambda)$, for any sufficiently large λ.

Claim (Distributional Communication Complexity Lower Bound for f). For any $\lambda \in \mathbb{N}$,

$$\mathcal{D}^{A \rightarrow B}\left(f, (X, Y), \frac{1}{2} - 2^{-\lambda}\right) = 2\lambda$$

Proof. Take $\lambda \in \mathbb{N}$. Let H be a matrix such that $H(x, y) = (-1)^{<x,y>}$. It is easy to check that the matrix H satisfies $HH^\top = H^\top H = 2^{\lambda^2} I$. Therefore, $\|H\| = \sqrt{2^{\lambda^2}}$. Let $R = S \times T$ be a rectangle on (X_λ, Y_λ). We have that

$$\mathsf{Disc}(f_\lambda; S \times T) \underset{(1)}{=} \left| \sum_{(x,y) \in S \times T} \Pr[x, y \in (X, Y)] (-1)^{<x,y>} \right|$$

$$\underset{(2)}{\leq} \left| \sum_{(x,y) \in S \times T} \frac{1}{\left(\frac{\lambda^2}{\frac{2\lambda}{\log \lambda}}\right)} \frac{1}{2^{\lambda^2}} H(x, y) \right|$$

$$= \frac{1}{\left(\frac{\lambda^2}{\frac{2\lambda}{\log \lambda}}\right)} \frac{1}{2^{\lambda^2}} |\mathbb{1}_S \cdot H \cdot \mathbb{1}_T|$$

$$\underset{(3)}{\leq} \frac{1}{\left(\frac{\lambda^2}{\frac{2\lambda}{\log \lambda}}\right)} \frac{1}{2^{\lambda^2}} \|\mathbb{1}_S\| \cdot \|H\| \cdot \|\mathbb{1}_T\|$$

$$\underset{(4)}{\leq} \frac{1}{\left(\frac{\lambda^2}{\frac{2\lambda}{\log \lambda}}\right)} \frac{1}{2^{\lambda^2}} \sqrt{\left(\frac{\lambda^2}{\frac{2\lambda}{\log \lambda}}\right)} \cdot 2^{\frac{\lambda^2}{2}} \cdot 2^{\frac{\lambda^2}{2}}$$

$$= \frac{1}{\sqrt{\left(\frac{\lambda^2}{\frac{2\lambda}{\log \lambda}}\right)}},$$

where (1) is by definition, (2) is since X_λ and Y_λ are independent and distributed uniformly over vectors with Hamming weight $\frac{2\lambda}{\log \lambda}$ in $\mathbb{F}_2^{\lambda^2}$ and over $\mathbb{F}_2^{\lambda^2}$ respectively, (3) is by Cauchy-Schwarz and (4) is since $\|H\| = \sqrt{2^{\lambda^2}}$ and since S and T can contain at most $\binom{\lambda^2}{\frac{2\lambda}{\log \lambda}}$ and 2^{λ^2} elements respectively. Therefore, by Theorem 7 we have for error-rate $\epsilon(\lambda) = \frac{1}{2} - 2^{-\lambda}$ the following,

$$
\begin{aligned}
\mathcal{D}^{A \to B}(f) &\geq \log\left(\frac{1 - 2\epsilon(\lambda)}{\mathsf{Disc}(f,(X,Y))}\right) \\
&\geq \frac{1}{2}\log\left(\frac{\lambda^2}{\frac{2\lambda}{\log \lambda}}\right) - \lambda \\
&\underset{(*)}{=} \frac{\lambda}{\log \lambda} \cdot \log\left(\frac{1}{2}\lambda \log \lambda\right) - \lambda \\
&\geq 2\lambda
\end{aligned}
$$

where $(*)$ is since $\binom{n}{k} \geq (\frac{n}{k})^k$ for any n and k.

Acknowledgments. We thank Aayush Jain and the TCC reviewers for their helpful comments. Y. Ishai was supported in part by ERC Project NTSC (742754), BSF grant 2018393, and ISF grant 2774/20. R. Rothblum is funded by the European Union (ERC, FASTPROOF, 101041208). Views and opinions expressed are however those of the author(s) only and do not necessarily reflect those of the European Union or the European Research Council. Neither the European Union nor the granting authority can be held responsible for them.

References

1. Alamati, N., Montgomery, H., Patranabis, S.: Symmetric primitives with structured secrets. In: Boldyreva, A., Micciancio, D. (eds.) CRYPTO 2019. LNCS, vol. 11692, pp. 650–679. Springer, Cham (2019). https://doi.org/10.1007/978-3-030-26948-7_23

2. Alamati, N., Montgomery, H., Patranabis, S., Roy, A.: Minicrypt primitives with algebraic structure and applications. In: Ishai, Y., Rijmen, V. (eds.) EUROCRYPT 2019. LNCS, vol. 11477, pp. 55–82. Springer, Cham (2019). https://doi.org/10.1007/978-3-030-17656-3_3

3. Alekhnovich, M.: More on average case vs approximation complexity. In: Proceedings of the 44th Symposium on Foundations of Computer Science, FOCS 2003, 11–14 October 2003, Cambridge, MA, USA, pp. 298–307. IEEE Computer Society (2003). https://doi.org/10.1109/SFCS.2003.1238204

4. Babai, L., Frankl, P., Simon, J.: Complexity classes in communication complexity theory. In: 27th Annual Symposium on Foundations of Computer Science, SFCS 1986, pp. 337–347. IEEE (1986)

5. Bellare, M., Hofheinz, D., Yilek, S.: Possibility and impossibility results for encryption and commitment secure under selective opening. In: Joux, A. (ed.) EUROCRYPT 2009. LNCS, vol. 5479, pp. 1–35. Springer, Heidelberg (2009). https://doi.org/10.1007/978-3-642-01001-9_1

6. Benaloh, J.: Dense probabilistic encryption. In: Selected Areas of Cryptography, May 1994. https://www.microsoft.com/en-us/research/publication/dense-probabilistic-encryption/

7. Bitansky, N., Freizeit, S.: Statistically sender-private OT from LPN and derandomization. In: Dodis, Y., Shrimpton, T. (eds.) Advances in Cryptology, CRYPTO 2022. LNCS, vol. 13509. Springer, Cham (2022). https://doi.org/10.1007/978-3-031-15982-4_21

8. Bogdanov, A., Lee, C.H.: Limits of provable security for homomorphic encryption. In: Canetti, R., Garay, J.A. (eds.) CRYPTO 2013. LNCS, vol. 8042, pp. 111–128. Springer, Heidelberg (2013). https://doi.org/10.1007/978-3-642-40041-4_7

9. Boneh, D., Goh, E.-J., Nissim, K.: Evaluating 2-DNF formulas on ciphertexts. In: Kilian, J. (ed.) TCC 2005. LNCS, vol. 3378, pp. 325–341. Springer, Heidelberg (2005). https://doi.org/10.1007/978-3-540-30576-7_18

10. Brakerski, Z., Lyubashevsky, V., Vaikuntanathan, V., Wichs, D.: Worst-case hardness for LPN and cryptographic hashing via code smoothing. In: Ishai, Y., Rijmen, V. (eds.) EUROCRYPT 2019. LNCS, vol. 11478, pp. 619–635. Springer, Cham (2019). https://doi.org/10.1007/978-3-030-17659-4_21

11. Brakerski, Z., Vaikuntanathan, V.: Efficient fully homomorphic encryption from (standard) LWE. SIAM J. Comput. **43**(2), 831–871 (2014). https://doi.org/10.1137/120868669

12. Cachin, C., Camenisch, J., Kilian, J., Müller, J.: One-round secure computation and secure autonomous mobile agents. In: Montanari, U., Rolim, J.D.P., Welzl, E. (eds.) ICALP 2000. LNCS, vol. 1853, pp. 512–523. Springer, Heidelberg (2000). https://doi.org/10.1007/3-540-45022-X_43

13. Cohen, S.P., Naor, M.: Low communication complexity protocols, collision resistant hash functions and secret key-agreement protocols. In: Dodis, Y., Shrimpton, T. (eds.) Advances in Cryptology, CRYPTO 2022. LNCS, vol. 13509, pp. 252–281. Springer, Cham (2022). https://doi.org/10.1007/978-3-031-15982-4_9

14. Di Crescenzo, G., Malkin, T., Ostrovsky, R.: Single database private information retrieval implies oblivious transfer. In: Preneel, B. (ed.) EUROCRYPT 2000. LNCS, vol. 1807, pp. 122–138. Springer, Heidelberg (2000). https://doi.org/10.1007/3-540-45539-6_10

15. Damgård, I., Jurik, M.: A generalisation, a simplification and some applications of Paillier's probabilistic public-key system. In: Kim, K. (ed.) PKC 2001. LNCS, vol. 1992, pp. 119–136. Springer, Heidelberg (2001). https://doi.org/10.1007/3-540-44586-2_9

16. Dwork, C., Naor, M., Reingold, O.: Immunizing encryption schemes from decryption errors. In: Cachin, C., Camenisch, J.L. (eds.) EUROCRYPT 2004. LNCS, vol. 3027, pp. 342–360. Springer, Heidelberg (2004). https://doi.org/10.1007/978-3-540-24676-3_21

17. ElGamal, T.: A public key cryptosystem and a signature scheme based on discrete logarithms. In: Blakley, G.R., Chaum, D. (eds.) CRYPTO 1984. LNCS, vol. 196, pp. 10–18. Springer, Heidelberg (1985). https://doi.org/10.1007/3-540-39568-7_2

18. Gentry, C.: A fully homomorphic encryption scheme. Ph.D. thesis, Stanford University, USA (2009). https://searchworks.stanford.edu/view/8493082

19. Gentry, C., Halevi, S., Vaikuntanathan, V.: i-hop homomorphic encryption and rerandomizable Yao circuits. In: Rabin, T. (ed.) CRYPTO 2010. LNCS, vol. 6223, pp. 155–172. Springer, Heidelberg (2010). https://doi.org/10.1007/978-3-642-14623-7_9

20. Gentry, C., Halevi, S., Vaikuntanathan, V.: A simple BGN-type cryptosystem from LWE. In: Gilbert, H. (ed.) EUROCRYPT 2010. LNCS, vol. 6110, pp. 506–522. Springer, Heidelberg (2010). https://doi.org/10.1007/978-3-642-13190-5_26
21. Gentry, C., Sahai, A., Waters, B.: Homomorphic encryption from learning with errors: conceptually-simpler, asymptotically-faster, attribute-based. In: Canetti, R., Garay, J.A. (eds.) CRYPTO 2013. LNCS, vol. 8042, pp. 75–92. Springer, Heidelberg (2013). https://doi.org/10.1007/978-3-642-40041-4_5
22. Goldwasser, S., Micali, S.: Probabilistic encryption. J. Comput. Syst. Sci. **28**(2), 270–299 (1984). https://doi.org/10.1016/0022-0000(84)90070-9
23. Hemenway, B., Libert, B., Ostrovsky, R., Vergnaud, D.: Lossy encryption: constructions from general assumptions and efficient selective opening chosen ciphertext security. In: Lee, D.H., Wang, X. (eds.) ASIACRYPT 2011. LNCS, vol. 7073, pp. 70–88. Springer, Heidelberg (2011). https://doi.org/10.1007/978-3-642-25385-0_4
24. Holenstein, T., Renner, R.: One-way secret-key agreement and applications to circuit polarization and immunization of public-key encryption. In: Shoup, V. (ed.) CRYPTO 2005. LNCS, vol. 3621, pp. 478–493. Springer, Heidelberg (2005). https://doi.org/10.1007/11535218_29
25. Horvitz, O., Katz, J.: Universally-composable two-party computation in two rounds. In: Menezes, A. (ed.) CRYPTO 2007. LNCS, vol. 4622, pp. 111–129. Springer, Heidelberg (2007). https://doi.org/10.1007/978-3-540-74143-5_7
26. Ishai, Y., Kushilevitz, E., Ostrovsky, R.: Sufficient conditions for collision-resistant hashing. In: Kilian, J. (ed.) TCC 2005. LNCS, vol. 3378, pp. 445–456. Springer, Heidelberg (2005). https://doi.org/10.1007/978-3-540-30576-7_24
27. Ishai, Y., Kushilevitz, E., Ostrovsky, R., Prabhakaran, M., Sahai, A.: Efficient non-interactive secure computation. In: Paterson, K.G. (ed.) EUROCRYPT 2011. LNCS, vol. 6632, pp. 406–425. Springer, Heidelberg (2011). https://doi.org/10.1007/978-3-642-20465-4_23
28. Ishai, Y., Paskin, A.: Evaluating branching programs on encrypted data. In: Vadhan, S.P. (ed.) TCC 2007. LNCS, vol. 4392, pp. 575–594. Springer, Heidelberg (2007). https://doi.org/10.1007/978-3-540-70936-7_31
29. Kushilevitz, E., Nisan, N.: Communication Complexity. Cambridge University Press (1997)
30. Kushilevitz, E., Ostrovsky, R.: Replication is NOT needed: SINGLE database, computationally-private information retrieval. In: 38th Annual Symposium on Foundations of Computer Science, FOCS 1997, Miami Beach, Florida, USA, 19–22 October 1997, pp. 364–373. IEEE Computer Society (1997). https://doi.org/10.1109/SFCS.1997.646125
31. Lipmaa, H.: An oblivious transfer protocol with log-squared communication. In: Zhou, J., Lopez, J., Deng, R.H., Bao, F. (eds.) ISC 2005. LNCS, vol. 3650, pp. 314–328. Springer, Heidelberg (2005). https://doi.org/10.1007/11556992_23
32. Liu, T., Vaikuntanathan, V.: On basing private information retrieval on NP-hardness. In: Kushilevitz, E., Malkin, T. (eds.) TCC 2016. LNCS, vol. 9562, pp. 372–386. Springer, Heidelberg (2016). https://doi.org/10.1007/978-3-662-49096-9_16
33. Matsui, M.: Linear cryptanalysis method for DES cipher. In: Helleseth, T. (ed.) EUROCRYPT 1993. LNCS, vol. 765, pp. 386–397. Springer, Heidelberg (1994). https://doi.org/10.1007/3-540-48285-7_33
34. Paillier, P.: Public-key cryptosystems based on composite degree residuosity classes. In: Stern, J. (ed.) EUROCRYPT 1999. LNCS, vol. 1592, pp. 223–238. Springer, Heidelberg (1999). https://doi.org/10.1007/3-540-48910-X_16

35. Peikert, C., Vaikuntanathan, V., Waters, B.: A framework for efficient and composable oblivious transfer. In: Wagner, D. (ed.) CRYPTO 2008. LNCS, vol. 5157, pp. 554–571. Springer, Heidelberg (2008). https://doi.org/10.1007/978-3-540-85174-5_31

36. Rao, A., Yehudayoff, A.: Communication Complexity: and Applications. Cambridge University Press (2020)

37. Razborov, A.A.: On the distributional complexity of disjointness. In: Paterson, M.S. (ed.) ICALP 1990. LNCS, vol. 443, pp. 249–253. Springer, Heidelberg (1990). https://doi.org/10.1007/BFb0032036

38. Regev, O.: On lattices, learning with errors, random linear codes, and cryptography. In: Gabow, H.N., Fagin, R. (eds.) Proceedings of the 37th Annual ACM Symposium on Theory of Computing, Baltimore, MD, USA, 22–24 May 2005, pp. 84–93. ACM (2005). https://doi.org/10.1145/1060590.1060603

39. Rivest, R.L., Adleman, L., Dertouzos, M.L.: On data banks and privacy homomorphisms. Foundations of Secure Computation, pp. 169–179. Academia Press (1978)

40. Rothblum, R.: Homomorphic encryption: from private-key to public-key. In: Ishai, Y. (ed.) TCC 2011. LNCS, vol. 6597, pp. 219–234. Springer, Heidelberg (2011). https://doi.org/10.1007/978-3-642-19571-6_14

41. Sander, T., Young, A.L., Yung, M.: Non-interactive cryptocomputing for nc^1. In: 40th Annual Symposium on Foundations of Computer Science, FOCS 1999, 17–18 October, 1999, New York, NY, USA, pp. 554–567. IEEE Computer Society (1999). https://doi.org/10.1109/SFFCS.1999.814630

42. Stern, J.P.: A new and efficient all-or-nothing disclosure of secrets protocol. In: Ohta, K., Pei, D. (eds.) ASIACRYPT 1998. LNCS, vol. 1514, pp. 357–371. Springer, Heidelberg (1998). https://doi.org/10.1007/3-540-49649-1_28

43. Yao, A.C.C.: Some complexity questions related to distributive computing (preliminary report). In: Proceedings of the Eleventh Annual ACM Symposium on Theory of Computing, pp. 209–213 (1979)

44. Yu, Yu., Zhang, J., Weng, J., Guo, C., Li, X.: Collision resistant hashing from sub-exponential learning parity with noise. In: Galbraith, S.D., Moriai, S. (eds.) ASIACRYPT 2019. LNCS, vol. 11922, pp. 3–24. Springer, Cham (2019). https://doi.org/10.1007/978-3-030-34621-8_1

Security with Functional Re-encryption from CPA

Yevgeniy Dodis[1]($\boxtimes$), Shai Halevi[2], and Daniel Wichs[3]

[1] New York University, New York, USA
dodis@cs.nyu.edu
[2] AWS, Los Angeles, USA
[3] Northeastern University and NTT Research, Boston, USA

Abstract. The notion of *functional re-encryption security (funcCPA)*
for public-key encryption schemes was recently introduced by Akavia *et
al.* (TCC'22), in the context of homomorphic encryption. This notion
lies in between CPA security and CCA security: we give the attacker a
functional re-encryption oracle instead of the decryption oracle of CCA
security. This oracle takes a ciphertext ct and a function f, and returns
fresh encryption of the output of f applied to the decryption of ct; in symbols, $ct' = Enc(f(Dec(ct)))$. More generally, we even allow for a multi-
input version, where the oracle takes an arbitrary number of ciphertexts
$ct_1, \ldots ct_\ell$ and outputs $ct' = Enc(f(Dec(ct_1), \ldots, Dec(ct_\ell)))$.

In this work we observe that funcCPA security may have applications
beyond homomorphic encryption, and set out to study its properties. As
our main contribution, we prove that funcCPA is "closer to CPA than
to CCA"; that is, funcCPA secure encryption can be constructed in a
black-box manner from CPA-secure encryption. We stress that, prior to
our work, this was not known even for basic re-encryption queries corresponding to the identity function f.

At the core of our result is a new technique, showing how to handle
adaptive functional re-encryption queries using tools previously developed in the context of non-malleable encryption, which roughly corresponds to a single *non-adaptive* parallel decryption query.

1 Introduction

The notion of functional re-encryption *FuncCPA* security for encryption schemes
was recently introduced by Akavia *et al.* [1], and shown to be useful in the context of homomorphic encryption schemes. This notion is similar to CCA security,
except that the attacker is given a *re-encryption oracle* rather than a decryption oracle. Roughly, the oracle replies to a query ciphertext ct with another

Y. Dodis—Research Supported by NSF grant CNS-2055578, and gifts from JP Morgan,
Protocol Labs and Algorand Foundation.
S. Halevi—Work was done while at the Algorand Foundation
D. Wichs—Research supported by NSF grant CNS-1750795, CNS-2055510 and the JP
Morgan faculty research award.

G. Rothblum and H. Wee (Eds.): TCC 2023, LNCS 14370, pp. 279–305, 2023.
https://doi.org/10.1007/978-3-031-48618-0_10

ciphertext $ct' = Enc(Dec(ct))$, corresponding to a fresh encryption of the message contained in ct. More generally, the definition even permits *"functional" re-encryption queries*: the attacker also specifies a function f, and the oracle returns $ct' = Enc(f(Dec(ct)))$. Or even more generally, we can consider *"multi-input functional" re-encryption queries*, where the oracle takes an arbitrary number of ciphetexts $ct_1, \ldots ct_\ell$ and outputs $ct' = Enc(f(Dec(ct_1), \ldots, Dec(ct_\ell)))$. Below, when we say FuncCPA, we refer to the strongest notion with multi-input functional queries by default, unless we explicitly restrict to single-input functional re-encryption or non-functional re-encryption.

At first glance, the FuncCPA-oracle may seem quite useless to the attacker, as it only returns properly encrypted ciphertexts. One may even be tempted to assume that every CPA-secure scheme is also FuncCPA-secure. Surprisingly, this is not the case: Akavia *et al.* described in [1] a CPA-secure scheme where a single (non-functional) re-encryption query allows the adversary to recover the secret key. This example makes FuncCPA an interesting notion to study, as it lies "somewhere in between" CPA and CCA security.

FuncCPA for Non-Homomorphic Schemes. Although Akavia *et al.* only considered FuncCPA in the context of homomorphic encryption, we note that it makes sense also for schemes that are not homomorphic. For example, consider using a "secure enclave" (such as a secure hardware or trusted execution environment) to address the same client-server delegation scenario. In this setting there could be an "analyst" that wants to perform various studies on sensitive data, multiple clients who are willing to donate their data to those studies (as long as their privacy is respected), and a worker server on which the studies are computed, endowed by a secure enclave. The analyst will have a secret-public key pair, they will send the secret key over a secure channel to the enclave, and publish the corresponding public key. Clients who want to donate their data to the studies will encrypt it under the analyst's public key, and send the ciphertext to the server. The server will collect the data (possibly more and over time), and occasionally will ask the enclave to compute something on the encrypted data. The enclave will decrypt the given pieces of data, compute the required function, encrypt the result, and return to the server.[1] When each study is over, the server will send the end-result back to the analyst, to be decrypted and used.

In that setting, we note that the queries made by the server to its secure enclave are exactly the type of re-encryption queries that we consider: The server sends encrypted data and some function, and the enclave decrypts, computes the function, re-encrypts, and return to the server.

Our Main Question. In this work we set out to study the properties of FuncCPA security. For starters, we give a simple proof that every CCA-secure scheme is also FuncCPA -secure.[2] Having established that FuncCPA security is implied

---

[1] Notice, this application requires FuncCPA security for queries consisting of multiple ciphertexts, which is why this will be our default notion of FuncCPA security.

[2] In fact, we show (see Lemma A.1) that FuncCPA security is implied by CCA security against "lunchtime attacks", known as CCA1.

by CCA security and implies CPA security, the main question that we address in this work is whether FuncCPA is "more like" CPA or CCA. Specifically we ask:

> Can one construct a FuncCPA-secure encryption scheme from any CPA-secure one?

We stress that the answer to this question is unknown even if we restrict to basic ("non-functional") re-encryption queries Enc(Dec(ct)), corresponding to a single ciphertext with the identity function f.

The relation between CPA-secure schemes and CCA-secure ones was studied extensively in the literature, and many construction of the latter are known. However, all these constructions either require making extra assumptions beyond just the existence of CPA-secure schemes [8–10, 12], or are carried out in idealized models (e.g., [7]). In particular, whether one can construct a CCA secure scheme generically from any CPA secure one, is considered a major open problem in cryptography.

As for standard model constructions from CPA encryption without extra assumptions, it is known that the existence of CPA-secure encryption can generically be upgraded to weaker variants of CCA security, such as non-malleability [3,4,11], bounded CCA security [6], or security against self-destruct attacks [5]. Of particular interest to us, non-malleable encryption corresponds to a "non-adaptive" variant of CCA-security, where the adversary can only issue one set of non-adaptive decryption queries in parallel. Pass *et al.* [11] showed how to generically transform CPA-security to non-malleability, and Choi *et al.* [3,4] showed that this can even be done while using the underlying CPA-secure scheme as a black box.

1.1 Our Main Result

We show that FuncCPA is "more like CPA than CCA", specifically we prove:

Theorem 1.1. *If CPA-secure encryption schemes exist, then so do FuncCPA-secure encryption schemes. Moreover, the transformation can be made black-box in the underlying CPA-secure scheme.*

Perhaps surprisingly, the transformation that we describe here is identical to the CPA-to-non-malleable transformation of Choi *et al.* from [3], except that *we need to start with a scheme which is already non-malleable.* Therefore, one way to get FuncCPA from CPA in a black-box way is to apply the transformation from [3] once to get non-malleability, then apply it again to get FuncCPA -security.[3]

---

[3] Our transformation in Theorem 1.1 is not only FuncCPA-secure, but also non-malleable. See Remark 3.8.

Our Technique. For simplicity of notation, we describe our technique for the case of single-input functional re-encryption queries, but everything trivially generalizes to multi-input functional re-encryption queries as well. The main difficulty of a reduction from CPA to FuncCPA security is that we need to simulate adaptive queries to a functional re-encryption oracle, which involves decryption. How do we do this without a decryption oracle? We use the transformation from [3], which was designed to allow a simulation of a batch of non-adaptive queries to a decryption oracle, and show that the same approach also allows us to simulate adaptive queries to a functional re-encryption oracle.

The high-level structure of the transformation from [3] is to encode the message with an appropriate error-correcting code, then encrypt the resulting codeword symbols multiple times under different keys, and check on decryption that the decrypted words are close enough to each other. Thinking of the encrypted symbols as a matrix, with the rows corresponding to multiple encryptions and the columns corresponding to positions in the codeword, Choi *et al.* observed that checking closeness can be done just by verifying that the codewords agree on some small randomly chosen subset of the columns. Hence the decryptor only needs to know the secret keys for one row to do the actual decryption, and for that small subset of columns to do the checks. Security is then proven by reduction to the security of the keys for which the decryptor does not know the secret keys.

For our purposes, we consider a "bad event" in which the attacker submits a query ciphertext for which not all the rows are close to each other, but this "is not caught" by the checks on decryption. As long as this bad event does not happen, we can show that the decryption procedure will always give the same answer, no matter which row or columns are used in it. Hence, as long as this bad event does not happen, one can simulate the attacker's view without knowing too many keys. Moreover, we also show that as long as the bad event did not happen so far, the adversary does not have enough information to cause it to happen in the next query. This allows us to describe a reduction using "almost-functional" keys, where the reduction can decrypt all the attacker's queries *except the one that it will use for its challenge ciphertext*. This, in turn, lets us switch from $\mathrm{Enc}(f(\mathrm{Dec}(\mathsf{ct})))$ to $\mathrm{Enc}(0)$, one query at a time.

Importantly, to turn the advantage of the FuncCPA attacker into an advantage in attacking the underlying scheme, the reduction algorithms that we describe must know if the bad event occurred on *any* of the re-encrypted ciphertexts ct_i. The key novelty here is the observation that the reduction does not need to know this at the time of each (functional) re-encryption query. Instead, it can run the attacker until the end, and check if the bad event had occurred on any of the ciphertexts $(\mathsf{ct}_1, \ldots, \mathsf{ct}_q)$ only then. This check requires access to the decryption oracle, which is where we use the *non-malleability* of the underlying encryption scheme (rather than mere CPA security). Namely, non-malleability allows us to make one such parallel decryption query to know precisely when any bad event happened.[4] Hence, the reduction to non-malleability will use a single, *non-adaptive* parallel decryption query to check whether or not the bad event occurred in any of the attacker's queries, despite the attacker making many *adaptive* functional re-encryption queries. See more details in Sect. 3.

We note that Choi *et al.* later described a more efficient CPA-to-non-malleability transformation [4], and that the same line of reasoning probably works for that transformation as well. But since we do not focus on efficiency in this work, we use the (arguably simpler) transformation from [3].

Do we Really Need Two Transformations? Seeing how we need to apply the same transformation twice, once to move from CPA to non-malleability and a second time to get FuncCPA, it is natural to ask if we can spare one of them – can't we just apply this transformation once?

While we don't know the answer, our proof technique completely breaks down without the assumption that the underlying scheme is already non-malleable. In fact, our intuition is that CPA security of the underlying scheme is not enough to ensure FuncCPA of the result, and one should be able to exhibit a counter-example using strong enough homomorphic properties of it. We note, however, that such counter-example "cannot be too simple", since the transformation encrypts different codeword positions with different keys, meaning that any such example will be at least as hard as showing that bit-encryption does not imply FuncCPA. Still, we conjecture that non-malleability is really needed for our proof.

Variations of FuncCPA. As we mentioned above, there are different variants of FuncCPA -security, with one or more ciphertexts, and with or without functional queries. Akavia *et al.* have shown in [1] that these notion are all equivalent for homomorphic encryption schemes,[5] but generally they may differ.

In fact, for our purposes it is convenient to use a possibly-stronger formal definition than the one from [1]. (This stronger definition was also considered by Akavia and Vald [2].) Roughly, instead of only requiring that functional re-encryption queries cannot help the attacker break semantic security, we require that these queries are indistinguishable from fresh encryptions of some fixed message (e.g. 0). This clearly implies that such queries cannot help break semantic security, but the converse may not hold. We denote this potentially stronger notion by FuncCPA+.

We note that, prior to the current work, constructing FuncCPA from CPA-secure encryption is challenging even for the weakest of these notions (non-functional re-encryption queries not helping break semantic security), while our positive result applies even to the strongest of them (functional re-encryption

---

[4] This aspect was not needed in the analysis of [3], as they did not have any re-encryption queries.

[5] Intuitively, multiple-ciphertext functional re-encryption oracle can be simulated by a single-ciphertext non-functional re-encryption oracle, by first homomorphically applying the function f "inside the encryption", and then calling the simpler oracle to ensure the resulting encryption is "fresh".

queries with multiple ciphertexts look like encryptions of 0). We discuss implications and separations between many of these variants in Sect. 2.1 and in Sect. A.

Organization

In Sect. 2 we recall the basic definitions and prove some simple properties of FuncCPA-security. Our main result Theorem 1.1 is proved in Sect. 3, and we state a few open problems in Sect. 4. Finally, in appendix A we prove some relations between various security notions.

2 Definitions

Signatures. A signature scheme $S = (\mathsf{Gen}, \mathsf{Sig}, \mathsf{Ver})$ consists of randomized key generation $(\mathsf{sk}, \mathsf{vk}) \leftarrow \mathsf{Gen}(1^\lambda)$, signing $\sigma \leftarrow \mathsf{Sig}(\mathsf{sk}, m)$, and verification, $0/1 \leftarrow \mathsf{Ver}(\mathsf{vk}, \sigma, m)$. The (error-free) correctness condition asserts that for all λ and all messages m, we have

$$\Pr\left[(\mathsf{sk}, \mathsf{vk}) \leftarrow \mathsf{Gen}(1^\lambda), \ \sigma \leftarrow \mathsf{Sig}(\mathsf{sk}, m) : \mathsf{Ver}(\mathsf{vk}, \sigma, m) = 1\right] = 1.$$

Definition 2.1 (Secure   one-time   Signatures).   *A   scheme* $S = (\mathsf{Gen}, \mathsf{Sig}, \mathsf{Ver})$ *is strongly existentially unforgeable under one-time attack if any PPT adversary $A = (A_1, A_2)$ has at most a negligible probability $\mathsf{negl}(\lambda)$ of winning the following game:*

1. $(\mathsf{sk}, \mathsf{vk}) \leftarrow \mathsf{Gen}(1^k)$;
2. $(m, \mathsf{state}) \leftarrow A_1(\mathsf{vk})$;
3. $\sigma \leftarrow \mathsf{Sig}(\mathsf{sk}, m)$;
4. $(m', \sigma') \leftarrow A_2(\mathsf{state}, \sigma)$.

A wins the game if $(m', \sigma') \neq (m, \sigma)$ but $\mathsf{Ver}(\mathsf{vk}, \sigma', m') = 1$.

Encryption Schemes. We recall below different notions of security for public-key encryption schemes. Such a scheme $\mathcal{E} = (\mathsf{Gen}, \mathsf{Enc}, \mathsf{Dec})$ (over message space M which could depend on the security parameter) consists of:

- Key Generation algorithm $(\mathsf{dk}, \mathsf{ek}) \leftarrow \mathsf{Gen}(1^\lambda)$. Here dk is the secret key and ek is the public key.
- Encryption algorithm $\mathsf{ct} \leftarrow \mathsf{Enc}(\mathsf{ek}, \mathsf{pt})$ converting message $\mathsf{pt} \in M$ into ciphertext ct; and
- Decryption algorithm $\mathsf{pt} \leftarrow \mathsf{Dec}(\mathsf{dk}, \mathsf{ct})$ recovering the plaintext $\mathsf{pt} \in M \cup \{\bot\}$ from the ciphertext ct, where $\bot$ denotes a decryption failure.

The (error-free[6]) correction condition asserts that for all λ and all $\mathsf{pt} \in M$, we have

$$\Pr\left[(\mathsf{dk}, \mathsf{ek}) \leftarrow \mathsf{Gen}(1^\lambda), \ \mathsf{ct} \leftarrow \mathsf{Enc}(\mathsf{ek}, \mathsf{pt}) : \mathsf{Dec}(\mathsf{dk}, \mathsf{ct}) = \mathsf{pt}\right] = 1.$$

---

[6] All the results in this work apply out-of-the-box also to schemes with decryption errors, as long as they only occur with negligible probability. Otherwise one can amplify correctness of the underlying CPA-secure scheme before applying our transformation.

Definition 2.2 ((nm)CPA/CCA1/CCA2/(multi)FuncCPA Security).
An encryption scheme $\mathcal{E} = (\text{Gen}, \text{Enc}, \text{Dec})$ *is X-secure for security notion*

$$X \in \{CPA,\ CCA1,\ CCA2,\ FuncCPA,\ 1\text{-}FuncCPA,\ ReEncCPA,\ nmCPA\},$$

if any PPT adversary $A = (A_1, A_2)$ *with access to oracles* $(\mathcal{O}_1, \mathcal{O}_2)$ *below has at most a negligible advantage* $\mathsf{negl}(\lambda)$ *in the following game:*

1. $b \leftarrow \{0,1\}$; $(\text{dk}, \text{ek}) \leftarrow \text{Gen}(1^\lambda)$;   2. $(\text{pt}_0, \text{pt}_1, \text{state}) \leftarrow A_1^{\mathcal{O}_1}(\text{ek})$;
3. $\text{ct} \leftarrow \text{Enc}(\text{ek}, \text{pt}_b)$;   4. $b' \leftarrow A_2^{\mathcal{O}_2}(\text{state}, \text{ct})$.

The advantage is defined as $|\Pr[b' = 1|b = 1] - \Pr[b' = 1|b = 0]|$, *where the oracles* $(\mathcal{O}_1, \mathcal{O}_2)$ *are instantiated as follows for each notion X:*

<u>*CPA*</u>: $\mathcal{O}_1, \mathcal{O}_2$ *always return* $\perp$.
<u>*CCA1*</u>: $\mathcal{O}_1(\text{ct}') = \text{Dec}(\text{dk}, \text{ct}')$ *is decryption oracle, and* $\mathcal{O}_2$ *always returns* $\perp$.
<u>*CCA2*</u>: $\mathcal{O}_1(\text{ct}') = \text{Dec}(\text{dk}, \text{ct}')$ *is decryption oracle, and* $\mathcal{O}_2$ *is the same as* $\mathcal{O}_1$,
   except it returns $\perp$ *on the challenge* ct *from Step 3 above.*
<u>*FuncCPA*</u>: $\mathcal{O}_1(\text{ct}'_1, \ldots, \text{ct}'_\ell, f) = \mathcal{O}_2(\text{ct}'_1, \ldots, \text{ct}'_\ell, f) =$
   $\text{Enc}(\text{ek}, f(\text{Dec}(\text{dk}, \text{ct}'_1), \ldots, \text{Dec}(\text{dk}, \text{ct}'_\ell)))$
   are multi-input functional re-encryption oracles, where $\ell \in \mathbb{Z}$ *can be arbitrary and* $f : (M \cup \{\perp\})^\ell \to M$ *is any function (specified as a circuit).*
<u>*1-FuncCPA*</u>: *Same as FuncCPA, but all functions* f *are single input* ($\ell = 1$);
   $\mathcal{O}_1(\text{ct}', f) = \mathcal{O}_2(\text{ct}', f) = \text{Enc}(\text{ek}, f(\text{Dec}(\text{dk}, \text{ct}')))$.
<u>*ReEncCPA*</u>: *Same as FuncCPA, but all functions* f *are the identity* $f(\text{pt}) = \text{pt}$;
   $\mathcal{O}_1(\text{ct}') = \mathcal{O}_2(\text{ct}') = \text{Enc}(\text{ek}, \text{Dec}(\text{dk}, \text{ct}'))$
<u>*nmCPA*</u>: $\mathcal{O}_1$ *always returns* $\perp$, *while* $\mathcal{O}_2$ *accepts a single "parallel" query* $\{(\text{ct}'_i)\}$,
   and returns $\{\text{pt}'_i\}$, *after which it returns* $\perp$ *for all subsequent queries. As with CCA2 notion,* $\text{pt}'_i = \perp$, *if* $\text{ct}'_i = \text{ct}$ *from Step 3; and otherwise it is the regular decryption oracle* $\text{pt}'_i = \text{Dec}(\text{dk}, \text{ct}'_i)$.

Multiple-Keys Tag-Based Non-Malleability. For our transformation, it will be slightly more convenient to use a slight extension of nmCPA security notion, which is easily seen equivalent to the traditional nmCPA security given in Definition 2.2.

First, we will use a *tagged* nmCPA encryption, where the encryption and decryption routines are also given a tag tg, and correctness in only ensured when the same tag is used in both.

$$\Pr\left[(\text{dk}, \text{ek}) \leftarrow \text{Gen}(1^\lambda),\ \text{ct} \leftarrow \text{Enc}(\text{ek}, \text{tg}, \text{pt}) : \text{Dec}(\text{dk}, \text{tg}, \text{ct}) = \text{pt}\right] = 1.$$

Furthermore, the non-malleability security game is modified so that the adversary submits a set of tag/ciphertext pairs $\{(\text{tg}'_i, \text{ct}'_i)\}$ in parallel, such that each pair $(\text{tg}'_i, \text{ct}'_i) \neq (\text{tg}, \text{ct})$ differs from the challenge tag/ciphertext pai from Step 3, and the oracle responds with $\text{pt}'_i = \text{Dec}(\text{dk}, \text{tg}'_i, \text{ct}'_i)$. Notice, a tagged scheme can always be converted into a non-tagged scheme by just omitting the tag. Conversely, non-tagged scheme for large message space can be made to support tags, by viewing the tag as part of the message, and then checking that the decrypted tag matches the declared one.

Second, we will use a multiple-keys/multiple-message nmCPA which will be slightly more convenient for our proof. This is known to be equivalent to the notion from Definition 2.2, e.g., [11, Thm 4]. The full definition is given below.

Definition 2.3 (tag-nmCPA Security). *A tagged scheme* $\mathcal{E} = (\mathsf{Gen}, \mathsf{Enc}, \mathsf{Dec})$ *is tag-non-malleable secure if for any polynomial* $p(\cdot)$, *a conforming PPT adversary* $A = (A_1, A_2, A_3)$ *has at most a negligible advantage* $\mathsf{negl}(\lambda)$ *in the following game:*

1. $b \leftarrow \{0,1\}$; $(\mathsf{dk}_i, \mathsf{ek}_i) \leftarrow \mathsf{Gen}(1^\lambda)$ *for* $i = 1, 2, \ldots, p(\lambda)$;
2. $((i_1, \mathsf{pt}_1^0, \mathsf{pt}_1^1, \mathsf{tg}_1), \ldots, (i_m, \mathsf{pt}_m^0, \mathsf{pt}_m^1, \mathsf{tg}_m), \mathsf{state}) \leftarrow A_1(\{\mathsf{ek}_i\})$;
3. $\mathsf{ct}_j \leftarrow \mathsf{Enc}(\mathsf{ek}_{i_j}, \mathsf{tg}_j, \mathsf{pt}_j^b)$ *for* $j = 1, \ldots, m$;
4. $((k_1, \mathsf{ct}_1', \mathsf{tg}_1'), \ldots, (k_n, \mathsf{ct}_n', \mathsf{tg}_n'), \mathsf{state}') \leftarrow A_2(\mathsf{state}, \mathsf{ct}_1, \ldots, \mathsf{ct}_m)$;
5. $\mathsf{pt}_\ell' \leftarrow \mathsf{Dec}(\mathsf{dk}_{k_\ell}, \mathsf{tg}_\ell', \mathsf{ct}_\ell')$ *for* $\ell = 1, \ldots, n$;
6. $b' \leftarrow A_3(\mathsf{state}', \mathsf{pt}_1', \ldots, \mathsf{pt}_n')$.

A is conforming if the pairs $\{(k_\ell, \mathsf{tg}_\ell', \mathsf{ct}_\ell') : \ell = 1, \ldots, n\}$ *are disjoint from* $\{(i_j, \mathsf{tg}_j, \mathsf{ct}_j) : j = 1, \ldots, m\}$. *The advantage is defined as*

$$|\Pr[b' = 1 | b = 1] - \Pr[b' = 1 | b = 0]|.$$

2.1 An Alternative Definition of FuncCPA

When proving the FuncCPA security of our construction, it is convenient to use a possibly-stronger notion than Definition 2.2, that we call FuncCPA⁺. Rather than requiring that the functional re-encryption oracle does not help in breaking semantic security, this definition states that functional re-encryption oracle does not help because it cannot by distinguished from fresh encryptions of 0 (which the attacker can do itself).[7]

Definition 2.4 (FuncCPA⁺ Security). *A (non-tagged) scheme* $\mathcal{E} = (\mathsf{Gen}, \mathsf{Enc}, \mathsf{Dec})$ *is FuncCPA⁺-secure if any PPT adversary* A *with access to a re-encryption oracle has at most a negligible advantage* $\mathsf{negl}(\lambda)$ *in the following game:*

1. $b \leftarrow \{0,1\}$; $(\mathsf{dk}, \mathsf{ek}) \leftarrow \mathsf{Gen}(1^\lambda)$;   2. $b' \leftarrow A^{\mathsf{reEnc}_b(\mathsf{dk}, \mathsf{ek}, \cdot, \cdot)}(\mathsf{ek})$.

where the re-encryption oracle takes an arbitrary ℓ *and* $f : (M \cup \{\bot\})^\ell \to M$ *(given as a circuit):*

$$\mathsf{reEnc}_b(\mathsf{dk}, \mathsf{ek}, \mathsf{ct}_1, \ldots, \mathsf{ct}_\ell, f) = \begin{cases} \mathsf{E}(\mathsf{ek}, f(\mathsf{Dec}(\mathsf{dk}, \mathsf{ct}_1), \ldots, \mathsf{Dec}(\mathsf{dk}, \mathsf{ct}_\ell))) & \textit{if } b = 1 \\ \mathsf{E}(\mathsf{ek}, 0) & \textit{if } b = 0 \end{cases}$$

---

[7] Having two such flavors is reminiscent of definitions of circular security: Over there one notion asserts that an encryption of the secret key does not help the attacker violate semantic security, and the other requires that the attacker cannot distinguish such encryption from an encryption of zero.

The advantage is defined as $|\Pr[b' = 1|b = 1] - \Pr[b' = 1|b = 0]|$. *We can also define restricted notions* 1-*FuncCPA*$^+$ *and ReEncCPA*$^+$, *corresponding to single input* f $(\ell = 1)$ *and the identity function* f, *respectively.*

First, we show that this notion indeed implies FuncCPA security.

Lemma 2.5. *Any scheme which is FuncCPA*$^+$-*secure, is also FuncCPA-secure. (Analogously, the same holds for restricted notions* 1-*FuncCPA and ReEnc-CPA.)*

Proof. We first recall that the "left-or-right" notion from Definition 2.2 where the attacker chooses $\mathsf{pt}_0, \mathsf{pt}_1$ and gets an encryption of one of them, is known to be equivalent to a "real-or-zero" notion of security where the attacker only chooses pt_1, and gets either an encryption of pt_1 or an encryption of zero. (These are equivalent upto a factor of 2 in the advantage.) It is therefore sufficient to show that Definition 2.4 implies this real-or-zero notion.

Let $\mathcal{E}$ be a scheme satisfying Definition 2.4, and we want to show that it also satisfy the (real-or-zero variant of) Definition 2.2. Let A be an adversary with access to a functional re-encryption oracle, and we want to show that it only has a negligible advantage in the real-or-zero game against $\mathcal{E}$. Consider the probability of A outputting 1 in the following four experiments:

1. A's oracle is implemented by a true functional re-encryption oracle, and its challenge-ciphertext query is answered by an encryption of pt_1.
2. A's oracle is implemented by a zero-encrypting oracle, and its challenge-ciphertext query is answered by an encryption of pt_1.
3. A's oracle is implemented by a zero-encrypting oracle, and its challenge-ciphertext query is answered by an encryption of 0.
4. A's oracle is implemented by a true functional re-encryption oracle, and its challenge-ciphertext query is answered by an encryption of 0.

The probabilities in Experiments 1 vs. 2 are close (upto a negligible difference) by the FuncCPA$^+$-security of $\mathcal{E}$, and the same holds for the probabilities in Experiments 3 vs. 4. Moreover, the probabilities in Experiments 2 vs. 3 are close (upto a negligible difference) by the CPA-security of $\mathcal{E}$, which is implied by FuncCPA$^+$-security. Hence the probability of A outputting 1 in experiments 1 vs. 4. are close upto a negligible difference, as needed.

The proof for restricted variants follows identically.

Are These Definitions Equivalent? Lemma 2.5 says that FuncCPA$^+$ implies FuncCPA, but we do not know if there is also an implication in the other direction. One piece of evidence that points toward FuncCPA$^+$ being strictly stronger than FuncCPA, is that we can show a separation for the analogous notions with a *non-functional* re-encryption oracle; namely, *ReEncCPA* notion. In this notion, a re-encryption query consists of only a ciphertexts ct (without the function f) and it is answered by $\mathsf{ct}' = \mathsf{Enc}(\mathsf{Dec}(\mathsf{ct}))$. See Lemma A.3.

Other (non-)Relations. In Appendix A we also have several other observations of interest. In Lemma A.1, we also show that a CCA1-secure scheme is always FuncCPA$^+$-secure. In Lemma A.4 we also show that a (single-input) 1-FuncCPA$^+$-secure scheme is not always (multi-input) FuncCPA-secure, while in Lemma A.2 we show that nmCPA-security of a given scheme is incomparable with any of the FuncCPA/1-FuncCPA/ReEncCPA-securities (enhanced or not) of that scheme.

3   From CPA to FuncCPA

This section is devoted to proving our main Theorem 1.1. As mentioned, we will actually prove (potentially) stronger FuncCPA$^+$ security; namely:

Theorem 3.1. *If CPA-secure encryption schemes exist, then so do FuncCPA$^+$-secure encryption schemes. Moreover, the transformation can be made black-box in the underlying CPA-secure scheme.*

As described in the introduction, we show that applying the CPA-to-nmCPA black-box transformation of Choi *et al.* [3], to a scheme *which is already nmCPA-secure*, results in a FuncCPA$^+$ scheme. As the existence of CPA-secure schemes implies the existence of nmCPA-secure ones [11], even with a black-box transformation [3], the theorem follows.

For simplicity of notation (e.g., to avoid double indices), we first describe our proof for single-input re-encryption queries (i.e., 1-FuncCPA notion, corresponding to single-input function f with arity $\ell = 1$). However, there is basically no difference in extending the proof to support multiple ciphertext queries (e.g., general $\ell \geq 1$), and we sketch the extension from 1-FuncCPA$^+$ to full FuncCPA$^+$ security of our transformation in Sect. 3.5.

3.1   Technical Overview

Before describing the CDMW construction itself, we highlight the abstract properties that it satisfies, and how they are used to prove FuncCPA security. We rely on the following properties:

1. We have a notion of valid/invalid ciphertexts, and all ciphertexts output by encryption are valid.
2. For any challenge ciphertext ct*, the reduction is able to find an alternate "somewhat defective" secret key, which decrypts *all valid ciphertexts except the challenge ciphertext* ct* identically to the original key, but is incapable of breaking the semantic security of ct*.
3. An adversary who only sees the public key, cannot produce an invalid ciphertext that decrypts to anything but 0, via either the original key or any defective key.

Non-Malleability. Let us briefly outline how the above properties are used in CDMW to show non-malleability: First, they switch to using an alternate "somewhat defective" decryption key from (2) to answer decryption queries. They argue that all decryption queries are answered identically with this change. As per (2), this is true for decryption queries with a valid ciphertext, and as per (3), queries with invalid ciphertext are always answered by 0 in both cases. We note that this step crucially relies on the adversary making only one (parallel) decryption query rather than many adaptive queries; i.e. it only provides non-malleability rather than CCA security. Indeed, an adversary making multiple adaptive decryption queries (with valid ciphertexts) can learn information about the secret key from answers to previous decryption queries, so can no longer rely on (3).[8] Second, after switching to using a "somewhat defective" decryption key, they can switch the challenge ciphertext ct^* from an encryption of pt_0 to an encryption of pt_1 by relying on property (2) that semantic security of ct^* is preserved even given the alternate decryption key.

FuncCPA+ Security. Now we show how to use the above properties to prove FuncCPA+ security. We define a *bad* event that the adversary submits an invalid ciphertext that does not decrypt to 0 (either by the original or any alternate decryption key) during the course of the game. As long as the bad event does not happen, we can replace the output of each functional re-encryption query (one by one) by an encryption of 0 via the same argument as above. On the other hand, we argue that the probability of the bad event occurring is negligible: To cause the bad event to happen for the first time on functional re-encryption query i, the adversary would have needed to learn something about the secret key from the first $i - 1$ functional re-encryption queries. But because the bad event did not occur during those queries yet, we can replace their outputs by encryptions of 0 (by the same argument as above) and argue that this cannot change the probability of the bad event occurring for the first time in the i'th query. Once the first $i - 1$ queries return 0 and do not induce the bad event, we know that they do not reveal anything about the secret key, which ensures that probability of the bad event happening on the ith query is negligible.

Formalizing this argument, however, requires handling the following subtle point: when changing a ciphertext to an encryption of 0 in each step, we must show this change is not only imperceptible to the adversary, but it also does not affect the probability of the bad event. In particular, the reduction must check if the bad event occurred at the very end of the game, which requires checking if various ciphertexts submitted by the adversary during the game were valid or invalid. Therefore, we need a stronger version of property (2) to hold: the semantic security of ct^* holds even given the alternate decryption key *and a single parallel query to a valid/invalid ciphertext check*. To achieve this stronger property, we need the underlying component scheme used by this transformation to already be non-malleable.

---

[8] Valid ciphertexts are not necessarily correctly generated and may decrypt differently depending on the secret key.

3.2 Building Blocks

Non-malleability. Recall from Definition 2.2 that (tagged) non-malleable encryption is a weaker variant of (tagged) CCA-secure encryption, where the adversary only gets to make a single non-adaptive query to the decryption oracle (but that query can ask to decrypt many ciphertexts). Below it will be convenient to use the multi-key/multi-message variant of this notion (cf. Definition 2.3). As mentioned earlier, this is known to be equivalent to the single-key variant from Definition 2.2 (e.g., [11, Thm 1]).[9]

One-Time Signatures. Our main construction also uses (one-time) signatures, which are strongly existentially unforgeable, as per Definition 2.1.

Secret Sharing Encoding Schemes. We will also use the notion of secret-sharing encoding scheme $\mathcal{C} = (\mathsf{E}, \mathsf{D})$, similar to the notion of linear error-correcting secret-sharing [5]. Such a scheme comes with efficient randomized encoding E and decoding D, and is parameterized by underlying symbol space Σ, as well as integers k (dimension), n (length), d (decoding radius), and t (privacy parameter). We sometimes abuse notations, denoting by $\mathcal{C}$ the resulting code itself (i.e., the image of the encoding routine).

Let $\left[\binom{n}{t}\right]$ denote the collection of all the subsets $S \subset [n]$ of cardinality t, the code $\mathcal{C}$ has the following features:

- The encoding is $\mathsf{E} : \Sigma^k \times \mathcal{R} \to \Sigma^n$, where $\mathcal{R}$ is the randomness space.
  The decoding is $\mathsf{D} : \Sigma^n \to ((\Sigma^k \times \mathcal{R}) \cup \{\bot\})$, such that $\forall x \in \Sigma^k, r \in \mathcal{R}$, we have $\mathsf{D}(\mathsf{E}(x, r)) = (x, r)$.
  Below when we say "decoding to a codeword", we mean a procedure $\mathsf{D}' : \Sigma^n \to (\Sigma \cup \{\bot\})^n$ which is defined as

$$\mathsf{D}'(z \in \Sigma^n) = \begin{cases} \bot^n & \text{if } \mathsf{D}(z) = \bot \\ \mathsf{E}(\mathsf{D}(z)) & \text{otherwise.} \end{cases}$$

- The decoding radius of $\mathcal{C}$ is at least some large enough d (see below). Namely, for any $x \in \Sigma^k, r \in \mathcal{R}$ and any word $z \in \Sigma^n$ of Hamming distance at most d from $\mathsf{E}(x, r)$, it holds that $\mathsf{D}(z) = (x, r)$.
- There is an efficient extension procedure $\mathsf{Extend} : \Sigma^k \times \Sigma^t \times \left[\binom{n}{t}\right] \to \Sigma^n$ that take as input $x \in \Sigma^k, y \in \Sigma^t$, and a size-$t$ subset $S \subset [n], |S| = t$, and outputs a codeword $z \in \mathcal{C}$ such that $\mathsf{D}(z) = (x, r)$ for some r, and $z|_S = y$ (i.e., the symbols of z in positions from S are exactly y).
  Moreover, for any $x \in \Sigma^k$ and any $S \in \left[\binom{n}{t}\right]$, the following two distributions are equal:

$$\{r \leftarrow \mathcal{R} : \text{output } \mathsf{E}(x, r)\} \text{ and } \{y \leftarrow \Sigma^t : \text{output } \mathsf{Extend}(x, y, S)\}.$$

The parameters of $\mathcal{C}$ are set to ensure that $(1 - \frac{d}{n})^t \leq 2^{-\lambda}$.[10]

---

[9] The theorem in [11, Thm 4] is stated for a non-tagged scheme, but it holds equally for the tagged version.

[10] We note that the requirements from Extend imply that t cannot be too close to n, at the very least we need $n \geq t + k$ so that any t-symbol string can be extended to an encoding of any k-symbol information word.

Some examples of such codes: using Shamir secret-sharing we can get a construction over a large enough field $\Sigma = \mathbb{F}_{2^\ell}$ with (say) $k = 1$, $t = 2\lambda$, $n = 3t$ and $d = t$. Or we can encode the Shamir-based constructions in binary, using $\Sigma = \{0,1\}$, $k \geq 3 + \log\lambda$, $t = 2\lambda k$, $n = 3t$ and $d = t$. A more general use of Reed-Solomon codes (still with large enough $\Sigma = \mathbb{F}_{2^\ell}$) could be an arbitrary k, $t = 2\lambda$ and $n = 3(t + k - 1)$, and $d = t + k - 1$. One can also get better efficiency using Algebraic-Geometric codes as described in [5].

3.3 The CDMW Transformation

We start by describing the CDMW transformation, using an abstraction similar to Coretti *et al.* [5]. Denote the security parameter by λ, and we want to construct an encryption scheme with message space Σ^k. Below we assume that $0 \in \Sigma$, and we sometimes think of Σ as a large enough field. The construction uses the following components

- An underlying encryption scheme $\mathcal{E} = (\text{Gen}_E, \text{Enc}, \text{Dec})$ with message space Σ, satisfying tag-nmCPA security (Definition 2.3). Below we sometimes call it the *component encryption scheme*.
- A one-time signature scheme $\mathcal{S} = (\text{Gen}_S, \text{Sig}, \text{Ver})$, satisfying strong existential unforgeability (Definition 2.1). We denote by $\kappa = \kappa(\lambda)$ the size of the verification key.
- A secret-sharing encoding scheme $\mathcal{C} = (\text{E}, \text{D})$, with underlying symbol space Σ, dimension k, length n, decoding radius d, and privacy parameter t.

The CDMW construction is an encryption scheme for messages $\text{pt} \in \Sigma^k$, $\mathcal{E}' = (\text{Gen}', \text{Enc}', \text{Dec}')$ as follows:

Key generation $\text{Gen}'(1^\lambda)$.

1. Generate $2\kappa n$ key pairs $(\text{ek}_{i,j,b}, \text{dk}_{i,j,b}) \leftarrow \text{Gen}_E(1^\lambda)$ with $i \in [\kappa], j \in [n]$, and $b \in \{0,1\}$;
2. Choose at random a size-t subset $S^* \in \left[\binom{n}{t}\right]$, and a random row $i^* \leftarrow [\kappa]$;

The public key consists of all the $2\kappa n$ component public keys, and the secret key consists of the $2(n + (\kappa - 1)t)$ component secret keys for the designated row i^* and columns $j \in S^*$,

$$\text{ek}' = \left\{\text{ek}_{i,j,b} : b \in \{0,1\}, i \in [\kappa], j \in [n], \right\}$$

$$\text{dk}' = \left(i^*, S^*, \left\{\text{dk}_{i,j,b} : b \in \{0,1\}, i = i^* \text{ or } j \in S^*\right\}\right).$$

Encryption $\text{Enc}'(\text{ek}', \text{pt})$, $\text{pt} \in \Sigma^k$.

1. Choose a signature key pair $(\text{sk}, \text{vk}) \leftarrow \text{Gen}_S(1^\lambda)$, with $|\text{vk}| = \kappa$. Denote the i'th bit in vk by v_i.
2. Choose encoding randomness $r \leftarrow \mathcal{R}$ and compute the codeword $c := \text{E}(\text{pt}, r) \in \mathcal{C}$.

3. For all $i \in [\kappa], j \in [n]$ encrypt $c_j \in \Sigma$ under ek_{i,j,v_i} with tag vk: $\mathsf{ct}_{i,j} \leftarrow \mathsf{Enc}(\mathsf{ek}_{i,j,v_i}, \mathsf{vk}, c_j)$.

   Denote the concatenation of all these κn component ciphertexts by $\vec{\mathsf{ct}} = (\mathsf{ct}_{i,j} : i \in [\kappa], j \in [n])$.
4. Compute the signature $\sigma \leftarrow \mathsf{Sig}(\mathsf{sk}, \vec{\mathsf{ct}})$.

The compound ciphertext is $\mathsf{ct}' = (\vec{\mathsf{ct}}, \mathsf{vk}, \sigma)$.

Decryption $\mathsf{Dec}'(\mathsf{dk}', \mathsf{ct}')$. Parse $\mathsf{ct}' = (\vec{\mathsf{ct}}, \mathsf{vk}, \sigma)$.

1. Check the signature, if $\mathsf{Ver}(\mathsf{vk}, \vec{\mathsf{ct}}, \sigma) = 0$ then output 0^k and halt.
2. Decrypt all the component ciphertexts for which you have keys, $\gamma'_{i,j} \leftarrow \mathsf{Dec}(\mathsf{dk}_{i,j,v_i}, \mathsf{vk}, \mathsf{ct}_{i,j})$ for $i = i^*$ or $j \in S^*$.
3. Let $c' = (\gamma'_{i^*,j} : j \in [n])$ be the word encoded in row i^*, and correct c' to a codeword, setting $\bar{c} = D'(c')$.
4. Check that all the columns in S^* agree with $\bar{c}$: For all $i \in [\kappa], j \in S^*, \gamma'_{i,j} = \bar{c}_j$.
   If any of these checks fails then output 0^k and halt.
5. Decode $(x, r) := D(\bar{c})$ and output x.

Connection to Technical Overview. Before giving a formal proof of security, we briefly discuss how this construction satisfies the abstract properties (1)-(3) from the technical overview in Sect. 3.1.

For (1), we define valid ciphertexts as ones where there is a single codeword $\bar{c} \in \mathcal{C}$ such that the component ciphertexts in each row i decrypt to a value sufficiently close (within distance d) to $\bar{c}$. Otherwise ciphertexts are invalid.

For (2), we can consider different decryption secret keys depending on the row i^* they decrypt. The original key picks one fixed row i^* in which it knows all the component secret keys for both bits $b \in \{0, 1\}$. The alternate "somewhat defective" decryption keys will only know all the secret keys for either $b = 0$ or $b = 1$ (but not both) in each row i. In particular, for a challenge ciphertext ct^* with verification vk^* we will pick a somewhat defective decryption key such that, for each row i, it only knows the secret keys with bit $b = 1 - v_i^*$ where v_i^* is the i'th bit of vk^*. It will decrypt each ciphertext with verification key $\mathsf{vk} \neq \mathsf{vk}^*$ using the first row i in which the verification key bits differ $v_i \neq v_i^*$. In both cases, we also keep all the component secret keys in the special columns S^* and perform the same checks as the original decryption procedure. This ensures that: (a) the somewhat defective decryption key is incapable of breaking the semantic security of ct^* since it is only capable of decrypting the component ciphertexts of ct^* is the columns S^*, but these don't reveal anything about the message by the hiding of the secret sharing encoding, (b) the somewhat defective decryption key decrypts every valid ciphertext $\mathsf{ct} \neq \mathsf{ct}^*$ (having $\mathsf{vk} \neq \mathsf{vk}^*$) identically to the original key, since the row i it decrypts will decode to the same codeword $\bar{c}$ as in the original decryption and the checks performed are identical.

For (3), in order for the adversary to produce an invalid ciphertext that decrypts to anything but 0, (via either the original key or any defective key), there must be some row i that decrypts to a value c that decodes to some codeword $\bar{c}$, and some row i' (possibly $i' = i$) that decrypts to a value c' such that c' is too far (more than d distance) from $\bar{c}$. But in that case, the decryption procedure will output 0 with overwhelming probability over the choice of S^*; it only fails to do so if none of the columns of S^* overlap with any of the positions in which c' differs from $\bar{c}$, but this only happens with probability $\leq (1 - \frac{d}{n})^t \leq 2^{-\lambda}$.

3.4 Proof of Security

Recall, we first give our main proof for 1-FuncCPA$^+$ security (i.e., a single-input functional re-encryption oracle). However, as we then discuss in Sect. 3.5, the proof extends directly to general FuncCPA$^+$ security (with a multi-input functional re-encryption oracle), with only minimal changes.

Lemma 3.2. *If the component encryption scheme $\mathcal{E}$ satisfies tag-nmCPA security (Definition 2.3) and the signature $\mathcal{S}$ satisfies strong existential unforgeability (Definition 2.1), then the compound scheme $\mathcal{E}'$ above is 1-FuncCPA$^+$ secure.*

Namely we show that under the stated assumptions, the view of a FuncCPA$^+$ attacker A in the "real world" is indistinguishable from its view in an "ideal world", in which all the functional re-encryption queries are answered by encrypting the all-zero plaintext word 0^k.

Simplifying Assumptions. Consider some 1-FuncCPA$^+$ adversary A. We sometimes refer to ciphertexts that A submits to the functional re-encryption oracle as *input ciphertexts*, and the ones returned from the oracle are called *output ciphertexts*.

Firstly, without loss of generality, we can assume that A never submits an input ciphertext which is equal to a prior output ciphertext. Indeed, if a previous functional re-encryption query (ct, f) returned some ct', then a new query (ct', f') could just as well be replaced by $(\mathsf{ct}, f' \circ f)$: By definition these two queries have identical answers.

Secondly, we will assume that A never queries the oracle on an input ciphertext $\mathsf{ct}' = (\vec{\mathsf{ct}}, \mathsf{vk}, \sigma)$ in which the signature fails to verify $\mathsf{Ver}(\mathsf{vk}, \vec{\mathsf{ct}}, \sigma) = 0$. This is because we can test this property efficiently given only ct' and can replace any such query (ct', f) with (ct'', f) where ct'' is a fresh (correctly generated) encryption of 0^k.

Thirdly, given the above assumptions, we can also assume (by reduction to the signature security) that the sets of verification keys in the input ciphertexts is disjoint from that in the output ciphertexts: To use the same verification key vk as in previous output ciphertext, the adversary will need to forge a signatures on the new $\vec{\mathsf{ct}}$ relative to that previous vk (or a new signature σ on the same $\vec{\mathsf{ct}}$), which can only happen with negligible probability.

We call an adversary for which the above three assumptions hold a *conforming adversary*. The arguments above imply that conforming adversaries have as much of an advantage as general ones in distinguishing the real game from the "ideal" one (upto negligible difference due to forgery of the signatures). Below we therefore fix one conforming adversary A and analyze its advantage. Important concepts in our analysis are *valid/invalid* ciphertexts and bad events, which are defined next.

Valid Ciphertext. A compound ciphertext $\mathsf{ct}' = (\vec{\mathsf{ct}}, \mathsf{vk}, \sigma)$ is valid — *relative to all the component public/secret key pairs*, $\{(\mathsf{ek}_{i,j,b}, \mathsf{dk}_{i,j,b}) : b \in \{0,1\}, i \in [\kappa], j \in [n]\}$ — if the following condition holds:

- There exists a unique codeword $\bar{c} \in \mathcal{C}$ such that for all $i \in [\kappa]$, using the i'th row for decryption yields a word which is at most d away from $\bar{c}$. Namely, setting $\gamma_{i,j} := \mathsf{Dec}(\mathsf{dk}_{i,j,v_i}, \mathsf{vk}, \mathsf{ct}_{i,j})$ and denoting $c_i = (\gamma_{i,1}, \ldots, \gamma_{i,n})$ for all i, all the c_i's are of Hamming distance at most d from $\bar{c}$.

A ciphertext is *invalid* if it is not valid.

Bad Events. A big part of the analysis below is devoted to bounding the probability of the bad event in which A submits an invalid ciphertext to the functional re-encryption oracle, but this invalid ciphertext "is not caught".

Consider the set S^* and all the component public/secret key pairs $\{(\mathsf{ek}_{i,j,b}, \mathsf{dk}_{i,j,b}) : b \in \{0,1\}, i \in [\kappa], j \in [n]\}$. We denote by Bad the event in which A makes a functional re-encryption query with an *invalid ciphertext* $\mathsf{ct}' = (\vec{\mathsf{ct}}, \mathsf{vk}, \sigma)$, but the check in step (4) of the decryption procedure does not trigger. Namely, for all $i \in [\kappa]$, denote by $c_i = (\gamma_{i,1}, \ldots, \gamma_{i,n})$ the decryption of the i'th row (as in the definition of valid ciphertexts above). Then the event Bad occurs if there is a codeword $\bar{c} = (\bar{\gamma}_1, \ldots, \bar{\gamma}_n) \in \mathcal{C}$ such that:

- There are indices $i_1, i_2 \in [\kappa]$, such that $\mathsf{D}'(c_{i_1}) = \bar{c}$, but c_{i_2} is at Hamming distance more than d from $\bar{c}$.
- All the c_i's agree with $\bar{c}$ on all the symbols in the columns $j \in S^*$: $\forall i \in [\kappa], \forall j \in S^* : \gamma_{i,j} = \bar{\gamma}_j$.

Let q be a polynomial upper bound on the number of functional re-encryption queries made by A. For all $u \in [q]$ denote by Bad_u the event in which the u'th functional re-encryption query causes the above bad event to occur. Also, for any $v \in [q]$, denote by $\mathsf{1stBad}_v$ the event where the first query to cause the bad event to occur is the v'th query i.e.:

$$\mathsf{1stBad}_v = \overline{\mathsf{Bad}_1} \,\&\, \ldots \,\&\, \overline{\mathsf{Bad}_{v-1}} \,\&\, \mathsf{Bad}_v.$$

Hybrids. With the same bound q on the number of decryption queries, we consider a set of $q+1$ hybrid experiments, $H_0, H_1, \ldots, H_q$. In the hybrid H_u the first u functional re-encryption queries are answered by encrypting the all-zero plaintext, and all the queries from $u+1$ and on are answered as in the real 1-FuncCPA$^+$ game. (Note that the notions of valid/invalid input ciphertexts and bad events apply to all these hybrids.) The real 1-FuncCPA$^+$ game is therefore H_0, the ideal game is H_q, and proving Lemma 3.2 boils down to showing that

$$\left| \Pr_{H_q}[A \to 1] - \Pr_{H_0}[A \to 1] \right| \leq \mathsf{negl}(\lambda), \tag{1}$$

for some negligible function $\mathsf{negl}(\cdot)$, where $A \to 1$ is the event of A halting after outputting 1. To establish Eq. (1), we first note that

$$\left| \Pr_{H_q}[A \to 1] - \Pr_{H_0}[A \to 1] \right| \le \left| \Pr_{H_q}[A \to 1 \ \overline{\mathsf{Bad}}] - \Pr_{H_0}[A \to 1 \ \overline{\mathsf{Bad}}] \right|$$
$$+ \Pr_{H_0}[\mathsf{Bad}] + \Pr_{H_q}[\mathsf{Bad}].$$

The heart of proof below consists of the following three lemmas, whose proofs are provided later in this section:

Lemma 3.3. *For all $u, v \in [q]$ there is a negligible function $\mathsf{negl}(\cdot)$ such that*

$$\left| \Pr_{H_{u-1}}[\mathsf{1stBad}_v] - \Pr_{H_u}[\mathsf{1stBad}_v] \right| < \mathsf{negl}(\lambda).$$

Lemma 3.4. *For all $v \in [q]$ there is a negligible function $\mathsf{negl}(\cdot)$ such that $\Pr_{H_q}[\mathsf{Bad}_v] < \mathsf{negl}(\lambda)$.*

Lemma 3.5. *For all $u \in [q]$ there is a negligible function $\mathsf{negl}(\cdot)$ such that*

$$\left| \Pr_{H_u}[A \to 1 \ \& \ \overline{\mathsf{Bad}}] - \Pr_{H_{u-1}}[A \to 1 \ \& \ \overline{\mathsf{Bad}}] \right| \le \mathsf{negl}(\lambda).$$

Given these three lemmas, we complete the proof as follows:

$$\left| \Pr_{H_q}[A \to 1] - \Pr_{H_0}[A \to 1] \right| \le \left| \Pr_{H_q}[A \to 1 \ \& \ \overline{\mathsf{Bad}}] - \Pr_{H_0}[A \to 1 \ \& \ \overline{\mathsf{Bad}}] \right|$$
$$+ \Pr_{H_0}[\mathsf{Bad}] + \Pr_{H_q}[\mathsf{Bad}]$$
$$\le \sum_{u=1}^{q} \left| \Pr_{H_u}[A \to 1 \ \& \ \overline{\mathsf{Bad}}] - \Pr_{H_{u-1}}[A \to 1 \ \& \ \overline{\mathsf{Bad}}] \right|$$
$$+ \sum_{v=1}^{q} \Pr_{H_0}[\mathsf{1stBad}_v] + \sum_{v=1}^{q} \Pr_{H_q}[\mathsf{Bad}_v]$$
$$\le 2q \cdot \mathsf{negl}(\lambda) + \sum_{v=1}^{q} \Pr_{H_0}[\mathsf{1stBad}_v], \tag{2}$$

where in the first inequality we rely on $\mathsf{Bad} = \bigvee_{u \in [q]} \mathsf{Bad}_u = \bigvee_{u \in [q]} \mathsf{1stBad}_u$ and the last inequality is due to Lemmas 3.4 and 3.5. Moreover, for any $v \in [q]$ we have

$$\Pr_{H_0}[\mathsf{1stBad}_v] = \Pr_{H_q}[\mathsf{1stBad}_v] + \sum_{u=1}^{q} \left(\Pr_{H_{u-1}}[\mathsf{1stBad}_v] - \Pr_{H_u}[\mathsf{1stBad}_v] \right)$$
$$\le \Pr_{H_q}[\mathsf{Bad}_v] + \sum_{u=1}^{q} \left| \Pr_{H_{u-1}}[\mathsf{1stBad}_v] - \Pr_{H_u}[\mathsf{1stBad}_v] \right|$$
$$\le (q+1) \cdot \mathsf{negl}(\lambda), \tag{3}$$

with the last inequality due to Lemmas 3.3 and 3.4. Plugging the expression from Eq. (3) into Eq. (2), we get

$$\left| \Pr_{H_q}[A \to 1] - \Pr_{H_0}[A \to 1] \right| \le 2q \cdot \mathsf{negl}(\lambda) + q \cdot ((q+1) \cdot \mathsf{negl}(\lambda)) = (q^2 + 3q) \cdot \mathsf{negl}(\lambda).$$

Since $\mathsf{negl}(\cdot)$ is negligible and q is polynomial, then also $(q^2 + 3q) \cdot \mathsf{negl}(\cdot)$ is negligible, completing the proof of Lemma 3.2.   □

Proving Lemmas 3.3 **through** 3.5. The proofs make use of the following two easy observations:

Fact 3.6 *For any $u \ge v$, the v'th oracle query in hybrid H_u is answered in a way that does not depend of the index i^* or the set S^* in the secret key.*

Proof. By definition of H_u, the v'th output ciphertext consists of just encryption of the all-zero plaintext, regardless of anything else.

Fact 3.7 *For any $u, v \in [q]$, if the event Bad_v does not occur in the hybrid H_u, then the v'th oracle query is answered in a way that does not pendent of the index i^* in the secret key.*

Proof. Follows by definition of the bad event Bad_v. If Bad_v does not occur, the v'th input ciphertext is either a valid ciphertext (does not satisfy the first condition of the bad event), or an invalid ciphertext that triggers one of the checks on decryption (does not satisfy the second condition of the bad event). In the first case, all the rows i are decrypted to a word c_i within the decoding radius d of the code from the same codeword $\bar{c}$, so the recovered value $\bar{c}$ in step (3) of decryption will be the same no matter which row i is used, and the rest of the decryption procedure does not depend on i. On the other hand, in the second case, the checks in step (4) of decryption will be triggered and cause the decrypted value to be 0^k no matter which row i is used.

Truncated Hybrids. When analyzing the events Bad_v or $\mathsf{1stBad}_v$, it is convenient to consider *truncated hybrids*, where the game is aborted as soon as A makes the v'th query, indeed whether or not Bad_v or $\mathsf{1stBad}_v$ happen is fully determined as soon as A made that query, so there is no reason to continue the game. Below we denote by $H_u|_v$ the hybrid H_u, truncated immediately after A's v'th functional re-encryption query.

Proof of Lemma 3.3. *For all $u, v \in [q]$ there is a negligible function $\mathsf{negl}(\cdot)$ such that*

$$\left| \Pr_{H_{u-1}}[\mathsf{1stBad}_v] - \Pr_{H_u}[\mathsf{1stBad}_v] \right| < \mathsf{negl}(\lambda).$$

Proof. By definition of the truncated hybrids, for any $u, v \in [q]$ we have that $\Pr_{H_u|_v}[\mathsf{1stBad}_v] = \Pr_{H_u}[\mathsf{1stBad}_v]$. Moreover, we note that when $u \ge v$, all the functional re-encryption queries in $H_u|_v$ are answered with encryption of the all-zero plaintext. It follows that when $u > v$ then the hybrids $H_{u-1}|v$ and $H_u|v$ are identical, and therefore

$$\Pr_{H_{u-1}}[\mathsf{1stBad}_v] = \Pr_{H_{u-1}|v}[\mathsf{1stBad}_v] = \Pr_{H_u|v}[\mathsf{1stBad}_v] = \Pr_{H_u}[\mathsf{1stBad}_v].$$

It remains to prove Lemma 3.3 for $u \leq v$, which we do by reduction to the tag-nmCPA security of the component encryption scheme $\mathcal{E}$. Before giving a detailed reduction, let us start with a high level description. We need to switch the u'th output ciphertext from real to an encryption of 0^k. First, let us switch how the u'th output ciphertext is generated, by always choosing the codeword symbols c_j in positions $j \in S^*$ uniformly at random and then choosing the remaining codeword symbols via the Extend procedure to ensure that the codeword encodes the intended plaintext – by definition, this yields an identically distributed codeword. Second, let vk^* be the verification key in the u'th output ciphertext. We switch how all the oracle queries are answered: instead of decrypting with the real secret key, we will decrypt each input ciphertext that has verification key vk' using some row i in which the i'th bit of vk^* and vk' differ. By Fact 3.7, if the bad event does not occur before the v'th query, then all the oracle queries are answered identically independent of which row i is used, and therefore this change cannot affect the probability of the event $\mathsf{1stBad}_v$ occurring. With the above changes, the oracle queries are answered without any knowledge the component secret keys $\mathsf{dk}_{i,j,\mathsf{vk}_i^*}$ for $i \in [\kappa], j \notin S^*$. Intuitively this lets us replace the encrypted value in the u'th output ciphertext from real to an encryption of 0^k, since the only component ciphertexts that depend on the plaintext are those encrypted under component public keys $\mathsf{ek}_{i,j,\mathsf{vk}_i^*}$ for $i \in [\kappa], j \notin S^*$, for which the secret keys are no longer used by the oracle. However, although these secret keys are not used by the oracle, they are needed to check if the event $\mathsf{1stBad}_v$ occurred, since this depends on all the components of all input ciphertexts in oracle queries $1, \ldots, v$. The key insight is that we can rely on non-malleability security of the component scheme to check if the event $\mathsf{1stBad}_v$ occurred by making one parallel decryption query on all these ciphertexts at the very end of the game.

To make the above formal, fix some $u \leq v \in [q]$, and we describe a tag-nmCPA attacker against the component encryption $\mathcal{E}$, whose advantage is equal to $\left|\Pr_{H_{u-1}|v}[\mathsf{1stBad}_v] - \Pr_{H_u|v}[\mathsf{1stBad}_v]\right| = \left|\Pr_{H_{u-1}}[\mathsf{1stBad}_v] - \Pr_{H_u}[\mathsf{1stBad}_v]\right|$.

The Reduction. The tag-nmCPA attacker, denoted B, begins by choosing at random a signature key-pair $(\mathsf{sk}^*, \mathsf{vk}^*) \leftarrow \mathsf{Gen}_S(1^\lambda)$ and a size-t subset $S^* \subset [n]$. It also chooses at random $\kappa(n + t)$ key-pairs for the component encryption scheme, setting $(\mathsf{dk}_{i,j,b}, \mathsf{ek}_{i,j,b}) \leftarrow \mathsf{Gen}_E(1^\lambda)$ for every $i \in [\kappa], j \in [n]$ and $b = \overline{\mathsf{vk}_i^*}$, and also for every $i \in [\kappa], j \in S^*$ and $b = \mathsf{vk}_i^*$. In words, B chooses one of every pair of keys (i, j, b) for $j \notin S^*$ (corresponding to the bit $b = \overline{\mathsf{vk}_i^*}$), and both keys $(i, j, 0), (i, j, 1)$ for $j \in S^*$.

B then receives $\kappa(n - t)$ public keys from its challenger, and assigns them to the missing positions (i, j, b) for $j \notin S^*$ and $b = \mathsf{vk}_i^*$. This completes the public key for the compound scheme, $\mathsf{ek}' = \{\mathsf{ek}_{i,j,b} : b \in \{0,1\}, i \in [\kappa], j \in [n], \}$, which B sends to the 1-FuncCPA$^+$ attacker A.

We note that component secret keys that B knows allow it to decrypt all input ciphertext queries, *except those with verification key* vk^*. Indeed for every other verification key $\mathsf{vk} \neq \mathsf{vk}^*$ there is at least one index i^* with $\mathsf{vk}_{i^*} \neq \mathsf{vk}^*_{i^*}$, and therefore B has a full functioning compound secret key

$$\mathsf{dk}' = \left(i^*, S^*, \{\mathsf{dk}_{i,j,b} : b \in \{0,1\}, i = i^* \text{ or } j \in S^*\}\right),$$

that it can use to decrypt. (Moreover, by Fact 3.7, if Bad_v doesn't happen then A will not be able to tell which row was used to answer that query.)

Next, B needs to answer the functional re-encryption queries that A makes. Let (ct'_k, f_k) be the k'th functional re-encryption query of A. We can assume that the verification keys in all the input ciphertexts ct'_k are different from vk^* since (a) for $k \leq u$ A has no information yet on vk^* and therefore $\mathsf{vk}_u \neq \mathsf{vk}^*$ except with a negligible probability, and (b) for $k > u$ we get $\mathsf{vk}_k \neq \mathsf{vk}^*$ since A is a conforming adversary. Hence, by the observation above B can decrypt all these queries. Let pt_k be the plaintext that B decrypts for the k'th query. B replies to the functional re-encryption queries as follows:

- For $k = 1, 2, \ldots, u-1$, B answer these queries simply by encrypting the all-zero plaintext.
- For $k = u+1, \ldots, v$, B replies to the k'th query by encrypting $f_k(\mathsf{pt}_k)$.
- For $k = u$, B uses its challenge-ciphertext oracle for the component scheme: B first chooses at random some $y \leftarrow \Sigma^t$ and extends it to get separate encodings of both the all-zero plaintext as well as the plaintext $f_k(\mathsf{pt}_k)$. Namely it sets $c^{k,0} := \mathrm{Extend}(0^k, y, S^*)$ and $c^{k,1} := \mathrm{Extend}(f_k(\mathsf{pt}_k), y, S^*)$. (Note again that $c^{k,0}, c^{k,1}$ agree on all the columns in S^*, $c^{0,k}|_{S^*} = c^{1,k}|_{S^*} = y$.)

B makes a call to its challenge-ciphertext oracle, relative to all the $\kappa(n-t)$ component public keys that it received from its challenger, specifying the words $(c_j^{0,k} : j \notin S^*)$ and $(c_j^{0,k} : j \notin S^*)$ for each "row" i of public keys. It receives back the ciphertexts $\{\mathsf{ct}_{i,j,b} : i \in [\kappa], j \notin S^*, b = \mathsf{vk}_i^*\}$, encrypting one of these two words in all the rows. B extends them to a full compound ciphertext by encrypting the symbols in y for the columns in S^* (which are the same between $c^{k,0}$ and $c^{k,1}$), relative to the appropriate public keys $\mathsf{ek}_{i,j,b}$ for all $i \in [\kappa], j \in S^*$ and $b = \mathsf{vk}_i^*$.

Concatenating all these component ciphertexts to a vector $\vec{\mathsf{ct}}$, B uses the signing key vk^* to generate a signature σ^*, and replies to A with the output ciphertext $\mathsf{ct}'_u = (\vec{\mathsf{ct}}, \mathsf{vk}^*, \sigma^*)$.

Depending on the answer from the challenge-ciphertext oracle of B, this is indeed a valid encryption of either the all-zero plaintext or the plaintext $f_k(\mathsf{pt}_k)$. Moreover, since $\mathrm{Extend}(\cdots)$ yields the same distribution on code-words as $\mathsf{E}(\cdots)$, then we also get the right distribution for this output ciphertext.

Finally, after A makes its v'th functional re-encryption query, B uses its parallel decryption query to determine if the event $\mathsf{1stBad}_v$ happened. This decryption query includes all the component ciphertexts in all the functional re-encryption queries $k = 1, 2, \ldots, v$, for which B is missing the component secret key.

Importantly, the tags in all these queries are different than the tag vk^* that B used for the query to its challenge-ciphertext oracle, hence this is a valid decryption query that B is allowed to make. Also, we note that a single decryption query at the end is sufficient, B does not need to make adaptive queries. Given these decryptions, B can determine if the event $\mathsf{1stBad}_v$ occurred or not, outputting 1 if it occurred and 0 if not.

Analysis of the Reduction. Denote by H'_{u-1} the reduction experimenter where B's challenge-ciphertext oracle encrypts the encoded all-zero plaintext, and by H'_u the reduction where the oracle encrypts the encoded $f_u(\mathsf{pt}_u)$. Note that the only difference between H'_{u-1} and the hybrid H_{u-1} is that in H_{u-1} the same row is used to decrypt all the queries, whereas B uses different rows for different queries in H'_{u-1} (and the same holds for H'_u vs. H_u).[11]

However, due to Fact 3.7, as long as none of the bad events $\mathsf{Bad}_1, \ldots, \mathsf{Bad}_{v-1}$ happen, the view of A is independent of the row that was used to decrypt. And as soon as any of these events happen, we are ensured that $\mathsf{1stBad}_v$ does not happen (in any of H'_{u-1}, H_{u-1}, H'_u, and H_u). It follows that $\Pr_{H'_{u-1}}[\mathsf{1stBad}_v] = \Pr_{H_{u-1}}[\mathsf{1stBad}_v]$ and $\Pr_{H'_u}[\mathsf{1stBad}_v] = \Pr_{H_u}[\mathsf{1stBad}_v]$. Hence the advantage of B in the tag-nmCPA game is exactly

$$\left| \Pr_{H'_{u-1}}[\mathsf{1stBad}_v] - \Pr_{H'_u}[\mathsf{1stBad}_v] \right| = \left| \Pr_{H_{u-1}}[\mathsf{1stBad}_v] - \Pr_{H_u}[\mathsf{1stBad}_v] \right|,$$

as needed. This completes the proof of Lemma 3.3.

Proof of Lemma 3.4. *For all $v \in [q]$ there is a negligible function $\mathsf{negl}(\cdot)$ such that $\Pr_{H_q}[\mathsf{Bad}_v] < \mathsf{negl}(\lambda)$.*

Proof. Recall that in the hybrid H_q, all functional re-encryption queries are answered with a fresh encryption of the all-zero plaintext, regardless of the input ciphertext. Hence, the view of A in that hybrid is independent of the set S^* of columns that is used to check the ciphertext during decryption. We can therefore analyze the probability of the event Bad_v in a modified game, in which the set S^* is chosen at random after the v'th decryption query.

Let $\mathsf{ct}' = (\vec{\mathsf{ct}}, \mathsf{vk}, \sigma)$ be the input ciphertext in the v'th query, and denote by $c_i \in \{0, 1, \perp\}^n$ the word obtained by decrypting the i'th ciphertext row. To trigger the bad event Bad_v, the first conditions says that ct' must be an invalid ciphertext, so there are indices $i_1, i_2 \in [\kappa]$, such that $\mathsf{D}'(c_{i_1}) = \bar{c} = (\bar{\gamma}_1, \ldots, \bar{\gamma}_n)$, but $c_{i_2} = (\gamma_{i_2,1}, \ldots, \gamma_{i_2,n})$ is at Hamming distance more than d from $\bar{c}$. But in that case the probability (over S^* chosen as a random size-t subset of $[n]$) of the second condition holding, $\gamma_{i_2,j} = \bar{\gamma}_j$ for all $j \in S^*$, is bounded by $(1 - \frac{d}{n})^t \leq 2^{-\lambda}$.

---

[11] An "invisible" difference is that u'th output ciphertext is computed using Extend rather than applying the encoding $\mathsf{E}(\cdots)$, but this produces the same distribution over the codewords.

Proof of Lemma 3.5. *For all $u \in [q]$ there is a negligible function $\mathsf{negl}(\cdot)$ such that*

$$\left| \Pr_{H_u}[A \to 1 \;\&\; \overline{\mathsf{Bad}}] - \Pr_{H_{u-1}} [A \to 1 \;\&\; \overline{\mathsf{Bad}}] \right| \leq \mathsf{negl}(\lambda).$$

Proof. The proof is nearly identical to Lemma 3.3, by reduction to the tag-nmCPA-security of the component encryption scheme $\mathcal{E}$. The only differences are (a) the reduction continues all the way to the end of the game (rather than aborting it after the v'th functional re-encryption query), and (b) the reduction algorithm's output at the end is calculated differently.

Specifically, the tag-nmCPA attacker B begins exactly the same as in the proof of Lemma 3.3, and answers functional re-encryption queries of A in exactly the same way. Once A halts with some output bit b, the attacker B uses its parallel decryption query to determine if the event Bad happened. This decryption query includes all the component ciphertexts in all the functional re-encryption queries $k = 1, 2, \ldots, q$, for which B is missing the component secret key. (As before, the tags in all these queries are different than the tag vk^* that B used for the query to its challenge-ciphertext oracle, hence this is a valid decryption query that B is allowed to make.) Given these decryptions, B can determine if the event Bad occurred or not. B then outputs 1 if A *returned 1 and* Bad *did not occur*, and 0 otherwise.

As in the proof of Lemma 3.3, the view of A in the reduction is identical to its view in the hybrids H_{u-1} or H_u as long as the event Bad did not occur, and therefore the advantage of B is equal to $|\Pr_{H_u}[A \to 1 \;\&\; \overline{\mathsf{Bad}}] - \Pr_{H_{u-1}}[A \to 1 \;\&\; \overline{\mathsf{Bad}}]|$.

Remark 3.8. We note that since we applied the CDMW transformation to a non-malleable scheme (which is in particular CPA secure), then the resulting $\mathcal{E}'$ is also non-malleable, not just 1-FuncCPA$^+$ secure. In fact, it can simultaneously withstand any number of adaptive functional re-encryption queries <u>and</u> a single parallel decryption query at the end of the game.

On the other hand, it is easy to see that this scheme is not CCA-secure (not even CCA1-secure). This is true for the same reason that the original CDMW transformation fails to produce a CCA-secure scheme: An attacker with adaptive access to a decryption oracle can use that oracle to detect the columns in the special subset S^*, then figure out the special row i^*, and then completely break the scheme.

3.5 Extension to General FuncCPA-Security

The proof of Lemma 3.2 extends easily to show multi-input FuncCPA$^+$ security, and not just 1-FuncCPA$^+$ security. In fact, the proof is essentially identical with minor syntactical modifications:

- The simplifying assumptions on the adversary remain the same, but now there are multiple input ciphertexts for each query. In particular, without loss of generality, we can assume that (a) *none* of the input ciphertexts in any query are equal to any previous output ciphertext, (b) the signatures of *all* of the

input ciphertexts verify correctly, (c) the sets of verification keys in the input ciphertexts is disjoint from that in the output ciphertexts.
- We define the Bad event for a multi-input query is triggered if any of the ciphertexts in that query satisfy the original definition of the Bad event.
- The rest of the proof proceeds identically. In the proof of Lemma 3.4, we need to take an additional union bound over all ℓ input ciphertexts in the v'th query.

4   Conclusions and Open Problems

In this work we proved that FuncCPA secure encryption can be constructed from any CPA scheme, essentially by *applying twice* the CPA-to-mnCPA transformation of Choi *et al.* [3]. A remaining open problem is to come up with simpler constructions, and in particular to resolve the question of whether a single application of this transformation suffices.

A similar question can be asked about non-functional re-encryption oracles, if it is easier to construct a secure scheme against non-functional re-encryption oracles from CPA than one secure against functional re-encryption? We remark that sometimes it is easier to withstand non-functional re-encryption. For example, ElGamal encryption is easily seen to be secure against non-functional re-encryption. However, we do not know if it can be proven secure against functional re-encryption under a reasonable assumption (or, conversely, if there is some surprising attack). More generally, it might be interesting to build natural number-theoretic FuncCPA$^+$-secure scheme which are not CCA1-secure.

Another open problem is the relation between FuncCPA and FuncCPA$^+$: we have shown implication in one direction (and separation for non-functional re-encryption oracles), but the other direction for functional re-encryption oracles remains open. If the general separation is found, it would be interesting to see if there are any real-world applications which require the stronger form of FuncCPA$^+$ security, and could be insecure with FuncCPA security.

More generally, it would be good to find more applications of FuncCPA and FuncCPA$^+$ encryption schemes.

A   Direct Implications and Separations

It follows directly from the definitions above that every CCA2-secure scheme is also nmCPA-secure, which is in turn also CPA secure. Additionally, in Lemma 2.5 we prove that every FuncCPA$^+$-secure scheme is also FuncCPA-secure, which is in turn CPA secure by definition. Here we study the other (non-)implications.

First, while our intuition tells us that every CCA2-secure scheme should also be FuncCPA$^+$ secure, we note that this implication is not completely straightforward, because the FuncCPA attacker is allowed to copy the challenge ciphertext for its re-encryption queries, while the CCA2-attacker is not allowed to do so. Nonetheless, we show that our intuition is still correct. In fact, we show that already (weaker) CCA1-security implies FuncCPA$^+$ security.

302   Y. Dodis et al.

Lemma A.1. *Every CCA1-secure encryption scheme is also FuncCPA$^+$-secure. (In particular, CCA2-security implies the original FuncCPA-security.)*

Proof. Let q be the overall number of re-encryption queries made by the FuncCPA$^+$-attacker A. For $0 < i \leq q$, we define hybrid H_i where the first i re-encryption queries $(\vec{ct}, f)$ by A return $\mathsf{E}(\mathsf{ek}, f(\mathsf{Dec}(\mathsf{dk}, \vec{ct})))$, and the remaining $(q - i)$ queries return $\mathsf{E}(\mathsf{ek}, 0)$. By hybrid argument it is enough to prove that H_i is indistinguishable from H_{i+1}, for every $0 < i \leq q$, as H_0 and H_q corresponding to $b = 0$ and $b = 1$ experiments, respectively.

For the latter, we have the following almost immediate reduction to CCA1-security from Definition 2.2. To simulate the j-th query (ct_j, f_j) of an attacker A claiming to distinguish H_i from H_{i+1}, the CCA1 attacker B does the following:

- For $j < i$, query its decryption oracle $\mathcal{O}_1$ on the ciphertexts in $\vec{ct}_j$, obtaining plaintexts $\vec{pt}_j$.
  Compute $\mathsf{pt}'_j = f_j(\vec{pt}_j)$, and return to A an honestly generated $\mathsf{ct}'_j = \mathsf{Enc}(\mathsf{ek}, \mathsf{pt}'_j)$.
- For $j = i$, query its decryption oracle $\mathcal{O}_1$ on the ciphertexts in $\vec{ct}_i$, obtaining plaintexts $\vec{pt}_i$.
  Compute $\mathsf{pt}^* = f_i(\vec{pt}_i)$, and submit the tuple $(\mathsf{pt}^*, 0)$ as its challenge.
  Finally, return to A the resulting challenge ciphertext ct^* to the attacker.
- For $j > i$, ignore $(\vec{ct}_j, f_j)$, and return $\mathsf{E}(\mathsf{ek}, 0)$ to A.

For $b = 0$, this run of B is a perfect simulation of H_i, while for $b = 1$ it is a perfect simulation of H_{i+1}, completing the proof.

In the opposite direction, Akavia et al. demonstrated in [1] that (somewhat surprisingly) CPA security of a scheme *does not* imply even the most basic ReEncCPA security of the same scheme. Below we extend their example to show that non-malleability (i.e., nmCPA-security) of a scheme also does not imply even ReEncCPA security. We also demonstrate that even FuncCPA$^+$ security does not imply nmCPA-security.

Lemma A.2. *If nmCPA-secure encryption schemes exist, then there exists a nmCPA-secure encryption scheme which is not ReEncCPA-secure. Conversely, if FuncCPA$^+$-secure encryption schemes exist, then there exists a FuncCPA$^+$-secure encryption scheme which is not nmCPA-secure.*

Proof. Starting from the easy separation, we can append 0 to all honestly produced ciphertexts in a FuncCPA$^+$-secure encryption scheme, and have the decryption oracle simply ignore this appended bit. This clearly does not change FuncCPA$^+$-security, as all honestly re-encrypted ciphertexts will still end with 0. However, the scheme is obviously malleable, by flipping the last bit of the challenge ciphertext from 0 to 1, and calling the decryption oracle of the resulting (formally "distinct") ciphertext.

For the other separation, let $\mathcal{E} = (\mathsf{Gen}, \mathsf{Enc}, \mathsf{Dec})$ be a scheme which is nmCPA-secure according to Definition 2.2, and we modify it into a scheme $\mathcal{E}' = (\mathsf{Gen}', \mathsf{Enc}', \mathsf{Dec}')$ as follows:

- Gen$'$ just runs Gen twice, outputting the two pairs $((dk, dk'), (ek, ek'))$. Roughly, dk, ek are the "real keys" for decryption and encryption, whereas dk', ek' are used for signalling various events.
- The new encryption $Enc'((ek, ek'), pt)$ checks if pt is the secret key corresponding to either ek or ek':
  - If pt is the secret key corresponding to ek or ek' then output $1|pt$,
  - Otherwise output $0|Enc(ek, pt)$.
- The new decryption $Dec((dk, dk'), ct')$ parses $ct' = b|ct$ with $b \in \{0, 1\}$, then proceeds as follows:
  - If $b = 1$ and $ct = dk'$ then output dk,
  - If $b = 1$ and $ct \neq dk'$ then output dk',
  - Otherwise output $Dec(dk, ct)$.

It is easy to see that the modified $\mathcal{E}'$ is still nmCPA-secure: An nmCPA attack on $\mathcal{E}'$ can be turned into nmCPA attack on the underlying $\mathcal{E}$ by having the reduction generate (dk', ek') itself, then simulate the sole decryption query to $\mathcal{E}'$ using its decryption oracle to $\mathcal{E}$: Unless the $\mathcal{E}'$ attacker guesses dk' (on which it has no information other than seeing ek'), then it cannot trigger the 1st bullet on decryption above.

On the other hand, it is easy to see that a ReEncCPA attacker can break this scheme completely, first making a query with $ct = 11 \ldots 1$ to get $1|dk'$, then making a second query with $1|dk'$ to get "the real key" dk.

Next, we show separation between ReEncCPA and ReEncCPA$^+$ notions (and conjecture that similar separations hold for FuncCPA and 1-FuncCPA notions).

Lemma A.3. *If ReEncCPA-secure encryption schemes exist, then there exists a ReEncCPA-secure encryption scheme which is not ReEncCPA$^+$-secure.*

Proof. Let $\mathcal{E} = (Gen, Enc, Dec)$ be a scheme which is ReEncCPA-secure according to Definition 2.2, and we modify it into a scheme $\mathcal{E}' = (Gen', Enc', Dec')$ as follows: The key generation remains unchanged, $Gen' = Gen$. Encryption is modified by setting

$$Enc'(ek, pt) = \begin{cases} 11 \ldots 1 & \text{if } pt \text{ is a decryption key corresponding to } ek \\ 0|Enc(ek, pt) & \text{otherwise.} \end{cases}$$

(Note that it is possible to check efficiently whether the condition above holds.) Decryption is also modified, as follows:

$$Dec'(dk, ct') = \begin{cases} dk & \text{if } ct' \text{ begins with a } 1 \\ Dec(dk, ct) & \text{if } ct' = 0|ct. \end{cases}$$

It is easy to see that $\mathcal{E}'$ is still ReEncCPA-secure according to Definition 2.2 (with a non-functional decryption oracle), since access to the oracle for $\mathcal{E}'$ can be perfectly simulated using access to the oracle for $\mathcal{E}$. (Indeed ciphertext beginning with 1 are answered with $11 \ldots 1$ and ciphertexts beginning with 0 are answered as in $\mathcal{E}$, with a zero prepended to the reply.) On the other hand, it is easy to distinguish a true re-encryption oracle from a zero-encrypting one, just by querying it on any ciphertext that begins with a 1.

Finally, we show that a 1-FuncCPA$^+$-secure scheme is not necessarily FuncCPA-secure (and, thus, not necessarily FuncCPA$^+$-secure), assuming the existence of CCA-secure schemes.

Lemma A.4. *If CCA-secure encryption schemes exist, then there exists a 1-FuncCPA$^+$-secure encryption scheme which is not FuncCPA-secure.*

Proof. Let $\mathcal{E} = (\mathsf{Gen}, \mathsf{Enc}, \mathsf{Dec})$ be a CCA-secure scheme, and let $OWF(\cdot)$ be a one-way function. (Recall that CCA-secure encryption implies the existence of one-way functions.) Consider the modified scheme $\mathcal{E}' = (\mathsf{Gen}', \mathsf{Enc}', \mathsf{Dec}')$, defined as follows:

- $\mathsf{Gen}'(1^\lambda)$ runs the underlying key-generation $(\mathsf{dk}, \mathsf{ek}) \leftarrow \mathsf{Gen}(1^\lambda)$, and in addition chooses two uniformly random and independent strings $r, s \leftarrow \{0,1\}^\lambda$ and sets $y = OWF(r \oplus s)$. The public key is $\mathsf{ek}' = (\mathsf{ek}, y)$ and the secret key is $\mathsf{dk}' = (\mathsf{dk}, r, s)$.
- $\mathsf{Enc}'(\mathsf{ek}', \mathsf{pt})$: If $y = OWF(\mathsf{pt})$ then output pt, else output $(0, \mathsf{Enc}(\mathsf{ek}, \mathsf{pt}))$.
- $\mathsf{Dec}'(\mathsf{dk}', (b, \mathsf{ct}))$: If $b = 0$ then output $\mathsf{Dec}(\mathsf{dk}, \mathsf{ct})$. If $b = 1$ then output r, if $b = 2$ then output s.

We show that $\mathcal{E}'$ is 1-FuncCPA$^+$-secure, but not FuncCPA-secure. To see that $\mathcal{E}'$ is 1-FuncCPA$^+$-secure, let us again consider only adversaries that never use the answers from previous re-encryption queries as inputs to future queries. (As we argued before, we can make this assumption without loss of generality.) Fixing one such adversary, we consider a sequence of hybrids, where in the i'th hybrid the first $i - 1$ queries are answered by encryption of 0, and the i'th query and later are answered by the single-ciphertext re-encryption oracle. Arguing that hybrid i is indistinguishable from hybrid $i + 1$ is done in two steps:

- We first argue that the i'th query will not decrypt to $r \oplus s$ (except with a negligible probability), by reduction to the one-wayness of $OWF(\cdot)$. Here, the reduction algorithm is given the secret key dk of the underlying encryption scheme Enc.
- Then we replace the i'th query answer by an encryption of zero, and argue indistinguishability by reduction to the CCA-security of the underlying scheme $\mathcal{E}$. Here the reduction algorithm is given access to the decryption oracle of $\mathcal{E}$, that allows it to simulate the answers to all future queries.

On the other hand, it is clear that $\mathcal{E}'$ is *not FuncCPA-secure*. The multi-ciphertext re-encryption oracle is easily distinguishable from a zero-encrypting oracle, because it enables easy extraction of a pre-image of y under $OWF(\cdot)$: The multi-ciphertext query $(\mathsf{ct}_1 = (1, 0^\lambda), \mathsf{ct}_2 = (2, 0^\lambda), f = \oplus)$ will decrypt ct_1 to r and ct_2 to s, then compute $x = f(r, s) = r \oplus s$, and applying the modified encryption procedure it will return the pre-image x. (As above, obtaining a pre-image of y is hard given a zero-encrypting oracle, by reduction to the one-wayness of $OWF(\cdot)$.)

References

1. Akavia, A., Gentry, C., Halevi, S., Vald, M.: Achievable CCA2 relaxation for homomorphic encryption. In: Kiltz, E., Vaikuntanathan, V. (eds.) Theory of Cryptography - 20th International Conference, TCC 2022, Chicago, IL, USA, November 7–10, 2022, Proceedings, Part II. Lecture Notes in Computer Science, vol. 13748, pp. 70–99. Springer (2022). https://doi.org/10.1007/978-3-031-22365-5_3, also available from https://ia.cr/2022/282
2. Akavia, A., Vald, M.: private communication, November 2022
3. Choi, S.G., Dachman-Soled, D., Malkin, T., Wee, H.: A black-box construction of non-malleable encryption from semantically secure encryption. J. Cryptol. $31(1)$, 172–201 (2017). https://doi.org/10.1007/s00145-017-9254-z
4. Choi, S.G., Dachman-Soled, D., Malkin, T., Wee, H.: Improved, black-box, non-malleable encryption from semantic security. Des. Codes Crypt. $86(3)$, 641–663 (2017). https://doi.org/10.1007/s10623-017-0348-2
5. Coretti, S., Dodis, Y., Maurer, U., Tackmann, B., Venturi, D.: Non-malleable encryption: simpler, shorter, stronger. J. Cryptol. $33(4)$, 1984–2033 (2020). https://doi.org/10.1007/s00145-020-09361-0
6. Cramer, R., Hanaoka, G., Hofheinz, D., Imai, H., Kiltz, E., Pass, R., Shelat, A., Vaikuntanathan, V.: Bounded cca2-secure encryption. In: Kurosawa, K. (ed.) Advances in Cryptology - ASIACRYPT 2007, 13th International Conference on the Theory and Application of Cryptology and Information Security, Kuching, Malaysia, December 2–6, 2007, Proceedings. Lecture Notes in Computer Science, vol. 4833, pp. 502–518. Springer (2007). https://doi.org/10.1007/978-3-540-76900-2_31
7. Fujisaki, E., Okamoto, T.: How to enhance the security of public-key encryption at minimum cost. In: Imai, H., Zheng, Y. (eds.) Public Key Cryptography, Second International Workshop on Practice and Theory in Public Key Cryptography, PKC '99, Kamakura, Japan, March 1–3, 1999, Proceedings. Lecture Notes in Computer Science, vol. 1560, pp. 53–68. Springer (1999). https://doi.org/10.1007/3-540-49162-7_5
8. Hohenberger, S., Koppula, V., Waters, B.: Chosen ciphertext security from injective trapdoor functions. In: Micciancio, D., Ristenpart, T. (eds.) CRYPTO 2020. LNCS, vol. 12170, pp. 836–866. Springer, Cham (2020). https://doi.org/10.1007/978-3-030-56784-2_28
9. Myers, S.A., Sergi, M., Shelat, A.: Black-box construction of a more than non-malleable CCA1 encryption scheme from plaintext awareness. J. Comput. Secur. $21(5)$, 721–748 (2013). https://doi.org/10.3233/JCS-130485
10. Naor, M., Yung, M.: Public-key cryptosystems provably secure against chosen ciphertext attacks. In: Ortiz, H. (ed.) Proceedings of the 22nd Annual ACM Symposium on Theory of Computing, May 13–17, 1990, Baltimore, Maryland, USA, pp. 427–437. ACM (1990). https://doi.org/10.1145/100216.100273
11. Pass, R., shelat, Vaikuntanathan, V.: Construction of a non-malleable encryption scheme from any semantically secure one. In: Dwork, C. (ed.) CRYPTO 2006. LNCS, vol. 4117, pp. 271–289. Springer, Heidelberg (2006). https://doi.org/10.1007/11818175_16
12. Sahai, A.: Non-malleable non-interactive zero knowledge and adaptive chosen-ciphertext security. In: 40th Annual Symposium on Foundations of Computer Science, FOCS '99, 17–18 October, 1999, pp. 543–553. IEEE Computer Society, New York (1999). https://doi.org/10.1109/SFFCS.1999.814628

Lower Bounds on Assumptions Behind Registration-Based Encryption

Mohammad Hajiabadi[1]([⊠]), Mohammad Mahmoody[2][iD], Wei Qi[2], and Sara Sarfaraz[1]

[1] University of Waterloo, Waterloo, Canada
{mdhajiabadi,ssarfaraz}@uwaterloo.ca
[2] University of Virginia, Charlottesville, USA
{mohammad,wq4sr}@virginia.edu

Abstract. Registration-based encryption (RBE) [11] is a primitive that aims to offer what identity-based encryption (IBE) [2] offers without the so-called key-escrow problem. In RBE parties who wish to join the system will generate their own secret and public keys and register their public keys to a transparent party called key curator (KC) who does not have any secret state.

The initial constructions of RBE made *non-black-box* use of building block primitives, due to their use of either indistinguishability obfuscation [11] or some garbling scheme [12]. More recently, it was shown [14,17] how to achieve *black-box* constructions of (variants of) RBE and even stronger primitives based on *bilinear maps* in which the RBE is relaxed to have a CRS whose length can *grow* with the number of registered identities. Making cryptographic constructions in general, and RBE in particular, black-box is an important step as it can play a significant role in its efficiency and potential deployment. Hence, in this work we ask: *what are the minimal assumptions for black-box constructions of RBE?* Particularly, can we black-box construct RBE schemes from the same assumptions used for public-key encryption or simpler algebraic assumptions that hold in the generic group model?

In this work, we prove the first black-box separation results for RBE beyond the separations that follow from the observation that RBE black-box implies public-key encryption. In particular, we answer both of the questions above negatively and prove that neither trapdoor permutations nor (even Shoup's) generic group model can be used as the sole source of hardness for building RBE schemes. More generally, we prove that a relaxation of RBE in which all the keys are registered and compressed at the same time is already too complex to be built from either of the above-mentioned primitives in a black-box way. At a technical level, using compression techniques, we prove lemmas in the TDP and GGM oracle settings that prove the following intuitive yet useful fact: that compact strings cannot signal too many trapdoors, even if their generation algorithm takes exponential time. Due to their generality, our lemmas could be of independent interest and find more applications.

Keywords: Registration-based encryption · Black-box separations · Trapdoor permutations · Generic group model

© International Association for Cryptologic Research 2023
G. Rothblum and H. Wee (Eds.): TCC 2023, LNCS 14370, pp. 306–334, 2023.
https://doi.org/10.1007/978-3-031-48618-0_11

1   Introduction

Registration-based encryption (RBE) [11] is a primitive that aims to offer what identity-based encryption (IBE) [2] offers while avoiding the key-escrow problem. Indeed, IBE suffers from the fact that the third party, (i.e., the private-key generator,) has a universal trapdoor, (i.e., the master secret key,) allowing it to decrypt all messages encrypted using the public parameter. However, in RBE, identities generate their own secret and public keys and then simply *register* their public keys to a transparent (public-state) entity, called the *key curator* (KC). All KC does is accumulating and compressing the registered public keys in an online fashion as more and more identities register in the system. Several works were proposed to add even more desirable properties to RBE. [12] showed how to base RBE on standard assumptions. [15] constructed verifiable RBE, where the KC can give succinct proof for the existence/non-existence of users in the system. In [24], blockchain was used to construct transparent RBE, making the system even more decentralized by letting the individual participants instead of the KC manage the keys. Inspired by RBE, more advanced primitives were defined and constructed, including registered attribute based encryption (ABE) [17] and registered functional encryption (FE) [6,10].

The initial constructions of RBE were all *non-black-box*, in the sense that implementing them required knowing the implementation details of *at least* one of the primitives that were used in those constructions. This was due to use of code obfuscation [11] and/or garbled circuits [12] in such constructions. This was an undesired state of affair, as non-black-box constructions are more likely to be inefficient for practical use, and indeed RBE is yet to become practical enough for real world deployment. This is in contrast with the closely-related primitive of IBE for which *black-box* constructions from pairing-based assumptions on bilinear maps exist [1,2].

More recently, the works of [14,17] showed how to achieve *black-box* constructions of RBE, provided that it is *relaxed* so that the common reference string (CRS) can grow as a function of the total number of registered identities.[1] These works suggest that perhaps even standard RBE could at some point be realized based on well-founded assumptions in a *black-box* manner. In the meantime, in this work, we focus on a tightly related question: if we could base RBE on black-box assumptions, how simple those assumptions need to be? In particular, *what are the black-box minimal assumptions for constructing RBE?* To answer this question, we also need to understand the *black-box barriers* that arise against building RBE from the *more desirable* type assumptions. In particular, prior to our work, it was not known whether RBE can be solely based on the assumption that public-key encryption (PKE) exists.[2] Moreover, it was not known whether simpler algebraic assumptions than those on bilinear maps (e.g., assumptions

---

[1] The work of [17] further generalizes the primitive to *attribute-based* encryption and constructs registered ABE, while further relaxing the primitive and allowing *interactive* registration.
[2] Note that PKE is indeed necessary for RBE in a black-box way.

that hold in the generic group model) may suffice for RBE in a black-box way. We emphasize that although it is known how to bootstrap RBE to IBE [4,7], black-box separations known for IBE [3] do not automatically carry over to RBE, as the bootstrapping is non-black-box.

1.1   Our Results

One approach to study the black-box complexity of RBE is to study the possibility of constructing it in idealized models that provide PKE or simple algebraic assumptions for free. In particular, the random trapdoor permutation (TDP) oracle model provides (CCA-secure) PKE (among other primitives such as collision-resistant hashing) as a black-box. Moreover, the generic group model (GGM) [18,23] is an idealized model in which assumptions such as hardness of discrete logarithm, CDH (computational Diffie-Hellman assumption), and even DDH (*decisional* Diffie-Hellman assumption) hold. Hence, it is a very natural model for studying the possibility of realizing RBE from those assumptions, which is the approach that we pursue as well.

In this work, we prove the first non-trivial black-box separations about the complexity of RBE. In particular, we prove the following theorem.

Theorem 1 (Main results – informal). *There is no black-box construction of RBEs in either of the idealized models of random trapdoor permutations (TDPs) or Shoup's generic group model. Our impossibility results hold even if the CRS in RBE can grow (polynomially) with the number of registered identities.*

In particular, what we prove is that there is no construction of RBEs whose security is *solely* based on the idealized models stated in Theorem 1. We do so by proving that such schemes can be broken by a polynomial-query attacker. This is sufficient for ruling out a fully black-box construction [20]. Ruling out constructions of RBE in the idealized model of TDPs would also rule out using any primitive $\mathcal{P}$ (or rather sets of primitives) that can be constructed from TDP oracles in a black-box way (e.g., collision-resistant hash functions and public-key encryption). Ruling out RBE in the GGM would also prove a black-box separation from concrete assumptions that hold in this model (e.g., DDH).

In Sect. 2, we give an in-depth technical overview of the proof of Theorem 1. However, here we present some high level discussions about Theorem 1 and why it does not follow from previous separations known for IBE.

Public-key Compression. We prove Theorem 1 by demonstrating a more general result about a primitive that is *weaker* than RBE and yet is black-box implied by RBE; we refer to that primitive as *public-key compression* (or PKCom, for short). PKCom can be thought of as a *static* variant of RBE. In PKCom a polynomial number of identities who have generated their own public and secret keys all arrive *at the same time*. Then, they send their public-keys $\mathsf{pk}_1, \ldots, \mathsf{pk}_n$ to be compressed by the key curator (KC) in "one shot". Then, the compressed public parameter pp is broadcast by the KC to the registered identities and can be used similarly to the public parameter of IBE to privately encrypt messages to registered identities. When it comes to decryption, all parties will have access to each other's *public* keys as well as their own secret key, but of course they do not have access to each others' secret keys. A very closely related primitive to PKCom (called *slotted registered* ABE, as a generalization of IBE) is also introduced in [17] and is shown to be black-box equivalent to RBE. However, our primitive is still weaker, as it works with the fixed identities set $\{1, 2, \dots\}$ rather than arbitrary strings. These limitations make our impossibility result stronger.

Main Challenge for Proving Separations for RBE. By now, multiple black-box separations are known for assumptions behind IBE. Boneh et al. [3] proved that IBE cannot be black-box constructed from random trapdoor permutations, and the works of [19,25] showed that IBE cannot be built in what is known as *Shoup's* generic group model [23].[3] However, we emphasize that, none of these works imply a separation for *registration* based encryption (and its relaxation PKCom). Below, we first describe the similarities between the two settings, and then we describe the major difference between them.

The core reason underlying both impossibilities for IBE and ours for RBE is that a compact public parameter (pp) cannot encode enough information for securely encrypting to more than an a priori bounded number of identities. However, when it comes to RBE, there is a big difference that makes the previous IBE separation techniques come short. The IBE separation proofs [3,25] proceed by crucially relying on the bounded *running time* of the setup algorithm: in an IBE scheme, the setup algorithm, which generates (pp, msk), makes a *fixed* polynomial q number of (pk, sk) (trapdoor) queries to its oracle. So, if one corrupts a sufficiently larger-than-q number of random identities and extracts their dedicated trapdoors (say by repeated decryptions), the attacker will then recover all the needed trapdoors and can decrypt the challenge ciphertext of a non-corrupted identity as well. This "combinatorial" argument, however, completely breaks down when we move to RBE. Indeed the *running time* of generating a public parameter of an n-user RBE *grows* with the parameter n itself, because this public parameter is generated through n registration steps. Therefore, the "setup" procedure (as analogous to IBE) that generates the public parameter might be asking n or more trapdoor queries.

Compression Techniques. To get around the above challenge, we introduce new compression techniques to prove exactly that a short pp still cannot encode enough information for all n users, *regardless* of how much time it takes to generate it (see more on this in the technical overview). In fact, our new compression tool, stated in Lemma 2, (i.e., a bounded-size message/pp cannot compress too many trapdoors no matter how long it takes to generate it) proves a basic and

---

[3] More specifically, [19] claimed the result in a model that is a mixture of Maurer's [18] and Shoup's [23] models. Then, [22] proved (a tight) separation in Murer's model, and finally, [25] proved the separation of IBE in Shoup's model.

intuitive fact that could potentially find other applications beyond RBE. For starters, it already allows us to rule out black-box construction of "leveled" IBE, where the number of users n is known during setup and the setup time is allowed to grow with n while the pp is compact, from the GGM. None of the previous IBE separation techniques allows for proving such an impossibility.

Shoup's GGM vs. Maurer's GGM. In Shoup's GGM [23] group elements do have (random-looking) representations. Therefore, impossibility results in this model imply further black-box separations (e.g., from public-key encryption). However, these corollaries do not automatically follow from results that the primitive is impossible in Maurer's model [18], in which group operations are outsourced to a black-box oracle. In fact, proving the impossibility of a primitive X in Maurer's model does not even imply that X is black-box impossible from PKE. In particular, some impossibility results in Maurer's GGM *cannot* be extended to Shoup's model; e.g., [21] ruled out sequential (delay) functions in Maurer's generic group, while such functions can be obtained from random oracles, which in turn can be obtained in Shoup's model. As another example, there exists natural DDH-based constructions of primitives such as rate-1 OT and private-information retrieval (PIR) in Shoup's model [8], yet these primitives can be proved impossible in Maurer's group. Thus, proving an impossibility in Shoup's model gives the stronger and more meaningful impossibility. See [25] for more discussion on this topic.

Limits of RBE in Maurer's GGM. For the reasons above, in this work we aim for proving impossibility of RBE (and PKCom) in Shoup's GGM. Having said that, we first show that a separation of RBE/PKCom in Maurer's GGM *can* indeed be proved as well. Our starting point for showing this barrier is the work of [22] that ruled out *identity* based encryption in Maurer's GGM. Despite focusing on IBE, their proof does *not* care about the exact running time that it takes to generate the public parameter, and it only relies on the *number* of group elements that are explicitly planted in the public parameter. This makes their result general enough to be basically applicable to our PKCom as well, if one opens up their proof to adapt it to RBE. One limitation of this result, however, is that it does not allow CRS to be present, and we particularly would like to even allow our PKCom (and RBE) schemes to have CRS that can *grow* with the number of identities. Such extensions would make our impossibility result *complement* the recent positive (black-box) results of [14,17] in which hardness assumptions in pairing-based groups are used to construct RBEs with polynomially long CRS. The follow-up works of [5,9] further generalized the initial impossibility of [22] to the point that we could use their results to formally obtain an impossibility of RBE from Maurer's GGM as corollary, even with polynomially long CRS. The reason is that RBEs, just like IBEs, can be used to obtain signature schemes using the so-called Naor's trick,[4] and the works of [5,9] do indeed rule out the

---

[4] This is done by interpreting the decryption keys as signatures over the identity's names interpreted as messages.

existence of digital signatures for a polynomially large message space in Maurer's GGM, even if the scheme has a polynomially long CRS.

2   Technical Overview

We prove that public-key compression schemes cannot be built in a black-box way from TDPs or in the Shoup generic group. Since RBE and PKCom are black-box equivalent, our impossibility results will also apply to RBE.[5]

We prove our two impossibility results by showing that relative to a random TDP oracle or a GGM oracle with explicit random labels (i.e., Shoup's model [23]), PKCom cannot exist so long as its security is solely based on the oracle model. More specifically, we show that any purported PKCom construction relative to either a random TDP oracle a GGM oracle can be broken by an adversary who makes a polynomial number of queries, while the adversary can do unbounded amount of computation independent of the oracle.

Outline. We follow the approach of Zhandry [25] for proving our impossibility results. Zhandry proved that a special type of signature schemes, simply called *restricted* signatures, defined in an oracle model, cannot be realized relative to any oracles. Thus, to prove an impossibility of a primitive X relative to an oracle O, it suffices to show how to black-box transform any purported construction of X relative to O into a restricted signature relative to O without losing correctness and security.[6] The rest follows by the impossibility of restricted signatures.

A restricted signature scheme relative to an oracle O has the normal algorithms $(\mathrm{Gen}^O, \mathrm{Sig}^O, \mathrm{Ver}^O)$ of a signature scheme, but the verification algorithm Ver^O is restricted in the following way: $\mathrm{Ver}^O(\mathrm{vrk}, m, \sigma) = \mathrm{Ver1}(\mathrm{Ver0}^O(\mathrm{vrk}, m), \sigma)$, where Ver1 makes no oracle calls and vrk, m, σ denote the verification key, message and signature, respectively. That is, the verification algorithm is restricted in that all oracle queries may be made prior to seeing the signature σ, and upon seeing σ no further queries are permitted. Zhandry proved that no restricted signatures exist relative to any oracle O by showing that any such construction can be broken by an adversary that makes a polynomial number of queries to O. As an example of a non-restricted scheme, consider Lamport's signatures from OWFs f. In that construction, σ corresponds to OWF pre-images, while vrk correspond to OWF image values. To verify a signature σ, one will check a number of image values against their corresponding pre-images by calling f, making the construction inherently non-restricted, as expected.

Zhandry proved that certain impossibility results, such as the impossibility of IBE from GGM [3,19,22], may be proved more naturally using the restricted signatures methodology. In particular, Zhandry showed that one can black-box transform any IBE construction $\mathsf{IBE}^{\mathsf{GGM}}$ relative to a GGM oracle into a restricted signature $\mathcal{E}^{\mathsf{GGM}}$, while preserving its correctness and security.

---

[5] The fact that RBE black-box implies PKCom is straightforward, due to PKCom being a special case. The converse is also true and is proved in [17].

[6] By security, here we refer to security against unbounded poly-query adversaries.

Target Restricted Signatures. For our impossibility results, we would need to further modify the notion of restricted signatures and work with a primitive which we call *target*-restricted signatures. A target restricted signature is defined over a message space $[n] = \{1, \ldots, n\}$ (think of n as the number of PKCom users), where the verification algorithm is restricted as it is in restricted signatures, but correctness and security only hold with respect to a random target message chosen as $h \leftarrow [n]$, where the verification and signing keys in turn may depend on h. That is, $\text{Gen}^O(1^n, h \in [n])$ outputs a pair of keys (vrk, sgk), and we require that the following holds. (a) δ-target correctness: for a signature σ derived for the target message h as $\sigma \leftarrow \text{Sig}^O(\text{sgk}, h)$ we have $\text{Ver}^O(\text{vrk}, h, \sigma) \geq \delta$, where Ver^O is restricted as above. (b) Zero-time unforgeability: given vrk (derived based on a random $h \leftarrow [n]$) and h, no poly-query adversary can forge a signature on h (Definition 4). We show that Zhandry's proof with almost no modifications also shows that target restricted signatures for non-negligible δ's are impossible.

Transformation. After establishing the notion of target-restricted signatures, the bulk of our technical work is as follows. For a TDP/GGM oracle O, we show how to black-box transform a purported PKCom construction CMP^O into a δ-correct target restricted signatures, where δ is non-negligible. This is where our new compression techniques come into play. Below, we first go over more details of our techniques for the case of TDP oracle, as it captures most of the challenges.

Warm-up: Restricted Oracle Calls. As a warm-up, first let us consider the case where the TDP oracles $(\mathbf{g}, \mathbf{e}, \mathbf{d})$ are used by the PKCom scheme $\text{PKCom}^{\mathbf{g}, \mathbf{e}, \mathbf{d}}$, in a special was as $\text{PKCom}^{\mathbf{g}, \mathbf{e}, \mathbf{d}} := (\text{Key}^{\mathbf{g}}, \text{Com}^{\mathbf{g}}, \text{Enc}^{\mathbf{e}}, \text{Dec}^{\mathbf{d}})$, where Key is the (public and secret) key generation algorithm, Com is the key compression algorithm, Enc is the encryption algorithm, and Dec is the decryption algorithm. Moreover, assume we do not have a CRS. This setting is already non-trivial, and helps us get our main insights across. The TDP oracles are defined randomly while inducing a permutation over the message space $\{0, 1\}^\kappa$ (Definition 4). Our goal is to black-box transform such $\text{PKCom}^{\mathbf{g}, \mathbf{e}, \mathbf{d}}$ constructions into a restricted signature relative to $(\mathbf{g}, \mathbf{e}, \mathbf{d})$ with comparable correctness and security.

Non-restricted Signatures from PKCom. A PKCom scheme over identities $[n]$ naturally induces a signature scheme using Naor's trick (that applies to IBE schemes but can be adapted to RBE as well). In that transformation, the secret keys of an identity are kept as the signature for that identity's string. The verification then proceeds by testing the quality of the decryption key (as the signature) through repeated encryption and decryptions. This scheme is clearly *not* restricted. Below, we first describe construction that is a modification of Naor's trick construction which is still *not* restricted. However, our scheme has the benefit that we can make it restricted with more modifications which we will explain below. Let $(\text{Key}^{\mathbf{g}}, \text{Com}^{\mathbf{g}}, \text{Enc}^{\mathbf{e}}, \text{Dec}^{\mathbf{d}})$ be the purported PKCom scheme relative to a TDP oracle $(\mathbf{g}, \mathbf{e}, \mathbf{d})$. A verification/signature key pair $(\text{vrk}, \text{sgk}) \leftarrow \text{Gen}^O(1^n, h \in [n])$ on a target message $h \in [n]$ is obtained as follows: generate n public/secret key pairs $\{(\text{pk}_i, \text{sk}_i)\}_{i \in [n]}$ by running $\text{Key}^{\mathbf{g}}(1^\kappa)$, and let

QGen_i denote the set of query-answer (Q-A for short) pairs obtained for generating $(\mathsf{pk}_i, \mathsf{sk}_i)$. Let $\mathsf{pp} := \mathsf{Com}^{\mathbf{g}}(\mathsf{pk}_1, \ldots, \mathsf{pk}_n)$. Output $\mathsf{vrk} := (\mathsf{pp}, \{\mathsf{QGen}_i\}_{i \neq h})$ and $\mathsf{sgk} := (\mathsf{sk}_h, \mathsf{QGen}_h).$[7] A signature on h is $(\mathsf{sk}_h, \mathsf{QGen}_h)$. Define $\mathsf{Ver}^O(\mathsf{vrk}, h, \sigma) =$ $\mathsf{Ver1}^O(\mathsf{Ver0}^O(\mathsf{vrk}, h), \sigma)$ as follows: $\mathsf{Ver0}^O(\mathsf{vrk}, h)$ generates a random ciphertext c for a random message m relative to identity h as $c \leftarrow \mathsf{Enc}^{\mathbf{e}}(\mathsf{pp}, h, m)$, lets QEnc contain the Q-A pairs (which are only of $\mathbf{e}$-type), and outputs $(m, c).$[8] Then, $\mathsf{Ver1}^O$, given $\sigma := (\mathsf{sk}_h, \mathsf{QGen}_h)$ and (m, c), simply decrypts $\mathsf{Dec}^{\mathbf{d}}(\mathsf{sk}_h, c)$ and outputs 1 iff the decryption outputs m. The signature correct, and is also secure: if an adversary can forge a signature on a target message h, it can also decrypt ciphertexts for that target index h under the PKCom scheme. (Under the PKCom scheme, the adversary can have the secret keys for all but the target index, since the public keys for all non-target indices are submitted by the adversary itself. Thus, a PKCom adversary can sample vrk itself.) The signature, however, is not restricted because $\mathsf{Ver1}^O$ makes queries in order to decrypt.

Making the Signature Restricted. A first (naive) idea in making $\mathsf{Ver1}$ oracle-free is to have $\mathsf{Ver0}^O$ pass QEnc, in addition to (vrk, m, c), onto $\mathsf{Ver1}$, and let $\mathsf{Ver1}((\mathsf{vrk}, m, c, \mathsf{QEnc}), \sigma)$, where $\sigma := (\mathsf{sk}_h, \mathsf{QGen}_h)$, decrypt $\mathsf{Dec}^{\mathbf{d}}(\mathsf{sk}_h, c)$ while using QEnc and $\{\mathsf{QGen}_i\}$ as hints, and respond to queries whose answers cannot be determined based on these hints with random values. In more detail, for an emerged query (which can only be of $\mathbf{d}$-type) $\mathsf{qu} := ((\mathsf{tk}, y) \xrightarrow{\mathbf{d}} ?)$ during $\mathsf{Dec}^{\mathbf{d}}(\mathsf{sk}_h, c)$ if both of the following hold then respond to qu with x:

(a) There exists a Q-A pair $(\mathsf{tk} \xrightarrow{\mathbf{g}} \mathsf{ik}) \in \cup_i \mathsf{QGen}_i$ for some ik; and
(b) there exists $((\mathsf{ik}, x) \xrightarrow{\mathbf{e}} y) \in \mathsf{QEnc}$ for some x.

Otherwise (i.e., if at least one of the above does not hold), pick a random answer. We claim we have correctness. This is because $(\mathsf{pk}_i, \mathsf{sk}_i)$ pairs are all generated honestly by running $\mathsf{Key}^{\mathbf{g}}$, with $\{\mathsf{QGen}_i\}$ being their underlying Q-A pairs, and that all of $\mathbf{d}$ queries during Dec are responded to consistently with those of $\{\mathsf{QGen}_i\}$ and QEnc.

However, we cannot reduce the security of the signature to that of the original PKCom (so to argue security). For example, suppose the PKCom's user public-secret key pairs $(\mathsf{pk}_i, \mathsf{sk}_i)$ are simply random index/trapdoor key pairs $(\mathsf{ik}_i, \mathsf{tk}_i)$ generated by calling $\mathbf{g}$ (i.e., $\mathsf{pk}_i = \mathsf{ik}_i$). An adversary $\mathcal{A}$ may then forge a signature as $\sigma' := (\tilde{\mathsf{tk}}_h, (\tilde{\mathsf{tk}}_h \xrightarrow{\mathbf{g}} \mathsf{ik}_h))$, where $\tilde{\mathsf{tk}}_h$ is just a 'junk' value. By Conditions (A) and (b) above, $\mathsf{Ver1}((\mathsf{vrk}, m, c, \mathsf{QEnc}), \sigma')$ will always decrypt c to m, outputting 1. But the forger $\mathcal{A}$ has not done anything clever, so we cannot use it in a reduction to break the security of $\mathsf{PKCom}^{\mathbf{g},\mathbf{e},\mathbf{d}}$. The reason we cannot prove a security reduction (for arguing the signature is as secure as the base PKCom)

---

[7] The Q-A sets QGen_i's will not be used in this simple construction, but later one they will be used when we make the signature restricted.

[8] Again, the set QEnc will not be used in this (flawed) construction, but will be used later when we discuss the fixes.

is that the verification provides 'free lunch' to a forger: inverting images with respect to an ik_h whose trapdoor key may not be known to the forger.

Compression to the Rescue. So far, we have not used the fact that pp is compact (of size $\ll n$), so it is not a surprise we cannot establish a security reduction from the signature to the PKCom. In other words, by plugging in a trivial PKCom scheme whose pp contains all public keys, we get a restricted signature against which there exists a generic attack, but the base PKCom is secure! We should use the fact that $|\mathsf{pp}|$ is compact in order to avoid giving free lunch to a forger in the above sense. Call an ik valid if $\mathsf{ik} \in \mathbf{g}(*)$. Assume $\mathbf{g}$ is sufficiently length increasing so the only way to produce a valid ik is to call $\mathbf{g}$ on a preimage. Our main idea is as follows: letting QGen_i be as above (all formed honestly), there must exist an index $h \in [n]$ such that the set of all valid ik's that emerge as $((\mathsf{ik}, *) \xrightarrow{\mathbf{e}} ?)$ queries during a random PKCom encryption $\mathsf{Enc}^{\mathbf{e}}(\mathsf{pp}, h, *)$ to index h are a subset of those ik's for which we have $(* \xrightarrow{\mathbf{g}} \mathsf{ik}) \in \cup_{i \neq h}\mathsf{QGen}_i$. Call this Condition cover. We will show in a moment why this condition holds, but let us sketch how to modify $\mathsf{Ver}^{\mathcal{O}}(\mathsf{vrk}, h, \sigma) = \mathsf{Ver1}(\mathsf{Ver0}^{\mathcal{O}}(\mathsf{vrk}, h), \sigma)$ in light of this fact. First, $\mathsf{Ver0}^{\mathcal{O}}(\mathsf{vrk}, h)$ outputs (m, c, QEnc), as before. Now $\mathsf{Ver1}((\mathsf{vrk}, m, c, \mathsf{QEnc}), \sigma)$, where $\sigma := (\mathsf{sk}_h, \mathsf{QGen}_h)$, proceeds exactly as before, except in response to a query $\mathsf{qu} := ((\mathsf{tk}, y) \xrightarrow{\mathbf{d}} ?)$, Condition (a) above will change to

(A) there exists a Q-A pair $(\mathsf{tk} \xrightarrow{\mathbf{g}} \mathsf{ik}) \in \cup_{i \neq h}\mathsf{QGen}_i$ for some ik.

Now correctness still holds, thanks to Condition cover. (Any $((\mathsf{ik}, x) \xrightarrow{\mathbf{e}} y)$ for a valid ik has a matching trapdoor key $(\mathsf{tk} \xrightarrow{\mathbf{g}} \mathsf{ik}) \in \cup_{i \neq h}\mathsf{QGen}_i$. All other decryption queries may be responded to randomly, without creating inconsistencies.) We should now have security (at least intuitively), because we do not provide free lunch to a forger anymore: Ver1 inverts images only for ik's already covered in $(\mathsf{tk} \xrightarrow{\mathbf{g}} \mathsf{ik}) \in \cup_{i \neq h}\mathsf{QGen}_i$, but this information is already available to the adversary itself (as part of vrk). Making this intuition formal, however, requires some delicate reasoning, which we skip here.

Proving Condition cover via a compression technique. Recall that $\mathsf{Enc}^{\mathbf{e}}(\mathsf{pp}, *, *)$ only calls $\mathbf{e}$, and the only information it gets regarding $\mathbf{g}$ is via pp which in turn has size $\ll n$. It is not hard to see if Condition cover does not hold, then by performing random encryptions for all indices $\mathsf{Enc}^{\mathbf{e}}(\mathsf{pp}, 1, *), \ldots, \mathsf{Enc}^{\mathbf{e}}(\mathsf{pp}, n, *)$, we will end up calling $\mathbf{e}(\mathsf{ik}, *)$ upon at least n different valid ik's. To see this let Q_i contain any ik such that $(* \xrightarrow{\mathbf{g}} \mathsf{ik}) \in \mathsf{QGen}_i$. If $\overline{\mathsf{cover}}$ holds, during $\mathsf{Enc}^{\mathbf{e}}(\mathsf{pp}, u, *)$, for any $u \in [n]$, we will make a query $((\mathsf{ik}_u, *) \xrightarrow{\mathbf{e}} ?)$ for a valid ik_u where $\mathsf{ik}_u \notin \cup_{i \neq u}\mathsf{QGen}_i$. We claim all ik_i are distinct, so we will have n distinct valid id_i's. Assume the contrary and that $\mathsf{ik}_1 = \mathsf{ik}_2$. We know both $\mathsf{ik}_1, \mathsf{ik}_2 \in \cup_i Q_i$, because a valid ik cannot come out of thin air. We also know $\mathsf{ik}_1 \notin \cup_{i \neq 1}Q_i$, and so $\mathsf{ik}_1 \in Q_1 \setminus \cup_{i \neq 1}Q_i$. So, if $\mathsf{ik}_1 = \mathsf{ik}_2$, then $\mathsf{ik}_2 \in Q_1 \setminus \cup_{i \neq 1}Q_i$, but this contradicts the fact that $\mathsf{ik}_2 \notin \cup_{i \neq 2}Q_i$.

Theorem 2 (Compression, informal). *Let* pp *be any advice string of size* $\ll n$ *generated based on* $(\mathbf{g}, \mathbf{e}, \mathbf{d})$*. For any poly-query adversary* $\mathcal{A}^{\mathbf{g},\mathbf{e},\mathbf{d}}(\mathsf{pp})$*, the probability that* $\mathcal{A}$ *can output a list* L *of* ik*'s satisfying the following two conditions is negligible: (a)* L *has at least* n *distinct valid* ik*'s, and (b) no* ik *in* L *was generated as a result of a* $\mathbf{g}$ *query by* $\mathcal{A}$ *itself.*

We show if there exists an adversary in the sense of the above theorem, then one can compress the oracle $\mathbf{g}$. We prove this via Gennaro-Trevisan style compression techniques [13], later generalized by Haitner *et al.* [16]. In our theorem description, the adversary $\mathcal{A}$ does not need to know which of the n ik's are valid: as long as at least n of them are valid we will prove a compression. Our theorem description holds even if the adversary makes an exponential number of queries (for a carefully selected exponential). We believe this technique employed within black-box separations might find other applications.

Allowing a CRS. We will now sketch how things will be different, still in the limited-access setting $(\mathsf{Key}^{\mathbf{g}}, \mathsf{Com}^{\mathbf{g}}, \mathsf{Enc}^{\mathbf{e}}, \mathsf{Dec}^{\mathbf{d}})$, by allowing in a CRS. Suppose the CRS is generated as crs $\leftarrow$ $\mathsf{CRS}(1^{\kappa}, 1^n)$, and is used in key generation $(\mathsf{pk}, \mathsf{sk}) \leftarrow \mathsf{Key}^g(\mathsf{crs})$. Let us first explain what will go wrong if we leave the above approach unmodified. Recall that $\mathrm{Ver1}((m, c, \mathsf{QEnc}), \sigma)$, where $\sigma := (\mathsf{sk}_h, \mathsf{QGen}_h)$, decrypts $\mathsf{Dec}^{\mathbf{d}}(\mathsf{sk}_h, c)$ and handles a query qu: $((\mathsf{tk}, c) \xrightarrow{\mathbf{d}} ?)$ via Conditions (A) and (b) above. We were able to argue correctness because for some index h with all but negligible probability, all valid ik's upon which we have a query $((\mathsf{ik}, *) \xrightarrow{\mathbf{e}} ?)$ must have been collected in $\cup_i \mathsf{QGen}_{i \neq h}$. However, this fact breaks down in the CRS case, because $\mathsf{Enc}^{\mathbf{e}}(\mathsf{pp}, h, *)$ might call $\mathbf{e}$ upon an ik that comes from crs, and whose trapdoor key is not collected in any of $\cup_i \mathsf{QGen}_i$. Thus, responding to inversion queries relative to $\mathbf{e}(\mathsf{ik}, *)$ with random values during decryption will create an inconsistency, destroying correctness. Since we aim to argue correctness, suppose $(\mathsf{sk}_h, \mathsf{QGen}_h)$ were generated honestly. Our solution is based on the following intuition: If a query $((\mathsf{tk}, *) \xrightarrow{\mathbf{d}} ?)$, where $\mathbf{g}(\mathsf{tk}) = \mathsf{ik}$, emerges during decryption of a random encryption relative to $\mathsf{Enc}^{\mathbf{e}}(\mathsf{pp}, h, *)$ with good probability, then by choosing many $(\mathsf{sk}_h, \mathsf{QGen}_h)$ and forming random encryptions as $\mathsf{Enc}^{\mathbf{e}}(\mathsf{pp}, h, *)$ and decrypting them back (all using the real oracles) we should collect these tk values. This encrypt-decrypt process will be performed by $\mathsf{Gen}^{O}(1^n, h \in [n])$ (the key generation algorithm of the signature scheme) and all the Q-A pairs are appended to a list T, put in the final vrk. Back to the above discussion, $\mathrm{Ver1}((m, c, \mathsf{QEnc}), \sigma)$ will decrypt $\mathsf{Dec}^{\mathbf{d}}(\mathsf{sk}_h, c)$ as per QEnc if (I) and (b) holds, where (b) is as above and (I) is as follows.

(I) There exists a Q-A pair $(\mathsf{tk} \xrightarrow{\mathbf{g}} \mathsf{ik}) \in \mathsf{T} \cup_{i \neq h} \mathsf{QGen}_i$ for some ik.

The proof of security is similar to the previous case, based on the intuition illustrated before.

Finally, for the general case in which oracle access is unrestricted (e.g., $\mathsf{Key}^{\mathbf{g},\mathbf{e},\mathbf{d}}$) we define the notion of 'free lunch' (which might make room for forgeries) as inversions $\mathbf{e}^{-1}(\mathsf{ik}, *)$, where $(* \xrightarrow{\mathbf{g}} \mathsf{ik})$ never appears in $\mathsf{QGen}_{i \neq h}$, nor in any safe lists (e.g., T as explained above, or any ik such that $(* \xrightarrow{\mathbf{g}} \mathsf{ik})$ is generated during $\mathsf{Enc}^{\mathbf{g},\mathbf{e},\mathbf{d}}(\mathsf{pp}, h, *))$. The chief challenge is to strike a delicate balance during the decryption performed by $\mathsf{Ver1}((m, c, \mathsf{QEnc}), \sigma)$ in between not overtly answering all $\mathbf{d}(\mathsf{tk}, y)$ queries as per QEnc (which will violate security) and not answering any queries at all (which will destroy correctness). The main techniques for establishing such a balance were sketched above, but the whole analysis for the general case requires more involved reasoning.

Impossibility in Shoup's GGM. We now describe how to derive a restricted signature scheme $\mathcal{E}^{\mathbb{G}_{RR}}$ from a PKCom construction $\mathsf{PKCom}^{\mathbb{G}_{RR}}$, where the oracle $\mathbb{G}_{RR} := (\mathbf{label}, \mathbf{add})$ comes with a labeling oracle $\mathbf{label}$ producing labels for exponents in $\mathbb{Z}_p$ (where p is the order of the group) and $\mathbf{add}$ adds two labels. We assume $\mathbf{label}$ produces labels of sufficiently large length, so that producing a label without calling $\mathbf{label}$ or $\mathbf{add}$ is effectively impossible. The general methodology is as follows, but we need some additional ideas to deal with the algebraic structure imposed bu groups. To illustrate our core ideas suppose we have no crs and that Com makes no $\mathbb{G}_{RR}$ queries, so the PKCom construction is as $(\mathsf{Key}^{\mathbb{G}}_{RR}, \mathsf{Com}, \mathsf{Enc}^{\mathbb{G}}_{RR}, \mathsf{Dec}^{\mathbb{G}}_{RR})$. Assume wlog all algorithms only have access to $\mathbf{add}$ (access to $\mathbf{label}$ can be simulated by including the generator as part of every input). The algorithms $\mathsf{Gen}^{\mathbb{G}}_{RR}$ and $\mathsf{Sig}^{\mathbb{G}}_{RR}$ and $\mathsf{Ver0}^{\mathbb{G}_{RR}}(\mathsf{vrk}, h)$ are defined exactly as before. A naive idea for $\mathsf{Ver1}(\mathsf{vrk}, m, \sigma)$, where $\sigma := ((\mathsf{sk}_h, \mathsf{QGen}_h))$, is to answer to an $\mathbf{add}$ query $((\ell_1, \ell_2) \xrightarrow{\mathbf{add}} ?)$ according to what can be inferred from the collective set of Q-A pairs in $\cup_i \mathsf{QGen}_i \cup \mathsf{QEnc}$. Namely, consider a matrix M with columns labeled according to labels present in output responses to queries in $\cup_i \mathsf{QGen}_i \cup \mathsf{QEnc}$. A given Q-A pair $((\ell, \ell') \xrightarrow{\mathbf{add}} \ell'')$ in $\cup_i \mathsf{QGen}_i \cup \mathsf{QEnc}$ is embedded into the matrix M by adding a row, which has a 1 on the ℓ-labelled column, a 1 on the ℓ' labeled column and a -1 on the ℓ''-labeled column. For brevity, we denote such a row with $x_\ell + x_{\ell'} - x_{\ell''}$. Having formed this matrix M, suppose $\mathsf{Ver1}$ given a query $((\ell_1, \ell_2) \xrightarrow{\mathbf{add}} ?)$ checks if an answer is present in M: namely, if there exists a label ℓ^* such that $x_{\ell_1} + x_{\ell_2} - x_{\ell^*} \in \mathsf{Span}(M)$, where Span denotes row span; if so, respond with ℓ^*, otherwise with a random label. This restricted signature scheme is correct (similarly to how we argued before), but is not secure in the sense of having a security reduction from the signature to the base PKCom. We will now establish a balancing act (in the sense of before) as follows. Call a label Known if $\mathbf{label}^{-1}(\ell)$ (its discrete log) is recoverable given $\cup_{i \neq h} \mathsf{QGen}_i \cup \mathsf{QEnc}$. For GGMs, we will prove a compression theorem (stated later), which as a consequence implies the following covering condition: with all but negligible probability, there exists an index h such that during a random encryption $\mathsf{Enc}^{\mathbf{add}}(\mathsf{pp}, h, *)$, if there exists a Q-A pair $((\ell_1, \ell_2) \xrightarrow{\mathbf{add}} \ell^*)$ such that $\ell^* \neq \perp$, then $\ell_1, \ell_2 \in \mathsf{Known}$. That is, for $b \in \{0, 1\}$, ℓ_b is either already a label in $\cup_{i \neq h} \mathsf{QGen}_i$, or is obtained via a sequence of $\mathbf{add}$ operations on labels with known discrete logs. With this intuition mind, $\mathsf{Ver1}$ simulates the response to an **add** query $((\ell_1, \ell_2) \xrightarrow{\text{add}} ?)$ as follows: if there exists a Known label ℓ^* such that such that $x_{\ell_1} + x_{\ell_2} - x_{\ell^*} \in \mathsf{Span}(M)$, where Span denotes row span; if so, respond with ℓ^*, else with a random label. This relaxation enables us to prove that no security is lost in the process. Finally, we derive the covering condition above from a compression lemma that we develop and prove in GGMs, which states given a short advice string pp, one can extract a bounded number of valid ℓ labels (those in the output of **label**).

Theorem 3 (Informal). *Let* pp *be any advice string of size* $\ll n$ *generated based on* (**label, add**). *For any poly-query adversary* $\mathcal{A}^{\mathsf{label,add}}$, *the probability that* $\mathcal{A}$ *can output a list* L *of* ℓ*'s satisfying the following two conditions is negligible: (a)* L *has at least* n *distinct valid* ℓ*'s, and (b) no* ℓ *in the list was generated as a result of a* **label** *or a* **add** *query.*

All the statements mentioned after Theorem 2 also hold for Theorem 3. The proof of this is based on a generalization of the Gennaro-Trevisan compression techniques [13] to the GGM setting. The GGM setting, due to its algebraic nature, makes the compression argument more delicate and challenging. Our techniques may be of independent interest.

Why Going through Restricted Signature Instead of a Direct Proof. Even though we could write a direct proof that avoids going through the notion of restricted signatures, by using this approach we also get the benefits of the proof of [25] for free. In particular, a direct proof would involve the high-level approach of (1) learning useful information about the oracle, (2) doing a reverse sampling of the keys and faking a partial oracle to be used for decrypting the challenge, and (3) analyzing the attack through careful hybrids. However, using the restricted signature approach allows us to have a more modular proof. In particular, with this approach Step (2) above would not be needed; all we do is a black-box reduction between RBE and restricted signatures, and the attack on RBE follows from the poly-query attack on the signatures that is transformed into an attack on RBE through the black-box reduction between them. In addition to simplicity and modularity, as a bonus we could also better explain (in the next paragraph) the new challenges that arise for our separation proof for RBE, in comparison with IBE, and how we resolve them.

3 Preliminaries

Proofs. All omitted proofs can be found in the full version.

Notation. We use κ for the security parameter. We write $\mathsf{negl}(x)$ for a negligible function of x. For an integer n, $[n] := \{1, \ldots, n\}$. We write $x \leftarrow \mathcal{S}$ (resp., $x \leftarrow D$) to denote picking an element uniformly at random from a set $\mathcal{S}$ (resp., a distribution D). By $\Pr[E; D]$ we denote the probability of E where D is random space/process over which E is defined. In general, we use $*$ as a placeholder for an arbitrary value. For example, $(x, *, *)$ is a 3-tuple where the first value is x and the second and third values are two arbitrary values. For function f, then $f(*)$ could denote the range of f (we let the context clarify whether $f(*)$ refers to a set or a single unspecified value). For an oracle $O = (\mathbf{q}_1, \ldots, \mathbf{q}_n)$ consisting of n different types of queries, we use $(x \xrightarrow[\mathbf{q}_i]{} y)$ to denote one query of type $\mathbf{q}_i$ where the input is x and the output is y. Note that both x and y can be tuples. Also note that we do not use $*$ as a placeholder for y or any term of y since y is not arbitrary but depends on x and $\mathbf{q}_i$. Finally, we explain how we use $\subset$ in this paper. (Note that $\subseteq$ is used in a similar way.) Since a function is formally defined as a relation, which is a set, when we write $f \subset g$ for two functions f, g, we mean f (viewed as a relation) is a subset of g (also viewed as a relation), which means that the domain of f is a subset of the domain of g and it is defined similarly on those points. For two n-tuples $x = (x_1, \cdots, x_n)$ and $y = (y_1, \cdots, y_n)$, $x \subset y$ if and only if $x_i \subset y_i$ for every $i \in [n]$. Since an oracle can be viewed as an n-tuple of functions, the notation $O' \subset O$ is well defined for two oracles O, O'.

3.1 Public Key Compression

Here we define Public Key Compression (PKCom). This primitive allows n identities $\mathsf{id}_1, \ldots, \mathsf{id}_n$ to independently sample their public/secret key pairs $(\mathsf{pk}_1, \mathsf{sk}_1), \ldots, (\mathsf{pk}_n, \mathsf{sk}_n)$ and then broadcast $(\mathsf{id}_1, \mathsf{pk}_1), \ldots, (\mathsf{id}_n, \mathsf{pk}_n)$. There is then a compression algorithm Com that compresses all these public keys into a short public parameter pp. This pp together with id_i can be used to encrypt to id_i. Finally, user id_i can use her secret key sk_i and the set of all public keys $\mathsf{pk}_1, \ldots, \mathsf{pk}_n$ to decrypt any message encrypted to her. In the actual definition of RBE [11], of which PKCom is a special case [17], a user needs only a short public "decryption-update" string (which in turn is deterministically derived from $\mathsf{pk}_1, \ldots, \mathsf{pk}_n$) to be able to perform decryption. But since we aim to prove a lower-bound, by allowing the decryption algorithm to take in all of $\mathsf{pk}_1, \ldots, \mathsf{pk}_n$, our impossibility results will become only stronger. Also, we assume the n identities are $\{\mathsf{id}_1 = 1, \ldots, \mathsf{id}_n = n\}$ for simplicity, and state the scheme for a *key encapsulation* variant; again, both of these will only make our impossibility results stronger.

Definition 1. *A public key compression scheme consists of PPT algorithms* $(\mathsf{CRS}, \mathsf{Key}, \mathsf{Com}, \mathsf{Enc}, \mathsf{Dec})$:

- *CRS generation.* $\mathsf{CRS}(1^\kappa, 1^n) \to \mathsf{crs}$ *is a randomized algorithm that takes in a security parameter κ and an integer n (the number of parties), and outputs a CRS crs of length $\mathsf{poly}(\kappa, n)$. We allow crs to grow polynomially with the number of users.*
- *Key generation.* $\mathsf{Key}(1^\kappa, \mathsf{crs}) \to (\mathsf{pk}, \mathsf{sk})$ *takes in 1^κ and crs and outputs a pair of public and secret keys $(\mathsf{pk}, \mathsf{sk})$.*
- *Key compression.* $\mathsf{Com}(\mathsf{crs}, \{\mathsf{pk}_i\}_{i \in [n]}) \to \mathsf{pp}$ *takes in the security parameter, the crs, a list of public keys $\{\mathsf{pk}_i\}_{i \in [n]}$, and deterministically outputs pp as the compressed public key.*

- **Encryption.** $\mathsf{Enc}(\mathsf{pp}, \mathsf{id}) \to (\mathsf{m}, \mathsf{ct})$ *takes in* pp, *a recipient identity* $\mathsf{id} \in [n]$, *and outputs a random* $\mathsf{m} \leftarrow \{0,1\}^\kappa$ *and a corresponding ciphertext* ct.
- **Decryption.** $\mathsf{Dec}(\mathsf{crs}, \mathsf{id}, \mathsf{sk}, \{\mathsf{pk}_i\}_{i \in [n]}, \mathsf{ct}) \to \mathsf{m}$ *takes in* crs, *an identity* $\mathsf{id} \in [n]$, *a secret key* sk, *public keys* $\{\mathsf{pk}_i\}_{i \in [n]}$, *a ciphertext* ct, *and outputs a plaintext* m *or a special symbol* $\perp$.

We require completeness, compactness and security, as defined next.

- **Completeness:** *The decryption algorithm recovers the plaintext with all but negligible probability. For every* $n \in \mathbb{N}$, *any* $i \in [n]$, $\mathsf{crs} \leftarrow \mathsf{CRS}(1^\kappa, n)$, $(\mathsf{pk}_i, \mathsf{sk}_i) \leftarrow \mathsf{Key}(1^\kappa, \mathsf{crs})$, $(m, \mathsf{ct}) \leftarrow \mathsf{Enc}(\mathsf{pp}, \mathsf{id})$, *it holds that* $\Pr[\mathsf{Dec}(\mathsf{crs}, \mathsf{id}, \mathsf{sk}_i, \{\mathsf{pk}_i\}_{i \in [n]}, \mathsf{ct}) = m] \geq 1 - \mathsf{negl}(\kappa)$.
- **Compactness:** *There exists a fixed polynomial* poly *such that for all* n *and* pp *formed as above,* $|\mathsf{pp}| = o(n)\mathsf{poly}(\kappa)$. *We require sub-linear compactness, making our impossibility results stronger.*
- **Security:** *Any PPT adversary* $\mathcal{A}$ *has a negligible advantage in the following game.* $\mathcal{A}$ *is given* n *and a CRS* $\mathsf{crs} \leftarrow \mathsf{CRS}(1^\kappa, n)$, *and* $\mathcal{A}$ *outputs a challenge index* h *and* $n-1$ *public keys* $\{\mathsf{pk}_i\}_{i \neq h}$. *The challenger samples* $(\mathsf{pk}_h, *) \leftarrow \mathsf{Key}(1^\kappa, \mathsf{crs})$, *forms* $\mathsf{pp} := \mathsf{Com}(\mathsf{crs}, \{\mathsf{pk}_i\}_{i \in [n]})$, *and* $(m, \mathsf{ct}) \leftarrow \mathsf{Enc}(\mathsf{pp}, \mathsf{id})$. $\mathcal{A}$ *is given* ct, *and outputs* m' *and wins if* $m' = m$.

Note that we are making the security notion weaker (the adversary's job is more difficult); our impossibility results separates this weak notion of security, hence making our results stronger.

4 Impossibility of PKCom from TDPs

In this section, we show that there exists an oracle $\mathcal{O}$ relative to which TDPs exists but PKCom does not. We define a distribution on TDP oracles as follows.

Definition 2. *We define an oracle distribution* Ψ *whose samples are oracles of the form* $\mathbf{O} = (\mathbf{g}, \mathbf{e}, \mathbf{d})$. *The distribution is parameterized over a security parameter* κ, *but we keep it implicit for better readability.*

- $\mathbf{g}\colon \{0,1\}^\kappa \mapsto \{0,1\}^{3\kappa}$ *is a random injective length-tripling function, mapping a trapdoor key to an index key.*
- $\mathbf{e}\colon \{0,1\}^{3\kappa} \times \{0,1\}^\kappa \mapsto \{0,1\}^\kappa$ *is a random function under the following condition: for all* $\mathsf{ik} \in \{0,1\}^{3\kappa}$, *the function* $\mathbf{e}(\mathsf{ik}, \cdot)$ *is a permutation.*
- $\mathbf{d}\colon \{0,1\}^\kappa \times \{0,1\}^\kappa \mapsto \{0,1\}^\kappa$ *is the inversion oracle, where* $\mathbf{d}(\mathsf{tk}, y)$ *outputs* $x \in \{0,1\}^\kappa$ *iff* $\mathbf{e}(\mathbf{g}(\mathsf{tk}), x) = y$.

Definition 3 (Validity of partial oracles). *We say a partial oracle* $\mathbf{O}'$ *(defined only on a subset of all points) is* Ψ-*valid if for some* $\mathbf{O} \in \mathsf{Supp}(\Psi)$: $\mathbf{O}' \subseteq \mathbf{O}$, *where* Supp *denotes the support of a distribution. We say an oracle* $(\mathbf{g}, \mathbf{e}, \mathbf{d})$ *is TDP-valid if it satisfies TDP's perfect completeness. A partial TDP-valid oracle is one which is a subset of a TDP-valid oracle (i.e., a triple* (g, e, d) *that satisfies TDP correctness, but which may not be in the support of* Ψ*). Note that any* Ψ-*valid oracle is TDP-valid as well. We say a partial oracle* $\mathbf{O}'$ *is TDP-consistent with a set of Query/Answer (Q-A in short) pairs* S *if* $\mathbf{O}' \cup \mathsf{S}$ *is TDP-valid.*

4.1   Oracle-Based Target-Restricted Signatures

Toward proving our impossibility results, inspired by [25], we define the notion of oracle-aided target-restricted signatures. The signature's message space is $[n]$, and we require correctness and security to hold with respect to a single, random target point, based on which signing and verification keys are generated. We first present the definition and then compare it to that of [25].

Definition 4 (Target-Restricted signatures [25]**).** *Let* $n = \mathsf{poly}(\kappa)$. *An* n-*target restricted signature scheme* $(\mathrm{Gen}^O, \mathrm{Sig}^O, \mathrm{Ver}^O)$ *relative to an oracle* O *is defined as follows.* $\mathrm{Gen}^O(1^\kappa, m) \to (\mathsf{sgk}, \mathsf{vrk})$: *takes in a security parameter and a target message* $m \in [n]$, *and outputs a signing key* sgk *and a verification key* vrk. *The other algorithms are defined as in standard signature schemes. We require the following properties.*

- δ-*target correctness*:

$$\Pr[\mathrm{Ver}^O(\mathsf{vrk}, m, \mathrm{Sig}^O(\mathsf{sgk}, m)) = 1; m \leftarrow [n], (\mathsf{sgk}, \mathsf{vrk}) \leftarrow \mathrm{Gen}^O(1^\kappa, m)] \geq \delta,$$

  where the probability is taken over $m \leftarrow [n]$, $(\mathsf{sgk}, \mathsf{vrk}) \leftarrow \mathrm{Gen}^O(1^\kappa, m)$ *and the random coins used by* Sig^O *and* Ver^O.
- *Restricted structure: We have* $\mathrm{Ver}^O(\mathsf{vrk}, m, \sigma) = \mathrm{Ver}1(\mathrm{Ver}0^O(\mathsf{vrk}, m), \sigma)$, *where* $\mathrm{Ver}1$ *makes no oracle calls.*
- *Zero-time unforgeability: For any PPT adversary* $\mathcal{A}$,

$$\Pr[\mathrm{Ver}^O(\mathsf{vrk}, m, \sigma) = 1; m \leftarrow [n], (\mathsf{sgk}, \mathsf{vrk}) \leftarrow \mathrm{Gen}^O(1^\kappa, m), \sigma \leftarrow \mathcal{A}^O(\mathsf{vrk}, m)] \leq \mathsf{negl}(\kappa).$$

Zhandry [25] defined oracle-based restricted signatures, where signing and verification keys should work for all messages, and proved such signatures are impossible relative to any oracle. Namely, there exists an adversary that can forge a signature by making at most a polynomial number of queries to the oracle, and by performing possibly exponential-time computations independent of the oracle. In the setting of [25] the message space is of exponential size, but in our setting the message space is $[n]$ and the verification key is allowed to grow with $[n]$. These differences are useful for our setting as we will derive the existence of *target-restricted* signatures during our impossibility proofs. Despite these differences, the following lemma shows that Zhandry's proof, that restricted signatures do not exist, extends almost immediately to our target-restricted setting.

Lemma 1 (Adapted from Lemma 7.4 in [25]**).** *Let* $1 \geq \delta > 0$ *and* O *be an oracle. For any target-restricted signature* Λ *relative to* O *that has* δ *target correctness according to Definition 4, there exists a computationally unbounded adversary which makes only polynomially many queries to* O *that breaks* Λ *with advantage at least* $\delta^3/100$.

The proof of the above lemma is basically the same as the proof of Lemma 7.4 in [25]. At a high level, the proof crucially relies on the restricted structure of the verification algorithm. The key idea of the proof is that since $\mathrm{Ver}^O(\mathsf{vrk}, m, \sigma) =$

Ver1(Ver0^O(vrk, m), σ), a computationally unbounded adversary can first compute an intermediate value $v = \text{Ver0}^O(\text{vrk}, \text{m})$ by itself and then brute force search over the circuit Ver1($v, \cdot$) for a valid signature σ satisfying Ver1(v, σ) = 1. Since target-restricted signatures also have the same restricted structure of verification algorithm, the same proof works. For sake of completeness, in Appendix A we include a full of Lemma 1, which is heavily based on that of [25] and is simply adapted to our setting.

Equipped with Lemma 1, we show any TDP-oracle-based PKCom may be transformed into an oracle-based target-restricted signatures, hence obtaining an impossibility result. As a warm-up and to show our core techniques, we first present this transformation for the CRS-free case in Sect. 4.2 and then present the transformation for schemes with CRS in Sect. B.1.

4.2 Impossibility of CRS-Free PKCom from TDP

We first present the transformation to target-restricted signatures for the case in which the PKCom does not have a CRS. Recall the notions of correctness and security of PKCom given in Definition 1. These notions are defined analogously relative to any fixed oracle $O = (\mathbf{g}, \mathbf{e}, \mathbf{d})$.

Theorem 4. *For*
$\epsilon := \frac{1}{\text{poly}(\kappa)}$ *let* $\mathcal{E}^{\mathbf{g},\mathbf{e},\mathbf{d}} := (\text{Key}^{\mathbf{g},\mathbf{e},\mathbf{d}}, \text{Com}^{\mathbf{g},\mathbf{e},\mathbf{d}}, \text{Enc}^{\mathbf{g},\mathbf{e},\mathbf{d}}, \text{Dec}^{\mathbf{g},\mathbf{e},\mathbf{d}})$ *be a* $(1 - \epsilon)$-*correct PKCom scheme with respect to a random TDP oracle* $O = (\mathbf{g}, \mathbf{e}, \mathbf{d})$. *Suppose a public parameter* pp *under* $\mathcal{E}^{\mathbf{g},\mathbf{e},\mathbf{d}}$ *satisfies* $|\text{pp}| \leq \frac{(n-2)|\text{ik}|}{2}$, *where n is the number of users and* ik *is a base index key (recall* $|\text{ik}| = 3\kappa$, *Defintion 2). Then, there exists a* $(1 - \epsilon)^{\frac{(1-2^{-\kappa/3})}{n}}$-*correct target-restricted signature scheme relative to* $O = (\mathbf{g}, \mathbf{e}, \mathbf{d})$.

Note 1. For all oracle algorithms $A^{\mathbf{g},\mathbf{e},\mathbf{d}}$ considered throughout, we assume whenever a Q-A ((tk, y) $\xrightarrow{\mathbf{d}}$ x) is made by $A^{\mathbf{g},\mathbf{e},\mathbf{d}}$, two dummy queries ($\text{tk}$ $\xrightarrow{\mathbf{g}}$?) and ((ik, x) $\xrightarrow{\mathbf{e}}$?) are subsequently made, where ik = g(tk). Thus, whenever ((tk, y) $\xrightarrow{\mathbf{d}}$ x) is in A's Q-A list, so are (tk $\xrightarrow{\mathbf{g}}$ ik) and ((ik, x) $\xrightarrow{\mathbf{e}}$ y). Moreover, for any A as above, we assume whenever two Q-A pairs (tk $\xrightarrow{\mathbf{g}}$ $*$) and ((ik, x) $\xrightarrow{\mathbf{e}}$ y) are made first, then no subsequent query ((tk, y) $\xrightarrow{\mathbf{d}}$?) is ever made.

Bluebird View of the Proof of Theorem 4. We show how to transform PKComs into target restricted signatures. This is given in Construction 5. The construction is similar to Lamport's signatures from OWFs, adapted to the PKE setting. That is, we generate n public keys $\{\text{pk}_i\}$, put all public keys and all secret keys except the target (hth) one in the verification key. The signature σ on $h \in [n]$ is a secret key for pk_h. The verification function will encrypt a random message m relative to h (performed inside Ver0), and decrypts the ciphertext c inside Ver1 using a signature $\sigma := \text{sk}_h$ to see if it gets m back. First, it is clear that Ver0 can be performed before seeing σ. The most major step is to make sure Ver1 can decrypt c without making queries. To this end, we equip the verification key with Q-A pairs underlying $\{pk_i\}_{i \neq h}$ (called QGen_i in the construction), and we also let Ver0 pass on all Q-A pairs QEnc underlying c to Ver1. The algorithm Ver1 simulates responses to its queries using these sets. The main difficulty is to define the simulated decryption in such a way that we can establish both correctness and security. (For example, letting Ver1 invert any $\mathbf{d}(\mathsf{tk}, y)$ that is "captured" by QEnc and sk_h will make the scheme forgeable, as a forger can cook up some fake sk_h that might pass the test.)

Target-Restricted Signature Construction

We now present our Target-Restricted Signatures construction. In the next sections we argue its correctness and security based on those of the base PKCom.

Construction 5 (Target-Restricted signatures from PKCom) *Suppose we are given a PKCom scheme* $\mathcal{E}^{\mathbf{g,e,d}} := (\mathsf{Key}^{\mathbf{g,e,d}}, \mathsf{Com}^{\mathbf{g,e,d}}, \mathsf{Enc}^{\mathbf{g,e,d}}, \mathsf{Dec}^{\mathbf{g,e,d}})$. *We build an n-target-restricted signature scheme as follows. We assume all the algorithms satisfy the assumption in Note 1.*

- $\mathsf{Gen}^{\mathbf{g,e,d}}(1^\kappa, h)$ *where* $h \in [n]$ *is the message to be signed. For* $i \in [n]$ *let* $\mathsf{QGen}_i = \emptyset$.
    1. *For* $j \in [n]$, *run* $\mathsf{Key}^{\mathbf{g,e,d}}(1^\kappa) \to (pk_j, sk_j)$, *and add all* $\mathbf{g}/\mathbf{e}$ *Q-A pairs to* QGen_j.[9]
    2. *Run* $\mathsf{Com}^{\mathbf{g,e,d}}(pk_1, \ldots, pk_n) \to pp$ *and add all* $\mathbf{g}/\mathbf{e}$ *Q-A pairs to* QCMP.
    3. *Return* $\mathsf{vrk} = ((pk_1, \ldots, pk_n), \cup_{j \neq h} \mathsf{QGen}_j \cup \mathsf{QCMP} \cup \mathsf{L})$, $\mathsf{sgk} = (sk_h, \mathsf{QGen}_h)$.
- $\mathsf{Sig}(\mathsf{sgk}, h) \to \sigma$: *For* sgk *as above, return* $\sigma := (sk_h, \mathsf{QGen}_h)$.
- $\mathsf{Ver}^{\mathbf{g,e,d}}(\mathsf{vrk}, \sigma, h) = \mathsf{Ver1}(\mathsf{Ver0}^O(\mathsf{vrk}, h), \sigma)$: *Parse* $\mathsf{vrk} := ((pk_1, \ldots, pk_n), \mathsf{S})$ *and* $\sigma := (sk_h, \mathsf{QGen}_h)$.
    1. $\mathsf{Ver0}^{\mathbf{g,e,d}}(\mathsf{vrk}, h) \to \alpha := (\mathsf{vrk}, h, m, c, \mathsf{QEnc})$, *where* $(m, c) \leftarrow \mathsf{Enc}^{\mathbf{g,e,d}}(pp, h)$ *and* QEnc *is the set of all Q-A pairs made to* $\mathbf{g}$ *and* $\mathbf{e}$.
    2. $\mathsf{Ver1}(\alpha, \sigma)$: *Retrieve* QEnc *and* S *from* α. *(Recall* $\mathsf{S} = \cup_{j \neq h} \mathsf{QGen}_j \cup \mathsf{QCMP} \cup \mathsf{L}$ *is in* vrk.) *Parse* $\sigma := (sk_h, \mathsf{QGen}_h)$. *Let* $\mathsf{All} = \mathsf{S} \cup \mathsf{QEnc} \cup \mathsf{QGen}_h$. *Run* $\mathsf{DecSim}(h, sk_h, \{pk_i\}, c, (\mathsf{All}, \mathsf{QEnc}, \mathsf{QGen}_h))$, *which simulates the execution of* $\mathsf{Dec}^O(h, sk_h, \{pk_i\}, c)$ *by rendering queries via* $(\mathsf{All}, \mathsf{QEnc}, \mathsf{QGen}_h)$, *as follows:*
        (a) *For a given* $\mathbf{g}$ *or* $\mathbf{e}$ *query, if the answer is already provided in* All, *reply with that answer; else, with a random string z of appropriate length. In case of answering with a random response, add the Q-A pair to* Fake *(initially empty).*[10]
        (b) *For a query* $\mathsf{qu} := ((\mathsf{tk}, y) \xrightarrow{\mathbf{d}} ?)$, *if* $(\mathsf{tk} \xrightarrow{\mathbf{g}} \mathsf{ik}) \in \mathsf{QGen}_h \setminus (\mathsf{S} \cup \mathsf{QEnc})$ *and* $((\mathsf{ik}, x) \xrightarrow{\mathbf{e}} y) \in (\mathsf{All} \setminus \mathsf{QEnc}) \cup \mathsf{Fake}$ *for some* ik *and* x, *respond to*

---

[9] We do not keep track of $\mathbf{d}$ queries because of Note 1.

[10] Duplicate queries will be replied to with the same random response.

qu *with* x. *Else if* $(\mathsf{tk} \xrightarrow{\mathsf{g}} \mathsf{ik}) \in \mathsf{All} \cup \mathsf{Fake}$ *for some* ik, *and* $((\mathsf{ik}, x) \xrightarrow{\mathsf{e}}$
$y) \in \mathsf{All} \cup \mathsf{Fake}$ *for some* x, *respond to* qu *with* x. *Else, respond to* qu
with a random $r \leftarrow \{0,1\}^{\kappa}$.[11]
Letting m' *be the output of* DecSim, *output 1 if* $m' = m$ *and 0 otherwise.*

Proof Overview. Our goal is to show that Construction 5 provides both correctness and security. We first discuss correctness. For that we have to argue that if $(\mathsf{sk}_h, \mathsf{QGen}_h)$ are produced honestly, then DecSim run by Ver1 will output m with high probability. For this we have to argue that DecSim respond to all $\mathbf{g}$, $\mathbf{e}$ and $\mathbf{d}$ queries consistently with how they were responded to before (if ever). For example, if a query qu was previously asked during the generation of, say, pk_i, if the same query is asked again by DecSim, it should receive the same response. It is easy to see that this is the case for both $\mathbf{g}$ and $\mathbf{e}$ queries qu. In particular, in Step 2a of Construction 5 we check if qu is in All, which contains all Q-A pairs up to that point. The challenging case is when qu is a $\mathbf{d}$ query: Step 2b Construction 5 responds to $\mathbf{d}$ queries only in some some special cases: in other cases it gives a random response. One scenario in which this happens is when (a) a Q-A pair $((* \xrightarrow{\mathsf{g}} \mathsf{ik})) \in \mathsf{QGen}_h$; and (b) $((\mathsf{ik}, *) \xrightarrow{\mathsf{e}} ?)* \in \mathsf{QEnc}$ and (c) $((* \xrightarrow{\mathsf{g}} \mathsf{ik})) \notin \cup_i \mathsf{QGen}_{i \neq h} \cup \mathsf{QCMP} \cup \mathsf{QEnc}$. This means that pp brings some ik information from index h (more specifically, from pk_h). We will prove that the probability that this happens is small; our proof makes use of the fact that $|\mathsf{pp}|$ is compact. In particular, given pp, for at least one index i, pp cannot bring ik information about pk_i that is not present in any other pk_j's. We present and prove the compression statement in Lemma 2. This statement is of independent interest and may find applications in some other impossibility results. We will then make use of this compression theorem to formalize and prove the above statement that pp loses 'ik-information' for some index i. Finally, we use this statement to give the correctness proof.

Compression Lemma for TDP Oracles

We present the compression lemma below.

Lemma 2. *Let* $\mathcal{A}^{\mathbf{g},\mathbf{e},\mathbf{d}}(1^{\kappa}) \to z$ *be an arbitrary algorithm (not necessarily poly-query) that outputs a string* z *while calling* $\mathbf{O} = (\mathbf{g}, \mathbf{e}, \mathbf{d})$. *Let* $w := \lceil \frac{2|z|}{3\kappa} + \frac{1}{3} \rceil$. *Let* $\mathcal{B}^{\mathbf{g},\mathbf{e},\mathbf{d}}(z)$ *be an adversary that takes as input* z, *makes at most* $2^{\kappa} - w$ *queries to* $\mathbf{g}$ *and* $\mathbf{d}$ *(in total), and an unlimited number of queries to* $\mathbf{e}$, *and outputs a set* $\mathsf{Chal} = \{\mathsf{ik}_1, \ldots, \mathsf{ik}_t\}$, *where* $w \leq t \leq 2^{\kappa/3}$. *Also, assume* B *satisfies the assumptions in Note 1. Let* Q *be the set of all queries/responses made by* $\mathcal{B}$. *We say* Chal *is non-trivial if for no* $i \in [t]$, $(* \xrightarrow{\mathsf{g}} \mathsf{ik}_i) \in Q$. *We say the event* $\mathsf{Success}$

---

[11] By Note 1, any decryption query is followed by two subsequent $\mathbf{g}$ and $\mathbf{e}$ dummy queries. In the last case where a random response r for (tk, y) is generated, we reply to the subsequent dummy $\mathbf{e}$ query with y.

holds if (i) all index keys in Chal are different, (ii) Chal is non-trivial and (iii) for at least w indices $i_1, \ldots, i_w \in [t]$, $\mathsf{ik}_{i_j} \in \mathbf{g}(*)$ for $j \in [w]$.

We then have $\Pr[\mathsf{Success}] \leq 2^{-\kappa/2}$, where the probability is taken over $(\mathbf{g}, \mathbf{e}, \mathbf{d}) \leftarrow \Psi$ and the random coins of $\mathcal{A}$ and $\mathcal{B}$.

Proof. Assume wlog that both $\mathcal{A}$ and $\mathcal{B}$ are deterministic. We will prove the lemma for any fixing of the oracle $\mathbf{e}$ (note that the oracles $\mathbf{g}$ and $\mathbf{e}$ are independent), obtaining a stronger result.

Since both $\mathcal{A}$ and $\mathcal{B}$ are deterministic, for any fixed oracle $\mathbf{g}$ (in addition to $\mathbf{e}$ already fixed) the event Sucess either holds or not; i.e., the probability of Success is either zero or one with respect to any fixed $\mathbf{g}$. Let $K = 2^\kappa$. We prove that any fixed oracle $\mathbf{g}$ for which Success holds can be uniquely described with

$$f := \log \left(2^{|z|} \binom{K}{w} w! \binom{t}{w} \frac{(K^3 - w)!}{(K^3 - K)!} \right) \tag{1}$$

bits. This means that there exists at most 2^f different Successful oracles. Using the inequalities $(a/b)^b \leq \binom{a}{b} \leq (ae/b)^b$, the fraction of $\mathbf{g}$ oracles for which Success holds is at most the following.

$$\leq \frac{\overbrace{2^{|z|} \binom{K}{w} w! \binom{t}{w} \frac{(K^3 - w)!}{(K^3 - K)!}}^{2^f}}{\underbrace{\frac{K^3!}{(K^3 - K)!}}_{\text{number of } L \text{ oracles}}} = \frac{2^{|z|} \binom{K}{w} \binom{t}{w}}{\binom{K^3}{w}}$$

$$\leq \frac{2^{|z|} (\frac{Ke}{w})^w (\frac{te}{w})^w}{(\frac{K^3}{w})^w} = 2^{|z|} (\frac{e^2 t}{K^2 w})^w \leq 2^{|z|} w! (\frac{8 \times 2^{\kappa/3}}{2^{2\kappa} w})^w$$

$$\leq 2^{|z|} (\frac{1}{2^{(3/2)\kappa} w})^w \qquad (\text{because } \frac{8 \times 2^{\kappa/3}}{2^{2\kappa}} \leq \frac{1}{2^{(3/2)\kappa}} \text{ for large } \kappa)$$

$$\leq 2^{|z|} (\frac{1}{2^{(3/2)\kappa}})^w = \frac{1}{2^{(3/2)\kappa w - |z|}} \leq \frac{1}{2^{\kappa/2}}.$$

The last inequality follows from $\frac{3}{2}kw - |z| \geq k/2$ implied by $w \geq \frac{2|z|}{3\kappa} + \frac{1}{3}$.

We now prove Eq. 1. Fix a Successful oracle $\mathbf{g}$. Let $\mathsf{Chal} = \{\mathsf{ik}_1, \ldots, \mathsf{ik}_t\}$ and wlog assume $\mathsf{ik}_1 <_{\mathsf{lex}} \mathsf{ik}_2 <_{\mathsf{lex}} \cdots <_{\mathsf{lex}} \mathsf{ik}_t$, where $<_{\mathsf{lex}}$ denotes lexicographical ordering. Let $(\mathsf{ik}_{i_1}, \ldots, \mathsf{ik}_{i_w})$ be the w lexicographically smallest elements in Chal that have a pre-image under $\mathbf{g}$, and let $(\mathsf{tk}_{i_1}, \ldots, \mathsf{tk}_{i_w})$ be their pre-images. By Condition (iii) of the lemma such a sequence exists. Let $\mathsf{Chal}_\mathsf{x} := (\mathsf{tk}_{i_1}, \ldots, \mathsf{tk}_{i_w})$. Let U be the set of trapdoor keys tk such that $(\mathsf{tk} \xrightarrow{\mathbf{g}} ?)$ was queried by $\mathcal{B}^{\mathbf{g}, \mathbf{e}, \mathbf{d}}(z)$.

By definition, for any Successful $\mathbf{g}$, we have $\mathsf{U} \cap \mathsf{Chal}_\mathsf{x} = \emptyset$, and hence $\mathsf{U} \subseteq \{0, 1\}^\kappa \setminus \mathsf{Chal}_\mathsf{x}$.

Given $\mathcal{B}$ we claim that any Successful oracle $\mathbf{g}$ can be fully described by z, Chal_x, the index set $\{i_1, \ldots, i_w\}$ and the output of $\mathbf{g}$ on all input points in $\{0, 1\}^\kappa \setminus \mathsf{Chal}_\mathsf{x}$. Indeed, for any $\mathsf{tk} \notin \mathsf{Chal}_\mathsf{x}$, the value $\mathbf{g}(\mathsf{tk})$ is already given. We determine the $\mathbf{g}$ outputs on inputs in Chal_x as follows: Run $\mathcal{B}^{\mathbf{g}, \mathbf{e}, \mathbf{d}}(z)$ to get Chal. We first explain how to reply to $\mathcal{B}$ queries using the provided information.

1. Answering $\mathbf{g}$ queries of $\mathcal{B}$: Since $\mathsf{U} \subseteq \{0, 1\}^\kappa \setminus \mathsf{Chal}_\mathsf{x}$ (recall that U contains the set of $\mathcal{B}$'s queries to $\mathbf{g}$) and that $\mathbf{g}$ is fully determined on $\{0, 1\}^\kappa \setminus \mathsf{Chal}_\mathsf{x}$, we can successfully answer all of $\mathcal{B}$'s $\mathbf{g}$ queries.

2. Answering $\mathbf{e}$ queries of $\mathcal{B}$: the oracle $\mathbf{e}$ is fixed and independent of $\mathbf{g}$.
3. Answering $\mathbf{d}$ queries: for any query $((\mathsf{tk}, y) \xrightarrow{\mathbf{d}} ?)$, by Note 1, $\mathsf{tk} \in \mathsf{U}$, and hence $\mathsf{tk} \in \{0,1\}^\kappa \setminus \mathsf{Chal}_x$. Thus, the value of $\mathsf{ik} := \mathbf{g}(\mathsf{tk})$ can be determined via the provided information. Once ik is known, since $\mathbf{e}$ is also known, we can compute $\mathbf{d}(\mathsf{tk}, y)$.

Thus, the set Chal can be retrieved. After that, sort its elements lexicographically to get $(\mathsf{ik}_1, \dots, \mathsf{ik}_t)$, and use the provided indices $(i_1, \dots, i_w)$ to retrieve $(\mathsf{ik}_{i_1}, \dots, \mathsf{ik}_{i_w})$. Assuming $\mathsf{Chal}_x = (\mathsf{tk}_1, \dots, \mathsf{tk}_w)$ we have $\mathbf{g}(\mathsf{tk}_h) = \mathsf{ik}_{i_h}$ for $h \in [w]$. Thus, $\mathbf{g}$ can be reconstructed on inputs in Chal_x, and hence on all inputs.

We now count f the number of bits sufficient to describe Chal_x, the index set $\{i_1, \dots, i_w\}$ and the output of $\mathbf{g}$ on all of $\{0,1\}^\kappa \setminus \mathsf{Chal}_x$. We can describe the ordered set Chal_x with $\log(\binom{K}{w} w!)$ bits. For describing the (unordered) index set $\{i_1, \dots, i_w\}$, note that all the indices are distinct and each is in $[t]$. Thus, we can describe the index set with $\log \binom{t}{w}$ bits. Finally, we can describe the function $\mathbf{g} : \{0,1\}^\kappa \to \{0,1\}^{3\kappa}$ on $\{0,1\}^\kappa \setminus \mathsf{Chal}_x$ with $\log \frac{(K^3 - w)!}{(K^3 - K)!}$ bits. Equation 1 now follows. $\square$

5   Impossibility in Shoup's Generic Group Model

In this section, we show that there exists a Shoup's GGM oracle relative to which PKCom does not exist. First, we recall Shoup's generic group model [23].

Definition 5. *Let $p \in \mathbb{N}$ be a positive integer and let $S = \{0,1\}^w$ be a set of strings where $w \geq \log p + \kappa$. A random injection* $\mathbf{label} : \mathbb{Z}_p \to S$ *is chosen, which we will call the labeling function. All parties have access to the oracle* $\mathbb{G}_{RR} = (\mathbf{label}, \mathbf{add})$, *defined in the following way.*

- $\mathbf{label}$: *The party submits $x \in \mathbb{Z}_p$, and receives the label of x.*
- $\mathbf{add}$: *The party submits $(\ell_1, \ell_2) \in S^2$. If there exists $x_1, x_2 \in \mathbb{Z}_p$ such that* $\mathbf{label}(x_1) = \ell_1$ *and* $\mathbf{label}(x_2) = \ell_2$, *then the party receives* $\mathbf{label}(x_1 + x_2)$. *Otherwise, the party receives $\perp$. Note that* $\mathbf{label}$ *completely determines* $\mathbf{add}$ *and thus also determines the whole oracle.*

In this section, we will assume that $p \in [2^\kappa, 2^{\kappa+1}]$ and $S = \{0,1\}^{3\kappa}$.

Lemma 3. *Let $\mathcal{A}^{\mathbf{label},\mathbf{add}}(1^\kappa) \to z$ be an arbitrary algorithm (not necessarily poly-query) that outputs a string z while calling $\mathbb{G}_{RR} = (\mathbf{label}, \mathbf{add})$. Let $\mathcal{B}^{\mathbf{label},\mathbf{add}}(z)$ be an adversary that takes as input the advice z, makes at most u queries to* $\mathbf{label}$ *and* $\mathbf{add}$ *in total, and outputs a set of labels* $\mathsf{Chal} = \{\ell_1, \dots, \ell_t\}$ *where $t = 2^{\kappa/3}$. Let $w := \lceil \frac{2(|z|+u)}{3\kappa} + \frac{1}{3} \rceil$. Let Q be the set of all labels that appear in the responses to the queries made by $\mathcal{B}$. We say the event* Success *holds if (i) all ℓ_i's are different, (ii) for no $i \in [t]$, $\ell_i \in Q$, and (iii) for at least w indices $i_1, \dots, i_w \in [t]$, $\ell_{i_j} \in \mathbf{label}(*)$ for $j \in [w]$. We then have* $\Pr[\mathsf{Success}] \leq 2^{-\kappa/2} = \mathsf{negl}(\kappa)$, *where the probability is taken over $L \leftarrow \Psi$ and the random coins of $\mathcal{A}$ and $\mathcal{B}$.*

The proof of Lemma 3 is very similar to the proof of Lemma 2 and thus it is moved to the appendix.

5.1   Impossibility of CRS-Free PKCom in Shoup's GGM

Similar to Sect. 4.2, we first present the transformation to target-restricted signatures for the case in which the PKCom does not have a CRS.

Definition 6. *Let x_ℓ be the variable that is either $\perp$ or x where x is the element in $\mathbb{Z}_p$ whose label is ℓ. If ℓ is invalid label, then x_ℓ is $\perp$.*

Definition 7. *Suppose Q is a set of group operation Q-A pairs. We define $\mathsf{Eq}(\mathsf{Q})$ to be the set of homogeneous linear equations that are directly implied by Q. In other words, for a query $((\ell_1, \ell_2) \xrightarrow{\mathrm{add}} \ell_3) \in \mathsf{Q}$, if $\ell_3 \neq \perp$, we add to $\mathsf{Eq}(\mathsf{Q})$ the equation $x_{\ell_1} + x_{\ell_2} - x_{\ell_3} = 0$.*

Definition 8. *For a set of Q-A pairs Q, define $\mathsf{Var}(\mathsf{Q})$ to be the set of all labels $\ell \neq \perp$ such that $((*, *) \xrightarrow{\mathrm{add}} \ell) \in \mathsf{Q}$.*

Definition 9. *Let LS be the set of all possible labels $\ell \in S = \{0, 1\}^*$ such that $\ell = \mathbf{label}(x)$ for some $x \in \mathbb{Z}_p$. Also, let $\upsilon = \mathbf{label}(1)$.*

Definition 10 (Updating the Known function). *Given a list L of add Q-A pairs, update $\mathsf{Known} \leftarrow \mathsf{Upd}(L)$ as follows. Do the following until no further updates are possible: if there exists $((\ell_1, \ell_2) \xrightarrow{\mathrm{add}} \ell_3) \in L$ such that $\mathsf{Known}(\ell_1) = \top$ or $\mathsf{Known}(\ell_2) = \top$, update $\mathsf{Known}(\ell_3) = \top$.*

Theorem 6. *If there exists a $(1 - \epsilon)$-correct PKCom scheme $(\mathsf{Key}^{\mathbb{G}_{RR}}, \mathsf{Com}^{\mathbb{G}_{RR}}, \mathsf{Enc}^{\mathbb{G}_{RR}}, \mathsf{Dec}^{\mathbb{G}_{RR}})$ in the RR generic group model, then there exists a δ-correct target-restricted signature scheme in the same model where $\delta = (1 - \epsilon)\frac{(1 - 2^{-\kappa/3})}{n}$.*

Construction 7 *Let $(\mathsf{Key}^{\mathbb{G}_{RR}}, \mathsf{Com}^{\mathbb{G}_{RR}}, \mathsf{Enc}^{\mathbb{G}_{RR}}, \mathsf{Dec}^{\mathbb{G}_{RR}})$ be a PKCom scheme. We will assume all queries made to $\mathbb{G}_{RR}$ are add queries since label queries can be answered using add queries given $\upsilon = \mathbf{label}(1)$. We construct a target-restricted signature scheme defined over messages in $[n]$ from the PKCom scheme. We let $\mathsf{Known}\colon \mathsf{LS} \to \{\perp, \top\}$, initially set to $\mathsf{Known}(\upsilon) = \top$, and $\perp$ for all other labels.*

- $\mathsf{Gen}^{\mathbb{G}_{RR}}(1^\kappa, h) \to (\mathsf{sgk}, \mathsf{vrk})$ *where $h \in [n]$ is the message to be signed. For $i \in [n]$ let $\mathsf{QGen}_i = \emptyset$.*
    1. *For $1 \leq j \leq n$, run $\mathsf{Key}^{\mathbb{G}_{RR}}(1^\kappa) \to (\mathsf{pk}_j, \mathsf{sk}_j)$ and add all Q-A pairs made to $\mathbb{G}_{RR}$ to QGen_j.*
    2. *Run $\mathsf{Com}^{\mathbb{G}_{RR}}(\mathsf{pk}_1, \ldots, \mathsf{pk}_n) \to \mathsf{pp}$ and let QCMP be the set of all Q-A pairs made to $\mathbb{G}_{RR}$.*
    3. *Update $\mathsf{Known} \leftarrow \mathsf{Upd}(\cup_{i \neq h}\mathsf{QGen}_i \cup \mathsf{QCMP})$ (Definition 10).*

4. Return $\mathsf{vrk} = ((\mathsf{pk}_1, \ldots, \mathsf{pk}_n), \cup_{j \neq h} \mathsf{QGen}_j \cup \mathsf{QCMP}, \mathsf{Known}, \upsilon)$, $\mathsf{sgk} = (\mathsf{sk}_h, \mathsf{QGen}_h)$.

- $\mathsf{Sig}(\mathsf{sgk}, h) \to \sigma$: For sgk as above, return $\sigma := (\mathsf{sk}_h, \mathsf{QGen}_h)$.
- $\mathsf{Ver}^{\mathbb{G}_{RR}}(\mathsf{vrk}, \sigma, h) \qquad = \qquad \mathsf{Ver1}(\mathsf{Ver0}^{\mathbb{G}_{RR}}(\mathsf{vrk}, h), \sigma) \qquad : \qquad$ *Parse* $\mathsf{vrk} := ((\mathsf{pk}_1, \ldots, \mathsf{pk}_n), \mathsf{A}, \mathsf{Known}, \upsilon)$ and $\sigma := (\mathsf{sk}_h, \mathsf{QGen}_h)$.

1. $\mathsf{Ver0}^{\mathbb{G}_{RR}}(\mathsf{vrk}, h) \rightarrow \alpha := (\mathsf{vrk}, h, m, c, \mathsf{QEnc})$, where $(m, c) \leftarrow \mathsf{Enc}^{\mathbb{G}_{RR}}(\mathsf{pp}, h)$ and QEnc is the set of all Q-A pairs made to $\mathbb{G}_{RR}$.

2. $\mathsf{Ver1}(\alpha, \sigma)$: *Retrieve* QEnc, A and Known from α. Recall $\mathsf{A} = \cup_{j \neq h} \mathsf{QGen}_j \cup \mathsf{QCMP}$. Update $\mathsf{Known} \leftarrow \mathsf{Upd}(\mathsf{QEnc})$. Let $\mathsf{All} = \cup_{j \neq h} \mathsf{QGen}_j \cup \mathsf{QCMP} \cup \mathsf{QEnc}$. Run DecSim which simulates the execution of $\mathsf{Dec}^{\mathbb{G}_{RR}}(h, \mathsf{sk}_h, \{\mathsf{pk}_i\}, c)$ by rendering queries via $(\mathsf{All}, \mathsf{QGen}_h)$, as follows: Initialize two sets $\mathsf{E} = \mathsf{Eq}(\mathsf{All})$ and $\mathsf{V} = \mathsf{Var}(\mathsf{All})$. For a given query $\mathbf{add}(\ell_1, \ell_2)$ do the following:

   (a) If $\ell_1 \notin \mathsf{V} \cup \mathsf{Var}(\mathsf{QGen}_h)$ or $\ell_2 \notin \mathsf{V} \cup \mathsf{Var}(\mathsf{QGen}_h)$, respond to the query with $\perp$.

   (b) Else if both $\ell_1, \ell_2 \in \mathsf{V}$, if there exists $\ell \in \mathsf{V} \cup \mathsf{Var}(\mathsf{QGen}_h)$ such that $x_{\ell_1} + x_{\ell_2} - x_\ell \in \mathsf{Span}(\mathsf{E} \cup \mathsf{Eq}(\mathsf{QGen}_h))$, return ℓ. If no such an ℓ is found, respond with a random label ℓ', add $x_{\ell_1} + x_{\ell_2} - x_{\ell'}$ to E and add ℓ' to V. Also, set $\mathsf{Known}(\ell') = \top$.

   (c) Else if there exists a label ℓ such that $x_{\ell_1} + x_{\ell_2} - x_{\ell'} \in \mathsf{Span}(\mathsf{Eq}(\mathsf{QCMP} \cup_i \mathsf{QGen}_i))$, return ℓ;

   (d) Else, if there exists a label ℓ such that $\mathsf{Known}(\ell) = \top$ and $x_{\ell_1} + x_{\ell_2} - x_\ell \in \mathsf{Span}(\mathsf{E} \cup \mathsf{Eq}(\mathsf{QGen}_h))$, return ℓ. Else, respond with a random label ℓ', add $x_{\ell_1} + x_{\ell_2} - x_{\ell'}$ to E, and add ℓ' to V. Also, set $\mathsf{Known}(\ell') = \top$.

Let m' be the output of DecSim, output 1 if $m = m'$ and 0 otherwise.

Security

Lemma 4 (Security of Construction 7). *Construction 7 is one-time unforgeable if the PKCom scheme is secure.*

Acknowledgements. Mahmoody and Wei were supported by NSF grants CCF-1910681 and CNS1936799. Mohammad Hajiabadi and Sara Sarfaraz were supported by an NSERC Discovery Grant RGPIN-03270, and a Meta Research Award.

A Omitted Proofs

For sake of completeness, here we include a full of Lemma 1, which is heavily based on that of [25] and is simply adapted to our setting.

Proof (of Lemma 1 - adapted from [25]). Consider choosing an oracle O, a random m, and $(\mathsf{sgk}, \mathsf{vrk}) \leftarrow \mathsf{Gen}^O(1^\kappa, m)$, and then fixing them. We will say that σ is "good" if $\Pr[\mathsf{Ver}^O(\mathsf{vrk}, m, \sigma) = 1] \geq \delta/2$, where the probability is taken over the random coins of Ver. By correctness, with probability at least $\delta/2$ over $m, (\mathsf{sgk}, \mathsf{vrk}) \leftarrow \mathsf{Gen}^O(1^\kappa, m)$, there will exist at least one good σ, namely the output of $\sigma \leftarrow \mathsf{Sig}^O(\mathsf{sgk}, m)$.

Suppose Ver0 was deterministic. Then we could compute $v \leftarrow \text{Ver0}^O(\text{vrk}, m)$, and consider the oracle-free probabilistic circuit $C(\sigma) = \text{Ver1}(v, \sigma)$. Then an input σ is good if and only if $C(\sigma)$ accepts with probability at least $\delta/2$. Since C is oracle-free, we can brute-force search for such a σ, finding it with probability at least $\delta/2$. The forgery will then be (m, σ), which is accepted by the challenger with probability $\delta/2$, giving an overall advantage $\delta^2/4$.

For a potentially randomized Ver0, we have to work slightly harder. For a good σ, we have that $\Pr_{v \leftarrow \text{Ver0}^O(\text{vrk}, m)}[\Pr[\text{Ver1}(v, \sigma) = 1] \geq \delta/4] \geq \delta/4$. Meanwhile, we will call a σ "bad" if $\Pr_{v \leftarrow \text{Ver0}^O(\text{vrk}, m)}[\Pr[\text{Ver1}(v, \sigma) = 1] \geq \delta/4] \leq \delta/8$.

For a parameter t chosen momentarily, we let $v_1, \ldots, v_t \leftarrow \text{Ver0}^O(\text{vrk}, m)$, and construct circuits $C_i(\sigma) = \text{Ver1}(v_i, \sigma)$. We then brute-force search for a σ such that $\Pr_{i \leftarrow [t]}[\Pr[C_i(\sigma) = 1] \geq \delta/4] \geq 3\delta/8$. By Hoeffding's inequality, any good σ will be a solution with probability $1 - 2^{-\Omega(\delta^2 t)}$. Meanwhile, any bad σ will be a solution with probability $2^{-\Omega(\delta^2 t)}$. By setting t such that t/δ^2 is sufficiently longer than the bit-length of signatures, we can union bound over all bad δ, showing that there will be no bad solutions except with negligible probability. We will therefore find a not-bad solution with probability at least $\delta/2 - \text{negl} \geq \delta/3$. In this case, with probability at least $\delta/8$ over the choice of v by the verifier, $\Pr[\text{Ver1}(v, \sigma) = 1] \geq \delta/4$. Hence, the overall success probability is at least $(\delta/3) \times (\delta/8) \times (\delta/4) \geq \delta^3/100$. $\qquad\square$

We now present proof of Lemma 3.

Proof (Proof of Lemma 3). Let $s = |\mathcal{S}| = 2^{3\kappa}$. Assume wlog that both $\mathcal{A}$ and $\mathcal{B}$ are deterministic. We prove that any fixed labeling function **label** for which Success holds can be uniquely described with

$$f := \log\left(2^{|z|}\binom{p}{w}w!\binom{t}{w}\frac{(s-w)!}{(s-p)!}2^u w!\right) \qquad (2)$$

bits.

This means that there exists at most 2^f different Successful oracles. Using the inequalities $(a/b)^b \leq \binom{a}{b} \leq (ae/b)^b$, the fraction of g oracles for which Success holds is at most

$$\frac{2^f}{\text{number of } L \text{ oracles}} \leq \frac{2^{|z|+u}w!\binom{p}{w}w!\binom{t}{w}\frac{(s-w)!}{(s-p)!}}{\frac{s!}{(s-p)!}} = \frac{2^{|z|+u}w!\binom{p}{w}\binom{t}{w}}{\binom{s}{w}}$$

$$\leq \frac{2^{|z|+u}w!(\frac{pe}{w})^w(\frac{te}{w})^w}{(\frac{s}{w})^w} = 2^{|z|+u}w!(\frac{e^2 tp}{sw})^w \leq 2^{|z|+u}w!(\frac{16 \times 2^{\kappa/3}}{2^{2\kappa}w})^w$$

$$\leq 2^{|z|+u}w!(\frac{1}{2^{(3/2)\kappa}w})^w \qquad \text{because } \frac{16 \times 2^{\kappa/3}}{2^{2\kappa}} \leq \frac{1}{2^{(3/2)\kappa}} \text{ for large } \kappa$$

$$\leq 2^{|z|+u}(\frac{1}{2^{(3/2)\kappa}})^w = \frac{1}{2^{(3/2)\kappa w - |z| - u}} \leq \frac{1}{2^{\kappa/2}},$$

as desired. The last inequality follows from $\frac{3}{2}kw - |z| - u \geq k/2$, in turn obtained from $w \geq \frac{2(|z|+u)}{3\kappa} + \frac{1}{3}$.

We now prove Eq. 2. Fix a Successful labelling function **label**. Let Chal $=$ $\{\ell_1, \ldots, \ell_t\}$ and wlog assume $\ell_1 <_{\text{lex}} \ell_2 <_{\text{lex}} \cdots <_{\text{lex}} \ell_t$, where $\leq_{\text{lex}}$ denotes lexicographical ordering. Let $(\ell_{i_1}, \ldots, \ell_{i_w})$ be the w lexicographically smallest elements in Chal that have a pre-image under **label**, and let $(x_{i_1}, \ldots, x_{i_w})$ be their pre-images. Let $\text{Chal}_x := \{x_{i_1}, \ldots, x_{i_w}\}$.

We say a query to **add** is *new* for $\mathcal{B}$ if it satisfies the following requirements: (1) the answer to this query is not $\bot$; (2) at least one of the input labels has not been input to queries to **add** made by $\mathcal{B}$ before and the label belongs to Chal. Such labels are called *new* labels. Let New be the list of pre-images to the new labels in the order as they appear in the queries. Let v be a bit string of length u that records the new queries of $\mathcal{B}$ such that the ith bit of v is 1 if and only if the ith query made by $\mathcal{B}$ is a *new* **add** query.

Given $\mathcal{B}$ we claim that any Successful labeling function **label** can be fully described by z, Chal_x, the index set $\{i_1, \ldots, i_w\}$, v, New and the outputs of **label** on all input points in $\mathbb{Z}_p \setminus \text{Chal}_x$. Indeed, for any $x \notin \text{Chal}_x$, the value **label**(x) is already given. We determine the labels of $x \in \text{Chal}_x$ as follows: run $\mathcal{B}^{\textbf{label}, \textbf{add}}(g, z)$ to get Chal. We first explain how to reply to $\mathcal{B}$'s queries using the provided information.

1. Answering **label** queries of $\mathcal{B}$: By condition (ii), we know the answer does not appear in Chal, which means the input of the query does not appear in Chal_x. Since **label** is completely determined on $\mathbb{Z}_p \setminus \text{Chal}_x$, we can successfully answer such queries.
2. Answering **add** queries of $\mathcal{B}$: First note that by assumption, if the answer to the query is not $\bot$, then its pre-image must be in Chal_x, which means we can answer correctly assuming we know the pre-images to the input labels. In the following, we show how to find pre-images with the provided information. Using v, one can tell if the query is new.
   - Suppose the query is new. We then know both of the input labels are valid.
     • If one of the labels has pre-image in $\mathbb{Z}_p \setminus \text{Chal}_x$ or has been seen before, we can retrieve the pre-image of the other label in New.
     • Otherwise, it must be the case that both labels are new and we can retrieve the pre-images in New.
   - Suppose the query is not new.
     • If the answer query to this query is not $\bot$, it must be the case that the labels either have pre-images in $\mathbb{Z}_p \setminus \text{Chal}_x$ or have been seen before, we can answer the queries directly.
     • Otherwise, it must be the case that the answer to this query is $\bot$.

Thus, the set Chal can be retrieved. Once Chal is retrieved, sort its elements to get $(\ell_1, \ldots \ell_t)$ and use the provided $(i_1, \ldots, i_w)$ to retrieve $(\ell_{i_1}, \ldots, \ell_{i_w})$. Assuming $\text{Chal}_x = (x_{i_1}, \ldots, x_{i_w})$, we have **label**$(x_{i_h}) = \ell_{i_h}$ for $h \in [w]$.

We now count f the number of bits required to describe Chal_x, the indices $\{i_1, \ldots, i_w\}$ and **label**'s outputs on all of $\mathbb{Z}_p \setminus \text{Chal}_x$. We can describe the sorted set Chal_x with $\log(\binom{p}{w} w!)$ bits. We can describe the index set with $\log\binom{t}{w}$ bits.

We can describe the function **label** on $\mathbb{Z}_p \setminus \text{Chal}_x$ with $\log \frac{(s-w)!}{(s-p)!}$ bits. The string v has length u. The list New can be described with $\log w!$ bits because we can choose a permutation of the w pre-images whose initial items form the list New. $\square$

B   Attacks on RBE with CRS

B.1   TDP-Impossibility of PKCom with CRS

Theorem 8. *For* $\epsilon := \frac{1}{\text{poly}(\kappa)}$ *let* $\mathcal{E}^{\mathbf{O}} := (\text{CRS}^{\mathbf{O}}, \text{Key}^{\mathbf{O}}, \text{Com}^{\mathbf{O}}, \text{Enc}^{\mathbf{O}}, \text{Dec}^{\mathbf{O}})$ *be a* $(1 - \epsilon)$*-correct PKCom scheme with respect to a random TDP oracle* $\mathbf{O} = (\mathbf{g}, \mathbf{e}, \mathbf{d})$. *Suppose a public parameter* pp *under* $\mathcal{E}^{\mathbf{g}, \mathbf{e}, \mathbf{d}}$ *satisfies* $|\text{pp}| \leq \frac{(n-2)|\text{ik}|}{2}$, *where* n *is the number of users and* ik *is a base index key (recall* $|\text{ik}| = 3\kappa$, *Defintion 2). Also, let* α *be the number of queries made by* $\text{CRS}^{\mathbf{O}}(1^{\kappa}, 1^n)$ *to the oracle* $\mathbf{O}$. *Then, there exists a* $(1 - \epsilon)(1 - \frac{1}{\alpha})^{\frac{(1-2^{-\kappa/3})}{n}}$*-correct target-restricted signature scheme relative to* $\mathbf{O} = (\mathbf{g}, \mathbf{e}, \mathbf{d})$.

We give the construction in Construction 9.

Construction 9. *We construct a* n*-target-restricted signature scheme from any PKCom scheme* $\mathcal{E}^{\mathbf{O}} = (\text{CRS}^{\mathbf{O}}, \text{Key}^{\mathbf{O}}, \text{Com}^{\mathbf{O}}, \text{Enc}^{\mathbf{O}}, \text{Dec}^{\mathbf{O}})$. *The construction is parameterized over an integer* s, *which will be parameterized later; this parameter will only affect the size of the verification key. We assume all the algorithms satisfy the assumption in Note 1.*

- $\text{Gen}^{\mathbf{O}}(1^{\kappa}, h) \rightarrow (\text{sgk}, \text{vrk})$ *where* $h \in [n]$ *is the message to be signed:*
    1. *Run* $\text{CRS}^{\mathbf{O}}(1^{\kappa}, 1^n) \rightarrow \text{crs}$ *and let* QCRS *be the set of all Q-A pairs made to* $\mathbf{g}$ *and* $\mathbf{e}$.[12]

Algorithm 1. SampleKeys(s)

Require: $h \in [n], \text{crs}, \{\text{pk}_i\}_{i \neq h}$
 $\mathsf{K} \leftarrow \phi$
 $j \leftarrow 0$
 while $j < s$ **do**
   $j \leftarrow j + 1$
   $(\text{pk}_h, \text{sk}_h) \leftarrow \text{Key}(1^{\kappa}, \text{crs})$
   $\text{pp} \leftarrow \text{Com}(\text{crs}, \text{pk}_1, \ldots, \text{pk}_h, \ldots, \text{pk}_n)$
   $(m, \text{ct}) \leftarrow \text{Enc}(\text{pp}, h)$
   run $\text{Dec}(\text{crs}, \text{sk}_h, \text{ct})$:
   for qu $= \mathbf{d}(\text{tk}, y)$ **do:**
     $\text{ik} \leftarrow \mathbf{g}(\text{tk})$
     add (tk, ik) to K
   end for
 end while
 return K

---

[12] We do not keep track of $\mathbf{d}$ queries because of Note 1.

2. For $1 \leq j \leq n$, run $\mathsf{Key}^O(1^\kappa, \mathsf{crs}) \to (\mathsf{pk}_j, \mathsf{sk}_j)$. Let QGen_j be the set of all Q-A pairs made to $\mathbf{g}$ and $\mathbf{e}$.

3. Run $\mathsf{Com}^O(\mathsf{crs}, \mathsf{pk}_1, \dots, \mathsf{pk}_n) \to \mathsf{pp}$ and let QCMP be the set of all query response pairs made to $\mathbf{g}$ and $\mathbf{e}$.

4. Run $\mathsf{SampleKeys}(\mathsf{crs}, h, \{\mathsf{pk}_i\}_{i \neq h})$ as defined in Algorithm 1 to obtain a set K.

5. Return $\mathsf{vrk} = ((\mathsf{pk}_1, \dots, \mathsf{pk}_n), \cup_{j \neq h} \mathsf{QGen}_j \cup \mathsf{QCMP}, \mathsf{K})$, $\mathsf{sgk} = (\mathsf{sk}_h, \mathsf{QGen}_h, \mathsf{QCRS})$.

- $\mathsf{Sig}(\mathsf{sgk}, h) \to \sigma$: For sgk as above, return $\sigma = (\mathsf{sk}_h, \mathsf{QGen}_h, \mathsf{QCRS})$.
- $\mathsf{Ver}^{\mathbf{g,e,d}}(\mathsf{vrk}, \sigma, h) = \mathsf{Ver1}(\mathsf{Ver0}^O(\mathsf{vrk}, h), \sigma)$: Parse $\mathsf{vrk} := ((\mathsf{pk}_1, \dots, \mathsf{pk}_n), S, K)$ and $\sigma := (\mathsf{sk}_h, \mathsf{QGen}_h, \mathsf{QCRS})$.

1. $\mathsf{Ver0}^{\mathbf{g,e,d}}(\mathsf{vrk}, h) \to \alpha := (\mathsf{vrk}, h, m, c, \mathsf{QEnc})$, where $(m, c) \leftarrow \mathsf{Enc}^{\mathbf{g,e,d}}(\mathsf{pp}, h)$ and QEnc is the set of all Q-A pairs made to $\mathbf{g}$ and $\mathbf{e}$.

2. $\mathsf{Ver1}(\alpha, \sigma)$: Retrieve QEnc, S and K from α. (Recall $S = \cup_{j \neq h} \mathsf{QGen}_j \cup \mathsf{QCMP} \cup \mathsf{K}$ is in vk.) Parse $\sigma := (\mathsf{sk}_h, \mathsf{QGen}_h, \mathsf{QCRS})$. Let $\mathsf{All} = S \cup \mathsf{QEnc} \cup \mathsf{QGen}_h \cup \mathsf{QCRS}$. Run $\mathsf{DecSim}(\mathsf{crs}, h, \mathsf{sk}_h, \{\mathsf{pk}_i\}, c, (\mathsf{All}, \mathsf{QEnc}, \mathsf{QGen}_h, \mathsf{QCRS}))$,
   which simulates the execution of $\mathsf{Dec}^O(\mathsf{crs}, h, \mathsf{sk}_h, \{\mathsf{pk}_i\}, c)$ by rendering queries via $(\mathsf{All}, \mathsf{QEnc}, \mathsf{QGen}_h, \mathsf{QCRS})$, as follows:

   (a) For a given $\mathbf{g}$ or $\mathbf{e}$ query, if the answer is already provided in All, reply with that answer; else, with a random string z of appropriate length. In case of answering with a random response, add the Q-A pair to Fake (initially empty).[13]

   (b) For a given query $\mathsf{qu} := ((\mathsf{tk}, y) \xrightarrow{\mathbf{d}} ?)$, if for some ik, $(\mathsf{tk} \xrightarrow{\mathbf{g}} \mathsf{ik}) \in (\mathsf{All} \cup \mathsf{Fake})/(\mathsf{QGen}_h \cup \mathsf{QCRS})$ and $((\mathsf{ik}, x) \xrightarrow{\mathbf{e}} c) \in \mathsf{All}$ for some x, respond to the query with x. Else, if for some ik, $(\mathsf{tk} \xrightarrow{\mathbf{g}} \mathsf{ik}) \in \mathsf{QGen}_h \cup \mathsf{QCRS}$ and $((\mathsf{ik}, x) \xrightarrow{\mathbf{e}} y) \in (\mathsf{All}/\mathsf{QEnc}) \cup \mathsf{Fake}$ for some x, respond to the query with x. Else, respond to the query with a random value $r \leftarrow \{0, 1\}^\kappa$.
   Letting m' be the output of DecSim, output 1 if $m' = m$ and 0 otherwise.

B.2 Impossibility of PKCom with CRS in Shoup's GGM

Now, we present the transformation of PKCom to target-restricted signatures while allowing CRS.

Theorem 10. If there exists a $(1-\epsilon)$-correct PKCom scheme ($\mathsf{CRS}^{\mathcal{G}_{RR}}$, $\mathsf{Key}^{\mathcal{G}_{RR}}$, $\mathsf{Com}^{\mathcal{G}_{RR}}$, $\mathsf{Enc}^{\mathcal{G}_{RR}}$, $\mathsf{Dec}^{\mathcal{G}_{RR}}$) in the RR generic group model, then there exists a δ-correct target-restricted signature scheme in the same model where $\delta = (1 - \epsilon)\frac{(1-2^{-\kappa/3})}{n}$.

Construction 11. We construct a target-restricted signature scheme defined over messages in $[n]$ from any PKCom scheme in the following way.

---

[13] Duplicate queries will be replied to with the same random response.

- $\text{Gen}^{\mathbb{G}_{RR}}(1^{\kappa}, h) \rightarrow (\text{sgk}, \text{vrk})$ *where* $h \in [n]$ *is the message to be signed. For* $i \in [n]$ *let* $\text{QGen}_i = \emptyset$.
    1. *Run* $\text{CRS}^{\mathbb{G}_{RR}}(1^{\kappa}, 1^n) \rightarrow \text{crs}$ *and all Q-A pairs made to* $\mathbb{G}_{RR}$ *to* QCRS.
    2. *For* $1 \leq j \leq n$, *run* $\text{Key}^{\mathbb{G}_{RR}}(1^{\kappa}, \text{crs}) \rightarrow (\text{pk}_j, \text{sk}_j)$ *and add all Q-A pairs made to* $\mathbb{G}_{RR}$ *to* QGen_j.
    3. *Run* $\text{Com}^{\mathbb{G}_{RR}}(\text{crs}, \text{pk}_1, \dots, \text{pk}_n) \rightarrow \text{pp}$ *and let* QCMP *be the set of all Q-A pairs made to* $\mathbb{G}_{RR}$.
    4. *Update* $\text{Known} \leftarrow \text{Upd}(\cup_{i \neq h} \text{QGen}_i \cup \text{QCMP} \cup \text{QCRS})$ *(Definition 10)*.
    5. *Return* $\text{vrk} = ((\text{pk}_1, \dots, \text{pk}_n), \cup_{j \neq h} \text{QGen}_j \cup \text{QCMP}, \text{Known}, v)$, $\text{sgk} = (\text{sk}_h, \text{QGen}_h, \text{QCRS})$.
- $\text{Sig}(\text{sgk}, h) \rightarrow \sigma$: *For* sgk *as above, return* $\sigma := (\text{sk}_h, \text{QGen}_h, \text{QCRS})$.
- $\text{Ver}^{\mathbb{G}_{RR}}(\text{vrk}, \sigma, h) = \text{Ver1}(\text{Ver0}^{\mathbb{G}_{RR}}(\text{vrk}, h), \sigma)$: *Parse* $\text{vrk} := ((\text{pk}_1, \dots, \text{pk}_n), A, \text{Known}, v)$ *and* $\sigma := (\text{sk}_h, \text{QGen}_h, \text{QCRS})$.
    1. $\text{Ver0}^{\mathbb{G}_{RR}}(\text{vrk}, h) \rightarrow \alpha := (\text{vrk}, h, m, c, \text{QEnc})$, *where* $(m, c) / \leftarrow \text{Enc}^{\mathbb{G}_{RR}}(\text{pp}, h)$ *and* QEnc *is the set of all Q-A pairs made to* $\mathbb{G}_{RR}$.
    2. $\text{Ver1}(\alpha, \sigma)$: *Retrieve* QEnc, A *and* Known *from* α. *Recall* $A = \cup_{j \neq h} \text{QGen}_j \cup \text{QCMP}$. *Update* $\text{Known} \leftarrow \text{Upd}(\text{QEnc})$. *Let* $\text{All} = \cup_{j \neq h} \text{QGen}_j \cup \text{QCMP} \cup \text{QEnc}$. *Run* DecSim *which simulates the execution of* $\text{Dec}^{\mathbb{G}_{RR}}(\text{crs}, h, \text{sk}_h, \{\text{pk}_i\}, c)$ *by rendering queries via* $(\text{All}, \text{QGen}_h, \text{QCRS})$, *as follows: Initialize two sets* $\text{E} = \text{Eq}(\text{All})$ *and* $\text{V} = \text{Var}(\text{All})$. *For a given query* $\text{add}(\ell_1, \ell_2)$ *do the following:*
        (a) *If* $\ell_1 \notin \text{V} \cup \text{Var}(\text{QGen}_h \cup \text{QCRS})$ *or* $\ell_2 \notin \text{V} \cup \text{Var}(\text{QGen}_h \cup \text{QCRS})$, *respond to the query with* $\bot$.
        (b) *Else if both* $\ell_1, \ell_2 \in \text{V}$, *if there exists* $\ell \in \text{V} \cup \text{Var}(\text{QGen}_h \cup \text{QCRS})$ *such that* $x_{\ell_1} + x_{\ell_2} - x_{\ell} \in \text{Span}(\text{E} \cup \text{Eq}(\text{QGen}_h \cup \text{QCRS}))$, *return* ℓ. *If no such an* ℓ *is found, respond with a random label* ℓ', *add* $x_{\ell_1} + x_{\ell_2} - x_{\ell'}$ *to* E *and add* ℓ' *to* V. *Also, set* $\text{Known}(\ell') = \top$.
        (c) *Else if there exists a label* ℓ *such that* $x_{\ell_1} + x_{\ell_2} - x_{\ell'} \in \text{Span}(\text{Eq}(\text{QCMP} \cup_i \text{QGen}_i \cup \text{QCRS}))$, *return* ℓ;
        (d) *Else, if there exists a label* ℓ *such that* $\text{Known}(\ell) = \top$ *and* $x_{\ell_1} + x_{\ell_2} - x_{\ell} \in \text{Span}(\text{E} \cup \text{Eq}(\text{QGen}_h \cup \text{QCRS}))$, *return* ℓ. *Else, respond with a random label* ℓ' *and add* $x_{\ell_1} + x_{\ell_2} - x_{\ell'}$ *to* E, *and add* ℓ' *to* V. *Also, set* $\text{Known}(\ell') = \top$.

References

1. Boneh, D., Boyen, X.: Secure identity based encryption without random oracles. In: Franklin, M. (ed.) CRYPTO 2004. LNCS, vol. 3152, pp. 443–459. Springer, Heidelberg (2004). https://doi.org/10.1007/978-3-540-28628-8_27
2. Boneh, D., Franklin, M.: Identity-based encryption from the weil pairing. In: Kilian, J. (ed.) CRYPTO 2001. LNCS, vol. 2139, pp. 213–229. Springer, Heidelberg (2001). https://doi.org/10.1007/3-540-44647-8_13
3. Boneh, D., Papakonstantinou, P.A., Rackoff, C., Vahlis, Y., Waters, B.: On the impossibility of basing identity based encryption on trapdoor permutations. In: 49th Annual Symposium on Foundations of Computer Science, pp. 283–292. IEEE Computer Society Press, Philadelphia, PA, USA, 25–28 Oct 2008. https://doi.org/10.1109/FOCS.2008.67

4. Brakerski, Z., Lombardi, A., Segev, G., Vaikuntanathan, V.: Anonymous IBE, leakage resilience and circular security from new assumptions. In: Nielsen, J.B., Rijmen, V. (eds.) EUROCRYPT 2018. LNCS, vol. 10820, pp. 535–564. Springer, Cham (2018). https://doi.org/10.1007/978-3-319-78381-9_20

5. Catalano, D., Fiore, D., Gennaro, R., Giunta, E.: On the impossibility of algebraic vector commitments in pairing-free groups. In: Kiltz, E., Vaikuntanathan, V. (eds.) Theory of Cryptography. TCC 2022. LNCS, Part II, vol. 13748, pp. 279–299. Springer, Cham (2022). https://doi.org/10.1007/978-3-031-22365-5_10

6. Datta, P., Pal, T.: Registration-based functional encryption. Cryptology ePrint Archive, Paper 2023/457 (2023). https://eprint.iacr.org/2023/457

7. Döttling, N., Garg, S.: From selective IBE to full IBE and selective HIBE. In: Kalai, Y., Reyzin, L. (eds.) TCC 2017, Part I. LNCS, vol. 10677, pp. 372–408. Springer, Cham (2017). https://doi.org/10.1007/978-3-319-70500-2_13

8. Döttling, N., Garg, S., Ishai, Y., Malavolta, G., Mour, T., Ostrovsky, R.: Trapdoor hash functions and their applications. In: Boldyreva, A., Micciancio, D. (eds.) CRYPTO 2019, Part III. LNCS, vol. 11694, pp. 3–32. Springer, Cham (2019). https://doi.org/10.1007/978-3-030-26954-8_1

9. Döttling, N., Hartmann, D., Hofheinz, D., Kiltz, E., Schäge, S., Ursu, B.: On the impossibility of purely algebraic signatures. In: Nissim, K., Waters, B. (eds.) TCC 2021, Part III. LNCS, vol. 13044, pp. 317–349. Springer, Cham (2021). https://doi.org/10.1007/978-3-030-90456-2_11

10. Francati, D., Friolo, D., Maitra, M., Malavolta, G., Rahimi, A., Venturi, D.: Registered (inner-product) functional encryption. Cryptology ePrint Archive, Paper 2023/395 (2023). https://eprint.iacr.org/2023/395

11. Garg, S., Hajiabadi, M., Mahmoody, M., Rahimi, A.: Registration-based encryption: removing private-key generator from IBE. In: Beimel, A., Dziembowski, S. (eds.) TCC 2018, Part I. LNCS, vol. 11239, pp. 689–718. Springer, Cham (2018). https://doi.org/10.1007/978-3-030-03807-6_25

12. Garg, S., Hajiabadi, M., Mahmoody, M., Rahimi, A., Sekar, S.: Registration-based encryption from standard assumptions. In: Lin, D., Sako, K. (eds.) PKC 2019. LNCS, vol. 11443, pp. 63–93. Springer, Cham (2019). https://doi.org/10.1007/978-3-030-17259-6_3

13. Gennaro, R., Trevisan, L.: Lower bounds on the efficiency of generic cryptographic constructions. In: 41st Annual Symposium on Foundations of Computer Science, pp. 305–313. IEEE Computer Society Press, Redondo Beach, CA, USA, 12–14 Nov 2000. https://doi.org/10.1109/SFCS.2000.892119

14. Glaeser, N., Kolonelos, D., Malavolta, G., Rahimi, A.: Efficient registration-based encryption. Cryptology ePrint Archive, Paper 2022/1505 (2022). https://eprint.iacr.org/2022/1505, https://eprint.iacr.org/2022/1505

15. Goyal, R., Vusirikala, S.: Verifiable registration-based encryption. In: Micciancio, D., Ristenpart, T. (eds.) CRYPTO 2020, Part I. LNCS, vol. 12170, pp. 621–651. Springer, Cham (2020). https://doi.org/10.1007/978-3-030-56784-2_21

16. Haitner, I., Hoch, J.J., Reingold, O., Segev, G.: Finding collisions in interactive protocols - a tight lower bound on the round complexity of statistically-hiding commitments. In: 48th Annual Symposium on Foundations of Computer Science, pp. 669–679. IEEE Computer Society Press, Providence, RI, USA, 20–23 Oct 2007. https://doi.org/10.1109/FOCS.2007.27

17. Hohenberger, S., Lu, G., Waters, B., Wu, D.J.: Registered attribute-based encryption. In: Hazay, C., Stam, M. (eds.) Advances in Cryptology - EUROCRYPT 2023, pp. 511–542. Springer Nature Switzerland, Cham (2023). https://doi.org/10.1007/978-3-031-30620-4_17

18. Maurer, U.: Abstract models of computation in cryptography. In: Smart, N.P. (ed.) Cryptography and Coding 2005. LNCS, vol. 3796, pp. 1–12. Springer, Heidelberg (2005). https://doi.org/10.1007/11586821_1
19. Papakonstantinou, P.A., Rackoff, C.W., Vahlis, Y.: How powerful are the DDH hard groups? Cryptology ePrint Archive, Report 2012/653 (2012), https://eprint.iacr.org/2012/653
20. Reingold, O., Trevisan, L., Vadhan, S.: Notions of reducibility between cryptographic primitives. In: Naor, M. (ed.) TCC 2004. LNCS, vol. 2951, pp. 1–20. Springer, Heidelberg (2004). https://doi.org/10.1007/978-3-540-24638-1_1
21. Rotem, L., Segev, G., Shahaf, I.: Generic-group delay functions require hidden-order groups. In: Canteaut, A., Ishai, Y. (eds.) EUROCRYPT 2020. LNCS, vol. 12107, pp. 155–180. Springer, Cham (2020). https://doi.org/10.1007/978-3-030-45727-3_6
22. Schul-Ganz, G., Segev, G.: Generic-group identity-based encryption: a tight impossibility result. In: 2nd Conference on Information-Theoretic Cryptography (ITC 2021). Schloss Dagstuhl-Leibniz-Zentrum für Informatik (2021)
23. Shoup, V.: Lower bounds for discrete logarithms and related problems. In: Fumy, W. (ed.) EUROCRYPT 1997. LNCS, vol. 1233, pp. 256–266. Springer, Heidelberg (1997). https://doi.org/10.1007/3-540-69053-0_18
24. Wang, Q., Li, R., Wang, Q., Galindo, D., Chen, S., Xiang, Y.: Transparent registration-based encryption through blockchain. Distrib. Ledger Technol. **2**(1) (2023). https://doi.org/10.1145/3568315
25. Zhandry, M.: To label, or not to label (in generic groups). In: Advances in Cryptology – CRYPTO 2022, Part III. pp. 66–96. Lecture Notes in Computer Science, Springer, Heidelberg, Germany, Santa Barbara, CA, USA (Aug 2022). https://doi.org/10.1007/978-3-031-15982-4_3

Secret Sharing, PIR and Memory Checking

Proactive Secret Sharing with Constant Communication

Brett Hemenway Falk$^{(\boxtimes)}$ ⓘ, Daniel Noble ⓘ, and Tal Rabin ⓘ

University of Pennsylvania, Philadelphia, USA
{fbrett,dgnoble,talr}@seas.upenn.edu

Abstract. This paper presents the first protocols for Proactive Secret Sharing (PSS) that only require constant (in the number of parties, n) communication per party per epoch. By harnessing the power of expander graphs, we are able to obtain strong guarantees about the security of the system. We present the following PSS protocols:
- A PSS protocol that provides *privacy* (but no robustness) against an adversary controlling $\mathcal{O}(n)$ parties per epoch.
- A PSS protocol that provides *robustness* (but no privacy) against an adversary controlling $\mathcal{O}(n)$ parties per epoch.
- A PSS protocol that provides privacy against an adversary controlling $\mathcal{O}(n^a)$ parties per epoch and provides robustness against an adversary controlling $\mathcal{O}(n^{1-a})$ parties per epoch, for any constant $0 \leq a \leq 1$. Instantiating this with $a = \frac{1}{2}$ gives a PSS protocol that is proactively secure (private and robust) against an adversary controlling $\mathcal{O}(\sqrt{n})$ parties per epoch.

Additionally, we discuss how secure channels, whose existence is usually assumed by PSS protocols, are challenging to create in the mobile adversary setting, and we present a method to instantiate them from a weaker assumption.

1 Introduction

Most multiparty protocols provide security as long as no more than a certain threshold of the parties are corrupted, e.g. the Shamir secret-sharing provides security as long as no more than m-out-of-n of the parties are corrupted. These protocols implicitly assume that adversarial corruptions are *static*, i.e., the subset of corrupted parties does not change over time.

The notion of *proactive* security [OY91], considers a *mobile* adversary that can adaptively corrupt different parties, subject to a maximum corruption threshold at a given time. More formally, the model considers a multiparty protocol with n parties, where time is divided into epochs. In each epoch the adversary can corrupt up to m of the n parties, learning their state (and in the malicious model completely controlling their behavior). In the next epoch, the adversary adaptively chooses a new subset of m parties to corrupt, and this continues indefinitely. A protocol that can achieve privacy (or robustness) in the face of this type of mobile adversary is said to be *proactively secure*.

© International Association for Cryptologic Research 2023
G. Rothblum and H. Wee (Eds.): TCC 2023, LNCS 14370, pp. 337–373, 2023.
https://doi.org/10.1007/978-3-031-48618-0_12

When considering proactive security, it is sufficient to consider Proactive Secret Sharing (PSS), i.e., secret-sharing schemes that can achieve privacy (and/or robustness) in the face of a mobile adversary. This is because any MPC protocol that computes on secret shares can be made proactively secure by simply assuming that each round of the MPC protocol happens *within* a single epoch. With this assumption, the adversary is essentially static with respect to the MPC protocol, and security follows immediately from the proactive security of the underlying secret sharing scheme together with the (static) security of the MPC protocol. Thus, previous works focused on building proactive secret sharing protocols, with the understanding that PSS protocols can be used as the substrate for general secure multiparty computation secure against mobile adversaries.

In addition to the design of the secret sharing protocol, i.e., the refreshing of shares, there is an orthogonal issue which needs to be addressed: the creation and re-establishing of the secure communication channels between the parties after (potential) adversarial corruptions. Previous works either simply assume that an infrastructure for secure channels exists, or have solutions to create secure channels that require (at least) $\Theta(n)$ communication per party per epoch, where n is the number of parties. We detail the prior art in Appendix A with an abridged version in Sect. 2.

Our Results

Given the communication complexity of prior constructions, the natural question to ask is whether this $O(n)$ communication for PSS is inherent or whether there exist protocols with sublinear communication. In this work, assuming a synchronous network, we present the first PSS protocol for single (unbatched) secrets that achieves sublinear communication. Surprisingly, we show that PSS is possible against passive mobile adversaries corrupting $\Theta(n)$ parties per epoch with only constant (in n) communication per party! Furthermore, we present a PSS protocol that is secure against *active* mobile adversaries corrupting $\Theta(\sqrt{n})$ parties per epoch that also has constant (in n) communication.

Assuming the existence of secure communication channels we show three PSS protocols with constant communication per party. Our first protocol provides secrecy for the shared value, but offers no robustness, i.e. it works only against a passive adversary (Sect. 5). The second provides robustness but no privacy, that is a malicious adversary cannot corrupt the secret (Sect. 6). Finally, we combine the first two protocols to provide both secrecy and robustness (Sect. 7). Our first two protocols are secure against an adversary corrupting $\Theta(n)$ parties per epoch while our third is only secure against an adversary corrupting $\Theta(\sqrt{n})$ parties per epoch. We note, however, that because our per-epoch communication cost is so low, we can set our epoch times to be *much* shorter than existing PSS protocols, which would reduce the number of parties that an adversary can corrupt during an epoch (see Appendix C).

Note that while the number of messages sent per party per epoch is constant, and the size of each message is independent of n, the message sizes do depend on two other parameters. Like any other PSS protocol, our message sizes depend on the size of the secret, $|\mathbb{F}|$. For notational simplicity we assume $|\mathbb{F}| = \mathcal{O}(1)$. Messages sizes may also depend on the computational security parameter, κ. Assuming secure channels, our first and second protocols do not depend on κ, while our third protocol has messages of size $\mathcal{O}(\kappa)$. Note that some works use batching to combine many secrets to obtain low communication cost per secret. We *do not use batching*; our results hold even if there is only a single secret.

Secure communication channels are required for PSS, so we also develop a method for establishing secure channels between parties that requires only $\mathcal{O}(\kappa)$ communication per party per epoch (Sect. 8). Using this protocol to instantiate secure channels (instead of simply assuming secure channels exist) increases the communication complexity of our first and second PSS protocols to $\mathcal{O}(\kappa)$ while our third PSS protocol remains $\mathcal{O}(\kappa)$. Our method requires a minimal trusted hardware assumption: that each party has access to a secure signing oracle. The adversary may make the oracle sign arbitrary messages when the party is corrupted, but cannot learn the secret key. This is a *much* weaker assumption than that of secure hardware channels, and is implemented by many common devices such as Yubikeys or iOS Secure Enclaves.

Our third PSS protocol can be easily modified to achieve a different cryptographic primitive called Proactive Pseudorandomness (PP), that is a protocol which enables a set of parties to preserve the ability to generate pseudorandomness in the face of a mobile adversary, despite no access to true randomness. Our protocol requires only $\mathcal{O}(\kappa)$ communication per-party per epoch and maintains (global) pseudorandomness against a mobile adversary controlling $\Theta(n)$ parties per epoch. Note that previous protocols required $\mathcal{O}(n)$ communication. This is presented in Sect. 9.

Our PSS protocols rely on expander graphs and in Sect. 4 we provide the properties and theorems for these graphs that we need in our design. Instead of requiring that each party communicate with every other party, each party communicates with only a constant number of neighbors, where the assignment of neighbors is chosen according to an expander graph.

Because each party only communicates with a constant number of other parties, it is possible that an honest party be entirely surrounded by corrupt parties. As such, the adversary may learn the honest party's state (by knowing all messages sent to it) or may cause an honest party to behave incorrectly (by sending it incorrect messages). Our security guarantees therefore will not be local: they will not necessarily apply to every honest party. Instead we prove *global* security properties that hold over the entire system, e.g. that the adversary is not able to learn a secret that has been shared between all parties, or that the adversary cannot cause most parties to behave incorrectly. Intuitively, these global security properties will hold because the expansion property of the communication network ensures that the set of honest parties at different times remain generally well-connected to each other.

2   Related Work

A full related work section appears in Appendix A. Table 1 shows the communication complexity of the works discussed there, as well as our own results. Here we only provide details of a few of the works.

Table 1. m-out-of-n PSS schemes. ℓ: batch size. $\epsilon > 0$ is a constant.

Work	Communication	Threshold	Synchrony
[HJKY95]	$O(n)$	$n = 2m + 1$	sync
[CKLS02]	$O(n^3)$	$n = 3m + 1$	async
[SLL10]	$O(n)$	$n = 3m + 1$	async
[ZSVR05]	$\exp(n)$	$n = 3m + 1$	async
[BEDLO14]	$O(n/\ell)$	$n = 2(m + \ell) + 1$	sync
[ELL20]	$O(n^2/\ell)$	$n = m + \sqrt{\ell} + 1$	sync
[MZW+19]	$O(n^2)$	$n = 2m + 1$	sync
[YXD22]	$O(n^2 \log n)$	$n = 4m + 1$	async
Protocol 1 (passive adversary)	$O(1)$	$n = (1 + \epsilon)m$	sync
Protocol 3	$O(\kappa)$	$n = (2 + \epsilon)m^2$	sync

Proactive secret sharing considers the problem of maintaining the *privacy* and *robustness* of a shared secret in the presence of a *mobile* adversary [OY91]. In the mobile-adversary model, time is divided into "epochs," and the adversary is allowed to corrupt a new subset of parties in every epoch.

In order for PSS to be feasible, we must assume that parties can be securely "rebooted," an operation which leaves them in a fresh (uncorrupted) state. We must also assume that parties can securely delete information, otherwise an adversary corrupting a party in one epoch could learn their shares from previous epochs, which would make it impossible to maintain privacy.

Essentially all PSS protocols are built around the idea of "refreshing" the parties' shares at every epoch. One method of refreshing shares is to simply have all parties generate a random sharing of zero, and then add these shares to the shares of the original secret [HJKY95]. This effectively re-randomizes the shares, and ensures that shares the adversary learns from different epochs cannot be combined. An alternative strategy for refreshing is to have each party re-share their share, then use the linearity of the secret-sharing protocol to have each party locally reconstruct a new share of the original secret [CKLS02]. Other works [ELL20, MZW+19, YXD22] share using bivariate polynomials. To achieve privacy against *malicious* adversaries, the underlying secret sharing protocol can be replaced with a Verifiable Secret Sharing protocol (e.g. [Fel87]).

Some PSS protocols (e.g. [SLL10, BDLO15]) consider *dynamic committees*, i.e., they assume that committees in different epochs may contain different (possibly disjoint) sets of parties, and that the threshold may also change between epochs. Some PSS protocols (e.g. [CKLS02, ZSVR05, SLL10, YXD22]) consider an *asynchronous* model of communication, meaning that although parties are synchronized across epochs, messages can be arbitrarily delayed by the adversary *within* an epoch. In this work, we consider *synchronous communication*.

The goals of PSS protocols are to tolerate a higher corruption threshold (usually $n/2$ or $n/3$) and to reduce communication complexity. Every previous PSS protocol requires all-to-all communication during the refresh phase, and thus every PSS protocol has at least $O(n)$ communication per party per epoch (and many have $O(n^2)$ or even $O(n^3)$).

One way to improve *amortized* communication complexity is to consider batches of secrets, which can then be refreshed simultaneously [BDLO15, BDLO15, ELL20]. By considering batches of $O(n)$ secrets, some PSS protocols are able to achieve *amortized* constant in n communication complexity per party per epoch. This work is the first to achieve communication complexity that is constant in n *without amortization* (see Sect. 7). In some applications, batching is appropriate, but in others the secret is inherently short. For instance, one of the most common applications of (proactive) secret-sharing is to store private keys for cryptocurrency wallets. In this case, the secret is a single private signing key, usually of size 256 bits. This would be much too small to benefit from batching.

One interesting feature of the mobile-adversary model is the problem of how secure channels are created and maintained between the parties. Essentially all multiparty protocols assume the parties are connected via secure, authenticated channels. In most situations, these secure channels can be achieved via a PKI – each party has a key pair for an authenticated encryption scheme. Unfortunately, in the mobile-adversary setting the existence of a PKI can no longer create secure channels, since once an adversary has corrupted a party, they would learn the party's long-term secret keys and would be able to impersonate that party and decrypt all messages to that party in future epochs. This problem was explored in depth in [CHH97], but their solution is rather cumbersome and re-establishing secure channels every epoch requires at least $O(n)$ communication per party. Many PSS protocols (e.g. [OY91, CKLS02, BEDLO14, MZW+19, YXD22]) still assume that all parties are connected via secure channels.

In Sect. 8 we give a simple solution to the problem of reinstating secure channels in the mobile adversary model, assuming each party has access to a lightweight signing oracle (such as can be found in any modern smartphone or hardware-based cryptocurrency wallet). Our solution for regenerating channel keys can be used with any existing PSS protocol. It is very light—it only requires $\mathcal{O}(\kappa)$ communication to establish a channel—so is compatible with our low-communication PSS protocols.

3   Model

Secrets and Shares. We assume that there is a single secret, denoted s, from some group $\mathbb{F}$, that is (honestly) distributed by a trusted dealer before the protocol begins, resulting in each party holding a share. In addition, we require that the dealer distributes initial PRG keys.

Epochs. We divide time into *epochs* consisting of two phases, *refresh* and *retain*. The PSS protocol describes the *refresh* phase, while the *retain* phase encompasses what parties do with their share outside of the PSS protocol.

1. **Refresh:**
   (a) Reboot
   (b) Establish secure channels
   (c) Send messages
   (d) Securely delete old share (everything except current private key)
   (e) Receive messages and compute new share
   (f) Securely delete keys (everything except new share)
2. **Retain:** Parties may use their share, e.g. in the context of an MPC protocol.

Mobile Adversaries. The set of parties in the protocol is denoted $\{P\}_{i=1}^{n}$, and communication is *synchronous*.

The adversary, $\mathcal{A}$, is *mobile*, which means that it can corrupt m(out of n) parties in each epoch, where m is a function of n. When $\mathcal{A}$ corrupts a party, it is allowed to see all its messages. If $\mathcal{A}$ is malicious, it can cause the party to deviate from the protocol. Furthermore, $\mathcal{A}$ is *rushing*: it can wait to receive all incoming messages before sending any messages.

We assume parties can securely delete data and have access to fresh randomness. We instantiate secure, authenticated channels between parties using a (hardware-based) signing oracle. Alternatively, we can simply assume the existence of secure channels.

Reboots. To handle such an adversary, we assume that it is possible to remove the adversary's control of a party by a *reboot* operation. Rebooting a party will cause the adversary to lose all access to new information and will cause the party to return to executing the correct program.

A party is *corrupted* if it has been corrupted, but not (yet) been rebooted. It is *honest* otherwise. By periodically applying reboots, we can limit the number of parties that are corrupted at any time.

Counting Corruptions. A party which is corrupted during the retain portion of epoch t is considered corrupt, and counted against the budget of the adversary in epoch t. As in [HJKY95], we consider that when an adversary corrupts a party during the *refresh* phase of epoch t, this counts towards the adversary's corruption budget of epoch t *and* epoch $t - 1$.

When the committee in epoch $t + 1$ is disjoint from the committee in epoch t, there is no need to double count parties who are corrupted during the refresh phrase. Thus it is typical, when considering dynamic committees, to give the adversary the power to corrupt up to m-out-of-n parties in the old committee as well as m-out-of-n of parties in the new committee.

Security. Most PSS protocols simultaneously achieve both *privacy* and *robustness*. *Privacy* ensures that the adversary gains no advantage in guessing the secret. *Robustness* ensures that the adversary cannot cause the reconstructed value to differ from the secret which was shared. In this work, we will sometimes consider these two properties separately.

For both private and robust protocols, we will show protocols secure against *malicious* (active) adversaries. Our protocols will either provide *perfect* security, ensuring that a property (privacy or robustness) always holds, or they will provide *computationally* security, ensuring that a property holds except with non-negligible probability against a computationally bounded adversary.

Reconstruction. In our protocols it is impossible to guarantee that *every* honest party holds a valid share at every step of the protocol. This is because each party communicates with only a constant number of other parties, so it is possible that an honest party is entirely surrounded by corrupted parties. Since this type of "eclipse attack" is unavoidable in our model, we consider a slightly different form of correctness in our constructions. We consider a PSS protocol robust if, in any given epoch, there exists a reconstruction protocol, which would allow the (honest) parties to reconstruct the original secret. The key distinction here is that the reconstruction procedure may require linear communication (e.g. all parties send their shares to every other party), but since the reconstruction procedure is not actually run in each epoch, the amortized communication per epoch can still be sub-linear.

4 Expander Graphs

The key tool in our protocols is expander graphs. These are graphs which, despite a small number of edges, remain well connected, for certain metrics of connectedness. In particular we will examine *bipartite* graphs, that is $G = (L \cup R, E)$ where $E \subset L \times R$. Our graphs will be *balanced*, that is $|L| = |R| = n$. Furthermore, our graphs will be *d-regular*, that is every vertex (whether in the "left" side L, or the "right" side R) will have exactly d neighbors, where d is a constant.[1]

The metric of connectedness that is most relevant to our work is *vertex expansion*, which is formally defined below:[2]

Definition 1 (Vertex expansion). *A bipartite graph $G = (L \cup R, E)$, is called a (γ, α)-expander if for every set $S \subset L$, with $|S| \leq \gamma n$, and letting $N(S)$ represent the set of neighbors of vertices in S, we have*

$$|N(S)| \geq \alpha |S|$$

Concretely, we use bipartite d-regular Ramanujan graphs. These are expander graphs that are essentially optimal according to another metric: spectral expansion. Appendix B contains a more detailed explanation of Ramanujan graphs and spectral expansion, as well as standard proofs that they have the properties we require (Theorems 1 and 2 below). Bipartite d-regular Ramanujan graphs

---

[1] A d-regular bipartite graph is always balanced since, $|E| = d|L| = d|R| \Rightarrow |L| = |R|$.
[2] While this definition is valid for the case $\alpha \leq 1$, we will only be interested in the case where $\alpha > 1$, i.e. there is actual *expansion*.

can be constructed in polynomial time for all degrees and sizes [MSS13] [MSS18] [Coh16]. Since Ramanujan graphs have optimal spectral expansion, they also have good vertex expansion:

Theorem 1. *A Ramanujan graph is a* $\left(\gamma, \frac{1}{(1-\gamma)\frac{4}{d}+\gamma}\right)$ *expander* $\forall\ \gamma \in [0,1]$.

Essentially, the property above will be useful when, if a party has one good neighbor, it will also be good, for some definition of good to be defined later. In other situations, a party will only be good if it has a *majority* of good neighbors. In such cases, we will need the following property of Ramanujan graphs.

Theorem 2. *Ramanujan graphs have the following property. Let S be a set of size at most δn vertices on the left. Then at most*

$$\frac{4\delta n}{(\frac{1}{2} - \delta)^2 d}$$

right-hand vertices have at least $\frac{1}{2}$ of their neighbors in S.

5 $\mathcal{O}(n)$-Private PSS with Constant Communication

In this section we present a PSS protocol that is perfectly private (but not robust) in the presence of an adversary that can corrupt up to δn parties per epoch, for some constant $0 < \delta < 1$.

Remark 1. In the case of *passive* adversaries, the privacy-only PSS protocol described is actually a full-blown PSS protocol, since passive adversaries cannot modify the shares. In this section, we prove a slightly stronger result, that the protocol achieves privacy in the face of an active (malicious) adversary.

As a warmup, consider the following simple (private-only) PSS protocol. The secret, s, is additively distributed among the players. That is, in epoch t, party P_i holds $s_i^{(t)}$ where $\sum_{i=1}^{n} s_i^{(t)} = s$. To refresh each party additively reshares its share to all other parties. Then, by summing the shares-of-shares it receives, each party gains a new re-randomized share of the secret original secret.

In our protocol, instead of each party additively resharing its share to all other parties, it only reshares to a constant number of neighbors. These neighbors are chosen according to an expander graph.

Definition 2 (Choosing Neighbors according to a Graph). *Let $G = (V, E)$ be a bipartite graph, with parts $L = \{L_1, \ldots, L_n\}$ and $R = \{R_1, \ldots, R_n\}$. If a protocol with parties $P_1, \ldots, P_n$, chooses neighbors according to G it means that P_j is a neighbor of P_i iff $(L_i, R_j) \in E$. Note that the neighborhood relation is not reflexive. Let $N(i)$ return the indices of the neighbors of P_i, and $N^{-1}(j)$ return the indices of parties that P_j is a neighbor of.*

Remark 2 (Fixed graph). The graph G will always be public and fixed. Thus, the attacker can therefore choose its corruptions with full knowledge of G.

At the beginning of each epoch, each party holds an additive share of the secret, $s \in \mathbb{F}$. For each epoch t, party P_i will hold a single share $s_i^{(t)} \in \mathbb{F}$, where $\sum_{1 \leq i \leq n} s_i^{(t)} = s$. The secret is reshared according to a constant-degree bipartite expander. This makes it very efficient, as each party only has to send a constant number of messages.[3] The expansion property of the underlying graph, G, will guarantee that a mobile adversary (controlling a constant fraction of the parties in each epoch) will not learn enough shares to reconstruct the secret.

Protocol 1 describes a scheme that achieves $\Theta(n)$ proactive privacy with only $\Theta(1)$ communication per player, yet it does not provide robustness.

Protocol 1: Private Efficient PSS

Parameters:
Let $G = (L \cup R, E)$ be a d-regular bipartite Ramanujan (γ, α) expander, with parts $L = \{L_1, \ldots, L_n\}$ and $R = \{R_1, \ldots, R_n\}$. We choose neighbors according to graph G.

1. **Setup:**
   The dealer divides the secret using an additive secret sharing, i.e., P_i receives $s_i^{(1)}$ for $1 \leq i \leq n$, where $s_i^{(1)}$ are chosen uniformly at random from $\mathbb{F}$ subject to the constraint that $\sum_{i=1}^{n} s_i^{(1)} = s$.
2. **Resharing:**
   (a) At the start of epoch t, party P_i generates a share-of-share $s_{i,j}^{(t)}$ for each neighbor P_j and sends the message to P_j. The shares are chosen uniformly at random subject to the constraint $\sum_{j \in N(i)} s_{i,j}^{(t)} = s_i^{(t)}$. P_i sends $s_{i,j}^{(t)}$ to P_j.
   (b) P_j receives values $s_{i,j}^{(t)}$ for each $i \in N^{-1}(j)$. It computes:
   $s_j^{(t+1)} = \sum_{i \in N^{-1}(j)} s_{i,j}^{(t)}$.

Theorem 3. *Protocol 1 is a correct resharing, i.e., the constructed secret would remain the same if all parties follow the protocol.*

Proof. By induction. For epoch 1, $\sum_{i=1}^{n} s_i^{(1)} = s$.
Assume for epoch t, $\sum_{i=1}^{n} s_i^{(t)} = s$. Then for epoch $t+1$,

$$\sum_{j=1}^{n} s_j^{(t+1)} = \sum_{j=1}^{n} \sum_{i \in N^{-1}(j)} s_{i,j}^{(t)} = \sum_{(L_i, R_j) \in E} s_{i,j}^{(t)} = \sum_{i=1}^{n} \sum_{j \in N(i)} s_{i,j}^{(t)} = \sum_{i=1}^{n} s_i^{(t)} = s.$$

---

[3] In order to instantiate secure channels as described in Sect. 8, each party will also have to send messages to its neighboring parties, but this will not change the fact that each party only communicates with $O(1)$ other parties in each epoch.

We now demonstrate that this protocol maintains privacy against a mobile adversary who can corrupt $\mathcal{O}(n)$ parties per epoch. There are essentially three ways that a mobile adversary can learn a party's share in a given epoch: it can corrupt a party in the current epoch, or it corrupts all the party's neighbors in the previous epoch, or all of the party's neighbors in the subsequent epoch.

To prove the privacy of Protocol 1, let us consider the communication graph, H. We will represent parties as vertices and messages as edges. Since whether a party is corrupt or honest depends on the epoch, we will actually have a different vertex for every party in every epoch. Vertex $H_i^{(t)}$ will represent P_i in epoch t. If P_i is corrupted in epoch t, we also call vertex $H_i^{(t)}$ corrupted; otherwise we call the vertex honest. We let $H^{(t)} = \{H_1^{(t)}, \ldots, H_n^{(t)}\}$, i.e. all vertices that represent parties from epoch t. We call $H^{(t)}$, *layer* t of the graph H. There are therefore at most δn corrupted vertices in each layer of H.

We put a directed edge[4] from $H_i^{(t)}$ to $H_j^{(t+1)}$ if P_i sends a message to P_j in epoch $t+1$. Since communication is according to expander G, edge $(H_i^{(t)}, H_j^{(t+1)})$ exists in H if and only if (L_i, R_j) is an edge in G. To make the graph finite, we set some arbitrarily large upper limit, T on the number of epochs.

We will be able to prove privacy of Protocol 1 by examining *paths* in H. In particular, we are concerned with *honest* paths, which are paths in which every vertex is honest. Recall that edges are directed; paths will follow the same orientation as edges. Since all edges are from a vertex from some layer t to a vertex in layer $t + 1$, the vertices in a path will be from contiguous layers. We call a path *ancient* if the first vertex in the path is in $H^{(1)}$.

We now prove some properties of the graph H. This will later allow us to prove the desired security properties of Protocol 1.

Lemma 1. *Let γ and α be constants such that G is a (γ, α) expander. Let H be defined as above. If there are at most δn corrupted vertices per layer, and $\delta \leq \gamma(\alpha - 1)$ then for every t, there exist at least γn vertices in $H^{(t)}$ that are part of ancient honest paths.*

Proof. First, note that for any expander, $\gamma\alpha \leq 1$, so $\delta \leq \gamma(\alpha - 1)$ also implies:

$$\delta \leq \gamma\alpha - \gamma \Rightarrow \delta \leq 1 - \gamma \Rightarrow \gamma \leq 1 - \delta$$

We show by induction that for any $1 \leq t \leq T$, there exist at least γn vertices in layer t that are part of ancient honest paths.

For $t = 1$, any honest vertex is on an ancient honest path consisting only of itself. There are at least $(1 - \delta)n$ honest vertices, and $(1 - \delta) \geq \gamma$.

Assume for epoch t. We now show it holds for epoch $t + 1$. If $H_i^{(t+1)}$ is honest, and is a neighbor of some vertex $H_j^{(t)}$ that is part of an ancient honest

---

[4] This assumes a secure channel is already established between P_i and P_j. If Protocol 4 is used to re-establish a secure channel, P_j will also need to send messages to P_i, but we do not represent this on the graph. Also, if a corrupted P_i *should* send a message to P_j but doesn't, we consider this as P_i sending some default message.

path, then appending $H_i^{(t+1)}$ to this path results in a path that is still ancient and honest and includes $H_i^{(t+1)}$. By induction, there are at least γn vertices in epoch $H^{(t)}$ that are part of ancient honest paths. Due to the expansion property, there must be at least $\alpha \gamma n$ vertices in epoch $H^{(t+1)}$ that are neighbors of these vertices, at most δn of which are corrupted. Therefore, there are at least $(\alpha\gamma - \delta)n$ vertices in $H^{(t+1)}$ are part of ancient honest paths. $\delta \leq \gamma(\alpha - 1)$, so $(\alpha\gamma - \delta)n \geq (\alpha\gamma - (\alpha - 1)\gamma)n \geq \gamma n$. Thus, by induction, at least γn vertices in $H^{(t+1)}$ are part of honest ancient paths.

Note that if vertex $H_i^{(t)}$ is on an honest ancient path, this does not guarantee that $\mathcal{A}$ does not learn P_i's share in epoch t. It guarantees that $\mathcal{A}$ did not learn P_i's share directly by corrupting it or by learning all messages it received. However, if $\mathcal{A}$ corrupts all of P_i's neighbors in epoch $t+1$ it will learn all messages P_i sent and thus learn P_i's share in epoch t.

However, the fact that there are honest paths to all future epochs $t' > t$, implies that there is at least 1 vertex in epoch t which is part of these paths, and for which $\mathcal{A}$ did not learn the outgoing messages. This is essentially sufficient to show that privacy is preserved. Formally, Lemma 1 implies the following:

Corollary 1. *If $\delta \leq \gamma(\alpha - 1)$ there exists an honest path from $H^{(1)}$ to $H^{(T)}$.*

We will now use this property of H to prove the security of Protocol 1.

Lemma 2. *If there exists an honest path from $H^{(1)}$ to $H^{(T)}$, then for all possible secrets $s_A, s_B \in \mathbb{F}$, the probability that $\mathcal{A}$ guesses output s_A when $s = s_A$ is the same as the probability that $\mathcal{A}$ guesses s_A when $s = s_B$.*

Proof. Recall that H represents the communication network of the protocol. Therefore, the existence of an honest path from $H^{(1)}$ to $H^{(T)}$ means that there are a sequence of parties, $P_{f(1)}, \ldots P_{f(T)}$ such that $P_{f(t)}$ is honest in epoch t and that $P_{f(t+1)}$ is a neighbor of $P_{f(t)}$. This means that $\mathcal{A}$ does not see the shares that these parties hold in the epochs in which they are honest: $s_{f(1)}^{(1)}, \ldots, s_{f(T)}^{(T)}$. Nor does $\mathcal{A}$ see the messages sent between these parties in the epochs in which they are honest: $s_{f(1),f(2)}^{(1)}, \ldots, s_{f(T-1),f(T)}^{(T-1)}$.

Since $\mathcal{A}$ cannot see these messages and shares, it is possible for them to be modified without $\mathcal{A}$ being able to detect it. Clearly, consistency has to be maintained: a share must be the sum of all messages received in that epoch. Likewise the messages sent in an epoch must sum to the share. If these shares and messages were all incremented by some value Δ, consistency would be maintained. Each party on the path would receive one message that was Δ larger, would hold a share that was Δ larger and would send one message that was Δ larger.

We can therefore consider 2 executions. In one, the secret is s_A. In another the secret is s_B and all messages and shares along the path are incremented by $\Delta = s_B - s_A \neq 0$. All other messages and shares are the same in both executions. Therefore, the information available to $\mathcal{A}$ is the same in both executions.

The probability of the first execution occurring when $s = s_A$ is exactly the same as the probability of the second execution occurring when $s = s_B$. Most parties will have the same inputs and outputs in both executions, and so both events will occur with the same probability. Likewise, $\mathcal{A}$ is not able to see anything different in the two executions, so all actions chosen by $\mathcal{A}$, including the behavior of parties it controls, will be the same in both executions. This is true whether $\mathcal{A}$ sends correct outputs or not, i.e., it holds true even for a malicious $\mathcal{A}$. The only parties that receive or send different messages are the dealer and $P^{(1)}_{f(1)}, \ldots, P^{(T)}_{f(T)}$.

The dealer generates shares randomly subject to the sum being equal to the secret. Therefore, the probability that it chooses any sequence of initial shares to send to all parties other than $P_{f(1)}$ is equal ($|\mathbb{F}|^{-(n-1)}$) in both executions. The final share, sent to $P_{f(1)}$ is determined by the other shares chosen. Likewise, each honest party on the path chooses shares-of-shares randomly subject to the sum being equal to their secret share. Therefore, the probability of the party choosing any sequence of shares-of-shares to send to parties that are not on the path (namely $|\mathbb{F}|^{-(d-1)}$) is the same in both executions. The share-of-share sent on to the next honest party on the path will be uniquely determined by the other shares-of-shares.

Therefore, for every execution where $s = s_A$ and $\mathcal{A}$ outputs s_A, there is another execution that when $s = s_B$ causes $\mathcal{A}$ to output s_B with the same probability. Summing over the finite set of all possible executions, we have that for all $s_A, s_B \in \mathbb{F}$, $Pr(\mathcal{A}$ outputs $s_A|s = s_A) = Pr(\mathcal{A}$ outputs $s_A|s = s_B)$.

Lemma 2 implies that $\mathcal{A}$ obtains no advantage in determining the secret by participating in the protocol. This holds provided there is an honest path from $H^{(1)}$ to $H^{(T)}$, which from Corollary 1 we know happens if $\delta \leq \gamma(\alpha - 1)$. Furthermore, since we instantiate with a Ramanujan graph, Theorem 1 shows that $\gamma(\alpha - 1) \geq (1 - \gamma)\frac{d-4}{d-4+\frac{4}{\gamma}}$. Some basic calculus shows that that this is maximized by $\gamma = \frac{2}{\sqrt{d}+2}$, for which the value is $\frac{\sqrt{d}-2}{\sqrt{d}+2}$. This shows that Protocol 1 provides the following privacy guarantee:

Theorem 4. *If $\delta \leq \frac{\sqrt{d}-2}{\sqrt{d}+2}$, Protocol 1 provides perfect privacy against (malicious) adversaries controlling at most δn parties per epoch.*

Table 2 presents some example values of δ and the smallest necessary value of d that ensures privacy given δn corruptions per epoch. For instance, for $d = 22$ it is possible to tolerate 40% of parties being corrupted per epoch.

Table 2. Corruption threshold, δ, as a function of the bandwidth cost, d for the privacy-only construction (Theorem 4).

δ	0.1	0.2	0.3	0.4	0.5	0.6	0.7
γ	0.45	0.40	0.35	0.30	0.25	0.20	0.15
d	6	9	14	22	36	64	129

6 $\mathcal{O}(n)$-Robust only PSS with Constant Communication

The privacy-only construction (Sect. 5) can be adapted to provide *robustness*, but not *privacy*. In this scheme, the "secret" message, s, is known in the clear. The scheme aims to ensure that the message is not changed despite a large number of malicious parties and a small amount of communication per party.

Recall that time is divided into epochs. As before, the adversary is allowed to corrupt δn of the parties from each epoch. In this setting, each party P_i, in each epoch t, holds a value, $s_i^{(t)}$. Our protocol will ensure that the majority of nodes in a committee hold the correct value.

Note that (as discussed in Sect. 3) because of "eclipse attacks" we cannot guarantee that *all* honest parties hold $s_i^{(t)} = s$ in every epoch t. Instead, we ensure that the *majority* of parties hold the correct value. This allows the true value to be reconstructed by a simple majority vote.

We define *deceived* nodes to be nodes that are honest but hold and send incorrect values because they have received incorrect values. This is a departure from standard PSS and Byzantine models. Due to this relaxation, we are able to obtain asymptotically optimal ($\Theta(n)$) robustness with only $\mathcal{O}(1)$ communication per party. Specifically, we guarantee that the number of *compromised* nodes, that is nodes that are either deceived or corrupt, remains a minority.

Since we guarantee that the majority of nodes are always uncompromised, it is always possible to use an $\mathcal{O}(n)$-communication reconstruction step which will allow each honest node to receive the correct value. If every node broadcasts its value to every other node, then the majority of values any node receives will be correct. If each honest party then sets its value to the most common value it received then every honest party will have the correct value. This step only needs to occur when we wish to return to a situation where every honest node holds the correct value. For the sake of simplicity we omit further discussion of the standard model and will focus on the model where we only need a majority of uncompromised nodes.

The scheme is shown in detail in Protocol 2. It achieves $\Theta(n)$ proactive robustness with only $\Theta(1)$ communication per player. However, it does not provide any privacy as the "secret" is seen by every node.

Protocol 2: Robust (only) Efficient PSS

Parameters:
Let $\hat{G}$ be a $\hat{d}$-regular Ramanujan bipartite expander graph with n vertices in each part. Choose neighbors according to $\hat{G}$.

1. **Setup:** s is the "secret". Dealer sends each party P_i the value $s_i^{(1)} = s$.
2. **Resharing:**
   (a) At the start of epoch t, party P_i sends its share to all of its neighbors. Let $s_{i,j}^{(t)}$ denote the message P_i sends to neighbor P_j in epoch t.

(b) P_j sets its new share to the majority of messages it received, i.e. $s_j^{(t+1)} = \text{majority}_{i \in N^{-1}(j)}(s_{i,j}^{(t)})$. If there is no majority, $s_j^{(t+1)} \overset{\text{def}}{=} \perp$.

The fact that the protocol has $\Theta(1)$ communication per player is evident from the fact that each player sends a single message to each of its $\hat{d}$ neighbors in the expander and that $\hat{d}$ is constant. We will now show that the protocol provides robustness against a *malicious proactive* adversary controlling δn parties in each epoch, for any constant $0 < \delta < \frac{1}{2}$.

First we will formalize our terminology. A node P_i is *deceived* in epoch t if it is honest in epoch t, but $s_i^{(t)} \neq s$. A node is *compromised* if it is either malicious or deceived.

Theorem 5 (Security of Protocol 2). *Protocol 2 guarantees that in each epoch, there is a majority of uncompromised nodes, provided $\mathcal{A}$ corrupts at most δn nodes in each epoch, for some constant $\delta < \frac{1}{2}$.*

Proof. Select some constant ϵ such that $\delta < \epsilon < \frac{1}{2}$. We show there exists some constant $\hat{d}$ such that, if $\hat{G}$ is a $\hat{d}$-regular Ramanujan bipartite expander, then the number of compromised nodes in any epoch is at most ϵn.

By induction. In epoch 1, there are δn corrupt nodes and no deceived nodes, so there are $\delta n < \epsilon n$ compromised nodes.

Assume that the statement holds until epoch t. Let X be the set of compromised nodes in epoch t. By the inductive hypothesis $|X| \leq \epsilon n$. Let Y be the set of deceived nodes in epoch $t + 1$. A node will be deceived only if at least half of the messages it received were incorrect.

Applying Theorem 2, where S is the nodes that are compromised, we obtain:

$$|Y| \leq \frac{4\epsilon n}{\hat{d}\left(\frac{1}{2} - \epsilon\right)^2}$$

The number of corrupt nodes in epoch $t+1$ is at most δn, so the total number of compromised nodes in epoch $t + 1$ is at most:

$$\frac{4\epsilon n}{\hat{d}\left(\frac{1}{2} - \epsilon\right)^2} + \delta n$$

If $\hat{d} \geq \frac{4\epsilon}{\left(\frac{1}{2} - \epsilon\right)^2(\epsilon - \delta)}$ then the number of compromised nodes in epoch $t+1$ is at most $(\epsilon - \delta)n + \delta n \leq \epsilon n$. Thus, by induction there are at most ϵn compromised nodes in every epoch. Since $\epsilon < \frac{1}{2}$, most nodes in each epoch are uncompromised.

The above proof works for every ϵ satisfying $\delta < \epsilon < \frac{1}{2}$. A simple calculus proof, delegated to Supplemental Material D, shows that the expression is minimized by $\epsilon = \frac{1}{4}\left(\delta + \sqrt{\delta^2 + 4\delta}\right)$. For instance, for $\delta = 0.1$ this yields the requirement that $\hat{d} \geq 88$.

7 $\mathcal{O}(n^a)$-Private, $\mathcal{O}(n^{1-a})$-Robust PSS with $\mathcal{O}(\kappa)$ Communication

The PSS protocols presented in Sects. 5 and 6 are extremely limited in that the first protocol does not provide any robustness (a malicious adversary can modify the secret) and the second does not provide any privacy (every party knows the "secret"). In this section we combine the two protocols to create a protocol that has both privacy and robustness, but still has the desired constant (in n) communication per party per epoch. Specifically, the protocol has privacy against a proactive adversary corrupting $\Theta(n^a)$ nodes each epoch, robustness against a proactive adversary corrupting $\Theta(n^{1-a})$ nodes per epoch, and requires $\Theta(\kappa)$ communication per party per epoch, where κ is a security parameter. The protocol is perfectly robust, and computationally private, such that the adversary's advantage in guessing the secret is negligible in κ. Setting $a = \frac{1}{2}$ provides a constant-communication PSS with both privacy and robustness against a proactive adversary corrupting $\Theta(\sqrt{n})$ nodes per epoch.

At a high-level, we start our construction with the private protocol (Protocol 1) and replicate each party, say P_i, of that protocol some number of times. We consider this set of replicas of P_i as if they are simulating P_i's actions. However, they will do it with a twist; they will utilize the robust protocol (Protocol 2) when they send a message on behalf of P_i. The robust protocol will ensure that no messages or shares are lost and the underlying private protocol will ensure that there is privacy for the global secret, delivering the desired result.

However, things are not straightforward; there are two obstacles which need to be overcome. The first is that for this general idea to work we need to guarantee that the replicas in fact work as replicas. That is, if they are not compromised (i.e. not corrupted or deceived) then they will execute the same steps with the same inputs and randomness, otherwise the replicas will be sending different messages. This is a challenging requirement to satisfy in the proactive setting. The second issue is that we cannot have a replica of one party send message to all the replicas of another party as this will increase the communication complexity beyond our goals. Thus, to deliver a solution we need to address these two problems.

Recall that in Protocol 1, the parties use fresh randomness to generate the shares-of-shares. As described the fresh randomness is unique to each party and is generated locally at the time it is needed. Note that we cannot generate randomness from long-term shared PRG keys, as a proactive adversary can learn all such keys and know the pseudorandomness being used by every party. Thus, it seems that, as we require fresh randomness and at the same time need replicas to have the same randomness, we are stuck in a bind.

To solve this, parties refresh the PRG keys of their neighbors in every epoch. That is, each party, each epoch, sends their neighbors both a share-of-share, and a string, called a re-randomizer. A party combines the re-randomizers it receives to generate a new PRG key. How does a party generate these re-randomizers? It uses its own PRG key for that epoch. This may seem circular since an adversary who corrupts a party will learn the re-randomizers that it sends. Security comes from combining multiple re-randomizers to create the new key, and choosing neighbors using an expander graph. Like Protocol 1 ensured a constant fraction of shares remained private each epoch, this will ensure a constant fraction of keys remain private. Our solution is therefore also Proactive Pseudorandomness (PP) protocol, that is a protocol that generates pseudorandomness in a way that is indistinguishable from random to a mobile adversary. See Sect. 9 for more details on PP and a simplified version of our protocol that just provides Proactive Pseudorandomness.

Since pseudorandomness is generated according to PRG keys, we can consider a *correct* execution in which parties always generate their messages according to the keys. This execution is deterministic given the dealer's initial distribution of keys and secret shares. We can consider the shares and messages of this correct execution as the *correct* shares and messages. To show the robustness of the protocol, we will show that, every epoch, for any party in the privacy-only protocol, most of its replicas hold the correct share.

Having resolved the randomness issue, we have made a step forward towards making replication possible. Now we need to address the issue of not having a replica send messages to all the replicas of its neighbor. To attain robustness, at a low communication cost we will have a replica of a party send its messages only to a small subset of its neighbor's replicas. We will show that robustness is maintained despite this dramatically lower communication.

Concretely, we instantiate Protocol 1 with n^a parties, but in our protocol each of these will be simulated by n^{1-a} replicas. These replicas will be the actual parties running the protocol; the fact that they are simulating an execution of Protocol 1 is a useful abstraction. We label the parties as if they were in a n^a by n^{1-a} grid, with row i holding the replicas of P_i from Protocol 1. $P_{i,j}$ denotes the party in row i and column j. We denote the set of parties in row i as row_i and the set of parties in column j as col_j. If we wish to specify that we are referring to a row (resp. column) in a specific epoch t, we use the notation $row_i^{(t)}$ (resp. $col_j^{(t)}$).

In more detail, examine party P_i from the private protocol that is replicated some number of times. If P_i sent $P_{i'}$ share-of-share $s_{i,i'}^{(t)}$ in epoch t in Protocol 1, then each uncompromised replica of P_i will also send replicas of $P_{i'}$, the share $s_{i,i'}^{(t)}$ in epoch t of the new protocol. We will ensure the majority of replicas of P_i will send the correct share-of-share. Thus, the replicas of P_i in row_i will send messages to the replicas of $P_{i'}$ in $row_{i'}$. Unfortunately, making every party in row_i communicate to every party in $row_{i'}$ causes the communication complexity to scale linearly in the amount of replication.

How many parties do they need to communicate to in order to ensure that the majority of parties in any row always hold the correct share? Surprisingly, a constant number suffices. The argument is almost identical to that of the robustness of Protocol 2. To explain this, let's restrict our view to one replica of P_i, say $P_{i,\ell}$. Examine the replicas of party $P_{i'}$ of which it needs to choose a subset to communicate with. The expander graph of the robust protocol will tell us with which replicas of $P_{i'}$ the replica $P_{i,\ell}$ should talk to, i.e. the columns that identify the subset of the replicas of $P_{i'}$. We state two important points that will aid in the proofs. The replica of P_i also needs to talk to replicas of a party $P_{i''}$, as P_i communicates with $P_{i''}$ in the private protocol. The subset of replicas of $P_{i''}$ will be in exactly the same columns as the replicas of $P_{i'}$. Furthermore, assume that P_j also communicates with $P_{i'}$ in the private protocol. Then, the replica $P_{j,\ell}$ of P_j will talk to the subset of the same columns as the replica $P_{i,\ell}$. Saying this abstractly we have that *column* col_j will only communicate with column $col_{j'}$ if, in an instantiation of Protocol 2 with n^{1-a} parties, P_j would communicate with $P_{j'}$. $P_{i,j}$ only communicates with $P_{i',j'}$ if row row_i communicates with $row_{i'}$ and column col_j communications with $col_{j'}$.

One final challenge is that malicious adversaries can choose to send incorrect randomness in an attempt to create related keys for a Related-Key Attack (RKA) on the PRG. To solve this, we use a PRF that is secure against additive RKAs to securely combine the randomness sent to a party. This ensures that if any of the messages is unknown to the adversary, it will be unable to distinguish the PRG seeds from ones that were truly generated at random. We instantiate with the additive-RKA-secure PRF of Bellare and Cash [BC10], which was proven secure under DDH by [ABPP14]. This PRF is a variant of the Naor-Reingold PRF, and like Naor-Reingold it has $\Theta(\kappa^2)$ bits per key ($\Theta(\kappa)$ values from a group where DDH is hard). A simple solution would be for each party to send $\Theta(\kappa^2)$-bit rerandomizers which would be added to form a key for an additive-RKA-secure PRF. However, it is not actually necessary for each party to send $\Theta(\kappa^2)$ bits. In our protocol each party instead sends a κ-bit PRG seed, which the recipient expands to generate the $\Theta(\kappa^2)$-bit rerandomizers, which are then added to create the key for the additive-RKA-secure PRF.

We set the parameters of the protocol as follows: a is a constant such that $0 < a < 1$. n is the number of parties, and n^a and n^{1-a} are both integers. The parties are arranged in an n^a by n^{1-a} grid, and are labeled $P_{i,j}$ for $1 \le i \le n^a$ and $1 \le j \le n^{1-a}$, such that $P_{i,j}$ is in row i and column j. $P_{i,j}$ in epoch t is represented as $P_{i,j}^{(t)}$. The labels are public.

There are two bipartite expanders of constant degree, G which has n^a nodes in each part and will be used for the private portion, and H which has n^{1-a} nodes in each part and will be used for the robust portion. d_G (d_H) is the degree of G (H), respectively. GR_i (HR_j) represent the sets of indices of right-neighbors of L_i (L_j) in G (H) respectively. Likewise GL_i (HL_j) represent the sets of indices of left-neighbors of R_i (R_j) in G (H) respectively. Expanders are fixed and public.

$\mathbb{F}$ is a group from which the secret is chosen. K_1 is a group from which PRG seeds are chosen, $|K_1| = 2^\kappa$. K_2 is a group from which PRG re-randomizers are chosen, $|K_1| = 2^{\Theta(\kappa^2)}$. $F : K_2 \times X \to K_1$ is a Φ_{add}-RKA-PRF where X can be any PRF input set.

Protocol 3: Private and Robust Efficient PSS

1. **Setup:**
   The dealer picks $s_1^{(1)}, \ldots, s_{n^a}^{(1)}$ uniformly at random from $\mathbb{F}$ subject to $\sum_{i=1}^{n^a} s_i = s$, where s is the secret.
   The dealer picks $k_1^{(1)}, \ldots, k_{n^a}^{(1)}$ uniformly at random from K_1.
   The dealer sends $(s_i^{(1)}, k_i^{(1)})$ to $P_{i,j}$ for all $1 \le i \le n^a$, $1 \le j \le n^{1-a}$.
   $P_{i,j}$ sets $(s_{i,j}^{(1)}, k_{i,j}^{(1)})$ to the received value.

2. **Resharing:**
   (a) At the start of epoch t each party $P_{i,j}$ does the following:
   Uses $k_{i,j}^{(t)}$ as a PRG seed to pseudorandomly generate $r_{i,i',j}^{(t)} \leftarrow K_1$,
   $s_{i,i',j}^{(t)} \leftarrow \mathbb{F}$, for all $i' \in GR_i$, chosen uniformly at random, subject
   only to $\sum_{i' \in GR_i} s_{i,i',j}^{(t)} = s_{i,j}^{(t)}$.
   Sets $r_{i,i',j,j'}^{(t)} = r_{i,i',j}^{(t)}$, $s_{i,i',j,j'}^{(t)} = s_{i,i',j}^{(t)}$ for all $i' \in GR_i$, $j' \in HR_j$.
   Sends $(r_{i,i',j,j'}^{(t)}, s_{i,i',j,j'}^{(t)})$ to $P_{i',j'}$ for all $i' \in GR_i$, $j' \in HR_j$.
   (b) Each party $P_{i',j'}$ then does the following:
   Receives $(r_{i,i',j,j'}^{(t)}, s_{i,i',j,j'}^{(t)})$ from all $i \in GL_{i'}$, $j \in HL_{j'}$.
   Sets $\hat{r}_{i,i',j'}^{(t)} = \mathrm{majority}_{j \in HL_{j'}} \, r_{i,i',j,j'}^{(t)}$
   Sets $\hat{s}_{i,i',j'}^{(t)} = \mathrm{majority}_{j \in HL_{j'}} \, s_{i,i',j,j'}^{(t)}$.
   Use $\hat{r}_{i,i',j'}^{(t)}$ as a PRG seed to generate rerandomizers $\hat{k}_{i,i',j'}^{(t)} \leftarrow K_2$ for all $i \in GL_{i'}$.
   Computes a new PRG seed from the provided randomness:
   $\hat{k}_{i',j'}^{(t)} = \sum_{i \in GL_{i'}} \hat{k}_{i,i',j'}^{(t)}$
   $k_{i',j'}^{(t+1)} = F(\hat{k}_{i',j'}^{(t)}, 1)$
   Combines shares-of-shares to get a new share of the secret:
   $s_{i',j'}^{(t+1)} = \sum_{i \in GL_{i'}} s_{i,i',j'}^{(t)}$.

Before proving properties of the protocol, we provide some definitions. A *corrupted row* is one in which there is at least one corrupted party, i.e. row $row_i^{(t)}$ is corrupted if there exists $j \in \{1, \ldots, n^{1-a}\}$ such that $P_{i,j}^{(t)}$ is corrupted. Two rows $row_i^{(t)}$ and $row_{i'}^{(t+1)}$ are *neighbors* if there exist $P_{i,j}^{(t)} \in row_i^{(t)}$, $P_{i',j'}^{(t+1)} \in row_{i'}^{(t+1)}$ such that $P_{i,j}^{(t)}$ sends a message to $P_{i',j'}^{(t+1)}$. This happens exactly when $(i, i') \in G$. We say that $row_{i_w}^{(w)}, row_{i_{w+1}}^{(w+1)}, \ldots, row_{i_{w+x}}^{(w+x)}$ is a *row path* if $row_{i_y}^{(y)}$ and $row_{i_{y+1}}^{(y+1)}$ are neighbors for all $w \le y \le w+x-1$. If a row path consists only of rows that are not corrupted, we say that it is an *honest row path*. Lastly, we call a row path *full* if it stretches from the first epoch (epoch 1) to the last epoch (epoch T), i.e. $row_{i_1}^{(1)}, \ldots, row_{i_T}^{(T)}$ is a full row path for any length-T index set,

$i_1, \ldots, i_T$, where $i_t \in \{1, \ldots, n^a\}$ for $1 \leq t \leq T$. We sometimes refer to a full row path $row_{i_1}^{(1)}, \ldots, row_{i_T}^{(T)}$ simply by the sequence of indices it uses: $i_1, \ldots, i_T$.

These definitions are intentionally analogous to those in the proof of privacy for Protocol 1. The proof of security will also be similar, in that it will be shown that if an honest row path exists throughout the entire protocol execution, then the privacy is preserved. However, the proof first needs to demonstrate that the adversary is not able to undermine security by using the fact that resharings are generated pseudorandomly.

We prove this by first comparing the adversary's view in two different executions. The first is an execution of Protocol 3. The second is an execution in which all PRG seeds in a full row path are generated truly at random. Now, they cannot be all generated independently. If $\mathcal{A}$ is a passive adversary the PRG seeds in a row will all be the same, but if $\mathcal{A}$ is malicious, the PRG seeds may differ, since $\mathcal{A}$ may provide nodes in the row with different randomness. Thus, we want the alternative execution to have nodes use the same PRG seeds exactly when they would have the same seeds in the original execution. We thus define the executions, or games, as follows.

Let $Game_{Real}$ denote an execution of Protocol 3. Given a full row path $R = row_{R_1}^{(1)}, \ldots, row_{R_T}^{(T)}$, $Game_{1,R}$ denotes an execution almost identical to Protocol 3 except for the way $k_{i',j'}^{(t+1)}$ is generated in part (b) of the Resharing step. If $P_{i',j'}^{(t+1)} \notin row_{R_{t+1}}^{(t+1)}$, it generates $k_{i',j'}^{(t+1)}$ in the normal way. However, if $P_{i',j'}^{(t+1)} \in row_{R_{t+1}}^{(t+1)}$, it communicates with all other parties in $row_{R_{t+1}}^{(t+1)}$ to identify the set of parties which have the same value for $\hat{k}_{i',j'}^{(t)}$. It then collaborates with the parties in this set to generate a new truly random value which all parties in this set then use for their PRG seeds $k_{i',j'}^{(t+1)}$.

Lemma 3. *If $R = R_1, \ldots, R_T$ is a full honest row path then any probabilistic polytime adversary, $\mathcal{A}$, is unable to distinguish $Game_{Real}$ from $Game_{1,R}$ except with negligible probability.*

Proof. By induction on the epoch t. The induction invariant is that $\mathcal{A}$ will know, at most, which parties from a row in the given epoch use the same PRG seeds, but will have a negligible advantage at guessing these values.

The setup does not differ between $Game_{Real}$ and $Game_{1,R}$. So initially the views are identical. Note that $\mathcal{A}$ knows that all values of $k_{R_1,j}^{(1)}$ are identical, but the value was chosen truly at random by the dealer, so $\mathcal{A}$ has no advantage in guessing it.

We now show that a Resharing step followed by a Reconstruct step preserves the invariant. We have that $\mathcal{A}$ knows which parties in $row_{R_t}^{(t)}$ have identical PRG keys. At worst, she learns the result of all messages sent by $row_{R_t}^{(t)}$ except those that are sent to $row_{R_{t+1}}^{(t+1)}$. However, by the security of the PRG, the portion of the PRG output $\mathcal{A}$ observes will give $\mathcal{A}$ negligible advantage in learning the seed. Therefore, this information provides negligible assistance in allowing $\mathcal{A}$ to distinguish the case where the PRG seed, $k_{i',j'}^{(t+1)}$ was generated using the PRF ($Game_{Real}$) and the case where it was generated truly at random ($Game_{1,R}$).

Additionally, the security of the PRG provides her no advantage in guessing the randomness sent from parties in $row_{R_t}^{(t)}$ to those in $row_{R_{t+1}}^{(t+1)}$. Specifically $\hat{k}_{R_t,R_{t+1},j'}^{(t)}$ is generated from a PRG seeded with $r_{R_t,R_{t+1},j'}^{(t)}$. This, in turn was taken as the most common value of $r_{R_t,R_{t+1},j,j'}^{(t)}$ for $j \in HL_{j'}$. In $Game_{Real}$, these are generated by a PRG on $k_{R_t,j}^{(t)}$, whereas in $Game_{1,R}$ these are generated using a fresh random value (which is the same for any party holding an identical $k_{R_t,j}^{(t)}$). By our inductive hypothesis, these cases are indistinguishable to $\mathcal{A}$. Therefore, by the security of the PRG, the outputs $r_{R_t,R_{t+1},j,j'}^{(t)}$ are indistinguishable from uniformly random to $\mathcal{A}$ except that $\mathcal{A}$ knows (at worst) which are identical, and likewise are the computed values $r_{R_t,R_{t+1},j'}^{(t)}$. Therefore, again by the security of the PRG, the rerandomizer $\hat{k}_{R_t,R_{t+1},j'}^{(t)}$ is indistinguishable from uniformly random (except that $\mathcal{A}$ may learn which parties hold the same value).

Note that $\mathcal{A}$ may, in the worst case, know and be able to influence all other rerandomizers that a given party in $row_{R_{t+1}}^{(t+1)}$ receives. Thus, $P_{R_{t+1},j'}^{(t)}$ computes

$$\hat{k}_{R_{t+1},j'}^{(t)} = \hat{k}_{R_t,R_{t+1},j'}^{(t)} + \sum_{i \in GL_{i'}/\{R_t\}} \hat{k}_{i,R_{t+1},j'}^{(t)}$$

The second term is, at worst, known and controllable by $\mathcal{A}$. However, we have shown that the first term is indistinguishable from uniformly at random to $\mathcal{A}$. Multiple parties in $row_{R_{t+1}}^{(t+1)}$ may receive the same value as the first term, but $\mathcal{A}$ could introduce different values for the second term. This is equivalent to a Related-Key Attack, where the first term is the original key and the second term is an additive modification to the key chosen by $\mathcal{A}$. However, since F is a Φ_{add}-RKA-PRF, the outputs of F on different, additively-related keys are indistinguishable from random outputs. Thus, $\mathcal{A}$ will not be able to distinguish the seeds $k_{i',j'}^{(t+1)}$ in $Game_{Real}$ from the truly randomly generated seeds in $Game_{1,R}$. The outputs of F on identical keys will be the same, and again in $Game_{1,R}$, parties that received the same values of $\hat{k}_{R_{t+1},j'}^{(t)}$ will generate and use the same PRG seeds. Thus the indistinguishability of the two games is preserved after an epoch, and in particular the adversary may learn (at worst) which parties in the honest row path in that epoch have the same PRG seeds, but has no advantage in learning the seeds themselves.

Now, let $Game_{2,R}$ be equivalent to $Game_{1,R}$ except that rather than choosing a truly random seed for the PRG, parties that have the same value for $\hat{k}_{i',j'}^{(t)}$ generate a truly random string in place of the PRG output.

Lemma 4. *A probabilistic polytime adversary is unable to distinguish $Game_{2,R}$ from $Game_{1,R}$, except with negligible probability.*

Proof. This follows immediately from the definition of a PRG. In $Game_{1,R}$ the PRG seeds are chosen truly at random, and the outputs generated from this seed. A PRG has the property that an output of such a PRG is computationally indistinguishable from a truly random output, and thus $Game_{1,R}$ is computationally indistinguishable from $Game_{2,R}$.

We are now essentially in the same position as the proof of Protocol 1. The only difference is that replicas in an honest row may not agree on the same randomness to generate their messages (if $\mathcal{A}$ sends them inconsistent randomizers). Nevertheless, this does not undermine privacy, and we can proceed to prove privacy similar to as for Protocol 1 by considering the case that the secret-shares on the honest path, and all secret-share messages on the honest path, are incremented by some value $s_B - s_A$.

Lemma 5. *If there exists a full honest row path, R, then in $Game_{2,R}$, for all possible secrets $s_A, s_B \in \mathbb{F}$, the probability that $\mathcal{A}$ guesses output s_A when $s = s_A$ is the same as the probability that $\mathcal{A}$ guesses s_A when $s = s_B$.*

Proof. For every execution of $Game_{2,R}$ in which $\mathcal{A}$ outputs s_A when $s = s_A$, there is an execution in which $\mathcal{A}$ outputs s_A when $s = s_B$ that occurs with equal probability.

Let us examine an execution in which $\mathcal{A}$ outputs s_A when $s = s_A$. Now we will examine another execution in which:

- The true secret is s_B, not s_A.
- The initial share sent to $row_{R_1}^{(1)}$ by the dealer was incremented by $s_B - s_A$.
- For all nodes not on path $row_{R_1}^{(1)}, \ldots, row_{R_T}^{(T)}$, the messages received, data held, and messages sent are the same as the original execution. (This means that the data seen by $\mathcal{A}$ and its behavior are identical in the two executions.)
- All secret-shares held by parties in path R are incremented by $s_B - s_A$.
- All shares of secret-shares sent from parties in R to other parties in R are incremented by $s_B - s_A$.

All parties except for the dealer and those in path R view the same thing in both executions and make the same choices, so the probability of them doing so is the same in both executions. This includes $\mathcal{A}$. It remains to show that this is a valid execution for honest parties on the path. The sum of the messages sent by the dealer is equal to the true secret, so this is a valid execution by the dealer. For each party in R, all of the messages they receive from parties in R is incremented by $s_B - s_A$, so, even if these messages disagree, the message they choose as the "correct" message will also be incremented by $s_B - s_A$. Thus the secret share they compute will be incremented by $s_B - s_A$ as required. Lastly, all output messages are the same except those sent to parties in R, and shares-of-shares sent to R are incremented by $s_B - s_A$, so the sum of shares-of-shares output will still equal the share held by the parties. Thus this is a valid execution by honest parties. Since each valid execution by honest parties is equally likely, the probability that this execution occurs is just as likely as the original. Finally, the random choices of all parties on the path R are made independently of all parties not on the path, and in particular of $\mathcal{A}$, so the combined probability of the modified execution occurring is the same as that of the original.

Theorem 6. *If a full honest row path exists, then $\mathcal{A}$ has negligible advantage in guessing the secret.*

Proof. If such a path, R, exists, then there is some game $Game_{1,R}$ which, by Lemma 3 is indistinguishable from $Game_{Real}$ to $\mathcal{A}$. By Lemma 4 this, in turn, is indistinguishable from $Game_{2,R}$ to $\mathcal{A}$. Now, $\mathcal{A}$'s behavior in $Game_{2,R}$ has the same probability if the secret is modified. Thus, $Game_{2,R}$ is (perfectly) indistinguishable to $\mathcal{A}$ from an execution of $Game_{2,R}$ with a modified secret. This in turn is indistinguishable from an execution of $Game_{1,R}$ with a modified secret, which in turn is indistinguishable from an execution of $Game_{Real}$ with a modified secret. Since the indistinguishable relation is transitive, this means that any real execution is indistinguishable to $\mathcal{A}$ from another real execution with a modified secret. Thus, $\mathcal{A}$ has negligible advantage in guessing the secret.

Finally, the proofs about the existence of honest paths for Protocol 1 apply immediately to the case of honest row paths. In particular, as has already been proven in Corollary 1, if a fixed portion δ of the rows are honest, and $\delta \leq \gamma(\alpha-1)$, (where constants γ and α depend on G) then a full honest row-path exists. Since a dishonest row requires at least one dishonest party, and there are n^a rows, we get the following result:

Corollary 2. *If there are at most δn^a malicious nodes, then there exists a full honest row path.*

Theorem 7. *There exists some constant δ, such that the protocol is computationally-private against a malicious proactive adversary corruption at most δn^a nodes per epoch.*

Now we show that the protocol also has robustness. The approach is very similar to that of Protocol 2, though in this case we show that a constant proportion of *columns* in the grid are holding and sending correct values.

Again, before proceeding we need to introduce some terminology. A *column* is a set of nodes in a given time-step that are in the same column in the grid, i.e. column $col_j^{(t)} = \cup_{i=1}^{n^a} P_{i,j}^{(t)}$. If the adversary corrupts any party in a column (in a given time step), then the column is *corrupt*. Otherwise a column is *honest*. Note that, except for the dealer, all (honest) parties' actions are deterministic. Therefore, given a certain setup by the dealer, we can consider the *correct* value for a data element held, or for a message sent, to be the value that would be sent if all parties follow the protocol. A column is *correct* if all of the data held and messages sent by all parties in the column are correct, and *incorrect* otherwise. Column $col_j^{(t)}$ is a *before-neighbor* of column $col_{j'}^{(t+1)}$ exactly if there exists i, i' such that $P_{i,j}^{(t)}$ is meant to send a message to $P_{i',j'}^{(t+1)}$. This occurs exactly when $(j, j') \in H$.

Lemma 6. *If the majority of an honest column's before-neighbors are correct, then the column will also be correct.*

Proof. Let $col_{j'}^{(t+1)}$ be a column with a majority of correct before-neighbors. Then, for every node $P_{i',j'}^{(t+1)} \in col_{j'}^{(t+1)}$, for every $i \in GL_{i'}$, the majority of messages $s_{i,i',j,j'}^{(t)}$ it receives are correct. Thus it will compute the correct value for $\hat{s}_{i,i',j'}^{(t)}$ for all $i \in GL_{i'}$ and thus it will also compute the correct value for $s_{i',j'}^{(t+1)}$. Likewise, for every $i \in GL_{i'}$, the majority of messages $\hat{k}_{i,i',j,j'}^{(t)}$ that it receives will be correct, so it will compute the correct value for $\hat{k}_{i,i',j}^{(t)}$ for every $i \in GL_{i'}$ and thus compute the correct value for $k_{i',j'}^{(t+1)}$. Thus all data held by $P_{i',j'}^{(t+1)}$ is correct. Since $s_{i',j'}^{(t+1)}$ and $k_{i',j'}^{(t+1)}$ are both correct, the messages that $P_{i',j'}^{(t+1)}$ sends in the next resharing step will also be correct. Since this is true for all $P_{i',j'}^{(t+1)} \in col_{j'}^{(t+1)}$, then column $col_{j'}^{(t+1)}$ is itself correct.

Theorem 8. *If $\mathcal{A}$ corrupts δn^{1-a} nodes in each epoch, for some constant $\delta < \frac{1}{2}$, then for any constant ϵ satisfying $\delta < \epsilon < \frac{1}{2}$ there exists some constant d such that if H is a d-regular Ramanujan bipartite expander, then at most ϵn^{1-a} columns in every epoch are not correct.*

Proof. By induction. For the first epoch, there are at most δn^{1-a} corrupt columns. The remaining nodes are correct, since they received messages only from the dealer, who is honest. Therefore, the total number of incorrect columns is $\delta n^{1-a} < \epsilon n^{1-a}$.

Now, assume at most ϵn^{1-a} columns are incorrect in epoch t. By Lemma 9, the definition of a Ramanujan d-regular expander and Lemma 6, this means that the number of honest columns in epoch $t+1$ that are incorrect is at most:

$$\frac{4\epsilon n^{1-a}}{d\left(\frac{1}{2} - \epsilon\right)^2}$$

A further δn^{1-a} columns may be corrupt. Therefore, the total number of incorrect columns in epoch $t+1$ is at most

$$\frac{4\epsilon n^{1-a}}{d\left(\frac{1}{2} - \epsilon\right)^2} + \delta n^{1-a} = \left(\delta + \frac{4\epsilon}{d\left(\frac{1}{2} - \epsilon\right)^2}\right) n^{1-a}$$

If $d \geq \frac{4\epsilon}{\left(\frac{1}{2} - \epsilon\right)^2 (\epsilon - \delta)}$ then this is at most ϵn^{1-a}.

Setting a concrete value of ϵ leads immediately to the robust security guarantee for Protocol 3.

Theorem 9. *Protocol 3 provides robustness against a proactive adversary corrupting $\Theta(n^{1-a})$ nodes in each epoch.*

8   Securing Channels Using Signing Oracles

Our solution for establishing secure channels requires a simple piece of trusted hardware, a secure signing oracle. The secure signing oracle has a (persistent) public verification key, and can be used to sign arbitrary messages. The only trust assumption is that the private key cannot be extracted from the device. In addition to the signing oracle, we assume that each party has a trusted random number generator, i.e., every party that is not corrupted in the current epoch can generate random numbers that are unpredictable to the adversary.

Such devices are commonly available as external devices (e.g. Yubikeys, or cryptocurrency wallets like the Ledger or Trezor), and are implemented by Apple's Secure Enclave on the iOS.[5]. Suppose, in addition, that the verification keys corresponding to these signing oracles are baked into the read-only memory of every other party.

When a party is corrupted by the adversary, we assume that the adversary has unfettered access to the signing oracle, and can sign arbitrary messages of their choosing.

Secure signing oracles do not immediately yield persistent secure channels on their own, since (1) they do not provide *private* channels, and (2) since the adversary (with access to a signing oracle), can always sign additional messages and inject them into the channels at a later date.

In our solution, we use the persistent key in the signing oracle to bootstrap new keys for each epoch of the protocol. It is not sufficient to simply use the signing oracle to sign new epoch-specific keys, because if an adversary corrupts a party at time t (and gains access to the signing oracle), the adversary can sign new key material, and hold onto these signed keys until after a reboot.

We can eliminate this attack vector with a simple challenge-response protocol. In epoch t, party i will reboot, and generate a new key, $pk_{i,t}, sk_{i,t}$. At the beginning of epoch t, party j will send a challenge $r_{i,j,t}$, to party i. Party i will then sign the pair $(pk_{i,t}, r_{i,j,t})$, using their signing oracle, and then return the signed key to party j. This allows party j to ensure that the new key $pk_{i,t}$ was generated by party i in epoch t (or later).

The formal protocol is described in Protocol 4.

Protocol 4: Establishing Secure Channels

Party i holds a secure signing oracle $SO_i(\cdot)$, and verification keys $\{VK_j\}_{j\in[N]}$.

- **Challenge:**
  - **Peer-to-peer messaging:** Player i generates a random challenge $r_{i,j,t} \leftarrow_r \{0,1\}^\kappa$ for each party, j, with whom they plan to communicate in epoch t.

---

[5] https://support.apple.com/guide/security/secure-enclave-sec59b0b31ff/web.

- **Randomness beacon:** In the presence of a trusted randomness beacon that generates a random nonce, $r_t \leftarrow_r \{0,1\}^\kappa$ every epoch, can use this to avoid communication. Instead, every players sets $r_{i,j,t} = r_t$, and players do *not* need to exchange challenges. Thus the presence of a trusted randomness beacon can reduce the communication and round complexity. The rest of protocol proceeds in the same way, whether the challenges $r_{i,j,t}$ were generated and exchanged by the players or provided by the randomness beacon.
- **Key generation:** Player i uses its random number generator to generate a key pair, $pk_{i,t}, sk_{i,t}$, for an *authenticated* encryption scheme.
- **Signing:** Player i uses their trusted signing oracle, SO_i to produce the signature $\sigma_{i,j,t} = \mathsf{SO}_i(i||pk_{i,t}||r_{i,j,t})$
- **Communication:** Player i sends $pk_{i,t}, \sigma_{i,j,t}$ to every player j that the wish to communicate with in epoch t.
- **Verification:** Player j checks that the signature $\sigma_{i,j,t}$ is a valid signature on the message $i||pk_{i,t}||r_{i,j,t}$ using the (persistent) verification key VK_i.

Theorem 10. *Protocol 4 is a secure method for establishing channel keys in the mobile adversary model. Specifically, consider a PPT mobile adversary who is allowed to corrupt a (possibly) different subset of parties at every epoch. Then if j is an uncorrupted party in epoch t, and j accepts $pk_{i,t}$, then (with all but negligible probability) $pk_{i,t}$ was generated by party i in epoch t.*

Proof. If party j is honest, and accepts a public key, $pk_{i,t}$ from party i in epoch t, then the signature $\sigma_{i,j,t}$ is valid signature of $pk_{i,t}||r_{i,j,t}$ under party i's persistent verification key, VK_i.

If $pk_{i,t}$ was *not* generated in epoch t, then either (i) the signature $\sigma_{i,j,t}$ was generated by an adversary *with* access to the signing oracle in a prior epoch, or (ii) the signature $\sigma_{i,j,t}$ was generated by an adversary *without* access to the signing oracle in the current epoch.

For case (i), an adversary with access to the signing oracle, would have to guess the challenge $r_{i,j,t}$ (which was generated uniformly at random from $\{0,1\}^\kappa$ in epoch t. Any polynomial-time adversary can make at most a polynomial number of queries to the signing oracle (and store the resulting signatures until epoch t), and thus has at most a negligible probability of querying the oracle with the challenge $r_{i,j,t}$.

For case (ii), an adversary who never had access to the signing oracle would have to guess the signature $\sigma_{i,j,t}$. A polynomial-time adversary can guess at most a polynomial number of signatures $\sigma'_{i,j,t}$ and check (using the public verification key VK_i) whether the signature is valid on $pk'||r_{i,j,t}$. Since the adversary can only make a polynomial number of guesses, the adversary's success probability in this scenario is also negligible.

Thus an adversary (who has not corrupted party i in epoch t) has only a negligible probability of getting party j to accept a public key.

9 $\mathcal{O}(n)$-secure Proactive Pseudorandomness with $\mathcal{O}(\kappa)$ Communication

In Sect. 7, we required replicas to have local PRG keys which were generally indistinguishable from random to $\mathcal{A}$. Using pseudorandomness rather than fresh, local randomness was necessary to allow replicas to send identical messages.

A simplified version of Protocol 3 can instead be used for a different objective, replacing the need for fresh, local randomness altogether. In [CH94], Canetti and Herzberg presented the problem of generating *Proactive Pseudorandomness* (PP). They argued that sometimes a source of fresh, local randomness is not available. They presented a protocol that replaces randomness by pseudorandomness generated by PRGs. In order to ensure that the pseudorandomness remains indistinguishable from random to a mobile adversary, each party, every epoch, sends every other party a randomizer. Each party combines the randomizers it receives to construct a new PRG seed. As long as the adversary is unaware of any one of these randomizers, a party's new PRG key will be indistinguishable from random to $\mathcal{A}$. [CH94] argue that this removes the need for local, fresh randomness in Proactive protocols.

Like [CH94] we present a protocol that removes the need for fresh, local randomness in proactive protocols *provided secure hardware channels exist*. Unlike [CH94], each party communicates with only $\Theta(1)$ parties per epoch rather than all n parties. Since each party only communicates with a constant number of other parties in each epoch, honest parties are susceptible to "eclipse attacks," where the adversary corrupts all of the party's communication partners. Thus, we consider a slightly more relaxed notion of PP security than [CH94]. The original PP protocol guarantees that every party that is honest in a given epoch has pseudorandomness that is unpredictable to the adversary. Our protocol will instead guarantee that in every epoch, at least γn parties will have pseudorandomness that is unpredictable to the adversary, where γ is a constant.

The protocol is obtained by simplifying Protocol 3 as follows. We no longer need replication, so we set $a = 1$. We are concerned only with keys and key re-randomizers, so we remove all messages and variables related to shares. Additionally, since there are no replicas, we do not need to worry about related-key attacks. We therefore do not need a Φ_{add}-RKA secure PRF to combine the re-randomizers, simply adding the re-randomizers to generate a new key suffices. The resulting protocol is presented in Protocol 5.

Protocol 5: Proactive Pseudorandomness

Parameters:
Let $G = (L \cup R, E)$ be a d-regular bipartite (γ, α) expander, with parts $L = \{L_1, \ldots, L_n\}$ and $R = \{R_1, \ldots, R_n\}$. We choose neighbors according to graph G. (See Section 5 for the definition of choosing neighbors.)

1. **Setup:**
   Each party, P_i, is provided an initial truly random seed k_i^1 from a trusted source.
2. **Re-randomizing:**
   (a) At the start of epoch t, each party P_i, for each of its neighbors P_j, generates re-randomizer $r_{i,j}^t = F(k_i^{t-1}, j)$ and sends it to P_j.
   (b) P_j receives a re-randomizer from each party of which it is a neighbor. It computes its new key as: $k_j^t = \bigoplus_{i \in N^{-1}(j)} r_{i,j}^t$.
   It computes a new PRG seed as: $\hat{k}_j^t = F(k_j^t, 0)$

To prove the security of this protocol, we first observe that the communication pattern in Protocol 5 is identical to that of Protocol 1. Thus as in the proof of security of Protocol 1, we can define a layered graph H, where vertex $H_i^{(t)}$ represents P_i at epoch t. We likewise re-use the definitions of an *honest vertex*, *honest path* and *honest ancient path*. We now establish the following lemma.

Lemma 7. *If $H_i^{(t)}$ is part of some honest ancient path, $H_{f(1)}^{(1)}, \ldots, H_{f(t)}^{(t)}$, then $F(k_i^t, x)$ is indistinguishable from random to $\mathcal{A}$ for all $x \notin N(i)$.*

Proof. We show this by induction using the following slightly stronger inductive hypothesis:

$\mathcal{A}$ *is unable to distinguish the real execution, from an execution in which $F(k_{f(u)}^u, \cdot)$ is replaced by a truly random function for all $1 \le u \le v$.*

For the base case, the key $k_{f(1)}^1$ is generated uniformly at random by a trusted dealer and sent to an honest party $P_{f(1)}$ using a secure (hardware) channel. (Note it is deleted from $P_{f(1)}$'s memory during the refresh phase of epoch 2, while $P_{f(1)}$ is still honest, so $\mathcal{A}$ can never observe it.) Therefore, the outputs of the PRF on key $k_{f(1)}^1$ will be indistinguishable from those of a random function.

Now assume the statement holds up to some value $v \in [t-1]$. Since $F(k_{f(v)}^v, \cdot)$ is indistinguishable from a random function to $\mathcal{A}$, the value $r_{f(v),f(v+1)}^v$ is indistinguishable from a random value to $\mathcal{A}$. (This value is generated, sent over a secure hardware channel, and deleted from the memory of both parties in the refresh phase of epoch $v + 1$, during which both $P_{f(v)}$ and $P_{f(v+1)}$ are honest, so $\mathcal{A}$ can never observe it.) Therefore, even if $\mathcal{A}$ knows all other re-randomizers sent to $P_{f(v+1)}$ in round $v + 1$, $r_{f(v),f(v+1)}^v$ will act as a one-time pad, so from $\mathcal{A}$'s perspective $k_{f(v+1)}^{v+1}$ will be distributed according to the uniform distribution. (Also, it will be deleted by $P_{f(v+1)}$ before $\mathcal{A}$ can observe it.) Thus, by the security of the PRF, $F(k_{f(v+1)}^{v+1}, \cdot)$ is indistinguishable from a random function.

Therefore, $F(k_{f(t)}^t, \cdot)$ is indistinguishable from a random function to $\mathcal{A}$. $\mathcal{A}$ may corrupt $P_{f(t)}$'s neighbors in epoch $t + 1$, which would allow $\mathcal{A}$, at most, to learn $F(k_{f(t)}^t, j)$ for $j \in N(f(t))$. However, for other inputs, the output will be indistinguishable from random to $\mathcal{A}$.

We can now prove that the random value generated is truly random:

Theorem 11. *Let there be a malicious mobile adversary that controls at most δn parties per epoch, where $\delta \leq \gamma(\alpha - 1)$. Protocol 5 ensures that γn of the PRG seeds in each epoch are indistinguishable from uniformly random seeds to $\mathcal{A}$.*

Proof. Lemma 1 in Sect. 5 states that when $\delta \leq \gamma(\alpha - 1)$, there will always be at least γn ancient honest paths to $H^{(t)}$. Thus, by Lemma 7, for γn of the parties in epoch t, $F(k_i^i, \cdot)$ is indistinguishable from a random function. $\mathcal{A}$ may receive $F(k_i^i, j)$ for all $j \in N(i) \subset \{1, \ldots, n\}$ in the next epoch, but will never receive the output of this function on input 0. Thus, at least γn parties will have PRG seeds that are indistinguishable from uniformly random to $\mathcal{A}$.

Remark 3 (Malicious adversaries). Recall that Protocol 1 provided only privacy, but not robustness, so $\mathcal{A}$ could *change* the secret by sending an incorrect message, but could not *learn* the secret. In our PP protocol, a corrupted party can similarly send incorrect re-randomizers. This will change the PRG seeds generated in later epochs, but it will not help $\mathcal{A}$ *learn* these seeds or undermine the pseudorandomness they generate. Therefore, our PP protocol has security guarantees that are still useful in practice against malicious, mobile adversaries.

Remark 4 (Secure channels). As discussed in Supplemental Material A.2, channels with proactive security cannot be instantiated with static cryptographic keys, since a mobile adversary could learn the channel keys in one epoch, and then continue to read messages on the channel in future epochs. Sect. 8 shows that proactively-secure channels *can* easily be instantiated using a trusted (hardware) signing oracle. It might seem that PP could also be used to instantiate proactively-secure channels. Unfortunately this is not possible.

To see this, note that $\mathcal{A}$ is able to see all (potentially encrypted) messages sent to a party P_i (even when P_i is not corrupted). Suppose P_i is corrupted and $\mathcal{A}$ learns the complete state of P_i, and then P_i is rebooted. Now, if P_i performs some local operation, $\mathcal{A}$ can simulate this since $\mathcal{A}$ learnt P_i's state and P_i has no fresh randomness. If P_i receives an encrypted message from another party, $\mathcal{A}$ can observe the encrypted message, decrypt the message as P_i would, and continue to simulate P_i. This is true even if the message is sent using a channel that is authenticated (by hardware) but is not private. Thus, if $\mathcal{A}$ corrupts P_i at any time and observes all messages P_i receives, $\mathcal{A}$ can simulate P_i's state indefinitely. This inherent limitation applies to all proactive protocols. Thus, without private (hardware) channels or fresh local randomness, it is impossible to attain any privacy in the mobile adversary model.

Furthermore, even if parties do have access to fresh local randomness, if there are no trusted hardware or authenticated hardware channels, once $\mathcal{A}$ corrupts a party, that party will never be able to authenticate itself. When $\mathcal{A}$ corrupts a party, it learns the entire state of the party at that point in time, and can therefore pretend to be the party in all future interactions. While the party may generate fresh local randomness, $\mathcal{A}$ can choose randomness from an identical distribution. Other parties will thus be unable to distinguish $\mathcal{A}$ from the real party.

Therefore, without (hardware) authenticated channels or local secure hardware, it is impossible to authenticate parties in the mobile adversary model.

Acknowledgements. This research was sponsored in part by ONR grant (N00014-15-1-2750) "SynCrypt: Automated Synthesis of Cryptographic Constructions" and a gift from Ripple Labs, Inc.

Supplemental Material

A   Previous Work

The Mobile adversary model is particularly challenging, because eventually a mobile adversary will have corrupted *all* the parties (but not all simultaneously). This means that an adversary who corrupts a party should (1) not be able to read the party's historical state, and (2) should not be able to predict the party's randomness in the future.

This means that at minimum parties need *secure deletes*, since otherwise an adversary who corrupted a party at time t, could read all of the messages received by the party during all previous rounds of the protocol, as well as *fresh randomness*, so that an adversary cannot predict the behavior of parties it has corrupted in the past.

In the original work introducing the mobile adversary [OY91], they imagined removing an adversary (and securely deleting previous state) by imagining a "clean" version of the program sitting in read-only memory, a piece of trusted hardware that would periodically "reboot" the machine to remove the adversary (as well as the history). They also assumed that either "each coin-flip is generated online (which is the practical assumption on generating randomness from physical devices), or, more abstractly, that the entire random tape of the machine is replaced with a new one during reboot."

Our works, like essentially all prior works in the PSS literature assume parties can securely delete state variables, and can be securely "rebooted" to obtain a clean copy of the PSS program.

A.1   PSS Protocols

The *mobile-adversary* model was introduced in [OY91], where they provided an information-theoretic protocol for secure computation. Proactive secret sharing has been widely studied e.g. [OY91, HJKY95, FGMY97, Rab98, CKLS02, ZSVR05] [BHNS99, SLL10, BEDLO14, MZW+19, YXD22] and some works (e.g. [FGMY97, Rab98]) focused on proactive secret sharing of keys for specific cryptosystems (e.g. RSA).

The main challenge in developing a PSS protocol is how to refresh the shares. In the semi-honest model, the linearity of secret sharing schemes like Shamir's scheme [Sha79] make it straightforward to re-randomize shares when parties are *semi-honest*. One method is to have each party generate a fresh sharing of zero, then each party locally adds all the shares they received. So the secret, s, can be shared according to a polynomial $f(x)$, where party i holds $f(i)$, and $f(0) = s$. In this method of refreshing, party i generates a polynomial $g_i(x)$, such that $g_i(0) = 0$, and gives $g_i(j)$ to party j, and party j calculates their new share as $f(j) + \sum_i g_i(j)$. This is the refresh method laid out in [HJKY95].

Another method is to have party i *re-share* their share, i.e., party i generates a new polynomial $g_i(x)$ such that $g_i(0) = f(i)$, and gives $g_i(j)$ to party j. This re-sharing technique is widely used in Secure Multiparty Computation [GRR98]. Since polynomial interpolation is a linear operation, party j can compute a new sharing of the original secret, s, by doing local, linear operations on the shares $\{g_j\}_i$. This is the refresh method laid out in [CKLS02].

Other works [ELL20, MZW+19, YXD22] share using bivariate polynomials. To obtain security against malicious adversaries (instead of semi-honest adversaries), these simple refresh protocols were combined with Verifiable Secret Sharing (like Feldman VSS [Fel87]), as well as BFT consensus.

The mobile adversary model relies on "epochs" – the adversary is static *within* an epoch – and this introduces some amount of synchrony into the model. It is possible to consider an *asynchronous* model of PSS, where there is still a global notion of epochs, but communication *within* an epoch is asynchronous (and adversarially controlled). PSS protocols that can tolerate asynchronous communication within an epoch include [CKLS02, ZSVR05, SLL10, YXD22]. Some PSS schemes have been implemented [SLL10, MZW+19, YXD22].

As is evident from the brief description of prior works, they all require for each party to carry out a secret sharing in the refresh phase, even in the semi-honest model. This results in an all-to-all communication between the parties during the share refresh. In our work, parties do not have all-to-all communication every epoch, instead they communicate according to an *expander graph*. Expander graphs have been used to build Robust Secret Sharing schemes [HO18], but those constructions only consider a static adversary.

To reduce communication, some protocols can handle batches of independent secrets, which can reduce *amortized* communication complexity. Batched PSS protocols include [BEDLO14, BDLO15, ELL20].

A.2   Refreshing Secure Channels

Most secure multiparty protocols assume that parties can communicate using "secure, authenticated channels." In practice, however, these secure channels are usually secured using public-key encryption, and authenticated using digital signatures. This works well in the *static* adversary model.

In the mobile adversary model, parties cannot use *persistent* keys to secure and authenticate their channels, because once an adversary has corrupted a party (and in doing so learned their private keys), the adversary can read *all* messages sent to that party during future rounds of the protocol (using the party's decryption key) and impersonate the party in all future rounds of the protocol (using the party's signing key).

This problem is *not* readily solved. If a party is securely rebooted (and generates new key material), how can they communicate their new public encryption and verification keys to the other parties? They cannot simply sign their new key using their old key, since an adversary (who had corrupted the party in the previous round) could generate a competing key, and sign it using the party's old, valid key.

One way to side-step this problem is to assume that parties are connected via persistent, secure authenticated channels (e.g. secure hardware channels), thus eliminating the need for key management. This is the approach taken in [OY91] as well as many subsequent works including [CKLS02,BEDLO14, MZW+19,YXD22].

In [HJKY95] they addressed this problem by assuming that all parties had access to an *uncensorable* broadcast channel. When a party was rebooted, they would generate new key material, and sign the new key using their old key, and broadcast their new (signed) key. As noted above, the adversary could do the same, by generating a new (adversarially controlled) key, and signing this key with the old key. In this case, however, since the broadcast channel is uncensorable, honest parties would see *two* new keys broadcast after the reboot. They would not be able to distinguish which one was valid, but they could refuse to use *either* key until the offending party was rebooted again. This provides a method whereby an adversary could halt the network (by continually broadcasting false keys after a reboot), but could never violate security.

This problem was explored in depth in [CHH97], where they propose a solution involving proactive, threshold signature schemes. Essentially, the construction of [CHH97] works as follows: At the start of the protocol, it is assumed that all parties hold a *share* of a private signing key, and the corresponding verification key is baked into their read-only memory. This persistent verification key will then be used to authenticate all short term secrets as follows. When a party reboots, and generates new key material, they will send their new public keys to all parties, at which point the parties will run a byzantine agreement protocol to agree on the party's public key. Then they will use their long-term key shares to generate a threshold signature on the party's new signing key. Unfortunately, this construction rests on a proactive threshold signature scheme, to avoid circularity, they show how to convert any proactive threshold signature scheme (that requires authenticated channels) to one that does not require authenticated channels, using byzantine agreement.

Some PSS protocols (e.g. [SLL10]) consider a *dynamic* committee model, where there is a completely new committee in each epoch (and the public keys of all the new committee members are known in advance), so there is no need to refresh channel keys. This model does allow members from *old* committees to be corrupted (even after their role on a committee is done), so parties use a *forward-secure* cryptosystem [CHK03]. This means that an adversary who corrupts a party cannot decrypt ciphertexts sent to that party in *previous* epochs. Unfortunately, forward-secure cryptosystems do *not* prevent the adversary from learning messages sent in *future* epochs.

[ZSVR05] suggests a few possible approaches for creating persistent secure channels between parties. One approach is to use trusted hardware to implement a signing oracle with a monotonically increasing counter. Every time the oracle signs a message, it would include the counter (that is incremented every epoch), that ensures that the message was sent during the current epoch. They also suggest an alternative approach with a trusted administrator (with a static public key), who can identify each party and sign their new keys after each refresh. They do not, however, describe how a party can authenticate themself to the trusted administrator after a reboot.

[CKLS02] suggests that if each party has a trusted co-processor (e.g. Intel SGX [MAA+16]), then the co-processor can have a trusted clock (that is timed to the epochs), as well as a persistent signing key. Then the co-processor can generate new session keys every epoch, and sign these new epoch-keys together with the epoch number (from its trusted clock), using its persistent signing key. Now that these trusted co-processors are prevalent in commodity hardware, this is a promising approach. Below (Sect. 8) we show how to eliminate the need for a full-blown trusted co-processor with a tamper-proof clock.

The assumption that persistent, trusted channels exist (e.g. [OY91, CKLS02, BEDLO14, MZW+19, YXD22]) is an extremely strong assumption, which we would like to avoid. Weaker assumptions, assuming a censorship resistant broadcast channel as in [HJKY95], or byzantine agreement and threshold secret sharing (as in [CHH97]) are unsatisfactory in our setting because they require *all-to-all* $O(n)$ communication per-party, something that we wish to avoid in our protocol.

In Sect. 8, we outline a novel solution for re-establishing secure, authenticated channels in the presence of a mobile adversary. Our solution is compatible with any other proactive secret sharing scheme that requires secure channels and has the added benefit that it is compatible with essentially any communication pattern, i.e., it only requires communication between the sender and receiver in order to set up a secure channel between the two parties.

B   Ramanujan Expanders

Ramanujan expanders are expanders with essentially optimal spectral expansion. The spectral expansion of a graph is the largest absolute value of an eigenvalue of the adjacency matrix (apart from the trivial eigenvalues $\pm d$). Ramanujan graphs have spectral expansion at most $2\sqrt{d-1}$. This is optimal in the sense that for any $\epsilon > 0$, any infinite family of d-regular graphs contains at least some graphs with spectral expansion greater than $(2\sqrt{d-1} - \epsilon)$ [Nil91].

Definition 3. *A d-regular graph, G, is called a* Ramanujan Graph *if the spectral radius of G is bounded by $2\sqrt{d-1}$, i.e., for every eigenvalue λ of the adjacency matrix of G, if $|\lambda| < d$, then $|\lambda| < 2\sqrt{d-1}$.*

In particular, we use balanced bipartite Ramanujan expanders. Balanced bipartite Ramanujan graphs can be efficiently computed for all degrees and sizes [MSS13, MSS18, Coh16].

Ramanujan graphs do not necessarily have *optimal* vertex expansion. It is an open problem to find explicit general constructions of bipartite graphs with near-optimal vertex expansion (see Open Question 6 of Paredes [Par21]). Constructing such graphs would improve the concrete results of this paper. Nevertheless, Ramanujan graphs provide good vertex expansion, which is sufficient for the purposes of this paper.

Below we demonstrate that Ramanujan graphs have the properties our protocols require. Concretely, we prove Theorems 1 and 2. We start with a standard theorem relating spectral and vertex expansion:

Theorem 12 (Spectral expansion implies vertex expansion [Vad12] **[Theorem 4.6]).** *If G is a d-regular graph with second largest eigenvalue λ, then for every $\gamma \in [0,1]$, G is a (γ, α) expander where*

$$\alpha = \frac{1}{(1-\gamma)\frac{\lambda^2}{d^2} + \gamma} \tag{1}$$

Combining Definition 3 and Theorem 12 gives our first required property:

Theorem 1 *A Ramanujan graph is a $\left(\gamma, \frac{1}{(1-\gamma)\frac{4}{d} + \gamma}\right)$ expander $\forall\ \gamma \in [0,1]$.*

We now prove the second property. We are given a d-regular, bipartite expander graph with two sets L and R each of size n. We have a subset $S \subset L$ of nodes of size δn on the left and a value ϵ_1. We want to calculate how many nodes on the right have more that ϵ_1 fraction of their edges connected to the set S.

Lemma 8 (Bipartite Expander Mixing [Hae95][**Theorem 5.1]).** *Let G be a d-regular bipartite graph with spectral radius λ. Suppose, $S \subset L$, and $T \subset R$, with $|S| = \alpha |L|$, and $|T| = \beta |R|$. Let $e(X,Y) \stackrel{\text{def}}{=} |\{(x,y) \in E \mid x \in X, y \in Y\}|$ then*

$$\left|\frac{e(S,T)}{e(L,R)} - \alpha\beta\right| \leq \frac{\lambda}{d}\sqrt{\alpha\beta} \tag{2}$$

Note, that $e(L,R)$ are all the edges in the graph, i.e. $d|L|$.

Lemma 9. *Given a d-regular bipartite expander with spectral radius λ, suppose a set of δn vertices on the left are in S then at most*

$$\frac{\lambda^2 \delta n}{(\epsilon_1 - \delta)^2 d^2} \tag{3}$$

right vertices have at least an ϵ_1 fraction of left-neighbors in S.

Proof. Let T denote the set of right-hand vertices that have at least an ϵ_1-fraction of left-neighbors in S. Since G has right-degree d, we have $e(S,T) \geq d\epsilon_1 |T|$.

On the other hand, the expander mixing lemma (Lemma 8) tells us that for $\alpha = |T|/n$ and $\beta = \delta$,

$$\left| \frac{e(S,T)}{nd} - \delta \frac{|T|}{n} \right| \le \frac{\lambda}{d} \sqrt{\delta \frac{|T|}{n}} \quad \Rightarrow \quad \frac{e(S,T)}{d} - \delta |T| \le \frac{\lambda}{d} \sqrt{n\delta |T|} \qquad (4)$$

On the other hand, $e(S,T) \ge d\epsilon_1 |T|$, so we have

$$\epsilon_1 |T| - \delta |T| \le \frac{\lambda}{d} \sqrt{n\delta |T|} \quad \Rightarrow \quad |T| \le \frac{\lambda^2 \delta n}{(\epsilon_1 - \delta)^2 d^2} \qquad (5)$$

Since Ramanujan graphs have spectral radius at most $2\sqrt{d-1}$, this implies our required property:

Theorem 2. *Ramanujan graphs have the following property. Let S be a set of size at most δn vertices on the left. Then at most*

$$\frac{4\delta n}{(\frac{1}{2} - \delta)^2 d}$$

right-hand vertices have at least $\frac{1}{2}$ of their neighbors in S.

C   Epoch Length

We present a maliciously-secure PSS protocol in Sect. 7 that can only tolerate $\Theta(\sqrt{n})$ corruptions per epoch, which may seem low compared to existing PSS protocols (e.g. [HJKY95] and [SLL10]) that can tolerate $\Theta(n)$ corruptions per epoch.

What this comparison hides is we are free to choose the length of an epoch by choosing how frequently we run the refresh protocol. Decreasing the length of an epoch will increase the communication cost (per unit time), but should decrease the number of parties an adversary can corrupt in a given epoch.

To see this in play, imagine that instead of allowing the adversary to corrupt $\delta \cdot n$ parties per epoch (as is standard in the PSS literature), we assumed the adversary had a fixed corruption *rate*, i.e., the adversary could corrupt one party every $t(n)$ units of time. A traditional PSS protocol (tolerating δn corruptions per epoch), would be secure in this model by setting the epoch length $T = \delta \cdot n \cdot t(n)$.

But now, consider the communication cost. A traditional PSS protocol, tolerating δn corruptions per epoch, and requiring $\Theta(n)$ communication per refresh, would have amortized communication cost of $\Theta\left(\frac{1}{t(n)}\right)$ per unit time. By contrast, our protocol, which requires only $\Theta(\kappa)$ communication per epoch, but can "only" tolerate $\Theta(\sqrt{n})$ corruptions could set a much lower epoch time, $T = \Theta(t(n) \cdot \sqrt{n})$, which would make the amortized communication cost of our protocol $\Theta\left(\frac{\kappa}{t(n)\sqrt{n}}\right)$ per unit time, which is much lower for sufficiently large n.

Furthermore, this ignores the costs of establishing secure channels in the (normal) case that secure hardware channels do not exist. Authentication between parties requires $\Omega(\kappa)$ communication (see Sect. 8 for our instantiation). This would increase the amortized communication cost of traditional protocols to $\Theta\left(\frac{\kappa}{t(n)}\right)$ per unit time, but the amortized cost of our maliciously-secure PSS protocol would remain $\Theta\left(\frac{\kappa}{t(n)\sqrt{n}}\right)$.

What this means is that (for sufficiently large n) we can achieve a *lower* amortized communication cost per unit time, while achieving the *same* level of security.

D   Proof of Lemma 10

Lemma 10. *The equation* $f(x) = \frac{4x}{(\frac{1}{2}-x)^2(x-a)}$ *where* $0 < a < \frac{1}{2}$ *is minimized over the range* $a < x < \frac{1}{2}$ *by* $x = \frac{1}{4}(a + \sqrt{a^2 + 4a})$.

Proof. First, observe that over the range $a < x < \frac{1}{2}$, $f(x)$ is continuous, differentiable and positive. Therefore, any minimum point of $f(x)$ over $a < x < \frac{1}{2}$ is also a maximum point of $g(x) = \frac{4}{f(x)}$ over the same range. So we will now instead find the maximum point(s) of $g(x)$ over this range.

$$g(x) = \frac{(\frac{1}{2}-x)^2(x-a)}{x} = \frac{x^3 - ax^2 - x^2 + ax + \frac{1}{4}x - \frac{1}{4}a}{x} = x^2 - (a+1)x + (a + \frac{1}{4}) - \frac{1}{4}\frac{a}{x}$$

Now $g(a) = 0$, $g(\frac{1}{2}) = 0$ and $g(x)$ is positive over $a < x < \frac{1}{2}$, so $g(x)$ is not maximized over $a < x < \frac{1}{2}$ at the end-points. It must be maximum at a point, v, where the first derivative is 0.

$$g'(v) = 2v - (a+1) + \frac{a}{4v^2} = 0 \Rightarrow 2v^3 - (a+1)v^2 + \frac{a}{4} = 0 \Rightarrow (v - \frac{1}{2})(2v^2 - a - \frac{a}{2}) = 0$$

The solutions are $v = \frac{1}{2}$, and $v = \frac{a \pm \sqrt{a^2 + 4a}}{4}$. Only $v = \frac{a + \sqrt{a^2 + 4a}}{4}$ is in the range $a < x < \frac{1}{2}$, so this value minimizes $g(x)$ and maximizes $f(x)$ over this range.

References

ABPP14. Abdalla, M., Benhamouda, F., Passelègue, A., Paterson, K.G.: Related-key security for pseudorandom functions beyond the linear barrier. In: Garay, J.A., Gennaro, R. (eds.) CRYPTO 2014. LNCS, vol. 8616, pp. 77–94. Springer, Heidelberg (2014). https://doi.org/10.1007/978-3-662-44371-2_5

BC10. Bellare, M., Cash, D.: Pseudorandom functions and permutations provably secure against related-key attacks. In: Rabin, T. (ed.) CRYPTO 2010. LNCS, vol. 6223, pp. 666–684. Springer, Heidelberg (2010). https://doi.org/10.1007/978-3-642-14623-7_36

BDLO15. Baron, J., Defrawy, K.E., Lampkins, J., Ostrovsky, R.: Communication-optimal proactive secret sharing for dynamic groups. In: Malkin, T., Kolesnikov, V., Lewko, A.B., Polychronakis, M. (eds.) ACNS 2015. LNCS, vol. 9092, pp. 23–41. Springer, Cham (2015). https://doi.org/10.1007/978-3-319-28166-7_2

BEDLO14. Baron, J., Defrawy, K.E., Lampkins, J., Ostrovsky, R.: How to withstand mobile virus attacks, revisited. In: PODC, pp. 293–302 (2014)

BHNS99. Barak, B., Herzberg, A., Naor, D., Shai, E.: The proactive security toolkit and applications. In: CCS, pp. 18–27 (1999)

CH94. Canetti, R., Herzberg, A.: Maintaining security in the presence of transient faults. In: Desmedt, Y.G. (ed.) CRYPTO 1994. LNCS, vol. 839, pp. 425–438. Springer, Heidelberg (1994). https://doi.org/10.1007/3-540-48658-5_38

CHH97. Canetti, R., Halevi, S., Herzberg, A.: Maintaining authenticated communication in the presence of break-ins. In: PODC, pp. 15–24 (1997)

CHK03. Canetti, R., Halevi, S., Katz, J.: A forward-secure public-key encryption scheme. In: Biham, E. (ed.) EUROCRYPT 2003. LNCS, vol. 2656, pp. 255–271. Springer, Heidelberg (2003). https://doi.org/10.1007/3-540-39200-9_16

CKLS02. Cachin, C., Kursawe, K., Lysyanskaya, A., Strobl, R.: Asynchronous verifiable secret sharing and proactive cryptosystems. In: CCS, pp. 88–97 (2002)

Coh16. Cohen, M.B.: Ramanujan graphs in polynomial time. In: 2016 IEEE 57th Annual Symposium on Foundations of Computer Science (FOCS), pp. 276–281. IEEE (2016)

ELL20. Eldefrawy, K., Lepoint, T., Leroux, A.: Communication-efficient proactive secret sharing for dynamic groups with dishonest majorities. In: Conti, M., Zhou, J., Casalicchio, E., Spognardi, A. (eds.) ACNS 2020. LNCS, vol. 12146, pp. 3–23. Springer, Cham (2020). https://doi.org/10.1007/978-3-030-57808-4_1

Fel87. Feldman, P.: A practical scheme for non-interactive verifiable secret sharing. In: FOCS, pp. 427–438. IEEE (1987)

FGMY97. Frankel, Y., Gemmell, P., MacKenzie, P.D., Yung, M.: Optimal-resilience proactive public-key cryptosystems. In: FOCS, pp. 384–393. IEEE (1997)

GRR98. Gennaro, R., Rabin, M.O., Rabin, T.: Simplified VSS and fast-track multiparty computations with applications to threshold cryptography. In: PODC, pp. 101–111 (1998)

Hae95. Haemers, W.H.: Interlacing Eigenvalues and graphs. Appl. Cryptography Network Secur. 226, 593–616 (1995)

HJKY95. Herzberg, A., Jarecki, S., Krawczyk, H., Yung, M.: Proactive secret sharing or: how to cope with perpetual leakage. In: Coppersmith, D. (ed.) CRYPTO 1995. LNCS, vol. 963, pp. 339–352. Springer, Heidelberg (1995). https://doi.org/10.1007/3-540-44750-4_27

HO18. Hemenway, B., Ostrovsky, R.: Efficient robust secret sharing from expander graphs. Cryptogr. Commun. 10(1), 79–99 (2018)

MAA+16. McKeen, F., et al.: Intel® software guard extensions (Intel® SGX) support for dynamic memory management inside an enclave. In: Proceedings of the Hardware and Architectural Support for Security and Privacy 2016, pp. 1–9 (2016)

MSS13. Marcus, A., Spielman, D.A., Srivastava, N.: Interlacing families I: bipartite Ramanujan graphs of all degrees. In: FOCS, pp. 529–537. IEEE (2013)

MSS18. Marcus, A.W., Spielman, D.A., Srivastava, N.: Interlacing families IV: bipartite Ramanujan graphs of all sizes. SIAM J. Comput. **47**(6), 2488–2509 (2018)

MZW+19. Maram, S.K.D., et al.: CHURP: dynamic-committee proactive secret sharing. In: CCS, pp. 2369–2386 (2019)

Nil91. Nilli, A.: On the second eigenvalue of a graph. Discret. Math. **91**(2), 207–210 (1991)

OY91. Ostrovsky, R., Yung, M.: How to withstand mobile virus attacks. In: PODC, pp. 51–59 (1991)

Par21. Paredes, P.: On the Expansion of Graphs. Ph.D. thesis, Princeton (2021)

Rab98. Rabin, T.: A simplified approach to threshold and proactive RSA. In: Krawczyk, H. (ed.) CRYPTO 1998. LNCS, vol. 1462, pp. 89–104. Springer, Heidelberg (1998). https://doi.org/10.1007/BFb0055722

Sha79. Shamir, A.: How to share a secret. Commun. ACM **22**(11), 612–613 (1979)

SLL10. Schultz, D., Liskov, B., Liskov, M.: MPSS: mobile proactive secret sharing. TISSEC **13**(4), 1–32 (2010)

Vad12. Vadhan, S.: Pseudorandomness, vol. 7. Now Delft (2012)

YXD22. Yan, Y., Xia, Y., Devadas, S.: Shanrang: fully asynchronous proactive secret sharing with dynamic committees. IACR ePrint 2022/164 (2022)

ZSVR05. Zhou, L., Schneider, F.B., Van Renesse, R.: APSS: proactive secret sharing in asynchronous systems. TISSEC **8**(3), 259–286 (2005)

Improved Polynomial Secret-Sharing Schemes

Amos Beimel[1]($\boxtimes$)(ID), Oriol Farràs[2](ID), and Or Lasri[1](ID)

[1] Ben-Gurion University of the Negev, Be'er-Sheva, Israel
beimel@bgu.ac.il, orshlomo@post.bgu.ac.il
[2] Universitat Rovira i Virgili, Tarragona, Spain
oriol.farras@urv.cat

Abstract. Despite active research on secret-sharing schemes for arbitrary access structures for more than 35 years, we do not understand their share size – the best known upper bound for an arbitrary n-party access structure is $2^{O(n)}$, while the best known lower bound is $\Omega(n/\log(n))$. Consistent with our knowledge, the share size can be anywhere between these bounds. To better understand this question, one can study specific families of secret-sharing schemes. For example, linear secret-sharing schemes, in which the sharing and reconstruction functions are linear mappings, have been studied in many papers, e.g., it is known that they require shares of size at least $2^{0.5n}$. Secret-sharing schemes in which the sharing and/or reconstruction are computed by low-degree polynomials have been recently studied by Paskin-Cherniavsky and Radune [ITC 2020] and by Beimel, Othman, and Peter [CRYPTO 2021]. It was shown that secret-sharing schemes with sharing and reconstruction computed by polynomials of degree 2 are more efficient than linear schemes (i.e., schemes in which the sharing and reconstruction are computed by polynomials of degree one).

Prior to our work, it was not known if using polynomials of higher degree can reduce the share size. We show that this is indeed the case, i.e., we construct secret-sharing schemes for arbitrary access structures with reconstruction by degree-d polynomials, where as the reconstruction degree d increases, the share size decreases. As a step in our construction, we construct conditional disclosure of secrets (CDS) protocols. For example, we construct 2-server CDS protocols for functions $f : [N] \times [N] \to \{0, 1\}$ with reconstruction computed by degree-d polynomials with message size $N^{O(\log \log d/ \log d)}$. Combining our results with a lower bound of Beimel et al. [CRYPTO 2021], we show that increasing the degree of the reconstruction function in CDS protocols provably reduces the message size. To construct our schemes, we define *sparse* matching vectors, show constructions of such vectors, and design CDS protocols and secret-sharing schemes with degree-d reconstruction from sparse matching vectors.

The full version of this work is available at [11].

G. Rothblum and H. Wee (Eds.): TCC 2023, LNCS 14370, pp. 374–405, 2023.
https://doi.org/10.1007/978-3-031-48618-0_13

1   Introduction

Secret sharing is a method by which a dealer holding a secret distributes shares to parties such that only pre-defined authorized subsets of parties can reconstruct the secret and unauthorized subsets should not learn any information about the secret. The collection of authorized sets is called the access structure. Originally, secret sharing was motivated by the problem of secure information storage; nowadays secret-sharing schemes have found numerous other applications in cryptography, distributed computing, and complexity theory (see, e.g., [9] for such applications). A major problem with secret-sharing schemes is that the best known schemes for general n-party access structures have shares of size $2^{O(n)}$ [4,6,34,37], making the known constructions for general access structures impractical. On the other hand, the best known lower bound on the total share size of secret-sharing schemes realizing an arbitrary n-party access structure, proved by Csirmaz [19,20], is $\Omega(\frac{n^2}{\log n})$. Despite active research on secret-sharing schemes for more than 35 years, determining the share size for arbitrary access structures is a major open problem.

To better understand this question, one can study specific families of secret-sharing schemes. Such study can shed light on general secret-sharing schemes, e.g., provide new techniques for constructing efficient secret-sharing schemes or provide new lower bound techniques. For example, linear secret-sharing schemes, in which the sharing and reconstruction are computed by linear mappings, have been studied in many papers [4,6,8,17,35,37,41], and it is known that they require shares of size at least $2^{0.5n}$ [8] and every n-party access structure can be realized by a secret-sharing scheme with share size $2^{0.757n}$ [6]. Secret-sharing schemes in which the sharing and/or reconstruction are computed by low-degree polynomials have been recently studied by Paskin-Cherniavsky and Radune [40] and by Beimel, Othman, and Peter [15]. It was shown in [15] that every n-party access structure can be realized by a secret-sharing scheme with sharing and reconstruction computed by polynomials of degree 2 and share size $2^{0.705n}$, that is, secret-sharing schemes with degree-2 sharing and reconstruction are more efficient than the best known linear schemes (i.e., schemes in which the sharing and reconstruction are computed by polynomials of degree one). Prior to this work, it was not known if secret-sharing schemes with constant reconstruction degree $d > 2$ are more efficient than secret-sharing schemes with reconstruction degree 2.

In this paper we continue the study of polynomial secret-sharing schemes, i.e., schemes in which the reconstruction of the secret from the shares of an authorized set is done by polynomials of constant degree. Our main result in this paper is showing that the increasing the degree results in better share size, as described in the next theorem.

Theorem 1.1 (Informal). *Every n-party access structure can be realized by a secret-sharing scheme with reconstruction by polynomials of degree d and share size $2^{(0.585+O(\frac{\log\log d}{\log d}))n}$.*

In particular, for an arbitrary access structure, we get a secret-sharing scheme with share size $2^{0.6731n+o(n)}$ and reconstruction degree 243. As $\lim\limits_{d\to\infty} \frac{\log\log d}{\log d} = 0$, the share size approaches $2^{0.585n+o(n)}$, which is the share size of the best known secret-sharing scheme [15]. In comparison, Beimel et al. [15] constructed a degree-2 secret-sharing scheme with share size $2^{0.705n+o(n)}$, and Applebaum and Nir [6] constructed a linear secret-sharing scheme with share size $2^{0.7575n+o(n)}$.

Beimel and Farràs [10] proved that most access structures can be realized with secret-sharing schemes that are much more efficient than the best known schemes for the worst access structures. Beimel et al. [15] showed a similar result for schemes with reconstruction of degree 2. We generalize this result to arbitrary reconstruction degrees.

Theorem 1.2 (Informal). *Almost all n-party access structures can be realized by a secret-sharing scheme with reconstruction by polynomials of degree d and 1-bit secrets and with share size $2^{O\left(\frac{\log\log d}{\log d}\right)n}$.*

The previous results and our results on secret-sharing schemes with polynomial reconstruction are summarized in Table 1.

Table 1. Summary of the best upper and lower bounds on the share size for secret-sharing schemes. The contributions of this work are Corollary 7.3 and Corollary 7.5.

	Linear	Degree-2	Degree-d	Unrestricted
Lower bound for the worst access structures	$\Omega(2^{n/2-o(n)})$ [8]	$\Omega(2^{n/3-o(n)})$ [15]	$\Omega(2^{n/(d+1)-o(n)})$ [15]	$\Omega(n^2/\log(n))$ [19]
Upper bound for all access structures	$2^{0.7576n+o(n)}$ [6]	$2^{0.705n+o(n)}$ [15]	$2^{\left(0.585+O\left(\frac{\log\log d}{\log d}\right)\right)n+o(n)}$ Corollary 7.3	$2^{0.585n+o(n)}$ [6]
Upper bound for *almost* all access structures	$2^{n/2+o(n)}$ [10]	$2^{n/3+o(n)}$ [15]	$2^{O\left(\frac{\log\log d}{\log d}\right)n}$ Corollary 7.5	$2^{\tilde{O}(\sqrt{n})}$ [10]

Conditional disclosure of secrets (CDS) protocols were introduced by Gertner, Ishai, Kushilevitz, and Malkin [30]. These protocols are an important tool in the recent constructions of secret-sharing schemes for arbitrary access structures [3,4,6,37]. In a k-server CDS protocol for a Boolean function $f : [N]^k \to \{0,1\}$, there are k servers that hold a secret s and have a common random string. In addition, each server holds a private input $x_i \in [N]$. Each server sends one message to a referee such that the referee, who knows the private inputs of the servers but nothing more, learns the secret s if $f(x_1,\ldots,x_k) = 1$ and learns nothing otherwise. CDS protocols have been used recently in [3,4,6,15,37] to construct the best known secret-sharing schemes for arbitrary access structures. CDS protocols in which the reconstruction is done by polynomials of degree d have been studied in [28,38] prior to the works on polynomial secret-sharing schemes. Continuing this line of research, we construct k-server CDS protocols that are provably more efficient as the degree of d of the reconstruction grows. We use them to construct secret-sharing schemes for arbitrary access structures with reconstruction by polynomials of degree d; these schemes are more efficient than the *best known* linear secret-sharing schemes. Specifically, we prove the following result.

Theorem 1.3 (Informal). *For every $N > 0$, $d > 0, k > 1$, and function $f : [N]^k \rightarrow \{0,1\}$, there is a k-server CDS protocol for f, with degree-d reconstruction and communication complexity $N^{O((k-1) \cdot \frac{\log \log d}{\log d})}$.*

For example, we prove that for any function $f : [N]^2 \rightarrow \{0,1\}$ there is a 2-server CDS protocol over $\mathbb{F}_7$ with communication complexity $O(N^{1/4})$ and reconstruction degree 243. In comparison, the best previously known 2-server CDS protocol with constant degree reconstruction has degree-2 reconstruction and communication complexity $O(N^{1/3})$ [15].

Theorem 1.3 is proved by constructing a CDS protocol for the function INDEX_N^k, where for every $D \in \{0,1\}^{N^{k-1}}$ (called the database) and every $(i_2, \ldots, i_k) \in [N]^{k-1}$ (called the index), $\text{INDEX}_N^k(D, i_2, \ldots, i_k) = D_{i_2,\ldots,i_k}$. This strategy was used by Liu et al. in [38]. The 2-server CDS protocol of [38] (and our 2-server CDS protocol) uses the ideas of the 2-server private information retrieval (PIR) protocol of Dvir and Gopi [22]. Our techniques imply 2-server PIR protocols over $\mathbb{Z}_m$, for $m = p_1 p_2$ where p_1, p_2 are primes and $p_1 | p_2 - 1$, with communication complexity $N^{O_m(\sqrt{\log \log N / \log N})}$[1] (the protocol of [22] only works over $\mathbb{Z}_6$). Furthermore, we can construct 2-server PIR protocols, in which the answers of the servers can be computed by a degree-d polynomial, the reconstruction function is linear, and the communication complexity is $N^{O(\frac{\log \log d}{\log d})}$.

By a lower bound of Beimel et al. [15] (generalizing results of [28]), the message size of CDS protocols with degree-d reconstruction is $\Omega(N^{1/(d+1)})$. Thus, while the message size of our protocols does not match the lower bound, our results show that increasing the degree of the reconstruction in 2-server CDS protocols provably reduces the message size. The known and new results on the message size CDS protocols are described in Table 2.

1.1   Our Techniques

Our main result is a general construction of secret-sharing schemes for arbitrary access structures in which reconstruction is done by low degree polynomials. We construct it using the same steps as the constructions of the most efficient known secret-sharing schemes for arbitrary access structures. We start by constructing 2-server CDS protocols using matching vectors, following the footsteps of Liu, Vaikuntanathan, and Wee [38]. We use this 2-server CDS protocols to construct k-server CDS protocols using decomposable matching vectors, as in Liu et al. [39]. We then transform this CDS protocol into a robust k-server CDS protocol using the transformation of Applebaum, Beimel, Nir, and Peter [4]

---

[1] The notation $O_m(\cdot)$ allows the constant in the O notation to depend on m.

Table 2. Summary of best upper and lower bounds on the message size of CDS protocols for functions $f : [N]^k \to \{0,1\}$ and INDEX_N^k, according to different types of reconstruction functions. In the first row, we present the best lower bound on the message size of CDS protocols for the worst function $f : [N]^2 \to \{0,1\}$ and for INDEX_N^2. In the second row, we present the best upper bounds for all functions $f : [N]^2 \to \{0,1\}$ and for INDEX_N^2. In the third and four rows, we present the corresponding bounds for functions $f : [N]^k \to \{0,1\}$ and INDEX_N^k. The contributions of this work are Corollary 3.7 and Corollary 5.14.

	Linear	Degree-2	Degree-d	Unrestricted
INDEX_N^2 and functions $f : [N]^2 \to \{0,1\}$	$\Omega(N^{1/2})$ [12,28]	$\Omega(N^{1/3})$ [15]	$\Omega(N^{1/(d+1)})$ [15,28]	$\Omega(\log N)$ [2,5,7]
	$O(N^{1/2})$ [13,28]	$O(N^{1/3})$ [38]	$N^{O\left(\frac{\log\log d}{\log d}\right)}$ Corollary 3.7	$N^{O\left(\sqrt{\frac{\log\log N}{\log N}}\right)}$ [38]
INDEX_N^k and functions $f : [N]^k \to \{0,1\}$	$\Omega(N^{(k-1)/2})$ [12,16]	$\Omega(N^{(k-1)/3})$ [15]	$\Omega\left(N^{\frac{k-1}{d+1}}/k\right)$ [15]	$\Omega(\log N)$ [2,5,7]
	$O(N^{(k-1)/2})$ [16,38]	$O(N^{(k-1)/3})$ [15]	$N^{O\left((k-1)\cdot\frac{\log\log d}{\log d}\right)}$ Corollary 5.14	$N^{O\left(\sqrt{\frac{k}{\log N}}\log\log N\right)}$ [39]

(with the better analysis of Beimel, Othoman, and Peter [15]), and finally use a transformation of [6] to construct secret-sharing schemes for arbitrary access structures. The technical contribution of this paper is in the first two steps. We show that if the matching vectors are sparse (i.e., the number of non-zero entries in them is small), then the degree of the reconstruction is low. We construct such matching vectors and show how to use them to construct 2-server and k-server CDS protocols with low-degree reconstruction, as explained below.

Matching Vectors and CDS Protocols. We start by recalling that a family of pairs of vectors $((\mathbf{u}_i, \mathbf{v}_i))_{i=1}^N$, where $\mathbf{u}_i, \mathbf{v}_i \subseteq \mathbb{Z}_m^h$, is a family S-matching vectors over $\mathbb{Z}_m$ if $\langle \mathbf{u}_i, \mathbf{v}_i \rangle \equiv 0 \pmod{m}$ for $i \in [N]$ and $\langle \mathbf{u}_i, \mathbf{v}_j \rangle \bmod m \in S$ for $i \neq j \in [N]$ (where $m = p_1 \cdot p_2$ is a product of two distinct primes $p_1 < p_2$, $S \subseteq \mathbb{Z}_m \setminus \{0\}$, and $\langle \mathbf{u}_i, \mathbf{v}_j \rangle$ is the inner product modulo m, i.e., $\sum_{\ell=1}^h \mathbf{u}_i[\ell] \cdot \mathbf{v}_j[\ell] \bmod m$). Matching vectors were used by Efremenko [24] and Dvir and Gopi [22] to construct 3-server and 2-server private information retrieval (PIR) protocols, respectively. Liu et al. [38] used the ideas in [22] to construct 2-server CDS protocols. In [22,38], they used matching vectors over $\mathbb{Z}_6$. We generalize these constructions and show that one can use matching vectors over $\mathbb{Z}_{p_1 p_2}$, where p_1 and p_2 are primes such that p_1 divides $p_2 - 1$. Furthermore, we observe that one can use S-matching vectors for sets S that are larger than the ones used in previous constructions on PIR and CDS protocols. Namely, one can take $S_{\text{one}} = \{a \in \mathbb{Z}_m : a \equiv 1 \pmod{p_1} \vee a \equiv 1 \pmod{p_2}\}$ instead of $S_{\text{can}} = \{a \in \mathbb{Z}_m : (a \equiv 0,1 \pmod{p_1}) \wedge (a \equiv 0,1 \pmod{p_1})\} \setminus \{0\}$, which was used in previous works.[2] E.g., over $\mathbb{Z}_{21}$ we can use $S_{\text{one}} = \{1, 4, 7, 8, 10, 13, 15, 16, 19\}$ instead of $S_{\text{can}} = \{1, 7, 15\}$. We use this observation to construct better CDS protocols with degree-d reconstruction. The construction of S_{one}-matching vectors that are shorter than the known S_{can}-matching vectors may lead to CDS protocols that are better than the currently best ones.

Sparse Matching Vectors. The most expensive part of computing the reconstruction function of the CDS protocol over $\mathbb{Z}_m$ (when considering the degree of the reconstruction) is computing $a^{\langle \mathbf{v}_i, \mathbf{m} \rangle} \mod p_2$, where a is an element of order p_1 in $\mathbb{F}_{p_2}$, $1 \leq i \leq N$ is an index, and $\mathbf{m}$ is a vector sent to the referee by the second server. Note that

$$a^{\langle \mathbf{v}_i, \mathbf{m} \rangle} \equiv \prod_{\ell=1}^{h} a^{\mathbf{v}_i[\ell] \cdot \mathbf{m}[\ell]} \pmod{p_2}, \tag{1}$$

where $\mathbf{v}_i, \mathbf{m} \in \mathbb{Z}_m^h$, and $\mathbf{v}_i[\ell], \mathbf{m}[\ell]$ are the ℓ-th coordinates of $\mathbf{v}_i$ and $\mathbf{m}$, respectively. If the server sends $a^{b \cdot \mathbf{m}[\ell]} \mod p_2$ for every $1 \leq \ell \leq h$ and every $b \in \mathbb{Z}_{p_1}$ (this only increases the communication complexity by a factor of p_1), then the referee can compute this value with a polynomial of degree h. In the best constructions of matching vectors, the length of the vectors h is $2^{\Theta(\sqrt{\log(N) \log\log(N)})}$ (over $\mathbb{Z}_6$). Thus, we get a CDS protocol with communication complexity and reconstruction degree $2^{\Theta(\sqrt{\log(N) \log\log(N)})}$.

The starting point of the construction with lower reconstruction degree is to recall that the order of a is p_1 and to write the product in (1) as

$$\prod_{\substack{\ell \in \{1,\ldots,h\}, \\ \mathbf{v}_i[\ell] \not\equiv 0 \pmod{p_1}}} a^{\mathbf{v}_i[\ell] \cdot \mathbf{m}[\ell]} \pmod{p_2}.$$

This implies that the degree of reconstruction is the number of coordinates in the matching vectors that are non-zero modulo p_1. To get a 2-server CDS protocol with degree-d reconstruction, we need a family of matching vectors in which each $\mathbf{v}_i$ contains at most d coordinates that are non-zero modulo p_1; we say that such family is a d-sparse family.

Constructions of Sparse Matching Vectors. Our goal is to construct a family of N matching vectors over $\mathbb{Z}_{p_1 \cdot p_2}$ that are d-sparse with respect to p_1 and their length h is as short as possible. By the lower bound of [15] their length is at least $h = \Omega(N^{1/(d+1)})$ for a constant d. We present 3 constructions in which $h = d^{O(\frac{\log d}{\log\log d})^{4.18}} N^{O(\frac{\log\log d}{\log d})}$. The first construction is due to Efremenko [24]; the construction as described in [24, Appendix A] is sparse. In the second construction, we show how to improve Efremenko's construction. For concrete parameters, our construction achieves the smallest length h compared to the other 2

---

[2] In [22], they also have a construction that uses a $\mathbb{Z}_6 \setminus \{0\}$-matching vectors family over $\mathbb{Z}_6$. It is unclear how to use this construction to improve the communication complexity of PIR and CDS protocols.

constructions. The downside of our construction is that they are S_{one}-matching vectors (compared to S_{can} in the other two constructions). S_{one}-matching vectors suffice for constructing 2-server private information retrieval (PIR) protocols [22], k-CDS protocols, and secret-sharing schemes for arbitrary access structures. However, they cannot be used in the 3-server PIR protocols of Efremenko [24]. The third construction we describe is a construction by Kutin [36]; in this case we need to decouple two of the parameters in the construction to achieve sparse matching vectors. The advantage of Kutin's construction compared to the other two constructions is that every m that is a product of two distinct primes (e.g., $m = 6$) can be used to achieve every sparsity d. In contrast, in Efremenko's construction and in our construction, to get smaller sparsity we need to use bigger m's. We remark that we can also use Grolmusz's construction of matching vectors [31] to construct sparse matching vectors (again by decoupling two parameters). This yields to a construction with similar features as Kutin's construction; we do not describe Grolmusz's construction in this paper.

We next describe the ideas of Efremenko's construction [24] and our improvement. Efremenko starts with a family of vectors $(\tilde{\mathbf{u}}_1, \ldots, \tilde{\mathbf{u}}_N)$ and $(\tilde{\mathbf{v}}_1, \ldots, \tilde{\mathbf{v}}_N)$ that are the characteristic vectors of N subsets in $\binom{[\tilde{h}]}{m-1}$. If $\tilde{\mathbf{u}}_i$ and $\tilde{\mathbf{v}}_j$ are the characteristic vectors of A_i and A_j, respectively, then $\langle \tilde{\mathbf{u}}_i, \tilde{\mathbf{v}}_j \rangle = |A_i \cap A_j|$ mod m. Thus, $\langle \tilde{\mathbf{u}}_i, \tilde{\mathbf{v}}_i \rangle = m - 1$ and $\langle \tilde{\mathbf{u}}_i, \tilde{\mathbf{v}}_j \rangle \in \{0, \ldots, m - 2\}$ for $i \neq j$. By adding a first coordinate that is 1 in all vectors, Efremenko constructs $\mathbb{Z}_m \setminus \{0\}$-matching vectors, where $\binom{\tilde{h}}{m-1} > N$ (since there must be at least N distinct subsets of size $m - 1$). The sparsity of these vectors is m. To construct S_{can}-matching vectors, Efremenko uses the tensor product, Fermat's little theorem, and the Chinese reminder theorem (CRT). The length of the resulting vectors is $\tilde{h}^{p_2-1}$ and their sparsity with respect to p_1 is m^{p_1}. We modify this construction by starting with characteristic vectors of sets of size p_1^2 (since $p_1 < p_2$, this is smaller than in Efremenko's construction). We use Fermat's little theorem only with respect to p_1 and use a polynomial of degree p_1 to deal with the vectors modulo p_2. The length of the vectors in our construction is $\tilde{h}^{p_1}$, where $\tilde{h}$ is bigger than in Efremenko's construction; however, our construction yields vectors with roughly the same length as Efremenko's construction and smaller sparsity.

k-Server CDS Protocols with Polynomial Decoding. We use 2-server CDS protocols to construct a k-server CDS protocols. Following [39], the first server in the k-server CDS protocol will simulate the first server in the 2-server CDS protocol and the last $k - 1$ servers in the k-server CDS protocol will simulate the second server in the 2-server CDS protocol. In the simulation, the last $k-1$ servers need to send a message depending on their collective inputs, but each server only sees its input. As in [39], we use decomposable matching vectors to enable the simulation, that is, matching vectors such that every vector $\mathbf{u}_i$ can be computed from $k-1$ vectors $\mathbf{u}_{2,i_2}, \ldots, \mathbf{u}_{k,i_k}$, where each vector $\mathbf{u}_{t,i_t}$ can be computed from the input of the t-th server. To construct k-server CDS protocols with polynomial decoding using this approach, we have two challenges. First, we need to show that the constructions of sparse matching vectors are decomposable. This is done by changing the basic construction; instead of taking characteristic vectors of arbitrary sets of size $m-1$, we partition the universe into $m-1$ parts (i.e., subsets) and take sets of size $m-1$ that contain exactly one party from each part. The second challenge is to implement the simulation of the second server's message in the 2-server CDS protocol using a protocol in which the referee reconstructs the message using a low-degree polynomial. Liu et al. [39] use a private simultaneous message (PSM) protocol of [33] for this task; however, it is not clear how to reconstruct the message with low-degree polynomials in this protocol. We design a special purpose protocol for this task exploiting the fact that in CDS protocols the referee knows the inputs (but not the secret).

From k-Server CDS Protocols with Polynomial Decoding to Secret-Sharing with Polynomial Reconstruction. We transform our k-server CDS protocol into a robust k-server CDS protocol using the transformation of Applebaum, Beimel, Nir, and Peter [4] (using the better analysis of Beimel, Othoman, and Peter [15]). In a robust CDS protocol (abbreviated as RCDS protocol) for a function f, a server can send messages for more than one input using the same randomness. The security of the protocol should hold as long as the messages correspond to zero-inputs (i.e., inputs for which f evaluates to zero). We finally use a transformation of [6] from RCDS protocols to secret-sharing schemes for arbitrary access structures. This last transformation is similar to the one in previous papers.

Summary of the Construction. The main conceptual contribution of this paper is defining sparse matching vectors and showing that they imply CDS protocols with polynomial reconstruction. Towards this good, we generalize the CDS protocol of [38] to work over arbitrary $m = p_1 \cdot p_2$ where p_1 and p_2 are primes such that p_1 divides $p_2 - 1$. We observe that in this case, we can use a more relaxed notion of matching vectors (i.e., S_{one}-matching vectors). Constructing S_{one}-matching vectors that are shorter than the known constructions of S_{can}-matching vectors will lead to better CDS protocols and secret-sharing schemes. Our most important technical contribution is constructing a new family of sparse matching vectors that for concrete parameters are shorter than the matching vectors of Efremenko [23], which are sparse and sparse generalizations of the constructions of Grolmusz [31] and Kutin [36]. Our contribution of secret-sharing schemes with polynomial reconstruction follows the steps of previous constructions [4,6,39]; however, in many steps we encountered technical difficulties and needed to change the constructions to enable polynomial reconstruction.

Due to the space restrictions of this publication, we omitted all the proofs and many intermediate results, comments, and remarks. The full version of this work is available at [11].

1.2   Previous Works

Secret-Sharing Schemes. Secret-sharing schemes were introduced by Shamir [42] and Blakley [18] for the threshold case, and by Ito, Saito, and Nishizeki [34] for the general case. Ito et al. presented two secret-sharing schemes with share size

2^n for every access structure. The best currently known secret-sharing schemes for general n-party access structure are highly inefficient with total share size of $2^{0.585n}$ [3,4,6,37]. The best known lower bound for the total share size of a secret-sharing scheme is $\Omega(\frac{n^2}{\log n})$ [19,20]; there is an exponential gap between the lower bound and the upper bound.

Polynomial Secret-Sharing Schemes. Paskin-Cherniavsky and Radune [40] defined secret-sharing schemes with polynomial sharing; in these schemes the sharing is computed by constant degree polynomials (there are no restrictions on the reconstruction functions). They showed limitations of various sub-classes of secret-sharing schemes with polynomial sharing. Specifically, they showed that the subclass of schemes for which the sharing is linear in the randomness (and the secret can be with arbitrary degree) is equivalent to multi-linear schemes up to a multiplicative factor of $O(n)$ in the share size. This implies that schemes in this subclass cannot significantly reduce the known share size of multi-linear schemes. In addition, they showed that the subclass of schemes over finite fields with odd characteristic such that the degree of the randomness in the sharing function is exactly 2 or 0 in any monomial of the polynomial can efficiently realize only access structures whose all minimal authorized sets are singletons. They also studied the randomness complexity of schemes with polynomial sharing and showed an exponential upper bound on the randomness complexity (as a function of the share size).[3] Beimel, Othman, and Peter [15] defined and studied secret-sharing schemes and CDS protocols with polynomial reconstruction and secret-sharing schemes with polynomial sharing and reconstruction. They constructed a k-server CDS protocols with degree 2 sharing and reconstruction with message size $O(N^{1/3})$ and proved a lower bound of $\Omega(N^{1/(d+1)})$ for every 2-server CDS protocol with degree-d reconstruction. They also prove that (under plausible assumptions) secret-sharing-schemes with polynomial sharing are more efficient than secret-sharing schemes with polynomial reconstruction.

Conditional Disclosure of Secrets Protocols. CDS protocols were introduced by Gertner et al. [29]. 2-server CDS are equivalent to secret-sharing for forbidden graph access structures [43]. Beimel et al. [13] showed a construction of 2-server CDS protocols with communication complexity of $O(\sqrt{N})$. Later, Gay et al. [28] showed a construction of 2-server CDS protocol for INDEX_N^2 and for every function $f : [N] \times [N] \to \{0,1\}$ with linear reconstruction and communication complexity $O(\sqrt{N})$. They also proved a lower bound of $\Omega(N^{1/d+1})$ on the communication complexity of 2-server CDS protocols for INDEX_N^2 in which the reconstruction is computed by a degree-d polynomial. In particular, they proved that their linear 2-server CDS protocol for INDEX_N^2 with communication complexity $O(\sqrt{N})$ is optimal. Beimel et al. [12] proved a lower bound of $\Omega(\sqrt{N})$ on the communication complexity of CDS protocols with linear reconstruction for almost all functions $f : [N] \times [N] \to \{0,1\}$; Beimel et al. [15] generalized the

---

[3] For linear and multi-linear schemes, there is a tight linear upper bound on the randomness complexity.

lower bound on the communication complexity of 2-server CDS protocols with degree-d reconstruction for almost all functions $f : [N] \times [N] \rightarrow \{0, 1\}$. Constructions and lower bounds for k-server CDS protocols appear in [12,15,16,30,38]; see Table 2.

Matching Vectors. We next discuss the most relevant results on matching vectors. The study of matching vectors families dates back to the study of set systems with restricted intersections modulo an integer m, that is, a system of sets whose size modulo m is some number μ_0 and the sizes of the intersection of any two sets in the system modulo m is in some set L. Such system implies a family of matching vectors by taking the characteristic vectors of the sets in the system. Frankl and Wilson [27] initiated the study of this question and proved upper bounds on the size of such set systems when the moduli is a prime. Using matching vector terminology, they proved that for any prime p if there is an S-matching vector family $((\mathbf{u}_i, \mathbf{v}_i))_{i=1}^{N}$ over $\mathbb{Z}_p^h$, then $N \le \binom{h}{|S|}$. They asked if the same lower bounds apply to composite numbers. Frankl [26] showed that this is not true; his result implies that for every N there is an S_{one}-matching vectors family over $\mathbb{Z}_6$ with N vectors of length $h = O(N^{1/3})$ (where $N > \binom{h}{3}$). Grolmusz [31] showed that working over composite numbers can drastically reduce the length of the matching vectors, i.e., his result implies that there is an S_{one}-matching vectors family over $\mathbb{Z}_m$, where $m = p_1 p_2$ for two primes $p_1 \ne p_2$, with N vectors and length $h = 2^{O(p_2 \sqrt{\log N \log \log N})}$. Kutin [36] showed that for every pair of primes $p_1 \ne p_2$ and for infinitely many values of N there are S_{one}-matching vectors families over $\mathbb{Z}_{p_1 p_2}$ of length $h = 2^{O(\sqrt{\log N \log \log N})}$ (notice that he removed the dependency of p_2 in the exponent). Efremenko [24] used matching vectors to construct locally decodable codes and 3-server private information retrieval protocols. He also provided another construction of S_{one}-matching vectors with length $h = 2^{O(\sqrt{\log N \log \log N})}$. Dvir, Gopalan, and Yekhanin [21] continued the study of matching vector codes, i.e., locally decodable codes based on matching vectors. Dvir and Gopi [22] used matching vectors to construct 2-server private information retrieval protocols and Liu, Vaikuntanathan, and Wee [38,39] used them to construct CDS protocols, robust CDS protocols, and matching vectors families. See [11] for more details.

2 Preliminaries

In this section, we will present the definitions needed for this paper. We will start with some notations, continue by defining secret-sharing schemes for general access structures, in particular secret-sharing with polynomial reconstruction. Afterwards, we define conditional disclosure of secrets (CDS) protocols. See the full version of this work [11] for more formal definitions and more details.

2.1 Notations

For a natural number $n \in \mathbb{N}$, we denote $[n] \triangleq \{1, \ldots, n\}$. We denote log the logarithmic function with base 2. For $\alpha \in [0, 1]$, we denote the binary entropy of α by $H_2(\alpha)$, where $H_2(\alpha) = -\alpha \log \alpha - (1-\alpha)\log(1-\alpha)$ for $\alpha \in (0,1)$, and $H_2(0) = H_2(1) = 0$.

For a set A and a positive integer k, we denote by $\binom{A}{k}$ the family of subsets of A of size k, i.e., $\{B \subseteq A : |B| = k\}$.

If two integers a and b are congruent modulo m, we denote $a \equiv b \pmod{m}$. If a is the reduction of b modulo m, then we denote $a \leftarrow b \bmod m$.

We use the $\widetilde{O}$ notation, called *soft-O*, as a variant of big O notation that ignores logarithmic factors, that is, $f(n) \in \widetilde{O}(g(n))$ if $f(n) \in O(g(n)\log^k g(n))$ for some constant k.

We next define three vector operations that are used to construct matching vectors. We define the first two over the ring $\mathbb{Z}_m$ and the last product over a field $\mathbb{F}$ as this is the way that they are used in this paper.

Definition 2.1 (Pointise and dot product). *Let $m, h > 0$ be two positive integers and let $\mathbf{x}, \mathbf{y} \in \mathbb{Z}_m^h$. The point-wise product (or Hadamard product) of $\mathbf{x}, \mathbf{y}$, denoted by $\mathbf{x} \odot \mathbf{y}$, is a vector in $\mathbb{Z}_m^h$ whose ℓ-th element is the product of the ℓ-th elements of $\mathbf{x}, \mathbf{y}$, i.e. $(\mathbf{x} \odot \mathbf{y})[\ell] = \mathbf{x}[\ell] \cdot \mathbf{y}[\ell] \bmod m$. The dot product (or inner product) of $\mathbf{x}$ and $\mathbf{y}$ is $\langle \mathbf{x}, \mathbf{y} \rangle = \sum_{\ell \in [h]} \mathbf{x}[\ell] \cdot \mathbf{y}[\ell] \bmod m$.*

Definition 2.2 (Tensor product). *Let $\mathbb{F}$ be a field, let N be an integer, and let $\mathbf{x}, \mathbf{y} \in \mathbb{F}^N$. The tensor product of $\mathbf{x}, \mathbf{y}$, denoted by $\mathbf{x} \otimes \mathbf{y} \in \mathbb{F}^{N^2}$, is defined by $(\mathbf{x} \otimes \mathbf{y})[i,j] := \mathbf{x}[i] \cdot \mathbf{y}[j]$, (where we identify $[N^2]$ with $[N]^2$). Similarly, we define the ℓ-th tensor power $\mathbf{x}^{\otimes \ell} \in \mathbb{F}^{N^\ell}$ as $\mathbf{x}^{\otimes \ell} = \mathbf{x}^{\otimes \ell-1} \otimes \mathbf{x}$.*

Theorem 2.3 (Chinese reminder theorem (CRT)). *Let $n_1, n_2, \ldots, n_k$ be pairwise relatively prime natural numbers, $N = n_1 n_2 \ldots n_k$, and $b_1, b_2, \ldots, b_k \in \mathbb{Z}$. Then there is a unique $x \in \mathbb{Z}_N$ such that $x \equiv b_i \pmod{n_i}$ for all $1 \le i \le k$.*

2.2 Access Structures and Secret-Sharing Schemes

The definitions in this section are mainly based on [9]. See the full version of this work [11] for more formal definitions and more details.

Definition 2.4 (Access structures). *Let $P = \{p_1, \ldots, p_n\}$ be a finite set of n parties. A collection $\mathcal{A} \subseteq 2^P$ is monotone if for every set $A \in \mathcal{A}$ and for every $C \subseteq P$ such that $A \subseteq C$ it must be that $C \in \mathcal{A}$. An access structure is a monotone collection $\mathcal{A} \subseteq 2^P \setminus \emptyset$. A set of parties is called authorized if it is in $\mathcal{A}$ and unauthorized otherwise.*

Definition 2.5 (Secret-sharing schemes—Syntax). *Let $P = \{p_1, \ldots, p_n\}$ be a set of n parties. A secret-sharing scheme with domain of secrets S, set of random strings R, and domain of shares $S_1, S_2, \cdots, S_n$ for the parties $p_1, p_2, \ldots, p_n$, is a mapping $\Pi : S \times R \to S_1 \times S_2 \times \cdots \times S_n$. For a set $A \subseteq P$, we denote $\Pi_A(s; r)$ as the restriction of Π to its A-entries. We define the size of the secret in Π as $\log |S|$, and the share size of party p_j as $\log |S_j|$, the maximum share size as $\max_{1 \le j \le n} \log |S_j|$, and the total share size as $\sum_{j=1}^{n} \log |S_j|$.*

Definition 2.6 (Secret-sharing schemes—Correctness and security). *A secret-sharing scheme Π with finite domain S, where $|S| \geq 2$, realizes an access structure $\mathcal{A}$ if the following two requirements hold:*

CORRECTNESS. *The secret s can be reconstructed by any authorized set of parties, that is, for any set $A \in \mathcal{A}$ (where $A = \{p_{i_1}, \ldots, p_{i_{|A|}}\}$), there exists a reconstruction function $\mathrm{RECON}_A : S_{i_1} \times \cdots \times S_{i_{|A|}} \to S$ such that $\mathrm{RECON}_A(\Pi_A(s; r)) = s$ for every $s \in S$ and every $r \in R$.*

SECURITY. *Every unauthorized set cannot learn anything about the secret from its shares (in the information theoretic sense).*

All the secret-sharing schemes presented in this paper are with the domain of secrets $S = \{0, 1\}$, unless stated otherwise.

2.3   Conditional Disclosure of Secrets

Informally, in a CDS protocol there are k servers $Q_1, \ldots, Q_k$, each holding a private input x_i, the secret s, and a common random string r, and there is a referee holding $x_1, \ldots, x_k$. Each server Q_i sends the message $m_i = Enc(x_i, s; r)$ to the referee, and the referee can reconstruct s if and only if $f(x_1, \ldots, x_n) = 1$. In a Robust CDS protocols (RCDS), the security is guaranteed even if the referee receives a certain amount of messages that correspond to different inputs.

Definition 2.7 (Conditional disclosure of secrets (CDS) protocols). *Let $f : X_1 \times \cdots \times X_k \to \{0, 1\}$ be a k-input function. A k-server CDS protocol $\mathcal{P}$ for f, with domain of secrets S, domain of common random strings R, and finite message domains $M_1, \ldots, M_k$, consists of k encoding functions $Enc_1, \ldots, Enc_k$, where $Enc_i : X_i \times S \times R \to M_i$ for every $i \in [k]$. For an input $x = (x_1, \ldots, x_k) \in X_1 \times \cdots \times X_k$, secret $s \in S$, and randomness $r \in R$, we let $Enc(x, s; r) = (Enc_1(x_1, s; r), \ldots, Enc_k(x_k, s; r))$. We say that $\mathcal{P}$ is a CDS protocol for f if it satisfies the following properties:*

CORRECTNESS. *There is a deterministic reconstruction function $Dec : X_1 \times \cdots \times X_k \times M_1 \times \cdots \times M_k \to S$ such that for every input $x = (x_1, \ldots, x_k) \in X_1 \times \cdots \times X_k$ for which $f(x_1, \ldots, x_k) = 1$, every secret $s \in S$, and every common random string $r \in R$, it holds that $Dec(x, Enc(x, s; r)) = s$.*

SECURITY. *For every input $x = (x_1, \ldots, x_k) \in X_1 \times \cdots \times X_k$ with $f(x_1, \ldots, x_k) = 0$ and for every pair of secrets $s, s' \in S$, the encodings $Enc(x, s; r)$ and $Enc(x, s'; r)$ are equally distributed.*

The message size *of a CDS protocol $\mathcal{P}$ is defined as the size of the largest message sent by the servers, i.e., $\max_{1 \leq i \leq k} \log |M_i|$.*

In two-server CDS protocols, we sometimes refer to the servers as Alice and Bob (instead of Q_1 and Q_2, respectively) and to the referee as Charlie.

Similarly to secret-sharing schemes, all the CDS protocols presented in this paper are with domain of secrets $S = \{0, 1\}$, unless stated otherwise.

Definition 2.8 (The predicate INDEX_N^k). *We define the k-input function* $\text{INDEX}_N^k : \{0,1\}^{N^{k-1}} \times [N]^{k-1} \to \{0,1\}$ *where for every $D \in \{0,1\}^{N^{k-1}}$ (a $(k-1)$ dimensional array called the database) and every $(i_2, \ldots, i_k) \in [N]^{k-1}$ (called the index), $\text{INDEX}_N^k(D, i_2, \ldots, i_k) = D_{i_2, \ldots, i_k}$.*

Observation 2.9 ([28]). *If there is a k-server CDS protocol for INDEX_N^k with message size M, then for every $f : [N]^k \to \{0,1\}$ there is a k-server CDS protocol with message size M.*

Definition 2.10 (Zero sets). *Let $f : X_1 \times X_2 \times \cdots \times X_k \to \{0,1\}$ be a k-input function. We say that a set of inputs $Z \subseteq X_1 \times X_2 \times \cdots \times X_k$ is a zero set of f if $f(x) = 0$ for every $x \in Z$. For sets $Z_1, \ldots, Z_k$, we denote $\text{Enc}(Z, s; r) = (\text{Enc}(x, s; r))_{x \in Z_1 \times \cdots \times Z_k}$.*

Definition 2.11 (t-RCDS protocols). *Let $\mathcal{P}$ be a k-server CDS protocol for a k-input function $f : X_1 \times X_2 \times \cdots \times X_k \to \{0,1\}$ and $Z = Z_1 \times Z_2 \times \cdots \times Z_k \subseteq X_1 \times X_2 \times \cdots \times X_k$ be a zero set of f. We say that $\mathcal{P}$ is robust for the set Z if for every pair of secrets $s, s' \in S$, it holds that $\text{Enc}(Z, s; r)$ and $\text{Enc}(Z, s'; r)$ are identically distributed. For an integer t, we say that $\mathcal{P}$ is a t-RCDS protocol if it is robust for every zero set $Z_1 \times Z_2 \times \cdots \times Z_k$ such that $|Z_i| \leq t$ for every $i \in [k]$.*

2.4 Degree-d Secret Sharing and Degree-d CDS Protocols

We next quote the definition of [15] of secret-sharing with polynomial reconstruction and CDS with polynomial decoding.

Definition 2.12 (Degree of polynomial). *The degree of a multivariate monomial is the sum of the degree of all its variables; the degree of a polynomial is the maximal degree of its monomials.*

Definition 2.13 Degree-d mapping over $\mathbb{F}$). *A function $f : \mathbb{F}^\ell \to \mathbb{F}^m$ can be computed by degree-d polynomials over $\mathbb{F}$ if there are m polynomials $Q_1, \ldots, Q_m : \mathbb{F}^\ell \to \mathbb{F}$ of degree at most d such that $f(x_1, \ldots, x_\ell) = (Q_1(x_1, \ldots, x_\ell), \ldots, Q_m(x_1, \ldots, x_\ell))$.*

Definition 2.14 (Secret-sharing schemes with degree-d reconstruction). *We say that the scheme Π with domain of secrets S has a degree-d reconstruction over a finite field $\mathbb{F}$ if there are integers $\ell, \ell_1, \ldots, \ell_n$ such that $S \subseteq \mathbb{F}^\ell$ and $S_i = \mathbb{F}^{\ell_i}$ for every $i \in [N]$, and Recon_B, the reconstruction function of the secret, can be computed by degree-d polynomials over $\mathbb{F}$ for every $B \in \mathcal{A}$.*

Definition 2.15 (CDS Protocols with Degree-d Decoding). *A CDS protocol $\mathcal{P}$ with domain of secrets S has a degree-d decoding over a finite field $\mathbb{F}$ if there are integers $\ell, \ell_1, \ldots, \ell_k \geq 1$ such that $S \subseteq \mathbb{F}^\ell$ and $M_i = \mathbb{F}^{\ell_i}$ for every $1 \leq \ell \leq k$, and for every inputs $x_1, \ldots, x_k$ the function $\text{Dec}_{x_1, \ldots, x_k} : \mathbb{F}^{\ell_1 + \cdots + \ell_k} \to S$ can be computed by degree-d polynomials over $\mathbb{F}$, where $\text{Dec}_{x_1, \ldots, x_k}(m_1, \ldots, m_k) = \text{Dec}(x_1, \ldots, x_k, m_1, \ldots, m_k)$.*

2.5   Matching Vectors

We next define matching vectors (MV), which are vectors whose inner product lies in a small set $S \cup \{0\}$. These vectors were used in [27,31] to construct a family of sets whose intersection lies in a small set. They were used in [24] to construct efficient PIR protocols and in [38] to construct efficient CDS protocols.

Definition 2.16 (Matching vector family [24]). *Let $m, h > 0$ be integers, and let $S \subseteq \mathbb{Z}_m \setminus \{0\}$ be a set. The family of vectors $((\mathbf{u}_i, \mathbf{v}_i))_{i=1}^N$, where $\mathbf{u}_i, \mathbf{v}_i \in \mathbb{Z}_m^h$, is called S-matching vectors if:*

1. *$\langle \mathbf{u}_i, \mathbf{v}_i \rangle \mod m = 0$ for $i \in [N]$, and*
2. *$\langle \mathbf{u}_i, \mathbf{v}_j \rangle \mod m \in S$ for $i \neq j \in [N]$.*

Let $m = p_1 p_2$ for some primes p_1, p_2. In previous works, they mainly considered the set $S_{\mathrm{can}} = \{a \in \mathbb{Z}_m : (a \bmod p_1 \in \{0,1\}) \wedge (a \bmod p_2 \in \{0,1\})\} \setminus \{0\}$.

In this work, we consider a bigger set

$$S_{\mathrm{one}} = \{a \in \mathbb{Z}_m : a \equiv 1 \ (\mathrm{mod} \ p_1) \vee a \equiv 1 \ (\mathrm{mod} \ p_2)\}.$$

3   A Polynomial 2-Server CDS Protocol

In this section, we present a 2-server CDS protocol with degree-d decoding for the INDEX_N^2 predicate with $N^{O(\frac{\log \log d}{\log d})}$ communication. This CDS protocol is a generalization of the CDS protocol from [38], which is based on a PIR protocol presented in [22]. In [38], they use matching vector families over $m = 3 \cdot 2$; We generalize this protocol and use matching vector families over $m = p_1 p_2$, for primes p_1, p_2 such that $p_1 | p_2 - 1$. We will first present the protocol and prove its correctness and security. We will then define sparse matching vectors and show that if we use sparse matching vectors in the CDS protocols, then we get a CDS protocol with degree-d decoding. In Sect. 4, we will show how to construct sparse matching vectors.

3.1   The CDS Protocol over $m = p_1 p_2$

In Fig. 1, we present the 2-server CDS protocol; in the protocol we use an element $a \in \mathbb{F}_{p_2}^*$ whose order is p_1, i.e., p_1 is the smallest positive integer such that $a^{p_1} \equiv 1 \ (\mathrm{mod} \ p_2)$. An element of order p_1 exists if and only if $p_1 | p_2 - 1$. This generalizes the CDS protocol of [38], which uses matching vectors over $m = 2 \cdot 3$ and the element $a = -1$.

Theorem 3.1. *Let p_1, p_2 be two primes such that $p_1 | p_2 - 1$, and let $m = p_1 p_2$. Given an S_{one}-matching vector family $((\mathbf{u}_i, \mathbf{v}_i))_{i=1}^N$ over $\mathbb{Z}_m^h$, the protocol in Fig. 1 is a 2-server CDS protocol over $\mathbb{F}_{p_2}$ for INDEX_N^2 with message size $h \cdot \log m$.*

A polynomial 2-server CDS protocol for INDEX$_N^2$

Public Knowledge: An S_{one}-matching vector family $((\mathbf{u}_i, \mathbf{v}_i))_{i=1}^N$ over $\mathbb{Z}_m^h$ for $m = p_1 p_2$ s.t. $p_1 | p_2 - 1$, and $h \in \mathbb{N}$. An element $a \in \mathbb{F}_{p_2}^*$ of order p_1 in $\mathbb{F}_{p_2}^*$.
Alice's Input: $D \in \{0,1\}^N$.
Bob's Input: $i \in [N]$.
The secret: $s \in \{0,1\}$.
Shared Randomness: $\mathbf{r}_1 \in \mathbb{F}_{p_1}^h$, $\mathbf{r}_2 \in \mathbb{F}_{p_2}^h$, $r_3 \in \mathbb{F}_{p_2}$.

Define $C : \mathbb{F}_{p_1}^h \to \mathbb{F}_{p_2}$ as $C(\mathbf{b}) = \sum_{j=1}^N D_j a^{\langle \mathbf{b}, \mathbf{v}_j \rangle} \mod p_2$.
Define $V : \mathbb{F}_{p_1}^h \to \mathbb{F}_{p_2}^h$ as $V(\mathbf{b}) = \sum_{j=1}^N D_j \mathbf{v}_j a^{\langle \mathbf{b}, \mathbf{v}_j \rangle} \mod p_2$.

- Alice sends $m_A^1 \leftarrow ((1-a)s - 1)C(\mathbf{r}_1) - r_3 \in \mathbb{F}_{p_2}$ and
  $\mathbf{m}_A^2 \leftarrow \mathbf{r}_2 + ((1-a)s - 1)V(\mathbf{r}_1) \in \mathbb{F}_{p_2}^h$.
- Bob sends $\mathbf{m}_B^1 \leftarrow (s\mathbf{u}_i + \mathbf{r}_1 \mod p_1) \in \mathbb{F}_{p_1}^h$ and
  $m_B^2 \leftarrow (\langle \mathbf{u}_i, \mathbf{r}_2 \rangle + r_3 \mod p_2) \in \mathbb{F}_{p_2}$.
- Charlie outputs 1 if

$$\langle \mathbf{u}_i, \mathbf{m}_A^2 \rangle - m_A^1 - m_B^2 - C(\mathbf{m}_B^1) + \langle \mathbf{u}_i, V(\mathbf{m}_B^1) \rangle \neq 0, \qquad (2)$$

and 0 otherwise.

Fig. 1. A polynomial CDS protocol using a matching vector family over $\mathbb{Z}_m$ where $m = p_1 p_2$ for primes p_1, p_2 such that $p_1 | p_2 - 1$.

3.2 Sparse Matching Vectors

In order to analyze the degree of the reconstruction function we will introduce a new definition regarding matching vector families. This new definition is one of our most important contributions in this paper.

Definition 3.2. ((d, p)-sparse matching vectors). *Let $((\mathbf{u}_i, \mathbf{v}_i))_{i=1}^N$ be an S-matching vector family over $\mathbb{Z}_m^h$ for some $m, h \in \mathbb{N}$. We say that $((\mathbf{u}_i, \mathbf{v}_i))_{i=1}^N$ is a d-sparse S-matching vector family if for all $i \in [N]$,*

$$|\{\ell \in [h] : \mathbf{v}_i[\ell] \neq 0\}| \leq d,$$

i.e., the number of non-zero entries in $\mathbf{v}_i$ is at most d.

For a prime p such that $p|m$, we say that $((\mathbf{u}_i, \mathbf{v}_i))_{i=1}^N$ is (d, p)-sparse if for all $i \in [N]$,

$$|\{\ell \in [h] : \mathbf{v}_i[\ell] \not\equiv 0 \ (\mathrm{mod}\ p)\}| \leq d.$$

We could have defined the sparsity property to be over $\mathbf{u}_i$ as well, and our constructions in Sect. 4 would satisfy this stronger requirement. However, for the reconstruction degree, sparsity solely for the $\mathbf{v}_i$'s suffices.

Next, we use the definition above for the reconstruction degree analysis.

Lemma 3.3. *Let p_1, p_2 be two primes such that $p_1 | p_2 - 1$, and let $m = p_1 p_2$. Given a (d, p_1)-sparse S_{one}-matching vector family over $\mathbb{Z}_m^h$, the reconstruction of the CDS protocol in Fig. 1 can be computed by a degree-$p_1 d$ polynomial over $\mathbb{F}_{p_2}$.*

Now, we present two theorems that state the existence of sparse matching vector families.

Theorem 3.4. *For every $N, d > 0$, there exists primes p_1, p_2 where $p_1 | p_2 - 1$, and $p_1 \leq \frac{2 \log d}{\log \log d}$ for which there is a (d, p_1)-sparse S_{one}-matching vector family $((\mathbf{u}_i, \mathbf{v}_i))_{i=1}^N$ over $\mathbb{Z}_m^h$, where $m = p_1 p_2$, and $h \leq 2 d^{1 + \frac{2}{\log \log d}} N^{\frac{16 \log \log d}{\log d}}$.*

Theorem 3.5. *For every $N, d > 0$, there is a $(d, 2)$-sparse S_{can}-matching vector family $((\mathbf{u}_i, \mathbf{v}_i))_{i=1}^N$ over $\mathbb{Z}_6^h$ with $h \leq d^{O(1)} N^{O(\frac{\log \log d}{\log d})}$.*

Combining Fig. 1 and Theorem 3.5 with the CDS protocol in Fig. 1, we get CDS protocols with various trade-offs between the decoding degree and the communication complexity.

Theorem 3.6. *For every $N, d > 0$, there is a 2-server CDS protocol over $\mathbb{F}_3$ or over $\mathbb{F}_{p_2}$ for some prime $p_2 = polylog(d)$ for $INDEX_N^2$, with degree-d reconstruction and communication complexity $d^{O(1)} N^{O(\frac{\log \log d}{\log d})}$.*

Corollary 3.7. *For every constant $d > 0$, $N > 0$, and function $f : [N]^2 \to \{0, 1\}$, there is a 2-server CDS protocol for f, with degree-d reconstruction and communication complexity $d^{O(1)} N^{O(\frac{\log \log d}{\log d})}$.*

4 Constructions of d-Sparse Matching Vector Families

In this section, we present three different constructions of (d, p_1)-sparse matching vector families over $\mathbb{Z}_m^h$ where $m = p_1 p_2$ and $h = d^{O(1)} N^{O(\frac{\log \log d}{\log d})}$. The main differences between the constructions are the constraints of choosing the primes p_1, p_2 as N grows.

In the three constructions of matching vector families, we use a basic construction of an $\tilde{S}$-matching vectors family for a large set $\tilde{S}$. To avoid repetition, we will present it here, and use it in the constructions with different choices of $\tilde{S}$.

Claim 4.1. *Let $N, t, w > 0$ be integers, where $0 < w < t$. There is a $(w + 1)$-sparse $\tilde{S}$-matching vector family $((\tilde{\mathbf{u}}_i, \tilde{\mathbf{v}}_i))_{i=1}^N$ over $\mathbb{Z}_t^{\tilde{h}}$, for $\tilde{S} = \{t - w, \ldots, t - 1\}$, and $\tilde{h} = \lceil N^{1/w} \rceil \cdot w + 1$.*

4.1 Efremenko's Construction

The first matching vector family we present is the Efremenko's [24, Appendix A]. We observe that Efremenko's construction is sparse. This construction takes the basic construction from Claim 4.1 and uses Fermat's little theorem and the Chinese reminder theorem in order to construct an S_{can}-matching vector family.

Construction 4.2. *Let $p_1 < p_2$ be two primes, $m = p_1 p_2$, and $\tilde{S} = \{1, \ldots, m - 1\}$. Let $((\tilde{\mathbf{u}}_i, \tilde{\mathbf{v}}_i))_{i=1}^N$, where $\tilde{h} = \lceil N^{1/(m-1)} \rceil \cdot (m-1) + 1$ be the $\tilde{S}$-matching vector family over $\mathbb{Z}_t^{\tilde{h}}$ of Claim 4.1 where $t = m$ (i.e., $w = m - 1$). For every $i \in [N]$, we define*

- $\mathbf{u}_{p_1,i} = \tilde{\mathbf{u}}_i^{\otimes(p_1-1)} \bmod p_1$, $- \mathbf{v}_{p_1,i} = \tilde{\mathbf{v}}_i^{\otimes(p_1-1)} \bmod p_1$,
- $\mathbf{u}_{p_2,i} = \tilde{\mathbf{u}}_i^{\otimes(p_2-1)} \bmod p_2$, $- \mathbf{v}_{p_2,i} = \tilde{\mathbf{v}}_i^{\otimes(p_2-1)} \bmod p_2$.

Construct $((\mathbf{u}_i, \mathbf{v}_i))_{i=1}^N$ over $\mathbb{Z}_m^h$, where $h = \tilde{h}^{p_2}$, using the CRT per entry, where we pad $\mathbf{u}_{p_1,i}$ and $\mathbf{v}_{p_1,i}$ with zeros to be of length $\tilde{h}^{p_2}$. That is, we define $\mathbf{u}_i[k] \in \mathbb{Z}_m$ for $k \in [\tilde{h}^{p_2}]$ as the unique element that satisfies

- $\mathbf{u}_i[k] \equiv \mathbf{u}_{p_1,i}[k] \pmod{p_1}$, *and*
- $\mathbf{u}_i[k] \equiv \mathbf{u}_{p_2,i}[k] \pmod{p_2}$.

These elements can be computed as

$$\mathbf{u}_i[k] = \left(\mathbf{u}_{p_1,i}[k] \cdot p_2(p_2^{-1} \mod p_1) + \mathbf{u}_{p_2,i}[k] \cdot p_1(p_1^{-1} \mod p_2)\right) \mod m.$$

We define $\mathbf{v}_i$ analogously using $\mathbf{v}_{p_1,i}$ and $\mathbf{v}_{p_2,i}$.

Efremenko [24] proves that $((\mathbf{u}_i, \mathbf{v}_i))_{i=1}^N$ is an S_{can}-matching vector family (recall that $S_{\text{can}} = \{a \in \mathbb{Z}_m : a \mod p_1, a \mod p_2 \in \{0,1\}\} \setminus \{0\}$).

We now will analyze the sparsity of the matching vectors family $((\mathbf{u}_i, \mathbf{v}_i))_{i=1}^N$. From Claim 4.1, the sparsity of $((\tilde{\mathbf{u}}_i, \tilde{\mathbf{v}}_i))_{i=1}^N$ is m. Thus, the family is (d, p_1)-sparse where $d = m^{p_1-1}$, since the number of entries k where $\mathbf{v}_i[k] \not\equiv 0 \pmod{p_1}$, by the CRT, is the number of entries k where $\mathbf{v}_{p_1,i}[k] \not\equiv 0 \pmod{p_1}$, which is m^{p_1-1}. The same applies to $\mathbf{v}_i$.

For the CDS protocol provided in Fig. 1, we need that $p_1 | p_2 - 1$. The next result assures that for every prime p_1 there is a fairly small prime p_2 such that $p_1 | p_2 - 1$.

Theorem 4.3 ([44]). *There exists a constant c such that for every integer $d \geq 2$ and every $a \in \mathbb{Z}$ relatively prime to d, there exists a prime $p < cd^{5.18}$ such that $p \equiv a \pmod{d}$.*

Using Theorem 4.3 for a prime p_1, we can take the least prime p_2 such that $p_2 \equiv 1 \pmod{p_1}$ and get that $p_2 \leq cp_1^{5.18}$, thus $p_1^2 \leq m \leq cp_1^{6.18}$. It can be proved (see [11]) that

$$h \leq \left(2cp_1^{6.18}\right)^{cp_1^{5.18}} N^{2/p_1}.$$

Since $d = m^{p_1}$, we have that $p_1^{2p_1} = (p_1^2)^{p_1} \leq d \leq (cp_1^{6.18})^{p_1}$, which implies that

$$2p_1 \log p_1 \leq \log d \leq p_1 \log c + 6.18 p_1 \log p_1.$$

We take p_1 as the smallest prime such that $p_1 > \frac{\log d}{\log \log d}$. From Bertrand's postulate (see, e.g., [1]) that states that for every integer $k > 0$ there is a prime p such that $k \leq p \leq 2k$, we take such $p_1 < 2 \cdot \frac{\log d}{\log \log d}$.

Combining this with the upper bound on h and on p_1, we obtain the following bound (see [11])

$$h \leq d^{O\left(\frac{\log d}{\log \log d}\right)^{4.18}} N^{O\left(\frac{\log \log d}{\log d}\right)} = 2^{\text{polylog}(d)} N^{O\left(\frac{\log \log d}{\log d}\right)}.$$

4.2 Our Construction

In this section, we will prove Theorem 3.4 by showing a construction of a matching vector family generalizing the construction in Sect. 4.1. The matching vector family in this section will be for a larger set S_{one}; in return, we will get a more efficient protocol and more freedom in choosing the pairs of primes p_1, p_2.

Construction 4.4. *Let p_1, p_2 be primes, and let $m = p_1 p_2$. Let $0 < w < m$ be a weight that will be chosen later. We start with the basic matching vector family $((\tilde{\mathbf{u}}_i, \tilde{\mathbf{v}}_i))_{i=1}^{N}$ over $\mathbb{Z}_t^{\tilde{h}}$ from Claim 4.1 with $t = m$ and $\tilde{h} = w\lceil N^{1/w} \rceil + 1$. Define $\mathbf{u}_{p_1,i} = \tilde{\mathbf{u}}_i^{\otimes p_1 - 1}$, and $\mathbf{v}_{p_1,i} = \tilde{\mathbf{v}}_i^{\otimes p_1 - 1}$, thus for every $i, j \in [N]$*

$$\langle \mathbf{u}_{p_1,i}, \mathbf{v}_{p_1,j} \rangle \equiv \langle \tilde{\mathbf{u}}_i^{\otimes p_1-1}, \tilde{\mathbf{v}}_j^{\otimes p_1-1} \rangle \equiv \langle \tilde{\mathbf{u}}_i, \tilde{\mathbf{v}}_j \rangle^{p_1-1} \equiv \mathbb{1}_{\langle \tilde{\mathbf{u}}_i, \tilde{\mathbf{v}}_j \rangle \not\equiv 0 \pmod{p_1}} \pmod{p_1}.$$

Next, we define the set $A = \{a \in \{m - w, \ldots, m - 1\} : a \equiv 0 \pmod{p_1}\}$. Since $m \equiv 0 \pmod{p_1}$, the size of A is $\lfloor \frac{w}{p_1} \rfloor$. We consider the polynomial $R : \mathbb{F}_{p_2} \to \mathbb{F}_{p_2}$ (of degree at most $\lfloor \frac{w}{p_1} \rfloor$) such that

1. $R(0) \equiv 0 \pmod{p_2}$, *and*
2. $R(a) \equiv 1 \pmod{p_2}$ *for all $a \in A$.*

This polynomial is equal to

$$R(x) = x \left(\sum_{a \in A} \prod_{b \in A, b \neq a} \frac{x - b}{a - b} \right).$$

Since $a, b \equiv 0 \pmod{p_1}$ and $0 < a, b < m$, then $a \not\equiv b \pmod{p_2}$, therefore the inverse of $a - b$ exists. Note that $\deg(R) = d_R = |A| = \lfloor \frac{w}{p_1} \rfloor$. Let $R(x) \equiv \sum_{k=1}^{d_R} a_k x^k \pmod{p_2}$ be the explicit representation of R (as $R(0) = 0$, its free coefficient is 0). Define $\mathbf{u}_{p_2,i} = \left(a_1 \tilde{\mathbf{u}}^{\otimes 1}, \ldots, a_{d_R} \tilde{\mathbf{u}}^{\otimes d_R} \right)$ and $\mathbf{v}_{p_2,j} = \left(\tilde{\mathbf{v}}^{\otimes 1}, \ldots, \tilde{\mathbf{v}}^{\otimes d_R} \right)$.

For every $i, j \in [N]$,

$$\langle \mathbf{u}_{p_2,i}, \mathbf{v}_{p_2,j} \rangle \equiv \sum_{k=1}^{d_R} a_k \langle \tilde{\mathbf{u}}_i^{\otimes k}, \tilde{\mathbf{v}}_j^{\otimes k} \rangle \equiv \sum_{k=1}^{d_R} a_k \langle \tilde{\mathbf{u}}_i, \tilde{\mathbf{v}}_j \rangle^k \equiv R(\langle \tilde{\mathbf{u}}_i, \tilde{\mathbf{v}}_j \rangle) \pmod{p_2}.$$

We pad either $\mathbf{u}_{p_1,i}$ and $\mathbf{v}_{p_1,i}$ or $\mathbf{u}_{p_2,i}$ and $\mathbf{v}_{p_2,i}$ such that they will have the same length. We construct $((\mathbf{u}_i, \mathbf{v}_i))_{i=1}^{N}$ over $\mathbb{Z}_m^h$, where $h = \tilde{h}^{\max\{\lfloor \frac{w}{p_1} \rfloor, p_1 - 1\}}$ using the CRT per entry, i.e., $\mathbf{u}_i[k]$ is the unique element in $\mathbb{Z}_m$ such that

- $\mathbf{u}_i[k] \equiv \mathbf{u}_{p_1,i}[k] \pmod{p_1}$, *and*
- $\mathbf{u}_i[k] \equiv \mathbf{u}_{p_2,i}[k] \pmod{p_2}$;

we define $\mathbf{v}_i$ the same way with $\mathbf{v}_{p_1,i}$ and $\mathbf{v}_{p_2,i}$.

Claim 4.5. *Let p_1, p_2 be primes and let $m = p_1 p_2$. The family $((\mathbf{u}_i, \mathbf{v}_i))_{i=1}^{N}$ over $\mathbb{Z}_m^h$ as in Construction 4.4 with $\lfloor \frac{w}{p_1} \rfloor = p_1 - 1$ is a (d, p_1)-sparse S_{one}-matching vector family with $h \leq 4d \cdot N^{\frac{2 \log \log d}{\log d}}$ and $\sqrt{2} p_1 \log (p_1/\sqrt{2}) \leq \log d \leq 2 p_1 \log p_1$.*

Remark 4.6. We next consider a specific choice of parameters in Construction 4.4 and analyze the resulting properties of the matching vector family. Take $p_1 = 3$, $p_2 = 7$, and choose $w = 8$. Then the length of the resulting matching vectors from Construction 4.4 is $h = \tilde{h}^{\max\{\lfloor \frac{8}{3} \rfloor, 2\}}$, where $\tilde{h} = O(N^{1/8})$, i.e., the length is $O(N^{1/4})$. The sparsity is $(8+1)^2 = 81$. Using this matching vector family, the protocol in Fig. 1 is a 2-server CDS protocol over $\mathbb{F}_7$, with reconstruction degree p_1 times the sparsity of the matching vectors, i.e. 243, and communication complexity $O(N^{1/4})$.

This 2-server CDS protocol has better communication complexity than the quadratic 2-server CDS protocol from [15] (whose communication complexity is $O(N^{1/3})$).

The following lemma proves Theorem 3.4.

Lemma 4.7. *For every $N, d > 0$, there exist primes p_1, p_2 where $p_1 | p_2 - 1$ such that the matching vectors from Construction 4.4 is a $(d, p_1) - sparse$ S_{one}-matching vector family over $\mathbb{Z}_m^h$, where $m = p_1 p_2$, and $h \leq 2d^{1 + \frac{2}{\log \log d}} N^{\frac{16 \log \log d}{\log d}}$.*

4.3   Kutin's Construction

In this section, we will prove Theorem 3.5 by presenting a variant of the construction of matching vector family of Kutin [36]. Let $p_1 < p_2$ be two primes, $m = p_1 p_2$, and $t = p_1^{e_1} p_2^{e_2}$ for some $e_1, e_2 > 0$. By Claim 4.1 there is an $\tilde{S}$-matching vector family $((\tilde{u}_i, \tilde{v}_i))_{i=1}^N$ over $\mathbb{Z}_t^{\tilde{h}}$, where $\tilde{S} = \{1, \ldots, t-1\}$, and $\tilde{h} = \lceil N^{1/(t-1)} \rceil \cdot (t-1) + 1$ (i.e., $w = t - 1$).

Next we define BBR polynomials, which will be used in the construction.

Theorem 4.8 (*[36]*). *Let $p_1 < p_2$ be two primes, $m = p_1 \cdot p_2$, and $t = p_1^{e_1} p_2^{e_2}$ for two positive integers e_1, e_2. There exists a polynomial $Q_{m,t}(x)$ over $\mathbb{Q}$ such that:*

1. *$Q_{m,t}(x) = \sum_{i=1}^{d_Q} b_i \binom{x}{i}$, where $b_i \in \mathbb{Z}_m$.*
2. *$Q_{m,t}(x) \equiv 0 \pmod{m}$ if and only if $x \equiv 0 \pmod{t}$.*
3. *$\deg Q_{m,t} = d_Q = \max\{p_1^{e_1}, p_2^{e_2}\} - 1$.*
4. *If $x \not\equiv 0 \pmod{t}$ then $Q_{m,t}(x) \bmod m \in S_{\text{can}}$.*

Note that the coefficients of Q are not necessarily integers, and yet for every input x, it evaluates to an integer when x is an integer.

Construction 4.9. *Let $t = p_1^{e_1} p_2^{e_2}$, and let $Q_{m,t}$ be the polynomial from Theorem 4.8. We use Claim 4.1 with t and $w = t - 1$. In this case, $\tilde{u}_i = \tilde{v}_i$, since by definition its first entry is $t - w = 1$, and $\tilde{u}_i$ is a binary vector. Let $A_i \subseteq [\tilde{h}]$ be the subset defined by $\tilde{u}_i$, i.e., $A_i = \{\ell \in [h] : \tilde{u}_i[\ell] = 1\}$; as the sparsity of $\tilde{u}_i$ is $w + 1 = t$, $|A_i| = t$. We define vectors u_i, v_i of length $\sum_{i=1}^{d_Q} \binom{h}{i}$, where for every $\emptyset \neq S \subseteq [\tilde{h}]$ of size at most d_Q we have the following coordinate in the vectors*

- *$u_i[S] = b_{|S|} \cdot \mathbb{1}_{S \subseteq A_i}$, and*

- $\mathbf{v}_i[S] = \mathbb{1}_{S \subseteq A_i}$.

The sparsity of this family is the number of non-empty subsets of A_i of size at most d_Q, i.e., at most $\sum_{i=1}^{d_Q} \binom{t}{i}$.

Our construction is based on Kutin's construction [36]. Kutin uses $\tilde{h} = t^{1.5}$ in Claim 4.1, and gets shorter vectors of length $N^{O\left(\sqrt{\frac{\log \log N}{\log N}}\right)}$; however, his vectors are dense. We get longer vectors that are sparser.

Lemma 4.10. *Let* $((\tilde{\mathbf{u}}_i, \tilde{\mathbf{v}}_i))_{i=1}^{N}$, $Q_{m,t}$, *and* $((\mathbf{u}_i, \mathbf{v}_i))_{i=1}^{N}$ *be as defined in Construction 4.9. Then, for all* $i, j \in [N]$,

$$\langle \mathbf{u}_i, \mathbf{v}_j \rangle = Q_{m,t}(\langle \tilde{\mathbf{u}}_i, \tilde{\mathbf{v}}_j \rangle).$$

Claim 4.11. *For every two primes* p_1, p_2 *and an integer* $e_1 > 0$, *there exists an integer* $e_2 > 0$ *such that for* $t = p_1^{e_1} p_2^{e_2}$, *the family* $((\mathbf{u}_i, \mathbf{v}_i))_{i=1}^{N}$ *as defined in Construction 4.9 is a* (d, p_1)-*sparse* S_{can}-*matching vector family over* $\mathbb{Z}_m^h$, *such that* $h \leq d^{O(p_1)} \cdot N^{\frac{2p_1 \log \log d}{\log d}}$, *and* $\sqrt{t/p_1} \leq \log d \leq \sqrt{p_1 t}$.

The following lemma proves Theorem 3.5.

Lemma 4.12. *For every* $N, d > 0$, *there exists integers* e_1, e_2 *such that the matching vectors from Construction 4.9 is a* $(d, 2)$-*sparse* S_{can}-*matching vector family over* $\mathbb{Z}_6^h$, *and* $h \leq d^{O(1)} N^{O\left(\frac{\log \log d}{\log d}\right)}$.

4.4   Comparison of the Three Constructions

We described three constructions of sparse matching vectors. These constructions have the same asymptotic behavior: For every d there is a d-sparse matching vector family with vectors of length $O_d\left(N^{O\left(\frac{\log \log d}{\log d}\right)}\right)$. The one based on Kutin's construction is the most interesting as the vectors can be over $\mathbb{Z}_m^h$ for $m = p_1 \cdot p_2$ for every two primes p_1, p_2, e.g., we can take $m = 2 \cdot 3$. In the construction we provide and Efremenko's construction, the value of m increases as d increases (e.g., as the length of the vectors decreases). Our construction yields shorter matching vectors that can be used to construct CDS protocols and secret-sharing schemes that are better than the degree-2 construction of [15]. Efremenko's and Kutin's constructions are for the S_{can}-matching vector family, whereas our construction yields only an S_{one}-matching vector family.

For every two primes p_1, p_2, and $m = p_1 p_2$, the length of Efremenko's matching vectors is $m^{p_2} N^{1/p_1}$, and are (m^{p_1}, p_1)-sparse. The length in our matching vector family is $p_1^{2p_1} \cdot N^{1/p_1}$ and they are $(p_1^{2p_1}, p_1)$-sparse. Thus, the sparsity and length in our matching vector family is much better since $p_2 > p_1$ and $p_1^{2p_1} < (p_1 \cdot p_2)^{p_1} = m^{p_1}$, and is independent of the choice of p_2. Recall that as we need that p_1 divides $p_2 - 1$, we only know that $p_2 \leq c \cdot p_1^{5.18}$.

5   A Polynomial k-Server CDS Protocol

In this section, we describe a construction of k-server CDS protocol for INDEX_N^k with polynomial reconstruction. Our protocol is a generalization of the k-server CDS protocol from [39]. It relies on two components. The first is a matching vector family with a special property of k-decomposability (see Definition 5.1). Thus, we need to prove that the constructions of sparse matching vectors are decomposable. The second is simulation of Bob in the 2-server CDS protocol by $k-1$ servers. We need to modify the simulation of [39] such that it can be computed by a linear function. Towards this goal, we describe a selection protocol that will be used as a black box in the k-server CDS protocol.

Definition 5.1 (k-decomposability). *Let $N' = \sqrt[k]{N}$. A family of vectors $(\mathbf{u}_i)_{i=1}^N$ over $\mathbb{Z}_m^h$ is k-decomposable if there exist vector families $(\mathbf{u}_{1,i})_{i=1}^{N'}, \dots,$ $(\mathbf{u}_{k,i})_{i=1}^{N'}$ over $\mathbb{Z}_m^h$ such that under the natural mapping $i \mapsto (i_1, \dots, i_k) \in [N']^k$*

$$\mathbf{u}_i = \mathbf{u}_{1,i_1} \odot \cdots \odot \mathbf{u}_{k,i_k} \mod m$$

for all $i \in [N]$.

Definition 5.2 (Decomposable Matching Vector Families). *For integers $N, m, h, k > 0$ and $S \subseteq \mathbb{Z}_m \setminus \{0\}$, a collection of vectors $((\mathbf{u}_i, \mathbf{v}_i))_{i=1}^N$ over $\mathbb{Z}_m^h$ is a k-decomposable S-matching vector family if it is an S-matching vector family and $(\mathbf{u}_i)_{i=1}^N$, $(\mathbf{v}_i)_{i=1}^N$ are k-decomposable (as in Definition 5.1).*

5.1   The Selection Protocol

In this section, we will describe an important component of our k-server CDS protocol. In our k-CDS protocol there will be k servers, the first server will simulate Alice in the 2-server CDS protocol described in Sect. 3, and the other $k-1$ servers will simulate Bob, i.e., each server Q_j for $2 \leq j \leq k$, holding an index i_{j-1}, sends a message such that the referee can reconstruct the messages of Bob with input $i = (i_1, \dots, i_{k-1})$ in the 2-server CDS protocol. This should be done in such a way that the referee will not learn any additional information. Furthermore, the referee should reconstruct the message of Bob using a linear function. We will formulate these requirements as a special case of private simultaneous message (PSM) protocols [25,32].

Definition 5.3 (PSM protocols). *Let $\mathcal{X}_t$ be a t-th input space and let $\mathcal{Y}$ be the output space. A private simultaneous messages (PSM) protocol $\mathcal{P}$ consists of*

- *A finite domain $\mathcal{R}$ of common random inputs, and k finite message domains $\mathcal{M}_1, \dots, \mathcal{M}_k$, denote $\mathcal{M} = \mathcal{M}_1 \times \cdots \times \mathcal{M}_k$.*
- *Message encoding algorithms $Enc_1, \dots, Enc_k$, where $Enc_t : \mathcal{X}_t \times \mathcal{R} \to \mathcal{M}_t$.*
- *A decoding algorithm $Dec : \mathcal{M} \to \mathcal{Y}$.*

We say that a PSM protocol computes a k-argument function $f : \mathcal{X}_1 \times \cdots \times \mathcal{X}_k \to \mathcal{Y}$, if it satisfies the following two properties:

CORRECTNESS. *For all $x_1 \in \mathcal{X}_1, \ldots, x_k \in \mathcal{X}_k$, and $r \in \mathcal{R}$:*

$$Dec(Enc_1(x_1; r), \ldots, Enc_k(x_k; r)) = f(x_1, \ldots, x_k),$$

that is, the referee always reconstructs the output of f.

SECURITY. *For every $\mathbf{m} = (m_1, \ldots, m_k) \in \mathcal{M}_1 \times \cdots \times \mathcal{M}_k$, $\mathbf{x} = (x_1, \ldots, x_k)$ and $\mathbf{x}' = (x_1', \ldots, x_k')$ in $\mathcal{X}$ satisfying $f(\mathbf{x}) = f(\mathbf{x}')$, it holds that*

$$\Pr_{r \sim U(R)} [(Enc_1(x_1; r), \ldots, Enc_k(x_k; r)) = \mathbf{m}]$$

$$= \Pr_{r \sim U(R)} [(Enc_1(x_1'; r), \ldots, Enc_k(x_k'; r)) = \mathbf{m}],$$

that is, the referee cannot distinguish between two inputs with the same output, i.e., the referee only learns the output of f.

The communication complexity of a PSM protocol is defined as $\log |\mathcal{M}|$.

Next, we define a function, simulating Bob's messages, and we design a PSM for it. In the function, we need the following selection function: each server holds an input $x_i \in \mathbb{F}_p$ and all servers hold a vector $\mathbf{s} = (s_0, \ldots, s_{p-1}) \in \mathbb{Z}_q^p$. The inputs of the servers define a selection index $b = \prod_{i=1}^{k} x_i \mod p$; the referee, which knows $x_1, \ldots, x_k$, should learn s_b without learning any additional information on $\mathbf{s}$.

Definition 5.4 (The selection function). *Let q be a positive integer, p be a prime, and let $\mathbf{s} = (s_0, \ldots, s_{p-1}) \in \mathbb{Z}_q^p$ be a vector of length p. Let $\mathbb{Z}_q^p \times \mathbb{F}_p$ be the input space for each server; each server holds the common input $\mathbf{s}$, and a private input x_t. The SELECTION function is defined as follows*

$$f_{\text{SELECTION}}(\mathbf{s}, x_1, \ldots, x_k) = (s_b, x_1, \ldots, x_k)$$

where $b = \prod_{t=1}^{k} x_t \mod p$.

In Protocol SELECTION, we assume that the referee knows $x_1, \ldots, x_k$; this is the case when we use it in a CDS protocol. For the purpose of analyzing Protocol SELECTION in Fig. 2 as a PSM protocol (where the referee has no input), we assume that each server Q_j also sends x_j and the referee also outputs $x_1, \ldots, x_k$. Furthermore, in the definition of $f_{\text{SELECTION}}$ we assume that all servers have a common input $\mathbf{s}$. We can modify Protocol SELECTION in a way that only Q_k holds $\mathbf{s}$.

Claim 5.5. *Let p be a prime and let k, q be integers. The PSM $(Enc_1, \ldots, Enc_k, Dec)$ described in Fig. 2 is a PSM protocol for $f_{\text{SELECTION}}$ with communication complexity $(2p - 2) \log p$.*

5.2 Protocols for the Simulation of Bob's Messages

In this section, we present the polynomial k-server CDS protocol for INDEX_N^k (hence for every function $f : [N]^k \to \{0, 1\}$). In this protocol, the first server Q_1

Protocol SELECTION

Private input: The input of server Q_i is $x_i \in \mathbb{F}_p$.
Common input: A vector $\mathbf{s} = (s_0, \ldots, s_{p-1}) \in \mathbb{Z}_q^p$.
Shared Randomness: $\mathbf{r} = (r_{j,a})_{j \in [k-1], a \in \mathbb{F}_p^*}$ where $r_{j,a} \in \mathbb{Z}_q$. Let $r_{k,a} = s_a$
for $a \in \mathbb{F}_p^*$.

The message of server Q_1:
If $x_1 = 0$ sends $m_1 \leftarrow s_0$, otherwise sends $m_1 \leftarrow r_{1,x_1}$.

The message of server Q_j, for $2 \le j \le k$:
If $x_j = 0$ sends $m_j \leftarrow s_0$ otherwise sends $(m_{j,1}, \ldots, m_{j,p-1})$, where

$$m_{j,a} = (r_{j,a} - r_{j-1, a \cdot x_j^{-1} \mod p}) \mod q.$$

Referee:
Denote $b_1 = x_1, b_2 = x_1 \cdot x_2 \mod p, \ldots, b_k = \prod_{i=1}^k x_i \mod p = b$. The referee
computes:

- If there exists j for which $x_j = 0$, then the referee outputs m_j.
- Otherwise, outputs $m_1 + \sum_{j=2}^k m_{j,b_j}$.

Fig. 2. A PSM protocol for the SELECTION function.

holds the database and the $k - 1$ servers $Q_2, \ldots, Q_k$ collectively hold the index.
In this protocol, the servers that hold the index will simulate Bob in the 2-server
CDS protocol described in Fig. 1, using the PSM protocol SELECTION from
Sect. 5.1. Server Q_1 will simulate Alice.

In the CDS protocol of Fig. 1, Bob sends $\mathbf{m}_B^1 = s\mathbf{u}_i + \mathbf{r}_1$. In the implementation of the protocol as a polynomial protocol, Bob sends $\mathbf{m'}_B^1 = (a^{\mathbf{m}_B^1[1]}$
$\mod p_2, \ldots, a^{\mathbf{m}_B^1[h]} \mod p_2)$ where $a^{\mathbf{m}_B^1[\ell]} \equiv a^{s\mathbf{u}_i[\ell] + \mathbf{r}_1[\ell]} \pmod{p_2}$. Recall that
we use decomposable matching vectors, so for $i = (i_1, \ldots, i_{k-1})$ we have $\mathbf{u}_i[\ell] \equiv$
$\prod_{t \in [k-1]} \mathbf{u}_{t,i_t}[\ell] \pmod{m}$. In particular, $\mathbf{u}_i[\ell] = \prod_{t \in [k-1]} \mathbf{u}_{t,i_t}[\ell] \pmod{p_1}$. Thus,
the ℓ-th coordinate of $\mathbf{m'}_B^1$ is

$$a^{\mathbf{m}_B^1[\ell]} \equiv a^{\left(s \prod_{t \in [k-1]} \mathbf{u}_{t,i_t}[\ell]\right) + \mathbf{r}_1[\ell] \mod p_1} \equiv a^{s \cdot b + \mathbf{r}_1[\ell]} \pmod{p_2}, \qquad (2)$$

where $b = \prod_{t \in [k-1]} \mathbf{u}_{t,i_t}[\ell] \mod p_1$. Consider the vector

$$(a^{\mathbf{r}_1[\ell]}, a^{s + \mathbf{r}_1[\ell]}, \ldots, a^{(p_1 - 1)s + \mathbf{r}_1[\ell]});$$

the referee should learn the $(b+1)$-th coordinate of this vector without learning
any other information. Therefore, each coordinate of the vector can be sent by
$Q_2, \ldots, Q_k$ using the selection protocol. A formal description of a protocol for
this task appears in Fig. 3.

In addition, Bob sends

$$m_B^2 \equiv \langle \mathbf{u}_i, \mathbf{r}_2 \rangle + r_3 \pmod{p_2}$$

$$\equiv \left(\sum_{\ell \in [h]} \mathbf{u}_i[\ell] \cdot \mathbf{r}_2[\ell] \right) + r_3 \equiv \left(\sum_{\ell \in [h]} \prod_{t=1}^{k-1} \mathbf{u}_{t,i_t}[\ell] \cdot \mathbf{r}_2[\ell] \right) + r_3 \pmod{p_2}. \quad (3)$$

This can be done by executing ℓ copies of Protocol SELECTION and summing the results. As we only want to disclose the sum of the executions, we mask each with a random element such that the sum of the masks is zero. A formal description of a protocol for this task appears in Fig. 4. We next describe the functionality computed by these protocols and prove their correctness and security.

Definition 5.6. (The function SEND$_1$). *Let $((\mathbf{u}_i, \mathbf{v}_i))_{i=1}^{N^{k-1}}$ be a decomposable matching vector family. For $i \in [N]$, we denote $i = (i_1, \ldots, i_{k-1})$, where $i_t \in [N^{1/(k-1)}]$ for every $t \in [k-1]$. Let $\mathbf{r}_1 \in \mathbb{F}_{p_1}^h$ be the server's common input and let $i \in [N]$. We define the PSM functionality SEND$_1$ as*

$$f_{\mathrm{SEND}_1}(s, i, \mathbf{r}_1) = (i, (a^{s\mathbf{u}_i[\ell] + \mathbf{r}_1[\ell]} \mod p_2)_{\ell \in [h]}).$$

Notice that $\mathbf{r}_1$ is an input of f_{SEND_1}, thus a PSM protocol for this function should hide it (i.e., the referee should not distinguish between $s = 1$, i, $\mathbf{r}_1$ and $s = 0, i, \mathbf{r}_1' = \mathbf{u}_i + \mathbf{r}_1$).

Protocol Send $\mathbf{m}_B^1$

Common input: $\mathbf{r}_1 \in \mathbb{F}_{p_1}^n$.
Private input of Q_{t+1} for $1 \le t \le k-1$: $i_t \in [N^{1/(k-1)}]$.

- For $\ell = 1$ to h:
  - $Q_2, \ldots, Q_k$ execute protocol SELECTION, where the vector is $\mathbf{s}^\ell = (a^{s \cdot b + r_1[\ell]} \mod p_2)_{b \in \mathbb{F}_{p_1}}$ and the input of the server Q_{t+1} for $1 \le t \le k-1$ is $x_t^\ell = \mathbf{u}_{t,i_t}[\ell] \mod p_1$.
- The referee reconstructs:

$$\mathbf{m}_B^1 \leftarrow (s_{b^1}^1, \ldots, s_{b^h}^h)$$

where $b^\ell = \prod_{t=1}^{k-1} \mathbf{u}_{t,i_t}[\ell] \mod p_1$ for every $\ell \in [h]$.

Fig. 3. A protocol simulating Bob's message $\mathbf{m}_B^1$.

Lemma 5.7. *Protocol **Send** $\mathbf{m}_B^1$ described in Fig. 3 is a PSM protocol for the function f_{SEND_1}.*

Definition 5.8 (The function SEND$_2$). *Let* $((\mathbf{u}_i, \mathbf{v}_i))_{i=1}^{N^{k-1}}$ *be a decomposable matching vector family. Let* $\mathbf{r}_2 \in \mathbb{F}_{p_2}^h, r_3 \in \mathbb{F}_{p_2}$ *be the servers' common input, and let* $i = (i_1, \ldots, i_{k-1})$, *where* $i_t \in [N^{1/(k-1)}]$ *for every* $t \in [k-1]$. *We define function* SEND$_2$ *as*

$$f_{\text{SEND}_2}(i, \mathbf{r}_2, r_3) = (i, \langle \mathbf{u}_i, \mathbf{r}_2 \rangle + r_3 \bmod p_2).$$

Protocol Send m$_B^2$

Common input: $\mathbf{r}_2 \in \mathbb{F}_{p_2}^h$, $r_3 \in \mathbb{F}_{p_2}$.
Private input of Q_{t+1} **for** $1 \le t \le k-1$: $i_t \in [N^{1/(k-1)}]$.
Shared randomness: $(r_3^\ell)_{\ell \in [h-1]}$. Define $r_3^h = r_3 - \sum_{\ell \in [h-1]} r_3^\ell \bmod p_2$.

- For $\ell = 1$ to h:
  - $Q_2, \ldots, Q_k$ execute Protocol SELECTION, where the vector is $\mathbf{s}^\ell = (b \cdot r_2[\ell] + r_3^\ell \bmod p_2)_{b \in \mathbb{F}_{p_2}}$, and the input of Q_{t+1} for $1 \le t \le k-1$ is $x_t^\ell = \mathbf{u}_{t,i_t}[\ell] \bmod p_2$.
- The referee reconstructs:

$$m_B^2 \leftarrow \sum_{\ell \in [h]} (b^\ell r_2[\ell] + r_3^\ell) \bmod p_2$$

where for every $\ell \in [h]$, $b^\ell = \prod_{t=1}^{k-1} \mathbf{u}_{t,i_t}[\ell] \bmod p_2$.

Fig. 4. A protocol simulating Bob's message m_B^2.

Lemma 5.9. *Protocol **Send m$_B^2$** described in Fig. 4 is a PSM protocol for the function* f_{SEND_2}.

5.3 The k-Server CDS Protocol

In Fig. 5, we describe the k-server CDS protocol for INDEX$_N^k$. This is an implementation of the 2-server CDS protocol from Fig. 1, where the index i is distributed between $Q_2, \ldots, Q_k$ and they send Bob's messages using protocols **Send m$_B^1$** and **Send m$_B^2$**.

Theorem 5.10. *Let* p_1, p_2 *be primes such that* $p_1 | p_2 - 1$, $m = p_1 \cdot p_2$ *and* $((\mathbf{u}_i, \mathbf{v}_i))_{i=1}^{N^{k-1}}$ *be a decomposable* (d, p_1)-*sparse* S_{one}-*matching vector family over* $\mathbb{Z}_m^h$. *The protocol in Fig. 5 is a k-server CDS protocol over* $\mathbb{F}_{p_2}$ *for* INDEX$_N^k$ *with message size* $h \cdot 2m \log m$ *and reconstruction by polynomial of degree* $d \cdot p_1$.

In Sect. 6, we will see how to decompose the matching vector families we have seen in Sect. 4, yielding a decomposable matching vector families as summarized in the next two theorems.

The Polynomial CDS Protocol for INDEX_N^k

Parameters: A decomposable S_{one}-matching vector family $((\mathbf{u}_i, \mathbf{v}_i))_{i=1}^{N^{k-1}}$ over $\mathbb{Z}_m^h$ for $m = p_1 p_2$ s.t. $p_1 | p_2 - 1$, and $h \in \mathbb{N}$, where for every $i \in [N^{k-1}]$ the decomposition of $\mathbf{u}_i$ is $\mathbf{u}_{i_1}, \ldots, \mathbf{u}_{i_{k-1}}$, and an element $a \in \mathbb{F}_{p_2}^*$ of order p_1 in $\mathbb{F}_{p_2}^*$.

Input of Q_1: $D \in \{0,1\}^{N^{k-1}}$.
Inputs of $Q_2, \ldots, Q_k$: $i_1, \ldots, i_{k-1} \in [N]$.
The secret: $s \in \{0,1\}$.
Shared Randomness: $\mathbf{r}_1 \in \mathbb{F}_{p_1}^h$, $\mathbf{r}_2 \in \mathbb{F}_{p_2}^h$, $r_3 \in \mathbb{F}_{p_2}$, $\mathbf{r}_1^\ell \in \mathbb{F}_{p_1}^{(k-1)\cdot(p_1-1)}$, $\mathbf{r}_2^\ell \in \mathbb{F}_{p_2}^{(k-1)\cdot(p_2-1)}$ for every $\ell \in [h]$, and the randomness of the protocols **Send $\mathbf{m}_B^1$** and **Send m_B^2**.

Define $C : \mathbb{F}_{p_1}^h \to \mathbb{F}_{p_2}$, as $C(\mathbf{b}) = \sum_{j=1}^N D_j a^{\langle \mathbf{b}, \mathbf{v}_j \rangle} \mod p_2$.
Define $V : \mathbb{F}_{p_1}^h \to \mathbb{F}_{p_2}^h$, as $V(\mathbf{b}) = \sum_{j=1}^N D_j \mathbf{v}_j a^{\langle \mathbf{b}, \mathbf{v}_j \rangle} \mod p_2$.

- Q_1 sends $m_A^1 \leftarrow ((1-a)s-1)C(\mathbf{r}_1) - r_3 \in \mathbb{F}_{p_2}$ and $\mathbf{m}_A^2 \leftarrow \mathbf{r}_2 + ((1-a)s-1)V(\mathbf{r}_1) \in \mathbb{F}_{p_2}^h$.
- Charlie and $Q_2, \ldots, Q_k$:
  - Execute protocol **Send $\mathbf{m}_B^1$** described in Figure 3 with inputs $(s, i, \mathbf{r}_1)$.
  - Execute protocol **Send m_B^2** described in Figure 4 with inputs $(i, \mathbf{r}_2, r_3)$.
- Charlie outputs 1 if

$$\langle \mathbf{u}_i, \mathbf{m}_A^2 \rangle - m_A^1 - m_B^2 - C(\mathbf{m}_B^1) + \langle \mathbf{u}_i, V(\mathbf{m}_B^1) \rangle \neq 0, \tag{5}$$

and 0 otherwise.

Fig. 5. A polynomial k-server CDS protocol using a decomposable matching vector family over $\mathbb{Z}_m$, where $m = p_1 p_2$ for primes p_1, p_2 such that $p_1 | p_2 - 1$.

Theorem 5.11. *For every $N, d > 0$, there exist primes p_1, p_2 where $p_1 | p_2 - 1$, and $p_1 \leq \frac{2\log d}{\log\log d}$ such that there is a decomposable (d, p_1)-sparse S_{one}-matching vector family over $\mathbb{Z}_m^h$ where $m = p_1 p_2$ and $h \leq 2d^{1+\frac{2}{\log\log d}} N^{\frac{2\log\log d}{\log d}}$.*

Theorem 5.12. *For every $N, d > 0$, there is a decomposable $(d, 2)$-sparse S_{can}-matching vector family over $\mathbb{Z}_6^h$, where $h \leq d^{O(1)} N^{O(\frac{\log\log d}{\log d})}$.*

Combining Theorems 5.11 and 5.12 with Theorem 5.10, we get the following theorem, which can be proved similarly as Theorem 3.6

Theorem 5.13. *For every $N, d > 0$, and $k > 1$, there is a k-server CDS protocol over $\mathbb{F}_3$ or over $\mathbb{F}_{p_2}$ for some prime $p_2 = polylog(d)$ for INDEX_N^k with degree-d reconstruction and communication complexity $d^{O(1)} N^{O((k-1)\cdot\frac{\log\log d}{\log d})}$.*

Corollary 5.14. *For every $N, d > 0$, $k > 1$, and function $f : [N]^k \to \{0,1\}$, there is a k-server CDS protocol for f, with degree-d reconstruction and communication complexity $d^{O(1)} N^{O\left((k-1) \cdot \frac{\log \log d}{\log d}\right)}$.*

Remark 5.15. Using the construction of the matching vector family over $\mathbb{Z}_{21}$ from Remark 4.6 (in the next section we will show that it is decomposable), we get a k-server CDS protocol over $\mathbb{F}_7$ with reconstruction degree 243 and communication complexity $O(N^{(k-1)/4})$. Previously, the best known k-server CDS protocol with polynomial reconstruction had communication complexity $O(N^{(k-1)/3})$ and degree 2 [15].

6   Construction of Decomposable Matching Vector Families

In this section, we show that the three construction we have seen in Sect. 4 are decomposable. First, we show a decomposition of the basic matching vector family in Claim 4.1.

Claim 6.1. *Let $N', m, \alpha, h' > 0$, and let $\mathbf{u} = (e_{i_1,\ldots,i_\alpha})_{i_1,\ldots,i_\alpha \in [N']}$ be the standard basis of $\mathbb{Z}_m^{h'}$. Then there is a decomposition $\mathbf{u}^1, \ldots, \mathbf{u}^\alpha$ of $\mathbf{u}$.*

Claim 6.2. *Let $N, m, w, k \geq 0$ where $0 \leq w \leq m$. There is a decomposable $(w+1)$-sparse $\tilde{S}$-matching vector family $((\tilde{\mathbf{u}}_i, \tilde{\mathbf{v}}_i))_{i=1}^N$ over $\mathbb{Z}_m^{\tilde{h}}$ for $\tilde{S} = \{m - w, \ldots, m - 1\}$, where $\tilde{h} = \lceil N^{1/w} \rceil \cdot w + 1$.*

6.1   Decomposability of Efremenko's and Our MVs

Now, we will show a decomposition for our matching vector family from Construction 4.4; since our construction uses the same techniques as in Construction 4.2, using polynomials and CRT per entry, the decomposition of our matching vector family will yield a decomposition of Efremenko's construction.

Construction 6.3. *Let $N, m, w, k \geq 0$ where $0 \leq w \leq m$, and $m = p_1 p_2$, for two primes $p_1 < p_2$. Let $((\tilde{\mathbf{u}}_i, \tilde{\mathbf{v}}_i))_{i=1}^N$ be the basic matching vector family over $\mathbb{Z}_m^{\tilde{h}}$ from Claim 4.1 For every $i = (i_1, \ldots, i_k) \in [N]$, let $(\tilde{\mathbf{u}}_{1,i_1}, \ldots, \tilde{\mathbf{u}}_{k,i_k})$, and $(\tilde{\mathbf{v}}_{1,i_1}, \ldots, \tilde{\mathbf{v}}_{k,i_k})$ be the decompositions for $\tilde{\mathbf{u}}_i$, and $\tilde{\mathbf{v}}_i$ respectively from Claim 6.2.*

Recall that in Construction 4.4 we defined $\mathbf{u}_{p_1,i} = \tilde{\mathbf{u}}_i^{\otimes p_1 - 1}$ and $\mathbf{u}_{p_2,i} = (a_1 \tilde{\mathbf{u}}_i^{\otimes 1}, \ldots, a_{d_R} \tilde{\mathbf{u}}_i^{\otimes d_R})$ for some polynomial $R(x) = \sum_{j=0}^{d_R} a_j x^j$; we also defined $\mathbf{v}_{p_1,i}, \mathbf{v}_{p_2,i}$ similarly. For every $t \in [k]$, we define

- $\mathbf{u}_{p_1,t,i_t} = \tilde{\mathbf{u}}_{t,i_t}^{\otimes p_1 - 1}$

- $\mathbf{u}_{p_2,t,i_t} = \begin{cases} (\tilde{\mathbf{u}}_{t,i_t}^{\otimes 1}, \ldots, \tilde{\mathbf{u}}_{t,i_t}^{\otimes d_R}) & \text{if } t < k, \\ (a_1 \tilde{\mathbf{u}}_{t,i_t}^{\otimes 1}, \ldots, a_{d_R} \tilde{\mathbf{u}}_{t,i_t}^{\otimes d_R}) & \text{if } t = k. \end{cases}$

Similarly, we define $\mathbf{v}_{p_1,t,i_t}, \mathbf{v}_{p_2,t,i_t}$. *Now, for every* $i \in [N]$, $t \in [k]$, *we define* $\mathbf{u}_{t,i_t}$ *using the CRT per entry similarly to Construction 4.4, and as in the construction in Construction 4.4, (we pad with zeros all vectors of length less than* h). *For every* $\ell \in [h]$ *for* $h = \tilde{h}^{\max\{\lfloor \frac{w}{p_1}\rfloor, p_1 - 1\}}$, $\mathbf{u}_{t,i_t}[\ell]$ *is the unique element in* $\mathbb{Z}_m$ *satisfying*

- $\mathbf{u}_{t,i_t}[\ell] \equiv \mathbf{u}_{p_1,t,i_t}[\ell] \pmod{p_1}$, *and*
- $\mathbf{u}_{t,i_t}[\ell] \equiv \mathbf{u}_{p_2,t,i_2}[\ell] \pmod{p_2}$.

We define $\mathbf{v}_{t,i_t}$ *in the same way.*

Claim 6.4. *Let* $N, k, m, h > 0$, *and let* $(\mathbf{u}_i)_{i=1}^N$ *be a decomposable vector family over* $\mathbb{Z}_m^h$, *where for every* $i = (i_1, \ldots, i_k) \in [N]$ *the decomposition of* $\mathbf{u}_i$ *is* $(\mathbf{u}_{1,i_1}, \ldots, \mathbf{u}_{k,i_k})$. *Then the* r-*th tensor power operation preserves decomposability, i.e.*

$$\mathbf{u}_i^{\otimes r} = (\mathbf{u}_{1,i_1}^{\otimes r} \odot \cdots \odot \mathbf{u}_{k,i_k}^{\otimes r}).$$

The next result proves Theorem 5.11.

Lemma 6.5. *Let* $((\mathbf{u}_i, \mathbf{v}_i))_{i=1}^N$, *be the matching vector family over* $\mathbb{Z}_m^h$ *from Construction 4.4. For every* $i \in [N]$, $(\mathbf{u}_{1,i_1}, \ldots, \mathbf{u}_{k,i_k})$ *and* $(\mathbf{v}_{1,i_1}, \ldots, \mathbf{v}_{k,i_k})$ *from Construction 6.3 are decomposition of* $\mathbf{u}_i$, $\mathbf{v}_i$, *respectively.*

6.2 Decomposability of Kutin's MVs

In this section, we will show that the techniques used in Construction 4.9 to construct S_{can}-matching vector family from the basic matching vector from Claim 4.1 preserve decomposability, and thus will yield a decomposition of the matching vectors in Construction 4.9.

Construction 6.6. *Let* $N, k, m > 0$, *such that* $m = p_1 p_2$ *for two primes* $p_1 < p_2$, *and let* $t = p_1^{e_1}, p_2^{e_2}$ *for some integers* $e_1, e_2 > 0$. *Let* $((\tilde{\mathbf{u}}_i, \tilde{\mathbf{v}}_i))_{i=1}^N \mathbb{Z}_m^{\tilde{h}}$ *be the basic matching vector family over* $\mathbb{Z}_m^{\tilde{h}}$ *from Claim 4.1, and for every* $i = (i_1, \ldots, i_k) \in [N]$, *let* $(\tilde{\mathbf{u}}_{1,i_1}, \ldots, \tilde{\mathbf{u}}_{k,i_k})$ *be the decomposition of* $\tilde{\mathbf{u}}_i$ *from Claim 6.2.*

Let $Q_{m,t}(x) = \sum_{i=1}^{d_Q} b_i \binom{x}{i}$ *be the BBR polynomial from Theorem 4.8. For every* $t \in [k]$, *let* $A_{t,i_t} \subseteq [\tilde{h}]$ *be the subset defined by* $\tilde{\mathbf{u}}_{t,i_t}$, *i.e.*, $A_{t,i_t} = \{\ell \in [h] : \tilde{\mathbf{u}}_{t,i_t}[\ell] = 1\}$. *We define the vectors* $\mathbf{u}_{t,i_t}, \mathbf{v}_{t,i_t}$ *of length* $\sum_{i=1}^{d_Q} \binom{h}{i}$ *where for every* $\emptyset \neq S \subseteq [\tilde{h}]$ *of size at most* d_Q *we have the following coordinate in the vectors*

- $\mathbf{u}_{t,i_t}[S] = \begin{cases} \mathbb{1}_{S \subseteq A_{t,i_t}} & \text{if } t < k, \\ b_{|S|} \cdot \mathbb{1}_{S \subseteq A_{t,i_t}} & \text{if } t = k. \end{cases}$
- $\mathbf{v}_{t,i_t}[S] = \mathbb{1}_{S \subseteq A_{t,i_t}}$.

Claim 6.7. *Let* $((\mathbf{u}_i, \mathbf{v}_i))_{i=1}^N$ *be the matching vector family over* $\mathbb{Z}_m^h$ *from Construction 4.2. For every* $i = (i_1, \ldots, i_k) \in [N]$, *the vectors* $(\mathbf{u}_{1,i_1}, \ldots, \mathbf{u}_{k,i_k})$ *and* $(\mathbf{v}_{1,i_1}, \ldots, \mathbf{v}_{k,i_k})$ *from Construction 6.6 are a decomposition of* $\mathbf{u}_i$ *and* $\mathbf{v}_i$, *respectively.*

7   A Polynomial Secret Sharing Scheme for General Access Structures

CDS protocols were used in [4,6,15,37] to construct secret-sharing schemes for arbitrary access structures. Similarly to Applebaum et al. [4], we construct a secret-sharing scheme from k-server CDS protocols in two steps, first constructing robust CDS protocols, and then constructing secret-sharing scheme for arbitrary access structures, while preserving the reconstruction degree throughout the steps. Specifically, we use an improved analysis of this transformation given in [15].

Beimel et al. [15] show a construction of a quadratic (i.e., degree 2) t-RCDS protocol based on a quadratic k-server CDS protocol. Combining that result with Theorem 5.13, we get the following result.

Corollary 7.1. *Let $t < \min\{N/2k, 2^{\sqrt{N}/k}\}$. Then there is a degree-d k-server t-RCDS protocol with message size*

$$O(N^{(k-1)\cdot O\left(\frac{\log\log d}{\log d}\right)} \cdot t^k \cdot k^{3k} \cdot \log^2 N \cdot \log^{2k}(t)) = \tilde{O}(N^{(k-1)\cdot\frac{\log\log d}{\log d}} \cdot t^k \cdot k^{3k}).$$

Next, we present an upper bound on the share size for secret-sharing schemes for all access structures. For that, we use results on RCDS from [15] and techniques for general constructions from [6].

Theorem 7.2. *Assume that there is a k-server CDS protocol, with degree-d reconstruction, with communication complexity $c(k, N, d) = N^{(k-1)/\xi(d)}$, for some function $\xi(d) \geq 2$, then there is a secret-sharing scheme realizing an arbitrary n-party access structure with share size*

$$\max\left\{2^{0.5n(1+1/\xi(d))}, 2^{n(\log(2^{1/\xi(d)}+2)-1)}\right\} \cdot 2^{o(n)}.$$

Combining Theorem 5.13 with Theorem 7.2, we get the following result.

Corollary 7.3. *Let $d > 2$. Every n-party access structure can be realized by a secret-sharing scheme with degree-d reconstruction over $\mathbb{F}_3$ or over $\mathbb{F}_{p_2}$ for some prime $p_2 = polylog(d)$ and share size $2^{n(0.585+O\left(\frac{\log\log d}{\log d}\right))}$.*

Remark 7.4. Applying Theorem 7.2 with the k-server CDS protocol from Remark 5.15 with communication complexity $O(N^{(k-1)/4})$ and reconstruction degree 243, we get a secret-sharing scheme for an arbitrary access structure with share size $2^{0.6731n+o(n)}$, and reconstruction degree 243.

In comparison, Beimel et al. [15] constructed a quadratic (i.e., degree-2) secret-sharing scheme with share size $2^{0.705n+o(n)}$, and Applebaum and Nir [6] constructs a linear secret-sharing scheme with share size $2^{0.7575n+o(n)}$ and a general (non-polynomial) secret-sharing scheme with share size $2^{0.585n+o(n)}$. As d increases, the share size in our secret-sharing scheme approaches $2^{0.585n}$, i.e., it approaches the share size of the scheme of Applebaum and Nir [6], the best known secret-sharing scheme for an arbitrary access structure.

Almost all access structures admit a secret-sharing scheme with shares of size $2^{o(n)}$ and by a linear secret-sharing scheme with share size $2^{n/2+o(n)}$ [10]. Moreover, almost all access structures can be realized by a quadratic secret-sharing scheme over $\mathbb{F}_2$ with share size $2^{n/3+o(n)}$ [15]. We use the same techniques as in these previous works and we construct secret-sharing schemes with polynomial reconstruction and smaller share size for almost all access structures. Using our polynomial k-server CDS protocols with message size $c(k, N, d) = N^{O((k-1)\cdot \frac{\log \log d}{\log d})}$ from Theorem 5.13, we get the following result.

Corollary 7.5. *Almost all access structures can be realized by secret-sharing scheme with degree-d reconstruction over $\mathbb{F}_3$ or over $\mathbb{F}_{p_2}$ for some prime $p_2 = polylog(d)$ and share size $2^{O(n \log \log d/\log d)+o(n)}$.*

As d grows, we get share size $2^{\epsilon n}$ for every constant $\epsilon > 0$. If we take $d - O(\log n)$ (or even $d = o(1)$), then the share size is $n^{o(1)}$, however larger than the share size of [10], where the degree of reconstruction is not bounded.

Acknowledgement. The first and the third authors are supported by the ISF grant 391/21. The first author is also supported by the ERC grant 742754 (project NTSC). The second author is supported by the grant 2021SGR 00115 from the Government of Catalonia, the project ACITHEC PID2021-124928NB-I00 from the Government of Spain, and the project HERMES, funded by INCIBE and NGEU/PRTR.

References

1. Aigner, M., Ziegler, G.M.: Bertrand's postulate. In: Proofs from THE BOOK, pp. 7–12. Springer, Heidelberg (2010). https://doi.org/10.1007/978-3-642-00856-6_2
2. Applebaum, B., Arkis, B., Raykov, P., Vasudevan, P.N.: Conditional disclosure of secrets: amplification, closure, amortization, lower-bounds, and separations. In: Katz, J., Shacham, H. (eds.) CRYPTO 2017. LNCS, vol. 10401, pp. 727–757. Springer, Cham (2017). https://doi.org/10.1007/978-3-319-63688-7_24
3. Applebaum, B., Beimel, A., Farràs, O., Nir, O., Peter, N.: Secret-sharing schemes for general and uniform access structures. In: Ishai, Y., Rijmen, V. (eds.) EURO-CRYPT 2019. LNCS, vol. 11478, pp. 441–471. Springer, Cham (2019). https://doi. org/10.1007/978-3-030-17659-4_15
4. Applebaum, B., Beimel, A., Nir, O., Peter, N.: Better secret sharing via robust conditional disclosure of secrets. In: 52nd STOC, pp. 280–293 (2020)
5. Applebaum, B., Holenstein, T., Mishra, M., Shayevitz, O.: The communication complexity of private simultaneous messages, revisited. In: Nielsen, J.B., Rijmen, V. (eds.) EUROCRYPT 2018. LNCS, vol. 10821, pp. 261–286. Springer, Cham (2018). https://doi.org/10.1007/978-3-319-78375-8_9
6. Applebaum, B., Nir, O.: Upslices, downslices, and secret-sharing with complexity of 1.5^n. In: Malkin, T., Peikert, C. (eds.) CRYPTO 2021. LNCS, vol. 12827, pp. 627–655. Springer, Cham (2021). https://doi.org/10.1007/978-3-030-84252-9_21
7. Applebaum, B., Vasudevan, P.N.: Placing conditional disclosure of secrets in the communication complexity universe. In: 10th ITCS, pp. 4:1–4:14 (2019)

8. Babai, L., Gál, A., Wigderson, A.: Superpolynomial lower bounds for monotone span programs. Combinatorica **19**(3), 301–319 (1999)
9. Beimel, A.: Secret-sharing schemes: a survey. In: Chee, Y.M., et al. (eds.) IWCC 2011. LNCS, vol. 6639, pp. 11–46. Springer, Heidelberg (2011). https://doi.org/10.1007/978-3-642-20901-7_2
10. Beimel, A., Farràs, O.: The share size of secret-sharing schemes for almost all access structures and graphs. In: Pass, R., Pietrzak, K. (eds.) TCC 2020. LNCS, vol. 12552, pp. 499–529. Springer, Cham (2020). https://doi.org/10.1007/978-3-030-64381-2_18
11. Beimel, A., Farràs, O., Lasri, O.: Improved polynomial secret-sharing schemes (2023). https://eprint.iacr.org/2023/1158
12. Beimel, A., Farràs, O., Mintz, Y., Peter, N.: Linear secret-sharing schemes for forbidden graph access structures. In: Kalai, Y., Reyzin, L. (eds.) TCC 2017. LNCS, vol. 10678, pp. 394–423. Springer, Cham (2017). https://doi.org/10.1007/978-3-319-70503-3_13
13. Beimel, A., Ishai, Y., Kumaresan, R., Kushilevitz, E.: On the cryptographic complexity of the worst functions. In: Lindell, Y. (ed.) TCC 2014. LNCS, vol. 8349, pp. 317–342. Springer, Heidelberg (2014). https://doi.org/10.1007/978-3-642-54242-8_14
14. Beimel, A., Ishai, Y., Kushilevitz, E.: General constructions for information-theoretic private information retrieval. J. Comput. Syst. Sci. **71**(2), 213–247 (2005)
15. Beimel, A., Othman, H., Peter, N.: Quadratic secret sharing and conditional disclosure of secrets. In: Malkin, T., Peikert, C. (eds.) CRYPTO 2021. LNCS, vol. 12827, pp. 748–778. Springer, Cham (2021). https://doi.org/10.1007/978-3-030-84252-9_25
16. Beimel, A., Peter, N.: Optimal linear multiparty conditional disclosure of secrets protocols. In: Peyrin, T., Galbraith, S. (eds.) ASIACRYPT 2018. LNCS, vol. 11274, pp. 332–362. Springer, Cham (2018). https://doi.org/10.1007/978-3-030-03332-3_13
17. Bertilsson, M., Ingemarsson, I.: A construction of practical secret sharing schemes using linear block codes. In: Seberry, J., Zheng, Y. (eds.) AUSCRYPT 1992. LNCS, vol. 718, pp. 67–79. Springer, Heidelberg (1993). https://doi.org/10.1007/3-540-57220-1_53
18. Blakley, G.R.: Safeguarding cryptographic keys. In: Proceedings of the 1979 AFIPS National Computer Conference, volume 48, pages 313–317 (1979)
19. Csirmaz, L.: The dealer's random bits in perfect secret sharing schemes. Studia Sci. Math. Hungar. **32**(3–4), 429–437 (1996)
20. Csirmaz, L.: The size of a share must be large. J. Cryptol. **10**(4), 223–231 (1997)
21. Dvir, Z., Gopalan, P., Yekhanin, S.: Matching vector codes. SIAM J. Comput. **40**(4), 1154–1178 (2011)
22. Dvir, Z., Gopi, S.: 2-server PIR with sub-polynomial communication. In: 47th STOC, pp. 577–584 (2015)
23. Efremenko, K.: 3-query locally decodable codes of subexponential length. In: STOC 2009, pp. 39–44 (2009)
24. Efremenko, K.: 3-query locally decodable codes of subexponential length. SIAM J. Comput. **41**(6), 1694–1703 (2012)
25. Feige, U., Kilian, J., Naor, M.: A minimal model for secure computation. In: 26th STOC, pp. 554–563 (1994)
26. Frankl, P.: Constructing finite sets with given intersections. In: Combinatorial Mathematics, Proceedings of the International Colloquium on Graph Theory and Combinatorics 1981, vol. 17 of Annals of Discrete Mathematics, pp. 289–291 (1983)

27. Frankl, P., Wilson, R.M.: Intersection theorems with geometric consequences. Combinatorica **1**(4), 357–368 (1981)
28. Gay, R., Kerenidis, I., Wee, H.: Communication complexity of conditional disclosure of secrets and attribute-based encryption. In: Gennaro, R., Robshaw, M. (eds.) CRYPTO 2015. LNCS, vol. 9216, pp. 485–502. Springer, Heidelberg (2015). https://doi.org/10.1007/978-3-662-48000-7_24
29. Gertner, Y., Ishai, Y., Kushilevitz, E., Malkin, T.: Protecting data privacy in private information retrieval schemes. In: Proceedings of the 30th ACM Symposium on the Theory of Computing, pp. 151–160 (1998). Journal version: J. of Computer and System Sciences, 60(3), 592–629, 2000
30. Gertner, Y., Ishai, Y., Kushilevitz, E., Malkin, T.: Protecting data privacy in private information retrieval schemes. JCSS **60**(3), 592–629 (2000)
31. Grolmusz, V.: Superpolynomial size set-systems with restricted intersections mod 6 and explicit Ramsey graphs. Combinatorica **20**, 71–86 (2000)
32. Ishai, Y., Kushilevitz, E.: Improved upper bounds on information theoretic private information retrieval. In: Proceedings of the 31st ACM Symposium on the Theory of Computing, pp. 79–88 (1999). Journal version in [14]
33. Ishai, Y., Kushilevitz, E.: Perfect constant-round secure computation via perfect randomizing polynomials. In: Automata, Languages and Programming, 29th International Colloquium, ICALP 2002, pp. 244–256 (2002)
34. Ito, M., Saito, A., Nishizeki, T.: Secret sharing schemes realizing general access structure. In: Globecom 87, pp. 99–102 (1987). Journal version: Multiple assignment scheme for sharing secret. J. of Cryptology, 6(1), 15–20, 1993
35. Karchmer, M., Wigderson, A.: On span programs. In: 8th Structure in Complexity Theory, pp. 102–111 (1993)
36. Kutin, S.: Constructing large set systems with given intersection sizes modulo composite numbers. Combinatorics, Probability Computing (2002)
37. Liu, T., Vaikuntanatha, V.: Breaking the circuit-size barrier in secret sharing. In: 50th STOC, pp. 699–708 (2018)
38. Liu, T., Vaikuntanathan, V., Wee, H.: Conditional disclosure of secrets via nonlinear reconstruction. In: Katz, J., Shacham, H. (eds.) CRYPTO 2017. LNCS, vol. 10401, pp. 758–790. Springer, Cham (2017). https://doi.org/10.1007/978-3-319-63688-7_25
39. Liu, T., Vaikuntanathan, V., Wee, H.: Towards breaking the exponential barrier for general secret sharing. In: Nielsen, J.B., Rijmen, V. (eds.) EUROCRYPT 2018. LNCS, vol. 10820, pp. 567–596. Springer, Cham (2018). https://doi.org/10.1007/978-3-319-78381-9_21
40. Paskin-Cherniavsky, A., Radune, A.: On polynomial secret sharing schemes. In: ITC 2020, vol. 163 of LIPIcs, pp. 12:1–12:21 (2020)
41. Pitassi, T., Robere, R.: Lifting Nullstellensatz to monotone span programs over any field. In: 50th STOC, pp. 1207–1219 (2018)
42. Shamir, A.: How to share a secret. Commun. ACM **22**, 612–613 (1979)
43. Sun, H.-M., Shieh, S.-P.: Secret sharing in graph-based prohibited structures. In: INFOCOM 1997, pp. 718–724. IEEE (1997)
44. Xylouris, T.: On the least prime in an arithmetic progression and estimates for the zeros of Dirichlet l-functions. Acta Arith **150**(1), 65–91 (2011)

Near-Optimal Private Information Retrieval with Preprocessing

Arthur Lazzaretti[✉] and Charalampos Papamanthou

Yale University, New Haven, USA
{arthur.lazzaretti,charalampos.papamanthou}@yale.edu

Abstract. In Private Information Retrieval (PIR), a client wishes to access an index i from a public n-bit database without revealing any information about i. Recently, a series of works starting with the seminal paper of Corrigan-Gibbs and Kogan (EUROCRYPT 2020) considered PIR with *client preprocessing* and *no additional server storage*. In this setting, we now have protocols that achieve $\widetilde{O}(\sqrt{n})$ (amortized) server time and $\widetilde{O}(1)$ (amortized) bandwidth in the two-server model (Shi et al., CRYPTO 2021) as well as $\widetilde{O}(\sqrt{n})$ server time and $\widetilde{O}(\sqrt{n})$ bandwidth in the single-server model (Corrigan-Gibbs et al., EURO-CRYPT 2022). Given existing lower bounds, a single-server PIR scheme with $\widetilde{O}(\sqrt{n})$ (amortized) server time and $\widetilde{O}(1)$ (amortized) bandwidth is still feasible, however, to date, no known protocol achieves such complexities. In this paper we fill this gap by constructing the first single-server PIR scheme with $\widetilde{O}(\sqrt{n})$ (amortized) server time and $\widetilde{O}(1)$ (amortized) bandwidth. Our scheme achieves near-optimal (optimal up to polylogarithmic factors) asymptotics in every relevant dimension. Central to our approach is a new cryptographic primitive that we call an *adaptable pseudorandom set*: With an adaptable pseudorandom set, one can represent a large pseudorandom set with a succinct fixed-size key k, and can both add to and remove from the set a constant number of elements by manipulating the key k, while maintaining its concise description as well as its pseudorandomness (under a certain security definition).

1 Introduction

In private information retrieval (PIR), a server holds a public database DB represented as an n-bit string and a client wishes to retrieve $\mathsf{DB}[i]$ without revealing i to the server. PIR has many applications in various systems with advanced privacy requirements [2,3, 28,31,38] and comprises a foundational computer science and cryptography problem, with connections to primitives such as oblivious transfer [19] and locally-decodable codes [29,40], among others. PIR can be naively realized by downloading the whole DB for each query, which is prohibitive for large databases. PIR is classically considered within the two-server model [11,12,14], where DB is replicated on two, non-colluding servers. *For the rest of the paper we use* **1PIR** *to refer to single-server PIR* [32] *and* **2PIR** *to refer to two-server PIR.* Clearly, 1PIR is much more challenging than 2PIR, but also more useful; it is hard to ensure two servers do not collude and remain both synchronized and available in practice [6,36].

© International Association for Cryptologic Research 2023
G. Rothblum and H. Wee (Eds.): TCC 2023, LNCS 14370, pp. 406–435, 2023.
https://doi.org/10.1007/978-3-031-48618-0_14

Sublinear Time 2PIR. Preliminary PIR works [4,13,20–22,25,30,32,34,35,39] featured linear server time and sublinear bandwidth. To reduce server time, several works [1,5,17,18,23,28] proposed *preprocessing PIR*. These approaches require a prohibitive amount of server storage due to large server-side data structures. Recently a new type of preprocessing PIR with *offline client-side preprocessing* was proposed by Corrigan-Gibbs and Kogan [16]. Introduced as 2PIR, their scheme has sublinear server time and *no additional server storage* — the preprocessing phase outputs just a few bits to be stored at the client, which is modeled as stateful. A simplified, stripped-down[1] version of their protocol, involving three parties, **client**, **server$_1$** and **server$_2$**, is given below.

- *Offline phase.* **client** sends $S_1, \ldots, S_{\sqrt{n}}$ to **server$_1$**. Each S_i is independent and contains $\sqrt{n}$ elements sampled uniformly from $\{0, \ldots, n-1\}$ without replacement. **server$_1$** returns database parities $p_1, \ldots, p_{\sqrt{n}}$, where $p_i = \oplus_{j \in S_i} \mathsf{DB}[j]$. These database parities, along with the respective index sets, are then stored by **client** locally.
- *Online phase (query to index i).* In Step 1, **client** finds a local set S_j that contains i and sends $S_j' = S_j \setminus \{i\}$ to **server$_2$**. In Step 2, **server$_2$** returns parity p_j' of S_j', and **client** computes $\mathsf{DB}[i] = p_j \oplus p_j'$. In Step 3, **client** generates a fresh random set S_j^* that contains i, sends $S_j^* \setminus \{i\}$ to **server$_1$**, gets back its parity p_j^*, and replaces (S_j, p_j) with $(S_j^*, p_j^* \oplus \mathsf{DB}[i])$. (We note that this last step is crucially needed to maintain the distribution of the sets at the client side and ensure security of future queries.)

The complexities of the above protocol are linear (such as client storage and bandwidth), but Corrigan-Gibbs and Kogan [16] achieved $\widetilde{O}(\sqrt{n})$ time and communication complexities by introducing the notion of *pseudorandom sets*: Instead of sending the sets in plaintext, the client sends a Pseudorandom Permutation (PRP) key so that the server can regenerate the sets as well as check membership efficiently. However, the first step of the online phase above requires removing element i from the set S_j. This cannot be done efficiently with a PRP key, so prior work sends $S_j \setminus \{i\}$ in plaintext, incurring $O(\sqrt{n} \log n)$ online bandwidth. In a followup work, Shi et al. [37] addressed this issue. They use no PRPs and construct their sets via *privately-puncturable pseudorandom functions* [7,10]. Their primitive allows element removal without key expansion in the online phase, thus keeping a short set description, yielding $\widetilde{O}(1)$ bandwidth.

Compiling 2PIR into 1PIR. The original protocol by Corrigan-Gibbs and Kogan [16], their follow-up work [31], as well as Shi et al.'s polylog bandwidth protocol [37], are all 2PIR protocols. Corrigan-Gibbs et al. [15] showed how to port the 2PIR protocols by Corrigan-Gibbs and Kogan [16,31] into a 1PIR scheme with the same (amortized[2]) $\widetilde{O}(\sqrt{n})$ complexities. Their main technique, is to transform their initial 2PIR

---

[1] In particular, in Step 1 of the actual protocol's online phase, the client sends $S_j \setminus \{i\}$ with probability $1 - 1/\sqrt{n}$ and $S_j \setminus \{r\}$, for a random element r, with probability $1/\sqrt{n}$, to ensure no information is leaked about i. Also, $\omega(\log \lambda)$ parallel executions are required to guarantee overwhelming correctness in λ, to account for puncturing 'fails' and when a set S_j that contains i cannot be found.

[2] Amortization is over $\sqrt{n}$ queries.

Table 1. Comparison with related work. Server time and bandwidth are amortized (indicated with a *). All schemes presented have $\tilde{O}(\sqrt{n})$ client time, $\tilde{O}(\sqrt{n})$ client space and no additional server space. The amortization kicks in after $\sqrt{n}$ queries.

scheme	model	server time*	bandwidth*	assumption
[15]	1PIR	$\tilde{O}(\sqrt{n})$	$\tilde{O}(\sqrt{n})$	LWE
[37]	2PIR	$\tilde{O}(\sqrt{n})$	$\tilde{O}(1)$	LWE
Theorem 52	1PIR	$\tilde{O}(\sqrt{n})$	$\tilde{O}(1)$	LWE

scheme [15] into another 2PIR scheme that *avoids communication with* **server**$_1$ in the online phase. We call such a 2PIR protocol 2PIR+. Then, they use fully-homomorhpic encryption (FHE) [24] to execute both offline and online phases on the same server, yielding 1PIR. To build the crucial 2PIR+ protocol, they make two simple modifications of the high-level protocol presented before: (i) In the offline phase, instead of preprocessing $\sqrt{n}$ sets, they preprocess $2\sqrt{n}$ sets, where $\sqrt{n}$ is the number of queries they wish to support; (ii) In the final step of the online phase, instead of picking a fresh random set S_j^* and then communicating with **server**$_1$, they use a preprocessed set S_h from above, *avoiding communication with* **server**$_1$ *in the online phase*. Crucially, S_h must then be updated to contain i, so that the primary sets maintain the same distribution after each query. After $\sqrt{n}$ queries there are no more preprocessed sets left and the offline phase is run again, maintaining the same amortized complexity.[3]

Based on the above, it seems that a natural approach to construct a sublinear-time, polylog-bandwidth 1PIR scheme (which is the central contribution of this paper) would be to apply the same trick of preprocessing an additional $\sqrt{n}$ random sets to the Shi et al. protocol [37]. But this strategy runs into a fundamental issue: We would have to ensure that, in Step 3 of the online phase, when we use one of the preprocessed sets, S_h, to replace the set that was just consumed to answer query i, the set key corresponding to S_h *would have to be updated to contain* i. However, this is not supported in the current construction of pseudorandom sets by Shi et al. [37]—one can only remove elements, but not add. Our work capitalizes on this observation.

Technical Highlight: Adaptable Pseudorandom Sets. A substantial part of our contribution is to define and construct an *adaptable pseudorandom set* supporting *both* element removal and addition. In fact, our technique can support addition and removal of a logarithmic number of elements. At a high level, our primitive can be used as follows. Key generation outputs a succinct key sk representing the set. Along with algorithms for enumeration of sk and membership checking in sk, we define algorithms for removing an element x from the set defined by sk and adding an element x into the set defined by sk, both of which output the updated set's new key sk'. We believe that this primitive can also be of independent interest outside of PIR.

Our construction of adaptable PRSets is simple. First, we show how previous puncturable pseudorandomsets can be modified to support a single addition (instead of a

---

[3] We pick $\sqrt{n}$ concretely for exposition. Looking ahead, our scheme achieves a same smooth tradeoff where by preprocessing $O(Q)$ sets achieves $O(n/Q)$ amortized online time.

single removal). Then, we show that given both capabilities, one can compose pseudorandom set keys to support any number of additions and removals. For the usecase of PIR, it is sufficient to support exactly one removal and one addition, but the technique can be extended further.

Our Final 2PIR+ and 1PIR Protocols. Armed with adaptable pseudorandom sets, a high-level description of our new 2PIR+ scheme is as follows. Below, APRS denotes "adaptable pseudorandom set".

- *Offline phase.* **client** sends $\sqrt{n} + Q$ APRS keys $sk_1, \ldots, sk_{\sqrt{n}+Q}$ to **server**$_1$ and **server**$_1$ returns database parities $p_1, \ldots, p_{\sqrt{n}+Q}$ where $p_i = \oplus_{j \in sk_i} \mathsf{DB}[j]$. The database parities are then stored locally by **client**, together with the respective APRS keys.
- *Online (query to index i).* First, **client** finds APRS key sk_j that contains i, **removes** i from sk_j and sends sk'_j to **server**$_2$. Then **server**$_2$ returns parity p'_j of sk'_j, and **client** computes $\mathsf{DB}[i] = p_j \oplus p'_j$. Finally, **client adds** i into key sk_h (for some $h > \sqrt{n}$) and replaces (sk_j, p_j) with $(sk_h, p_h \oplus \mathsf{DB}[i])$.

The above 2PIR+ protocol requires more work to ensure a small probability of failure and that the server's view is uniform. Also, again, we can convert the above 2PIR+ protocol to 1PIR with sublinear complexities, using FHE [15]. Note that using FHE naively for 1PIR would incur $\widetilde{O}(n)$ server time—thus combining FHE with our above 2PIR+ protocol yields a much better (sublinear) FHE-based 1PIR instantiation.

Our Result and Comparison with Related Work. As we discussed, if we require the server time to be sublinear (with no additional storage), the most bandwidth-efficient 2PIR protocol is the one by Shi et al. [37]. However, the most efficient 1PIR construction, by Corrigan-Gibbs et al. [15], incurs bandwidth on the order of $O(\sqrt{n} \log n)$.

In this paper, we fill this gap. Our result (Theorem 52) provides the first 1PIR protocol with *sublinear amortized server time and polylogarithmic amortized bandwidth*.

We note that our scheme is optimal up to polylogarithmic factors in every relevant dimension, given known lower bounds for client-dependent preprocessing PIR where the server stores only the database [5, 15, 16]. For a comparison with prior sublinear-server-time-no-additional-server-storage schemes, see Table 1.

Concurrent Work. We note independently and concurrently, the notion of 1PIR with polylogarithmic bandwidth and sublinear server time was studied by Zhou et al. [41]. Their work requires use of a privately *programmable* PRF, and the sets constructed do not enjoy the same strong security properties as our adaptable pseudorandom sets. Specifically, our adaptable sets are defined more generally. One can pick $\mathsf{L} = O(\log(N))$ (for sets of size N) additions or removals to support when generating the set key, and the set will support any number between 0 and L of adaptive additions/removals, maintaining a concise description, and with each intermediate key satisfying our security definitions. Our adaptable PRSets could therefore have more applications due to their higher flexibility. With respect to the final PIR scheme, the asymptotics achieved in their scheme are the same as the asymptotics achieved here in every dimension (what we define as near-optimality).

Notation. We use the abbreviation PPT to refer to probabilistic polynomial time. Unless otherwise noted, we define a negligible function $\mathsf{negl}(\cdot)$ to be a function such that for every polynomial $p(\cdot)$, $\mathtt{negl}(\cdot)$ is less than $1/p(\cdot)$. We fix $\lambda \in \mathbb{N}$ to be a security parameter. We will also use the notation 1^z or 0^z to represent 1 or 0 repeated z times. For any vector or bitstring V, we index V using the notation $V[i]$ to represent the i-th element or i-th bit of V, indexed from 0. We will also use the notation $V[i :]$ to denote V from the i-th index onwards. We use $x\|y$ to denote the concatenation of bitsring x and bitstring y. We use $S \sim D$ to denote that S is "sampled from distribution" D. We use the notation $[x, y]$ to represent the set $\{x, x + 1, \ldots, y - 1\}$. Finally, we use $\tilde{O}(\cdot)$ to denote the big-O notation that ignores polylogarithmic terms and any polynomial terms in the security parameter λ.

2   Background: PIR, Puncturable Functions and Puncturable Sets

We now introduce definitions for 2PIR. We consider 2PIR protocols where only one server (the second one) participates in the online phase. We refer to these protocols as 2PIR+. We also formally introduce privately-puncturable PRFs [7] and privately-puncturable pseudorandom sets [16,37], both crucial for our work. Moving forward, "PRF" stands for "pseudorandom function" and "PRS" stands for "pseudorandom set".

Definition 21 (2PIR+ scheme). *A 2PIR+ scheme consists of three stateful algorithms* (**server**$_1$, **server**$_2$, **client**) *with the following interactions.*

- *Offline:* **server**$_1$ *and* **server**$_2$ *receive the security parameter* 1^λ *and an n-bit database* DB. *client receives* 1^λ. **client** *sends one message to* **server**$_1$ *and* **server**$_1$ *replies with one message.*
- *Online: For any query* $x \in \{0, \ldots, n-1\}$, **client** *sends one message to* **server**$_2$ *and* **server**$_2$ *responds with one message. In the end,* **client** *outputs a bit b.*

Definition 22 (2PIR+ correctness). *A 2PIR+ scheme is correct if its honest execution, with any database* DB $\in \{0,1\}^n$ *and any polynomial-sized sequence of queries* $x_1, \ldots, x_Q$, *returns* DB$[x_1], \ldots,$ DB$[x_Q]$ *with probability* $1 - \mathtt{negl}(\lambda)$.

Definition 23 (2PIR+ privacy). *A 2PIR+ scheme* (**server**$_1$, **server**$_2$, **client**) *is private if there exists a PPT simulator* Sim, *such that for any algorithm* serv$_1$, *no PPT adversary* $\mathcal{A}$ *can distinguish the experiments below with non-negligible probability.*

- *Expt$_0$:* **client** *interacts with* $\mathcal{A}$ *who acts as* **server**$_2$ *and* **server**$_1^*$ *who acts as the* **server**$_1$. *At every step t,* $\mathcal{A}$ *chooses the query index* x_t, *and* **client** *is invoked with input* x_t *as its query and outputs its query.*
- *Expt$_1$:* Sim *interacts with* $\mathcal{A}$ *who acts as* **server**$_2$ *and* **server**$_1^*$ *who acts as the* **server**$_1$. *At every step t,* $\mathcal{A}$ *chooses the query index* x_t, *and* Sim *is invoked with no knowledge of* x_t *and outputs a query.*

We note that in the above definition our adversary $\mathcal{A}$ can deviate arbitrarily from the protocol. Intuitively the privacy definition implies that queries made to **server**$_2$ will appear random to **server**$_2$, assuming servers do not collude (as is the case in our model). Also, note that the above definition only captures privacy for **server**$_2$ since by Definition 21, **server**$_1$ interacts with **client** *before* the query indices are picked.

Privately-puncturable PRFs. A puncturable PRF is a PRF F whose key k can be punctured at some point x in the domain of the PRF, such that the output punctured key k_x reveals nothing about $F_k(x)$ [27]. A privately-puncturable PRF is a puncturable PRF where the punctured key k_x also reveals *no* information about the punctured point x (by re-randomizing the output $F_k(x)$). Privately-puncturable PRFs can be constructed from standard LWE (learning with errors assumption) [7,8,10] and can be implemented to allow puncturing on m points at once [7]. We now give the formal definition.

Definition 24 (Privately-puncturable PRF [7]). *A privately-puncturable PRF with domain $\{0,1\}^*$ and range $\{0,1\}$ has four algorithms: (i) $\mathsf{Gen}(1^\lambda, L, m) \to sk$: Outputs secret key sk, given security parameter λ, input length L and number of points to be punctured m; (ii) $\mathsf{Eval}(sk, x) \to b$: Outputs the evaluation bit $b \in \{0,1\}$, given sk and input x; (iii) $\mathsf{Puncture}(sk, P) \to sk_P$: Outputs punctured key sk_P, given sk and set P of m points for puncturing; (iv) $\mathsf{PEval}(sk_P, x) \to b$: Outputs the evaluation bit $b \in \{0,1\}$, given sk_P and x.*

There are three properties we require from a privately-puncturable PRF: First, *functionality preservation*, meaning that $\mathsf{PEval}(sk_P, x)$ equals $\mathsf{Eval}(sk, x)$ for all $x \notin P$. Second, *pseudorandomness*, meaning that the values $\mathsf{Eval}(sk, x)$ at $x \in P$, appear pseudorandom to the adversary that has access to sk_P *and* oracle access to $\mathsf{Eval}(sk, \cdot)$ (as long as the adversary cannot query $\mathsf{Eval}(sk, x)$ for $x \in P$, in which case it is trivial to distinguish). Third, *privacy with respect to puncturing*, meaning that the punctured key sk_P does not reveal anything about the set of points that was punctured. Formal definitions are given in [7,37]. (We include these only in the full version of the paper [33, Definitions E1, E2, E3].).

It is important to note here that we will be using a privately-puncturable PRF with a *randomized* puncturing algorithm. Although initial constructions were deterministic [7], Canetti and Chen [10] show how to support randomized puncturing without extra assumptions and negligible extra cost. Any of the constructions can be extended in the manner shown in [10] to achieve a randomized puncturing. The randomization will be important since our add functionality uses rejection sampling.

Privately-puncturable PRSs. A privately-puncturable PRS is a set that contains elements drawn from a given distribution $\mathbb{D}_n$. (We define a $\mathbb{D}_n$ to be used in this work in Sect. 3.) The set can be represented succinctly with a key sk. Informally, one can "puncture" an element x, producing a new key that represents a set without x. Privately-puncturable PRSs were first introduced by Corrigan-Gibbs and Kogan [16] and were further optimized by Shi et al. [37]. The formal definition is as follows.

Definition 25 (Privately-puncturable PRS [16,37]). *A privately-puncturable PRS has four algorithms: (i) $\mathsf{Gen}(1^\lambda, n) \to (msk, sk)$: Outputs a set key sk and a master key msk, given security parameter λ and the set domain $\{0, \ldots, n-1\}$; (ii) $\mathsf{EnumSet}(sk) \to S$: Outputs set S given sk; (iii) $\mathsf{InSet}(sk, x) \to b$: Outputs a bit b denoting whether $x \in \mathsf{EnumSet}(sk)$; (iv) $\mathsf{Resample}(msk, x) \to sk_x$: Outputs a secret key sk_x for a set generated by sk, with x's membership resampled.*[4]

---

[4] Previously this was called "puncture". We rename it to "resample" for ease of understanding and consistency with our work.

We require three properties from a privately-puncturable PRS: First, *pseudorandom-ness with respect to a distribution* $\mathbb{D}_n$, meaning that $\mathsf{Gen}(1^\lambda, n)$ generates a key that represents a set whose distribution is indistinguishable from $\mathbb{D}_n$. Second, *functionality preservation with respect to resampling*, informally meaning that the set resulting from resampling should be a subset of the original set. This means we can only resample elements already in the set. Third, *security in resampling*, states that for any (msk, sk) output by $\mathsf{Gen}(1^\lambda, n)$, sk is computationally indistinguishable from a key sk'_x where (msk', sk') is a key output by calling $\mathsf{Gen}(1^\lambda, n)$ until $\mathsf{InSet}(sk', x) \to 1$ and sk'_x is the output of $\mathsf{Resample}(msk', x)$. Formal definitions can be found in [16,37]. (We also include these in Appendix A, Definitions A3, A1, A2.)

Privately-puncturable PRSs from Privately-puncturable PRFs. Shi et al. [37] constructed a privately-puncturable PRS from a privately-puncturable PRF. Let F be a privately-puncturable PRF and let $x \in \{0,1\}^{\log n}$ be an element of the set domain. We provide the intuition behind the construction. Consider that we require both concise description and fast membership testing. One first approach to constructing a PRS could be to define $x \in S$ to be $F.\mathsf{Eval}(sk, x)$ equals 1. Resampling x would then be equivalent to puncturing F's key at point x. Given $x \in \{0,1\}^{\log n}$, this approach creates sets proportional to the size of $n/2$ in expectation, which is undesirable for our application; we want sets of size approximately $\sqrt{n}$. To deal with this problem, one can add additional constraints with respect to suffixes of x. In other words, define $x \in S$ iff $F.\mathsf{Eval}(sk, x[i :])$ equals 1, for all $i = [0, \log n/2]$. Recall $x[i :]$ denotes the suffix of bitstring x starting at position i. Puncturing in this case would require puncturing at $\log n/2$ points. While this approach generates sets of expected size $\sqrt{n}$, it introduces too much dependency between elements in the set: Elements with shared suffixes are very likely to be together in the set. To deal with this, Shi et al. [37] changed the construction as follows. Let B be an integer greater than 0. Then, let $z = 0^B || x$. We say that $x \in S$ iff

$$F.\mathsf{Eval}(sk, z[i :]) = 1, \text{ for all } i = [0, \log n/2 + B].$$

For clarity we provide a small example here. Suppose $n = 16$ and that we want to check the membership of element 7 for set S. First, we represent 7 with $\log 16 = 4$ bits, $7_2 = 0111$. Next, we append $B = 4$ zeros to the front of the bitstring, so that we have the string 00000111. Now, we say that $7 \in S$ iff

$$F.\mathsf{Eval}(sk, 00000111) = 1 \wedge F.\mathsf{Eval}(sk, 0000111) = 1 \wedge F.\mathsf{Eval}(sk, 000111) = 1$$
$$\wedge F.\mathsf{Eval}(sk, 00111) = 1 \wedge F.\mathsf{Eval}(sk, 0111) = 1 \wedge F.\mathsf{Eval}(sk, 111) = 1.$$

Note that adding these B extra checks decreases dependency of set membership between elements proportional to 2^B, since it adds bits unique to each element. As a tradeoff, it decreases the size of the set proportional to 2^B. By picking $B = \lceil 2 \log \log n \rceil$, we maintain the set size to be $\sqrt{n}/\log^2 n$ while having small dependency between elements—which can be addressed. We give an overview of our remaining algorithms:

Set Enumeration. Let $m = \log n/2 + B$. Naively, set enumeration would take linear time, since membership for each $x \in \{0, \ldots, n-1\}$ must be checked. Shi et al. [37]

observed that due to the dependency introduced, the set can be enumerated in expected time $\widetilde{O}(\sqrt{n})$.

Resampling. To resample an element x from the set S, we puncture the PRF key at the $m = \log n/2 + 2\log\log n$ points that determine x's membership by running

$$sk_x \leftarrow F.\mathsf{Puncture}(sk, \{z[i :]\}_{i=[0,m]}) \, .$$

By the pseudorandomness of F, this will resample x's membership in S and x will not be in the set defined by sk_x with probability $1 - 1/2^m = 1 - 1/\sqrt{n}\log^2 n$. Clearly, we do not remove elements from the set with overwhelming probability. Aside from that, there is still dependency among elements, and puncturing x may also remove other elements in S with some small probability. Shi et al. [37] resolve this by bounding these probabilities to less than $1/2$ and running λ parallel executions of the protocol and taking a majority. Looking ahead, we will require this too.

Key Generation. By Definition 25, key generation for a privately-puncturable PRS outputs two keys, key sk that represents the initial set and key msk that is used for puncturing. To output msk, we simply call $F.\mathsf{Gen}(1^\lambda, L, m)$. To output sk, we pick a set P of m "useless" strings of $L = \log n + B$ bits that start with the 1 bit and output a second key $sk \leftarrow F.\mathsf{Puncture}(msk, P)$. The reason for that is to ensure that resampled keys are indistinguishable from freshly sampled keys as required by the "security in resampling" property. Therefore we artificially puncture msk in a way that does not affect the set of elements represented by it, yet we change its format to be the same as a set key resampled at a given point.

Efficiency and Security. To summarize, the scheme described above by Shi et al. [37] has the following complexities: Algorithms Gen, InSet and Resample run in $\widetilde{O}(1)$ time. All keys have $\widetilde{O}(1)$ size. Algorithm EnumSet runs in expected $\widetilde{O}(\sqrt{n})$ time. It satisfies Definitions A1 and A2 assuming privately-puncturable PRFs with the properties aforementioned (and shown feasible from LWE in previous works [7,10]).

3 Preliminary 2PIR+ Protocol

We first design a preliminary 2PIR+ protocol (Fig. 1) that helps with the exposition of our final protocol. In this preliminary 2PIR+ protocol the client has linear local storage and the communication is amortized $\widetilde{O}(\sqrt{n})$. Later, we will convert this 2PIR+ scheme into a space and communication-efficient 2PIR+ protocol (by using our PRS primitive of Sect. 4) that will yield our final 1PIR scheme. Crucially, the analysis of the preliminary protocol is almost the same as that of our final PIR protocol in Sect. 5.

Overview of our Preliminary Protocol. Our preliminary protocol works as follows. During the *preprocessing* phase, the client constructs a collection T of $\ell = \sqrt{n}\log^3 n$ "primary" sets and a collection Z of an additional $\sqrt{n}$ "reserve" sets. All sets are sampled from a fixed distribution $\mathbb{D}_n$ over the domain $\{0, \ldots, n-1\}$. While we can use any distribution for our preliminary protocol, we use a specific one that will serve the use of PRSs in Sect. 5. Both T and Z are sent to **server**₁ and client receives the hints back, as explained in the introduction. Client stores locally the collections T and Z along with the hints. This is the main difference with our final protocol, where we will be storing keys instead of the sets themselves. To query an index x during the *query* phase, the client finds some $T_j = (S_j, p_j)$ in T such that S_j contains x, "removes" x and sends the new set to $\mathbf{server}_2$. Then $\mathbf{server}_2$ computes the parity of the new set and sends the parity back, at which point the client can compute $\mathsf{DB}[x]$, by xoring $\mathbf{server}_2$'s response with p_j. As we will see, element removal in this context means resampling the membership of x via a Resample algorithm introduced below. To ensure the set distribution of T does not change across queries, our protocol has a *refresh* phase, where element x is "added", to the next available reserve set, via an Add algorithm introduced below. The protocol allows for $\sqrt{n}$ queries and achieves amortized sublinear server time over these $\sqrt{n}$ queries. After $\sqrt{n}$ queries, we re-run the offline phase.

The above protocol can fail with constant probability, as we will analyze in Lemma 31 below. To avoid this, as we indicate at the top of Fig. 1, we run $\log n \log \log n$ parallel instances of the protocol and take the majority bit as the output answer. We now continue with the detailed description of the building blocks (such as algorithms Resample and Add) that our protocol uses.

Sampling Distribution $\mathbb{D}_n$. For our preliminary protocol we are using the same distribution as the one induced by the PRS construction by Shi et al. [37] described in Sect. 2. This will help us seamlessly transition to our space-efficient protocol in Sect. 5. To sample a set S with elements from the domain $\{0, \dots, n-1\}$ we define, for all $x \in \{0, \dots, n-1\}$,

$$x \in S \Leftrightarrow \mathsf{RO}(z[i:]) = 1 \text{ for all } i \in [0, m],$$

where we recall that $m = \log n/2 + B, B = 2 \log \log n$ and $z = 0^B || x$. Also, RO : $\{0,1\}^* \to \{0,1\}$ denotes a random oracle. We use the random oracle for exposition only—our final construction does not need one. Note for our preliminary protocol, the adversary cannot call the RO function or otherwise all the sets would revealed. We also define $\mathbb{D}_n^x$ to be a distribution where a set S is sampled from $\mathbb{D}_n$ *until* $x \in S$.

Functions with Respect to $\mathbb{D}_n$. We define two functions with respect to the distribution $\mathbb{D}_n$ —these functions will be needed to describe our preliminary scheme. To define these functions, we first introduce what it means for two elements to be *related*.

Definition 31. *Function* Related(x, y), *where* $x, y \in \{0, \dots, n-1\}$, *returns a bit* $b \in \{0, 1\}$ *where* $b = 1$ *(in which case we say that* x *is* related *to* y*) iff* x *and* y *share a suffix of length* $> \log n/2$ *in their binary representation.*

For example Related$(1000001, 1100001) = 1$ and Related$(1000001, 1101111) = 0$. Equipped with this, we define our two functions.

- Resample$(S, x) \to S'$: Given $x \in S$ as input, define $z = 0^B || x$. We sample a uniform bit for each suffix of z, $z[i:]$, for $i \in [0, m]$. For each $y \in S$ such that Related(x, y) (including x), we check if any suffix of y was mapped to 0, and if so, remove it from S and return this new set.
- Add$(S, x) \to S'$: This function essentially "reprograms" the random oracle such that $\mathsf{RO}(z[i:]) = 1$ for all $i \in [0, m]$, where $z = 0^B || x$. This may also affect membership of other elements $y \in \{0, \dots, n-1\}$ that are not in S, but related to x

with some probability. For us it will suffice that for most of executions, $\text{Add}(S, x) = S \cup \{x\}$. We bound the probability of this formally in Appendix B.

- Run $\omega(\log \lambda)$ instances of the protocol below.
- Output the majority bit maj in Step 4 of **Query**.
- Use maj as $\text{DB}[x]$ in Step 2 of **Refresh**.

Offline phase: Preprocessing

1. **client** samples $\ell + \sqrt{n}$ sets from $\mathbb{D}_n$, $S_1, \ldots, S_{\ell+\sqrt{n}}$, where $\ell = \sqrt{n} \log^3 n$.
2. **client** sends sets $S_1, \ldots, S_{\ell+\sqrt{n}}$ to **server**$_1$ and **server**$_1$ returns a set of bits $p_1, \ldots, p_{\ell+\sqrt{n}}$, where

$$p_i = \oplus_{j \in S_i} \text{DB}[j].$$

3. **client** stores pairs of sets/hints

$$\mathsf{T} = \{T_j = (S_j, p_j)\}, \mathsf{Z} = \{Z_k = (S_k, p_k)\},$$

where $j \in [\ell]$ and $k \in [\ell+1, \ell+\sqrt{n}]$.

Online phase: Query (input is index $x \in \{0, \ldots, n-1\}$)

1. **client** finds the first $T_j = (S_j, p_j)$ in T such that $x \in S_j$. If such T_j is not found, set $j = |\mathsf{T}| + 1$ and $T_j = (S_j, p_j)$ where $S_j \sim \mathbb{D}_n$ and p_j is uniform bit.
2. **client** sends $S' = \text{Resample}(S_j, x)$ to **server**$_2$.
3. **server**$_2$ returns $r = \bigoplus_{k \in S'} \text{DB}[k]$.
4. **client** computes $\text{DB}[x] = r \oplus p_j$.

Online phase: Refresh (executed when $j \leq |\mathsf{T}|$)

1. Let $Z_0 = (S_0, p_0)$ be the first item from Z.
2. Let $S_0^* = \text{Add}(S_0, x)$, and

$$p_0^* = p_0 \oplus (\text{DB}[x] \wedge (x \notin S_0)).$$

3. **client** sets $T_j = (S_0^*, p_0^*)$, where T_j was consumed earlier, and removes Z_0 from Z.

Fig. 1. Our preliminary 2PIR+ protocol. With n we denote the size of DB and $[\ell] = [1, \ell]$.

Efficiency Analysis. Our preliminary protocol in Fig. 1 is inefficient: The online server time is $\widetilde{O}(\sqrt{n})$, client storage and computation is $\widetilde{O}(n)$ and bandwidth is $\widetilde{O}(\sqrt{n})$. It supports $\sqrt{n}$ queries, after which we need to re-run the offline phase.

Correctness Proof. As we mentioned before, our basic protocol without parallel instances, has constant failure probability, less than $1/2$. We prove this through Lemma 31.

Lemma 31 (Correctness of protocol with no repetitions). *Consider the protocol of Fig. 1 with no repetitions and fix a query x_i. The probability that the returned bit $\text{DB}[x_i]$*

in Step 4 of Query *is incorrect, assuming* DB$[x_{i-1}]$ *used in Step 2 of* Refresh *is correct with overwhelming probability, is less than* $1/2$.

We give an overview of the intuition of the proof here and defer the full proof of Lemma 31 to Appendix B. We distinguish two cases. For the first query x_1, there are three cases where our protocol can fail. The first failure occurs if we cannot find an index j in T such that $x \in S_j$ for $T_j = (S_j, p_j)$ (Step 1 of Query). We can bound this failure by $1/n$. The second failure occurs when our Resample function does not remove x. This happens with probability $1/\sqrt{n}\log^2 n$. The third failure case occurs when we remove x, but also remove an element other than x within Resample. This can bounded by $1/2\log n$.

For every other query x_i, i greater than 1, we must consider an additional failure case which occurs when, in the Refresh phase, we add an element other than x within Add—which we can also bound by $1/2\log n$. Computing the final bound requires more work. It requires showing that Refresh only incurs a very small additional error probability to subsequent queries, which can also be bounded at the query step. We argue this formally in our proof of Theorem 31.

Amplifying Correctness via Repetition. To increase correctness of our scheme, we run k parallel instances of our protocol and set the output bit in Step 3 of Query to equal the majority of DB$[x]$ over these k instance. We run Refresh with the correct DB$[x]$ computed in Query so that we can apply Lemma 31. Let C be the event, where, over k instances of our preliminary PIR scheme, more than $\frac{k}{2}$ instances output the correct DB$[x]$. Using a standard lower-tail Chernoff bound, we have that, if $p > 1/2$ is the probability DB$[x]$ is correct, C's probability $> 1 - \exp(-\frac{1}{2p}k(p - \frac{1}{2})^2)$ which is overwhelming for $k = \omega(\log n)$, satisfying Definition 22. The same technique is used in our final PIR scheme.

Privacy Proof. We now show that our preliminary PIR protocol satisfies privacy, per Definition 23. Proving privacy relies on two properties we define below. Both proofs are similar, so we provide only the proof of the less intuitive *Property 2*.

Property 1: Let $S \sim \mathbb{D}_n^x$ and $S' \sim \mathbb{D}_n$. Then Resample(S, x) and S' are statistically indistinguishable.

Property 2: Let $S \sim \mathbb{D}_n$ and $S' \sim \mathbb{D}_n^x$. Then Add(S, x) and S' are statistically indistinguishable.

Lemma 32. *Property 2 holds.*

Proof. Consider the set $S' \sim \mathbb{D}_n^x$ and the set S'' output as (i) $S \sim \mathbb{D}_n$; (ii) $S'' \leftarrow$ Add(S, x). For an arbitrary y in the domain we show that $\Pr[y \in S'] = \Pr[y \in S'']$. Recall $m = 1/2\log n + B$. We distinguish two cases.

1. y is not related to x.
   - **Computing** $\Pr[y \in S']$. Let F_i be the event that set S' is output in the i-th try, where $i = 1, 2, \ldots, \infty$. It is

$$\Pr[y \in S'] = \sum_{i=1}^{\infty} \Pr[y \in S'|F_i] \Pr[F_i] = \frac{1}{2^m} \sum_{i=1}^{\infty} \Pr[F_i] = \frac{1}{2^m}.$$

In the above, $\Pr[y \in S'|F_i] = 1/2^m$ since x being in S' **does not affect** y's membership. Therefore for y to be a member, all m membership-test suffixes of y must evaluate to 1 during the i-th try, hence the derived probability.

- **Computing** $\Pr[y \in S'']$. Since adding x to S after S is sampled from $\mathbb{D}_n$ **does not affect** y's membership, it is $\Pr[y \in S''] = 1/2^m$.

2. y is related to x. Assume there are k (out of m) shared membership-test suffixes of x and y.

   - **Computing** $\Pr[y \in S']$. Again, let F_i be the event that set S' is output in the i-th try, where $i = 1, 2, \ldots, \infty$. It is

$$\Pr[y \in S'] = \sum_{i=1}^{\infty} \Pr[y \in S'|F_i] \Pr[F_i] = \frac{1}{2^{m-k}} \sum_{i=1}^{\infty} \Pr[F_i] = \frac{1}{2^{m-k}} .$$

In the above, $\Pr[y \in S'|F_i] = 1/2^{m-k}$. This is because x being in S' **does affect** y's membership. Therefore for y to be a member, all remaining $m - k$ membership-test suffixes of y must evaluate to 1 during the i-th try, hence the derived probability.

- **Computing** $\Pr[y \in S'']$. Adding x to S after S is sampled from $\mathbb{D}_n$ sets k membership-test suffixes of y to 1. Therefore for y to be a member of S'', the remaining membership-test suffixes have to be set to 1 before x is added, meaning $\Pr[y \in S''] = 1/2^{m-k}$.

Therefore the distributions are identical.   □

Given these two properties, our proof sketch goes as follows. For the first query, we pick an entry $T_j = (S_j, p_j)$ from T whose S_j contains the index x we want to query. Since S_j is the first set in T to contain x, $S_j \sim \mathbb{D}_n^x$. By Property 1, since what $\mathbf{server}_2$ sees is $S' = \mathtt{Resample}(S_j, x)$, S' is indistinguishable from a random set drawn from $\mathbb{D}_n$, and therefore, the query reveals nothing about the query index x to $\mathbf{server}_2$.

For every other query, we argue that the $\mathsf{Refresh}$ step maintains the distribution of T. Note that after a given set S_j is used, re-using it for the same query *or* a different query could create privacy problems. That is why after each query, we must replace S_j with an identically distributed set. By Property 2, S_j and $\mathtt{Add}(S_0, x)$ are identically distributed. Then, the swap maintains the distribution of sets in T and therefore the view of $\mathbf{server}_2$ is also simulatable without x. These arguments form the crux of the proof of Theorem 31; we provide the full proof in Appendix B.

Theorem 31 (Preliminary 2PIR+ protocol). *The 2PIR+ scheme in Fig. 1 is correct (per Definition 22) and private (per Definition 23) and has: (i) $\widetilde{O}(n)$ client storage $\widetilde{O}(n)$ client time; (ii) $\widetilde{O}(\sqrt{n})$ amortized server time and no additional server storage; (iii) $\widetilde{O}(\sqrt{n})$ amortized bandwidth.*

4 Adaptable Pseudorandom Sets

In this section, we introduce the main primitive required for achieving our result, an *adaptable pseudorandom set*. The main difference from a privately-puncturable PRS introduced in Sect. 2 is the support for the "add" procedure, as well as any logarithmic (in the set size) number of additions or removals, as opposed to a single removal. This will eventually allow us to port the protocol from Sect. 3 into a 1PIR protocol that has much improved complexities, such as sublinear client storage and polylogarithmic communication. We now give the formal definition and then we present a construction that satisfies our definition.

Definition 41 (Adaptable PRS). *An adaptable PRS has five algorithms: (i)* $\mathsf{Gen}(1^\lambda, n) \to (msk, sk)$: *Outputs our set's key* sk *and master key* msk, *given security parameter* λ *and set domain* $\{0, \ldots, n-1\}$; *(ii)* $\mathsf{EnumSet}(sk) \to S$: *Outputs set* S *given* sk; *(iii)* $\mathsf{InSet}(sk, x) \to b$: *Outputs bit* 1 *iff* $x \in \mathsf{EnumSet}(sk)$; *(iv)* $\mathsf{Resample}(msk, sk, x) \to sk_x$: *Outputs secret key* sk_x *that corresponds to an updated version of the set (initially generated by* sk) *after element* x *is resampled; (v)* $\mathsf{Add}(msk, sk, x) \to sk^x$: *Outputs secret key* sk^x *that corresponds to an updated version of the set (initially generated by* sk) *after element* x *is added.*

Note that our interface differs from privately-puncturable PRSs introduced in Sect. 2 in that our resample and add operations are dependent on both msk and sk; we will see why below.

Security Definitions for Adaptable PRSs. Our adaptable PRS must satisfy five definitions. Three of them, *functionality preservation with respect to resampling, pseudorandomness with respect to a distribution* $\mathbb{D}_n$ *and security in resampling* are identical to the equivalent definitions from privately-puncturable PRSs, namely Definitions A3, A1, A2 in Appendix A. We give two additional definitions in Appendix A (definitions A5 and A4) that relate to addition. First, *functionality preservation with respect to addition*, meaning that adding always yields a superset of the original set and can only cause elements related to x (which are few) to be added to the set. Second, *security in addition*, meaning that generating fresh keys until we find one where x belongs to the set is equivalent to generating one fresh key and then adding x into it.

Intuition of Our Construction: Introduce an Additional Key. Our core idea is to use two keys $sk[0]$ and $sk[1]$ and define the evaluation on the suffixes that determines membership as the XOR of $F.\mathsf{Eval}(sk[0], \cdot)$ and $F.\mathsf{Eval}(sk[1], \cdot)$. In this way, we can add to one key, and resample the other, independently. Note that this idea can support any fixed number of additions or resamplings (removals), by adding extra PRF keys. This simple construction circumvents many problems related with trying to perform multiple operations on the same key. Each key has one well defined operation. This also makes showing security and privacy straight-forward to argue.

We present a summary of our construction below. The detailed implementation is in Fig. 3 in Appendix C.

Key Generation. Let F be a privately-puncturable PRF. For key generation, we run $\overline{F.\mathsf{Gen}}$ twice, outputting $msk[0]$ and $msk[1]$. After puncturing on m "useless" points (for reasons we explained in Sect. 2), we output $sk[0]$ and $sk[1]$. And finally we output $sk = (sk[0], sk[1])$ and $msk = (msk[0], msk[1])$.

Set Membership and Enumeration. For each $x \in \{0, \ldots, n-1\}$ we define

$$x \in S \Leftrightarrow F.\mathsf{Eval}(sk[0], z[i:]) \oplus F.\mathsf{Eval}(sk[1], z[i:]) = 1 \text{ for all } i \in [0, m],$$

where we recall $m = \log n/2 + B, B = 2\log\log n$ and $z = 0^B||x$. For enumeration, we use the same algorithm as Shi et al. [37], with the difference that evaluation is done as the XOR of two evaluations, as above.

Resampling. Resampling works exactly as resampling in privately-puncturable PRSs (by calling $F.\mathsf{Puncture}$) and uses, without loss of generality, $msk[1]$ as input. The output replaces only the second part of sk—thus we require sk as input so that we can output the first part intact.

Addition. To add an element x, we call $F.\mathsf{Puncture}$ on input $msk[0]$, and then check x's membership on the punctured key. If x was added, we output the punctured key, else, we try puncturing from the master key again, until x is resampled *into* the set. This is the reason why it is necessary to have a rerandomizable puncture operation. Naively, this algorithm takes $\widetilde{O}(\sqrt{n})$ time, but we show in the Appendix how to reduce this to $\widetilde{O}(1)$ by leveraging the puncturable PRF used. Our final theorem is Theorem 41, and the construction and proof can be found in Appendix C.

Theorem 41 (Adaptable PRS construction). *Assuming* LWE, *the scheme in Fig. 3 satisfies correctness, pseudorandomness with respect to* $\mathbb{D}_n$ *(Definition A1), functionality preservation in resampling and addition (Definitions A3 and A5), security in resampling and addition (Definitions A2 and A4), and has the following complexities: (i) keys* sk *and* msk *have* $\widetilde{O}(1)$ *size; (ii) membership testing, resampling and addition take* $\widetilde{O}(1)$ *time; (iii) enumeration takes* $\widetilde{O}(\sqrt{n})$ *time.*

5 More Efficient 2PIR+ and Near-Optimal 1PIR

We now use adaptable PRSs introduced in the previous section to build a more efficient 2PIR+ scheme (one with $\widetilde{O}(\sqrt{n})$ client storage and $\widetilde{O}(1)$ communication complexity) which can be compiled, using FHE, into a 1PIR scheme with the same complexities, as we explained in the introduction. The main idea is to replace the actual sets, stored by the client in their entirety in our preliminary protocol, with PRS keys that support succinct representation, addition and removal. In particular, our proposed protocol in Fig. 2 is identical to our preliminary protocol in Fig. 1 except for the following main points: (i) In the offline phase, instead of sampling sets from $\mathbb{D}_n$, we generate keys (msk, sk) for adaptable PRSs that correspond to sets of the same distribution $\mathbb{D}_n$. (ii) In the online phase, we run $\mathsf{Resample}$ and Add defined in the adaptable PRS. These have exactly the same effect in the output set, except the operations are done on the set key not the set. (iii) We can check membership efficiently using InSet. We now introduce Theorem 51.

Theorem 51 (Efficient 2PIR+ protocol). *Assuming* LWE, *the 2PIR+ scheme in Fig. 2 is correct (per Definition 22) and private (per Definition 23) and has: (i)* $\widetilde{O}(\sqrt{n})$ *client storage and* $\widetilde{O}(\sqrt{n})$ *client time; (ii)* $\widetilde{O}(\sqrt{n})$ *amortized server time and no additional server storage; (iii)* $\widetilde{O}(1)$ *amortized bandwidth.*

- Run $\omega(\log \lambda)$ instances of the protocol below.
- Output the majority bit maj in Step 4 of Query.
- Use maj as DB[x] in Step 2 of Refresh.

Offline phase: Preprocessing

1. **client** generates $\ell + \sqrt{n}$ PRSet keys

$$(msk_1, sk_1), \ldots, (msk_{\ell+\sqrt{n}}, sk_{\ell+\sqrt{n}})$$

   with $\mathsf{Gen}(1^\lambda, n), \ell = \sqrt{n}\log^3 n$.
2. **client** sends keys $sk_1, \ldots, sk_{\ell+\sqrt{n}}$ to **server**$_1$ and **server**$_1$ returns a set of bits $p_1, \ldots, p_{\ell+\sqrt{n}}$, where

$$p_i = \oplus_{j \in \mathsf{EnumSet}(sk_i)} \mathsf{DB}[j] .$$

3. **client** stores pairs of keys/hints

$$\mathsf{T} = \{T_j = (msk_j, sk_j, p_j)\}, \mathsf{Z} = \{Z_k = (msk_k, sk_k, p_k)\},$$

   where $j \in [\ell]$ and $k \in [\ell+1, \ell+\sqrt{n}]$.

Online phase: Query (input is index $x \in \{0, n-1\}$)

1. **client** finds the first $T_j = (msk_j, sk_j, p_j)$ in T such that $\mathsf{InSet}(sk_j, x) = 1$. If such T_j is not found, set $j = |\mathsf{T}| + 1$ and $T_j = (msk_j, sk_j, p_j)$ where $\mathsf{Gen}(1^\lambda, n) \to (msk_j, sk_j)$ and p_j is uniform bit.
2. **client** sends $sk' \leftarrow \mathsf{Resample}(msk_j, sk_j, x)$ to **server**$_2$.
3. **server**$_2$ returns $r = \bigoplus_{k \in \mathsf{EnumSet}(sk')} \mathsf{DB}[k]$.
4. **client** computes $\mathsf{DB}[x] = r \oplus p_j$.

Online phase: Refresh (executed when $j \leq |\mathsf{T}|$)

1. Let $Z_0 = (msk_0, sk_0, p_0)$ be the first item from Z.
2. Let $(msk_0^x, sk_0^*) \leftarrow \mathsf{Add}(msk_0, sk_0, x)$ and

$$p_0^* = p_0 \oplus (\mathsf{DB}[x] \wedge (\neg \mathsf{InSet}(x, sk_0))) .$$

3. **client** sets $T_j = (msk_0^x, sk_0^*, p_0^*)$, where T_j was consumed earlier, and removes Z_0 from Z.

Fig. 2. Our 2PIR+ for n-bit DB using adaptable PRS (Gen, EnumSet, InSet, Resample, Add).

Unlimited Queries. Our scheme can handle $\sqrt{n}$ queries but can be extended to unlimited queries: We just rerun the offline phase after all secondary sets are used. This maintains the complexities from Theorem 51.

Trade-offs in Client Space and Server Time. Our scheme enjoys a trade-off between client space and server time. One can increase the number of elements of each PRSet to n/Q. This would change the number of sets required for our scheme to Q, and consequently our scheme would enjoy Q client space, at the expense of requiring n/Q online server time. This tradeoff holds in the other direction as well (increasing client space reduces online server time). In any case, the product of client space and online server time must equal n, as shown by Corrigan-Gibbs et al. in [16].

From 2PIR+ to 1 PIR with Same Complexities. As detailed in [15], we can port our 2PIR+ to 1PIR by merging **server$_1$** and **server$_2$** and executing the work of **server$_1$** using FHE. We require a symmetric key FHE scheme that is *gate-by-gate* [15], where *gate-by-gate* means that encrypted evaluation runs in time $\widetilde{O}(|C|)$ for a circuit of size $|C|$. As noted in [15], this is a property of standard FHE based on LWE [9, 26]. With this, we can use a batch parity Boolean circuit C that, given a database of size n and l lists of size m, C computes the parity of the lists in $\widetilde{O}(l \cdot m + n)$ time [15]. The last consideration is how to perform the set evaluation under FHE. This can be done using slight modifications to our evaluation algorithm and using oblivious sorting. Our main result, Theorem 52, is as follows.

Theorem 52 (Near-Optimal 1PIR protocol). *Assuming* LWE, *there exists an 1PIR scheme that is correct (per Definition 22) and private (per Definition 23) and has: (i) $\widetilde{O}(\sqrt{n})$ client storage and $\widetilde{O}(\sqrt{n})$ client time; (ii) $\widetilde{O}(\sqrt{n})$ amortized server time and no additional server storage; (iii) $\widetilde{O}(1)$ amortized bandwidth.*

We discuss this further and include the proofs for both theorems in our paper's full version [33].

Acknowledgement. This work was supported by the NSF, VMware and Protocol Labs.

A   Definitions

A.1   Additional Definitions for Adaptable PRSs

Our adaptable PRS primitive will satisfy the following definitions.

Definition A1 (Pseudorandomness with respect to some distribution $\mathbb{D}_n$ for privately-puncturable PRSs [37]) *A privately-puncturable PRS scheme (*Gen, EnumSet, InSet, Resample*) satisfies* pseudorandomness with respect to some distribution $\mathbb{D}_n$ *if the distribution of* EnumSet(sk), *where sk is output by* Gen(λ, n), *is indistinguishable from a set sampled from $\mathbb{D}_n$.*

Definition A2 (Security in resampling for privately-puncturable PRSs [37]). *A privately-puncturable PRS scheme (*Gen, EnumSet, InSet, Resample*) satisfies security in resampling if, for any $x \in \{1, \ldots, n-1\}$, the following two distributions are computationally indistinguishable.*

- *Run* Gen$(\lambda, n) \rightarrow (sk, msk)$, *output sk.*
- *Run* Gen$(\lambda, n) \rightarrow (sk, msk)$ *until* InSet$(sk, x) \rightarrow 1$, *output $sk_x =$* Resample(msk, x).

Definition A3 (Functionality preservation in resampling for privately-puncturable PRSs *[37]*). *We say that a privately-puncturable PRS scheme (*Gen, EnumSet, InSet, Resample*) satisfies functionality preservation in resampling with respect to a predicate* Related *if, with probability* $1 - \mathrm{negl}(\lambda)$ *for some negligible function* $\mathrm{negl}(.)$, *the following holds. If* $\mathrm{Gen}(1^\lambda, n) \rightarrow (sk, msk)$ *and* $\mathrm{Resample}(msk, x) \rightarrow sk_x$ *where* $x \in \mathrm{InSet}(sk)$ *then*

1. $\mathrm{EnumSet}(sk_x) \subseteq \mathrm{EnumSet}(sk)$;
2. $\mathrm{EnumSet}(sk_x)$ *runs in time no more than* $\mathrm{EnumSet}(sk)$;
3. *For any* $y \in \mathrm{EnumSet}(sk) \setminus \mathrm{EnumSet}(sk_x)$, *it must be that* $\mathrm{Related}(x, y) = 1$.

Definition A4 (Security in addition for adaptable PRSs). *We say that an adaptable PRS scheme (*Gen, EnumSet, InSet, Resample, Add*) satisfies security in addition if, for any* $x \in \{0, \ldots, n-1\}$, *the following two distributions are computationally indistinguishable.*

- *Run* $\mathrm{Gen}(1^\lambda, n) \rightarrow (sk, msk)$ *until* $\mathrm{InSet}(sk, x) \rightarrow 1$. *Let* $msk[0] = null$ *and output* (msk, sk).
- *Run* $\mathrm{Gen}(1^\lambda, n) \rightarrow (sk, msk)$. *Output* $(msk^x, sk^x) \leftarrow \mathrm{Add}(msk, sk, x)$.

Definition A5 (Functionality preservation in addition for adaptable PRS). *We say that an adaptable PRS scheme (*Gen, EnumSet, InSet, Resample, Add*) satisfies functionality preservation in addition with respect to a predicate* Related *if, with probability* $1 - \mathrm{negl}(\lambda)$ *for some negligible function* $\mathrm{negl}(.)$, *the following holds. If* $\mathrm{Gen}(1^\lambda, n) \rightarrow (sk, msk)$ *and* $\mathrm{Add}(msk, sk, x) \rightarrow sk^x$ *then*

- $\mathrm{EnumSet}(sk) \subseteq \mathrm{EnumSet}(sk^x)$;
- *For all* $y \in \mathrm{EnumSet}(sk^x) \setminus \mathrm{EnumSet}(sk)$ *it must be that* $\mathrm{Related}(x, y) = 1$.

B   Correctness Lemmata

See below the proof of Lemma 31. We then use it to prove Theorem 31.

Proof. Recall that we fix $B = 2 \log \log n$. As alluded to in Sect. 3, we can split our failure probability in three cases:

- Case 1: x_i is not in any primary set that was preprocessed.
- Case 2: The resampling does not remove x_i.
- Case 3: Resampling removes *more* that just x_i from the set.

Case 1: We first note that, from our distribution $\mathbb{D}_n$, for any $x \in \{0, \ldots, n-1\}$, we have that, for $S \sim \mathbb{D}_n$,

$$\Pr[x \in S] = \left(\frac{1}{2}\right)^{\frac{1}{2}\log n + B} = \frac{1}{\sqrt{n}}\left(\frac{1}{2}\right)^B = \frac{1}{2^B\sqrt{n}}.$$

Then note that the expected size of S is the sum of the probability of each element being in the set, i.e.,

$$\mathbb{E}\left[|S|\right] = \mathbb{E}\left[\sum_{x=0}^{n-1} \frac{1}{2^B\sqrt{n}}\right] = \sum_{x=0}^{n-1} \mathbb{E}\left[\frac{1}{2^B\sqrt{n}}\right] = \frac{\sqrt{n}}{2^B} \leq \frac{\sqrt{n}}{(\log n)^2} \cdot$$

We can conclude that the desired probability is

$$\Pr[x \notin \cup_{i\in[1,l]} S_i] = \left(1 - \frac{1}{\sqrt{n}(\log n)^2}\right)^{\sqrt{n}(\log n)^3} \leq \left(\frac{1}{e}\right)^{\log n} \leq \frac{1}{n},$$

where $\ell = \sqrt{n}\log^3 n$ and $S_1, \ldots, S_\ell \sim (\mathbb{D}_n)^\ell$.

Case 2: Assuming there is a set S such that $x_i \in S$, by construction of `Resample`, it is easy to see that the probability that x_i is not removed from S is equivalent to a Bernoulli variable that is 1 with probability $p = \frac{1}{\sqrt{n}\cdot 2^B}$, since we toss $1/2\log n + B$ coins, and x is not removed only if all of these coins evaluate to 1. Therefore

$$\Pr[x_i \in \texttt{Resample}(S, x_i)] = \frac{1}{\sqrt{n}\cdot 2^B} \leq \frac{1}{\sqrt{n}\log^2 n} \cdot$$

Case 3: Note that for any k less than $\log n$, there are exactly $2^{\log n - k} - 1$, or less than $2^{\log n - k}$ strings in $\{0,1\}^{\log n}$, that are different than x share a suffix of length $\geq k$ with x. Note that since x is in the set, for any k, the probability that a string y that has a common suffix of length exactly k with x is included in the set is the chance that its initial B bits *and* its remaining bits not shared with x evaluate to 1, namely, for any k less than $\log n$ and $y = \{0,1\}^{\log n - k}||x[\log n - k :]$ we have that:

$$\Pr[y \in S] = \frac{1}{2^B 2^{\log n - k}} \cdot$$

Let N_k be the set of strings in the set that share a longest common suffix with x of length k. Then, since we know that there are at most $2^{\log n - k}$ such strings, we can say that for any k, the expected size of N_k is

$$\mathbb{E}\left[|N_k|\right] \leq \mathbb{E}\left[\sum_{x=1}^{2^{\log n - k}} \frac{1}{2^B 2^{\log n - k}}\right] = \sum_{x=1}^{2^{\log n - k}} \mathbb{E}\left[\frac{1}{2^B 2^{\log n - k}}\right] = \frac{2^{\log n - k}}{2^B 2^{\log n - k}} = \frac{1}{2^B}.$$

Then, for our construction, where we only check prefixes for k greater than $(1/2)\log n$, we can find that the sum of the expected size of N_k, for each such k is

$$\mathbb{E}\left[\sum_{k=\frac{1}{2}\log n+1}^{\log n-1} |N_k|\right] = \sum_{k=\frac{1}{2}\log n+1}^{\log n-1} \mathbb{E}\left[|N_k|\right] \leq \left(\frac{1}{2}\log n - 1\right)\frac{1}{2^B} \leq \frac{1}{2\log n}.$$

Clearly, we can bound the probability of removing an element along with x_i by the probability that there exists a related element to x_i in the set, by previous discussion in Sect. 3. Then, given each bound above, assuming that the previous query was correct and that the refresh phase maintains the set distribution, we see that the probability that the returned bit $DB[x_i]$ is incorrect for query step i is

$$\Pr[DB[x_i] \text{is incorrect}] \leq \frac{1}{n} + \frac{1}{\sqrt{n}\log^2 n} + \frac{1}{2\log n} \leq \frac{3}{2\log n} < \frac{1}{3},$$

for $n \geq 32$.   □

Now we introduce a new lemma that will help us prove Theorem 31. This lemma will bound the probability that Add does not work as expected. The intuition here is that, just like Resample can remove elements (already in the set) related to the resampled element, Add can add elements (not in the set) related to the added element. Below, we are bounding the number of elements *that are not x* and are expected to be added to the set when we add x. As we explained in Sect. 3, this is a "failure case", since it means that our set will not be what we expect.

Lemma B1 (Adding related elements). *For $S \sim \mathbb{D}_n$, and any $x \in \{0, \ldots, n-1\}$, the related set $S_{almost,x}$ is defined as*

$$S_{almost,x} = \{y \mid y \in Add(S,x) \setminus (S \cup \{x\})\}.$$

Then the expected size of $S_{almost,x}$ is at most $\frac{1}{2\log n}$.

Proof. Note that for any k less than $\log n$, there are less than $2^{\log n - k}$ strings in $\{0,1\}^{\log n}$ that share a suffix of length greater than or equal to k with x that do not equal x. The probability that a string y that has a common suffix of exactly k with x is included in $S_{almost,x}$ is the chance that its initial B bits *and* its remaining bits not shared with x evaluate to 1. Namely, let us say that

$$S_{almost,x} = \bigcup N_k,$$

for any $k \in \mathbb{N}$ that is less than $\log n$ and more than $(1/2)\log n$. We define each N_k as

$$N_k = \{y : y = \{0,1\}^{\log n - k} || x[\log n - k :]\}.$$

Since this is the same size as the N_k in Case 3 of Lemma 31, and we are iterating over the same k, the expected size of $S_{almost,x}$ is

$$\mathbb{E}[|S_{almost,x}|] \leq \frac{1}{2\log n}.$$

□

We are now equipped with all the tools we need to prove Theorem 31. We prove it below:

Proof. We first prove privacy of the scheme, then proceed to prove correctness. The asymptotics follow by construction and were argued in Sect. 3.

Privacy. Privacy for **server**$_1$ is trivial. It only ever sees random sets generated completely independent of the queries and is not interacted with online. We present the privacy proof for **server**$_2$ below.

Privacy with respect to **server**$_2$, as per our definition, must be argued by showing there exists a stateful algorithm Sim that can run without knowledge of the query and be indistinguishable from an honest execution of the protocol, from the view of any PPT adversary $\mathcal{A}$ acting as **server**$_2$ for any protocol **server**$_1^*$ acting as **server**$_1$. First, we note that the execution of the protocol between **client** and **server**$_2$ is independent of **client**'s interaction with **server**$_1$. **client** generates sets and queries **server**$_1$ in the offline phase for their parity. Although this affects correctness of each query, it does not affect the message sent to **server**$_2$ at each step of the online phase, since this is decided by the sets, generated by **client**. Then, we can rewrite our security definition, equivalently, disregarding **client**'s interactions with **server**$_1$.

We want to show that for any query q_t for $t \in [1, Q]$, q_t leaks no information about the query index x_t to **server**$_2$, or that interactions between **client** and **server**$_2$ can be simulated with no knowledge of x_t. To do this, we show, equivalently, that the following two experiments are computationally indistinguishable.

- **Expt**$_0$: Here, for each query index x_t that **client** receives, **client** interacts with **server**$_2$ as in our PIR protocol.
- **Expt**$_1$ In this experiment, for each query index x_t that **client** receives, **client** *ignores* x_t, samples a fresh $S \sim \mathbb{D}_n$ and sends S to **server**$_2$.

First we define an intermediate experiment **Expt**$_1^*$.

- **Expt**$_1^*$: For each query index x_t that **client** receives, **client** samples $S \sim \mathbb{D}_n^{x_t}$. **client** sends $S' = \text{Resample}(S, x_t)$ to the **server**$_2$.

By Property 1 defined in Sect. 3, S' is computationally indistinguishable from a fresh set sampled from $\mathbb{D}_n$. Therefore, we have that **Expt**$_1^*$ and **Expt**$_1$ are indistinguishable. Next, we define another intermediate experiment **Expt**$_0^*$ to help in the proof.

- **Expt**$_0^*$: Here, for each query index x_t that **client** receives, **client** interacts with **server**$_2$ as in our PIR protocol, except that on the refresh phase after each query, instead of picking a table entry $B_k = (S_k, P_k)$ from our secondary sets and running $S_k' = \text{Add}(S_k, x_t)$, we generate a new random set $S \sim \mathbb{D}_n^{x_t}$ and replace our used set with sk instead.

First, we note that by Property 2 defined in Sect. 3, it follows directly that **Expt**$_0$ and **Expt**$_0^*$ are computationally indistinguishable. Now, we continue to show that **Expt**$_0^*$ and **Expt**$_1^*$ are computationally indistinguishable. At the beginning of the protocol, right after the offline phase, the client has a set of $|T|$ primary sets picked at random. For the first query index, x_1, we either pick an entry $(S_j, p_j) \in T$ from these random sets where $x_1 \in S_j$ or, if the that fails, we run $S_j \sim \mathbb{D}_n^{x_1}$.

Then, we send to **server**$_2$ $S_j' = \text{Resample}(S_j, x)$. Note that the second case is trivially equivalent to generating a random set with x_1 and resampling it at x_1. But in the first case, note that T holds a sets sampled from $\mathbb{D}_n$ in order. As a matter of fact, looking at it in this way, S_j is the first output in a sequence of samplings that satisfies the constraint of x being in the set. Then, if we consider just the executions from 1 to j, this means that picking S_j is equivalent to sampling from $\mathbb{D}_n^{x_1}$, by definition. Then, by Property 1, it follows that the set that the server sees in the first query is indistinguishable from a freshly sampled set.

It follows from above that for the first query, q_1, $\mathbf{Expt}_0^*$ is indistinguishable from $\mathbf{Expt}_1^*$. To show that this holds for all q_t for $t \in [1, Q]$ we show, by induction, that after each query, we refresh our set table T to have the same distribution as initially. Then, by the same arguments above, it will follow that every query q_t in $\mathbf{Expt}_0^*$ is indistinguishable from each query in $\mathbf{Expt}_1^*$.

Base Case. Initially, our table T is a set of $|T|$ random sets sampled from $\mathbb{D}_n$ independently from the queries, offline.

Inductive Step. After each query q_t, the smallest table entry (S_j, p_j) such that $x_t \in S_j$ is replaced with a set sampled from $\mathbb{D}_n^{x_t}$. Since the sets are identically distributed, then it must be that the table of set keys T maintains the same distribution after each query refresh.

Since our set distribution is unchanged across all queries, then using the same argument as for the first query, each query q_t from **client** will be indistinguishable from a freshly sampled set to **server**$_2$. Then, we can say that $\mathbf{Expt}_1^*$ is indistinguishable from $\mathbf{Expt}_0^*$. This concludes our proof for experiment indistinguishability. Since we have defined a way to simulate our protocol *without* access to each x_t, it follows that we satisfy **server**$_2$ privacy for any PPT non-uniform adversary $\mathcal{A}$.

Correctness. To show correctness, we consider a slightly modified version of the scheme: After the refresh phase has used the auxiliary set (S_j, p_j), the client stores (S_j, p_j, z_j), where z_j is the element that was added to S_j as part of the protocol—for the sets that have not been used, we simply set $z_j = null$. Note that the rest of the scheme functions exactly as in Fig. 1 and therefore never uses z_j. It follows, then, that the correctness of this modified scheme is exactly equivalent to the correctness of the scheme we presented. Note that the query phase will fail to output the correct bit only on the following four occasions: *(Case 1).* x_i is not in any primary set that was preprocessed. *(Case 2).* The resampling does not remove x_i *(Case 3).* Resampling removes *more* that just x_i from the set. *(Case 4).* Parity is incorrect because Add added a related element during the refresh phase.

Case 1: From the privacy proof above, we know that refreshing the sets maintains the primary set distribution. Then, we can use the same argument as in Lemma 31 and say that, for a query x_i, for all $i \in \{1, \ldots, Q\}$, we have:

$$\Pr[x_i \notin \cup_{j \in [1,l]} S_j] = \left(\frac{1}{e}\right)^{\log n} \leq \frac{1}{n}.$$

Case 2: Since Resample is independent from the set (just tossing random coins), we can again re-use the proof of Lemma 31 and say that, for any x_i, for all $i \in \{1, .., Q\}$, we have:

$$\Pr[x_i \in \texttt{Resample}(S, x_i)] \leq \frac{1}{\sqrt{n}(\log n)^2}.$$

Case 3: Case 3 requires us to look into our modified scheme. For the initial primary sets, the probability of removing an element related to the query is exactly the same as in Case 3 for our Lemma 31. However, for sets that were refreshed, we need to consider the fact that these are not freshly sampled sets, in fact, they are sets that were sampled and then had an Add operation performed on them. For a given query x_i, let S_j be the first set in T that contains x_i. Let us denote PuncRel to be the event that we remove *more* than just x_i when resampling S_j on x_i. We split the probability of PuncRel as

$$\Pr[\texttt{PuncRel}] = \Pr[\texttt{PuncRel} \mid \texttt{Related}(x_i, z_j) = 1 \wedge x_i \neq z_j] \times \Pr[\texttt{Related}(x_i, z_j) = 1 \wedge x_i \neq z_j]$$
$$\cup \Pr[\texttt{PuncRel} \mid \texttt{Related}(x_i, z_j) = 0 \vee x_i = z_j] \times \Pr[\texttt{Related}(x_i, z_j) = 0 \vee x_i = z_j].$$

The first term corresponds to the case where the added element in a previous refresh phase, z_j, is related to the current query element, x_i. Note that if x_i equals z_j, we get the same distribution as the initial S_j by Property 2 in Sect. 3. Then, we consider only the case where z_j does not equal x_i. Note that we can bound

$$\Pr[\texttt{Related}(x_i, z_j) = 1 \wedge x_i \neq z_j] \leq \Pr[\texttt{Related}(S_j, z_j) = 1] \leq \frac{1}{2 \log n}.$$

Above, we use $\texttt{Related}(S_j, z_j)$ to denote the probability that there is any related element to z_j (not equal to z_j) in S_j. We can bound this event by Lemma 31 (see Case 3). Then, we have

$$\Pr[\texttt{PuncRel} \mid \texttt{Related}(x_i, z_j) = 1 \wedge x_i \neq z_j] \times \Pr[\texttt{Related}(x_i, z_j) = 1 \wedge x_i \neq z_j] \leq \frac{1}{2 \log n}.$$

For the second term of our initial equation, since $\texttt{Related}(x_i, z_j)$ is 0 or x_i equals z_j, note that our probability of resampling incorrectly is either *independent* of z_j, since z_j does not share any prefix with x_i and therefore the resampling cannot affect z_j or its related elements in any way, by definition; *or* it is identical to the probability of the initial set, by Property 2. Therefore, we have that the probability of removing a related element is at most the probability of removing a related element in the original set, which by Lemma 31 is

$$\Pr[\texttt{PuncRel} \mid \texttt{Related}(x_i, z_j) = 0 \vee x_i = z_j] \leq \frac{1}{2 \log n}.$$

And, therefore, it follows that

$$\Pr[\texttt{PuncRel} \mid \texttt{Related}(x_i, z_j) = 0 \vee x_i = z_j] \times \Pr[\texttt{Related}(x_i, z_j) = 0 \vee x_i = z_j] \leq \frac{1}{2 \log n}.$$

Finally, we have that $\Pr[\texttt{PuncRel}] \leq \frac{1}{2 \log n} + \frac{1}{2 \log n} \leq \frac{1}{\log n}$.

Case 4: Lastly, we have the case that query x_i is incorrect because the parity p_j from the set S_j where we found x_i is incorrect. This will only happen when we added elements related to z_j when adding z_j during the refresh phase. We denote this event AddRel. By Lemma B1, we have that

$$\Pr[\texttt{AddRel}] \leq \frac{1}{2 \log n}.$$

We can conclude that at each query x_i, $i \in \{1, \ldots, Q\}$, assuming the previous query was correct, it follows that the probability of a query being incorrect, such that the output of the query does not equal $\mathsf{DB}[x_i]$, is:

$$\Pr[\text{incorrect query}] \leq \frac{1}{n} + \frac{1}{\sqrt{n} \log^2 n} + \frac{1}{\log n} + \frac{1}{2 \log n} \leq \frac{2}{\log n} \leq \frac{1}{3} \text{ for } n > 405.$$

Because at each step we run a majority vote over $\omega(\log n)$ parallel instances, we can guarantee that, since our failure probability is less than $\frac{1}{2}$, each instance will get back the correct $\mathsf{DB}[x_i]$ with overwhelming probability. $\qquad \square$

C   PRS Constructions and Proofs

This section presents a construction and proof for the Adaptable PRS, as introduced and defined in Sect. 4. We present a construction of our Adaptable PRS in Fig. 3. In the proof, we use a function $\texttt{time}: f(\cdot) \to \mathbb{N}$ that takes in a function $f(\cdot)$ and output the number of calls made in $f(\cdot)$ to any PRF function. We also prove Theorem 41 for our construction in Fig. 3. We prove Theorem 41 below. In the proof, we use properties of the underlying PRF found only within the full version of the paper [33, Appendix E] or previous work [37].

Proof. We begin the proof by showing that our scheme in Fig. 3 satisfies the definitions in Appendix A. We then argue efficiencies.

Correctness and Pseudorandomness with Respect to $\mathbb{D}_n$. Correctness follows from our construction and functionality preservation of the underlying PRF. Pseudorandomness follows from pseudorandomness of the underlying PRF ([33, Definition E1]). Both incur a negligible probability of failure in λ, inherited from the underlying PRF.
Functionality preservation in resampling and addition. Assuming pseudorandomness and functionality preservation of the underlying PRF ([33, Definitions E1, E2]), our PRS scheme satisfies the properties of Functionality Preservation in Addition.
    For $(sk, msk) \leftarrow \mathsf{Gen}(1^\lambda, n)$ until $\mathsf{InSet}(sk, x)$, and $sk_x \leftarrow \mathsf{Punc}(msk, sk, x)$:

- From construction, $\mathsf{EnumSet}(sk_x) \subseteq \mathsf{EnumSet}(sk)$, since puncturing strings that evaluate to 1 can only reduce the size of the set (since we only resample elements in the set).
- From the point above, and construction of our $\mathsf{EnumSet}$, it follows that $\texttt{time}(\mathsf{EnumSet}(sk)) \geq \texttt{time}(\mathsf{EnumSet}(sk_x))$.
- By construction of our resampling operation and $\texttt{Related}$ function, it must be that

$$y \in \mathsf{EnumSet}(sk) \setminus \mathsf{EnumSet}(sk_x) \leftrightarrow \texttt{Related}(x, y) = 1.$$

Also, for any $n, \lambda \in \mathbb{N}$, $x \in \{0, \ldots, n-1\}$, for $(sk, msk) \leftarrow \mathsf{Gen}(1^\lambda, n)$, $sk^x \leftarrow \mathsf{Add}(msk, sk, x)$ we note that:

- By construction, $\mathsf{EnumSet}(sk) \subseteq \mathsf{EnumSet}(sk^x)$ since since we only ever make 0 s into 1 s.

Let $B = 2 \log \log n$, $m = \frac{1}{2} \log n + B$.

- $\mathsf{Gen}(1^\lambda, n) \to (sk, msk)$:

1. Let $msk_0 \leftarrow \mathsf{PRF.Gen}(1^\lambda, \log n + B, m)$, $msk_1 \leftarrow \mathsf{PRF.Gen}(1^\lambda, \log n + B, m)$.
2. Let P_1, P_2 be two sets of random $\left(\frac{1}{2}\log n + B\right)$ strings in $\{0,1\}^{\log n + B}$ that start with a 1-bit.
3. Let $sk_0 = \mathsf{PRF.Puncture}(msk_0, P_1)$, $sk_1 = \mathsf{PRF.Puncture}(msk_1, P_2)$.
4. output $(sk, msk) = ((sk_0, sk_1), (msk_0, msk_1))$.

- $\mathsf{Eval}(sk, x) \to b$:   % internal function used to simplify algorithms

1. Return $\mathsf{PRF.PEval}(sk[0], x) \oplus \mathsf{PRF.PEval}(sk[1], x)$.

- $\mathsf{EnumSet}(sk) \to S$:

1. Let $Z_{\frac{1}{2}\log n}$ be all bit-strings in $\ell \in \{0,1\}^{\frac{1}{2}\log n}$ such that $\mathsf{Eval}(sk, l) = 1$.
2. Then, For $i \in [\frac{1}{2}\log n + 1, \ldots, \log n]$:
   (a) Set Z_{i+1} to be any string of the form $b\|\ell$ where $b \in \{0,1\}$, $\ell \in Z_i$ and $\mathsf{Eval}(sk, b\|\ell) = 1$.
3. Return $S = \{\ell : \ell \in Z_{\log n} \wedge \mathsf{Eval}(sk, 0^k\|\ell) = 1 \text{ for } k \in [0, B]\}$.

- $\mathsf{InSet}(sk, x) \to b$:

1. Let $z = 0^B\|x$.
2. Output 1 if $\mathsf{Eval}(sk, z[i:]) = 1$ for $i \in [0, m]$, otherwise output 0.

- $\mathsf{Resample}(msk, sk, x) \to sk$:

1. Let $z = 0^B\|x$, $Z = \{z[i:]\}$ for $i \in [0, m]$.
2. Let $sk_x = \mathsf{PRF.Puncture}(msk[1], Z)$.
3. Return $(sk[0], sk_x)$.

- $\mathsf{Add}(msk, sk, x) \to (msk, sk)$:

1. Write $x \in \{0,1\}^{\log n}$ as a binary string.
2. Define $z = 0^B\|x$, $Z = \{z[i:]\}$ for $i \in [0, m]$.
3. While true: % puncture until we find sk_x such that $\mathsf{Eval}(sk, x)$ equals 1.
   (a) Let $sk_x = \mathsf{PRF.Puncture}(msk[0], Z)$.
   (b) If $\mathsf{InSet}((sk_x, sk[1]), x)$, break.
4. Output $((null, msk[1]), (sk_x, sk[1]))$

Fig. 3. Our Adaptable PRS Implementation.

- By the converse of same argument as Functionality Preservation in Resampling above, it follows that

$$y \in \mathsf{EnumSet}(sk^x) \setminus \mathsf{EnumSet}(sk) \leftrightarrow \texttt{Related}(x, y) = 1.$$

Therefore, our scheme satisfies Functionality preservation in resampling and addition. *Security in resampling.* We show that our scheme satisfies Definition A2 below, assuming pseudorandomness and privacy w.r.t. puncturing of the underlying PRF ([33, Definitions E1, E3], respectively).

To aid in the proof, we define an intermediate experiment, $\mathbf{Expt}_1^*$, defined as:

- $\mathbf{Expt}_1^*$: Run $\mathsf{Gen}(\lambda, n) \to (sk, msk)$, and return $sk_x \leftarrow \mathsf{Resample}(msk, sk, x)$.

For each sk output by Gen, $sk = (sk[0], sk[1])$, two keys of m-puncturable PRFs. First, we show indistinguishability between $\mathbf{Expt}_1^*$ and $\mathbf{Expt}_0$:

Assume that there exists a distinguisher D_0 than can distinguish $\mathbf{Expt}_1^*$ and $\mathbf{Expt}_0$. Let us say that D_0 outputs 0 whenever it is on $\mathbf{Expt}_0$ and 1 when it is on $\mathbf{Expt}_1^*$. Then, we can construct a D_0^* with access to D_0 that breaks the privacy w.r.t. puncturing of the PRF as follows. For any $x \in \{0, \dots, n-1\}$:

Let $m = \frac{1}{2}\log n + B$, $L = \log n + B$, $z = 0^B || x$.
$D_0^*(m, L, z)$:

1. Define $P_0 = \{z[i :]\}_{i \in [0,m]}$ and let P_1, P_2 be a set of m random points of length L starting with a 1-bit.
2. Send P_0, P_1 to the privacy w.r.t. puncturing experiment and get back sk_{P_b} and oracle access to $\mathsf{PRF.Eval}(sk, \cdot)$.
3. Run $\mathsf{PRF.Gen}(1^\lambda, L, m) \to sk$, $\mathsf{PRF.Puncture}(sk, P_2) \to sk_{P_2}$.
4. Set secret key $sk' = (sk_{P_2}, sk_{P_b})$.
5. Return $D_0(sk')$.

Note that in the case where b equals 0, the experiment is exactly equivalent to D_0's view of $\mathbf{Expt}_0$, since sk' is two random m-privately-puncturable PRF keys punctured and m points starting with a 1-bit. Also, when b is 1, D_0's view is exactly equivalent to $\mathbf{Expt}_1^*$, since we pass in two random m-privately-puncturable PRF keys, one punctured at m points starting with a 1-bit, and the other at $\{z[i :]\}_{i \in [0,m]}$, with no constraints on whether x was in the set before or after the puncturings. Then, since D_0's view is exactly the same as its experiment, it will distinguish between both with non-negligible probability, and whatever it outputs, by construction, will be the correct guess for b with non-negligible probability.

Now we proceed to show that $\mathbf{Expt}_1^*$ and $\mathbf{Expt}_1$ are indistinguishable, assuming pseudorandomness of the underlying PRF. Now, assume there exists a distinguisher D_1 that can distinguish between $\mathbf{Expt}_1^*$ and $\mathbf{Expt}_1$ with non-negligible probability. Then, we can construct a distinguisher D_1^* that uses D_1 to break the pseudorandomness of the underlying PRF as follows. For any $x \in \{0, \dots, n-1\}$:

Let $m = \frac{1}{2}\log n + B$, $L = \log n + B$, $z = 0^B\|x$.
$D_1^*(m, L, z)$:

1. Send $P = \{z[i\ :]\}_{i\in[0,m]}$ to the PRF pseudorandomness experiment, get back sk_P and a set of m bits $\{M_i\}_{i\in[0,m]}$.
2. Let P_1 be a set of m random bit strings of length L starting with a 1-bit. Run PRF.Gen$(1^\lambda, L, m) \to sk$, PRF.Puncture$(sk, P_1) \to sk_{P_1}$. Let $sk' = (sk_{P_1}, sk_P)$.
3. If $\forall i \in [0, m]$, PRF.PEval$(sk_{P_1}, z[i\ :]) \oplus M_i = 1$, output $D_1(sk')$, else output a random bit.

Note that in the case D_1's view in the case where the evaluations as described above all output 1 is exactly its view in distinguishing between our **Expt**$_1$ and **Expt**$_1^*$. With probability $\frac{1}{2}$, it is given a punctured key where x was an element of the original set, and with probability $\frac{1}{2}$ it is given a punctured key where x was sampled at random. Then, in this case, it will be able to distinguish between the two with non-negligible by assumption, and therefore distinguish between the real and random experiment for pseudorandomness of the PRF. Since the probability of having all the evaluations output 1 is non-negligible, then we break the pseudorandomness of the PRF. By contraposition, then, assuming pseudorandomness of the PRF, it must be that **Expt**$_1$ and **Expt**$_1^*$ are indistinguishable. This concludes our proof.

Security in Addition. We now show that our scheme satisfies Definition A4, assuming privacy w.r.t. puncturing of the underlying PRF. Assume there exists a distinguisher D that can distinguish between these two with non-negligible probability. Then, we can construct a distinguisher D^* that breaks privacy w.r.t. puncturing of the PRF as follows, for any $x \in \{0, \ldots, n-1\}$:

Let $m = \frac{1}{2}\log n + B$, $L = \log n + B$, $z = 0^B\|x$.
$D^*(m, L, z)$:

1. Define $P_0 = \{z[i\ :]\}_{i\in[0,m]}$ and let P_1, P_2 be two sets of random m points of length L starting with a 1-bit.
2. Send P_0, P_1, to the privacy w.r.t. puncturing experiment and get back sk_{P_b} and oracle access to PRF.Eval$(sk, \cdot)$.
3. Run PRF.Gen$(1^\lambda, L, m) \to (msk, sk)$, PRF.Puncture$(sk, P_2) \to sk_{P_2}$.
4. Set our secret key $sk' = (sk_{P_b}, sk_{P_2})$.
5. **If** InSet(sk', x), output $D(sk')$, **else** output a random bit.

Consider the case where $x \in$ EnumSet(sk'):

- If P_0 was punctured, D's view is exactly equivalent to **Expt**$_0$ in his experiment, since in Add we output a secret key $sk = (sk[0], sk[1])$ where $sk[0]$ is punctured at x, $sk[1]$ is punctured at m random points starting with a 1, and InSet(sk, x) returns true.
- If P_1 was punctured, D's view is exactly equivalent to **Expt**$_1$ in his experiment, by construction of Gen, P_1 and P_2, the sk outputted is equivalent to a key outputted by Gen$(1^\lambda, n)$ where InSet(sk, x) returns true.

We conclude that, conditioned on $\mathsf{InSet}(sk_{P_b}, x)$ returning true, D's view of the experiment is exactly equivalent to the experiment from our Definition A4, and therefore it will be able to distinguish between whether P_0 and P_1 was punctured with non-negligible probability. If we fix a random $sk[1]$, the probability:

$$\Pr\left[\mathsf{InSet}(sk', x) = true\right] = \frac{1}{\sqrt{n}} > \mathtt{negl}(n).$$

Then, the algorithm D^* we constructed will break the privacy w.r.t. puncturing of the PRF with non-negligible probability. By contraposition, assuming privacy w.r.t. puncturing, sk^x and sk are computationally indistinguishable. Following almost exactly the same argument as above, we can show that the tuples $(sk^x[0], msk^x[1])$ and $(sk[0], msk[1])$ are also indistinguishable. Also, in both tuples $(msk^x[1], sk^x[1])$ and $(msk[1], sk[1])$ the master key is just the unpunctured counterpart of the secret key. Finally, $msk^x[0] = msk[0] = null$. Then, since we have shown that assuming the privacy w.r.t. puncturing property, the keys involved are pairwise indistinguishable, by the transitive property, we see that assuming privacy w.r.t. puncturing, (msk^x, sk^x) and (msk, sk) are computationally indistinguishable and therefore, *security in addition* holds.

Efficiencies. Efficiency for our Gen, InSet and Resample follow from the construction and efficiencies for our underlying PRF. The two efficiencies which we will show are EnumSet and Add. Note that in EnumSet, the step 1 takes $\widetilde{O}(\sqrt{n})$ time to evaluate every string of size $\frac{\log n}{2}$, then, by pseudorandomness of the PRF, at each subsequent step we only ever keep $\sqrt{n}$ strings since half are eliminated. Since there are a logarithmic number of steps, we can say that EnumSet runs in probabilistic $\widetilde{O}(\sqrt{n})$ time. For Add, by pseudorandomness of the PRF, our construction will take probabilistic $\widetilde{O}(\sqrt{n})$ time. (We provide better, deterministic bounds in the full version of the paper [33]). □

References

1. Angel, S., Chen, H., Laine, K., Setty, S.: PIR with compressed queries and amortized query processing. In: 2018 IEEE Symposium on Security and Privacy (SP), pp. 962–979 (2018). https://doi.org/10.1109/SP.2018.00062. ISSN: 2375-1207
2. Angel, S., Setty, S.: Unobservable communication over fully untrusted infrastructure. In: Proceedings of the 12th USENIX conference on Operating Systems Design and Implementation, pp. 551–569. OSDI2016, USENIX Association, USA (2016)
3. Backes, M., Kate, A., Maffei, M., Pecina, K.: ObliviAd: provably secure and practical online behavioral advertising. In: 2012 IEEE Symposium on Security and Privacy, pp. 257–271 (2012). https://doi.org/10.1109/SP.2012.25. ISSN: 2375-1207
4. Beimel, A., Ishai, Y.: Information-theoretic private information retrieval: a unified construction. In: Orejas, F., Spirakis, P.G., van Leeuwen, J. (eds.) ICALP 2001. LNCS, vol. 2076, pp. 912–926. Springer, Heidelberg (2001). https://doi.org/10.1007/3-540-48224-5_74
5. Beimel, A., Ishai, Y., Malkin, T.: Reducing the servers computation in private information retrieval: PIR with preprocessing. In: Bellare, M. (ed.) CRYPTO 2000. LNCS, vol. 1880, pp. 55–73. Springer, Heidelberg (2000). https://doi.org/10.1007/3-540-44598-6_4
6. Bell, J.H., Bonawitz, K.A., Gascón, A., Lepoint, T., Raykova, M.: Secure single-server aggregation with (poly)logarithmic overhead. In: Proceedings of the 2020 ACM SIGSAC

Conference on Computer and Communications Security, pp. 1253–1269. CCS 2020, Association for Computing Machinery, New York, NY, USA (2020). https://doi.org/10.1145/3372297.3417885

7. Boneh, D., Kim, S., Montgomery, H.: Private puncturable PRFs from standard lattice assumptions. In: Coron, J.-S., Nielsen, J.B. (eds.) EUROCRYPT 2017. LNCS, vol. 10210, pp. 415–445. Springer, Cham (2017). https://doi.org/10.1007/978-3-319-56620-7_15

8. Brakerski, Z., Tsabary, R., Vaikuntanathan, V., Wee, H.: Private constrained PRFs (and more) from LWE. In: Kalai, Y., Reyzin, L. (eds.) TCC 2017. LNCS, vol. 10677, pp. 264–302. Springer, Cham (2017). https://doi.org/10.1007/978-3-319-70500-2_10

9. Brakerski, Z., Vaikuntanathan, V.: Fully homomorphic encryption from ring-LWE and security for key dependent messages. In: Rogaway, P. (ed.) CRYPTO 2011. LNCS, vol. 6841, pp. 505–524. Springer, Heidelberg (2011). https://doi.org/10.1007/978-3-642-22792-9_29

10. Canetti, R., Chen, Y.: Constraint-hiding constrained PRFs for NC^1 from LWE. In: Coron, J.-S., Nielsen, J.B. (eds.) EUROCRYPT 2017. LNCS, vol. 10210, pp. 446–476. Springer, Cham (2017). https://doi.org/10.1007/978-3-319-56620-7_16

11. Chor, B., Goldreich, O., Kushilevitz, E., Sudan, M.: Private information retrieval, p. 41. IEEE Computer Society (1995). https://doi.org/10.1109/SFCS.1995.492461. https://www.computer.org/csdl/proceedings-article/focs/1995/71830041/12OmNzYNNfi. ISSN: 0272-5428

12. Chor, B., Gilboa, N.: Computationally private information retrieval (extended abstract). In: Proceedings of the twenty-ninth annual ACM symposium on Theory of computing, pp. 304–313. STOC 1997, Association for Computing Machinery, New York, NY, USA (1997). https://doi.org/10.1145/258533.258609

13. Chor, B., Gilboa, N., Naor, M.: Private information retrieval by keywords (1998). https://eprint.iacr.org/1998/003. Report Number: 003

14. Chor, B., Kushilevitz, E., Goldreich, O., Sudan, M.: Private information retrieval. J. ACM 45(6), 965–981 (1998)

15. Corrigan-Gibbs, H., Henzinger, A., Kogan, D.: Single-server private information retrieval with sublinear amortized time. In: Dunkelman, O., Dziembowski, S. (eds.) Advances in Cryptology – EUROCRYPT 2022. EUROCRYPT 2022. LNCS, vol. 13276. Springer, Cham (2022). https://doi.org/10.1007/978-3-031-07085-3_1

16. Corrigan-Gibbs, H., Kogan, D.: Private information retrieval with sublinear online time. In: Canteaut, A., Ishai, Y. (eds.) EUROCRYPT 2020. LNCS, vol. 12105, pp. 44–75. Springer, Cham (2020). https://doi.org/10.1007/978-3-030-45721-1_3

17. Devadas, S., van Dijk, M., Fletcher, C.W., Ren, L., Shi, E., Wichs, D.: Onion ORAM: a constant bandwidth blowup oblivious ram. In: Kushilevitz, E., Malkin, T. (eds.) TCC 2016. LNCS, vol. 9563, pp. 145–174. Springer, Heidelberg (2016). https://doi.org/10.1007/978-3-662-49099-0_6

18. Di Crescenzo, G., Ishai, Y., Ostrovsky, R.: Universal service-providers for private information retrieval. J. Cryptol. 14(1), 37–74 (2001)

19. Di Crescenzo, G., Malkin, T., Ostrovsky, R.: Single database private information retrieval implies oblivious transfer. In: Preneel, B. (ed.) EUROCRYPT 2000. LNCS, vol. 1807, pp. 122–138. Springer, Heidelberg (2000). https://doi.org/10.1007/3-540-45539-6_10

20. Dong, C., Chen, L.: A fast single server private information retrieval protocol with low communication cost. In: Kutyłowski, M., Vaidya, J. (eds.) ESORICS 2014. LNCS, vol. 8712, pp. 380–399. Springer, Cham (2014). https://doi.org/10.1007/978-3-319-11203-9_22

21. Dvir, Z., Gopi, S.: 2-server PIR with subpolynomial communication. J. ACM 63(4), 1–15 (2016)

22. Efremenko, K.: 3-query locally decodable codes of subexponential length. SIAM J. Comput. 41(6), 1694–1703 (2012)

23. Garg, S., Mohassel, P., Papamanthou, C.: TWORAM: efficient oblivious ram in two rounds with applications to searchable encryption. In: Robshaw, M., Katz, J. (eds.) CRYPTO 2016. LNCS, vol. 9816, pp. 563–592. Springer, Heidelberg (2016). https://doi.org/10.1007/978-3-662-53015-3_20

24. Gentry, C.: Fully homomorphic encryption using ideal lattices. In: Proceedings of the 41st Annual ACM symposium on Symposium on Theory of Computing - STOC 2009, p. 169. ACM Press, Bethesda, MD, USA (2009). https://doi.org/10.1145/1536414.1536440

25. Gentry, C., Ramzan, Z.: Single-database private information retrieval with constant communication rate. In: Caires, L., Italiano, G.F., Monteiro, L., Palamidessi, C., Yung, M. (eds.) ICALP 2005. LNCS, vol. 3580, pp. 803–815. Springer, Heidelberg (2005). https://doi.org/10.1007/11523468_65

26. Gentry, C., Sahai, A., Waters, B.: Homomorphic encryption from learning with errors: conceptually-simpler, asymptotically-faster, attribute-based. In: Canetti, R., Garay, J.A. (eds.) CRYPTO 2013. LNCS, vol. 8042, pp. 75–92. Springer, Heidelberg (2013). https://doi.org/10.1007/978-3-642-40041-4_5

27. Goldreich, O., Goldwasser, S., Micali, S.: How to construct random functions (Extended Abstract). In: FOCS (1984). https://doi.org/10.1109/SFCS.1984.715949

28. Gupta, T., Crooks, N., Mulhern, W., Setty, S., Alvisi, L., Walfish, M.: Scalable and private media consumption with Popcorn. In: Proceedings of the 13th USENIX Conference on Networked Systems Design and Implementation, pp. 91–107. NSDI2016, USENIX Association, USA (2016)

29. Kazama, K., Kamatsuka, A., Yoshida, T., Matsushima, T.: A note on a relationship between smooth locally decodable codes and private information retrieval. In: 2020 International Symposium on Information Theory and Its Applications (ISITA), pp. 259–263 (2020). ISSN: 2689–5854

30. Kiayias, A., Leonardos, N., Lipmaa, H., Pavlyk, K., Tang, Q.: Optimal rate private information retrieval from homomorphic encryption. Proceed. Privacy Enhan. Technol. **2015**(2), 222–243 (2015)

31. Kogan, D., Corrigan-Gibbs, H.: Private blocklist lookups with checklist. In: 30th USENIX Security Symposium (USENIX Security 21), pp. 875–892. USENIX Association (2021). https://www.usenix.org/conference/usenixsecurity21/presentation/kogan

32. Kushilevitz, E., Ostrovsky, R.: Replication is not needed: single database, computationally-private information retrieval. In: Proceedings 38th Annual Symposium on Foundations of Computer Science, pp. 364–373. IEEE Comput. Soc, Miami Beach, FL, USA (1997). https://doi.org/10.1109/SFCS.1997.646125. https://ieeexplore.ieee.org/document/646125/

33. Lazzaretti, A., Papamanthou, C.: Near-optimal private information retrieval with preprocessing (2022). https://eprint.iacr.org/2022/830. Publication info: Preprint

34. Lipmaa, H.: An oblivious transfer protocol with log-squared communication. In: Zhou, J., Lopez, J., Deng, R.H., Bao, F. (eds.) ISC 2005. LNCS, vol. 3650, pp. 314–328. Springer, Heidelberg (2005). https://doi.org/10.1007/11556992_23

35. Lipmaa, H., Pavlyk, K.: A simpler rate-optimal CPIR protocol. In: Financial Cryptography and Data Security 2017 (2017). https://eprint.iacr.org/2017/722

36. Mughees, M.H., Chen, H., Ren, L.: OnionPIR: response efficient single-server PIR. In: Proceedings of the 2021 ACM SIGSAC Conference on Computer and Communications Security, pp. 2292–2306. CCS 2021, Association for Computing Machinery, New York, NY, USA (2021). https://doi.org/10.1145/3460120.3485381

37. Shi, E., Aqeel, W., Chandrasekaran, B., Maggs, B.: Puncturable pseudorandom sets and private information retrieval with near-optimal online bandwidth and time. In: Malkin, T., Peikert, C. (eds.) CRYPTO 2021. LNCS, vol. 12828, pp. 641–669. Springer, Cham (2021). https://doi.org/10.1007/978-3-030-84259-8_22

38. Singanamalla, S., et al.: Oblivious DNS over HTTPS (ODoH): a practical privacy enhancement to DNS. In: Proceedings on Privacy Enhancing Technologies **2021**(4), 575–592 (2021)
39. Yekhanin, S.: Towards 3-query locally decodable codes of subexponential length. J. ACM **55**(1), 1–16 (2008)
40. Yekhanin, S.: Locally decodable codes and private information retrieval schemes. Information Security and Cryptography, Springer, Heidelberg (2010). https://doi.org/10.1007/978-3-642-14358-8
41. Zhou, M., Lin, W.K., Tselekounis, Y., Shi, E.: Optimal single-server private information retrieval. ePrint IACR (2022)

Memory Checking for Parallel RAMs

Surya Mathialagan[✉][iD]

Massachusetts Institute of Technology, Cambridge, MA, USA
smathi@mit.edu

Abstract. When outsourcing a database to an untrusted remote server, one might want to verify the integrity of contents while accessing it. To solve this, Blum et al. [FOCS '91] propose the notion of *memory checking*. Memory checking allows a user to run a RAM program on a remote server, with the ability to verify integrity of the storage with small local storage.

In this work, we define and initiate the formal study of memory checking for *Parallel RAMs* (PRAMs). The parallel RAM model is very expressive and captures many modern architectures such as multi-core architectures and cloud clusters. When multiple clients run a PRAM algorithm on a shared remote server, it is possible that there are concurrency issues that cause inconsistencies. Therefore, integrity verification is even more desirable property in this setting.

Assuming only the existence of one-way functions, we construct an online memory checker (one that reports faults as soon as they occur) for PRAMs with $O(\log N)$ simulation overhead in both work and depth. In addition, we construct an offline memory checker (one that reports faults only after a long sequence of operations) with amortized $O(1)$ simulation overhead in both work and depth. Our constructions match the best known simulation overhead of the memory checkers in the RAM settings. As an application of our parallel memory checking constructions, we additionally construct the first *maliciously secure oblivious parallel RAM* (OPRAM) with polylogarithmic overhead.

1 Introduction

Consider a large database outsourced to an untrusted remote storage server. A fundamental cryptographic property one might hope to achieve in this setting is *integrity verification*, i.e., the ability to verify that the server has not tampered with the contents of the storage. For example, if a hospital stores its patients' medical records on a database, the reliability of the records is crucial. Moreover,

The author was supported in part by DARPA under Agreement No. HR00112020023, an NSF grant CNS-2154149, a grant from the MIT-IBM Watson AI, a grant from Analog Devices, a Microsoft Trustworthy AI grant, and a Thornton Family Faculty Research Innovation Fellowship from MIT. Any opinions, findings and conclusions or recommendations expressed in this material are those of the author(s) and do not necessarily reflect the views of the United States Government or DARPA.

G. Rothblum and H. Wee (Eds.): TCC 2023, LNCS 14370, pp. 436–464, 2023.
https://doi.org/10.1007/978-3-031-48618-0_15

the use of cloud servers to store personal information (e.g. email, digital photographs, etc.) is widespread. For all of these applications, it is important to guarantee the integrity of the contents of the storage.

In the setting where a user outsources a *static* database, they can simply authenticate the database to ensure integrity. However, when the user outsources a database which also has to *dynamically* support updates, integrity verification becomes more complicated. This is in fact the problem of *memory checking*, which was first introduced by Blum, Evans, Gemmel, Kannan and Naor [6].

In the memory checking setting, a user $\mathcal{U}$ would like to run a RAM program on a remote storage $\mathcal{S}$. A memory checker is a layer between the user $\mathcal{U}$ and remote storage $\mathcal{S}$, as shown in Fig. 1. The user $\mathcal{U}$ sends read and write requests to $\mathcal{M}$, and $\mathcal{M}$ then sends its own read and write requests to the unreliable storage $\mathcal{S}$. The checker $\mathcal{M}$ then uses the responses from the server and its own small private local storage to determine if $\mathcal{S}$ responded correctly and send the correct response to $\mathcal{U}$. If $\mathcal{S}$ sends an incorrect response, the checker $\mathcal{M}$ reports that $\mathcal{S}$ was faulty and aborts.

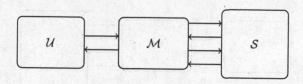

Fig. 1. Memory checking model for RAMs as defined by Blum et al. [6]. Here, user $\mathcal{U}$ is accessing a remote storage $\mathcal{S}$. Memory checker $\mathcal{M}$ is a layer between $\mathcal{C}$ and $\mathcal{S}$ that ensures the correctness of the responses from $\mathcal{S}$.

There are two main efficiency metrics for memory checking: the *work blowup* (the ratio of the number of physical accesses by $\mathcal{M}$ per underlying logical query made by $\mathcal{U}$), and the *space complexity* of the local private storage of $\mathcal{M}$. Using an authentication tree [6,27], it is possible to achieve $O(\log N)$ work blowup with $O(1)$ word space complexity.

The memory checking model of Blum et al. has been well studied [1,6,17,29, 30] and has found many real-world and theoretical applications. For example, many secure enclaves such as AEGIS and Intel SGX [14] support the integrity verification of external memory. On the theoretical side, memory checking has been used to obtain proofs of retrievability [33] and maliciously secure oblivious RAM (ORAM) constructions [26,32].

Integrity Verification with Multiple Users. One can also ask if integrity verification can be done in a setting where there are multiple users executing a *parallel RAM* (PRAM) algorithm on a shared remote storage. The PRAM model is a generalization of the RAM model that allows for parallel batches of operations to be made to the server. The PRAM model captures many emerging technologies. For example, it can model multiple users sharing a common cloud server to perform some shared computation, or multiple processors running within a single multicore system. One can also imagine multiple entities (e.g. hospitals) sharing a single shared database that they dynamically and independently update. Due to its generality, many recent works have studied cryptography in the PRAM setting, such as Oblivious PRAM (OPRAM), Garbled PRAM, and more [7,11,12,25].

Integrity verification can also be useful to ensure that the various entities have a *consistent* and most up-to-date view of remote storage. Therefore, it seems natural to extend memory checking to the parallel setting.

1.1 Our Contributions

In this work, we initiate the formal study of memory checking for PRAM programs. We first define memory checking notions for PRAMs by generalizing the definitions of Blum et al. Throughout this section, N is the size of shared remote storage with word size w, and $1 \leq m \leq N$ is the number of users.

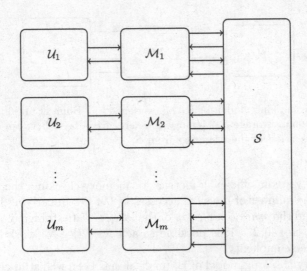

Fig. 2. Memory checking model for PRAMs. Here, $\mathcal{U}_1, \mathcal{U}_2, \ldots, \mathcal{U}_m$ are CPUs that simultaneously access a server $\mathcal{S}$. To ensure the correctness of the server's responses, we have memory checkers $\mathcal{M}_1, \mathcal{M}_2, \ldots, \mathcal{M}_m$ as an interface for the clients $\mathcal{U}_1, \ldots, \mathcal{U}_m$, and the memory checker communicates with the server $\mathcal{S}$ to ensure the correctness of the server's responses.

In this model, we assume that each user $\mathcal{U}_i$ interfaces with a checker $\mathcal{M}_i$ to interact with the server (see Fig. 2). For every batch of *logical* queries from $\{\mathcal{U}_i\}_i$, the checkers $\{\mathcal{M}_i\}_i$ produce batches of *physical* requests to the $\mathcal{S}$. While the checkers $\{\mathcal{M}_i\}_i$ can use shared private randomness to generate a secret state (e.g. authentication keys) before the start of the memory checking protocol, they are not allowed to communicate directly to each other after the start of the protocol. These users can still communicate with each other through the server in an authenticated manner. This is the most general setting because it does not require any reliable communication channels between the checkers. Note that however, our model does not prevent the users $\mathcal{U}_i$ from communicating with each other, but it is general enough to accomodate users that do not communicate with each other. We formalize this model in Sect. 4.

We focus on three main PRAM models: exclusive-read exclusive-write (EREW), concurrent-read exclusive-write (CREW) and concurrent-read concurrent-write (CRCW). In the first model, we assume that at most one user accesses any index of the remote storage at any parallel time step. In the CREW model, we allow concurrent read accesses to any location, but only one user can access any given location for a write. Finally, in the CRCW model we allow concurrent reand and write accesses to memory locations, where we resolve write-conflicts according to some pre-determined rule (e.g. an arbitrary user wins any write. See Sect. 3 for more examples). Our results apply to most natural conflict-resolution rules.

Efficiency Metrics. Like Blum et al., we are interested in minimizing *work blowup* (i.e. the ratio of the number of physical queries for every batch of logical queries) and *space complexity* of each $\mathcal{M}_i$. Moreover, an additional complexity measure we hope to minimize in the case of PRAMs is *depth* or *parallel complexity blowup*. In other words, for each parallel batch of instructions from the users $\{\mathcal{U}_i\}_i$, we hope to minimize the number of parallel batches of instructions from $\{M_i\}_i$. For all constructions in this work, the blowup in server space storage is $O(1)$.

The Problem with Concurrency. As we detail in Sect. 2, allowing concurrent reads and writes makes the memory checking problem more challenging. In the standard RAM setting (as in Fig. 1), the problem of memory checking boils down to checking whether a server returns corrupted data when $\mathcal{U}$ performs a read. In the CRCW PRAM setting, we also run into problems when multiple users execute writes. For example, if multiple users attempt to write to the same address, $\mathcal{S}$ essentially gets to choose which user wins the write. However, nothing prevents $\mathcal{S}$ from pretending that multiple different writes were accepted. For example, if $\mathcal{U}_1$ and $\mathcal{U}_2$ both write to some address addr, the server can now branch the memory into two versions - one with $\mathcal{U}_1$ winning the write, and one with $\mathcal{U}_2$ winning the write. Therefore, we need to ensure that $\mathcal{S}$ does not branch the memory and instead commits to a single consistent memory across all users.

Online Memory Checking for PRAMs. The notion of memory checking defined above is known as *online memory checking* since no $\mathcal{M}_i$ sends incorrect responses to its user, i.e. the correctness of responses is ensured in an *online* manner. In particular, if the server sends an incorrect response to some $\mathcal{M}_i$, there exists some $\mathcal{M}_j$ (possibly different from $\mathcal{M}_i$) which will abort before $\mathcal{M}_i$ sends any response to $\mathcal{U}_i$.

In the standard single-user RAM setting, one can implement online memory checkers with collision-resistant hash functions (CRHFs) following the Merkle-tree paradigm [27] with $O(\log N)$ work blowup. Blum et al. show a tree-based memory checker can also be instantiated with pseudorandom functions with $O(\log N)$ overhead. At a high level, the construction maintains a binary tree where the leaf nodes correspond to the elements of the underlying database. Every leaf node is given a counter value keeping track of the number of times the associated database entry is updated. Every internal node and the root node contains the sum of the counts of its children nodes. $\mathcal{M}$ keeps track of the value at the root node. Whenever $\mathcal{U}$ performs a read to some database entry, $\mathcal{M}$ traverses the path to the corresponding leaf node. While doing so, $\mathcal{M}$ verifies the consistency of the counts of the nodes on the path. Whenever $\mathcal{U}$ performs a write, the counts along the corresponding path are incremented. Since the binary tree has $O(\log N)$ height, this introduces an $O(\log N)$ simulation overhead. We refer the reader to Sect. 2 for more details on this construction.

There is no known construction known construction beating the $O(\log N)$ overhead. Moreover, Dwork, Naor, Rothblum and Vaikuntanathan [17] showed a $\Omega(\log N/\log\log N)$ lower bound on the blowup for memory checkers which are deterministic and non-adaptive - capturing most known memory checkers. Therefore, this is essentially the best work blowup one can hope for.

One can imagine that by serializing a given PRAM algorithm (i.e. at each time-step, exactly one user accesses the server), one can adapt a tree-based online memory checker such as the construction of Blum et al. [6] or a Merkle tree [27]. However, this gives a memory checking construction with $O(\log N)$ work blowup and $O(m \log N)$ depth blowup. While the work blowup matches that of memory checking for RAMs, the depth blowup is in fact equal to the total work, and does not capitalize on the parallelization capabilities of our model. Therefore, one can ask if it is also possible to also achieve an $O(\log N)$ depth blowup. In this work, we show that this is indeed possible.

Theorem 1 (Informal version of Theorem 7). *Assuming the existence of one-way functions, there exists an online memory checking protocol with $O(\log N)$ work blowup, $O(\log N)$ depth blowup and $O(1)$ local space complexity per checker.*

We remark that if the underlying algorithm is EREW or CREW, the access pattern of the resulting memory checking protocol is also EREW or CREW respectively when interacting with an honest server.

Naor and Rothblum [29] show that one-way functions are in fact necessary for online memory checking for RAM programs, and hence this assumption is also necessary for our result. Moreover, when we consider the special case where $m = 1$, our result reduces to memory checking for RAM programs, and our efficiency in fact matches the best known memory checkers [6,17,30].

The starting point of our construction is the authentication tree of Blum et al. [6]. However, there are two main technical difficulties that arise when directly implementing their construction. Firstly, since multiple elements of the database might be accessed in the same batch of queries, this could result in many read-write conflicts when updating the internal nodes of the tree. Secondly, if the underlying algorithm performs concurrent accesses, the database could potentially branch the history by showing multiple incompatible versions of the storage to different users. Therefore, we have to ensure that all the users view exactly one consistent copy of the authentication tree.

To solve the first problem, we simply introduce a simple tie-breaking rule. If two CPUs in charge of two children nodes want to update the parent node at the same time, we give the left node priority. This ensures that in an honest execution, at most one CPU attempts to update any given internal node of the authentication tree. To avoid the branching-history problem, we use a simple counting technique. Essentially, in addition to updating the counters of the leaf nodes of the authentication tree, each CPU also locally keeps track of whether it successfully executed a write (i.e. if its write won the conflict resolution rule). Once the counts are propagated through the authentication tree, we can then verify that the number of successful writes recorded at the root node corresponds to the total number of CPU writes. If the server tells more than one client that they "won", we argue that we will detect a discrepancy. We discuss our techniques in further detail in Sect. 2.

Offline Memory Checking for PRAMs. Blum et al. [6] also suggest a weaker notion of memory checking known as *offline* memory checking. An offline checker gives a weaker guarantee that after a long sequence of operations to the storage, it can detect whether there was any faulty response from the storage. To contrast with online memory checking, we note that it is possible that some $\mathcal{M}_i$ sent back an incorrect response to $\mathcal{U}_i$, but by the end of the algorithm, with high probability, some $\mathcal{M}_j$ (not necessarily the same as $\mathcal{M}_i$) reports that some mistake has occurred.

The main benefit of an offline checker is that it is possible to achieve an amortized work blowup of $O(1)$. In fact, Blum et al. showed that there exists a statistically secure offline memory checker with amortized $O(1)$ query complexity, i.e. even a computationally unbounded remote server S cannot fool the memory checker with high probability. To achieve this, they use ϵ-biased hash functions as constructed by Naor and Naor [28]. The work of Arasu et al. [2]

Table 1. Consider offline checking for a storage of size N with a m-user database. Here, we are given an underlying PRAM program with q queries and depth d over a database of size N, and the table represents the work and parallel complexity of the communication with the remote storage after applying an offline memory checker.

Model	CPUs	Total Work	Total Parallel Depth	Assumption	Reference
RAM	1	$O(q + N)$	–	None	[6,17]
RAM	1	$O(q + N)$	–	OWF	[26]
EREW	m	$O(q + N)$	$O(d + N/m + \log m)$	None	Theorem 8
CRCW/CREW	m	$O(q + N + dm \log m)$	$(d \log m + N/m + \log m)$	None	Corollary 1
CRCW/CREW	m	$O(q + N)$	$O(d + N/m + \log m)$	OWF	Theorem 10

alludes to the fact that this algorithm is parallelizable for EREW programs[1]. We give a formal exposition of the algorithm and prove that this is in fact the case.

Theorem 2 (Informal version of Theorem 8**).** *There exists a statistically secure offline memory checker for EREW PRAM algorithms with amortized $O(1)$ blowup in work and parallel complexity.*

Since all CREW and CRCW programs can be emulated in the EREW model with logarithmic overhead in work and parallel complexity, this additionally gives us a statistically secure memory checker for CREW and CRCW PRAM programs as well. However, the amortized blowup of such a scheme is $O(\log m)$ in terms of work and depth.

To achieve $O(1)$ amortized complexity, we instead draw inspiration from the offline memory checking construction of Mathialagan and Vafa [26] which relies on authentication.

Theorem 3 (Informal version of Theorem 10**).** *Assuming the existence of one-way functions, there exists an offline memory checker with amortized $O(1)$ work blowup and amortized $O(1)$ depth blowup.*

The main difficulty in obtaining this result once again is ensuring that the adversary does not branch the memory (i.e. by accepting different concurrent writes from the perspective of multiple users). To resolve this issue, we carefully extend our counting argument from our online memory checking construction to the offline setting as well. Additionally, authentication seems to be necessary to prevent any "spoofing" attacks from the server. We elaborate our techniques in Sect. 2. We state the exact work and parallel overhead of our offline checkers in Table 1.

Relaxing the Parallelization Requirements. Just like the RAM model, the PRAM model is rather idealized and abstracts out many practical considerations such as sychronization. In the respective sections (Remarks 2 and 3), we argue that the memory checking algorithms are flexible and can in fact be generalized to work with some notion of "rounds" without the need for synchronization.

Application to Oblivious Parallel RAM (OPRAM). Oblivious RAM is a primitive which takes a sequence of RAM queries to a server and transforms the access pattern to remove any information leakage to the server. As a general technique to ensure privacy of RAM computations, ORAM has many applications including cloud computing, multi-party protocols, secure processor design, and private contact discovery, the latter as implemented by the private messaging service Signal [5,13,15,20–24,34–36].

Boyle, Chung and Pass [7] extended this notion to the parallel RAM setting, and defined the notion of an *Oblivious Parallel RAM* (OPRAM). OPRAM is a

---

[1] Arasu et al. [2] ultimately instantiate the algorithm of Blum et al. [6] with pseudorandom functions.

compiler that allows multiple users to interact with a remote server in a privacy-preserving way. After a series of works [7–10], the work of Asharov et al. [3] constructed an OPRAM with $O(\log N)$ blowup.

Theorem 4 (Informal, [3]). *Assuming the existence of one-way functions, there exists an arbitrary CRCW OPRAM scheme with $O(\log N)$ blowup in both work and depth.*

Asharov et al. [3] additionally show that their construction is optimal when the number of CPUs $m = O(N^{0.99})$.

However, this OPRAM construction is only known to be secure in the *honest-but-curious* setting, where the adversary answers all read and write queries *honestly*. In reality, the adversary can do a lot more. If the adversary tampers with the database contents and returns corrupted responses, the OPRAM scheme may no longer be secure. We say that an OPRAM is maliciously secure if it is secure even against tampering adversaries.

Recently, Mathialagan and Vafa [26] noted that composing memory checkers with ORAM constructions is sufficient to obtain malicious security. By a similar argument, we can combine our PRAM memory checker with the optimal OPRAM of [3] to obtain the following result.

Theorem 5 (Informal version of Theorem 11). *Assuming the existence of one-way functions, there exists a maliciously secure arbitrary CRCW OPRAM scheme with $O(\log^2 N)$ blowup in both work and depth.*

To the best of our knowledge, this is the first maliciously secure OPRAM construction with polylogarithmic overhead.

In the case of ORAMs, Mathialagan and Vafa [26] were able to intricately interleave offline and online memory checking for RAMs with the optimal ORAM construction of Asharov et al. [4] to avoid the additional log factor from memory checking, and obtained a maliciously secure ORAM with optimal logarithmic overhead. We believe that our offline and online PRAM memory checking constructions can also be similarly used to obtain a more efficient maliciously secure OPRAM. We leave this for future work.

1.2 Related Work

We will compare our model and results to some related work.

Byzantine Agreement and Distributed Consensus. Our model differs from the traditional distributed algorithms setting for Byzantine agreement [31] crucially because our model has no reliable communication channels between the users. The only way the users can communicate with each other in our setting is through an unreliable remote server. We also assume that the users are trusted. On the other hand, the focus in many works in Byzantine agreement and consensus [16,18,19,31] in the presence of faulty/malicious users. For example, in work of Dolev and Strong [16], all communication channels are thought to be *reliable* (i.e. no spoofing attacks), but authentication is still useful in ensuring malicious users cannot introduce new messages in the information exchange.

Parallel Memory Checking. In the work of Papamanthou and Tamassia [30], they consider the parallel complexity of memory checking for a RAM program. In other words, a single user makes an update to the remote storage, but the memory checker itself is able to send parallel batches of requests to the remote storage. Instead, our work focuses on allowing many users to concurrently access a shared database.

1.3   Organization

In Sect. 2, we discuss the main technical challenges of memory checking with concurrency, and give an overview of our memory checking algorithms. In Sect. 3, we define the RAM and PRAM models, and introduce cryptographic primitives that we use in our construction. In Sect. 4, we formally define the memory checking model for parallel RAMs. In Sect. 5, we give our online memory checking construction. In Sect. 6, we construct statistically secure offline memory checkers for EREW algorithms with amortized $O(1)$ complexity. We then show a computationally secure offline memory checker for CRCW algorithms with amortized $O(1)$ complexity in Sect. 7. In Sect. 8, we show how we can apply memory checking to obtain a maliciously secure oblivious parallel RAM construction. Many details have been deferred to the full version of the paper [37].

2   Technical Overview

In this section, we give an overview of our constructions in the EREW setting. We then highlight the core difficulties that arise in the CRCW setting due to the concurrency, and describe how we deal with these issues.

2.1   Overview of Our Constructions

First, we give an overview of our algorithms. For simplicity, we first consider the case where the underlying PRAM program satisfies the EREW model.

Authentication Trees. For our online memory checking construction, we follow the authentication tree paradigm for RAM models [6,27]. We first recall the memory checking construction of [6] for RAMs. At a high level, an authentication tree stores the database at the leaves of a binary tree. At the leaves, the version number (i.e. the number of updates made) of every element is stored along with contents of the memory location. The parents of the leaf nodes then contain the sum of the version numbers of its two children. Every subsequent internal node contains the sum of the counts on both of its children. Every node is authenticated. The memory checker then keeps track of the count stored at the root node at any point in time. The main invariant maintained is that if the storage functions honestly, then the count stored at any internal node is the sum of the counts of its two children.

When a user wants to read a memory location, the checker verifies the counts of all the elements from the root to the corresponding leaf node, and ensures that the count is in fact the sum of the counts of its children. When a user writes to a memory location, it increments the counts of all nodes on the path from the leaf to the root. At a high level, this is secure because by the security of MACs, the server S can only present "stale" values with lower counts. Since we know the count of the root node reliably, one can always detect a replay attack.

Authentication Trees for PRAMs. When extending this construction to EREW or CREW PRAMs, we run into the issue that if many leaf values are updated in parallel, there will be many conflicts at the internal nodes of the tree. If we serialize the updates (i.e. one update is made at a time), the depth complexity of the algorithm blows up by $O(m \log N)$.

In order to update the tree in parallel, we instead carefully assign exactly one checker to update any internal node in the tree. For EREW/CREW algorithms, clearly at most one checker updates any leaf node. After updating the leaf nodes, we now have to propagate the updated counts to the rest of the tree. To ensure that the nodes at the next level have a unique CPU assigned, we always give priority to the CPU that updated the left child. In other words, the CPU associated to the right child first checks if the left child was updated (e.g. by checking a time-stamp). If so, the CPU in charge of the left node is now in charge of the parent node. Otherwise, the CPU in charge of the right node is now in charge of the parent. We use a similar rule to assign a checker to any parent. It is clear that this can be done in an EREW manner with $O(1)$ blowup in time-complexity.

At the end of each iteration, the algorithm then tallies the number of checkers that made updates to the database at a given time-step (can be done in $O(\log m)$ depth), and verifies that the root node count has in fact increased by that amount. This ensures that all internal nodes were in fact increased consistently. For a full exposition of this algorithm, see Sect. 5.

Offline Memory Checking. We now described our offline memory checking construction from one-way functions, once again in the context of EREW algorithms. We draw inspiration from the counting-based argument of Mathialagan and Vafa [26].

At a high level, every memory location stored on the server is tagged with a version number (i.e. the number of times that element was updated). Whenever a checker reads or writes to a memory location, it writes back to the memory location with the version number incremented. The checker also locally increments a counter. Note that we authenticate every read and write to this server. In the offline setting, since reads and writes both result in updates to a memory location, the CREW model and CRCW model both have CRCW offline-checkers.

At the end of the sequence of operations, the checkers sum the version numbers of all the elements on the server, and compares this to the sum of the local counters of all the checkers. By the security of MACs, we have that the sums are equal only if the server succeeds in forgery or if the server did not corrupt any of the responses. For a full exposition and proof of correctness, see Sect. 7.

2.2 Main Challenges with Concurrency

We now describe the subtleties that arise in the CRCW model that do not show up in the RAM or EREW/CREW PRAM model.

Concurrent Reads and Writes. In the *arbitrary* CRCW PRAM model, multiple users are able to write to the same location at any point in time. For example, suppose both U_1 and U_2 try to write values v_1 and v_2 respectively to some address addr. Then, a malicious storage server S could essentially branch the storage into two states: a state where location addr contains v_1, and a state where location addr contains v_2 instead. Therefore, our memory checking protocol must account for this, and force the server to commit to one consistent memory. Note that this may not be a problem for conflict resolution rules such as priority CRCW which uniquely determines the CPU that "win" the concurrent write.

Preventing Spoofing Attacks. On the other hand, one can also imagine that a server could block a memory location addr that some user U_i wishes to update, by "spoofing" some other user U_j. Therefore, the server can repeatedly do this and block every memory location. However, this attack can be prevented by using authentication. This fundamentally seems to be the reason we are unable to obtain a statistically secure CRCW offline memory checker with $O(1)$ amortized work blowup.

Note that both of the above attacks do not appear in the EREW PRAM algorithms, since every memory checker knows that there will be no conflict during a read or a write.

2.3 Our Techniques for Concurrency

Although dealing with memory branching seems like a daunting task, we show how one can use authentication along with a simple counting argument to prevent branching in both our offline and online memory checking constructions. We give a high-level overview of our counting technique.

In both of our online and offline checking constructions, every address is tagged with a version number count, initialized to 0 at the start of the algorithm. This version number keeps track of the number of times the location was accessed. We instantiate every write in a few phases. At parallel time-step t, we do the following:

1. *Test phase:* First, every user U_i reads from their desired location addr to retrieve the version number count of the location. Then, every M_i attempts to write to its desired address, with a test flag set. The M_i also tags their data with the time-step t, user ID i and increases the version number of count.

2. *Winner phase:* Now, every checker reads the same location again to determine if they "won" the concurrent write.
   - If $\mathcal{U}_i$ in fact "won" the write (i.e. the storage $\mathcal{S}$ reports back with their write), $\mathcal{M}_i$ writes back the contents with the test flag set to false.
   - If $\mathcal{U}_i$ did not "win" the write, $\mathcal{M}_i$ ensures that the winning user $\mathcal{U}_j$ in fact set the test flag to false, set the time-step to t, and has a consistent count value.

By authenticating all with a shared secret MAC key, one can be sure that the server is not spoofing fake writes. Additionally, the verification of the "test" flag ensures that there are no cycle of winners. In other words, we prevent the scenario where user U_{i_1} receives the signal that U_{i_2} won, U_{i_2} receives the signal that U_{i_1} won. While this prevents a spoofing attack, this does not yet prevent branching in memory.

Throughout the algorithm, every $\mathcal{M}_i$ keeps track of the number of concurrent writes it has won. Let C be the sum of the highest version numbers of all memory locations, and let M be the sum of the number of concurrent writes won by all $\mathcal{M}_1, \mathcal{M}_2, \ldots, \mathcal{M}_m$. Assuming unforgeability of MACs, our key observation is that $C = M$ if and only if the server responded with respect to a "consistent version" of the storage to all users. In fact, if the server lies at any point, it must be the case that at the end of the algorithm, $C < M$. We formalize this argument in the proofs of Theorem 7 and Theorem 10.

3 Preliminaries

Throughout this work, we let λ be the security parameter. In all of these constructions, we assume the adversary or the server $\mathcal{S}$ runs in time $\text{poly}[\lambda]$. We say that a function $\text{negl} : \mathbb{N} \to \mathbb{R}^+$ is negligible if for every constant c, there exists N_c such that $\text{negl}(\lambda) < \lambda^{-c}$ for all $\lambda > N_c$. For an integer $n \in \mathbb{N}$, we denote by $[n]$ the set $\{1, 2, \ldots, n\}$. We use the notation (x, y) or $(x\|y)$ to indicate string concatenation of x and y.

3.1 Parallel RAM Machines

RAM Machines. A RAM is an interactive turing machine with memory mem containing N logical addresses where each memory cell indexed by addr $\in [N]$ contains a word of size w. The RAM supports read and write operations. Read operations are of the form $(\text{read}, \text{addr}, \bot)$ where addr $\in [N]$, the RAM returns the contents of mem[addr]. Write operations are of the form $(\text{write}, \text{addr}, v)$, in which case the RAM updates the contents of mem[addr] to be v. As standard in previous works, we assume that word-level addition, Boolean operations and evaluating PRFs can be done in unit cost.

In this work, we generally set $w = \omega(\log \lambda)$. While this is not standard for the RAM model, many memory checking constructions implicitly operate in this setting since most construction use MACs or CRHFs, which need to be of size $\omega(\log \lambda)$ to be secure against $\text{poly}[\lambda]$ adversaries. For a detailed discussion, see Sect. 2.4 of [26].

Parallel RAM Machines. A parallel RAM (PRAM) is a generalization of a RAM but with multiple CPUs. In fact, a RAM is simply a PRAM with exactly 1 CPU. A PRAM comprises m CPUs and a shared memory mem containing N logical addresses where each memory cell indexed by addr $\in [N]$ contains a word of size w. Just like RAMs, we assume the word-level operations such as word-level addition, Boolean operations and evaluating PRFs can be done in $O(1)$ time.

At time step t of the execution, each CPU might compute some request $\vec{I}_i^{(t)} = (\text{op}, \text{addr}, \text{data})$. Then, the RAM receives a sequence of requests $\vec{I}^{(t)} := (I_i^{(t)} : i \subseteq [m])$ (i.e. a set of requests from a subset of the CPUs). If $\text{op}_i = \text{read}$, then CPU$_i$ receives the contents of mem[addr$_i$] at the start of time-step t. If $\text{op}_i = \text{write}$, then the contents of mem[addr$_i$] are updated to data$_i$.

Write Conflict Resolution. In the PRAM model, it is possible that multiple CPUs attempt to access a given address at the same time. If a PRAM algorithm guarantees that any address is accessed by at most one CPU at any given time-step, we say that the algorithm is exclusive-read exclusive-write (EREW). If CPUs can concurrently read any address but at most one CPU writes to an address at any given time-step, we say the algorithm is concurrent-read exclusive-write (CREW).

On the other hand, if there are multiple concurrent accesses to the same address for both reads and writes, we call this the concurrent-read concurrent-write (CRCW) model. Since many CPUs can perform a write to the same address, we need a conflict resolution rule so that the PRAM update operations are well-defined. Here are a few commonly used rules:

- Arbitrary CRCW: An arbitrarily chosen CPU wins a write.
- Priority CRCW: Processors are ordered by some fixed priority, and the processor with the highest priority wins any write.
- Maximum/Minimum CRCW: The write with the maximum or minimum value is accepted.

It is well known that a CREW or CRCW algorithm can be transformed into an EREW algorithm with a logarithmic slow-down.

Lemma 1. *Consider a (possibly randomized) CREW/CRCW algorithm with work q and depth d on a m-processor PRAM. Such an algorithm can be converted into an EREW algorithm with work $O(q + dm \log m)$ and depth $O(d \log m)$ on an m-processor PRAM.*

Throughout our paper, we often using the following fact about the parallel runtime of adding n numbers.

Lemma 2. *There is an m-CPU EREW algorithm that sums n numbers with $O(n)$ work and $O(n/m + \log m)$ depth.*

This is done as follows. First, each of the m processors sums n/m of the numbers. This step takes $O(n)$ work and $O(n/m)$ depth. Then, the m CPUs publish their current m values, and these are then summed up in a binary tree fashion. This step takes $O(m)$ work and $O(\log m)$ depth.

3.2 Authentication

In the full version of this paper, we define the cryptographic primitives we need, such as pseudorandom function families (PRFs) and message authentication codes (MACs).

4 Memory Checking Model

In this section, we first recall the notion of memory checking for RAMs as introduced by Blum et al. [6]. We then define our notion of memory checking for PRAMs.

4.1 Memory Checking for RAMs

We recall the notion of memory checking from Blum et al. [6]. A memory checker M can be defined as a probablistic RAM program that interacts with a user U and server S, where U is performing a RAM computation with memory held by S. Specifically, without a memory checker, U sends $(\mathsf{op}, \mathsf{addr}, \mathsf{data}) \in \{\mathsf{read}, \mathsf{write}\} \times [N] \times (\{0,1\}^w \cup \{\bot\})$ to S, who may or may not correctly follow the RAM command, i.e., may send the wrong word back to U when $\mathsf{op} = \mathsf{read}$. M now serves as an intermediary between U and S (see Fig. 1) that takes in each query from U and generates and sends (possibly multiple and adaptive) queries to S. Whenever $\mathsf{op} = \mathsf{read}$, U once again generates and sends (possibly multiple and adaptive) queries to S, and M is then required to either respond to U with some word or abort by sending $\bot$ to indicate a malicious S. Once the memory checker aborts, the protocol is done. This continues in rounds until U is done sending queries, of which there are at most $\mathsf{poly}[\lambda]$.

Definition 1 (Online Memory Checker). *We say that M is an* online *memory checker if for any U the following two properties hold:*

1. **Completeness**: *If S is honest, then M never aborts and the responses that M sends to U are all correct with probability $1 - \mathsf{negl}(\lambda)$.*
2. **Soundness**: *For all p.p.t. S, the probability that M ever sends some incorrect response to U is $\mathsf{negl}(\lambda)$. That is, for each request from U, if S sends an incorrect response to M, M can either independently recover the correct answer and send it to U, or it can abort by sending $\bot$ to U.*

We call such a memory checker "online" because the memory checker must be able to catch incorrect responses from M as soon they are sent. On the other hand, one can define the notion of an "offline" memory checker:

Definition 2 (Offline Memory Checker). *We say that M is an* offline *memory checker for U if the following two properties hold:*

1. **Completeness**: *If S is honest, then M never aborts, and the responses that M sends to U are all correct with probability $1 - \mathsf{negl}(\lambda)$.*

2. **Soundness:** *For all p.p.t. $\mathcal{S}$, if $\mathcal{M}$ ever sends an incorrect response to $\mathcal{U}$, it must abort by the end of the last request made by $\mathcal{U}$ (the user indicates this by sending $\perp$ to $\mathcal{M}$, for example) with probably at least $1 - \mathsf{negl}(\lambda)$.*

In other words, $\mathcal{M}$ may send many incorrect responses to $\mathcal{U}$, but if it does, by the end of the computation, $\mathcal{M}$ must detect that there was some error at some point. We emphasize that $\mathcal{M}$ does not need to know where or when an error occurred.

In both the offline and online memory checking setting, we consider security versus a malicious adversary $\mathcal{A}$ that controls all messages sent to $\mathcal{M}$, i.e., controls both $\mathcal{U}$ and the server responses to $\mathcal{M}$.

4.2 Memory Checking for Parallel RAMs

We now define the memory checking model for PRAMs. As pictured in Fig. 2, given a PRAM with m CPUs $\{\mathcal{U}_i\}_{i \in [m]}$, we have corresponding family of memory checkers $\{\mathcal{M}_i\}_{i \in [m]}$. Before the start of the protocol, there is a *set-up phase* where the memory checkers run a probabilistic key generation algorithm $(s_1, \ldots, s_m) \leftarrow \mathsf{Gen}(1^\lambda, 1^m)$, and obtain secret states based on shared randomness. Now, each $\mathcal{M}_i$ only locally stores s_i.

Each $\mathcal{M}_i$ acts as an intermediary between $\mathcal{U}_i$ and the $\mathcal{S}$. If $\{\mathcal{U}_i\}_i$ at parallel time-step t directly sends $\vec{I}^{(t)} = (I_i^{(t)} : i \subseteq [m])$ to the server, the server may not carry out the commands correctly or *consistently*. Instead, each $\mathcal{U}_i$ now sends $I_i^{(t)} = (\mathsf{op}_i, \mathsf{addr}_i, \mathsf{data}_i)$ to $\mathcal{M}_i$. Now, the family $\{\mathcal{M}_i\}_i$, in parallel, make multiple (possibly adaptive) queries in parallel $\vec{I}^{(t,1)}, \vec{I}^{(t,2)}, \ldots, \vec{I}^{(t,\ell_t)}$ for some $\ell_t \in \mathbb{N}$ to $\mathcal{S}$. Then, $\mathcal{M}_i$ needs to respond to $\mathcal{U}_i$ either with some word, or $\perp$ if it detects any malicious behavior from the adversary. This continues in rounds until $\{\mathcal{U}_i\}_i$ is done sending queries, of which there are at most $\mathsf{poly}[\lambda]$ batches of requests.

Definition 3 (Online memory checker for PRAMs). *We say that the family $\mathcal{M} = \{\mathcal{M}_i\}_i$ is an parallel online memory checker family if for all CPUs $\{\mathcal{U}_i\}_i$ where each $\mathcal{M}_i$ is an intermediary between $\mathcal{U}_i$ and $\mathcal{S}$, if the following two properties hold:*

- **Correctness:** *If $\mathcal{S}$ is honest, then no $\mathcal{M}_i$ aborts and the responses from $\mathcal{M}_i$ to $\mathcal{U}_i$ are all correct with probability $1 - \mathsf{negl}(\lambda)$.*
- **Soundness:** *For all p.p.t. $\mathcal{S}$ that $\mathcal{M}_i$ sends an incorrect response to $\mathcal{U}_i$ is $\mathsf{negl}(\lambda)$. In particular, if $\mathcal{S}$ sends an incorrect response to $\mathcal{M}_i$, either $\mathcal{M}_i$ recovers the correct answer and sends it to $\mathcal{U}_i$, or some $\mathcal{M}_j$ (not necessarily the same as $\mathcal{M}_i$) aborts with $1 - \mathsf{negl}(\lambda)$ probability.*

Similarly, we define offline memory checking for PRAMs as follows.

Definition 4 (Offline memory checker for PRAMs). *We say that the family $\mathcal{M} = \{\mathcal{M}_i\}_i$ is an parallel online memory checker if for any family $\{\mathcal{U}_i\}_i$, where each $\mathcal{M}_i$ is an intermediary between $\mathcal{U}_i$ and $\mathcal{S}$ if the following two properties hold:*

- **Correctness:** If S is honest, then no $\mathcal{M}_i$ aborts and the responses from $\mathcal{M}_i$ to $\mathcal{U}_i$ are all correct with probability $1 - \mathsf{negl}(\lambda)$.
- **Soundness:** For all p.p.t. S, if any $\mathcal{M}_i$ had sent back an incorrect response to $\mathcal{U}_i$, some $\mathcal{M}_j$ (not necessarily the same as $\mathcal{M}_i$) must abort by the end of the last request made by the clients with probability at least $1 - \mathsf{negl}(\lambda)$.

Concurrency. We sometimes distinguish a family of memory checkers as compatible with EREW, CREW or CRCW PRAM programs. If not explicitly stated, we generally default to the arbitrary CRCW model.

Efficiency Metrics. We recap the efficiency metrics as described in Sect. 1. The main metrics are work and depth blowup, space requirement of the memory checkers, and the server space blowup.

- Depth blowup: The value of ℓ_t (as defined in the first paragraph of this subsection). In other words, this is the ratio of the number of parallel steps conducted by $\{\mathcal{M}_i\}$ for every parallel step of $\{\mathcal{U}_i\}_i$.
- Work blowup: The ratio of $|\vec{I}^{(t,1)} + \vec{I}^{(t,1)} + \cdots + \vec{I}^{(t,\ell_t)}|$ to $\vec{I}^{(t)}$. In other words, is the ratio of the number of physical queries from $\{\mathcal{M}_i\}_i$ to the ratio of underlying logical queries from $\{\mathcal{U}_i\}_i$. We note that we are only charging the communication with S as work.
- Memory checker local space: This is the amount of secret local space stored by each $\mathcal{M}_i$.
- Server space blowup: This is the size of the server storage divided by Nw (the size of the underlying server storage). In our constructions, this will be $O(1)$ assuming $w = \omega(\log \lambda)$.

5   Efficient Parallel Online Checker

In this section, we present our online-memory checking construction achieving $O(\log N)$ blowup in work and depth. Without loss of generality, suppose m and N are powers of two.

Algorithm 6 Online memory checker for a PRAM with m CPUs sharing a work-tape of size N.

Set-up: A key $\mathsf{sk} \leftarrow \mathsf{MACGen}(1^\lambda)$ is sampled and distributed to all checkers $\{\mathcal{M}_i\}_{i \in [m]}$.

Initial State: The server S's memory is organized in a binary tree of size $2N$ of height $\log_2 N$. (Note that since the root is the node that is initialized, initialization only takes $O(1)$ time.)

- Initialize the root node r to contain $(r, \mathsf{count} := 0, \mathsf{time} := 0, \mathsf{test} := 0)$ (authenticated).
- Each internal node v is of the form $(v, \mathsf{count}, \mathsf{time})$ (if uninitialized or if authentication fails, treat the contents as $(v, 0, 0)$).

- The N leaf nodes of the binary tree correspond to the contents of the logical memory. The leaf node corresponding to addr in the work tape W will contain (addr, data, count, time, test). If uninitialized, treat the contents as (addr, data $:= \varnothing$, CPU $:= \varnothing$, count $:= 0$, time $:= 0$, test $:= 0$).
- Every $\mathcal{M}_i$ has a counter T initialized to 1.

Authentication: Every write is authenticated using $\mathsf{MAC_{sk}}$ and every read is verified with Verify. If a read fails authentication, we assume that it is an *uninitialized* node.

The algorithm: At iteration T:

- *All readers:* First, every $\mathcal{M}_i$ corresponding to CPUs performing *reads* proceeds as follows.
  - Every $\mathcal{M}_i$ verifies that the root node has time $= T - 1$ and test $= 0$. Record the count value at the root.
  - Each $\mathcal{M}_i$ traverses the tree along the path to the leaf associated with addr, in parallel. For each node v along the path with children u and w, verify that v.count $= u$.count $+ w$.count (i.e. the count values of the corresponding nodes add up). If this is not true for any node, abort and output $\perp$.
  - Once the leaf node is reached, $\mathcal{M}_i$ simply reads the contents of the leaf node corresponding to addr, and sends data to CPU i.
- *All writers:* Now, every $\mathcal{M}_i$ corresponding to CPUs with *writes* proceeds as follows.
  1. *Test phase:* Every $\mathcal{M}_i$ reads the leaf node corresponding to addr. Suppose addr has counter value count. Then, every $\mathcal{M}_i$ tries to write (addr, data$'$, i, count $+ 1$, time $:= T$, test $:= 1$) (in parallel) to the leaf node corresponding to addr.
  2. *Winner phase:* Each $\mathcal{M}_i$ reads the same entry to check if their corresponding write had "won" the concurrent write.
     - If yes, rewrite (addr, data$'$, i, count $+ 1$, time $:= T$, test $:= 0$) to the same address (i.e. indicate that the test phase is concluded).
     - Otherwise, verify that the count value has been incremented, and time $= T$, and test $= 1$.
     - Every $\mathcal{M}_i$ reads the corresponding leaf node again to ensure that it is updated with the "winning" entry with test $= 0$ [2].
  3. *Propagation phase:* Now, we propagate the counts from the leaves of the tree to the root of the tree in parallel one layer at a time, starting from the bottom, i.e. updating the nodes from $h = 0, 1, \ldots, \log_2 N$:
     - At $h = 0$ (i.e. leaf nodes), every $\mathcal{M}_i$ with a successful write is assigned to that node.
     - At $h \geq 1$, each node with children that are updated will be assigned a checker $\mathcal{M}_i$ as follows:
       * If the left child was updated at round T, the checker $\mathcal{M}_i$ assigned to the left child is assigned to the node.
       * Otherwise, the checker $\mathcal{M}_i$ assigned to the right child at round T is also assigned to the parent node.

         * Note that this can be checked in an *EREW manner* by simply having a time-step where any checker $\mathcal{M}_i$ assigned to a right node checks if the sibling left node was updated at time T. If yes, it will no longer update the values.

        • Every node v at level $h \leq \log_2 N - 1$ with an assigned CPU with children u and w is updated to $(v, u.\mathsf{count} + w.\mathsf{count}, T)$. At $h = \log_2 N$ (i.e. the root node), the root r is set to $(r, u.\mathsf{count} + w.\mathsf{count}, T, \mathsf{test} := 1)$.

  4. *Verification of the root:*

        • In a separate array of size m (i.e. the number of CPUs), every $\mathcal{M}_i$ writes a 1 if it performed a successful write operation (i.e. "won" in the "winner phase") to the database, and 0 otherwise.

        • Compute the sum of this array to be some W. Note that this can be done in $O(\log m)$ depth with $O(m)$ work with an EREW algorithm.

        • $\mathcal{M}_1$ verifies that the count value of the root of the tree was increased by W (note that W can be 0 if no writes were performed).

           * If the count count was in fact correct, update the root to be $(\mathsf{addr}, \mathsf{count}, T, 0)$.

           * Otherwise, abort and output $\bot$.

  – Every $\mathcal{M}_i$ locally increments T.

Remark 1. If the underlying algorithm is CREW, the access patterns of the memory checkers are also CREW if the server is honest. If the underlying algorithm is EREW, we can make the following modifications to ensure the memory checkers' access patterns are also EREW. One can treat every "read" also as a "write" where the same value is written back. Then, we can simply skip "All readers" phase of the above algorithm and execute the "All writers" phase. Since exactly one user is assigned to each internal node when the server is honest, the resulting memory checking algorithm is also EREW against honest servers.

Remark 2. We can relax the parallelization requirements of the model by instead having an agreed upon time for 'read rounds" and "write rounds" for the "All readers" and "All writers" phase. This ensures that all CPUs can agree on the time-stamp of the root of the tree. We can also assume that in practice, no writes happen concurrently (e.g. by adding randomness to the timing of an access), and the algorithm is essentially EREW. We also assume that any read followed by an immediate write to the same location is "atomic" and cannot be interfered (i.e. any read-write to update the counter will not be interleaved with another CPUs read-write, as this will result in inconsistent counters). The "read rounds" have no synchronization issues, as long as every CPU agrees on the counter at

---

[2] If there is a rule for conflict resolution that can be easily verified (e.g. the CPU with the highest priority wins, CPU with the maximum or minimum value write wins, etc.), then that can also be verified here.

the root of the tree. During the "write rounds", the protocol is consistent during leaf-update phase and propagation phases as long as read-writes are atomic. During the verification phase, we perform an EREW algorithm sum a set of values and compare it against the root. As long as this is done in a consistent and authenticated way, this phase can be done correctly and securely.

Theorem 7. *Assuming the existence of one-way functions, there exists an online memory checker for a m-CPU PRAM with $O(\log N)$ work blowup and $O(\log N)$ depth blowup. Each CPU locally needs to store $O(1)$ words and one PRF key of length $\ell(\lambda)$ (for authentication).*

Proof. We first start by mentioning some invariants preserved during the algorithm when the server is honest.

Invariants. The main invariant maintained is that the sum of the counts of every node is the sum of the counts of its children node. Moreover, we have the following invariants.

– Every $\mathcal{M}_i$ has the correct value T of the number of overall requests supported by the memory checker.
– Every entry is authenticated, unless uninitialized (we treat every entry which fails authentication as uninitialized). An uninitialized node is treated to have count $= 0$.
– Every leaf node v corresponding to addr contains (addr, data, CPU, count, time, test), where count is the number of times addr was updated, and the time was the last round when a given node was written to, and test is a boolean value indicating whether the write corresponds to a "test phase" (defined later).
– Every internal node v is of the form $(v, \mathsf{count}, \mathsf{time})$, where count is the *total* number of times the leaf nodes of the corresponding sub-tree rooted at v are updated, and time is the last iteration when any of the leaves of the sub-tree is updated.

Clearly, the invariants are met at the initialization phase of the algorithm.

Suppose that we are at time $T = t$ of the algorithm, and suppose that the server has functioned honestly so far and the invariants have been maintained. Now, we argue that at the end of iteration t, either:

– The memory functioned correctly and the invariant is preserved.
– The memory functions incorrectly and some $\mathcal{M}_i$ aborts and outputs $\perp$.

The former case is easy. Therefore, it suffices to consider the case where the memory functions incorrectly.

By unforgeability of MACs, every valid read corresponds to some authenticated write with probability $1 - \mathsf{negl}(\lambda)$. Therefore, for the rest of this proof, we limit the memory's attacks to only *replay attacks* (i.e. memory sends stale requests corresponding to each address). There are a few cases to consider when the memory functions incorrectly.

Case 1: Memory functions incorrectly during the traversal phase of either the reads or the writes.

First, notice that the T value of the root is monotone increasing with each iteration, and therefore any replay attack at on the root node will be detected. For every internal node and leaf node, notice that the count value is monotone increasing with every write if the memory functions correctly. Suppose the memory first performs a replay attack on node u while some $\mathcal{M}_i$ is traversing a path, we note that v.count $> u$.count $+ w$.count where v is the parent node of u, and w is a sibling node of u. Therefore, any such replay attack will be caught and $\mathcal{M}_i$ will immediately abort.

Case 2: Memory functions incorrectly during the test and/or winner phases.

Let W be the number of CPUs that "win" during the test phase, and let U be the number of leaf nodes that are updated with writes. Note that it is possible that multiple CPUs get the signal that they won the concurrent write. Let $w_1, w_2, \ldots, w_U$ denote the number of "wins" associated to each of the U nodes that are updated with writes, i.e. number of CPUs that get a signal that they won per updated leaf node. Since every $\mathcal{M}_i$ with a write verifies that some CPU has won that concurrent write (with test $= 0$), this ensures that $w_j \geq 1$. Moreover, equality holds if and only if there is exactly one CPU that won the arbitrary write.

Therefore, we have that $W = \sum_{j=1}^{U} w_j \geq U$, where equality holds if and only if exactly one CPU wins each concurrent write. In other words, if the memory functions incorrectly in this phase, we must have $W > U$. Recall that W is computed during the verification phase, and we argue in the next case that this inequality will be detected during the verification phase.

Case 1: Memory functions incorrectly during the traversal phase of either the reads or the writes.

First, notice that the T value of the root is monotone increasing with each iteration, and therefore any replay attack at on the root node will be detected. For every internal node and leaf node, notice that the count value is monotone increasing with every write if the memory functions correctly. Suppose the memory first performs a replay attack on node u while some $\mathcal{M}_i$ is traversing a path, we note that v.count $> u$.count $+ w$.count where v is the parent node of u, and w is a sibling node of u. Therefore, any such replay attack will be caught and $\mathcal{M}_i$ will immediately abort.

Case 2: Memory functions incorrectly during the test and/or winner phases.

Let W be the number of CPUs that "win" during the test phase, and let U be the number of leaf nodes that are updated with writes. Note that it is possible that multiple CPUs get the signal that they won the concurrent write. Let $w_1, w_2, \ldots, w_U$ denote the number of "wins" associated to each of the U nodes that are updated with writes, i.e. number of CPUs that get a signal that they won per updated leaf node. Since every $\mathcal{M}_i$ with a write verifies that some CPU has won that concurrent write (with test $= 0$), this ensures that $w_j \geq 1$. Moreover, equality holds if and only if there is exactly one CPU that won the arbitrary write.

Therefore, we have that $W = \sum_{j=1}^{U} w_j \geq U$, where equality holds if and only if exactly one CPU wins each concurrent write. In other words, if the memory functions incorrectly in this phase, we must have $W > U$. Recall that W is computed during the verification phase, and we argue in the next case that this inequality will be detected during the verification phase.

Case 3: Memory functions incorrectly during the propagation and/or the verification phases.

Consider an arbitrary internal node v of the tree. Let v.count be the count value at time $T - 1$ this is correct by the induction hypothesis), and let v.update be the number of leaf nodes of the sub-tree at v that were updated at time T. We argue by induction on the height of v that for any read to v, the counter value read is at most v.count + v.update. Moreover, equality holds if and only if the memory functioned correctly in the sub-tree rooted at v during the propagation phase.

At $h = 0$ (i.e. leaf nodes), the statement is clearly true because a replay attack can only show a smaller counter value than v.count by the monotonicity of the count values. Therefore, any read to v can only show a value of at most v.count if it was not updated, and v.count + 1 otherwise.

Now, consider a node v at height $h' \geq 1$. Suppose that u and w are the children of v, and that the node updating v receives counter values u.count$'$ and w.count$'$ when reading u and w respectively. Then, the new updated counter value of v is

$$u.\text{count}' + v.\text{count}'$$
$$\leq u.\text{count} + u.\text{update} + w.\text{count} + w.\text{update}$$
$$= v.\text{count} + v.\text{update}$$

where the first equality holds by the definition of v.count$'$, the second inequality holds by the induction hypothesis, and the last equality comes from the correctness of the memory at time $T-1$. Therefore, the largest possible count value associated to any read of v in this iteration is at most v.count+v.update, where equality holds if and only if the memory functioned correctly in the sub-tree rooted at v during the propagation phase.

In particular, at the root node r, we have that

$$r.\text{count}' \leq r.\text{count} + r.\text{update} \leq r.\text{count} + U$$

where equality holds if and only if the memory functioned correctly during the propagation phase. Moreover, combining this with Case 2, we have that

$$r.\text{count}' - r.\text{count} \leq U \leq W$$

where all the inequalities hold if and only if the memory functioned correctly at every point in the algorithm. Therefore, if the memory functions incorrectly at any point, the check at the verification phase will fail, thereby completing the proof.

Efficiency. Note that each $\mathcal{M}_i$ traverses a path to the desired leaf of CPU i, and therefore does a $O(\log N)$ depth traversal. Moreover, during the propagation phase, each CPU again updates only elements on the path from the root to its leaf of the tree, and hence will once again only update $O(\log N)$ elements.

Moreover, it is clear that each checker only requires $O(1)$ local space to keep track of the root of the tree as well as verify the count values of the nodes of the tree. Therefore, this gives us the desired and space complexity.

6   Statistically Secure EREW Parallel Offline Checker

In the full version of this paper, we show that the offline memory checking approach of Blum et al. can be naturally parallelized and extended to the EREW PRAM setting. We state the theorem here.

Theorem 8. *Consider* $w = \Theta(\log N)$. *Consider an EREW algorithm with work q and depth d. There is a statistically secure offline memory checker for a m-CPU EREW algorithm with total work $O(q + N + m)$ and depth $O(d + N/m + \log m)$. Each $\mathcal{M}_i$ has to locally store $O(\log N + \log(1/\epsilon))$ bits of memory, where $\epsilon = \mathsf{negl}(\lambda)$.*

We defer the proof and construction to the full version of this paper.

Corollary 1. *Consider* $w = \Theta(\log N)$. *Consider an arbitrary CRCW algorithm algorithm with work q and depth d. There is a statistically secure offline memory checker for a m-CPU EREW algorithm with total work $O(q + md \log m + N + m)$ and depth $O(d \log m + N/m + \log m)$. Each $\mathcal{M}_i$ has to locally store $O(\log N + \log(1/\epsilon))$ bits of memory, where $\epsilon = \mathsf{negl}(\lambda)$.*

Proof. Using Lemma 1, we have that the algorithm can be converted into an EREW algorithm with work $q + md \log m$ and depth $d \log m$. Now, we get our result by applying Theorem 8.

7   CRCW Parallel Offline Checker from One-Way Functions

In this section, we use authentication to construct an offline memory checker for CREW and CRCW PRAM programs with amortized $O(1)$ complexity in both work and depth. In this section, we are once again in the setting where the word size is $w = \omega(\log \lambda)$.

In our construction, every value on the server is stored with metadata **MD** representing the following:

- addr: Logical address
- data: Contents of logical address addr.
- count: Number of times this logical address accessed.
- CPU: Name of CPU that last accessed (could be either read or write).

- time: Last time CPU accessed addr.
- CPU$_{prev}$: Name of CPU that accessed addr before time.
- time$_{prev}$: Last time CPU$_{prev}$ accessed addr.
- test: A boolean bit indicating if the last write happened during the "test" phase.

We refer to the metadata **MD** as (count, CPU, time, CPU$_{prev}$, time$_{prev}$, test).

Algorithm 9 Offline memory checker for the arbitrary CRCW model

Setup:
- Fix a MAC family (MACGen, MAC, Verify). Sample sk ← MACGen(1^λ) and distribute sk to all $\mathcal{M}_i$.
- Each $\mathcal{M}_i$ associated to CPU i initializes a local counter t_i to 0.
- We abuse the notation $S[\text{addr}]$ to denote the underlying database entry at address addr along with the corresponding metadata. We also have additional $O(N)$ server space for the second phase of the algorithm.

Authentication: Every write is authenticated using MAC$_{sk}$ and every read is verfied with Verify$_{sk}$. If a read fails authentication, we abort.

Algorithm (query phase):
- Initialize $S[\text{addr}]$ to set addr := addr, count := 0, test := 0, and set all other fields, CPU, time, CPU$_{prev}$, time$_{prev}$ to $\varnothing$.
- For each batch of requests $\vec{I}^{(T)} = (I_i^{(T)} : i \subseteq [m])$ at time T:
  - *All readers:* First, we handle all requests which are *reads* to the database.
    * Each $\mathcal{M}_i$ reads their corresponding entries, and downloads and saves the contents. Abort if any of the test values are 1, or if any of the address values are inconsistent.
    * For CPU i that performed a read and downloaded (addr, data, CPU, count, CPU$_{prev}$, count$_{prev}$, test), update the metadata as follows:
      · Set CPU$_{prev}$:= CPU and time$_{prev}$ = time.
      · Set CPU := i and time := T.
      · Increment count := count + 1.
      · Set test := 1.
    * *Test phase:* All $\mathcal{M}_i$'s perform a write to the accessed address with updated metadata.
    * *Winner phase:* Each $\mathcal{M}_i$ performs a read to see if it "won" the arbitrary write. Note that when the memory is honest, there should be exactly one write that wins.
      · If   yes, write back (addr, data, count, CPU, time, CPU$_{prev}$, time$_{prev}$, test = 0), i.e. update the test value to be 0. Increment local counter t_i.
      · Else, verify that CPU$_{prev}$, time$_{prev}$ and count values are consistent with their own write attempt, and that the test value is updated to 0. [3]
    * Every $\mathcal{M}_i$ increments their locally stored global timer T.

- *All writers:* Same as read phase, except data is now updated with data′ during the test and winner phases.

Algorithm (after query phase):

- Compute $t := \sum_i t_i$, i.e. the sum of all local counters of all the CPUs.
- Denote $c_{\mathsf{addr}} := S[\mathsf{addr}].\mathrm{count}$. Compute $t' := \sum_{\mathsf{addr}} c_{\mathsf{addr}}$ in a tree-like manner.
- Accept if and only if $t = t'$, otherwise abort and output $\bot$.

Remark 3. As in the online memory checking case, we can relax the parallelization requirements of the model for this memory checking protocol. During the query phase, we assume that in practice, no reads or writes happen concurrently (e.g. by adding randomness to the timing of an access), and the algorithm is essentially EREW. We also assume that any read followed by an immediate write to the same location is "atomic" and cannot be interfered (i.e. any read-write to update the counter will not be interleaved with another CPUs read-write, as this will result in inconsistent counters). For the verification phase, every CPU needs to agree when the verification phase begins, and when to write their respective local counters on the server. After this, the CPUs have to sum two lists of numbers and compare them. Since summing a list is an EREW algorithm, as long as this is done in a consistent and authenticated way, we can ensure the security and correctness of our protocol.

Theorem 10. *Consider an honest-but-curious implementation with work q and depth d. Then, there is a post-verifiable offline memory checker with total work $O(q+N)$, total depth $O(d+N/m+\log m)$ and space complexity $O(1)$ words and one PRF key of length $\ell(\lambda)$.*

Proof. By unforgeability of MACs, every valid read corresponds to some authenticated write with probability $1 - \mathsf{negl}(\lambda)$. Therefore, for the rest of this proof, we limit the memory's attacks to only *replay attacks* (i.e. memory sends stale requests corresponding to each address).

History Graph. For each address $\mathsf{addr} \in S$, let S_{addr} be the set of $(\mathsf{count}, \mathsf{CPU}, \mathsf{time})$ tuples corresponding to contents written to addr with flag $\mathsf{test} = 0$. Construct the following directed acyclic graph G_{addr} on S_{addr}. Intuitively, this graph will represent the *history* of updates made to the values at addr.

- The root of the graph is $(0, \varnothing, 0)$.
- If something of the form $(\mathsf{addr}, *, \mathsf{count}, \mathsf{CPU}, \mathsf{time}, \mathsf{CPU}_{\mathsf{prev}}, \mathsf{time}_{\mathsf{prev}}, \mathsf{test} := 0)$ was ever written to addr, add an edge from $(\mathsf{count} - 1, \mathsf{CPU}_{\mathsf{prev}}, \mathsf{time}_{\mathsf{prev}})$ to $(\mathsf{count}, \mathsf{CPU}, \mathsf{time})$. Here, $*$ denotes that the data entry can be any arbitrary value.

---

[3] If there is a rule for conflict resolution that can be easily verified (e.g. the CPU with the lowest number wins), then that can also be verified here.

We abuse the notation $|G_{\mathsf{addr}}|$ to denote the number of vertices in G_{addr}.

Claim. If the memory functioned correctly, then $c_{\mathsf{addr}} = |G_{\mathsf{addr}}| - 1$. Otherwise, if the memory functioned incorrectly, for some $\mathsf{addr} \in \mathcal{S}$, we must have $c_{\mathsf{addr}} < |G_{\mathsf{addr}}| - 1$.

Proof. First, we argue that the history graph G_{addr} for each $\mathsf{addr} \in \mathcal{S}$ is connected. For all nodes with count value 1, clearly they are adjacent to the root node $(0, \varnothing, 0)$. For a node with $\mathsf{count} = k$, it must be adjacent to some node with $\mathsf{count} = k - 1$, and hence inductively, we must have that G_{addr} is connected.

Let h_{addr} denote the height of the graph G_{addr}. It is clear that c_{addr} must correspond to the count value of some node in the graph, and hence $c_{\mathsf{addr}} \leq h_{\mathsf{addr}}$. Note that $h_{\mathsf{addr}} = |G_{\mathsf{addr}}| - 1$ if and only if G_{addr} is a path. Hence, it suffices to show that G_{addr} is a path if and only if the memory functions correctly.

Clearly, if the memory functions correctly, for every $\mathsf{addr} \in \mathcal{S}$, the graph G_{addr} is a path. Moreover, the final version of the $\mathcal{S}[\mathsf{addr}]$ corresponds to the leaf node of G_{addr}, and hence has count $|G_{\mathsf{addr}}| - 1$, as desired.

Now, suppose the memory functions incorrectly at some address addr. There are three ways that the memory could have functioned incorrectly.

- The memory functioned correctly throughout, until the final read to $\mathcal{S}[\mathsf{addr}]$, where the memory does a replay attack. Then, $c_{\mathsf{addr}} < |G_{\mathsf{addr}}| - 1$ since the memory must have sent back a counter associated to a non-leaf node.
- The memory could have sent back a "stale" entry for some address addr. Consider the first such replay response. Note that because of the $\mathsf{test} = 0$ flag check, the "stale" request must correspond to some node on G_{addr}, say $(\mathsf{count}, \mathsf{CPU}, \mathsf{time})$. Moreover, since this is a stale request, it must mean that this node already has a child in G_{addr}. Note that the new update created must have the form $(\mathsf{addr}, *, \mathsf{count} + 1, \mathsf{CPU}', \mathsf{time}', \mathsf{CPU}, \mathsf{time})$. Therefore, $(\mathsf{count}, \mathsf{CPU}, \mathsf{time})$ has at least two children, and the graph is no longer a path.
- Alternatively, the memory could have accepted conflicting writes. In particular, some $\mathcal{M}_i$ and $\mathcal{M}_j$ concurrently write to some addr at time time, and both writes "win" in the winner phase. Then, the corresponding winning writes, $(\mathsf{count}_i, \mathsf{CPU}_i, \mathsf{time})$ and $(\mathsf{count}_j, \mathsf{CPU}_j, \mathsf{time})$, cannot lie on the same path from the root because they both have the same time value (because by construction, the time values are increasing on any directed path from the root).

If the memory functions correctly, note that $t = \sum t_i = \sum |G_{\mathsf{addr}}| - 1$ because this is the number of times each address is updated, and $t' = \sum_{\mathsf{addr}} c_{\mathsf{addr}} = \sum |G_{\mathsf{addr}}| - 1 = t$. Therefore, the memory checker accepts.

Otherwise, if the memory functions incorrectly, then for some address addr', $c_{\mathsf{addr}'} \leq |G_{\mathsf{addr}'}| - 2$. Therefore, $T' \leq \sum_{\mathsf{addr} \neq \mathsf{addr}'} (|G_{\mathsf{addr}}| - 1) + (|G_{\mathsf{addr}'}| - 2) < \sum(|G_{\mathsf{addr}}| - 1) = \sum t_i = T$, and hence will be rejected with probability $1 - \mathsf{negl}(\lambda)$.

Efficiency. During the query phase, it is easy to see that every underlying query generates $O(1)$ physical queries. Therefore, the work during the query phase is exactly $O(q)$, and the depth is $O(d)$. During the second phase of the algorithm, we are summing $O(N)$ counters, and this takes $O(N+m)$ time and $O(N/m+\log m)$ parallel steps. This gives us the desired efficiency.

8 Maliciously Secure Oblivious Parallel RAM

In this full version of this paper, we extend the notion of oblivious parallel RAM as defined by Boyle et al. [7] to also be secure against tampering adversaries. We call such an OPRAM construction *maliciously secure*. We refer the reader to the full version for a formal definition.

Following the argument of Mathialagan and Vafa [26], we argue that naturally composing our memory checking construction with existing OPRAM constructions gives us a maliciously secure ORAM.

Theorem 11. *Suppose $\{\mathcal{C}_i\}_{i \in [m]}$ is an honest-but-curious oblivious PRAM implementation. Let $\{\mathcal{M}_i\}_{i \in [m]}$ be a family of online memory checkers. Then the family $\{\mathcal{C}'_i\}_{i \in [m]}$ obtained by taking $\mathcal{C}'_i$ to be the natural composition of $\mathcal{M}_i$ with $\mathcal{C}_i$, i.e. $\mathcal{M}_i$ is an intermediary between $\mathcal{C}_i$ and the server. The family $\{\mathcal{C}'_i\}$ is a maliciously secure oblivious PRAM.*

Therefore, by choosing $\{\mathcal{C}_i\}_i$ to be the optimal OPRAM construction of [3] (as in Theorem 4) and $\{\mathcal{M}_i\}_i$ to be our construction from Sect. 5, we obtain the following result.

Theorem 12. *Assuming the existence of one-way functions, there exists a maliciously secure arbitrary CRCW OPRAM scheme with $O(\log^2 N)$ blowup in both work and depth.*

Acknowledgements. I would like to thank Vinod Vaikuntanathan and Virginia Vassilevska Williams for their enthusiasm and guidance, and for giving valuable feedback on this manuscript. I would like to thank Neekon Vafa and Wei Kai Lin for helpful discussions, and Rahul Ilango and Yael Kirkpatrick for giving feedback on the manuscript. I would like to thank Mohsen Ghaffari and Christoph Grunau for helpful discussions on PRAMs, and Nancy Lynch for helpful discussions about distributed systems and byzantine agreement. I would also like to thank the anonymous reviewers for their detailed comments on the manuscripts.

References

1. Ajtai, M.: The invasiveness of off-line memory checking. In: 34th ACM STOC, pp. 504–513. ACM Press (2002). https://doi.org/10.1145/509907.509981
2. Arasu, A., et al.: Concerto: a high concurrency key-value store with integrity. In: Proceedings of the 2017 ACM International Conference on Management of Data, pp. 251–266 (2017)

3. Asharov, G., Komargodski, I., Lin, W.K., Peserico, E., Shi, E.: Optimal oblivious parallel ram. In: Proceedings of the 2022 Annual ACM-SIAM Symposium on Discrete Algorithms (SODA), pp. 2459–2521. SIAM (2022)
4. Asharov, G., Komargodski, I., Lin, W.-K., Shi, E.: Oblivious RAM with *Worst-Case* logarithmic overhead. In: Malkin, T., Peikert, C. (eds.) CRYPTO 2021. LNCS, vol. 12828, pp. 610–640. Springer, Cham (2021). https://doi.org/10.1007/978-3-030-84259-8_21
5. Bindschaedler, V., Naveed, M., Pan, X., Wang, X., Huang, Y.: Practicing oblivious access on cloud storage: the gap, the fallacy, and the new way forward. In: Ray, I., Li, N., Kruegel, C. (eds.) ACM CCS 2015, pp. 837–849. ACM Press (2015). https://doi.org/10.1145/2810103.2813649
6. Blum, M., Evans, W.S., Gemmell, P., Kannan, S., Naor, M.: Checking the correctness of memories. In: 32nd FOCS, pp. 90–99. IEEE Computer Society Press (1991). https://doi.org/10.1109/SFCS.1991.185352
7. Boyle, E., Chung, K.-M., Pass, R.: Oblivious parallel RAM and applications. In: Kushilevitz, E., Malkin, T. (eds.) TCC 2016. LNCS, vol. 9563, pp. 175–204. Springer, Heidelberg (2016). https://doi.org/10.1007/978-3-662-49099-0_7
8. Chan, T.-H.H., Chung, K.-M., Shi, E.: On the depth of oblivious parallel RAM. In: Takagi, T., Peyrin, T. (eds.) ASIACRYPT 2017. LNCS, vol. 10624, pp. 567–597. Springer, Cham (2017). https://doi.org/10.1007/978-3-319-70694-8_20
9. Chan, T.-H.H., Guo, Y., Lin, W.-K., Shi, E.: Oblivious hashing revisited, and applications to asymptotically efficient ORAM and OPRAM. In: Takagi, T., Peyrin, T. (eds.) ASIACRYPT 2017. LNCS, vol. 10624, pp. 660–690. Springer, Cham (2017). https://doi.org/10.1007/978-3-319-70694-8_23
10. Hubert Chan, T.-H., Shi, E.: Circuit OPRAM: unifying statistically and computationally secure ORAMs and OPRAMs. In: Kalai, Y., Reyzin, L. (eds.) TCC 2017. LNCS, vol. 10678, pp. 72–107. Springer, Cham (2017). https://doi.org/10.1007/978-3-319-70503-3_3
11. Chen, B., Lin, H., Tessaro, S.: Oblivious parallel RAM: improved efficiency and generic constructions. In: Kushilevitz, E., Malkin, T. (eds.) TCC 2016. LNCS, vol. 9563, pp. 205–234. Springer, Heidelberg (2016). https://doi.org/10.1007/978-3-662-49099-0_8
12. Chen, Y.C., Chow, S.S.M., Chung, K.M., Lai, R.W.F., Lin, W.K., Zhou, H.S.: Cryptography for parallel RAM from indistinguishability obfuscation. In: Sudan, M. (ed.) ITCS 2016, pp. 179–190. ACM (2016). https://doi.org/10.1145/2840728.2840769
13. Connell, G.: Technology deep dive: Building a faster ORAM layer for enclaves. https://signal.org/blog/building-faster-oram/ (2022)
14. Costan, V., Devadas, S.: Intel SGX explained. Cryptology ePrint Archive, Report 2016/086 (2016). https://eprint.iacr.org/2016/086
15. Dauterman, E., Fang, V., Demertzis, I., Crooks, N., Popa, R.A.: Snoopy: surpassing the scalability bottleneck of oblivious storage. In: Proceedings of the ACM SIGOPS 28th Symposium on Operating Systems Principles, pp. 655–671 (2021)
16. Dolev, D., Strong, H.R.: Authenticated algorithms for byzantine agreement. SIAM J. Comput. **12**(4), 656–666 (1983). https://doi.org/10.1137/0212045
17. Dwork, C., Naor, M., Rothblum, G.N., Vaikuntanathan, V.: How efficient can memory checking be? In: Reingold, O. (ed.) TCC 2009. LNCS, vol. 5444, pp. 503–520. Springer, Heidelberg (2009). https://doi.org/10.1007/978-3-642-00457-5_30
18. Fischer, M.J., Lynch, N.A.: A lower bound for the time to assure interactive consistency. Inf. Process. Lett. **14**(4), 183–186 (1982). https://doi.org/10.

1016/0020-0190(82)90033-3,   https://www.sciencedirect.com/science/article/pii/
0020019082900333

19. Fischer, M.J., Lynch, N.A., Merritt, M.: Easy impossibility proofs for distributed consensus problems. Distrib. Comput. **1**, 26–39 (1986)

20. Fletcher, C.W., Dijk, M.V., Devadas, S.: A secure processor architecture for encrypted computation on untrusted programs. In: Proceedings of the Seventh ACM Workshop on Scalable Trusted Computing, pp. 3–8 (2012)

21. Fletcher, C.W., Ren, L., Kwon, A., van Dijk, M., Devadas, S.: Freecursive ORAM: [nearly] free recursion and integrity verification for position-based oblivious RAM. In: Proceedings of the Twentieth International Conference on Architectural Support for Programming Languages and Operating Systems. p. 103–116. ASPLOS 2015, Association for Computing Machinery, New York, NY, USA (2015). https://doi.org/10.1145/2694344.2694353

22. Gentry, C., Halevi, S., Jutla, C., Raykova, M.: Private database access with HE-over-ORAM architecture. In: Malkin, T., Kolesnikov, V., Lewko, A.B., Polychronakis, M. (eds.) ACNS 2015. LNCS, vol. 9092, pp. 172–191. Springer, Cham (2015). https://doi.org/10.1007/978-3-319-28166-7_9

23. Liu, C., Wang, X.S., Nayak, K., Huang, Y., Shi, E.: ObliVM: a programming framework for secure computation. In: 2015 IEEE Symposium on Security and Privacy, pp. 359–376. IEEE Computer Society Press (2015). https://doi.org/10.1109/SP.2015.29

24. Lu, S., Ostrovsky, R.: Distributed oblivious RAM for secure two-party computation. In: Sahai, A. (ed.) TCC 2013. LNCS, vol. 7785, pp. 377–396. Springer, Heidelberg (2013). https://doi.org/10.1007/978-3-642-36594-2_22

25. Lu, S., Ostrovsky, R.: Black-box parallel garbled RAM. In: Katz, J., Shacham, H. (eds.) CRYPTO 2017. LNCS, vol. 10402, pp. 66–92. Springer, Cham (2017). https://doi.org/10.1007/978-3-319-63715-0_3

26. Mathialagan, S., Vafa, N.: MacORAMa: Optimal oblivious RAM with integrity. In: To appear at CRYPTO 2023 (2023). https://eprint.iacr.org/2023/083

27. Merkle, R.C.: A certified digital signature. In: Brassard, G. (ed.) CRYPTO 1989. LNCS, vol. 435, pp. 218–238. Springer, New York (1990). https://doi.org/10.1007/0-387-34805-0_21

28. Naor, J., Naor, M.: Small-bias probability spaces: efficient constructions and applications. In: 22nd ACM STOC, pp. 213–223. ACM Press (1990). https://doi.org/10.1145/100216.100244

29. Naor, M., Rothblum, G.N.: The complexity of online memory checking. J. ACM (JACM) **56**(1), 1–46 (2009)

30. Papamanthou, C., Tamassia, R.: Optimal and parallel online memory checking. Cryptology ePrint Archive, Report 2011/102 (2011). https://eprint.iacr.org/2011/102

31. Pease, M., Shostak, R., Lamport, L.: Reaching agreement in the presence of faults. J. ACM **27**(2), 228–234 (1980). https://www.microsoft.com/en-us/research/publication/reaching-agreement-presence-faults/, 2005 Edsger W. Dijkstra Prize in Distributed Computing

32. Ren, L., Fletcher, C.W., Yu, X., van Dijk, M., Devadas, S.: Integrity verification for path oblivious-RAM. In: 2013 IEEE High Performance Extreme Computing Conference (HPEC), pp. 1–6 (2013). https://doi.org/10.1109/HPEC.2013.6670339

33. Shacham, H., Waters, B.: Compact proofs of retrievability. J. Cryptol. **26**(3), 442–483 (2013). https://doi.org/10.1007/s00145-012-9129-2

34. Shi, E., Chan, T.-H.H., Stefanov, E., Li, M.: Oblivious RAM with $O((\log N)^3)$ worst-case cost. In: Lee, D.H., Wang, X. (eds.) ASIACRYPT 2011. LNCS, vol. 7073, pp. 197–214. Springer, Heidelberg (2011). https://doi.org/10.1007/978-3-642-25385-0_11
35. Wang, X.S., Huang, Y., Chan, T.H.H., shelat, A., Shi, E.: SCORAM: oblivious RAM for secure computation. In: Ahn, G.J., Yung, M., Li, N. (eds.) ACM CCS 2014, pp. 191–202. ACM Press (2014). https://doi.org/10.1145/2660267.2660365
36. Zahur, S., et al.: Revisiting square-root ORAM: efficient random access in multi-party computation. In: 2016 IEEE Symposium on Security and Privacy, pp. 218–234. IEEE Computer Society Press (2016). https://doi.org/10.1109/SP.2016.21
37. Mathialagan, S.: Memory checking for parallel RAMs. Cryptology ePrint Archive, Paper 2023/1703 (2023). https://eprint.iacr.org/2023/1703

Author Index

© International Association for Cryptologic Research 2023
G. Rothblum and H. Wee (Eds.): TCC 2023, LNCS 14370, p. 465, 2023.
https://doi.org/10.1007/978-3-031-48618-0

Printed in the United States
by Baker & Taylor Publisher Services